BEN JONSON'S PLAYS AND MASQUES

TEXTS OF THE PLAYS AND MASQUES

JONSON ON HIS WORK

CONTEMPORARY READERS ON JONSON

CRITICISM

W. W. NORTON & COMPANY, INC.
also publishes

THE NORTON ANTHOLOGY OF AMERICAN LITERATURE
edited by Ronald Gottesman et al.

THE NORTON ANTHOLOGY OF ENGLISH LITERATURE
edited by M. H. Abrams et al.

THE NORTON ANTHOLOGY OF MODERN POETRY
edited by Richard Ellmann and Robert O'Clair

THE NORTON ANTHOLOGY OF POETRY
edited by Arthur M. Eastman et al.

THE NORTON ANTHOLOGY OF SHORT FICTION
edited by R. V. Cassill

THE NORTON ANTHOLOGY OF WORLD MASTERPIECES
edited by Maynard Mack et al.

THE NORTON FACSIMILE OF
THE FIRST FOLIO OF SHAKESPEARE
prepared by Charlton Hinman

THE NORTON INTRODUCTION TO LITERATURE
edited by Carl E. Bain, Jerome Beaty, and J. Paul Hunter

THE NORTON READER
edited by Arthur M. Eastman et al.

A NORTON CRITICAL EDITION

BEN JONSON'S PLAYS AND MASQUES

TEXTS OF THE PLAYS AND MASQUES
JONSON ON HIS WORK
CONTEMPORARY READERS ON JONSON
CRITICISM

Selected and Edited by

ROBERT M. ADAMS

PROFESSOR EMERITUS OF ENGLISH,
UNIVERSITY OF CALIFORNIA AT LOS ANGELES

W · W · Norton & Company
New York London

ACKNOWLEDGMENTS

Jonas A. Barish: "The Double Plot in *Volpone*," from *Modern Philology*, 51 (November 1953), pp. 83–92. © 1953 by The University of Chicago Press. Reprinted by permission of the University of Chicago Press and the author.
William Blissett: "The Venter Tripartite in *The Alchemist*," from *Studies in English Literature*, 8 (1968), pp. 323–334. Reprinted by permission of *Studies in English Literature* and the author.
Ian Donaldson: From *The World Upside-Down* (London, 1970) Chapter 2, pp. 24–45. (Originally published in the *Review of English Studies*.) © 1970 by Oxford University Press. Reprinted by permission of the publisher.
T. S. Eliot: "Ben Jonson," from *The Sacred Wood* (London: Methuen & Co., 1950), pp. 104–107, 113–122. Reprinted by permission of the publisher.
Harry Levin: "Jonson's Metempsychosis," from *Philological Quarterly*, XXII, 3 (March 1943). Reprinted by permission of the University of Iowa.
Stephen Orgel: "Conclusion: More Removed Mysteries," from *The Jonsonian Masque* (Cambridge, Mass.: Harvard University Press, 1965), pp. 186–202.
Edward B. Partridge: From *The Broken Compass* (New York: Columbia University Press; London: Chatto and Windus Ltd., 1958), pp. 114–120, 139–152, 156–160. Reprinted by permission of the publishers and the author.

Library of Congress Cataloging in Publication Data

Jonson, Ben, 1573?–1637.
Ben Jonson's plays and masques.
(A Norton critical edition)
Bibliography: p.
1. Jonson, Ben, 1573?–1637—Criticism and interpretation—Addresses, essays, lectures. I. Adams, Robert Martin, 1915– II. Title.
PR2602.A3 1979 822'.3 78-7325

Published simultaneously in Canada by George J. McLeod Limited, Toronto. Printed in the United States of America.

FIRST EDITION

1 2 3 4 5 6 7 8 9 0

Contents

Criticism

Preface

Ben Jonson wrote nineteen plays and had an assistant's hand in several others; he was the author of twenty-four masques and entertainments. To represent in reasonable compass the scope of his work for the stage and the court, one must select. The first choices are not at all difficult, since everyone agrees that his twin masterpieces for the stage are *Volpone* and *The Alchemist*, both in verse. *Epicoene*, in prose, is our third choice; it has a beautifully articulated plot and a set of characters whose manners and motives are relatively easy to grasp. In fact it is close kin to the sort of gentlemanly comedy that would come into full fashion at the Restoration —easy and fluent in its wit, full of the spirit of play, but tough too (as Jonson could always be tough) in its judgment of moral and social values.

All of these great and very successful plays are bunched in Jonson's miraculous decade of 1606–16, when the playwright was at the height of his powers. The plays he wrote in the last years of his life were not as successful, and some of them, it must be admitted, were downright bad; they have become known collectively by the cruel name of Jonson's "dotages." But, like most wholesale artistic judgments, this one is unfair and inaccurate in detail. *The Sad Shepherd*, which appeared in the world only after Jonson's death, is the mere torso of a play, but it is a strange and beautiful achievement; and it illustrates a special gift of Jonson's for combining unlikely elements into a harmonious poetic composition. Above all, it complements the other three plays, which are all urban in their setting, by displaying a broad, an almost romantic, strain of country feeling which dwelt within this most London of playwrights. As for the fact that the play is unfinished, well, that's just an interest the more. There have been two attempted completions already, and anyone else who feels suitably adventurous is free to try his hand.

Jonson's masques and courtly entertainments, as they have come down to us, vary enormously in size and "seriousness," depending on the social occasion that called them forth. They might help to welcome a distinguished visitor to a country house, to celebrate a wedding or a birthday, or to enliven the Christmas season at court, when merry-making and feasting were traditional. The persons participating might be of the very highest rank under the king, or of somewhat lower status; the amount of money spent might be slight or enormous. For the great court masques, in which the richest ladies in the land vied to outdo one another, thousands of pounds might be invested in costumes, musicians, and stage-machinery; and for such occasions, the poet as well might feel impelled to outdo himself. We are fortunate to have not only the text of the greatest of these, *The Masque of Queens*, but a set of Jonson's handwritten notes, which make evident how much scholarly substance lay hidden behind his use of a single name or theatrical prop. As for the other three masques, they were chosen on the basis of their poetry, their eloquent morality, their frequent wit; it's an editor's judgment that they are among the best, but the editor who made that judgment would be happy if there were room for six more masques, and doesn't think the additions would appreciably lower the general level.

The plays and masques selected for this volume can be supplemented, for the poetry and critical prose, by Hugh MacLean's Norton Critical Edition of *Ben Jonson and the Cavalier Poets*; and from there, the devotee of Ben is invited to move on to the *Complete Works* edited by Herford and Simpson in a classic 11-volume edition. Our texts here have been modernized for greater accessibility, but checked against the old-spelling versions of Herford and Simpson, according to principles outlined in the Note on the Text. The background materials contain hints toward Jonson's structure of esthetic values and glimpses of his informal personality; the appended critical essays provide a cross section of modern views as they relate particularly to the materials of this collection.

A note on the cover illustration: Jacques Callot, a younger contemporary of Ben Jonson, was born at Nancy, capitol of the French province of Lorraine, in 1592; his death occured in 1635. While still a boy, he ran away from France to Italy, where he rapidly rose to prominence as an engraver; his work is vivid, realistic, and boldly dramatic. Often it is funny, sometimes coming close to caricature; occasionally it is stark and tragic, or macabre. While he made many engravings of gypsies, soldiers, clowns, and grotesques, Callot is probably best known for his series based on the stylized characters of the Italian *commedia dell' arte*. Harlequin, Columbine, Pierrot, Scaramouche, Captain Fracasse, and Pantaloon are but a few of this zany, colorful tribe. Wearing fanciful masks and exaggerated but always identifiable costumes, they could be combined on stage into improvised dramatic sketches and comic routines of infinite variety. Callot was expert at capturing their capering gestures, their grotesque elegance.

Pantaloon (anglicized name of Pantaleone) is the jealous, suspicious, lecherous old man of these plots; because his costume always included a pair of long, baggy trousers, they took on his name, and survive, in modern abbreviation, as pants. A richly developed comic gaffer, Pantaloon probably contributed to Jonsonian characters like Corbaccio in *Volpone* or Morose in *Epicoene*. But, more than any specific persona, he serves to represent on our cover the verve, nerve, and vigor of Jonson's character drawing.

Robert M. Adams

The Texts of
The Plays

Volpone

or

The Fox

The Persons of the Play[1]

VOLPONE, *a magnifico*
MOSCA, *his parasite*
VOLTORE, *an advocate*
CORBACCIO, *an old gentleman*
CORVINO, *a merchant*
BONARIO, *son to Corbaccio*
SIR POLITIC WOULD-BE, *a knight*
PEREGRINE, *a gentleman traveller*
NANO, *a dwarf*
CASTRONE, *an eunuch*
ANDROGYNO, *an hermaphrodite*

GREGE (*or Mob*)

COMMENDATORI, *officers of justice*
MERCATORI, *three merchants*
AVOCATORI, *four magistrates*
NOTARIO, *the register*

LADY WOULD-BE, SIR POLITIC'S *Wife*
CELIA, CORVINO'S *Wife*
SERVITORI, *Servants, two* WAITING-WOMEN, *&c.*

THE SCENE: *Venice*

The Argument[2]

Volpone, childless, rich, feigns sick, despairs,
Offers his state to hopes of several heirs,

1. Most of the names are Italian, and in that language many of them signify animals. Volpone: "fox." "Magnifico" is not a formal title; it simply means "gentleman." Mosca: "fly." The figure of the parasite implies scavenging, as well as fawning dependence. The client-patron relationship in Rome fostered parasitical dependents, and Jonson saw something similar, not only around the English court, but around the big money-men of London city. Voltore: "vulture." Corbaccio: "raven." Corvino: "crow." Bonario: "good-natured." Sir Politic Would-be: in the 17th century the word "politic" carried overtones of devious and subtle calculation. His name spells out, almost too explicitly, Sir Politic's character; and in its abbreviation ("Pol") suggests further the parrot he is. Peregrine: in English, "a falcon," but the world also associates with "pilgrim," i.e., "traveller." Nano: "dwarf." Castrone: "gelding." Androgyno: from the Greek, "man-woman," i.e., "hermaphrodite." Grege: from the Latin, "mob" or "crowd." Commendatori: a not very distinguished title of honor: Jonson assigns them a function akin to sergeants or marshals of a court. Mercatori: "merchants." Avocatori: properly, in Italian, "prosecutors"; Jonson makes them judges. Notario: "recorder." Celia: literally, "heavenly."

2. A capsule summary of the plot.

Lies languishing; his parasite receives
Presents of all, assures, deludes; then weaves
Other cross plots, which ope themselves, are told.
New tricks for safety are sought; they thrive: when bold,
Each tempts the other again, and all are sold.[3]

Prologue

Now, luck yet send us, and a little wit
Will serve to make our play hit;
According to the palates of the season
Here is rhyme, not empty of reason.
This we were bid to credit from our poet,
Whose true scope, if you would know it,
In all his poems still hath been this measure,
To mix profit with your pleasure;[4]
And not as some, whose throats their envy failing,
Cry hoarsely, All he writes is railing;[5]
And when his plays come forth, think they can flout them,
With saying, he was a year about them.
To these there needs no lie,[6] *but this his creature,*
Which was two months since no feature;
And though he dares give them five lives to mend it,
'Tis known, five weeks fully penned it,
From his own hand, without a co-adjutor,
Novice, journey-man,[7] *or tutor.*
Yet thus much I can give you as a token
Of his play's worth, no eggs are broken,
Nor quaking custards with fierce teeth affrighted,[8]
Wherewith your rout[9] *are so delighted;*
Nor hales he in a gull,[1] *old ends reciting,*
To stop gaps in his loose writing;
With such a deal of monstrous and forced action,
As might make Bedlam[2] *a faction:*
Nor made he his play for jests stolen from each table,
But makes jests to fit his fable;
And so presents quick comedy refined,
As best critics have designed;
The laws of time, place, persons he observeth,[3]
From no needful rule he swerveth.

3. Deceived.
4. That the task of the poet is to mix profit with pleasure was an idea dating back to Horace's *Art of Poetry,* lines 343–44.
5. Abuse, invective.
6. "To give the lie" was to deny flatly; we would use here the word "denial."
7. Piece-worker, apprentice, or assistant.
8. Comic routines—thrown eggs or custard pies—which had popular success on the low Elizabethan stage. A giant custard pie was also served at city feasts inaugurating the Lord Mayor; sometimes an attendant fool jumped into it.
9. Mob, common herd.
1. Buffoon. Elizabethans were fond of wise saws and ancient adages, and often put characters into plays who recited them.
2. Bethlehem Hospital, the madhouse.
3. The so-called Aristotelian unities, actually imposed as prescripts by the Renaissance critics Castelvetro and Scaliger, placed limits of time and place on a dramatic action; the limitation on persons was less strict.

All gall and copperas from his ink he draineth,
Only a little salt remaineth,[4]
Wherewith he'll rub your cheeks, till, red with laughter,
They shall look fresh a week after.

Act I

SCENE 1. *A room in* VOLPONE's *house*

[*Enter* VOLPONE *and* MOSCA.]

VOLPONE. Good morning to the day; and next, my gold!
Open the shrine,[1] that I may see my saint.
[MOSCA *withdraws the curtain, and discovers piles of gold, plate, jewels, &c.*]
Hail the world's soul, and mine! more glad than is
The teeming earth to see the longed-for sun
Peep through the horns of the celestial ram,[2]
Am I, to view thy splendor darkening his;
That lying here, amongst my other hoards,
Show'st like a flame by night, or like the day
Struck out of chaos, when all darkness fled
Unto the center. O thou son of Sol,[3]
But brighter than thy father, let me kiss,
With adoration, thee, and every relic
Of sacred treasure in this blessèd room.
Well did wise poets, by thy glorious name,
Title that age which they would have the best;[4]
Thou being the best of things, and far transcending
All style of joy, in children, parents, friends,
Or any other waking dream on earth.
Thy looks when they to Venus did ascribe,
They should have given her twenty thousand Cupids;[5]
Such are thy beauties and our loves! Dear saint,
Riches, the dumb god, that givest all men tongues,

4. Gall and copperas (i.e., green vitriol) are traditional ingredients of ink: both are corrosive and bitter to the taste. Salt, though not an ingredient of ink, is a classical metaphor for wit, that which gives flavor to speech or writing.
1. Though there was no proscenium curtain in the Elizabethan theater, such as rises on a modern play, there was a small curtained inner area, and that is what Mosca unveils. By "the world's soul and mine" Volpone means the soul of the universe and his own immortal essence, both identified with gold.
2. The sun peeps through the horns of the constellation "Ram" in the zodiac about the middle of April; cf. Chaucer, at the opening of the *Canterbury Tales* (lines 5–8); "When Zephyrus eek with his sweete breeth / Inspired hath in every holt and heeth / The tendre croppes, and the yonge sonne / Hath in the Ram his halve cours yronne."
3. The circle of a gold coin is compared to the created cosmos, i.e., the world with sun, moon, and stars, created by God in Genesis i. When the sun illumined the outer universe, darkness "fled to the center," i.e., to hell, underground. Gold is said to be "the son of Sol" (the sun) because in Renaissance lore, the fertilizing rays of the sun, penetrating the ground, were supposed responsible for developing the "seeds of gold" naturally found there.
4. The "age of gold."
5. Lines 16–20 are translated from a fragment of Euripides; Seneca tells us that when they were pronounced onstage, the audience was so indignant that it would allow the play to continue only after Euripides provided assurance that the speakers would be badly punished in the course of the play. A traditional epithet of Venus is "golden"; but Volpone is not satisfied with her minting a single golden boy; he wants a lot of them.

That canst do nought, and yet mak'st men do all things;
The price of souls; even hell, with thee to boot,
Is made worth heaven. Thou art virtue, fame,
Honor and all things else. Who can get thee,
He shall be noble, valiant, honest, wise—

MOSCA. And what he will, sir. Riches are in fortune
A greater good than wisdom is in nature.

VOLPONE. True, my belovéd Mosca. Yet I glory
More in the cunning purchase[6] of my wealth
Than in the glad possession, since I gain
No common way; I use no trade, no venture;
I wound no earth with plough-shares, fat no beasts
To feed the shambles; have no mills for iron,
Oil, corn, or men, to grind them into powder;[7]
I blow no subtle glass, expose no ships
To threat'nings of the furrow-facéd sea;
I turn no moneys[8] in the public bank,
Nor usure private.

MOSCA. No, sir, nor devour
Soft prodigals. You shall have some will swallow
A melting heir as glibly as your Dutch
Will pills of butter, and ne'er purge[9] for it;
Tear forth the fathers of poor families
Out of their beds, and coffin them alive
In some kind clasping prison, where their bones
May be forth-coming, when the flesh is rotten.
But your sweet nature doth abhor these courses;
You loathe the widow's or the orphan's tears
Should wash your pavements, or their piteous cries
Ring in your roofs, and beat the air for vengeance.

VOLPONE. Right, Mosca; I do loathe it.

MOSCA. And besides, sir,
You are not like the thresher that doth stand
With a huge flail, watching a heap of corn,
And, hungry, dares not taste the smallest grain,
But feeds on mallows, and such bitter herbs;
Nor like the merchant, who hath filled his vaults
With Romagnía, and rich Candian wines,
Yet drinks the lees of Lombard's vinegar.[1]

6. I.e., acquisition.

7. As Jonson wrote, household industries were just starting to be converted, in a few places, to factory industries run by water power. Glass was a Venetian specialty, in Jonson's day as now, but in England it was just starting to be used for glazing.

8. I.e., take no interest. Banking and money-lending were more important in Venice, where long voyages were common mercantile practice, than in England.

9. Suffer indigestion. Many jokes were made in the 17th century on the Dutch appetite for butter. Loan-sharks swallowed up heirs by lending them money at exorbitant rates against their future inheritance.

1. Romagnía was a sweet wine from Greece; Candian is wine from Crete (Candia). During the Renaissance good wine was thought to come from the eastern Mediterranean, or else from Spain (sack and canary). French and Italian wines ("Lombard's vinegar") were not much appreciated, and the "lees" (dregs) were of course the worst part of any bottle.

You will lie not in straw, whilst moths and worms
Feed on your sumptuous hangings and soft beds.
You know the use of riches, and dare give now
From that bright heap, to me, your poor observer,
Or to your dwarf, or your hermaphrodite,
Your eunuch, or what other household trifle
Your pleasure allows maintenance.

VOLPONE. Hold thee, Mosca,
[*Gives him money.*]
Take of my hand; thou strik'st on truth in all,
And they are envious term thee parasite.
Call forth my dwarf, my eunuch, and my fool,
And let them make me sport. [*Exit* MOSCA.] What should I do,
But cocker up[2] my genius, and live free
To all delights my fortune calls me to?
I have no wife, no parent, child, ally,
To give my substance to, but whom I make
Must be my heir; and this makes men observe me.
This draws new clients daily to my house,
Women and men of every sex and age,
That bring me presents, send me plate, coin, jewels,
With hope that when I die (which they expect
Each greedy minute) it shall then return
Ten-fold upon them; whilst some, covetous
Above the rest, seek to engross me whole,[3]
And counter-work the one unto the other,
Contend in gifts, as they would seem in love.
All which I suffer, playing with their hopes,
And am content to coin them into profit,
And look upon their kindness, and take more,
And look on that; still bearing them in hand,
Letting the cherry knock against their lips,
And draw it by their mouths, and back again.[4]—How now!

SCENE 2

[*Enter* MOSCA *with* NANO, ANDROGYNO, *and* CASTRONE.]

NANO. *Now, room for fresh gamesters, who do will you to know,*
They do bring you neither play nor university show;
And therefore do entreat you, that whatsoever they rehearse,
May not fare a whit the worse, for the false pace of the verse.[5]
If you wonder at this, you will wonder more ere we pass,
For know, here[6] *is enclosed the soul of Pythagoras,*

2. Pamper, indulge.
3. An engrosser bought up an entire crop of grain, held it for hard times, then sold it at exorbitant prices.
4. "Chop-cherry" is a country game in which a cherry hung from a string is dangled before a player who tries to catch it with his teeth.
5. This little interlude tells us something about the tastes of the man for whom it is performed. The loose, jog-trot meter that the characters recite is reminiscent of the vices in the old morality plays.
6. He points at Androgyno. The Greek philosopher Pythagoras put forward the

That juggler divine, as hereafter shall follow;
Which soul, fast and loose, sir, came first from Apollo,
And was breathed into Æthalides,[7] *Mercurius his son,*
Where it had the gift to remember all that ever was done.
From thence it fled forth, and made quick transmigration
To goldy-locked Euphorbus,[8] *who was killed in good fashion,*
At the siege of old Troy, by the cuckold of Sparta.
Hermotimus was next (I find it in my charta)[9]
To whom it did pass, where no sooner it was missing,
But with one Pyrrhus of Delos it learned to go a fishing;
And thence did it enter the sophist of Greece.
From Pythagore, she went into a beautiful piece,
Hight Aspasia, the meretrix;[1] *and the next toss of her*
Was again of a whore, she became a philosopher,
Crates the cynic,[2] *as itself doth relate it:*
Since kings, knights, and beggars, knaves, lords, and fools gat it,
Besides ox and ass, camel, mule, goat, and brock,[3]
In all which it hath spoke, as in the cobbler's cock.
But I come not here to discourse of that matter,
Or his one, two, or three, or his great oath, BY QUATER!
His musics, his trigon, his golden thigh,[4]
Or his telling how elements shift; but I
Would ask, how of late thou hast suffered translation,
And shifted thy coat in these days of reformation.
ANDROGYNO. *Like one of the reformed, a fool, as you see,*
Counting all old doctrine heresy.
NANO. *But not on thine own forbid meats hast thou ventured?*
And. *On fish, when first a Carthusian I entered.*[5]
NANO. *Why, then thy dogmatical silence hath left thee?*
And. *Of that an obstreperous lawyer bereft me.*[6]
NANO. *O wonderful change, when sir lawyer forsook thee!*
For Pythagore's sake, what body then took thee?

---

doctrine of transmigration of souls, and fantastic lineages were a frequent comic exercise in the Renaissance. Nano's comic story is copied from the life of Pythagoras, by Diogenes Laertius.

7. Herald of the Argonauts.

8. Trojan hero, killed by Menelaus, "the cuckold of Sparta"; Pythagoras specifically claimed to have been Euphorbus, and to recall the event.

9. Hermotimus is indeed mentioned in Nano's "charta," i.e., the text of Diogenes Laertius, but hardly anywhere else. Pyrrhus of Delos is an equally obscure figure, a fisherman mentioned only in Diogenes. The "sophist of Greece" is Pythagoras himself.

1. Whore; but Aspasia was simply the mistress of Pericles.

2. Crates was a philosopher of the Cynic school, a follower of Diogenes who professed a particularly bitter brand of scepticism.

3. Badger. Lucian's comic dialogue, "Gallus, or the Cock," which reproduces much of this material about Pythagoras, is a dialogue between a cobbler and a chicken.

4. Pythagorean theories about music and numerology, the Pythagorean theorem about right triangles, and the myth that Pythagoras had a golden thigh are glanced at here. A trigon is a triangle; the oath "by Quater" (four) is reported in Plutarch, *On the Sayings of the Philosophers*.

5. As a Carthusian monk (of a particularly strict sect), he learned to eat fish, which as a Pythagorean was forbidden to him.

6. Having taken a vow of silence as a Carthusian, he became a lawyer and learned to blabber.

ANDROGYNO. *A good dull mule.*

NANO. *And how! by that means*
Thou wert brought to allow of the eating of beans?[7]

ANDROGYNO. *Yes.*

NANO. *But from the mule into whom didst thou pass?*

ANDROGYNO. *Into a very strange beast, by some writers called an ass;*
By others, a precise, pure, illuminate brother,[8]
Of those devour flesh, and sometimes one another;
And will drop you forth a libel, or a sanctified lie,
Betwixt every spoonful of a nativity-pie.[9]

NANO. *Now quit thee, for heaven, of that profanenation,*
And gently report thy next transmigration.

ANDROGYNO. *To the same that I am.*

NANO. *A creature of delight,*
And, what is more than a fool, an hermaphrodite!
Now, prithee, sweet soul, in all thy variation,
Which body wouldst thou choose, to keep up thy station?

ANDROGYNO. *Troth, this I am in, even here would I tarry.*

NANO. *Cause here the delight of each sex thou canst vary?*

ANDROGYNO. *Alas, those pleasures be stale and forsaken;*
No, 'tis your fool wherewith I am so taken,
The only one creature that I can call blessed;[1]
For all other form I have proved most distressed.

NANO. *Spoke true, as thou wert in Pythagoras still.*
This learned opinion we celebrate will,
Fellow eunuch, as behooves us, with all our wit and art,
To dignify that whereof ourselves are so great and special a part.

VOLPONE. Now, very, very pretty! Mosca, this
Was thy invention?

MOSCA. If it please my patron,
Not else.

VOLPONE. It doth, good Mosca.

MOSCA. Then it was, sir.

[NANO *and* CASTRONE *sing.*[2]]

Fools, they are the only nation
Worth men's envy or admiration;
Free from care or sorrow-taking,
Selves and others merry making,
All they speak or do is sterling.
Your fool he is your great man's darling,
And your ladies' sport and pleasure;

7. Pythagoras forbade the eating of beans. All these prohibitions and special observances were supposed to have occult or mystical meaning.

8. All these adjectives would be understood as pointing at the Puritans, for whom Jonson had a standing aversion.

9. The Puritans did not like the old word "Christmas" because it included the "idolatrous" word "mass," so they began using the neutral word "Nativity," which Jonson here derides.

1. Jonson is drawing here on one of the wellsprings of Renaissance thought, Erasmus's mock-oration, *The Praise of Folly*.

2. The song is a patchwork of passages from Erasmus.

Tongue and bauble are his treasure.
E'en his face begetteth laughter,
And he speaks truth free from slaughter;
He's the grace of every feast,
And sometimes the chiefest guest;
Hath his trencher[3] *and his stool.*
When wit waits upon the fool,
O, who would not be
He, he. he? [*Knocking without.*]

VOLPONE. Who's that? Away! [*Exeunt* NANO *and* CASTRONE.]
Look, Mosca.
MOSCA. Fool, begone! [*Exit* ANDROGYNO.] 'Tis signor Voltore, the advocate;
I know him by his knock.
VOLPONE. Fetch me my gown,
My furs, and night-caps; say, my couch is changing,
And let him entertain himself awhile
Without i' the gallery. [*Exit* MOSCA.] Now, now my clients
Begin their visitation! Vulture, kite,
Raven, and gor-crow, all my birds of prey,[4]
That think me turning carcass, now they come;
I am not for them yet.
[*Re-enter* MOSCA, *with the gown, &c.*]
How now? The news?
MOSCA. A piece of plate,[5] sir.
VOLPONE. Of what bigness?
MOSCA. Huge,
Massy, and antique, with your name inscribed,
And arms engraven.
VOLPONE. Good! and not a fox
Stretched on the earth, with fine delusive sleights
Mocking a gaping crow?[6] ha, Mosca!
MOSCA. Sharp, sir.
VOLPONE. Give me my furs. [*Puts on his sick dress.*]
Why dost thou laugh so, man?
MOSCA. I cannot choose, sir, when I apprehend
What thoughts he has without now, as he walks:—
That this might be the last gift he should give;
That this would fetch you; if you died to-day,
And gave him all, what he should be to morrow;
What large return would come of all his ventures;

3. Dish.
4. Volpone foresees his visitors precisely in the order they come: Lady Politic is the kite, Corvino the gor-crow ("gor": filth). They are not, however, birds of prey, but all carrion-eaters.
5. A solid silver platter. In those days, when banks were uncertain and display important, families often put much of their wealth in massive silver dinnerware.
6. Volpone imagines an allegorical device, taken from one of Aesop's fables, engraved on the piece of plate. In essence, the story tells how the fox flattered the crow, sitting safely in a treetop with a piece of cheese, into trying to sing. When the foolish bird opened its mouth, the cheese fell to the ground for the fox to devour.

How he should worshipped be, and reverenced;
Ride with his furs and foot-cloths;[7] waited on
By herds of fools and clients; have clear way
Made for his mule, as lettered as himself;
Be called the great and learned advocate:
And then concludes, there's nought impossible.
VOLPONE. Yes, to be learned, Mosca.
MOSCA. O, no; rich
Implies it. Hood an ass with reverened purple,
So you can hide his two ambitious ears,
And he shall pass for a cathedral doctor.[8]
VOLPONE. My caps, my caps, good Mosca. Fetch him in.
MOSCA. Stay, sir; your ointment for your eyes.
VOLPONE. That's true;
Dispatch, dispatch.[9] I long to have possession
Of my new present.
MOSCA. That, and thousands more,
I hope to see you lord of.
VOLPONE. Thanks, kind Mosca.
MOSCA. And that, when I am lost in blended dust,
And hundred such as I am, in succession—
VOLPONE. Nay, that were too much, Mosca.
MOSCA. You shall live,
Still, to delude these harpies.
VOLPONE. Loving Mosca!
'Tis well. My pillow now, and let him enter. [*Exit* MOSCA.]
Now, my feigned cough, my phthisic, and my gout,
My apoplexy, palsy, and catarrhs,
Help, with your forcéd functions, this my posture,
Wherein, this three year, I have milked their hopes.
He comes; I hear him—Uh! [*coughing*] uh! uh! uh! O—

SCENE 3

[*Enter* MOSCA, *introducing* VOLTORE *with a piece of plate.*]

MOSCA. You still are what you were, sir. Only you,
Of all the rest, are he commands his love,
And you do wisely to preserve it thus,
With early visitation, and kind notes
Of your good meaning to him, which, I know,
Cannot but come most grateful. Patron! sir!
Here's signor Voltore is come—
VOLPONE. [*faintly*] What say you?
MOSCA. Sir, signor Voltore is come this morning
To visit you.

7. Ornate tapestries, laid upon the beast, not his rider; the furs would be for the lawyer.
8. The power of money to make the stupid wise, the ugly beautiful, and, in general, black white had been a satiric commonplace since antiquity. "Cathedral doctor": a doctor of theology (with the implication that he's not only the most pompous but the most stupid of the lot).
9. Hurry.

VOLPONE. I thank him.
MOSCA. And hath brought
A piece of antique plate, bought of St. Mark,[1]
With which he here presents you.
VOLPONE. He is welcome.
Pray him to come more often.
MOSCA. Yes.
VOLTORE. What says he?
MOSCA. He thanks you, and desires you see him often.
VOLPONE. Mosca.
MOSCA. My patron!
VOLPONE. Bring him near, where is he?
I long to feel his hand.
MOSCA. The plate is here, sir.
VOLTORE. How fare you, sir?
VOLPONE. I thank you, signor Voltore;
Where is the plate? mine eyes are bad.
VOLTORE. [*putting it into his hands*] I'm sorry,
To see you still thus weak.
MOSCA. [*aside*] That he's not weaker.
VOLPONE. You are too munificent.
VOLTORE. No, sir; would to heaven,
I could as well give health to you, as that plate!
VOLPONE. You give, sir, what you can; I thank you. Your love
Hath taste in this, and shall not be unanswered;
I pray you see me often.
VOLTORE. Yes, I shall, sir.
VOLPONE. Be not far from me.
MOSCA. Do you observe that, sir?
VOLPONE. Hearken unto me still; it will concern you.
MOSCA. You are a happy man, sir; know your good.
VOLPONE. I cannot now last long—
MOSCA. You are his heir, sir.
VOLTORE. Am I?
VOLPONE. I feel me going; Uh! uh! uh! uh!
I'm sailing to my port, Uh! uh! uh! uh!
And I am glad I am so near my haven.
MOSCA. Alas, kind gentleman! Well, we must all go—
VOLTORE. But, Mosca—
MOSCA. Age will conquer.
VOLTORE. 'Pray thee, hear me:
Am I inscribed his heir for certain?
MOSCA. Are you!
I do beseech you, sir, you will vouchsafe
To write me in your family.[2] All my hopes
Depend upon your worship. I am lost,
Except the rising sun do shine on me.
VOLTORE. It shall both shine, and warm thee, Mosca.

1. I.e., bought in Saint Mark's square.
2. I.e., inscribe me on the list of your servants.

MOSCA. Sir,
I am a man, that hath not done your love
All the worst offices.[3] Here I wear your keys,
See all your coffers and your caskets locked,
Keep the poor inventory of your jewels,
Your plate and moneys; am your steward, sir,
Husband[4] your goods here.
VOLTORE. But am I sole heir?
MOSCA. Without a partner, sir; confirmed this morning.
The wax is warm yet, and the ink scarce dry
Upon the parchment.
VOLTORE. Happy, happy, me!
By what good chance, sweet Mosca?
MOSCA. Your desert, sir;
I know no second cause.
VOLTORE. Thy modesty
Is loath to know it; well, we shall requite it.
MOSCA. He ever liked your course, sir; that first took him.
I oft have heard him say, how he admired
Men of your large profession, that could speak
To every cause, and things mere contraries,
Till they were hoarse again, yet all be law;
That, with most quick agility, could turn,
And return; make knots, and undo them;
Give forkéd counsel;[5] take provoking gold
On either hand, and put it up. These men,
He knew, would thrive with their humility.
And, for his part, he thought he should be blessed
To have his heir of such a suffering spirit,
So wise, so grave, of so perplexed a tongue,
And loud withal, that would not wag, nor scarce
Lie still, without a fee; when every word
Your worship but lets fall, is a sequin!—[6]
[*Knocking without.*]
Who's that? one knocks; I would not have you seen, sir.
And yet—pretend you came, and went in haste;
I'll fashion an excuse—and, gentle sir,
When you do come to swim in golden lard,
Up to the arms in honey, that your chin
Is born up stiff, with fatness of the flood,
Think on your vassal; but remember me:
I have not been your worst of clients.
VOLTORE. Mosca—
MOSCA. When will you have your inventory brought, sir?
Or see a copy of the will? [*Knocking again.*] Anon![7]

3. Services.
4. Safeguard.
5. Ambiguous, ambivalent advice. This ironic praise of lawyers is probably from Cornelius Agrippa's book influential *On the uncertainty and vanity of the sciences and arts* (1531).
6. Zecchino, a gold coin.
7. Said in response to a sharp rap at the door; a modern Mosca would say, "Coming!" See the game played by Prince Hal and Poins with a waiter who says nothing but "Anon!" in *1 Henry IV* II.iv.

I'll bring them to you, sir. Away, be gone;
Put business in your face. [*Exit* VOLTORE.]

VOLPONE. [*springing up*]
Excellent Mosca!
Come hither, let me kiss thee.

MOSCA. Keep you still, sir.
Here is Corbaccio.

VOLPONE. Set the plate away.
The vulture's gone, and the old raven's come.

SCENE 4

MOSCA. Betake you to your silence and your sleep.
[*Puts the plate away.*] Stand there and multiply. Now shall we see
A wretch who is indeed more impotent
Than this can feign to be; yet hopes to hop
Over his grave. [*Enter* CORBACCIO.] Signor Corbaccio!
You're very welcome, sir.

CORBACCIO. How does your patron?

MOSCA. Troth, as he did, sir; no amends.

CORBACCIO. What! mends he?

MOSCA. No, sir, he's rather worse.

CORBACCIO. That's well. Where is he?

MOSCA. Upon his couch, sir, newly fallen asleep.

CORBACCIO. Does he sleep well?

MOSCA. No wink, sir, all this night.
Nor yesterday; but slumbers.[8]

CORBACCIO. Good! he should take
Some counsel of physicians. I have brought him
An opiate here, from mine own doctor.

MOSCA. He will not hear of drugs.

CORBACCIO. Why? I myself
Stood by while it was made, saw all the ingredients,
And know it cannot but most gently work.
My life for his, 'tis but to make him sleep.

VOLPONE. [*aside*] Ay, his last sleep, if he would take it.

MOSCA. Sir,
He has no faith in physic.

CORBACCIO. Say you, say you?

MOSCA. He has no faith in physic. He does think
Most of your doctors are the greater danger,
And worse disease, t'escape. I often have
Heard him protest, that your physician
Should never be his heir.

CORBACCIO. Not I his heir?

MOSCA. Not your physician, sir.

CORBACCIO. O, no, no, no,
I do not mean it.

8. Cat-naps.

MOSCA. No, sir, nor their fees
He cannot brook; he says, they flay a man,
Before they kill him.
CORBACCIO. Right, I do conceive you.
MOSCA. And then they do it by experiment;
For which the law not only doth absolve them,
But gives them great reward; and he is loath
To hire his death, so.
CORBACCIO. It is true, they kill
With as much license as a judge.
MOSCA. Nay, more;
For he but kills, sir, where the law condemns,
And these can kill him too.
CORBACCIO. Ay, or me,
Or any man. How does his apoplex?
Is that strong on him still?
MOSCA. Most violent.
His speech is broken, and his eyes are set,
His face drawn longer than 'twas wont—
CORBACCIO. How! how!
Stronger than he was wont?
MOSCA. No, sir: his face
Drawn longer than 'twas wont.
CORBACCIO. O, good!
MOSCA. His mouth
Is ever gaping, and his eyelids hang.
CORBACCIO. Good.
MOSCA. A freezing numbness stiffens all his joints,
And makes the color of his flesh like lead.
CORBACCIO. 'Tis good.
MOSCA. His pulse beats slow and dull.
CORBACCIO. Good symptoms still.
MOSCA. And from his brain—
CORBACCIO. Ha? how? not from his brain?
MOSCA. Yes, sir, and from his brain—
CORBACCIO. I conceive you; good.
MOSCA. Flows a cold sweat, with a continual rheum,
Forth the resolvéd corners of his eyes.
CORBACCIO. Is't possible? Yet I am better, ha!
How does he, with the swimming of his head?
MOSCA. O, sir, 'tis past the scotomy;[9] he now
Hath lost his feeling, and hath left to snort.
You hardly can perceive him, that he breathes.
CORBACCIO. Excellent, excellent! sure I shall outlast him!
This makes me young again, a score of years.
MOSCA. I was a coming for you, sir.
CORBACCIO. Has he made his will?
What has he given me?

9. Dizziness, with dimness of sight.

MOSCA. No, sir.
CORBACCIO. Nothing? ha!
MOSCA. He has not made his will, sir.
CORBACCIO. Oh, oh, oh!
What then did Voltore, the lawyer, here?
MOSCA He smelt a carcass, sir, when he but heard
My master was about his testament;
As I did urge him to it for your good.
CORBACCIO. He came unto him, did he? I thought so.
MOSCA. Yes, and presented him this piece of plate.
CORBACCIO. To be his heir?
MOSCA. I do not know, sir.
CORBACCIO. True,
I know it too.
MOSCA. [*aside*] By your own scale, sir.[1]
CORBACCIO. Well,
I shall prevent him, yet. See, Mosca, look,
Here, I have brought a bag of bright sequins,
Will quite weigh down his plate.
MOSCA. [*taking the bag*] Yea, marry, sir.
This is true physic, this your sacred medicine;
No talk of opiates, to this great elixir![2]
CORBACCIO. 'Tis *aurum palpabile*,[3] if not *potabile*.
MOSCA. It shall be ministered to him, in his bowl.
CORBACCIO. Ay, do, do, do.
MOSCA. Most blesséd cordial!
This will recover him.
CORBACCIO. Yes, do, do, do.
MOSCA. I think it were not best, sir.
CORBACCIO. What?
MOSCA. To recover him.
CORBACCIO. O, no, no, no; by no means.
MOSCA. Why, sir, this
Will work some strange effect, if he but feel it.
CORBACCIO. 'Tis true, therefore forbear; I'll take my venture.
Give me it again.
MOSCA. At no hand; pardon me.
You shall not do yourself that wrong sir. I
Will so advise you, you shall have it all.
CORBACCIO. How?
MOSCA All, sir, 'tis your right, your own; no man
Can claim a part; 'tis yours without a rival,
Decreed by destiny.
CORBACCIO. How, how, good Mosca?

1. The phrase seems to imply, "You think so because that's the sort of creature you are yourself."
2. No comparison of sedatives ("opiates") to this great medicine is possible. The exlixir was supposed to be the supreme, universal medicine, capable of prolonging life indefinitely as well as of transforming baser metals to gold.
3. I.e., palpable, material gold; *aurum potabile,* or drinkable gold, was the elixir.

MOSCA. I'll tell you, sir. This fit he shall recover—
CORBACCIO. I do conceive you.
MOSCA. And, on first advantage
Of his gained sense, will I re-importune him
Unto the making of his testament.
And show him this. [*Pointing to the money.*]
CORBACCIO. Good, good.
MOSCA. 'Tis better yet,
If you will hear, sir.
CORBACCIO. Yes, with all my heart.
MOSCA. Now, would I counsel you, make home with speed;
There, frame a will, whereto you shall inscribe
My master your sole heir.
CORBACCIO. And disinherit
My son?
MOSCA. Oh, sir, the better: for that color
Shall make it much more taking.[4]
CORBACCIO. O, but color?
MOSCA. This will, sir, you shall send it unto me.
Now, when I come to enforce, as I will do,
Your cares, your watchings, and your many prayers,
Your more than many gifts, your this day's present,
And last, produce your will; where, without thought,
Or least regard unto your proper issue,
A son so brave and highly meriting,
The stream of your diverted love hath thrown you
Upon my master, and made him your heir:
He cannot be so stupid, or stone-dead,
But out of conscience, and mere gratitude—
CORBACCIO. He must pronounce me his?
MOSCA. 'Tis true.
CORBACCIO. This plot.
Did I think on before.
MOSCA. I do believe it.
CORBACCIO. Do you not believe it?
MOSCA. Yes, sir.
CORBACCIO. Mine own project.
MOSCA. Which, when he hath done, sir—
CORBACCIO. Published me his heir?
MOSCA. And you so certain to survive him—
CORBACCIO. Ay.
MOSCA. Being so lusty a man—
CORBACCIO. 'Tis true.
MOSCA. Yes, sir—
CORBACCIO. I thought on that too. See, how he should be
The very organ to express my thoughts!
MOSCA. You have not only done yourself a good—
CORBACCIO. But multiplied it on my son?

4. That circumstance or appearance ("color") will make the trick more effective.

MOSCA. 'Tis right, sir.
CORBACCIO. Still, my invention.
MOSCA. 'Las, sir! heaven knows,
It hath been all my study, all my care
(I e'en grow gray withal), how to work things—
CORBACCIO. I do conceive, sweet Mosca.
MOSCA. You are he,
For whom I labor, here.
CORBACCIO. Ay, do, do, do:
I'll straight about it. [*Going.*]
MOSCA. Rook go with you, raven![5]
CORBACCIO. I know thee honest.
MOSCA. [*aside*] You do lie, sir!
CORBACCIO. And—
MOSCA. Your knowledge is no better than your ears, sir.
CORBACCIO. I do not doubt, to be a father to thee.
MOSCA. Nor I to gull my brother of his blessing.[6]
CORBACCIO. I may have my youth restored to me, why not?
MOSCA. Your worship is a precious ass!
CORBACCIO. What sayest thou?
MOSCA. I do desire your worship to make haste, sir
CORBACCIO. 'Tis done, 'tis done; I go. [*Exit.*]
VOLPONE. [*leaping from his couch*] O, I shall burst!
Let out my sides, let out my sides—
MOSCA. Contain
Your flux of laughter, sir; you know this hope
Is such a bait, it covers any hook.
VOLPONE. O, but thy working, and thy placing it!
I cannot hold; good rascal, let me kiss thee:
I never knew thee in so rare a humor.
MOSCA. Alas, sir, I but do as I am taught;
Follow your grave instructions; give them words;
Pour oil into their ears, and send them hence.
VOLPONE. 'Tis true, 'tis true. What a rare punishment
Is avarice to itself![7]
MOSCA. Ay, with our help, sir.
VOLPONE. So many cares, so many maladies,
So many fears attending an old age,
Yea, death so often called on, as no wish
Can be more frequent with them, their limbs faint,
Their senses dull, their seeing, hearing, going,
All dead before them; yea, their very teeth,
Their instruments of eating, failing them:
Yet this is reckoned life! nay, here was one,
Is now gone home, that wishes to live longer!

5. The rook is a common crowlike bird, raucous and thievish; but Mosca is playing on a secondary meaning—cheat or deception: "May you be deceived, you raven!"

6. Jacob robbed Esau of his blessing by impersonating him before blind old Isaac (Genesis xxvii).

7. Seneca, Epistle 115, par. 16. Volpone is liberated, at least intellectually, from the vices on which he plays.

Feels not his gout, nor palsy; feigns himself
Younger by scores of years, flatters his age
With confident belying it, hopes he may,
With charms, like Æson,[8] have his youth restored;
And with these thoughts so battens, as if fate
Would be as easily cheated on, as he,
And all turns air! [*Knocking within.*] Who's that there, now? a third!

MOSCA. Close, to your couch again; I hear his voice:
It is Corvino, our spruce merchant.

VOLPONE. [*Lies down as before.*] Dead.[9]

MOSCA. Another bout, sir, with your eyes. [*Anointing them.*] —Who's there?

SCENE 5

[*Enter* CORVINO.]

Signor Corvino! come most wished for! O,
How happy were you, if you knew it, now!

CORVINO. Why? what? wherein?

MOSCA. The tardy hour is come, sir.

CORVINO. He is not dead?

MOSCA. Not dead, sir, but as good:
He knows no man.

CORVINO. How shall I do then?

MOSCA. Why, sir?

CORVINO. I have brought him here a pearl.

MOSCA. Perhaps he has
So much remembrance left, as to know you, sir.
He still calls on you; nothing but your name
Is in his mouth. Is your pearl orient,[1] sir?

CORVINO. Venice was never owner of the like.

VOLPONE. [*faintly*] Signor Corvino!

MOSCA. Hark.

VOLPONE. Signor Corvino!

MOSCA. He calls you; step and give it him.—He's here, sir,
And he has brought you a rich pearl.

CORVINO. How do you, sir?
Tell him, it doubles the twelfth carat.[2]

MOSCA. Sir,
He cannot understand, his hearing's gone;
And yet it comforts him to see you—

CORVINO. Say,
I have a diamond for him, too.

MOSCA. Best show it, sir;
Put it into his hand; 'tis only there

8. Aeson, Jason's father, was restored to life by the charms of Medea the witch.

9. I.e., "Pretend that I'm dead." The "bout . . . with your eyes" is a dose of gummy medicine.

1. Lustrous.

2. I.e., weighs 24 carats, or more than a third of an ounce—a huge pearl. "24-carat" has other overtones, as a measure of perfect purity in gold.

He apprehends:[3] he has his feeling, yet.
See how he grasps it!

CORVINO. 'Las, good gentleman!
How pitiful the sight is!

MOSCA. Tut! forget, sir.
The weeping of an heir should still be laughter
Under a visor.[4]

CORVINO. Why, am I his heir?

MOSCA. Sir, I am sworn, I may not show the will
Till he be dead; but here has been Corbaccio,
Here has been Voltore, here were others too,
I cannot number 'em, they were so many,
All gaping here for legacies; but I,
Taking the vantage of his naming you,
Signor Corvino, Signor Corvino, took
Paper, and pen, and ink, and there I asked him,
Whom he would have his heir? *Corvino.* Who
Should be executor? *Corvino.* And,
To any question he was silent to,
I still interpreted the nods he made,
Through weakness, for consent; and sent home th' others,
Nothing bequeathed them, but to cry and curse.

CORVINO. O, my dear Mosca! [*They embrace.*] Does he not perceive us?

MOSCA. No more than a blind harper.[5] He knows no man,
No face of friend, nor name of any servant,
Who 'twas that fed him last, or gave him drink;
Not those he hath begotten, or brought up,
Can he remember.

CORVINO. Has he children?

MOSCA. Bastards,
Some dozen, or more, that he begot on beggars,
Gypsies, and Jews, and black-moors, when he was drunk.
Knew you not that, sir? 'tis the common fable,
The dwarf, the fool, the eunuch, are all his;[6]
He's the true father of his family,
In all save me; but he has given them nothing.

CORVINO. That's well, that's well! Art sure he does not hear us?

MOSCA. Sure, sir! why, look you, credit your own sense.
[*Shouts in* VOLPONE's *ear.*]
The pox approach, and add to your diseases,
If it would send you hence the sooner, sir.
For your incontinenence, it hath deserved it

3. In English "apprehends" means "to understand intellectually," but the root Latin sense is "to grasp physically."
4. An heir should look sad by way of concealing his jubilation.
5. Playing the harp and singing ballads to it were traditional devices of blind beggars; but blindness in poets is sometimes accompanied by second sight, and Mosca knows that Volpone sees the situation clearly.
6. The suggestion that Volpone's playmates are his own children is never really contradicted.

Throughly and throughly, and the plague to boot!—
You may come near, sir—Would you would once close
Those filthy eyes of yours, that flow with slime,
Like two frog-pits; and those same hanging cheeks,
Covered with hide instead of skin—Nay, help, sir—
That look like frozen dish-clouts set on end!
CORVINO. Or like an old smoked wall, on which the rain
Ran down in streaks!
MOSCA. Excellent, sir! speak out.
You may be louder yet; a culverin[7]
Dischargéd in his ear would hardly bore it.
CORVINO. His nose is like a common sewer, still running.
MOSCA. 'Tis good! And what his mouth?
CORVINO. A very draught.[8]
MOSCA. O, stop it up—
CORVINO. By no means.
MOSCA. 'Pray you, let me:
Faith I could stifle him rarely with a pillow,
As well as any woman that should keep him.[9]
CORVINO. Do as you will; but I'll be gone.
MOSCA. Be so;
It is your presence makes him last so long.
CORVINO. I pray you, use no violence.
MOSCA. No, sir! why?
Why should you be thus scrupulous, pray you, sir?
CORVINO. Nay, at your discretion.
MOSCA. Well, good sir, be gone.
CORVINO. I will not trouble him now, to take my pearl?
MOSCA. Puh! nor your diamond. What a needless care
Is this afflicts you? Is not all here yours?
Am not I here? whom you have made your creature?
That owe my being to you?
CORVINO. Grateful Mosca!
Thou art my friend, my fellow, my companion,
My partner, and shalt share in all my fortunes.
MOSCA. Excepting one.
CORVINO. What's that?
MOSCA. Your gallant wife, sir.—
[*Exit* CORVINO.]
Now is he gone: we had no other means
To shoot him hence, but this.
VOLPONE. My divine Mosca!
Thou hast today outgone thyself. [*Knocking within.*]—
Who's there?
I will be troubled with no more. Prepare
Me music, dances, banquets, all delights;
The Turk is not more sensual in his pleasures,
Than will Volpone. [*Exit* MOSCA.] Let me see; a pearl!

7. Horse-pistol.
8. Cesspool.
9. I.e., "I could smother him as well as a nurse."

A diamond! plate! sequins! Good morning's purchase.
Why, this is better than rob churches,[1] yet;
Or fat, by eating, once a month, a man—[*Enter* MOSCA.]
Who is't?

MOSCA. The beauteous Lady Would-be, sir,
Wife to the English knight, Sir Politic Would-be
(This is the style, sir, is directed me),[2]
Hath sent to know how you have slept tonight,
And if you would be visited?

VOLPONE. Not now:
Some three hours hence—

MOSCA. I told the squire so much.

VOLPONE. When I am high with mirth and wine, then, then.
'Fore heaven, I wonder at the desperate valor
Of the bold English, that they dare let loose
Their wives to all encounters!

MOSCA. Sir, this knight
Had not his name for nothing, he is *politic*,[3]
And knows, howe'er his wife affect strange airs,
She hath not yet the face to be dishonest:[4]
But had she Signor Corvino's wife's face—

VOLPONE. Has she so rare a face?

MOSCA. O, sir, the wonder,
The blazing star of Italy! a wench
Of the first year! a beauty ripe as harvest![5]
Whose skin is whiter than a swan all over,
Than silver, snow, or lilies! a soft lip,
Would tempt you to eternity of kissing!
And flesh that melteth in the touch to blood!
Bright as your gold, and lovely as your gold!

VOLPONE. Why had not I known this before?

MOSCA. Alas, sir,
Myself but yesterday discovered it.

VOLPONE. How might I see her?

MOSCA. O, not possible;
She's kept as warily as is your gold;
Never does come abroad, never takes air,
But at a window. All her looks are sweet,
As the first grapes or cherries, and are watched
As near as they are.

VOLPONE. I must see her.

MOSCA. Sir,
There is a guard of ten spies thick upon her,
All his whole household; each of which is set
Upon his fellow, and have all their charge,
When he goes out, when he comes in, examined.

1. I.e., easy money.
2. I.e., "this is the way I've been told to announce her."
3. Devious, subtle.
4. I.e., "she's not beautiful enough to be unchaste."
5. A blazing star is literally a comet, hence a heavenly object of special attention. "A wench of the first year" seems to be a metaphor from winemaking, implying that the first crop of grapes makes the best wine.

VOLPONE. I will go see her, though but at her window.
MOSCA. In some disguise, then.
VOLPONE. That is true; I must
Maintain mine own shape still the same; we'll think.
[*Exeunt*.]

Act II

SCENE 1. *St. Mark's Place, before* CORVINO'S *house*

[*Enter* SIR POLITIC WOULD-BE, *and* PEREGRINE.]

SIR POLITIC. Sir, to a wise man, all the world's his soil.
It is not Italy, nor France, nor Europe,
That must bound me, if my fates call me forth.
Yet, I protest, it is no salt[6] desire
Of seeing countries, shifting a religion,
Nor any disaffection to the state
Where I was bred, and unto which I owe
My dearest plots,[7] hath brought me out; much less,
That idle, antique, stale, gray-headed project
Of knowing men's minds and manners, with Ulysses![8]
But a peculiar humor of my wife's,
Laid for this height of Venice, to observe,
To quote, to learn the language, and so forth.—
I hope you travel, sir, with license?[9]
PEREGRINE. Yes.
SIR POLITIC. I dare the safelier converse—How long, sir,
Since you left England?
PEREGRINE. Seven weeks.
SIR POLITIC. So lately!
You have not been with my lord ambassador?
PEREGRINE. Not yet, sir.
SIR POLITIC. Pray you, what news, sir, vents our climate?[1]
I heard last night a most strange thing reported
By some of my lord's followers, and I long
To hear how 'twill be seconded.
PEREGRINE. What was't, sir?
SIR POLITIC. Marry, sir, of a raven that should build
In a ship royal of the king's.[2]
PEREGRINE. This fellow,
Does he gull me,[3] trow? or is gulled?—Your name, sir?
SIR POLITIC. My name is Politic Would-be.
PEREGRINE. [*aside*] O, that speaks him.—
A knight, sir?
SIR POLITIC. A poor knight, sir.
PEREGRINE. Your lady

6. Wanton, frivolous.
7. Projects, notions.
8. Ulysses (Homer says) knew the minds of many men and saw many cities. The "humor" of Sir Politic's wife was exactly calculated, he thinks, to bring her to Venice.
9. I.e., special permission to travel abroad.
1. I.e., "What news does our climate give off?"
2. A raven is a bird of ill omen.
3. To "gull" is constantly used in the sense of to fool or deceive; "trow?": do you think?

Lies here in Venice, for intelligence
Of tires and fashions, and behavior,
Among the courtesans?[4] the fine Lady Would-be?
SIR POLITIC. Yes, sir; the spider and the bee, oft-times
Suck from one flower.
PEREGRINE. Good Sir Politic,
I cry you mercy; I have heard much of you.
'Tis true, sir, of your raven.
SIR POLITIC. On your knowledge?
PEREGRINE. Yes, and your lion's whelping in the Tower.[5]
SIR POLITIC. Another whelp!
PEREGRINE. Another, sir.
SIR POLITIC. Now, heaven!
What prodigies be these? The fires at Berwick![6]
And the new star! these things concurring, strange
And full of omen! Saw you those meteors?
PEREGRINE. I did, sir.
SIR POLITIC. Fearful! Pray you, sir, confirm me,
Were there three porpoises seen above the bridge,
As they give out?[7]
PEREGRINE. Six, and a sturgeon, sir.
SIR POLITIC. I am astonished.
PEREGRINE. Nay, sir, be not so;
I'll tell you a greater prodigy than these.
SIR POLITIC. What should these things portend?
PEREGRINE. The very day
(Let me be sure) that I put forth from London,
There was a whale discovered in the river,
As high as Woolwich, that had waited there,
Few know how many months, for the subversion
Of the Stade fleet.[8]
SIR POLITIC. Is't possible? believe it,
'Twas either sent from Spain, or the Archduke's:
Spinola's whale, upon my life, my credit![9]
Will they not leave these projects? Worthy sir,
Some other news.
PEREGRINE. Faith, Stone the fool is dead,
And they do lack a tavern fool extremely.

4. Attires, costumes. Venetian prostitutes were for hundreds of years reputed to be the most desirable in Europe, perhaps because Pietro Aretino advertised them so flatteringly in his pornographic poems.
5. Lions were in fact kept caged in the Tower of London, and cubs were whelped from time to time. Most of the events to which Sir Politic alludes had in fact occurred shortly before the time of the play's first production, and would have been familiar to the audience.
6. A new star appeared in October, 1604, and the aurora borealis over Berwick in January, 1605, was said to resemble armies of men fighting in the sky.
7. It was unusual for deep-sea creatures to venture up the Thames, past London Bridge.
8. The Stade fleet was the Danish fleet at the mouth of the Elbe river. How a whale in the Thames could subvert it is not very clear.
9. Sir Politic's suggestions about the origin of the whale all involve Spain. It comes either from Spain itself, or from the Archduke Albert, ruler of the Spanish Netherlands in the name of Philip II, or from Ambrosio Spinola, general of the Spanish armies in Holland.

SIR POLITIC. Is Mas' Stone dead?[1]
PEREGRINE. He's dead, sir; why, I hope
You thought him not immortal?—O, this knight,
Were he well known, would be a precious thing
To fit our English stage. He that should write
But such a fellow, should be thought to feign
Extremely, if not maliciously.
SIR POLITIC. Stone dead!
PEREGRINE. Dead. Lord! how deeply, sir, you apprehend it!
He was no kinsman to you?
SIR POLITIC. That I know of.
Well! that same fellow was an unknown fool.
PEREGRINE. And yet you knew him, it seems?
SIR POLITIC. I did so. Sir,
I knew him one of the most dangerous heads
Living within the state, and so I held him.
PEREGRINE. Indeed, sir?
SIR POLITIC. While he lived, in action.
He has received weekly intelligence,
Upon my knowledge, out of the Low Countries,
For all parts of the world, in cabbages;[2]
And those dispensed again to ambassadors,
In oranges, musk-melons, apricots,
Lemons, pome-citrons, and such-like; sometimes
In Colchester oysters, and your Selsey cockles.[3]
PEREGRINE. You make me wonder.
SIR POLITIC. Sir, upon my knowledge.
Nay, I've observed him, at your public ordinary,[4]
Take his advertisement from a traveler
(A concealed statesman) in a trencher of meat;
And instantly, before the meal was done,
Convey an answer in a tooth-pick.
PEREGRINE. Strange!
How could this be, sir?
SIR POLITIC. Why, the meat was cut
So like his character, and so laid, as he
Must easily read the cipher.
PEREGRINE. I have heard,
He could not read, sir.
SIR POLITIC. So 'twas given out,
In polity,[5] by those that did employ him:
But he could read, and had your languages,
And to't,[6] as sound a noddle—
PEREGRINE. I have heard, sir,

1. Stone the fool was an actual figure, about whom various anecdotes survive. "Mas' ": short for Master, the common denomination of fools and boys.
2. Cabbages were a recent importation from Holland.
3. "Pomecitrons" we would call simply "citrons." The oysters and cockles specified were the best shellfish to be had in England, and were often served to royalty.
4. Common tavern. Advertisement: secret message, tip.
5. For political reasons, as part of his cover story.
6. In addition.

That your baboons were spies, and that they were
A kind of subtle nation near to China.

SIR POLITIC. Ay, ay, your Mamaluchi.[7] Faith, they had
Their hand in a French plot or two; but they
Were so extremely given to women, as
They made discovery of all; yet I
Had my advices here, on Wednesday last,
From one of their own coat, they were returned,
Made their relations, as the fashion is,
And now stand fair for fresh employment.

PEREGRINE. [*aside*] 'Heart!
This Sir Politic will be ignorant of nothing.
—It seems, sir, you know all.

SIR POLITIC. Not all, sir; but
I have some general notions. I do love
To note and to observe; though I live out,
Free from the active torrent, yet I'd mark
The currents and the passages of things,
For mine own private use; and know the ebbs
And flows of state,

PEREGRINE. Believe it, sir, I hold
Myself in no small tie unto my fortunes,
For casting me thus luckily upon you,
Whose knowledge, if your bounty equal it,
May do me great assistance, in instruction
For my behavior, and my bearing, which
Is yet so rude and raw.

SIR POLITIC. Why? came you forth
Empty of rules for travel?

PEREGRINE. Faith, I had
Some common ones, from out that vulgar grammar,
Which he that cried Italian to me, taught me.[8]

SIR POLITIC. Why this it is that spoils all our brave bloods,
Trusting our hopeful gentry unto pedants,
Fellows of outside, and mere bark.[9] You seem
To be a gentleman, of ingenuous race:
I not profess it, but my fate hath been
To be, where I have been consulted with,
In this high kind, touching some great men's sons,
Persons of blood and honor.—

PEREGRINE. [*seeing people approach*] Who be these, sir?

SCENE 2

[*Enter* MOSCA *and* NANO *disguised, followed by persons with materials for erecting a stage.*]

MOSCA. Under that window, there 't must be. The same.

7. Mameluchi is the Italian form of *mamelukes*, a group of slaves and warriors originally from Circassia, in Asia Minor, who held or controlled the throne of Egypt for many years.

8. Trained me in the pronunciation of Italian.

9. Superficial and ignorant teachers.

SIR POLITIC. Fellows, to mount a bank. Did your instructor
In the dear tongues, never discourse to you
Of the Italian mountebanks?[1]
PEREGRINE. Yes, sir.
SIR POLITIC. Why,
Here you shall see one.
PEREGRINE. They are quacksalvers,
Fellows that live by venting[2] oils and drugs?
SIR POLITIC. Was that the character he gave you of them?
PEREGRINE. As I remember.
SIR POLITIC. Pity his ignorance.
They are the only knowing men of Europe!
Great general scholars, excellent physicians,
Most admired statesmen, professed favorites,
And cabinet counselors to the greatest princes;
The only languaged men of all the world![3]
PEREGRINE. And, I have heard, they are most lewd impostors;
Made all of terms and shreds; no less beliers
Of great men's favors, than their own vile medicines;
Which they will utter upon monstrous oaths,
Selling that drug for two-pence, ere they part,
Which they have valued at twelve crowns before.
SIR POLITIC. Sir, calumnies are answered best with silence.
Yourself shall judge—Who is it mounts, my friends?
MOSCA. Scoto of Mantua, sir.[4]
SIR POLITIC. Is't he? Nay, then
I'll proudly promise, sir, you shall behold
Another man than has been phant'sied[5] to you.
I wonder yet, that he should mount his bank,
Here in this nook, that has been wont t'appear
In face of the Piazza!—Here he comes.
[*Enter* VOLPONE *disguised as a mountebank and followed by a crowd of people.*]
VOLPONE. [*to* NANO] Mount, zany.[6]
MOB. Follow, follow, follow, follow, follow!
SIR POLITIC. See how the people follow him! he's a man
May write ten thousand crowns in bank here. Note,
[VOLPONE *mounts the stage.*]
Mark but his gesture: I do use to observe
The state he keeps in getting up.

1. The word "mountebank" comes from the Italian *montambanco*, meaning "to mount the bench": other terms for the same fellow are *saltimbanco* and *charlatan*. They were a mixture of public entertainer and patent-medicine salesman who gave a very considerable semi-dramatic, improvised performance before delivering their pitch.
2. Vending.
3. The best talkers.
4. Scoto of Mantua was a real person, a juggler, magician, and performer at legerdemain; he actually visited England and performed before Queen Elizabeth, about a quarter of a century before *Volpone* had its first performance.
5. Described to you.
6. Zany: from the Italian name *Giovanni*; a generic term for a fool, clown, performer. The speech of the crowd is intended to mimic a confused hubbub.

PEREGRINE. 'Tis worth it, sir.

VOLPONE. *Most noble gentlemen, and my worthy patrons! It may seem strange, that I, your Scoto Mantuano, who was ever wont to fix my bank in face of the public Piazza, near the shelter of the Portico to the Procuratia,*[7] *should now, after eight months' absence from this illustrious city of Venice, humbly retire myself into an obscure nook of the Piazza.*

SIR POLITIC. Did not I now object the same?

PEREGRINE. Peace, sir.

VOLPONE. *Let me tell you: I am not, as your Lombard proverb saith, cold on my feet;*[8] *or content to part with my commodities at a cheaper rate, than I accustomed: look not for it. Nor that the calumnious reports of that impudent detractor, and shame to our profession (Alessandro Buttone, I mean), who gave out, in public, I was condemned a* sforzato *to the galleys, for poisoning the cardinal Bembo's—*[9] *cook, hath at all attached, much less dejected me. No, no, worthy gentlemen; to tell you true, I cannot endure to see the rabble of these ground ciarlitani,*[1] *that spread their cloaks on the pavement, as if they meant to do feats of activity, and then come in lamely, with their moldy tales out of Boccaccio,*[2] *like stale Tabarin, the fabulist: some of them discoursing their travels, and of their tedious captivity in the Turks' galley, when, indeed, were the truth known, they were the Christians' galleys, where very temperately they ate bread, and drunk water, as a wholesome penance, enjoined them by their confessors, for base pilferies.*[3]

SIR POLITIC. Note but his bearing, and contempt of these.

VOLPONE. *These turdy-facy-nasty-paty-lousy-fartical rogues, with one poor groat's-worth of unprepared antimony, finely wrapped up in several* scartoccios,[4] *are able, very well, to kill their twenty a week, and play; yet, these meager, starved spirits, who have half stopped the organs of their minds with earthy oppilations,*[5] *want not their favorers among your shrivelled salad-eating artisans, who are overjoyed that they may*

7. The arcade along the north side of Piazza San Marco, where the Procurators resided. Jonson takes great pains to make his Venetian details specific and accurate.

8. There is in fact an Italian proverb, "*Haver freddo a'piedi,*" meaning "to be so hard up that one has to sell one's goods at a loss."

9. Alessandro Buttone is an imaginary rival who has dreamed up a slander against Scoto—but the tale is most unlikely since Cardinal Bembo died in 1547, more than 50 years before the play is supposed to be taking place. A *sforzato* is a galley-slave; the dash before "cook" is supposed to indicate that the title of "cook" is just a euphemism.

1. Ground *ciarlatani* or charlatans put on their acts and sold their nostrums at street level.

2. Boccaccio told in the *Decameron* a great many popular stories; as he lived in the 14th century, the tales were "moldy" by the 17th. Like Scoto, Tabarine was an actual Italian comedian of the time who performed in France (not, so far as we know, in England) during the 1570's.

3. Venetian galleys required many oars, often operated by captive Turks or condemned criminals, chained to the bench, fed miserable food, and whipped mercilessly.

4. Antimony was the basis of most common emetics; *scartoccios* were little paper envelopes in which drugs were placed.

5. Obstructions.

have their half-p'orth of physic; though it purge them into another world, it makes no matter.

SIR POLITIC. Excellent! have you heard better language, sir?

VOLPONE. *Well, let them go. And, gentlemen, honorable gentlemen, know, that for this time, our bank, being thus removed from the clamors of the* canaglia,[6] *shall be the scene of pleasure and delight; for I have nothing to sell, little or nothing to sell.*

SIR POLITIC. I told you, sir, his end.

PEREGRINE. You did so, sir.

VOLPONE. *I protest, I, and my six servants, are not able to make of this precious liquor, so fast as it is fetched away from my lodging by gentlemen of your city; strangers of the Terra-*firma;[7] *worshipful merchants; ay, and senators too: who, ever since my arrival, have detained me to their uses, by their splendidous liberalities. And worthily; for, what avails your rich man to have his magazines stuffed with* moscadelli,[8] *or of the purest grape, when his physicians prescribe him, on pain of death, to drink nothing but water cocted*[9] *with aniseeds? O, health! health! the blessing of the rich! the riches of the poor! who can buy thee at too dear a rate, since there is no enjoying this world without thee? Be not then so sparing of your purses, honorable gentlemen, as to abridge the natural course of life—*

PEREGRINE. You see his end.

SIR POLITIC. Ay, is't not good?

VOLPONE. *For, when a humid flux, or catarrh, by the mutability of air, falls from your head into an arm or shoulder, or any other part; take you a ducat, or your sequin of gold, and apply to the place affected: see what good effect it can work.*[1] *No, no, 'tis this blessed* unguento, *this rare extraction, that hath only power to disperse all malignant humours, that proceed either of hot, cold, moist, or windy causes—*

PEREGRINE. I would he had put in dry too.[2]

SIR POLITIC. 'Pray you, observe.

VOLPONE. *To fortify the most indigest and crude stomach, ay, were it of one that, through extreme weakness, vomited blood, applying only a warm napkin to the place, after the unction and fricace;*[3]*—for the* vertigine *in the head, putting but a drop into your nostrils, likewise behind the ears; a most sovereign and approved remedy: the* Mal Caduco, *cramps, convulsions, paralyses, epilepsies,* Tremor-Cordia, *retired nerves, ill vapors of the spleen, stoppings of the liver, the stone, the stran-*

6. The common mob.
7. *Terra firma* is still the Venetian term for land across the lagoon, the mainland.
8. Muscadel or muscatel is wine made from certain grapes, in Italian *moscatini,* which seem to have the perfume of musk.
9. Flavored.
1. I.e., money won't cure your cold when you catch it (but my "blessed unguent" will).
2. Of the four "humours" or ingredients of a balanced human complexion, "Scoto" has left out one, as Peregrine drily observes.
3. Anointing and massage.

gury, Hernia Ventosa, Ilica Passio; *stops a* dysenteria *immediately; easeth the torsion of the small guts, and cures* Melancholia Hypocondriaca,[4] *being taken and applied, according to my printed receipt.* [Pointing to his bill and his vial.] *For, this is the physician, this the medicine; this counsels, this cures; this gives the direction, this works the effect; and, in sum, both together may be termed an abstract of the theoric and practic*[5] *in the Æsculapian art. 'Twill cost you eight crowns. And, Zan Fritada,*[6] *prithee sing a verse extempore in honor of it.*

SIR POLITIC. How do you like him, sir?

PEREGRINE. Most strangely, I!

SIR POLITIC. Is not his language rare?

PEREGRINE. But alchemy,[7]
I never heard the like; or Broughton's books.

[NANO *sings.*]

Had old Hippocrates, or Galen,[8]
That to their books put med'cines all in,
But known this secret, they had never
(Of which they will be guilty ever)
Been murderers of so much paper,
Or wasted many a hurtless taper;
No Indian drug had e'er been famed,
Tobacco, sassafras not named;
Ne yet, of guacum[9] *one small stick, sir,*
Nor Raymond Lully's great elixir.
Ne had been known the Danish Gonswart,
Or Paracelsus, with his long sword.[1]

PEREGRINE. All this, yet, will not do; eight crowns is high.

VOLPONE. *No more. Gentlemen, if I had but time to discourse to you the miraculous effects of this my oil, surnamed* oglio del Scoto;[2] *with the countless catalogue of those I have cured of the aforesaid, and many more diseases; the patents and privileges of all the princes and commonwealths of Christendom; or but the depositions of those that appeared on my part, before the signory of the Sanita*[3] *and most learned College of Physicians; where I was authorized, upon notice taken*

4. "*Melancholia Hypocondriaca*" is black depression. The other ailments are: *Mal Caduco,* falling sickness, epilepsy; *Tremor Cordia,* palpitations of the heart; strangury, painful urination; *Hernia Ventosa,* gassy hernia; *Iliaca Passio,* cramps of the small intestine.

5. Theory and practice. The Aesculapian art: medicine (from Aesculapius, Greek god of medicine).

6. Literally, "Johnny Omelet," obviously one of the mountebank's stooges.

7. Except for alchemy. Johnson had no use for the books of Hugh Broughton, a Puritan divine and rabbinical scholar.

8. Famous doctors of the Classical world.

9. Modern guaiacum, obtained from the bark of a South American tree.

1. Raymond Lully or Lull was a Spanish mystic philosopher of the 13th century who claimed to have discovered the elixir. "The Danish Gonswart": unidentifiable. Paracelsus, the famous German doctor of the 16th century, had a famous sword in the handle of which he kept, according to legend, familiar spirits, and according to history, medications and herbs.

2. Scoto's oil.

3. The Board of Medical Examiners in Venice.

of the admirable virtues of my medicaments, and mine own excellency in matter of rare and unknown secrets, not only to disperse them publicly in this famous city, but in all the territories, that happily joy under the government of the most pious and magnificent states of Italy. But may some other gallant fellow say, 'O, there be divers that make profession to have as good, and as experimented receipts as yours.' Indeed, very many have essayed, like apes, in imitation of that which is really and essentially in me, to make of this oil; bestowed great cost in furnaces, stills, alembics,[4] *continual fires, and preparation of the ingredients, (as indeed there goes to it six hundred several simples,*[5] *besides some quantity of human fat, for the conglutination, which we buy of the anatomists) but, when these practitioners come to the last decoction, blow, blow, puff, puff, and all flies in* fumo:[6] *ha, ha, ha! Poor wretches, I rather pity their folly and indiscretion, than their loss of time and money; for those may be recovered by industry: but to be a fool born, is a disease incurable.*

For myself, I always from my youth have endeavored to get the rarest secrets, and book them, either in exchange, or for money: I spared nor cost nor labor, where anything was worthy to be learned. And, gentlemen, honorable gentlemen; I will undertake, by virtue of chemical art, out of the honorable hat that covers your head, to extract the four elements; that is to say, the fire, air, water, and earth, and return you your felt without burn or stain. For, whilst others have been at the balloo,[7] *I have been at my book; and am now past the craggy paths of study, and come to the flowery plains of honor and reputation.*

SIR POLITIC. I do assure you, sir, that is his aim.

VOLPONE. *But to our price—*

PEREGRINE. And that withal, sir Pol.

VOLPONE. *You all know, honorable gentlemen, I never valued this* ampulla, *or vial, at less than eight crowns; but for this time, I am content to be deprived of it for six: six crowns is the price, and less in courtesy I know you cannot offer me; take it or leave it, howsoever, both it and I am at your service. I ask you not as the value of the thing, for then I should demand of you a thousand crowns; so the cardinals* Montalto, *Farnese, the great duke of Tuscany, my gossip,*[8] *with divers other princes, have given me; but I despise money. Only to show my affection to you, honorable gentlemen, and your illustrious state here, I have neglected the messages of these princes, mine own offices, framed my journey hither, only to*

4. Distilleries, retorts.
5. Herbs.
6. In smoke; "decoction": boiling down.
7. Balloon, ball; i.e., while others have been diverting themselves with ball games.
8. My good friend. Cardinal Montalto became Pope as Sixtus the Fifth in 1585; Alessandro Farnese had been Pope as Paul III in 1534; "the great duke of Tuscany" was Cosimo de Medici.

present you with the fruits of my travels. [*To* NANO.]—*Tune your voices once more to the touch of your instruments, and give the honorable assembly some delightful recreation.*

PEREGRINE. What monstrous and most painful circumstance
Is here, to get some three or four *gazettes*,[9]
Some three-pence in the whole! for that 'twill come to.

[NANO *sings.*]
You that would last long, list to my song,
Make no more coil,[1] *but buy of this oil.*
Would you be ever fair and young?
Stout of teeth, and strong of tongue?
Tart of palate? quick of ear?
Sharp of sight? of nostril clear?
Moist of hand and light of foot?
Or, I will come nearer to't,
Would you live free from all diseases?
Do the act your mistress pleases,
Yet fright all aches from your bones?
Here's a medicine for the nones.[2]

VOLPONE. *Well, I am in a humor at this time to make a present of the small quantity my coffer contains; to the rich in courtesy, and to the poor for God's sake. Wherefore, now mark: I asked you six crowns; and six crowns, at other times, you have paid me; you shall not give me six crowns, nor five, nor four, nor three, nor two, nor one; nor half a ducat; no, nor a* mocenigo.[3] *Sixpence it will cost you, or six hundred pound—expect no lower price, for, by the banner of my front, I will not bate a* bagatine,[4]*—that I will have, only, a pledge of your loves, to carry something from amongst you, to show I am not contemned by you. Therefore, now, toss your handkerchiefs, cheerfully, cheerfully;*[5] *and be advertised, that the first heroic spirit that deigns to grace me with a handkerchief, I will give it a little remembrance of something, beside, shall please it better, than if I had presented it with a double pistolet.*[6]

PEREGRINE. Will you be that heroic spark, sir Pol?

[CELIA *at a window above, throws down her handkerchief.*]

O, see! the window has prevented[7] you.

VOLPONE. *Lady, I kiss your bounty; and for this timely grace you have done your poor Scoto of Mantua, I will return you, over and above my oil, a secret of that high and inestimable nature,*

9. The smallest Venetian coins, worth less than an English penny.
1. Stir, fuss.
2. For the occasion.
3. A Venetian coin, worth about nine English pennies.
4. A tiny coin.
5. When business was brisk at the mountebank's stand, customers sometimes knotted their money in a handkerchief or glove and tossed it on stage; the money was taken out, replaced with the medicine, and the handkerchief tossed back to the purchaser.
6. A double pistolet was a Spanish coin of some value, worth not much less than an English pound.
7. Forestalled, anticipated.

shall make you for ever enamored on that minute, wherein your eye first descended on so mean, yet not altogether to be despised, an object. Here is a powder concealed in this paper, of which, if I should speak to the worth, nine thousand volumes were but as one page, that page as a line, that line as a word; so short is this pilgrimage of man (which some call life) to the expressing of it. Would I reflect on the price? why, the whole world were but as an empire, that empire as a province, that province as a bank, that bank as a private purse to the purchase of it. I will only tell you; it is the powder that made Venus a goddess, (given her by Apollo,) that kept her perpetually young, cleared her wrinkles, firmed her gums, filled her skin, colored her hair; from her derived to Helen, and at the sack of Troy unfortunately lost; till now, in this our age, it was as happily recovered, by a studious antiquary, out of some ruins of Asia, who sent a moiety[8] of it to the court of France, (but much sophisticated,) wherewith the ladies there now color their hair. The rest, at this present, remains with me; extracted to a quintessence, so that, wherever it but touches, in youth it perpetually preserves, in age restores the complexion; seats your teeth, did they dance like virginal jacks,[9] firm as a wall; makes them white as ivory, that were black as———

SCENE 3

[*Enter* CORVINO.]

CORVINO. Spite o' the devil, and my shame! come down, here;
Come down; [*To* VOLPONE.]—No house but mine to make your scene?
Signor Flaminio,[1] will you down, sir? down?
What, is my wife your Franciscina, sir?
No windows on the whole Piazza, here,
To make your properties, but mine? but mine? [*Beats away* VOLPONE, NANO, *&c.*]
Heart! ere to-morrow I shall be new-christened,
And called the *Pantalone di Bisognosi*,[2]
About the town.

PEREGRINE. What should this mean, sir Pol?

SIR POLITIC. Some trick of state, believe it; I will home.

PEREGRINE. It may be some design on you.

SIR POLITIC. I know not.
I'll stand upon my guard.

PEREGRINE. It is your best, sir.

SIR POLITIC. This three weeks, all my advices, all my letters,
They have been intercepted.

8. Fraction; "sophisticated": refined, purified.
9. The quills that pluck the strings of a harpsichord ("virginal").
1. Signor Flaminio was Flaminio Scala, a Venetian comic actor of the day; Franciscina is an always-available serving girl in popular Italian comedy (*commedia dell'arte*).
2. Pantaloon of the Paupers. Pantaloon, in the tradition of *commedia dell'arte*, is a doddering old fool in perpetual terror of being cuckolded.

PEREGRINE. Indeed, sir!
Best have a care.
SIR POLITIC. Nay, so I will.
PEREGRINE. This knight,
I may not lose him, for my mirth, till night. [*Exeunt.*]

SCENE 4. *A room in* VOLPONE'*s house*

[*Enter* VOLPONE *and* MOSCA.]

VOLPONE. O, I am wounded!
MOSCA. Where, sir?
VOLPONE. Not without;
Those blows were nothing; I could bear them ever.
But angry Cupid, bolting from her eyes,
Hath shot himself into me like a flame,
Where, now, he flings about his burning heat,
As in a furnace an ambitious[3] fire,
Whose vent is stopped. The fight is all within me.
I cannot live, except thou help me, Mosca;
My liver melts, and I, without the hope
Of some soft air, from her refreshing breath,
Am but a heap of cinders.
MOSCA. 'Las, good sir,
Would you had never seen her!
VOLPONE. Nay, would thou
Hadst never told me of her!
MOSCA. Sir, 'tis true;
I do confess I was unfortunate,
And you unhappy: but I'm bound in conscience,
No less than duty, to effect my best
To your release of torment, and I will, sir.
VOLPONE. Dear Mosca, shall I hope?
MOSCA. Sir, more than dear,
I will not bid you to despair of aught
Within a human compass.
VOLPONE. O, there spoke
My better angel. Mosca, take my keys,
Gold, plate, and jewels, all's at thy devotion;[4]
Employ them how thou wilt; nay, coin me too,
So thou, in this, but crown my longings. Mosca?
MOSCA. Use but your patience.
VOLPONE. So I have.
MOSCA. I doubt not
To bring success to your desires.
VOLPONE. Nay, then,
I not repent me of my late disguise.
MOSCA. If you can horn[5] him, sir, you need not.
VOLPONE. True:
Besides, I never meant him for my heir.—

3. Aspiring, growing. Most of Volpone's erotic torments are of the sort popularized 300 years before by Francesco Petrarca.
4. At your service.
5. Cuckold.

Is not the color of my beard and eyebrows
To make me known?

MOSCA. No jot.

VOLPONE. I did it well.

MOSCA. So well, would I could follow you in mine,
With half the happiness!—and yet I would
Escape your epilogue.[6]

VOLPONE. But were they gulled
With a belief that I was Scoto?

MOSCA. Sir,
Scoto himself could hardly have distinguished!
I have not time to flatter you now, we'll part:
And as I prosper, so applaud my art. [*Exeunt.*]

SCENE 5. *A room in* CORVINO'*s house*

[*Enter* CORVINO, *sword in his hand, dragging in* CELIA.]

CORVINO. Death of mine honor, with the city's fool!
A juggling, tooth-drawing, prating mountebank!
And at a public window! where, whilst he,
With his strained action, and his dole[7] of faces,
To his drug-lecture draws your itching ears,
A crew of old, unmarried, noted lechers,
Stood leering up like satyrs: and you smile
Most graciously, and fan your favors forth,
To give your hot spectators satisfaction!
What, was your mountebank their call?[8] their whistle?
Or were you enamored on his copper rings,
His saffron jewel, with the toad-stone in't?
Or his embroidered suit, with the cope-stitch,
Made of a hearse cloth?[9] or his old tilt-feather?
Or his starched beard? Well! you shall have him, yes!
He shall come home, and minister unto you
The fricace for the mother.[1] Or, let me see,
I think you'd rather mount;[2] would you not mount?
Why, if you'll mount, you may; yes, truly, you may:
And so you may be seen, down to the foot.
Get you a cittern,[3] lady Vanity,
And be a dealer with the virtuous man;
Make one: I'll but protest myself a cuckold,
And save your dowry.[4] I'm a Dutchman, I!
For, if you thought me an Italian,

6. Avoid the beating you got.
7. Guile, trickery; the suggestion is of false faces or masks.
8. I.e., did you arrange the appearance of Scoto deliberately to draw a crowd?
9. Copper rings and toad-stone jewelry are Corvino's sneers at the cheap and flashy dress of the mountebank, whose suit (he imagines) is made of coarse brown burlap ("hearse-cloth") prettied up with embroidery.
1. Massage for the womb.
2. I.e., both on the man and on the stage.
3. A kind of guitar, with which she could set up with the mountebank as whore and pimp ("dealer"). "Lady Vanity" is a stock figure out of the old morality plays.
4. In the event of her infidelity, Celia's dowry would be forfeited to her husband. "I'm a Dutchman": the stolidity, not to say complacency, of Dutch men was a common theme of satire—Italians, on the other hand, were reputed to be fiercely jealous.

You would be damned, ere you did this, you whore!
Thou'dst tremble, to imagine, that the murder
Of father, mother, brother, all thy race,
Should follow, as the subject of my justice.

CELIA. Good sir, have patience.

CORVINO. What couldst thou propose
Less to thyself, than in this heat of wrath,
And stung with my dishonor, I should strike
This steel into thee, with as many stabs,
As thou wert gazed upon with goatish eyes?

CELIA. Alas, sir, be appeased! I could not think
My being at the window should more now
Move your impatience, than at other times.

CORVINO. No? not to seek and entertain a parley
With a known knave, before a multitude?
You were an actor with your handkerchief,
Which he most sweetly kissed in the receipt,
And might, no doubt, return it with a letter,
And 'point the place where you might meet; your sister's,
Your mother's, or your aunt's might serve the turn.

CELIA. Why, dear sir, when do I make these excuses,
Or ever stir abroad, but to the church?
And that so seldom—

CORVINO. Well, it shall be less;
And thy restraint before was liberty
To what I now decree: and therefore mark me.
First, I will have this bawdy light dammed up;[5]
And till't be done, some two or three yards off,
I'll chalk a line, o'er which if thou but chance
To set thy desperate foot, more hell, more horror,
More wild remorseless rage shall seize on thee,
Than on a conjuror, that had heedless left
His circle's safety ere his devil was laid.[6]
Then here's a lock which I will hang upon thee,
And, now I think on't, I will keep thee backwards;
Thy lodging shall be backwards; thy walks backwards;
Thy prospect, all be backwards; and no pleasure,
That thou shalt know but backwards. Nay, since you force
My honest nature, know, it is your own,
Being too open, makes me use you thus.
Since you will not contain your subtle nostrils
In a sweet room, but they must snuff the air
Of rank and sweaty passengers. [*Knocking within.*]—One knocks.
Away, and be not seen, pain of thy life;
Nor look toward the window: if thou dost—
Nay, stay, hear this: let me not prosper, whore,

5. I.e., brick up the window.
6. When a warlock raised the devil, he was well advised to draw around himself a magic circle, over which the devil could not step.

But I will make thee an anatomy,[7]
Dissect thee mine own self, and read a lecture
Upon thee to the city, and in public.
Away!—[*Exit* CELIA.] Who's there? [*Enter* SERVANT.]
SERVANT. 'Tis signor Mosca, sir.

SCENE 6

CORVINO. Let him come in. [*Exit* SERVANT.] His master's dead: there's yet
Some good to help the bad. [*Enter* MOSCA.] My Mosca, welcome!
I guess your news.
MOSCA. I fear you cannot, sir.
CORVINO. Is't not his death?
MOSCA. Rather the contrary.
CORVINO. Not his recovery?
MOSCA. Yes, sir.
CORVINO. I am cursed,
I am bewitched, my crosses meet to vex me.
How? how? how? how?
MOSCA. Why, sir, with Scoto's oil!
Corbaccio and Voltore brought of it,
Whilst I was busy in an inner room——
CORVINO. Death! that damned mountebank! but for the law
Now, I could kill the rascal: it cannot be,
His oil should have that virtue.[8] Have not I
Known him a common rogue, come fiddling in
To the *ostería*,[9] with a tumbling whore,
And, when he has done all his forced tricks, been glad
Of a poor spoonful of dead wine, with flies in't?
It cannot be. All his ingredients
Are a sheep's gall, a roasted bitch's marrow,
Some few sod[1] earwigs, pounded caterpillars,
A little capon's grease, and fasting spittle:
I know them to a dram.
MOSCA. I know not, sir;
But some on't, there, they poured into his ears,
Some in his nostrils, and recovered him;
Applying but the fricace.[2]
CORVINO. Pox o' that fricace!
MOSCA. And since, to seem the more officious
And flattering of his health, there, they have had,
At extreme fees, the college of physicians
Consulting on him, how they might restore him;
Where one would have a cataplasm[3] of spices,
Another a flayed ape clapped to his breast,

7. A skeleton hung up in a medical laboratory for demonstration purposes.
8. Efficacy.
9. The Italian word for "tavern."
1. Boiled; fasting spittle: as it implies, spit taken from a hungry man.
2. I.e., all they had to do was rub it in.
3. Poultice.

A third would have it a dog, a fourth an oil,
With wild cats' skins; at last, they all resolved
That, to preserve him, was no other means,
But some young woman must be straight sought out,
Lusty, and full of juice, to sleep by him;
And to this service, most unhappily,
And most unwillingly, am I now employed,
Which here I thought to pre-acquaint you with,
For your advice, since it concerns you most,
Because I would not do that thing might cross
Your ends, on whom I have my whole dependence, sir.
Yet, if I do it not, they may delate[4]
My slackness to my patron, work me out
Of his opinion; and there all your hopes,
Ventures, or whatsoever, are all frustrate!
I do but tell you, sir. Besides, they are all
Now striving, who shall first present him; therefore—
I could entreat you, briefly conclude somewhat;
Prevent[5] them if you can.

CORVINO. Death to my hopes,
This is my villainous fortune! Best to hire
Some common courtesan.

MOSCA. Ay, I thought on that, sir;
But they are all so subtle, full of art,
And age again doting and flexible,
So as—I cannot tell—we may, perchance,
Light on a quean[6] may cheat us all.

CORVINO. 'Tis true.

MOSCA. No, no: it must be one that has no tricks, sir,
Some simple thing, a creature made unto it;
Some wench you may command. Have you no kinswoman?
God's so—Think, think, think, think, think, think, think, sir.
One o' the doctors offered there his daughter.

CORVINO. How!

MOSCA. Yes, signor Lupo,[7] the physician.

CORVINO. His daughter!

MOSCA. And a virgin, sir. Why, alas,
He knows the state of's body, what it is;
That nought can warm his blood, sir, but a fever;
Nor any incantation raise his spirit:
A long forgetfulness hath seized that part.
Besides, sir, who shall know it? some one or two—

CORVINO. I pray thee give me leave. [*Walks aside.*] If any man
But I had had this luck—The thing in itself,
I know, is nothing—Wherefore should not I
As well command my blood and my affections,
As this dull doctor? In the point of honor,
The cases are all one of wife and daughter.

4. Denounce, complain of.
5. Forestall.
6. Trollop.
7. Doctor Wolf.

MOSCA. [*aside*] I hear him coming.
CORVINO. She shall do't: 'tis done.
Slight! if this doctor, who is not engaged,
Unless 't be for his counsel, which is nothing,
Offer his daughter, what should I, that am
So deeply in? I will prevent him: Wretch!
Covetous wretch![8]—Mosca, I have determined.
MOSCA. How, sir?
CORVINO. We'll make all sure. The party you wot of[9]
Shall be mine own wife, Mosca.
MOSCA. Sir, the thing,
But that I would not seem to counsel you,
I should have motioned[1] to you, at the first:
And, make your count, you have cut all their throats.
Why, 'tis directly taking a possession!
And in his next fit, we may let him go.
'Tis but to pull the pillow from his head,
And he is throttled: it had been done before,
But for your scrupulous doubts.
CORVINO. Ay, a plague on't,
My conscience fools my wit! Well, I'll be brief,
And so be thou, lest they should be before us:
Go home, prepare him, tell him with what zeal
And willingness I do it; swear it was
On the first hearing, as thou mayst do truly,
Mine own free motion.
MOSCA. Sir, I warrant you,
I'll so possess him with it, that the rest
Of his starved clients shall be banished all,
And only you received. But come not, sir,
Until I send, for I have something else
To ripen for your good, you must not know it.
CORVINO. But do not you forget to send now.
MOSCA. Fear not. [*Exit* MOSCA.]

SCENE 7

CORVINO. Where are you, wife? my Celia! wife!
[*Enter* CELIA, *weeping.*]
What, blubbering?
Come, dry those tears. I think thou thought'st me in earnest?
Ha! by this light I talked so but to try thee.
Methinks, the lightness of the occasion
Should have confirmed thee.[2] Come, I am not jealous.
CELIA. No?
CORVINO. Faith I am not, I, nor never was;
It is a poor unprofitable humor.
Do not I know, if women have a will,

8. The words are spoken by Corvino to himself about himself.
9. Know about.
1. Suggested.
2. You should have seen I was joking because the occasion was so trivial.

They'll do 'gainst all the watches of the world,
And that the fiercest spies are tamed with gold?[3]
Tut, I am confident in thee, thou shalt see't;
And see, I'll give thee cause too, to believe it.
Come, kiss me. Go, and make thee ready straight,
In all thy best attire, thy choicest jewels,
Put them all on, and, with them, thy best looks:
We are invited to a solemn feast,
At old Volpone's, where it shall appear
How far I am free from jealousy or fear. [*Exeunt.*]

Act III

SCENE 1. *A street*

[*Enter* MOSCA.]

MOSCA. I fear, I shall begin to grow in love
With my dear self, and my most prosperous parts,
They do so spring and burgeon; I can feel
A whimsy in my blood: I know not how,
Success hath made me wanton. I could skip
Out of my skin, now, like a subtle snake,
I am so limber. O! your parasite[4]
Is a most precious thing, dropped from above,
Not bred 'mongst clods and clodpoles, here on earth.
I muse the mystery[5] was not made a science,
It is so liberally professed! almost
All the wise world is little else, in nature,
But parasites or sub-parasites. And, yet,
I mean not those that have your bare town-art,
To know who's fit to feed them; have no house,
No family, no care, and therefore mold
Tales for men's ears, to bait[6] that sense; or get
Kitchen-invention, and some stale receipts
To please the belly, and the groin; nor those,
With their court dog-tricks, that can fawn and fleer,
Make their revénue out of legs and faces,[7]
Echo my lord, and lick away a moth:
But your fine elegant rascal, that can rise,
And stoop, almost together, like an arrow;
Shoot through the air as nimbly as a star;
Turn short as doth a swallow; and be here,
And there, and here, and yonder, all at once;
Present to any humor, all occasion;
And change a visor,[8] swifter than a thought!

3. Immemorial commonplaces on the lust and treachery of women.
4. The comedies of Terence and Plautus, with which Jonson was thoroughly familiar, swarm with parasites; the very idea of the relationship was repugnant to his sturdy, Stoic independence of spirit.
5. Craft. Mosca is playing on the idea of the liberal arts and sciences.
6. The parasite who talks for a living "baits" (teases, gratifies) the sense of hearing; others gratify the bellies and groins of their patrons.
7. Scrapings and looks of admiration.
8. I.e., the mask of his expression.

This is the creature had the art born with him;
Toils not to learn it, but doth practice it
Out of most excellent nature: and such sparks
Are the true parasites, others but their zanies.

SCENE 2

[*Enter* BONARIO.]

MOSCA. Who's this? Bonario, old Corbaccio's son?
The person I was bound to seek.—Fair sir,
You are happily met.
BONARIO. That cannot be by thee.
MOSCA. Why, sir?
BONARIO. Nay, pray thee know thy way, and leave me:
I would be loath to interchange discourse
With such a mate as thou art.
MOSCA. Courteous sir,
Scorn not my poverty.
BONARIO. Not I, by heaven;
But thou shalt give me leave to hate thy baseness.
MOSCA. Baseness!
BONARIO. Ay; answer me, is not thy sloth
Sufficient argument? thy flattery?
Thy means of feeding?
MOSCA. Heaven be good to me!
These imputations are too common, sir,
And easily stuck on virtue when she's poor.
You are unequal to me, and howe'er
Your sentence may be righteous, yet you are not,
That, ere you know me, thus proceed in censure:
St. Mark bear witness 'gainst you, 'tis inhuman. [*Weeps.*]
BONARIO. [*aside*] What! does he weep! the sign is soft and good;
I do repent me that I was so harsh.
MOSCA. 'Tis true, that, swayed by a strong necessity
I am enforced to eat my careful bread
With too much obsequy;[9] 'tis true, beside,
That I am fain to spin mine own poor raiment
Out of my mere observance,[1] being not born
To a free fortune: but that I have done
Base offices, in rending friends asunder,
Dividing families, betraying counsels,
Whispering false lies, or mining men with praises,
Trained their credulity with perjuries,
Corrupted chastity, or am in love
With mine own tender ease, but would not rather
Prove the most rugged, and laborious course,
That might redeem my present estimation,
Let me here perish, in all hope of goodness.
BONARIO. [*aside*] This cannot be a personated passion.—

9. Flattery, obsequiousness.
1. Service.

I was to blame, so to mistake thy nature;
Prithee forgive me and speak out thy business.
MOSCA. Sir, it concerns you; and though I may seem,
At first to make a main offense in manners,
And in my gratitude unto my master;
Yet, for the pure love, which I bear all right,
And hatred of the wrong, I must reveal it.
This very hour your father is in purpose
To disinherit you—
BONARIO. How!
MOSCA. And thrust you forth,
As a mere stranger to his blood; 'tis true, sir.
The work no way engageth me, but, as
I claim an interest in the general state
Of goodness and true virtue, which I hear
T'abound in you; and, for which mere respect,
Without a second aim, sir, I have done it.
BONARIO. This tale hath lost thee much of the late trust
Thou hadst with me; it is impossible.
I know not how to lend it any thought,
My father should be so unnatural.
MOSCA. It is a confidence that well becomes
Your piety; and formed, no doubt, it is
From your own simple innocence: which makes
Your wrong more monstrous and abhorred. But, sir,
I now will tell you more. This very minute,
It is, or will be doing; and, if you
Shall be but pleased to go with me, I'll bring you,
I dare not say where you shall see, but where
Your ear shall be a witness of the deed;
Hear yourself written bastard, and professed
The common issue of the earth.[2]
BONARIO. I'm 'mazed.
MOSCA. Sir, if I do it not, draw your just sword,
And score your vengeance on my front and face;
Mark me your villain: you have too much wrong,
And I do suffer for you, sir. My heart
Weeps blood in anguish—
BONARIO. Lead; I follow thee. [*Exeunt.*]

SCENE 3. *A room in* VOLPONE*'s house*

[*Enter* VOLPONE.]
VOLPONE. Mosca stays long, methinks. Bring forth your sports,
And help to make the wretched time more sweet.
[*Enter* NANO, ANDROGYNO, *and* CASTRONE.]
NANO. *Dwarf, fool, and eunuch, well met here we be.*
A question it were now, whether of us three,
Being all the known delicates[3] *of a rich man,*

2. A man without recognized father was known to the Romans as a *filius terrae*, "son of earth."
3. Favorites.

In pleasing him, claim the precedency can?
CASTRONE. *I claim for myself.*
ANDROGYNO. *And so doth the fool.*
NANO. *'Tis foolish indeed: let me set you both to school.*
First for your dwarf, he's little and witty,
And every thing, as it is little, is pretty;
Else why do men say to a creature of my shape,
So soon as they see him, 'It's a pretty little ape?'
And why a pretty ape, but for pleasing imitation
Of greater men's actions, in a ridiculous fashion?
Beside, this feat[4] *body of mine doth not crave*
Half the meat, drink, and cloth, one of your bulks will have.
Admit your fool's face be the mother of laughter,
Yet, for his brain, it must always come after:
And though that do feed him, it's a pitiful case,
His body is beholding to such a bad face. [*Knocking within.*]
VOLPONE. Who's there? my couch; away! look, Nano, see: [*Exeunt* ANDROGYNO *and* CASTRONE.]
Give me my caps, first—go, enquire. [*Exit* NANO.] Now, Cupid
Send it be Mosca, and with fair return!
NANO. [*within*] It is the beauteous madam—
VOLPONE. Would-be—is it?
NANO. The same.
VOLPONE. Now torment on me! Squire her in;
For she will enter, or dwell here forever:
Nay quickly. [*Retires to his couch.*]—That my fit were past! I fear
A second hell too, that my loathing this
Will quite expel my appetite to the other:[5]
Would she were taking now her tedious leave.
Lord, how it threats me what I am to suffer!

SCENE 4

[*Enter* NANO *with* LADY POLITIC WOULD-BE.]

LADY POLITIC. I thank you, good sir. 'Pray you signify
Unto your patron, I am here. This band
Shows not my neck enough. I trouble you, sir.
Let me request you, bid one of my women
Come hither to me. In good faith, I am dressed
Most favorably to-day. It is no matter;
'Tis well enough.[6]
[*Enter 1st* WAITING-WOMAN.]
Look, see, these petulant[7] things,
How they have done this!

4. Trim.
5. I.e., his loathing for Lady Politic may destroy his appetite for Celia.
6. The theme of talkative women was ancient and traditional; Jonson got a lot of Lady Politic's chatter from a Syrian sophist of the 4th century A.D., Libanius, who wrote a talkative book all about talkative women.
7. Troublesome.

VOLPONE. [*aside*] I do feel the fever
Entering in at mine ears; O, for a charm,
To fright it hence!
LADY POLITIC. Come nearer: is this curl
In his right place? or this? Why is this higher
Than all the rest? You have not washed your eyes, yet!
Or do they not stand even in your head?
Where is your fellow? call her. [*Exit 1st* WOMAN.]
NANO. [*aside*] Now, St. Mark
Deliver us! anon, she'll beat her women,
Because her nose is red.
[*Re-enter 1st with 2nd* WOMAN.]
LADY POLITIC. I pray you, view
This tire,[8] forsooth: are all things apt, or no?
1 WOMAN. One hair a little, here, sticks out, forsooth.
LADY POLITIC. Does't so, forsooth! and where was your dear sight,
When it did so, forsooth![9] What now! bird-eyed?
And you, too? Pray you, both approach and mend it.
Now, by that light, I muse you're not ashamed!
I, that have preached these things so oft unto you,
Read you the principles, argued all the grounds,
Disputed every fitness, every grace,
Called you to counsel of so frequent dressings—
NANO. [*aside*] More carefully than of your fame or honor.
LADY POLITIC. Made you acquainted, what an ample dowry
The knowledge of these things would be unto you,
Able, alone, to get you noble husbands
At your return; and you thus to neglect it!
Besides, you seeing what a curious[1] nation
The Italians are, what will they say of me?
The English lady cannot dress herself.—
Here's a fine imputation to our country!
Well, go your ways, and stay in the next room.
This fucus[2] was too coarse too; it's no matter.
Good sir, you'll give them entertainment?
[*Exeunt* NANO *and* WAITING-WOMEN.]
VOLPONE. The storm comes toward me.
LADY POLITIC. [*Goes to the couch.*] How does my Volpone?
VOLPONE. Troubled with noise; I cannot sleep; I dreamt
That a strange fury entered, now, my house,
And, with the dreadful tempest of her breath,
Did cleave my roof asunder.
LADY POLITIC. Believe me, and I
Had the most fearful dream, could I remember't—
VOLPONE. [*aside*] Out on my fate! I have given her the occasion

8. Headdress, arrangement of hair.
9. She strikes at them both, and jeers at their flinching. "Bird-eyed": sharp of sight.
1. Fastidious, particular.
2. Makeup. The last sentence is spoken to Nano.

How to torment me: she will tell me hers.
LADY POLITIC. Methought, the golden mediocrity,[3]
Polite, and delicate—
VOLPONE O, if you do love me,
No more; I sweat, and suffer, at the mention
Of any dream: feel how I tremble yet.
LADY POLITIC. Alas, good soul! the passion of the heart.[4]
Seed-pearl were good now, boiled with syrup of apples,
Tincture of gold, and coral, citron-pills,
Your elecampane root, myrobalanes[5]—
VOLPONE. [*aside*] Ay me, I have ta'en a grass-hopper by the wing!
LADY POLITIC. Burnt silk, and amber; you have muscadel
Good in the house—
VOLPONE. You will not drink, and part?
LADY POLITIC. No, fear not that. I doubt we shall not get
Some English saffron, half a dram would serve;
Your sixteen cloves, a little musk, dried mints,
Bugloss,[6] and barley-meal—
VOLPONE. [*aside*] She's in again!
Before I feigned diseases, now I have one.
LADY POLITIC. And these applied with a right scarlet cloth.
VOLPONE. [*aside*] Another flood of words! a very torrent!
LADY POLITIC. Shall I, sir, make you a poultice?
VOLPONE. No, no, no;
I'm very well, you need prescribe no more.
LADY POLITIC. I have a little studied physic; but now,
I'm all for music, save, in the forenoons,
An hour or two for painting. I would have
A lady, indeed, to have all letters and arts,
Be able to discourse, to write, to paint,
But principal, as Plato holds, your music
(And so does wise Pythagoras, I take it)
Is your true rapture; when there is consent[7]
In face, in voice, and clothes: and is, indeed,
Our sex's chiefest ornament.
VOLPONE. The poet
As old in time as Plato, and as knowing,
Says, that your highest female grace is silence.[8]
LADY POLITIC. Which of your poets? Petrarch, or Tasso, or Dante?
Guarini? Ariosto? Aretine?
Cieco di Hadria?[9] I have read them all.

3. I.e., the golden rule or the golden mean.
4. Heartburn.
5. An Oriental drug used for diarrhea. "Elecampane": a stimulant.
6. A common herb used as a mild stimulant.
7. Harmony, concord.
8. The poet as old as Plato is Sophocles (*Ajax*, line 293).
9. All Lady Politic's poets are well known today except Cieco di Hadria ("the blind man of Adria"), Luigi Groto; he was an actor as well as a poet, and made a tremendous impression by playing Oedipus (in Giustiniani's version of Sophocles' play) at the opening of Palladio's Teatro Olimpico at Vicenza (1585).

VOLPONE [*aside*] Is everything a cause to my destruction?
LADY POLITIC. I think I have two or three of them about me.
VOLPONE. [*aside*] The sun, the sea, will sooner both stand still
Than her eternal tongue! nothing can 'scape it.
LADY POLITIC. Here's *Pastor Fido*—[1]
VOLPONE [*aside*] Profess obstinate silence;
That's now my safest.
LADY POLITIC. All our English writers,
I mean such as are happy in th' Italian,
Will deign to steal out of this author, mainly;
Almost as much as from Montagnié:[2]
He has so modern and facile a vein,
Fitting the time, and catching the court-ear!
Your Petrarch is more passionate, yet he,
In days of sonneting, trusted them with much:
Dante is hard, and few can understand him.
But, for a desperate wit, there's Aretine;[3]
Only, his pictures are a little obscene—
You mark me not?
VOLPONE. Alas, my mind's perturbed.
LADY POLITIC. Why, in such cases, we must cure ourselves,
Make use of our philosophy—
VOLPONE. Oh me!
LADY POLITIC. And as we find our passions do rebel,
Encounter them with reason, or divert them,
By giving scope unto some other humor
Of lesser danger; as in politic bodies,
There's nothing more doth overwhelm the judgment,
And cloud the understanding, than too much
Settling and fixing, and, as 'twere, subsiding
Upon one object. For the incorporating
Of these same outward things, into that part,
Which we call mental, leaves some certain fæces[4]
That stop the organs, and, as Plato says,
Assassinate our knowledge.
VOLPONE. [*aside*] Now, the spirit
Of patience help me!
LADY POLITIC. Come, in faith, I must
Visit you more a days, and make you well;
Laugh and be lusty.
VOLPONE. [*aside*] My good angel save me!
LADY POLITIC. There was but one sole man in all the world,
With whom I e'er could sympathize; and he
Would lie you, often,[5] three, four hours together
To hear me speak; and be sometime so rapt,

1. A pastoral by G. B. Guarini (1590), internationally popular.
2. Montaigne's name tended to be given three syllables by English tongues; his *Essays*, first published in 1580, were translated into English by Jonson's friend John Florio (1603).
3. Aretino's dirty poems, illustrated by Giulio Romano and engraved by M. Raimondi, were internationally notorious.
4. Traces. Lady Politic is into orthodox, but very verbose, psychology.
5. Would often lie (if you please).

As he would answer me quite from the purpose,
Like you, and you are like him, just. I'll discourse,
An't be but only, sir, to bring you asleep,
How we did spend our time and loves together,
For some six years.

VOLPONE. Oh, oh, oh, oh, oh, oh!

LADY POLITIC. For we were *coaetanei*,[6] and brought up—

VOLPONE. Some power, some fate, some fortune rescue me!

SCENE 5

[*Enter* MOSCA.]

MOSCA. God save you, madam!

LADY POLITIC. Good sir.

VOLPONE. Mosca! welcome,
Welcome to my redemption!

MOSCA. Why, sir?

VOLPONE. Oh,
Rid me of this my torture, quickly, there;
My madam, with the everlasting voice:
The bells, in time of pestilence, ne'er made
Like noise, or were in that perpetual motion!
The cock-pit comes not near it.[7] All my house,
But now, steamed like a bath with her thick breath.
A lawyer could not have been heard; nor scarce
Another woman, such a hail of words
She has let fall. For hell's sake, rid her hence.

MOSCA. Has she presented?

VOLPONE. O, I do not care;
I'll take her absence, upon any price,
With any loss.

MOSCA. Madam—

LADY POLITIC. I have brought your patron
A toy, a cap here, of mine own work.

MOSCA. 'Tis well.
I had forgot to tell you, I saw your knight,
Where you would little think it—

LADY POLITIC. Where?

MOSCA. Marry,
Where yet, if you make haste, you may apprehend him,
Rowing upon the water in a gondola,
With the most cunning courtesan of Venice.

LADY POLITIC. Is't true?

MOSCA. Pursue them, and believe your eyes:
Leave me to make your gift. [*Exit* LADY POLITIC *hastily*.]—I knew 'twould take:
For, lightly,[8] they that use themselves most license,
Are still most jealous.

6. Of an age.
7. When the plague struck, church bells were constantly tolling; at the cockpit spectators constantly shouted bets and encouragement to the birds.
8. Commonly (an old sense of the word).

VOLPONE. Mosca, hearty thanks,
For thy quick fiction, and delivery of me.
Now to my hopes, what sayest thou?
[*Re-enter* LADY POLITIC.]
LADY POLITIC. But do you hear, sir?—
VOLPONE. Again! I fear a paroxysm.
LADY POLITIC. Which way
Rowed they together?
MOSCA. Toward the Rialto.
LADY POLITIC. I pray you lend me your dwarf.
MOSCA. I pray you take him—
[*Exit* LADY POLITIC.]
Your hopes, sir, are like happy blossoms, fair,
And promise timely fruit, if you will stay
But the maturing; keep you at your couch,
Corbaccio will arrive straight, with the will;
When he is gone, I'll tell you more. [*Exit.*]
VOLPONE. My blood,
My spirits are returned; I am alive:
And, like your wanton gamester at primero,[9]
Whose thought had whispered to him, not go less,
Methinks I lie, and draw—for an encounter.
[*The bed-curtains close upon* VOLPONE.]

SCENE 6. *The passage leading to* VOLPONE'*s chamber*

[*Enter* MOSCA *and* BONARIO.]
MOSCA. Sir, here concealed, [*shows him a closet*] you may hear all. But, pray you,
Have patience, sir. [*Knocking within.*]—The same's your father knocks:
I am compelled to leave you. [*Exit.*]
BONARIO. Do so. Yet
Cannot my thought imagine this a truth. [*Goes into the closet.*]

SCENE 7. *Another part of the same*

[*Enter* MOSCA *and* CORVINO, CELIA *following.*]
MOSCA. Death on me! you are come too soon, what meant you?
Did not I say, I would send?
CORVINO. Yes, but I feared
You might forget it, and then they prevent us.
MOSCA. [*aside*] Prevent! did e'er man haste so, for his horns?
A courtier would not ply it so, for a place.
—Well, now there is no helping it, stay here;
I'll presently return. [*Crosses stage to* BONARIO.]
CORVINO. Where are you, Celia?
You know not wherefore I have brought you hither?

9. An early form of the Spanish card game later known as ombre (the game played in Pope's *Rape of the Lock*). The phrases "go less," "draw," and "encounter" are all used in primero.

CELIA. Not well, except you told me.
CORVINO. Now, I will: [*He leads her apart, and whispers to her.*]
Hark hither.
MOSCA. [*to* BONARIO] Sir your father hath sent word,
It will be half an hour ere he come;
And therefore, if you please to walk the while
Into that gallery—at the upper end,
There are some books to entertain the time;
And I'll take care no man shall come unto you, sir.
BONARIO. Yes, I will stay there. [*aside*]—I do doubt this fellow.
[*Exit* BONARIO.]
MOSCA. [*looking after him*] There; he is far enough; he can hear nothing:
And, for his father, I can keep him off. [*Exit.*]
CORVINO. [*to* CELIA] Nay, now, there is no starting back, and therefore,
Resolve upon it: I have so decreed.
It must be done. Nor would I move't afore,
Because I would avoid all shifts and tricks,
That might deny me.
CELIA. Sir, let me beseech you,
Affect not these strange trials;[1] if you doubt
My chastity, why, lock me up forever;
Make me the heir of darkness. Let me live,
Where I may please your fears, if not your trust.
CORVINO. Believe it, I have no such humor, I.
All that I speak I mean; yet I'm not mad;
Not horn-mad, see you? Go to, show yourself
Obedient, and a wife.
CELIA. O heaven!
CORVINO. I say it,
Do so.
CELIA. Was this the train?[2]
CORVINO. I've told you reasons;
What the physicians have set down; how much
It may concern me; what my engagements are;
My means; and the necessity of those means,
For my recovery:[3] wherefore, if you be
Loyal, and mine, be won, respect my venture.[4]
CELIA. Before your honor?
CORVINO. Honor! tut, a breath;[5]
There's no such thing in nature. A mere term
Invented to awe fools. What is my gold
The worse for touching, clothes for being looked on?

1. Don't tempt me so.
2. Is this what you had in mind all the time?
3. Corvino is evidently in financial straits.
4. In the sense of a commercial venture.
5. Like Falstaff (*1 Henry IV* V.i), Corvino disposes easily of honor.

Why, this's no more. An old decrepit wretch,
That has no sense, no sinew; takes his meat
With others' fingers; only knows to gape,
When you do scald his gums;[6] a voice; a shadow;
And what can this man hurt you?

CELIA. [*aside*] Lord! what spirit
Is this hath entered him?

CORVINO. And for your fame,
That's such a jig;[7] as if I would go tell it,
Cry it on the Piazza! who shall know it,
But he that cannot speak it, and this fellow,[8]
Whose lips are in my pocket? save yourself
(If you'll proclaim't, you may), I know no other
Should come to know it.

CELIA. Are heaven and saints then nothing?
Will they be blind or stupid?

CORVINO. How!

CELIA. Good sir,
Be jealous still, emulate them;[9] and think
What hate they burn with toward every sin.

CORVINO. I grant you; if I thought it were a sin,
I would not urge you. Should I offer this
To some young Frenchman, or hot Tuscan blood
That had read Aretine,[1] conned all his prints,
Knew every quirk within lust's labyrinth,
And were professed critic in lechery;
And I would look upon him, and applaud him,
This were a sin: but here, 'tis contrary,
A pious work, mere charity, for physic,
And honest polity, to assure mine own.[2]

CELIA. O heaven! canst thou suffer such a change?

VOLPONE. Thou art mine honor, Mosca, and my pride,
My joy, my tickling, my delight! Go bring them.

MOSCA. [*advancing*] Please you draw near, sir.

CORVINO. Come on, what—
You will not be rebellious? by that light—

MOSCA. Sir,
Signor Corvino, here, is come to see you—

VOLPONE. Oh!

MOSCA. And hearing of the consultation had,
So lately, for your health, is come to offer,
Or rather, sir, to prostitute—

CORVINO. Thanks, sweet Mosca.

6. I.e., the old man has to be fed by others, and doesn't even know enough to open his own mouth for food.
7. Farce, joke.
8. "He that cannot speak it": Volpone; "this fellow": Mosca.
9. I.e., God and the saints, who hate sin.
1 Aretino was a notorious pornographer.
2. "Pious work" means it's good for your soul, "mere charity" says it's kindness to the neighbor, "for physic" says it's for the benefit of his health, "honest policy" means it's prudent self-interest, and "to assure mine own" gets down to the basic motivation—greed.

MOSCA. Freely, unasked, or unentreated—
CORVINO. Well.
MOSCA. As the true fervent instance of his love,
His own most fair and proper wife, the beauty
Only of price in Venice—
CORVINO. 'Tis well urged.
MOSCA. To be your comfortress, and to preserve you.
VOLPONE. Alas, I'm past, already! Pray you, thank him
For his good care and promptness; but for that,
'Tis a vain labor e'en to fight 'gainst heaven;
Applying fire to stone—uh, uh, uh, uh! [*Coughing.*]
Making a dead leaf grow again. I take
His wishes gently, though; and you may tell him,
What I have done for him: marry, my state is hopeless.
Will him to pray for me; and to use his fortune
With reverence, when he comes to't.
MOSCA. Do you hear, sir?
Go to him with your wife.
CORVINO. Heart of my father!
Wilt thou persist thus? come, I pray thee, come.
Thou seest 'tis nothing. Celia! By this hand,
I shall grow violent. Come, do't, I say.
CELIA. Sir, kill me, rather: I will take down poison,
Eat burning coals, do anything.
CORVINO. Be damned!
Heart, I will drag thee hence, home, by the hair;
Cry thee a strumpet through the streets; rip up
Thy mouth unto thine ears; and slit thy nose,
Like a raw rochet![3]—Do not tempt me; come,
Yield, I am loath—Death! I will buy some slave
Whom I will kill, and bind thee to him, alive;
And at my window hang you forth, devising
Some monstrous crime which I, in capital letters,
Will eat into thy flesh with aquafortis,
And burning corsives,[4] on this stubborn breast.
Now, by the blood thou hast incensed, I'll do it!
CELIA. Sir, what you please you may, I am your martyr.
CORVINO. Be not thus obstinate, I have not deserved it:
Think who it is entreats you. 'Prithee, sweet;
Good faith, thou shalt have jewels, gowns, attires,
What thou wilt think, and ask. Do but go kiss him.
Or touch him, but. For my sake. At my suit.
This once. No? not! I shall remember this.
Will you disgrace me thus? Do you thirst my undoing?
MOSCA. Nay, gentle lady, be advised.
CORVINO. No, no.
She has watched her time. Ods precious, this is scurvy,[5]
'Tis very scurvy; and you are—

3. Like a fish.
4. With acids and corrosives.
5. I.e., by God's precious blood, this is villainous.

MOSCA. Nay, good sir.
CORVINO. An arrant locust, by heaven, a locust![6]
Crocodile, that hast thy tears prepared,
Expecting, how thou'lt bid them flow—
MOSCA. Nay, pray you, sir!
She will consider.
CELIA. Would my life would serve
To satisfy.
CORVINO. S'death! if she would but speak to him,
And save my reputation, it were somewhat;
But spitefully to effect my utter ruin!
MOSCA. Ay, now you have put your fortune in her hands.
Why, i'faith, it is her modesty; I must quit[7] her.
If you were absent, she would be more coming;
I know it, and dare undertake for her.
What woman can before her husband? Pray you,
Let us depart, and leave her here.
CORVINO. Sweet Celia,
Thou mayst redeem all, yet; I'll say no more:
If not, esteem yourself as lost Nay, stay there.
[*Shuts the door, and exit with* MOSCA.]
CELIA. O God, and his good angels! whither, whither,
Is shame fled human breasts? that with such ease,
Men dare put off your honors, and their own?
Is that, which ever was a cause of life,
Now placed beneath the basest circumstance,
And modesty an exile made, for money?
VOLPONE. Ay, in Corvino, and such earth-fed minds, [*leaping from his couch*]
That never tasted the true heaven of love.
Assure thee, Celia, he that would sell thee,
Only for hope of gain, and that uncertain,
He would have sold his part of Paradise
For ready money, had he met a cope-man.[8]
Why are thou 'mazed to see me thus revived?
Rather applaud thy beauty's miracle;
'Tis thy great work:[9] that hath, not now alone,
But sundry times raised me, in several shapes,
And, but this morning, like a mountebank,
To see thee at thy window. Ay, before
I would have left my practice for thy love,
In varying figures I would have contended
With the blue Proteus, or the hornéd flood.[1]
Now art thou welcome.

6. I.e., a destructive plague. The lore of the crocodile says it sheds deceitful tears.
7. Acquit; coming: forthcoming.
8. Buyer.
9. "The great work" is always the philosopher's stone, which converts base metals to gold.
1. Proteus was a sea god who could take any shape at will; Virgil calls him "blue Proteus." Achelous was a river god with whom Hercules fought for possession of Deianira; he fought first as a river, then as a snake, and finally as a bull (hence "the hornéd flood"), but was beaten in all three shapes (Ovid, *Metamorphoses* IX).

CELIA. Sir!

VOLPONE. Nay, fly me not.
Nor let thy false imagination
That I was bed-rid, make thee think I am so:
Thou shalt not find it. I am now as fresh,
As hot, as high, and in as jovial plight,
As when, in that so celebrated scene,
At recitation of our comedy,
For entertainment of the great Valois,[2]
I acted young Antinous; and attracted
The eyes and ears of all the ladies present,
To admire each graceful gesture, note, and footing.

Song[3]

Come, my Celia, let us prove,
While we can, the sports of love,
Time will not be ours for ever,
He, at length, our good will sever;
Spend not then his gifts in vain:
Suns that set may rise again;
But if once we lose this light,
'Tis with us perpetual night.
Why should we defer our joys?
Fame and rumor are but toys.
Cannot we delude the eyes
Of a few poor household spies?
Or his easier ears beguile,
Thus removéd by our wile?—
'Tis no sin love's fruits to steal;
But the sweet thefts to reveal,
To be taken, to be seen,
These have crimes accounted been.

CELIA. Some sérene[4] blast me, or dire lightning strike
This my offending face!

VOLPONE. Why droops my Celia?
Thou hast, in place of a base husband, found
A worthy lover: use thy fortune well,
With secrecy and pleasure. See, behold,
What thou art queen of; not in expectation,
As I feed others: but possessed and crowned.
See here a rope of pearl; and each, more orient
Than that the brave Egyptian queen caroused:[5]
Dissolve and drink them. See, a carbuncle[6]
May put out both the eyes of our St. Mark;

2. Henry of Valois, Duke of Anjou, visited Venice in 1574, and was entertained with splendid festivities. Antinous was the favorite (catamite) of Emperor Hadrian, in Roman antiquity.

3. The opening lines are adapted from Catullus, boldest and bawdiest of Latin lyricists, and the whole song emphasises the theme of "*carpe diem*" (clutch the fleeting moment), which is a common erotic incitement.

4. Mist from heaven, malignant influence.

5. According to a common story, Cleopatra dissolved a precious pearl in wine and during a banquet with Antony drank it up.

6. Ruby.

A diamond, would have bought Lollia Paulina,
When she came in like star-light, hid with jewels,
That were the spoils of provinces;[7] take these,
And wear, and lose them: yet remains an earring
To purchase them again, and this whole state.
A gem but worth a private patrimony,
Is nothing: we will eat such at a meal.
The heads of parrots, tongues of nightingales,
The brains of peacocks, and of ostriches,
Shall be our food: and, could we get the phoenix,[8]
Though nature lost her kind, she were our dish.

CELIA. Good sir, these things might move a mind affected
With such delights; but I, whose innocence
Is all I can think wealthy, or worth th'enjoying,
And which, once lost, I have nought to lose beyond it,
Cannot be taken with these sensual baits:
If you have conscience—

VOLPONE. 'Tis the beggar's virtue;
If thou hast wisdom, hear me, Celia.
Thy baths shall be the juice of gilly-flowers,[9]
Spirit of roses, and of violets,
The milk of unicorns, and panthers' breath
Gathered in bags, and mixed with Cretan wines.[1]
Our drink shall be preparéd gold and amber;
Which we will take, until my roof whirl round
With the vertigo: and my dwarf shall dance,
My eunuch sing, my fool make up the antic,
Whilst we, in changèd shapes, act Ovid's tales,[2]
Thou, like Europa now, and I like Jove,
Then I like Mars, and thou like Erycine:
So, of the rest, till we have quite run through,
And wearied all the fables of the gods.
Then will I have thee in more modern forms,
Attiréd like some sprightly dame of France,
Brave Tuscan lady, or proud Spanish beauty;
Sometimes, unto the Persian Sophy's wife,[3]
Or the Grand Signor's mistress; and, for change,
To one of our most artful courtesans,
Or some quick Negro, or cold Russian;
And I will meet thee in as many shapes:
Where we may so transfuse our wandering souls
Out at our lips, and score up sums of pleasures, [*sings*]

7. Lollia Paulina, wife of a Roman governor, is said by Pliny (*Natural History* IX.117) to have worn in her hair jewels enough to represent the loot of several provinces.
8. Only one phoenix is said to be alive at any one time; eating him would eradicate the species.
9. Clove-scented flowers used to flavor drinks and as a light perfume.
1. The most expensive known to Jonson's age.
2. I.e., to enact all the fables in the *Metamorphoses*. "Erycine" is one of the epithets of Venus.
3. The "Sophy" is the Shah of Persia, the "Grand Signor" the Sultan of Turkey.

That the curious shall not know
How to tell them as they flow;
And the envious, when they find
What their number is, be pined.[4]

CELIA. If you have ears that will be pierced; or eyes
That can be opened; a heart may be touched;
Or any part that yet sounds man about you;
If you have touch of holy saints, or heaven,
Do me the grace to let me 'scape. If not,
Be bountiful and kill me. You do know,
I am a creature, hither ill betrayed,
By one, whose shame I would forget it were.
If you will deign me neither of these graces,
Yet feed your wrath, sir, rather than your lust
(It is a vice comes nearer manliness),
And punish that unhappy crime of nature,
Which you miscall my beauty; flay my face,
Or poison it with ointments, for seducing
Your blood to this rebellion. Rub these hands,
With what may cause an eating leprosy,
E'en to my bones and marrow: any thing,
That may disfavor[5] me, save in my honor—
And I will kneel to you, pray for you, pay down
A thousand hourly vows, sir, for your health;
Report, and think you virtuous—
VOLPONE. Think me cold,
Frozen and impotent, and so report me?
That I had Nestor's hernia,[6] thou wouldst think.
I do degenerate, and abuse my nation,
To play with opportunity thus long;
I should have done the act, and then have parleyed.
Yield, or I'll force thee. [*Seizes her.*]
CELIA. O! just God!
VOLPONE. In vain—
BONARIO. [*rushing in*] Forbear, foul ravisher! libidinous swine!
Free the forced lady, or thou diest, impostor!
But that I'm loath to snatch thy punishment
Out of the hand of justice, thou shouldst yet
Be made the timely sacrifice of vengeance
Before this altar, and this dross, thy idol.
Lady, let's quit the place, it is the den
Of villainy; fear nought, you have a guard:
And he, ere long, shall meet his just reward. [*Exeunt* BONARIO *and* CELIA.]
VOLPONE. Fall on me, roof, and bury me in ruin!
Become my grave, that wert my shelter! O!

4. Envious, depressed. The verses, once again, are adapted from Catullus.
5. Disfigure.
6. Senile impotence; the phrase is from Juvenal's sixth satire.

I am unmasked, unspirited, undone,
Betrayed to beggary, to infamy—

SCENE 8

[*Enter* MOSCA, *wounded, and bleeding.*]

MOSCA. Where shall I run, most wretched shame of men,
To beat out my unlucky brains?

VOLPONE. Here, here.
What! dost thou bleed?

MOSCA. O that his well-driven sword
Had been so courteous to have cleft me down
Unto the navel, ere I lived to see
My life, my hopes, my spirits, my patron, all
Thus desperately engagéd, by my error!

VOLPONE. Woe on thy fortune!

MOSCA. And my follies, sir.

VOLPONE. Thou hast made me miserable.

MOSCA. And myself, sir.
Who would have thought he would have hearkened so?

VOLPONE. What shall we do?

MOSCA. I know not; if my heart
Could expiate the mischance, I'd pluck it out.
Will you be pleased to hang me? or cut my throat?
And I'll requite you, sir. Let's die like Romans,
Since we have lived like Grecians.[7] [*Knocking within.*]

VOLPONE. Hark! who's there?
I hear some footing; officers, the Saffi,[8]
Come to apprehend us! I do feel the brand
Hissing already at my forehead; now
Mine ears are boring.[9]

MOSCA. To your couch, sir, you,
Make that place good, however. [VOLPONE *lies down, as before.*]—Guilty men
Suspect what they deserve still. Signor Corbaccio!

SCENE 9

[*Enter* CORBACCIO.]

CORBACCIO. Why, how now, Mosca?

MOSCA. O, undone, amazed, sir.
Your son, I know not by what accident,
Acquainted with your purpose to my patron,
Touching your will, and making him your heir,
Entered our house with violence, his sword drawn,
Sought for you, called you wretch, unnatural,
Vowed he would kill you.

7. Greeks, especially Corinthians, were famous for living in luxury; Romans for committing suicide with dignity when life no longer appeared worthy of them.

8. Police officers, investigators.

9. Branding on the face and boring holes in the ears were common criminal punishments.

CORBACCIO. Me!

MOSCA. Yes, and my patron.

CORBACCIO. This act shall disinherit him indeed:
Here is the will.

MOSCA. 'Tis well, sir.

CORBACCIO. Right and well;
Be you as careful now for me.

[*Enter* VOLTORE *behind.*]

MOSCA. My life, sir,
Is not more tendered; I am only yours.

CORBACCIO. How does he? will he die shortly, think'st thou?

MOSCA. I fear
He'll outlast May.

CORBACCIO. Today?

MOSCA. No, last out May, sir.

CORBACCIO. Couldst thou not give him a dram?

MOSCA. O, by no means, sir.

CORBACCIO. Nay, I'll not bid you.

VOLTORE. [*coming forward*] This is a knave, I see.

MOSCA. [*seeing* VOLTORE, *aside*] How! signor Voltore! did he hear me?

VOLTORE. Parasite!

MOSCA. Who's that? O, sir, most timely welcome—

VOLTORE. Scarce,
To the discovery of your tricks, I fear.
You are his, *only?* and mine also, are you not?

MOSCA. Who? I, sir!

VOLTORE. You, sir. What device is this
About a will?

MOSCA. A plot for you, sir.

VOLTORE. Come,
Put not your foists[1] upon me; I shall scent them.

MOSCA. Did you not hear it?

VOLTORE. Yes, I hear Corbaccio
Hath made your patron there his heir.

MOSCA. 'Tis true,
By my device, drawn to it by my plot,
With hope—

VOLTORE. Your patron should reciprocate?
And you have promised?

MOSCA. For your good, I did, sir.
Nay more, I told his son, brought, hid him here,
Where he might hear his father pass the deed;
Being persuaded to it by this thought, sir,
That the unnaturalness, first, of the act,
And then his father's oft disclaiming in him,
(Which I did mean t'help on), would sure enrage him
To do some violence upon his parent,

1. Tricks, but also bad smells.

On which the law should take sufficient hold,
And you be stated[2] in a double hope:
Truth be my comfort, and my conscience,
My only aim was to dig you a fortune
Out of these two old rotten sepulchres—

VOLTORE. I cry thee mercy, Mosca.

MOSCA. Worth your patience,
And your great merit, sir. And see the change!

VOLTORE. Why, what success?[3]

MOSCA. Most hapless! you must help, sir.
Whilst we expected the old raven, in comes
Corvino's wife, sent hither by her husband—

VOLTORE. What, with a present?

MOSCA. No, sir, on visitation
(I'll tell you how anon); and staying long,
The youth he grows impatient, rushes forth,
Seizeth the lady, wounds me, makes her swear
(Or he would murder her, that was his vow)
To affirm my patron to have done her rape:
Which how unlike it is, you see! and hence,
With that pretext he's gone to accuse his father,
Defame my patron, defeat you—

VOLTORE. Where is her husband?
Let him be sent for straight.

MOSCA. Sir, I'll go fetch him.

VOLTORE. Bring him to the Scrutineo.[4]

MOSCA. Sir, I will.

VOLTORE. This must be stopped.

MOSCA. O, you do nobly, sir.
Alas, 'twas labored all, sir, for your good;
Nor was there want of counsel in the plot:
But fortune can, at any time, o'erthrow
The projects of a hundred learned clerks,[5] sir.

CORBACCIO. [*listening*] What's that?

VOLTORE. Will't please you, sir, to go along? [*Exit* CORBACCIO *followed by* VOLTORE.]

MOSCA. Patron, go in, and pray for our success.

VOLPONE. [*rising from his couch*] Need makes devotion: heaven your labor bless! [*Exeunt.*]

Act IV

SCENE 1. *A street*

[*Enter* SIR POLITIC WOULD-BE *and* PEREGRINE.]

SIR POLITIC. I told you, sir, it was a plot; you see
What observation is! You mentioned[6] me
For some instructions: I will tell you, sir

2. Installed.
3. Result, outcome.
4. The court of law. Jonson's court, like courts on the Continent generally, has power to look into abuses and investigate possible violations of the law, before any particular suit is filed.
5. Scholars.
6. Asked.

(Since we are met here in this height[7] of Venice),
Some few particulars I have set down,
Only for this meridian, fit to be known
Of your crude traveler; and they are these.
I will not touch, sir, at your phrase, or clothes,
For they are old.

PEREGRINE. Sir, I have better.

SIR POLITIC. Pardon,
I meant, as they are themes.

PEREGRINE. O, sir, proceed:
I'll slander you no more of wit, good sir.

SIR POLITIC. First, for your garb, it must be grave and serious,
Very reserved and locked; not tell a secret
On any terms, not to your father; scarce
A fable, but with caution; make sure choice
Both of your company, and discourse; beware
You never speak a truth—

PEREGRINE. How!

SIR POLITIC. Not to strangers,
For those be they you must converse with most;
Others I would not know, sir, but at distance,
So as I still might be a saver in them:[8]
You shall have tricks, else, passed upon you hourly.
And then, for your religion, profess none,
But wonder at the diversity of all;
And, for your part, protest, were there no other
But simply the laws o' th' land, you could content you.
Nick Machiavel, and Monsieur Bodin, both
Were of this mind.[9] Then must you learn the use
And handling of your silver fork at meals,[1]
The metal of your glass (these are main matters
With your Italian), and to know the hour
When you must eat your melons, and your figs.

PEREGRINE. Is that a point of state too?

SIR POLITIC. Here it is;
For your Venetian, if he see a man
Preposterous[2] in the least, he has him straight;
He has; he strips him. I'll acquaint you, sir.
I now have lived here, 'tis some fourteen months;
Within the first week of my landing here,
All took me for a citizen of Venice,
I knew the forms so well—

7. Climate, constitution.
8. The implication is clear: Don't lend anybody money.
9. The abbreviation "Nick Machiavel" implies casual familiarity; the sentiment attributed to Machiavelli shows complete ignorance of him. Sir Politic Would-be is more nearly right in his estimate of Jean Bodin, the French political philosopher, who did advocate religious toleration.
1. Handling a fork was a new experience for Englishmen who traveled abroad in Jonson's time; back home, fingers were still the preferred instruments. "The metal of your glass": literally, the composition of your glass (perhaps to know what could or couldn't be put in it).
2. In its literal Latin sense, getting things back to front.

PEREGRINE. [*aside*] And nothing else.
SIR POLITIC. I had read Contarine,[3] took me a house,
Dealt with my Jews to furnish it with movables—
Well, if I could but find one man, one man
To mine own heart, whom I durst trust, I would—
PEREGRINE. What, what, sir?
SIR POLITIC. Make him rich; make him a fortune;
He should not think again. I would command it.
PEREGRINE. As how?
SIR POLITIC. With certain projects[4] that I have
Which I may not discover.
PEREGRINE. [*aside*] If I had
But one to wager with, I would lay odds now,
He tells me instantly.
SIR POLITIC. One is (and that
I care not greatly who knows) to serve the state
Of Venice with red herrings for three years,
And at a certain rate, from Rotterdam,[5]
Where I have correspondence. There's a letter,
Sent me from one o' the States,[6] and to that purpose;
He cannot write his name, but that's his mark.
PEREGRINE. He is a chandler?
SIR POLITIC. No, a cheese monger.
There are some others too with whom I treat
About the same negotiation;
And I will undertake it: for, 'tis thus.
I'll do't with ease, I've cast it all. Your hoy[7]
Carries but three men in her, and a boy;
And she shall make me three returns a year.
So, if there come but one of three, I save;
If two, I can defalc[8]:—but this is now,
If my main project fail.
PEREGRINE. Then you have others?
SIR POLITIC. I should be loath to draw the subtle air
Of such a place, without my thousand aims.
I'll not dissemble, sir; where'er I come,
I love to be considerative; and 'tis true,
I have at my free hours thought upon
Some certain goods unto the state of Venice,
Which I do call my *Cautions*; and, sir, which
I mean, in hope of pension, to propound
To the Great Council, then unto the Forty,

3. Contarini wrote a book on Venetian government, which Sir Politic would be quick to know. "My Jews": in the indefinite sense—the usual Jews that everybody goes to for furniture to set up a Venetian apartment.
4. Schemes for social improvement or making money (or preferably both) were favorite targets of 17th-century satire. "Discover": disclose.
5. The Venetians have plenty of fresh fish in the Adriatic, and would not like salt herring in any case.
6. I.e., from one of the States-General in Holland.
7. A small North Sea fishing vessel; such a boat would have great trouble making a trip to Venice, let alone carrying a worthwhile cargo.
8. Reduce the amount, cut back, maybe even go into bankruptcy.

So to the Ten.[9] My means are made already—
PEREGRINE. By whom?
SIR POLITIC. Sir, one that, though his place be obscure,
Yet he can sway, and they will hear him. He's
A *commendatore.*
PEREGRINE. What! a common sergeant?
SIR POLITIC. Sir, such as they are, put it in their mouths,
What they should say, sometimes, as well as greater.
I think I have my notes to show you—[*Searching his pockets.*]
PEREGRINE. Good, sir.
SIR POLITIC. But you shall swear unto me, on your gentry,[1]
Not to anticipate—
PEREGRINE. I, sir!
SIR POLITIC. Nor reveal
A circumstance—My paper is not with me.
PEREGRINE. O, but you can remember, sir.
SIR POLITIC. My first is
Concerning tinder-boxes.[2] You must know,
No family is here without its box.
Now, sir, it being so portable a thing,
Put case, that you or I were ill affected
Unto the state, sir; with it in our pockets,
Might not I go into the Arsenal,[3]
Or you? come out again? and none the wiser?
PEREGRINE. Except yourself, sir.
SIR POLITIC. Go to, then. I therefore
Advertise to the state, how fit it were,
That none but such as were known patriots,
Sound lovers of their country, should be suffered
To enjoy them in their houses; and even those
Sealed at some office, and at such a bigness
As might not lurk in pockets.
PEREGRINE. Admirable!
SIR POLITIC. My next is, how to inquire, and be resolved
By present demonstration, whether a ship,
Newly arrived from Syria, or from
Any suspected part of all the Levant,[4]
Be guilty of the plague; and where they use
To lie out forty, fifty days, sometimes,
About the Lazaretto,[5] for their trial,
I'll save that charge and loss unto the merchant,
And in an hour clear the doubt.
PEREGRINE. Indeed, sir!

9. Representative legislative bodies, increasingly narrow and increasingly lofty, of the Venetian government. "My means": my approaches to these eminent bodies.
1. As you are a gentleman.
2. As we would say, matchboxes or cigarette lighters.
3. Venice being largely a maritime power, the Arsenal where ships were built and repaired was (and still is) an important part of the city.
4. The Middle East.
5. Quarantine. Bubonic plague, carried by lice living on shipboard rats, was a constant peril in Venice, where trade with the Middle East was particularly busy. Ships had to wait several months in port before debarking crew, passengers, or cargo.

SIR POLITIC. Or—I will lose my labor.
PEREGRINE. My faith, that's much.
SIR POLITIC. Nay, sir, conceive me. 'Twill cost me in onions,
Some thirty livres[6]—
PEREGRINE. Which is one pound sterling.
SIR POLITIC. Besides my water-works; for this I do, sir.
First, I bring in your ship 'twixt two brick-walls;
But those the state shall venture. On the one
I strain[7] me a fair tarpaulin, and in that
I stick my onions, cut in halves; the other
Is full of loop-holes, out at which I thrust
The noses of my bellows; and those bellows
I keep, with water-works,[8] in perpetual motion,
Which is the easiest matter of a hundred.
Now, sir, your onion, which doth naturally
Attract the infection, and your bellows blowing
The air upon him, will show instantly,
By his changed color, if there be contagion,
Or else remain as fair as at the first.
—Now it is known, 'tis nothing.
PEREGRINE. You are right, sir.
SIR POLITIC. I would I had my note.
PEREGRINE. Faith, so would I:
But you have done well for once, sir.
SIR POLITIC. Were I false,
Or would be made so, I could show you reasons
How I could sell this state now to the Turk,[9]
Spite of their galleys, or their—[*Examining his papers.*]
PEREGRINE. Pray you, sir Pol.
SIR POLITIC. I have them not about me.
PEREGRINE. That I feared.
They are there, sir?
SIR POLITIC. No, this is my diary,
Wherein I note my actions of the day.
PEREGRINE. Pray you let's see, sir. What is here?
Notandum,[1]
[*Reads.*]
A rat had gnawn my spur-leathers; notwithstanding,
I put on new, and did go forth; but first
I threw three beans over the threshold. Item,
I went and bought two tooth-picks, whereof one
I burst immediately, in a discourse
With a Dutch merchant, 'bout ragion del stato.[2]

6. A French coin of small value. Onions were reputed to be good against the plague; cut open, they supposedly absorbed the plague germs from the air.
7. Stretch.
8. Sir Politic's waterworks are apparently a water wheel arranged to operate a bellows. Of course there is no spot in the flat country around Venice where streams have enough impetus to turn a wheel.
9. Here Sir Politic is verging on real subversion, and Peregrine quickly shuts him off.
1. Take special note.
2. Literally, "reason of state," but also the title of a famous book by Giovanni Botero, presenting a diluted version of Machiavelli's thought.

From him I went and paid a mocenigo
For piecing my silk stockings; by the way
I cheapened sprats;[3] *and at St. Mark's I urined.*
Faith, these are politic notes!

SIR POLITIC. Sir, I do slip
No action of my life, thus, but I quote it.

PEREGRINE. Believe me, it is wise!

SIR POLITIC. Nay, sir, read forth.

SCENE 2

[*Enter, at a distance,* LADY POLITIC WOULD-BE, NANO, *and two* WAITING-WOMEN.]

LADY POLITIC. Where should this loose knight be, trow? sure he's housed.[4]

NANO. Why, then he's fast.

LADY POLITIC. Ay, he plays both with me.[5]
I pray you stay. This heat will do more harm
To my complexion, than his heart is worth.
(I do not care to hinder, but to take him.)
How it[6] comes off! [*Rubbing her cheeks.*]

1 WOMAN. My master's yonder.

LADY POLITIC. Where?

2 WOMAN. With a young gentleman.

LADY POLITIC. That same's the party,
In man's apparel! Pray you, sir, jog my knight;
I will be tender to his reputation,
However he demerit.

SIR POLITIC. [*seeing her*] My lady!

PEREGRINE. Where?

SIR POLITIC. 'Tis she indeed, sir; you shall know her. She is,
Were she not mine, a lady of that merit,
For fashion and behavior; and for beauty
I durst compare—

PEREGRINE. It seems you are not jealous,
That dare commend her.

SIR POLITIC. Nay, and for discourse—

PEREGRINE. Being your wife, she cannot miss that.

SIR POLITIC. [*introducing Peregrine*] Madam,
Here is a gentleman, pray you, use him fairly;
He seems a youth, but he is—

LADY POLITIC. None.

SIR POLITIC. Yes, one
Has put his face as soon into the world—

LADY POLITIC. You mean, as early? but today?

SIR POLITIC. How's this?

LADY POLITIC. Why, in this habit, sir; you apprehend me.
Well, Master Would-be, this doth not become you;

3. Bargained over some trifling fish; "piecing": mending.

4. Gone into somebody's house. "He's fast" implies that he's securely fastened and in fast company.

5. Both fast and loose.

6. I.e., her complexion.

I had thought the odor, sir, of your good name
Had been more precious to you; that you would not
Have done this dire massacre on your honor;
One of your gravity, and rank besides!
But knights, I see, care little for the oath
They make to ladies, chiefly, their own ladies.

SIR POLITIC. Now, by my spurs, the symbol of my knighthood[7]—

PEREGRINE [*aside*] Lord, how his brain is humbled for an oath!

SIR POLITIC. I reach you not.

LADY POLITIC. Right, sir, your polity
May bear it through thus. [*To* PEREGRINE.]—Sir, a word with you.
I would be loath to contest publicly
With any gentlewoman, or to seem
Froward, or violent, as the courtier says;[8]
It comes too near rusticity in a lady,
Which I would shun by all means; and however
I may deserve from Master Would-be, yet
T'have one fair gentlewoman thus be made
The unkind instrument to wrong another,
And one she knows not, ay, and to perséver;
In my poor judgment, is not warranted
From being a solecism in our sex,
If not in manners.

PEREGRINE. How is this!

SIR POLITIC. Sweet madam,
Come nearer to your aim.

LADY POLITIC. Marry, and will, sir.
Since you provoke me with your impudence,
And laughter of your light land-siren here,
Your Sporus,[9] your hermaphrodite—

PEREGRINE. What's here?
Poetic fury, and historic[1] storms!

SIR POLITIC. The gentleman, believe it, is of worth,
And of our nation.

LADY POLITIC. Ay, your Whitefriars[2] nation!
Come, I blush for you, Master Would-be, ay;
And am ashamed you should have no more forehead,[3]
Than thus to be the patron, or St. George,
To a lewd harlot, a base fricatrice,[4]
A female devil, in a male outside.

SIR POLITIC. Nay,

7. Because King James created knights indiscriminately at his accession, knighthood was a broad joke in early 17th-century England.

8. I.e., Castiglione.

9. Sporus was a favorite catamite of Nero, who dressed him in drag and married him.

1. With reference to the historical allusion (Sporus), but "hysteric" is not far away.

2. Disreputable quarter of London, inhabited by whores.

3. Sense of shame.

4. Prostitute.

An you be such a one, I must bid adieu
To your delights. The case appears too liquid. [*Exit.*]

LADY POLITIC. Ay, you may carry't clear, with your state-face![5]
But for your carnival concupiscence,
Who here is fled for liberty of conscience,
From furious persecution of the marshal,
Her will I dis'ple.[6]

PEREGRINE. This is fine, i'faith,
And do you use this often? Is this part
Of your wit's exercise, 'gainst you have occasion?
Madam——

LADY POLITIC. Go to, sir.

PEREGRINE. Do you hear me, lady?
Why, if your knight have set you to beg shirts,
Or to invite me home, you might have done it
A nearer way, by far.[7]

LADY POLITIC. This cannot work you
Out of my snare.

PEREGRINE. Why, am I in it, then?
Indeed your husband told me you were fair,
And so you are; only your nose inclines,
That side that's next the sun, to the queen-apple.[8]

LADY POLITIC. This cannot be endured, by any patience.

SCENE 3

[*Enter* MOSCA.]

MOSCA. What is the matter, madam?

LADY POLITIC. If the Senate
Right not my quest in this,[9] I will protest them
To all the world, no aristocracy.

MOSCA. What is the injury, lady?

LADY POLITIC. Why, the callet[1]
You told me of, here I have ta'en disguised.

MOSCA. Who? this! what means your ladyship? the creature
I mentioned to you is apprehended now,
Before the Senate; you shall see her—

LADY POLITIC. Where?

MOSCA. I'll bring you to her. This young gentleman,
I saw him land this morning at the port.

LADY POLITIC. Is't possible! how has my judgment wandered?
Sir, I must, blushing, say to you, I have erred;
And plead your pardon.

PEREGRINE. What, more changes yet!

LADY POLITIC. I hope you have not the malice to remember
A gentlewoman's passion. If you stay

5. A solemn expression.
6. Discipline; specifically, whip. In England at least (though not in Venice) the marshall was directly charged with catching and punishing prostitutes.
7. Peregrine implies that the whole situation is a setup, the knight pimping for his wife.
8. Lady Politic has a fiery red nose.
9. Don't do me justice.
1. Slut.

In Venice here, please you to use me, sir—
MOSCA. Will you go, madam?
LADY POLITIC. 'Pray you, sir, use me; in faith,
The more you see me, the more I shall conceive
You have forgot our quarrel.
[*Exeunt* LADY WOULD-BE, MOSCA, NANO, *and* WAITING-WOMEN.]
PEREGRINE. This is rare!
Sir Politic Would-be? no; Sir Politic Bawd!
To bring me thus acquainted with his wife!
Well, wise Sir Pol, since you have practiced thus
Upon my freshman-ship,[2] I'll try your salt-head,
What proof it is against a counterplot. [*Exit.*]

SCENE 4. *The Scrutineo*

[*Enter* VOLTORE, CORBACCIO, CORVINO, *and* MOSCA.]
VOLTORE. Well, now you know the carriage of the business,
Your constancy is all that is required
Unto the safety of it.
MOSCA. Is the lie[3]
Safely conveyed amongst us? is that sure?
Knows every man his burden?[4]
CORVINO. Yes.
MOSCA. Then shrink not.
CORVINO. [*aside to* MOSCA] But knows the advocate the truth?
MOSCA. O, sir,
By no means; I devised a formal tale
That salved your reputation. But be valiant, sir.
CORVINO. I fear no one but him, that this his pleading
Should make him stand for a co-heir—
MOSCA. Co-halter!
Hang him; we will but use his tongue, his noise,
As we do Croaker's[5] here.
CORVINO. Ay, what shall he do?
MOSCA. When we have done, you mean?
CORVINO. Yes.
MOSCA. Why, we'll think:
Sell him for mummia;[6] he's half dust already.
[*To* VOLTORE.] Do you not smile to see this buffalo,[7]
How he doth sport it with his head? [*Aside*]—I should,
If all were well and past. [*To* CORBACCIO.] Sir, only you
Are he that shall enjoy the crop of all,
And these know not for whom they toil.
CORBACCIO. Ay, peace.

2. Innocence, as of a freshman, but in opposition to Sir Politic's "salt-head": salacity.
3. Untruth, but also the shape of things, as in the lie or lay of the land.
4. "Part," as in part-singing. Mosca must be sure everyone has his story straight.
5. I.e., Corbaccio's.
6. Allegedly the powdered remains of the Pharaohs, popularly sold as medicine.
7. An allusion to the cuckold's horns worn by Corvino.

MOSCA. [*turning to* CORVINO] But you shall eat it. [*Aside.*]
Much![8] [*to* VOLTORE] Worshipful sir,
Mercury sit upon your thundering tongue,
Or the French Hercules,[9] and make your language
As conquering as his club, to beat along,
As with a tempest, flat, our adversaries;
But much more yours, sir.
VOLTORE. Here they come, have done.
MOSCA. I have another witness, if you need, sir,
I can produce.
VOLTORE. Who is it?
MOSCA. Sir, I have her.

SCENE 5

[*Enter* AVOCATORI *and take their seats;* BONARIO, CELIA, NOTARIO, COMMENDATORI, SAFFI, *and other* OFFICERS OF JUSTICE.]

1 AVOCATORE. The like of this the Senate never heard of.
2 AVOCATORE. 'Twill come most strange to them when we report it.
4 AVOCATORE. The gentlewoman[1] has been ever held
Of unreprovéd name,
3 AVOCATORE. So has the youth.[2]
4 AVOCATORE. The more unnatural part that of his father.
2 AVOCATORE. More of the husband.[3]
1 AVOCATORE. I not know to give
His act a name, it is so monstrous!
4 AVOCATORE. But the impostor,[4] he's a thing created
To exceed example!
1 AVOCATORE. And all after-times!
2 AVOCATORE. I never heard a true voluptuary
Described, but him.
3 AVOCATORE. Appear yet those were cited?
NOTARIO. All but the old magnifico, Volpone.
1 AVOCATORE. Why is not he here?
MOSCA. Please your fatherhoods,
Here is his advocate: himself's so weak,
So feeble—
4 AVOCATORE. What are you?
BONARIO. His parasite,
His knave, his pander: I beseech the court,
He may be forced to come, that your grave eyes
May bear strong witness of his strange impostures.
VOLTORE. Upon my faith and credit with your virtues,
He is not able to endure the air.
2 AVOCATORE. Bring him, however.

8. I.e., "fat chance!"
9. Both Mercury, god of thieves, and the French Hercules were patrons of eloquence; the latter is specifically discussed by the classical burlesque-writer, Lucian.
1. I.e., Celia.
2. I.e., Bonario.
3. I.e., Corvino.
4. I.e., Volpone.

3 AVOCATORE. We will see him.
4 AVOCATORE. Fetch him.
VOLTORE. Your fatherhoods' fit pleasures be obeyed; [*Exeunt* OFFICERS.]
But sure, the sight will rather move your pities
Than indignation. May it please the court,
In the meantime, he may be heard in me.
I know this place most void of prejudice,
And therefore crave it, since we have no reason
To fear our truth should hurt our cause.
3 AVOCATORE. Speak free.
VOLTORE. Then know, most honored fathers, I must now
Discover to your strangely abuséd ears,
The most prodigious and most frontless[5] piece
Of solid impudence and treachery,
That ever vicious nature yet brought forth
To shame the state of Venice. This lewd woman,
That wants[6] no artificial looks or tears
To help the visor she has now put on,
Hath long been known a close adulteress
To that lascivious youth there; not suspected,
I say, but known, and taken in the act
With him; and by this man, the easy husband,
Pardoned; whose timeless[7] bounty makes him now
Stand here, the most unhappy, innocent person,
That ever man's own goodness made accused.
For these not knowing how to owe a gift
Of that dear grace, but with their shame; being placed
So above all powers of their gratitude,
Began to hate the benefit; and, in place
Of thanks, devise to extirp[8] the memory
Of such an act. Wherein, I pray your fatherhoods
To observe the malice, yea, the rage of creatures
Discovered in their evils; and what heart
Such take, even from their crimes. But that anon
Will more appear. This gentleman, the father,
Hearing of this foul fact, with many others,
Which daily struck at his too tender ears,
And grieved in nothing more than that he could not
Preserve himself a parent (his son's ills
Growing to that strange flood), at last decreed
To disinherit him.
1 AVOCATORE. These be strange turns!
2 AVOCATORE. The young man's fame was ever fair and honest.
VOLTORE. So much more full of danger is his vice,
That can beguile so under shade of virtue.
But, as I said, my honored sires, his father

5. Shameless.
6. Lacks; "visor": artificial features, outward appearance.
7. Ill-timed.
8. Wipe out, extirpate.

Having this settled purpose, by what means
To him betrayed, we know not, and this day
Appointed for the deed; that parricide,
I cannot style him better, by confederacy[9]
Preparing this his paramour to be there,
Entered Volpone's house (who was the man,
Your fatherhoods must understand, designed
For the inheritance), there sought his father;
But with what purpose sought he him, my lords?
I tremble to pronounce it, that a son
Unto a father, and to such a father,
Should have so foul, felonious intent!
It was to murder him; when, being prevented
By his more happy absence, what then did he?
Not check his wicked thoughts; no, now new deeds
(Mischief doth never[1] end where it begins);
An act of horror, fathers! he dragged forth
The agéd gentleman that had there lain bed-rid
Three years and more, out of his innocent couch,
Naked upon the floor, there left him; wounded
His servant in the face; and, with this strumpet,
The stale[2] to his forged practice, who was glad
To be so active (I shall here desire
Your fatherhoods to note but my collections,[3]
As most remarkable), thought at once to stop
His father's ends, discredit his free choice
In the old gentleman, redeem themselves,
By laying infamy upon this man,[4]
To whom, with blushing, they should owe their lives.

1 AVOCATORE. What proofs have you of this?

BONARIO. Most honored fathers,
I humbly crave there be no credit given
To this man's mercenary tongue.

2 AVOCATORE. Forbear.

BONARIO. His soul moves in his fee.

3 AVOCATORE. O, sir.

BONARIO. This fellow,
For six sols more,[5] would plead against his maker.

1 AVOCATORE. You do forget yourself.

VOLTORE. Nay, nay, grave fathers,
Let him have scope; can any man imagine
That he will spare his accuser, that would not
Have spared his parent?

1 AVOCATORE. Well, produce your proofs.

CELIA. I would I could forget I were a creature,

VOLTORE. Signor Corbaccio! [CORBACCIO *comes forward.*]

9. Conspiracy.
1. Jonson's text reads "ever," and the sense is defensible, but the stronger meaning comes from "never."
2. Pretext.
3. Deductions.
4. I.e., Corvino.
5. Three pence.

4 AVOCATORE. What is he?
VOLTORE. The father.
2 AVOCATORE. Has he had an oath?
NOTARIO. Yes.
CORBACCIO. What must I do now?
NOTARIO. Your testimony's craved.
CORBACCIO. Speak to the knave?
I'll have my mouth first stopped with earth; my heart
Abhors his knowledge:[6] I disclaim in him.
1 AVOCATORE. But for what cause?
CORBACCIO. The mere portent of nature!
He is an utter stranger to my loins.
BONARIO. Have they made you to this?
CORBACCIO. I will not hear thee,
Monster of men, swine, goat, wolf, parricide!
Speak not, thou viper.[7]
BONARIO. Sir, I will sit down,
And rather wish my innocence should suffer,
Than I resist the authority of a father.
VOLTORE. Signor Corvino! [CORVINO *comes forward.*]
2 AVOCATORE. This is strange.
1 AVOCATORE. Who's this?
NOTARIO. The husband.
4 AVOCATORE. Is he sworn,
NOTARIO. He is.
3 AVOCATORE. Speak, then.
CORVINO. This woman, please your fatherhoods, is a whore
Of most hot exercise, more than a partridge,[8]
Upon record—
1 AVOCATORE. No more.
CORVINO. Neighs like a jennet.[9]
NOTARIO. Preserve the honor of the court.
CORVINO. I shall,
And modesty of your most reverend ears.
And yet I hope that I may say, these eyes
Have seen her glued unto that piece of cedar,
That fine well-timbered gallant; and that here[1]
The letters may be read, through the horn,
That make the story perfect.
MOSCA. Excellent! sir.
CORVINO. [*aside to* MOSCA] There is no shame in this now, is there?
MOSCA. None.
CORVINO. Or if I said, I hoped that she were onward
To her damnation, if there be a hell

6. Shudders to recognize him.
7. The parricide, as a creature wholly unnatural, was punished among the Romans by being whipped, sewed up in a sack with a dog, a cock, a viper, and an ape, and thrown into the sea.
8. The partridge vied with the sparrow as the most lustful of birds.
9. Mare.
1. Corvino holds two fingers over his head to make the horned sign of the cuckold.

Greater than whore and woman; a good catholic
May make the doubt.[2]

3 AVOCATORE. His grief hath made him frantic.

1 AVOCATORE. Remove him hence. [CELIA *swoons.*]

2 AVOCATORE. Look to the woman.

CORVINO. Rare!
Prettily feigned, again!

4 AVOCATORE. Stand from about her.

1 AVOCATORE. Give her the air.

3 AVOCATORE. [*to* MOSCA] What can you say?

MOSCA. My wound,
May it please your wisdoms, speaks for me, received
In aid of my good patron, when he missed
His sought-for father,[3] when that well-taught dame
Had her cue given her, to cry out, A rape!

BONARIO. O most laid impudence! Fathers—

3 AVOCATORE. Sir, be silent;
You had your hearing free, so must they theirs.

2 AVOCATORE. I do begin to doubt the imposture here.

4 AVOCATORE. This woman has too many moods.

VOLTORE. Grave fathers,
She is a creature of a most professed
And prostituted lewdness.

CORVINO. Most impetuous,
Unsatisfied, grave fathers!

VOLTORE. May her feignings
Not take your wisdoms: but this day she baited
A stranger, a grave knight, with her loose eyes,
And more lascivious kisses. This man saw them
Together on the water, in a gondola.

MOSCA. Here is the lady herself, that saw them too,
Without; who then had in the open streets
Pursued them, but for saving her knight's honor.

1 AVOCATORE. Produce that lady.

2 AVOCATORE. Let her come. [*Exit* MOSCA.]

4 AVOCATORE. These things,
They strike with wonder.

3 AVOCATORE. I am turned a stone.

SCENE 6

[*Enter* MOSCA *with* LADY WOULD-BE.]

MOSCA. Be resolute, madam.

LADY POLITIC. Ay, this same is she. [*Pointing to* CELIA.]
Out, thou chameleon[4] harlot! now thine eyes
Vie tears with the hyena. Dar'st thou look

2. If there's any hell worse than being a woman and a whore, Corvino thinks of saying Celia may be headed for it; because he doesn't say flatly that she *is* so headed, he can claim the virtue of charity, and remain a good Catholic. The 1607 quarto reads "Christian" instead of "catholic."

3. I.e., Corbaccio.

4. An animal that changes colors. The hyena is emblematic of treachery and an eater of carrion.

Upon my wrongéd face?—I cry your pardons,
I fear I have forgettingly transgressed
Against the dignity of the court—

2 AVOCATORE. No, madam.

LADY POLITIC. And been exorbitant[5]—

2 AVOCATORE. You have not, lady.

4 AVOCATORE. These proofs are strong.

LADY POLITIC. Surely, I had no purpose
To scandalize your honors, or my sex's.

3 AVOCATORE. We do believe it.

LADY POLITIC. Surely, you may believe it.

2 AVOCATORE. Madam, we do.

LADY POLITIC. Indeed you may; my breeding
Is not so coarse——

4 AVOCATORE. We know it.

LADY POLITIC. To offend
With pertinacy——

3 AVOCATORE. Lady—

LADY POLITIC. Such a presence!
No, surely.

1 AVOCATORE. We well think it.

LADY POLITIC. You may think it.

1 AVOCATORE. Let her o'ercome. [*to* BONARIO] What witnesses have you,
To make good your report?

BONARIO. Our consciences.

CELIA. And heaven, that never fails the innocent.

4 AVOCATORE. These are no testimonies.

BONARIO. Not in your courts,
Where multitude, and clamor overcomes.

1 AVOCATORE. Nay, then you do wax insolent.

[*Re-enter* OFFICERS, *bearing* VOLPONE *on a couch.*]

VOLTORE. Here, here,
The testimony comes, that will convince,
And put to utter dumbness their bold tongues!
See here, grave fathers, here's the ravisher,
The rider on men's wives, the great impostor,
The grand voluptuary! Do you not think
These limbs should affect venery?[6] or these eyes
Covet a concubine? pray you mark these hands;
Are they not fit to stroke a lady's breasts?
Perhaps he doth dissemble!

BONARIO. So he does.

VOLTORE. Would you have him tortured?

BONARIO. I would have him proved.

VOLTORE. Best try him then with goads, or burning irons;
Put him to the strappado.[7] I have heard

5. Lady Politic doubtless means "excessive."

6. Be disposed to lust.

7. A common torture of the time: a man's hands were tied behind his back, and he was hoisted by his wrists on a gallows, to the common effect of dislocating his shoulders.

The rack hath cured the gout; 'faith, give it him,
And help him of a malady; be courteous.
I'll undertake, before these honored fathers,
He shall have yet as many left diseases,
As she has known adulterers, or thou strumpets.
O, my most equal hearers, if these deeds,
Acts of this bold and most exorbitant strain,
May pass with sufferance, what one citizen
But owes the forfeit of his life, yea, fame,
To him that dares traduce him? which of you
Are safe, my honored fathers? I would ask,
With leave of your grave fatherhoods, if their plot
Have any face or color like to truth?
Or if, unto the dullest nostril here,
It smell not rank, and most abhorréd slander?
I crave your care of this good gentleman,
Whose life is much endangered by their fable;
And as for them, I will conclude with this,
That vicious persons, when they're hot, and fleshed
In impious acts, their constancy abounds:
Damned deeds are done with greatest confidence.

1 AVOCATORE. Take them to custody, and sever them. [CELIA *and* BONARIO *are taken out.*]

2 AVOCATORE. 'Tis pity two such prodigies should live.

1 AVOCATORE. Let the old gentleman be returned with care: [*Exeunt* OFFICERS *with* VOLPONE.]
I'm sorry our credulity hath wronged him.

4 AVOCATORE. These are two creatures!

3 AVOCATORE. I've an earthquake in me.[8]

2 AVOCATORE. Their shame, even in their cradles, fled their faces.

4 AVOCATORE. [*to* VOLTORE] You have done a worthy service to the state, sir,
In their discovery.

1 AVOCATORE. You shall hear, ere night,
What punishment the court decrees upon them.

VOLTORE. We thank your fatherhoods. [*Exeunt* AVOCATORI, NOTARIO, and OFFICERS.] [*to* MOSCA]—How like you it?

MOSCA. Rare.
I'd have your tongue, sir, tipped with gold for this;
I'd have you be the heir to the whole city;
The earth I'd have want men, ere you want living:
They're bound to erect your statue in St. Mark's.
Signor Corvino, I would have you go
And show yourself, that you have conquered.

CORVINO. Yes.

MOSCA. It was much better that you should profess
Yourself a cuckold thus, than that the other
Should have been proved.

8. I'm overwhelmed.

CORVINO. Nay, I considered that;
Now it is her fault.
MOSCA. Then it had been yours.
CORVINO. True; I do doubt this advocate still.
MOSCA. I'faith,
You need not, I dare ease you of that care.
CORVINO. I trust thee, Mosca. [*Exit.*]
MOSCA. As your own soul, sir.
CORBACCIO. Mosca!
MOSCA. Now for your business, sir.
CORBACCIO. How! have you business?
MOSCA. Yes, yours sir.
CORBACCIO. O, none else?
MOSCA. None else, not I.
CORBACCIO. Be careful then.
MOSCA. Rest you with both your eyes, sir.
CORBACCIO. Dispatch it.[9]
MOSCA. Instantly.
CORBACCIO. And look that all,
Whatever, be put in, jewels, plate, moneys,
Household stuff, bedding, curtains.
MOSCA. Curtain-rings, sir:
Only the advocate's fee must be deducted.
CORBACCIO. I'll pay him now; you'll be too prodigal.
MOSCA. Sir, I must tender it.
CORBACCIO. Two sequins is well.
MOSCA. No, six, sir.
CORBACCIO. 'Tis too much.
MOSCA. He talked a great while;
You must consider that, sir.
CORBACCIO. Well, there's three—
MOSCA. I'll give it him.
CORBACCIO. Do so, and there's for thee. [*Exit.*]
MOSCA. Bountiful bones! What horrid strange offense
Did he commit 'gainst nature, in his youth,
Worthy this age? [*To* VOLTORE.]—You see, sir, how I work
Unto your ends; take you no notice.
VOLTORE. No,
I'll leave you. [*Exit.*]
MOSCA. All is yours, the devil and all,
Good advocate!—Madam, I'll bring you home.
LADY POLITIC. No, I'll go see your patron.
MOSCA. That you shall not.
I'll tell you why. My purpose is to urge
My patron to reform his will;[1] and for
The zeal you have shown today, whereas before
You were but third or fourth, you shall be now

9. I.e., get the will made, with me in it.
1. Rewrite his testament, though always with the other connotation of improving his disposition.

Put in the first; which would appear as begged,
If you were present. Therefore—
LADY POLITIC. You shall sway me. [*Exeunt.*]

Act V

SCENE 1. *A room in* VOLPONE'S *house*

[*Enter* VOLPONE.]

VOLPONE. Well, I am here, and all this brunt[2] is past.
I ne'er was in dislike with my disguise
Till this fled moment:[3] here 'twas good, in private,
But in your public—*cave*[4] whilst I breathe.
'Fore God, my left leg 'gan to have the cramp,
And I apprehended[5] straight some power had struck me
With a dead palsy. Well! I must be merry,
And shake it off. A many of these fears
Would put me into some villainous disease,
Should they come thick upon me: I'll prevent 'em.
Give me a bowl of lusty wine, to fright
This humour from my heart. [*Drinks.*]—Hum, hum, hum!
'Tis almost gone already, I shall conquer.
Any device, now, of rare ingenious knavery,
That would possess me with a violent laughter,
Would make me up again. [*Drinks again.*]—So, so, so, so!
This heat is life; 'tis blood by this time! Mosca!

SCENE 2

[*Enter* MOSCA.]

MOSCA. How now, sir? does the day look clear again?
Are we recovered? and wrought out of error,
Into our way, to see our path before us?
Is our trade free once more?
VOLPONE. Exquisite Mosca!
MOSCA. Was it not carried learnedly?
VOLPONE. And stoutly.
Good wits are greatest in extremities.
MOSCA. It were a folly beyond thought, to trust
Any grand act unto a cowardly spirit.
You are not taken with it[6] enough, methinks.
VOLPONE. O, more than if I had enjoyed the wench;
The pleasure of all womankind's not like it.
MOSCA. Why now you speak, sir. We must here be fixed;
Here we must rest. This is our masterpiece;
We cannot think to go beyond this.
VOLPONE. True,
Thou'st played thy prize, my precious Mosca.
MOSCA. Nay, sir,

2. Trouble.
3. Moment just past.
4. Beware, watch out.
5. The word is printed and pronounced "apprended."
6. Pleased, satisfied with it.

To gull the court—
VOLPONE. And quite divert the torrent
Upon the innocent.
MOSCA. Yes, and to make
So rare a music out of discords—
VOLPONE. Right.
That yet to me's the strangest! how thou'st borne it
That these, being so divided 'mongst themselves,
Should not scent somewhat, or in me or thee,
Or doubt their own side.
MOSCA. True, they will not see't.
Too much light blinds them, I think.[7] Each of them
Is so possessed and stuffed with his own hopes,
That anything unto the contrary,
Never so true, or never so apparent,
Never so palpable, they will resist it—
VOLPONE. Like a temptation of the devil.
MOSCA. Right, sir.
Merchants may talk of trade, and your great signors
Of land that yields well; but if Italy
Have any glebe[8] more fruitful than these fellows,
I am deceived. Did not your advocate rare?[9]
VOLPONE. O—*My most honored fathers, my grave fathers,*
Under correction of your fatherhoods,
What face of truth is here? If these strange deeds
May pass, most honored fathers—I had much ado
To forbear laughing.
MOSCA. It seemed to me, you sweat, sir.
VOLPONE. In troth, I did a little.
MOSCA. But confess, sir,
Were you not daunted?
VOLPONE. In good faith, I was
A little in a mist, but not dejected;
Never, but still myself.
MOSCA. I think it, sir.
Now, so truth help me, I must needs say this, sir,
And out of conscience for your advocate,
He has taken pains, in faith, sir, and deserved,
In my poor judgment, I speak it under favor,
Not to contrary you, sir, very richly—
Well—to be cozened.
VOLPONE. Troth, and I think so too,
By that I heard him, in the latter end.
MOSCA. O, but before, sir: had you heard him first
Draw it to certain heads, then aggravate,
Then use his vehement figures[1]—I looked still
When he would shift a shirt;[2] and, doing this

7. An ancient adage.
8. Soil.
9. Did not your advocate (perform) rare(ly)?
1. Terms of legal oratory.
2. I.e., he sweated so much over his speech, it seemed he might have to change his linen.

Out of pure love, no hope of gain—
VOLPONE. 'Tis right.
I cannot answer him Mosca, as I would,
Not yet; but for thy sake, at thy entreaty,
I will begin e'en now to vex them all,
This very instant.
MOSCA. Good, sir.
VOLPONE. Call the dwarf
And eunuch forth.
MOSCA. Castrone, Nano!
[*Enter* CASTRONE *and* NANO.]
NANO. Here.
VOLPONE. Shall we have a jig now?
MOSCA. What you please, sir.
VOLPONE. Go,
Straight give out about the streets, you two,
That I am dead; do it with constancy,
Sadly, do you hear? impute it to the grief
Of this late slander. [*Exeunt* CASTRONE *and* NANO.]
MOSCA. What do you mean, sir?
VOLPONE. O,
I shall have instantly my vulture, crow,
Raven, come flying hither, on the news,
To peck for carrion, my she-wolf, and all,
Greedy, and full of expectation—
MOSCA. And then to have it ravished from their mouths!
VOLPONE. 'Tis true. I will have thee put on a gown,
And take upon thee, as thou wert mine heir;
Show them a will. Open that chest, and reach
Forth one of those that has the blanks; I'll straight
Put in thy name.
MOSCA. It will be rare, sir. [*Gives him a paper.*]
VOLPONE. Ay,
When they e'en gape, and find themselves deluded—
MOSCA. Yes.
VOLPONE. And thou use them scurvily! Dispatch,
Get on thy gown.
MOSCA. But what, sir, if they ask
After the body?
VOLPONE. Say, it was corrupted.
MOSCA. I'll say it stunk, sir; and was fain to have it
Coffined up instantly, and sent away.
VOLPONE. Anything, what thou wilt. Hold, here's my will.
Get thee a cap, a count-book,[3] pen and ink,
Papers afore thee; sit as thou wert taking
An inventory of parcels. I'll get up
Behind the curtain, on a stool, and hearken;
Sometime peep over, see how they do look,
With what degrees their blood doth leave their faces.

3. Ledger.

O, 'twill afford me a rare meal of laughter!
MOSCA. [*putting on a cap, and setting out the table, &c.*] Your advocate will turn stark dull upon it.
VOLPONE. It will take off his oratory's edge.
MOSCA. But your clarissimo, old round-back,[4] he
Will crump you like a hog-louse, with the touch.
VOLPONE. And what Corvino?
MOSCA. O, sir, look for him,
Tomorrow morning, with a rope and dagger,
To visit all the streets;[5] he must run mad.
My lady too, that came into the court
To bear false witness for your worship—
VOLPONE. Yes,
And kissed me 'fore the fathers, when my face
Flowed all with oils.
MOSCA. And sweat, sir. Why, your gold
Is such another medicine, it dries up
All those offensive savors; it transforms
The most deformed, and restores them lovely,
As 'twere the strange poetical girdle.[6] Jove
Could not invent t' himself a shroud more subtle
To pass Acrisius' guards.[7] It is the thing
Makes all the world her grace, her youth her beauty.
VOLPONE. I think she loves me.
MOSCA. Who? the lady, sir?
She's jealous of you.
VOLPONE. Dost thou say so? [*Knocking within.*]
MOSCA. Hark,
There's some already.
VOLPONE. Look.
MOSCA. It is the vulture;
He has the quickest scent.
VOLPONE. I'll to my place,
Thou to thy posture. [*Goes behind the curtain.*]
MOSCA. I am set.
VOLPONE. But, Mosca,
Play the artificer now, torture them rarely.

SCENE 3

[*Enter* VOLTORE.]
VOLTORE. How now, my Mosca?
MOSCA. [*writing*] *Turkey carpets, nine*[8]—

4. Corbaccio is a *clarissimo*, a distinguished man in Venice. "Crump you": curl up on you; there is a species of wood louse or hog louse (the names are interchangeable) which curls up in a ball when touched.
5. I.e., looking for a place to commit suicide.
6. The girdle of Venus (*cestus*) made any wearer irresistibly beautiful.
7. Acrisius was the father of Danae; he locked her up in a tower till Jove managed to get to her in the form of a shower of gold.
8. Turkey carpets (not necessarily from Turkey) were particularly thick and luxurious; cloth described as tissue often had threads of gold or silver interwoven.

VOLTORE. Taking an inventory? that is well.
MOSCA. *Two suits of bedding, tissue—*
VOLTORE. Where's the will?
Let me read that the while.
[*Enter* SERVANTS *with* CORBACCIO *in a chair.*]
CORBACCIO. So, set me down,
And get you home. [*Exeunt servants.*]
VOLTORE. Is he come now to trouble us?
MOSCA. *Of cloth of gold, two more—*
CORBACCIO. Is it done, Mosca?
MOSCA. *Of several velvets, eight—*
VOLTORE. I like his care.
CORBACCIO. Dost thou not hear?
[*Enter* CORVINO.]
CORVINO. Ha! is the hour come, Mosca?
VOLPONE. [*peeping over the curtain*] Ay, now they muster.
CORVINO. What does the advocate here,
Or this Corbaccio?
CORBACCIO. What do these here?
[*Enter* LADY POLITIC WOULD-BE.]
LADY POLITIC. Mosca!
Is his thread spun?
MOSCA. *Eight chests of linen—*
VOLPONE. O,
My fine dame Would-be, too!
CORVINO. Mosca, the will,
That I may show it these, and rid them hence.
MOSCA. *Six chests of diaper,*[9] *four of damask.*—There. [*Gives them the will carelessly, over his shoulder.*]
CORBACCIO. Is that the will?
MOSCA. *Down-beds, and bolsters—*
VOLPONE. Rare!
Be busy still. Now they begin to flutter:
They never think of me. Look, see, see, see!
How their swift eyes run over the long deed,
Unto the name, and to the legacies,
What is bequeathed them there—
MOSCA. *Ten suits of hangings—*[1]
VOLPONE. Ay, in their garters, Mosca. Now their hopes
Are at the gasp.
VOLTORE. Mosca the heir!
CORBACCIO. What's that?
VOLPONE. My advocate is dumb; look to my merchant,
He has heard of some strange storm, a ship is lost,
He faints; my lady will swoon. Old glazen-eyes,[2]
He hath not reached his despair yet.

9. Fine linen cloth; "damask" (from Damascus): a silk fabric woven with many figures.
1. Sets of tapestries on the walls. But Volpone suggests garters, traditional means of suicide.
2. I.e., Corbaccio.

CORBACCIO. All these
Are out of hope; I am, sure, the man. [*Takes the will.*]
CORVINO. But, Mosca—
MOSCA. *Two cabinets*—
CORVINO. Is this in earnest?
MOSCA. *One*
Of ebony—
CORVINO. Or do you but delude me?
MOSCA. *The other, mother of pearl*—I am very busy.
Good faith, it is a fortune thrown upon me—
Item, one salt[3] *of agate*—not my seeking.
LADY POLITIC. Do you hear, sir?
MOSCA. A *perfumed box*—'Pray you forbear,
You see I'm troubled—*made of an onyx*—
LADY POLITIC. How!
MOSCA. To-morrow or next day, I shall be at leisure
To talk with you all.
CORVINO. Is this my large hope's issue?
LADY POLITIC. Sir, I must have a fairer answer.
MOSCA. Madam!
Marry, and shall: pray you, fairly[4] quit my house.
Nay, raise no tempest with your looks; but hark you:
Remember what your ladyship offered me
To put you in an heir;[5] go to, think on it:
And what you said e'en your best madams did
For maintenance;[6] and why not you? Enough.
Go home, and use the poor Sir Pol, your knight, well,
For fear I tell some riddles; go, be melancholic. [*Exit* LADY POLITIC.]
VOLPONE. O, my fine devil!
CORVINO. Mosca, 'pray you a word.
MOSCA. Lord! will not you take your dispatch hence yet?
Methinks, of all, you should have been the example.
Why should you stay here? with what thought, what promise?
Hear you; do not you know, I know you an ass,
And that you would most fain have been a wittol,[7]
If fortune would have let you? that you are
A declared cuckold, on good terms? This pearl,
You'll say, was yours? Right. This diamond?
I'll not deny't, but thank you. Much here else?
It may be so. Why, think that these good works
May help to hide your bad. I'll not betray you;
Although you be but extraordinary,[8]
And have it only in title, it sufficeth;
Go home, be melancholic too, or mad. [*Exit* CORVINO.]

3. Salt-cellar.
4. Once and for all.
5. This aspect of Lady Politic Jonson has saved for the present moment.
6. Lady Politic would never say "for money."
7. A pimp for your own wife.
8. I.e., not a full-fledged pimp or cuckold, just one who did his best to be such.

VOLPONE. Rare Mosca! how his villainy becomes him!
VOLTORE. Certain he doth delude all these for me.
CORBACCIO. Mosca the heir!
VOLPONE. O, his four eyes have found it.[9]
CORBACCIO. I am cozened, cheated, by a parasite slave;
Harlot,[1] thou hast gulled me.
MOSCA. Yes, sir. Stop your mouth,
Or I shall draw the only tooth is left.
Are not you he, that filthy covetous wretch,
With the three legs,[2] that here, in hope of prey,
Have, any time this three years, snuffed about
With your most groveling nose, and would have hired
Me to the poisoning of my patron, sir?
Are not you he that have today in court
Professed the disinheriting of your son?
Perjured yourself? Go home, and die, and stink;
If you but croak a syllable, all comes out:
Away, and call your porters! [*Exit* CORBACCIO.]—
Go, go, stink.
VOLPONE. Excellent varlet!
VOLTORE. Now, my faithful Mosca,
I find thy constancy—
MOSCA. Sir?
VOLTORE. Sincere.
MOSCA. [*writing*] *A table*
Of porphyry—I mar'l you'll be thus troublesome.
VOLTORE. Nay, leave off now, they are gone.
MOSCA. Why, who are you?
What! Who did send for you? O, cry you mercy,
Reverend sir! Good faith, I am grieved for you,
That any chance of mine should thus defeat
Your (I must needs say) most deserving travails:
But I protest, sir, it was cast upon me,
And I could almost wish to be without it,
But that the will o' the dead must be observed.
Marry, my joy is that you need it not;
You have a gift, sir (thank your education),
Will never let you want, while there are men,
And malice, to breed causes. Would I had
But half the like, for all my fortune, sir!
If I have any suits (as I do hope,
Things being so easy and direct, I shall not)
I will make bold with your obstreperous aid—
Conceive me—for your fee, sir. In meantime,
You that have so much law, I know have the conscience
Not to be covetous of what is mine.
Good sir, I thank you for my plate; 'twill help

9. Corbaccio wears spectacles.
1. Frequently used of men, in the sense of "scoundrel."
2. I.e., two plus a cane or crutch.

To set up a young man.[3] Good faith, you look
As you were costive;[4] best go home and purge, sir. [*Exit* VOLTORE.]

VOLPONE. [*Comes from behind the curtain.*] Bid him eat lettuce well.[5] My witty mischief,
Let me embrace thee. O that I could now
Transform thee to a Venus!—Mosca, go,
Straight take my habit of clarissimo,[6]
And walk the streets; be seen, torment them more.
We must pursue, as well as plot. Who would
Have lost this feast?

MOSCA. I doubt it will lose them.

VOLPONE. O, my recovery shall recover all.
That I could now but think on some disguise
To meet them in, and ask them questions;
How I would vex them still at every turn!

MOSCA. Sir, I can fit you.

VOLPONE. Canst thou?

MOSCA. Yes, I know
One o' the commendatori, sir, so like you;
Him will I straight make drunk, and bring you his habit.[7]

VOLPONE. A rare disguise, and answering thy brain!
O, I will be a sharp disease unto them.

MOSCA. Sir, you must look for curses—

VOLPONE. Till they burst;
The fox fares ever best when he is cursed [*Exeunt.*]

SCENE 4. *A hall in* SIR POLITIC'S *house*

[*Enter* PEREGRINE *disguised, and three* MERCHANTS.]

PEREGRINE. Am I enough disguised?

1 MERCHANT. I warrant you.

PEREGRINE. All my ambition is to fright him only.

2 MERCHANT. If you could ship him away, 'twere excellent.

3 MERCHANT. To Zant, or to Aleppo?[8]

PEREGRINE. Yes, and have his
Adventures put i' the Book of Voyages,
And his gulled story[9] registered for truth.
Well, gentlemen, when I am in a while,
And that you think us warm in our discourse,
Know your approaches.

1 MERCHANT. Trust it to our care. [*Exeunt* MERCHANTS.]

[*Enter* WAITING WOMAN.]

3. I.e., himself.
4. Constipated; "purge": take a laxative.
5. In classical days, lettuce was thought to have mild purgative powers.
6. Mosca, in putting on the distinctive dress of a nobleman (clarissímo) is running a big risk—laws about wearing the costume of one's rank were strict and severe.
7. Volpone now assumes a common sergeant's uniform, and over it a loose black robe, with a red cap and two brass buttons.
8. Zant is Byzantium, Constantinople, or (now) Istanbul; Aleppo, in Syria, still carries its old name.
9. The story of his gulling.

PEREGRINE. Save you, fair lady! Is Sir Pol within?
WOMAN. I do not know, sir.
PEREGRINE. Pray you say unto him,
Here is a merchant, upon earnest business,
Desires to speak with him.
WOMAN. I will see, sir. [*Exit*]
PEREGRINE. Pray you.—
I see the family is all female here.
[*Re-enter* WAITING WOMAN.]
WOMAN. He says, sir, he has weighty affairs of state,
That now require him whole; some other time
You may possess him.
PEREGRINE. Pray you say again.
If those require him whole, these will exact him,
Whereof I bring him tidings. [*Exit* WOMAN.]—What might be
His grave affair of state now? How to make
Bolognian sausages[1] here in Venice, sparing
One o' the ingredients?
[*Re-enter* WAITING WOMAN.]
WOMAN. Sir, he says, he knows
By your word *tidings*, that you are no statesman,[2]
And therefore wills you stay.
PEREGRINE. Sweet, pray you return him;
I have not read so many proclamations,
And studied them for words, as he has done—
But—here he deigns to come. [*Exit* WOMAN.]
[*Enter* SIR POLITIC.]
SIR POLITIC. Sir, I must crave
Your courteous pardon. There hath chanced today
Unkind disaster 'twixt my lady and me;
And I was penning my apology,
To give her satisfaction, as you came now.
PEREGRINE. Sir, I am grieved I bring you worse disaster:
The gentleman you met at the port today,
That told you, he was newly arrived—
SIR POLITIC. Ay, was
A fugitive punk?[3]
PEREGRINE. No, sir, a spy set on you;
And he has made relation to the senate,
That you professed to him to have a plot
To sell the state of Venice to the Turk.[4]
SIR POLITIC. O me!
PEREGRINE. For which, warrants are signed by this time,
To apprehend you, and to search your study
For papers—

1. Sausages of Bologna were so famous that *baloney* is still a word in general use.
2. "Tidings" were what normal people received; a secret-service operative would get "intelligence."
3. A runaway pimp (the "gentleman" was, of course, Peregrine himself).
4. See above, IV.1.

SIR POLITIC. Alas, sir, I have none but notes
Drawn out of play-books[5]—
PEREGRINE. All the better, sir.
SIR POLITIC. And some essays. What shall I do?
PEREGRINE. Sir, best
Convey yourself into a sugar-chest;
Or, if you could lie round, a frail[6] were rare,
And I could send you aboard.
SIR POLITIC. Sir, I but talked so,
For discourse' sake merely. [*Knocking within.*]
PEREGRINE. Hark! they are there.
SIR POLITIC. I am a wretch, a wretch!
PEREGRINE. What will you do, sir?
Have you ne'er a currant-butt[7] to leap into?
They'll put you to the rack; you must be sudden.
SIR POLITIC. Sir, I have an engine—
3 MERCHANT. [*within*] Sir Politic Would-be!
2 MERCHANT. [*within*] Where is he?
SIR POLITIC. That I have thought upon before time.
PEREGRINE. What is it?
SIR POLITIC. I shall ne'er endure the torture.
Marry, it is, sir, of a tortoise-shell,
Fitted for these extremities: pray you, sir, help me.
Here I've a place, sir, to put back my legs,
Please you to lay it on, sir, [*Lies down while* PEREGRINE *places the shell upon him.*]—With this cap,
And my black gloves, I'll lie, sir, like a tortoise,
Till they are gone.
PEREGRINE. And call you this an engine?
SIR POLITIC. Mine own device—Good sir, bid my wife's women
To burn my papers. [*Exit* PEREGRINE.]
[*The* MERCHANTS *rush in.*]
1 MERCHANT. Where is he hid?
3 MERCHANT. We must,
And will sure find him.
2 MERCHANT. Which is his study?
[*Re-enter* PEREGRINE.]
1 MERCHANT. What
Are you, sir?
PEREGRINE. I am a merchant, that came here
To look upon this tortoise.
3 MERCHANT. How!
1 MERCHANT. St. Mark!
What beast is this?
PEREGRINE. It is a fish.
2 MERCHANT. Come out here!

5. Sir Pol's exotic information turns out to be very common stuff. Play-books in particular had then about the reputation of comic books now.
6. Flimsy fruit-basket.
7. Cask for holding currants.

PEREGRINE. Nay, you may strike him, sir, and tread upon him:
He'll bear a cart.
1 MERCHANT. What, to run over him?
PEREGRINE. Yes.
3 MERCHANT. Let's jump upon him.
2 MERCHANT. Can he not go?
PEREGRINE. He creeps, sir.
1 MERCHANT. Let's see him creep. [*Pokes him.*]
PEREGRINE. No, good sir, you will hurt him.
2 MERCHANT. Heart, I will see him creep, or prick his guts.
3 MERCHANT. Come out here!
PEREGRINE. Pray you, sir! [*aside to* SIR POLITIC]
—Creep a little.
1 MERCHANT. Forth.
2 MERCHANT. Yet farther.
Good sir! [*aside to* SIR POLITIC]
—Creep.
2 MERCHANT. We'll see his legs.
[*They pull off the shell and discover him.*]
3 MERCHANT. Gods' so, he has garters!
1 MERCHANT. Ay, and gloves!
2 MERCHANT. Is this
Your fearful tortoise?
PEREGRINE. [*discovering himself*] Now, Sir Pol, we are even;
For your next project I shall be prepared.
I am sorry for the funeral of your notes, sir.
1 MERCHANT. 'Twere a rare motion[8] to be seen in Fleet Street.
2 MERCHANT. Ay, in the Term.
1 MERCHANT. Or Smithfield, in the fair.
3 MERCHANT. Methinks 'tis but a melancholic sight.
PEREGRINE. Farewell, most politic tortoise! [*Exeunt* PEREGRINE *and* MERCHANTS.]
[*Re-enter* WAITING-WOMAN.]
SIR POLITIC. Where's my lady?
Knows she of this?
WOMAN. I know not, sir.
SIR POLITIC. Inquire.
O, I shall be the fable of all feasts,
The freight of the gazetti,[9] ship-boys' tale;
And, which is worst, even talk for ordinaries.
WOMAN. My lady's come most melancholic home,
And says, sir, she will straight to sea, for physic.[1]
SIR POLITIC. And I, to shun this place and clime forever,
Creeping with house on back, and think it well
To shrink my poor head in my politic shell. [*Exeunt.*]

8. Puppet show. "Fleet Street": then as now a busy street in central London. "Smithfield": where Bartholomew Fair was held. All fairs were especially busy in Term, when lawyers, and their clients, were in residence. These Venetian *mercatori* are remarkably conversant with London manners.
9. Subject of the newsletters; "talk for the ordinaries": tavern gossip.
1. For her health.

SCENE 5. *A room in* VOLPONE'S *house*

[*Enter* MOSCA *in the habit of a* clarissimo, *and* VOLPONE *in that of a* commendatore.]

VOLPONE. Am I then like him?

MOSCA. O, sir, you are he.
No man can sever[2] you.

VOLPONE. Good.

MOSCA. But what am I?

VOLPONE. 'Fore heaven, a brave *clarissimo*; thou becom'st it!
Pity thou wert not born one.

MOSCA. If I hold
My made one, 'twill be well.

VOLPONE. I'll go and see
What news first at the court. [*Exit*]

MOSCA. Do so. My fox
Is out of his hole,[3] and ere he shall re-enter,
I'll make him languish in his borrowed case,
Except he come to composition with me.—
Androgyno, Castrone, Nano!

[*Enter* ANDROGYNO, CASTRONE, *and* NANO.]

ALL. Here.

MOSCA. Go, recreate yourselves abroad; go, sport.— [*Exeunt.*]
So, now I have the keys, and am possessed.
Since he will needs be dead afore his time,
I'll bury him, or gain by him. I am his heir,
And so will keep me, till he share at least.
To cozen him of all, were but a cheat
Well placed; no man would cónstrue it a sin:
Let his sport pay for't. This is called the fox-trap. [*Exit.*]

SCENE 6. *A street*

[*Enter* CORBACCIO *and* CORVINO.]

CORBACCIO. They say the court is set.

CORVINO. We must maintain
Our first tale good, for both our reputations.

CORBACCIO. Why? mine's no tale; my son would there have killed me.

CORVINO. That's true, I had forgot. [*Aside.*]—Mine is, I'm sure.
But for your will, sir.

CORBACCIO. Ay, I'll come upon him
For that hereafter, now his patron's dead.

[*Enter* VOLPONE *in disguise.*]

VOLPONE. Signor Corvino! and Corbaccio! sir,
Much joy unto you.

CORVINO. Of what?

2. Distinguish.
3. Children play a game called Fox-in-the-Hole. "His borrowed case": his false costume.

VOLPONE. The sudden good
Dropped down upon you—
CORBACCIO. Where?
VOLPONE. And none knows how,
From old Volpone, sir.
CORBACCIO. Out, arrant knave!
VOLPONE. Let not your too much wealth, sir, make you furious.
CORBACCIO. Away, thou varlet.
VOLPONE. Why, sir?
CORBACCIO. Dost thou mock me?
VOLPONE. You mock the world, sir; did you not change[4] wills?
CORBACCIO. Out, harlot!
VOLPONE. O! belike you are the man,
Signor Corvino? Faith, you carry it well;
You grow not mad withal; I love your spirit.
You are not over-leavened[5] with your fortune.
You should have some would swell now, like a wine-vat.
With such an autumn—Did he give you all, sir?
CORVINO. Avoid, you rascal!
VOLPONE. Troth, your wife has shown
Herself a very woman;[6] but you are well,
You need not care, you have a good estate,
To bear it out, sir; better by this chance.
Except Corbaccio have a share.
CORBACCIO. Hence, varlet.
VOLPONE. You will not be a'known, sir; why, 'tis wise.
Thus do all gamesters, at all games, dissemble,
No man will seem to win. [*Exeunt* CORVINO *and* CORBACCIO.]
—Here comes my vulture,
Heaving his beak up in the air, and snuffing.

SCENE 7

[*Enter* VOLTORE.]

VOLTORE. Outstripped thus, by a parasite! a slave,
Would run on errands, and make legs[7] for crumbs!
Well, what I'll do—
VOLPONE. The court stays for your worship.
I' e'en rejoice, sir, at your worship's happiness,
And that it fell into so learnéd hands,
That understand the fingering—
VOLTORE. What do you mean?
VOLPONE. I mean to be a suitor to your worship
For the small tenement, out of reparations[8]—
That at the end of your long row of houses,
By the Pescheria[9]; it was, in Volpone's time,

4. Exchange.
5. Too puffed up (like a loaf of bread).
6. I.e., promiscuous.
7. Bow and scrape.
8. Repair.
9. The fish market on the Grand Canal.

Your predecessor, ere he grew diseased,
A handsome, pretty, customed[1] bawdy-house
As any was in Venice, none dispraised;
But fell with him. His body and that house
Decayed together.

VOLTORE. Come, sir, leave your prating.

VOLPONE. Why, if your worship give me but your hand
That I may have the refusal, I have done.
'Tis a mere toy to you, sir; candle-rents;[2]
As your learned worship knows—

VOLPONE. What do I know?

VOLPONE. Marry, no end of your wealth, sir; God decrease it!

VOLTORE. Mistaking knave! what, mock'st thou my misfortune?

VOLPONE. His blessing on your heart, sir; would 'twere more!—
[*Exit* VOLTORE.]
—Now to my first again, at the next corner. [*Exit.*]

SCENE 8. [*Another part of the street*]

[*Enter* CORBACCIO *and* CORVINO;—MOSCA *passes over the stage, before them.*]

CORBACCIO. See, in our habit![3] see the impudent varlet!

CORVINO. That I could shoot mine eyes at him, like gun-stones!

[*Enter* VOLPONE.]

VOLPONE. But is this true, sir, of the parasite?

CORBACCIO. Again, to afflict us! monster!

VOLPONE. In good faith, sir,
I'm heartily grieved, a beard of your grave length
Should be so over-reached. I never brooked[4]
That parasite's hair; methought his nose should cozen.
There still was somewhat in his look, did promise
The bane of a clarissimo.[5]

CORBACCIO. Knave—

VOLPONE. Methinks
Yet you, that are so traded in the world,
A witty merchant, the fine bird, Corvino,
That have such moral emblems on your name,
Should not have sung your shame, and dropped your cheese,
To let the fox laugh at your emptiness.[6]

CORVINO. Sirrah, you think the privilege of the place,
And your red saucy cap, that seems to me
Nailed to your jolt-head[7] with those two sequins,
Can warrant your abuses. Come you hither;
You shall perceive, sir, I dare beat you; approach.

VOLPONE. No haste, sir, I do know your valor well,

1. Well patronized; "none dispraised": without prejudice to any of the other splendid bawdy houses in Venice.
2. I.e., mere drippings and leftovers, enough to buy candles with.
3. I.e., in the clothes we aristocrats are accustomed to wear.
4. Could stand.
5. I.e., trouble for an aristocrat.
6. The recurrent refrain from Aesop's fable.
7. Blockhead.

Since you durst publish what you are, sir.[8]
CORVINO. Tarry,
I'd speak with you.
VOLPONE. Sir, sir, another time—
CORVINO. Nay, now.
VOLPONE. O lord, sir! I were a wise man,
Would stand the fury of a distracted cuckold [*As he is running off, re-enter* MOSCA.]
CORBACCIO. What, come again!
VOLPONE. Upon 'em, Mosca; save me.
CORBACCIO. The air's infected where he breathes.
CORVINO. Let's fly him.
[*Exeunt* CORVINO *and* CORBACCIO.]
VOLPONE. Excellent basilisk![9] turn upon the vulture.

SCENE 9

[*Enter* VOLTORE.]
VOLTORE. Well, flesh-fly, it is summer with you now;
Your winter will come on.
MOSCA. Good advocate,
Prithee not rail, nor threaten out of place thus;
Thou'lt make a solecism, as madam says.[1]
Get you a biggen[2] more; your brain breaks loose. [*Exit.*]
VOLTORE. Well sir.
VOLPONE. Would you have me beat the insolent slave,
Throw dirt upon his first good clothes?
VOLPONE. This same
Is doubtless some familiar.
VOLPONE. Sir, the court,
In troth, stays for you. I am mad, a mule
That never read Justinian,[3] should get up,
And ride an advocate. Had you no quirk
To avoid gullage,[4] sir, by such a creature?
I hope you do but jest; he has not done it;
This's but confederacy,[5] to blind the rest.
You are the heir?
VOLPONE. A strange, officious,
Troublesome knave! thou dost torment me.
VOLPONE. I know—
It cannot be, sir, that you should be cozened;
'Tis not within the wit of man to do it;
You are so wise, so prudent; and 'tis fit
That wealth and wisdom still should go together.
[*Exeunt.*]

8. A cuckold, liable to run "horn-mad."
9. Fishmarket.
1. The "solecism" of Lady Politic is above, IV 2.
2. A little skullcap worn by lawyers.
3. I.e., Mosca, wholly ignorant of the legal codes compiled by the Emperor Justinian.
4. Deceit.
5. Conspiracy, trickery.

SCENE 10. *The Scrutineo*

[*Enter* AVOCATORI, NOTARIO, BONARIO, CELIA, CORBACCIO, CORVINO, COMMENDATORI, SAFFI, *&c.*]

1 AVOCATORI. Are all the parties here?

NOTARIO. All but the advocate.

2 AVOCATORE. And here he comes.

[*Enter* VOLTORE *and* VOLPONE.]

1 AVOCATORE. Then bring them forth to sentence.

VOLTORE. O, my most honored fathers, let your mercy
Once win upon your justice, to forgive—
I am distracted——

VOLPONE. [*aside*] What will he do now?

VOLTORE. O,
I know not which to address myself to first;
Whether your fatherhoods, or these innocents—

CORVINO. [*aside*] Will he betray himself?

VOLPONE. Whom equally
I have abused, out of most covetous ends—

CORVINO. The man is mad!

CORBACCIO. What's that?

CORVINO. He is possessed

VOLTORE. For which, now struck in conscience, here I prostrate
Myself at your offended feet, for pardon.

1, 2 AVOCATORI. Arise.

CELIA. O heaven, how just thou art!

VOLPONE. [*aside*] I am caught
In mine own noose—

CORVINO. [*to Corbaccio*] Be constant, sir; nought now
Can help, but impudence.

1 AVOCATORE. Speak forward.

COMMENDATORE. Silence!

VOLTORE. It is not passion in me, reverend fathers,
But only conscience, conscience, my good sires,
That makes me now tell truth. That parasite,
That knave, hath been the instrument of all.

1 AVOCATORE. Where is that knave? fetch him.

VOLPONE. I go. [*Exit.*]

CORVINO. Grave fathers,
This man's distracted; he confessed it now;
For, hoping to be old Volpone's heir,
Who now is dead—

3 AVOCATORE. How!

2 AVOCATORE. Is Volpone dead?

CORVINO. Dead since, grave fathers.

BONARIO. O sure vengeance!

1 AVOCATORE. Stay,
Then he was no deceiver.

VOLTORE. O no, none;
The parasite, grave fathers.

CORVINO. He does speak
Out of mere envy, 'cause the servant's made
The thing he gaped for. Please your fatherhoods,
This is the truth, though I'll not justify
The other,[6] but he may be some-deal faulty.
VOLTORE. Ay, to your hopes, as well as mine, Corvino.
But I'll use modesty. Pleaseth your wisdoms,
To view these certain notes, and but confer them;
As I hope favor, they shall speak clear truth.
CORVINO. The devil has entered him!
BONARIO. Or bides in you.
4 AVOCATORE. We have done ill, by a public officer
To send for him, if he be heir.
2 AVOCATORE. For whom?
4 AVOCATORE. Him that they call the parasite.
3 AVOCATORE. 'Tis true,
He is a man of great estate, now left.[7]
4 AVOCATORE. Go you, and learn his name, and say, the court
Entreats his presence here, but to the clearing
Of some few doubts. [*Exit* NOTARIO.]
2 AVOCATORE. This same's a labyrinth!
1 AVOCATORE. Stand you unto your first report?
CORVINO. My state,
My life, my fame—
BONARIO. Where is it?
CORVINO. Are at the stake.
1 AVOCATORE. Is yours so too?
CORBACCIO. The advocate's a knave,
And has a forkéd tongue—
2 AVOCATORE. Speak to the point.
CORBACCIO. So is the parasite too.
1 AVOCATORE. This is confusion.
VOLTORE. I do beseech your fatherhoods, read but those—
[*Giving them papers.*]
CORVINO. And credit nothing the false spirit hath writ;
It cannot be, but he's possessed,[8] grave fathers.

SCENE 11. *A street*

[*Enter* VOLPONE.]

VOLPONE. To make a snare for mine own neck! and run
My head into it, wilfully! with laughter!
When I had newly 'scaped, was free, and clear!
Out of mere wantonness! O, the dull devil
Was in this brain of mine, when I devised it,
And Mosca gave it second; he must now

6. I.e., Mosca.
7. As an aristocrat (which he automatically is if he has a lot of money), Mosca is not to be summoned by a common official.
8. I.e., demonically possessed by a devil inside him (not wholly incredible in those days, when witchcraft was an accepted fact).

Help to sear up this vein,[9] or we bleed dead.
[*Enter* NANO, ANDROGYNO, *and* CASTRONE.]
How now! who let you loose? whither go you now?
What? to buy gingerbread, or to drown kitlings?
NANO. Sir, Master Mosca called us out of doors,
And bid us all go play, and took the keys.
ANDROGYNO. Yes.
VOLPONE. Did Master Mosca take the keys? why, so!
I'm farther in. These are my fine conceits!
I must be merry, with a mischief to me!
What a vile wretch was I, that could not bear
My fortune soberly! I must have my crotchets,
And my conundrums! Well, go you, and seek him.
His meaning may be truer than my fear.
Bid him, he straight come to me to the court;
Thither will I, and, if't be possible,
Unscrew my advocate, upon new hopes.
When I provoked him, then I lost myself. [*Exeunt.*]

SCENE 12. *The Scrutineo*

[AVOCATORI, BONARIO, CELIA, CORBACCIO, CORVINO, COMMENDATORI, SAFFI, *&c. as before.*]
1 AVOCATORE. [*showing the papers*] These things can ne'er be reconciled. He here
Professeth that the gentleman was wronged,
And that the gentlewoman was brought thither,
Forced by her husband, and there left.
VOLTORE. Most true.
CELIA. How ready is heaven to those that pray!
1 AVOCATORE. But that
Volpone would have ravished her, he holds
Utterly false, knowing his impotence.
CORVINO. Grave fathers, he's possessed; again, I say,
Possessed; nay, if there be possession and
Obsession, he has both.[1]
3 AVOCATORE. Here comes our officer.
[*Enter* VOLPONE, *still in disguise.*]
VOLPONE. The parasite will straight be here, grave fathers.
4 AVOCATORE. You might invent some other name, sir varlet.
3 AVOCATORE. Did not the notary meet him?
VOLPONE. Not that I know.
4 AVOCATORE. His coming will clear all.
2 AVOCATORE. Yet, it is misty.
VOLTORE. May't please your fatherhoods.
VOLPONE. [*Whispers to* VOLTORE.] Sir, the parasite
Willed me to tell you, that his master lives;
That you are still the man; your hopes the same;

9. Cautery was frequent medical procedure in the days before antisepsis.
1. Possession is a devil attacking the mind from within, obsession is the same temptation from without.

And this was only a jest—
VOLTORE. How?
VOLPONE. Sir, to try
If you were firm, and how you stood affected.
VOLTORE. Art sure he lives?
VOLPONE. Do I live, sir?
VOLTORE. O me!
I was too violent.
VOLPONE. Sir, you may redeem it.
They said you were possessed; fall down, and seem so.
I'll help to make it good. [VOLTORE *falls.*] —God bless the man!
[*aside*] Stop your wind hard, and swell.—See, see, see, see!
He vomits crooked pins![2] his eyes are set,
Like a dead hare's hung in a poulter's[3] shop!
His mouth's running away! Do you see, signor?
Now it is in his belly.
CORVINO. Ay, the devil!
VOLPONE. Now in his throat.
CORVINO. Ay, I perceive it plain.
VOLPONE. 'Twill out, 'twill out! stand clear!
See where it flies,
In shape of a blue toad with a bat's wings!
Do not you see it, sir?
CORBACCIO. What? I think I do.
CORVINO. 'Tis too manifest.
VOLPONE. Look! he comes to himself!
VOLTORE. Where am I?
VOLPONE. Take good heart, the worst is past, sir.
You are dispossessed.
1 AVOCATORE. What accident is this?
2 AVOCATORE. Sudden and full of wonder!
3 AVOCATORE. If he were
Possessed, as it appears, all this is nothing. [*He waves the notes.*]
CORVINO. He has been often subject to these fits.
1 AVOCATORE. Show him that writing. —Do you know it, sir?
VOLPONE. [*Whispers to* VOLTORE.] Deny it, sir, forswear it; know it not.
VOLTORE. Yes, I do know it well, it is my hand;
But all that it contains is false.
BONARIO. O practice![4]
2 AVOCATORE. What maze is this?
1 AVOCATORE. Is he not guilty then,
Whom you there name the parasite?
VOLTORE. Grave fathers,
No more than his good patron, old Volpone.

2. The symptoms that Volpone "sees," and persuades others to see, were standard. The "blue toad with bat's wings" below is the demon himself.
3. A dealer in fowl and small game.
4. Deceit.

4 AVOCATORE. Why, he is dead.
VOLTORE. O no, my honored fathers,
He lives—
1 AVOCATORE. How! Lives?
VOLTORE. Lives.
2 AVOCATORE. This is subtler yet!
3 AVOCATORE. You said he was dead.
VOLTORE. Never.
AVOCATORE. [*to* CORVINO] You said so!
CORVINO. I heard so.
4 AVOCATORE. Here comes the gentleman; make him way.[5]
[*Enter* MOSCA *as a* clarissimo.]
3 AVOCATORE. A stool.
4 AVOCATORE. [*aside*] A proper man; and, were Volpone dead,
A fit match for my daughter.
3 AVOCATORE. Give him way.
VOLPONE. [*aside to* MOSCA] Mosca, I was almost lost; the advocate
Had betrayed all; but now it is recovered;
All's on the hinge again—say, I am living.
MOSCA. What busy knave is this! Most reverend fathers,
I sooner had attended your grave pleasures,
But that my order for the funeral
Of my dear patron did require me—
VOLPONE. [*aside*] Mosca!
MOSCA. Whom I intend to bury like a gentleman.
VOLPONE. [*aside*] Ay, quick,[6] and cozen me of all.
2 AVOCATORE. Still stranger!
More intricate!
1 AVOCATORE. And come about again!
4 AVOCATORE. [*aside*] It is a match, my daughter is bestowed.
MOSCA. [*aside to* VOLPONE] Will you give me half?
VOLPONE. First, I'll be hanged.
MOSCA. I know
Your voice is good, cry not so loud.
1 AVOCATORE. Demand
The advocate.—Sir, did you not affirm
Volpone was alive?
VOLPONE. Yes, and he is;
This gentleman[7] told me so. [*aside to* MOSCA] Thou shalt have half.
MOSCA. Whose drunkard is this same? speak, some that know him:
I never saw his face. [*aside to* VOLPONE] I cannot now
Afford it you so cheap.
VOLPONE. No!
1 AVOCATORE. What say you?

5. Jonson's audience would be scandalized at the instant transformation of a parasite into a gentleman, partly because they had seen it happen frequently in their own land.
6. Alive.
7. I.e., Mosca.

VOLPONE. The officer told me.

VOLPONE. I did, grave fathers,
And will maintain he lives, with mine own life,
And that this creature [*points to* MOSCA] told me.
[*aside*] I was born.
With all good stars my enemies.

MOSCA. Most grave fathers,
If such an insolence as this must pass
Upon me, I am silent: 'twas not this
For which you sent, I hope.

2 AVOCATORE. Take him away.

VOLPONE. [*aside*] Mosca!

3 AVOCATORE. Let him be whipped.

VOLPONE. Wilt thou betray me?
Cozen me?

3 AVOCATORE. And taught to bear himself
Toward a person of his rank.
Away. [*The* OFFICERS *seize* VOLPONE.]

MOSCA. I humbly thank your fatherhoods.

VOLPONE. [*aside*] Soft, soft. Whipped!
And lose all that I have! If I confess,
It cannot be much more.

4 AVOCATORE. Sir, are you married?[8]

VOLPONE. They'll be allied anon; I must be resolute.
The fox shall here uncase.[9] [*Throws off his disguise.*]

MOSCA. Patron!

VOLPONE. Nay, now
My ruins shall not come alone; your match
I'll hinder sure: my substance shall not glue you
Nor screw you into a family.

MOSCA. Why, patron!

VOLPONE. I am Volpone, and this [*pointing to* MOSCA] is my knave;
This, [*to* VOLTORE] his own knave; this, [*to* CORBACCIO] avarice's fool;
This, [*to* CORVINO] a chimera[1] of wittol, fool, and knave.
And, reverend fathers, since we all can hope
Nought but a sentence, let's not now despair it.
You hear me brief.

CORVINO. May it please your fatherhoods—

COMMENDATORE. Silence!

1 AVOCATORE. The knot is now undone by miracle.

2 AVOCATORE. Nothing can be more clear.

3 AVOCATORE. Or can more prove
These innocent.

1 ADVOCATORE. Give them their liberty.

BONARIO. Heaven could not long let such gross crimes be hid.

8. The question is addressed to Mosca.
9. Remove his mask.
1. The chimera was an unnatural imaginary creature compounded of lion, goat, and serpent.

2 AVOCATORE. If this be held the highway to get riches,
May I be poor!
3 AVOCATORE. This is not gain, but torment.
1 AVOCATORE. These possess wealth, as sick men possess fevers.
Which trulier may be said to possess them.[2]
2 AVOCATORE. Disrobe that parasite.
CORVINO, MOSCA. Most honored fathers!
1 AVOCATORE. Can you plead aught to stay the course of justice?
If you can, speak.
CORVINO, VOLTORE. We beg favor.
CELIA. And mercy.
1 AVOCATORE. You hurt your innocence, suing for the guilty.
Stand forth; and first, the parasite. You appear
T'have been the chiefest minister, if not plotter,
In all these lewd impostures; and now, lastly,
Have with your impudence abused the court,
And habit of a gentleman of Venice,
Being a fellow of no birth or blood:[3]
For which our sentence is, first, thou be whipped;
Then live perpetual prisoner in our galleys.
VOLPONE. I thank you for him.
MOSCA. Bane[4] to thy wolfish nature!
1 AVOCATORE. Deliver him to the Saffi. [MOSCA *is led out.*]
—Thou, Volpone,
By blood and rank a gentleman, canst not fall
Under like censure; but our judgment on thee
Is, that thy substance all be straight confiscate
To the hospital of the Incurabili.[5]
And, since the most was gotten by imposture,
By feigning lame, gout, palsy, and such diseases,
Thou art to lie in prison, cramped with irons,
Till thou be'st sick and lame indeed. Remove him. [*He is taken away.*]
VOLPONE. This is called mortifying of a fox.
1 AVOCATORE. Thou, Voltore, to take away the scandal
Thou hast given all worthy men of thy profession,
Art banished from their fellowship, and our state.
Corbaccio!—bring him near—we here possess
Thy son of all thy state,[6] and confine thee
To the monastery of San Spirito;
Where, since thou knew'st not how to live well here,
Thou shalt be learned[7] to die well.

2. The aphorism is Seneca's (Epistle 119, par. 12).
3. Justice in Venice makes no pretense to equality; Mosca's sentence is most severe, and for snob reasons.
4. Poison. It was legitimate to poison wolves, not foxes. "Saffi": guards.
5. There was a Hospital of the Incurables in Venice, but the sentence carries an irony: these are the only people in Venice who can be trusted with money. The diseases to be picked up in Venetian jails were no joke; the Stinche, so called, were the most horrible dungeons in all Europe.
6. I.e., convey to your son your entire estate.
7. Taught.

CORBACCIO. Ha! what said he?
COMMENDATORE. You shall know anon, sir.
1 AVOCATORE. Thou, Corvino, shalt
Be straight embarked from thine own house, and rowed
Round about Venice, through the Grand Canal,
Wearing a cap with fair long ass's ears
Instead of horns; and so to mount, a paper
Pinned on thy breast, to the Berlina[8]——
CORVINO. Yes,
And have mine eyes beat out with stinking fish,
Bruised fruit, and rotten eggs—'Tis well. I'm glad
I shall not see my shame yet.
1 AVOCATORE. And to expiate
Thy wrongs done to thy wife, thou art to send her
Home to her father, with her dowry trebled:
And these are all your judgments—
ALL. Honored fathers.
1 AVOCATORE. Which may not be revoked. Now you begin,
When crimes are done, and past, and to be punished,
To think what your crimes are: away with them!
Let all that see these vices thus rewarded,
Take heart, and love to study 'em! Mischiefs feed
Like beasts, till they be fat, and then they bleed. [*Exeunt.*]
[VOLPONE *comes forward.*]
The seasoning of a play is the applause.
Now, though the fox be punished by the laws,
He yet doth hope, there is no suffering due,
For any fact which he hath done 'gainst you;
If there be, censure him; here he doubtful stands:
If not, fare jovially, and clap your hands. [*Exit.*]

THE END

1606

8. Pillory.

Epicoene

or

The Silent Woman

The Persons of the Play

MOROSE, *a gentleman that loves no noise.*
SIR DAUPHINE EUGENIE, *his nephew.*
CLERIMONT, *a gentleman, his friend.*
TRUEWIT, *another friend.*
EPICOENE, *supposed the Silent Woman.*
SIR JOHN DAW, *a Knight.*
SIR AMOROUS LA FOOLE, *a Knight.*
THOMAS OTTER, *a land- and sea-captain.*
CUTBEARD, *a barber*
MUTE, *one of* MOROSE'S *servants.*
PARSON.

LADY HAUGHTY, LADY CENTAUR, MISTRESS MAVIS — *Ladies Collegiates.*
MISTRESS OTTER, *the Captain's wife*; MISTRESS TRUSTY, *the* LADY HAUGHTY'S *woman* — *Pretenders.*[1]

PAGES, SERVANTS, &C.

THE SCENE: *London*

Prologue

Truth says, of old the art of making plays
Was to content the people; and their praise
Was to the poet money, wine, and bays.[2]
But in this age a sect of writers are,
That only for particular likings care,
And will taste nothing that is popular.
With such we mingle neither brains nor breasts;[3]
Our wishes, like to those make public feasts,
Are not to please the cook's taste, but the guests.
Yet if those cunning palates hither come,
They shall find guests' entreaty, and good room;
And though all relish not, sure there will be some,

1. I.e., Pretenders to learning, probationers in the bluestockings' academy.
2. Laurels, the poet's crown.
3. Hearts.

That when they leave their seats shall make them say,
Who wrote that piece, could so have wrote a play;
But that he knew this was the better way.
For, to present all custard or all tart,
And have no other meats to bear a part,
Or to want[4] *bread and salt, were but coarse art.*
The poet prays you then, with better thought
To sit; and when his cates[5] *are all in brought,*
Though there be none far-fet,[6] *there will dear-bought*
Be, fit for ladies: some for lords, knights, squires;
Some for your waiting-wench, and city-wires;[7]
Some for your men and daughters of Whitefriars.
Nor is it only while you keep your seat
Here, that his feast will last; but you shall eat
A week at ord'naries[8] *on his broken meat;*
If his muse be true,
Who commends her to you.

Another

OCCASIONED BY SOME PERSON'S IMPERTINENT EXCEPTION[9]

The ends of all, who for the scene do write,
Are, or should be, to profit and delight.
And still 't hath been the praise of all best times,
So persons were not touched, to tax the crimes.
Then in this play, which we present tonight,
And make the object of your ear and sight,
On forfeit of your selves, think nothing true;
Lest so you make the maker to judge you.
For he knows poet never credit gained
By writing truths, but things like truths, well feigned.
If any yet will, with particular sleight
Of application, wrest what he doth write,
And that he meant or him or her, will say;
They make a libel, which he made a play.

4. Lack.
5. Dishes.
6. Farfetched, exotic.
7. I.e., fancy ladies (from the wires holding up their ruffs). Whitefriars was the London district, named from a long-abolished monastery, where *Epicoene* was first performed.
8. Public taverns; "broken meats": leftovers.
9. *Epicoene* got into trouble, and may even have been suppressed on its first run, because of an allusion in Act V, Scene 1, to the Prince of Moldavia: he was a fraud who visited England in 1607, talked King James out of some money, and after his departure gave out that he was going to marry the King's cousin, Lady Arabella Stuart. Since Lady Arabella was, according to the lineage-experts, next in line for the throne of England to the King himself, both Elizabeth and James had long ago determined that she should not marry. Whether Jonson really alluded to the lady in Act V of *Epicoene*, Arabella thought he did; though out of the royal favor, she was strong enough to have steps taken against Jonson, and in response to them, he evidently wrote this second prologue.

Act I

SCENE 1. CLERIMONT'S *house*

[*Enter* CLERIMONT, *making himself ready, followed by his* PAGE.]

CLERIMONT. Have you got the song yet perfect I gave you, boy?

PAGE. Yes, sir.

CLERIMONT. Let me hear it.

PAGE. You shall, sir; but, i' faith, let nobody else.

CLERIMONT. Why, I pray?

PAGE. It will get you the dangerous name of a poet in town, sir, besides me a perfect deal of ill will at the mansion you wot of, whose lady is the argument of it; where now I am the welcom'st thing under a man that comes there.

CLERIMONT. I think; and above a man, too, if the truth were racked[1] out of you.

PAGE. No, faith, I'll confess before, sir. The gentlewomen play with me, and throw me o' the bed, and carry me in to my Lady; and she kisses me with her oiled face, and puts a peruke[2] o' my head, and asks me an I will wear her gown; and I say no. And then she hits me a blow o' the ear, and calls me Innocent! and lets me go.

CLERIMONT. No marvel if the door be kept shut against your master, when the entrance is so easy to you——Well, sir, you shall go there no more, lest I be fain to seek your voice in my lady's rushes a fortnight hence.[3] Sing, sir.

[PAGE *sings*.]

Still to be neat, still to be dressed——

[*Enter* TRUEWIT.]

TRUEWIT. Why, here's the man that can melt away his time, and never feels it! What between his mistress abroad and his ingle[4] at home, high fare, soft lodging, fine clothes, and his fiddle, he thinks the hours have no wings, or the day no post-horse.[5] Well, Sir Gallant, were you struck with the plague this minute, or condemned to any capital punishment tomorrow, you would begin then to think, and value every article o' your time, esteem it at the true rate, and give all for't.

CLERIMONT. Why, what should a man do?

TRUEWIT. Why, nothing; or that which, when 'tis done, is as idle. Hearken after the next horse-race or hunting-match, lay wagers, praise Puppy, or Peppercorn. Whitefoot, Franklin; swear upon Whitemane's party;[6] speak aloud, that my lords may hear you;

1. The rack was a common instrument of torture for dragging confessions out of criminals.
2. Wig, hairpiece.
3. Boy sopranos lose their elegant voices as they mature sexually; Clerimont is afraid precocious experience will leave his boy's voice on the "rushes," spread on the floor of the lady's bedroom.
4. Bosom friend, sometimes with the overtone of catamite.
5. The post-horse reminds one that time is passing—for the easy man, his only reminder.
6. Racehorses.

visit my ladies at night, and be able to give them the character of every bowler or better on the green.[7] These be the things wherein your fashionable men exercise themselves, and I for company.

CLERIMONT. Nay, if I have thy authority, I'll not leave yet. Come, the other are considerations when we come to have gray heads and weak hams, moist eyes and shrunk members. We'll think on 'em then; then we'll pray and fast.

TRUEWIT. Ay, and destine only that time of age to goodness, which our want of ability will not let us employ in evil?

CLERIMONT. Why, then 'tis time enough.

TRUEWIT. Yes; as if a man should sleep all the term,[8] and think to effect his business the last day. O, Clerimont, this time, because it is an incorporeal thing, and not subject to sense, we mock ourselves the fineliest out of it, with vanity and misery indeed; not seeking an end of wretchedness, but only changing the matter still.

CLERIMONT. Nay, thou'lt not leave now——

TRUEWIT. See but our common disease! With what justice can we complain that great men will not look upon us, nor be at leisure to give our affairs such dispatch as we expect, when we will never do it to our selves; nor hear, nor regard our selves?

CLERIMONT. Foh! thou hast read Plutarch's 'Morals,' now,[9] or some such tedious fellow, and it shows so vilely with thee, 'fore God, 'twill spoil thy wit utterly! Talk me of pins and feathers and ladies and rushes and such things, and leave this Stoicity alone till thou mak'st sermons.[1]

TRUEWIT. Well, sir, if it will not take, I have learned to lose as little of my kindness as I can. I'll do good to no man against his will, certainly. When were you at the College?

CLERIMONT. What college?

TRUEWIT. As if you knew not!

CLERIMONT. No, faith, I came but from court yesterday.

TRUEWIT. Why, is it not arrived there yet, the news? A new foundation, sir, here in the town, of ladies that call themselves the Collegiates, an order between courtiers and country madams, that live from their husbands and give entertainment to all the wits and braveries of the time, as they call them; cry down, or up, what they like or dislike in a brain or a fashion, with most masculine, or rather, hermaphroditical authority;[2] and every day gain to their college some new probationer.

CLERIMONT. Who is the president?

TRUEWIT. The grave and youthful matron, the Lady Haughty.

CLERIMONT. A pox of her autumnal face, her pieced beauty! There's no man can be admitted till she be ready nowadays, till

7. Bowling and betting on bowling were popular pastimes for Jacobean idlers.

8. Law-terms ran for several months while the judges held sittings; even by non-lawyers, the terms were commonly used as measures of time.

9. Plutarch's moral essays, the so-called *Moralia*, are his miscellaneous writings.

1. "Stoicity" is used in the loose sense of "solemn moralizing."

2. Bluestocking societies of literary ladies were novelties in the 17th century, and seemed to be encroachments on male privilege.

she has painted, and perfumed, and washed, and scoured, but the boy here; and him she wipes her oiled lips upon, like a sponge. I have made a song—I pray thee hear it—o' the subject.

[PAGE *sings*.]

'Still to be neat, still to be dressed
As you were going to a feast,
Still to be powdered, still perfumed;
Lady, it is to be presumed,
Thought art's hid cause are not found,
All is not sweet, all is not sound.

'Give me a look, give me a face,
That makes simplicity a grace;
Robes loosely flowing, hair as free—
Such sweet neglect more taketh me,
Than all the adulteries of art.
They strike mine eyes, but not my heart.'

TRUEWIT. And I am clearly on the other side; I love a good dressing before any beauty o' the world. O, a woman is then like a delicate garden, nor is there one kind of it. She may vary every hour, take often counsel of her glass, and choose the best. If she have good ears, show 'em; good hair, lay it out; good legs, wear short clothes; a good hand, discover if often; practice any art to mend breath, cleanse teeth, repair eyebrows; paint, and profess it.

CLERIMONT. How! publicly?

TRUEWIT. The doing of it, not the manner; that must be private. Many things that seem foul in the doing, do please done. A lady should, indeed, study her face, when we think she sleeps; nor, when the doors are shut, should men be inquiring; all is sacred within, then. Is it for us to see their perukes put on, their false teeth, their complexion, their eyebrows, their nails? You see gilders will not work, but enclosed.[3] They must not discover how little serves, with the help of art, to adorn a great deal. How long did the canvas hang afore Aldgate?[4] Were the people suffered to see the City's Love and Charity, while they were rude stone, before they were painted and burnished? No. No more should servants approach their mistresses, but when they are complete and finished.

CLERIMONT. Well said, my Truewit.

TRUEWIT. And a wise lady will keep a guard always upon the place, that she may do things securely. I once followed a rude fellow into a chamber, where the poor madam, for haste, and troubled, snatched at her peruke to cover her baldness, and put it on the wrong way.

CLERIMONT. O prodigy!

3. Men who work with gold leaf require closed rooms to keep the airy stuff from blowing around.

4. Aldgate, a gate in the city walls, was evidently hidden behind a canvas while being reworked: Love and Charity were two painted statues on the new structure.

TRUEWIT. And the unconscionable knave held her in compliment an hour with that reversed face, when I still looked when she should talk from the tother side.

CLERIMONT. Why, thou shouldst have relieved her.

TRUEWIT. No, faith, I let her alone, as we'll let this argument, if you please, and pass to another. When saw you Dauphine Eugenie?

CLERIMONT. Not these three days. Shall we go to him this morning? he is very melancholy, I hear.

TRUEWIT. Sick of the uncle, is he? I met that stiff piece of formality, his uncle, yesterday, with a huge turban of nightcaps on his head, buckled over his ears.

CLERIMONT. O, that's his custom when he walks abroad. He can endure no noise, man.

TRUEWIT. So I have heard. But is the disease so ridiculous in him as it is made? They say he has been upon divers treaties with the fishwives and orange-women, and articles propounded between them. Marry, the chimney-sweepers will not be drawn in.[5]

CLERIMONT. No, nor the broom-men; they stand out stiffly. He cannot endure a costermonger;[6] he swoons if he hear one.

TRUEWIT. Methinks a smith should be ominous.

CLERIMONT. Or any hammer-man. A brazier[7] is not suffered to dwell in the parish, nor an armorer. He would have hanged a pewterer's prentice once upon a Shrove Tuesday's riot,[8] for being of that trade, when the rest were quit.

TRUEWIT. A trumpet should fright him terribly, or the hautboys![9]

CLERIMONT. Out of his senses. The waits[1] of the City have a pension of him, not to come near that ward.[2] This youth practiced on him one night, like the bellman,[3] and never left till he had brought him down to the door with a long-sword, and there left him flourishing with the air.

PAGE. Why, sir, he hath chosen a street to lie in, so narrow at both ends that it will receive no coaches, nor carts, nor any of these common noises. And therefore we that love him devise to bring him in such as we may, now and then, for his exercise, to breathe him. He would grow resty[4] else, in his ease; his virtue would rust without action. I entreated a bear-ward[5] one day to come down with the dogs of some four parishes that way, and I thank him, he did; and cried his games under Master Morose's window, till he was sent crying away with his head made a most bleeding

5. All the jokes have to do with Morose's efforts to prevent street-cries in his area of town, or to muffle noisy workshops.
6. Pushcart salesman.
7. Worker in brass.
8. Shrove Tuesday, known in other cultures as Mardi Gras, was a day of license, especially for the tradesmen's helpers and shop-assistants called as a group prentices.
9. Oboes.
1. Bands of itinerant musicians.
2. District.
3. Bellmen wandered the streets by night, ringing their bells to indicate the hours, and shouting any spectacular news aloud.
4. Restive.
5. The keeper of the bears at the garden where they were baited often roamed the streets advertising future shows.

spectacle to the multitude. And another time, a fencer marching to his prize had his drum most tragically run through, for taking that street in his way, at my request.

TRUEWIT. A good wag! How does he for the bells?

CLERIMONT. O, in the Queen's time,[6] he was wont to go out of town every Saturday at ten o'clock, or on holiday eves. But now, by reason of the sickness,[7] the perpetuity of ringing has made him devise a room with double walls and treble ceilings, the windows close shut and caulked, and there he lives by candlelight. He turned away a man last week, for having a pair of new shoes that creaked. And this fellow waits on him now in tennis-court socks, or slippers soled with wool; and they talk each to other in a trunk.[8] See, who comes here!

SCENE 2

[*Enter* SIR DAUPHINE EUGENIE.]

DAUPHINE. How now! what ail you, sirs? dumb?

TRUEWIT. Struck into stone, almost, I am here, with tales o' thine uncle. There was never such a prodigy heard of.

DAUPHINE. I would you would once lose this subject, my masters, for my sake. They are such as you are, that have brought me into that predicament I am, with him.

TRUEWIT. How is that?

DAUPHINE. Marry, that he will disinherit me, no more. He thinks I and my company are authors of all the ridiculous acts and monuments[9] are told of him.

TRUEWIT. 'Slid, I would be the author of more to vex him; that purpose deserves it; it gives thee law of plaguing him. I'll tell thee what I would do. I would make a false almanac, get it printed, and then have him drawn out on a coronation day to the Tower Wharf, and kill him with the noise of the ordnance.[1] Disinherit thee! he cannot, man. Art not thou next of blood, and his sister's son?

DAUPHINE. Ay, but he will thrust me out of it, he vows, and marry.

TRUEWIT. How! that's a more portent. Can he endure no noise, and will venture on a wife?

CLERIMONT. Yes. Why, thou art a stranger, it seems, to his best trick yet. He has employed a fellow this half-year all over England to hearken him out a dumb woman, be she of any form or any quality, so she be able to bear children; her silence is dowry enough, he says.

TRUEWIT. But I trust to God he has found none.

6. Queen Elizabeth, who was strict about church attendance, had the bells pealed on Sunday mornings; James was less insistent on the point.

7. Frequent funerals during plague-time made for much tolling of bells.

8. Speaking tube.

9. George Foxe wrote the history of the Protestant martyrs under the title of *Acts and Monuments*: the title became proverbial.

1. On ceremonial occasions the cannon in London Tower were fired off.

CLERIMONT. No, but he has heard of one that's lodged in the next street to him, who is exceedingly soft-spoken, thrifty of her speech, that spends but six words a day. And her he's about now, and shall have her.

TRUEWIT. Is't possible! Who is his agent in the business?

CLERIMONT. Marry, a barber, one Cutbeard; an honest fellow, one that tells Dauphine all here.

TRUEWIT. Why, you oppress me with wonder: a woman and a barber, and love no noise!

CLERIMONT. Yes, faith. The fellow trims him silently, and has not the knack with his shears or his fingers;[2] and that continence in a barber he thinks so eminent a virtue, as it has made him chief of his counsel.

TRUEWIT. Is the barber to be seen, or the wench?

CLERIMONT. Yes, that they are.

TRUEWIT. I pray thee, Dauphine, let's go thither.

DAUPHINE. I have some business now; I cannot, i' faith.

TRUEWIT. You shall have no business shall make you neglect this, sir. We'll make her talk, believe it; or, if she will not, we can give out at least so much as shall interrupt the treaty. We will break it. Thou art bound in conscience, when he suspects thee without cause, to torment him.

DAUPHINE. Not I, by any means. I'll give no suffrage to't. He shall never have that plea against me, that I opposed the least fancy of his. Let it lie upon my stars to be guilty, I'll be innocent.

TRUEWIT. Yes, and be poor, and beg; do, innocent; when some groom of his has got an heir, or this barber, if he himself cannot. Innocent! I pray thee, Ned, where lies she? Let him be innocent still.

CLERIMONT. Why, right over against the barber's, in the house where Sir John Daw[3] lies.

TRUEWIT. You do not mean to confound me!

CLERIMONT. Why?

TRUEWIT. Does he that would marry her know so much?

CLERIMONT. I cannot tell.

TRUEWIT. 'Twere enough of imputation to her, with him.[4]

CLERIMONT. Why?

TRUEWIT. The only talking Sir in the town! Jack Daw! An he teach her not to speak—God b'w'you.[5] I have some business tooo.

CLERIMONT. Will you not go thither, then?

TRUEWIT. Not with the danger to meet Daw, for mine ears.

CLERIMONT. Why? I thought you two had been upon very good terms.

TRUEWIT. Yes, of keeping distance.

CLERIMONT. They say he is a very good scholar.

2. I.e., the art of snipping with scissors or cracking the knuckles.

3. The jackdaw is a notoriously raucous and noisy bird like a small crow; it is also a notorious coward.

4. I.e., if Morose knew she was acquainted with Daw, that would be enough for him.

5. The phrase *God be with you* was in the process, during the early 17th century, of being shortened to *Goodbye*.

TRUEWIT. Ay, and he says it first. A pox on him, a fellow that pretends only to learning, buys titles, and nothing else of books in him!

CLERIMONT. The world reports him to be very learned.

TRUEWIT. I am sorry the world should so conspire to belie him.

CLERIMONT. Good faith, I have heard very good things come from him.

TRUEWIT. You may. There's none so desperately ignorant to deny that; would they were his own! God b'w'you, gentlemen. [*Exit hastily.*]

CLERIMONT. This is very abrupt!

SCENE 3

DAUPHINE. Come, you are a strange, open man, to tell everything thus.

CLERIMONT. Why, believe it, Dauphine, Truewit's a very honest fellow.

DAUPHINE. I think no other; but this frank nature of his is not for secrets.

CLERIMONT. Nay then, you are mistaken, Dauphine. I know where he has been well trusted, and discharged the trust very truly and heartily.

DAUPHINE. I contend not, Ned; but with the fewer a business is carried, it is ever the safer. Now we are alone, if you'll go thither, I am for you.

CLERIMONT. When were you there?

DAUPHINE. Last night; and such a Decameron[6] of sport fallen out! Boccace never thought of the like. Daw does nothing but court her, and the wrong way. He would lie with her, and praises her modesty; desires that she would talk and be free, and commends her silence in verses, which he reads, and swears are the best that ever man made. Then rails at his fortunes, stamps, and mutines,[7] why he is not made a councillor, and called to affairs of state.

CLERIMONT. I pray thee, let's go. I would fain partake this.—Some water, boy. [Exit PAGE.]

DAUPHINE. We are invited to dinner together, he and I, by one that came thither to him, Sir La Foole.

CLERIMONT. O, that's a precious mannikin!

DAUPHINE. Do you know him?

CLERIMONT. Ay, and he will know you too, if e'er he saw you but once, though you should meet him at church in the midst of prayers. He is one of the braveries,[8] though he be none o' the wits. He will salute a judge upon the bench, and a bishop in the pulpit, a lawyer when he is pleading at the bar, and a lady when

6. A hundred comical and often bawdy tales by Boccaccio (14th century).

7. Complains.

8. Fine dressers, fops. "Putting a lady out" is embarrassing her by revealing her identity when she's wearing a mask to conceal it.

she is dancing in a masque, and put her out. He does give plays and suppers, and invites his guests to them aloud, out of his window, as they ride by in coaches. He has a lodging in the Strand for the purpose; or to watch when ladies are gone to the china-houses, or the Exchange,[9] that he may meet them by chance, and give them presents, some two or three hundred pounds worth of toys, to be laughed at. He is never without a spare banquet, or sweetmeats in his chamber, for their women to alight at, and come up to, for a bait.

DAUPHINE. Excellent! He was a fine youth last night, but now he is much finer! What is his Christian name? I have forgot.

[*Re-enter* PAGE.]

CLERIMONT. Sir Amorous La Foole.

PAGE. The gentleman is here below that owns that name.

CLERIMONT. Heart, he's come to invite me to dinner, I hold my life.

DAUPHINE. Like enough. Pray thee, let's have him up.

CLERIMONT. Boy, marshal[1] him.

PAGE. With a truncheon, sir?

CLERIMONT. Away, I beseech you. [*Exit* PAGE.] I'll make him tell us his pedigree now, and what meat he has to dinner, and who are his guests, and the whole course of his fortunes, with a breath.

SCENE 4

[*Enter* SIR AMOROUS LA FOOLE.]

LA FOOLE. Save, dear Sir Dauphine! honored Master Clerimont!

CLERIMONT. Sir Amorous! you have very much honested my lodging with your presence.

LA FOOLE. Good faith, it is a fine lodging! almost as delicate a lodging as mine.

CLERIMONT. Not so, sir.

LA FOOLE. Excuse me, sir, if it were in the Strand, I assure you. I am come, Master Clerimont, to entreat you to wait upon two or three ladies, to dinner, today.

CLERIMONT. How, sir! wait upon them? Did you ever see me carry dishes!

LA FOOLE. No, sir, dispense with me; I meant, to bear them company.

CLERIMONT. O, that I will, sir. The doubtfulness of your phrase, believe it, sir, would breed you a quarrel once an hour with the terrible boys,[2] if you should but keep them fellowship a day.

LA FOOLE. It should be extremely against my will, sir, if I contested with any man.

9. The New Exchange, where millinery was sold, and the china shops, where one might buy tableware, were fashionable shopping areas. They were also often places of assignation.

1. I.e., show him up. The Page plays on the word by asking for a regular marshal's staff, a truncheon.

2. Roughnecks-about-town.

CLERIMONT. I believe it, sir. Where hold you your feast?

LA FOOLE. At Tom Otter's, sir.

DAUPHINE. Tom Otter! What's he?

LA FOOLE. Captain Otter, sir; he is a kind of gamester, but he has had command both by sea and by land.

DAUPHINE. O, then he is *animal amphibium*?[3]

LA FOOLE. Ay, sir. His wife was the rich china-woman, that the courtiers visited so often, that gave the rare entertainment. She commands all at home.

CLERIMONT. Then she is Captain Otter.

LA FOOLE. You say very well, sir. She is my kinswoman, a La Foole by the mother side, and will invite any great ladies for my sake.

DAUPHINE. Not of the La Fooles of Essex?

LA FOOLE. No, sir, the La Fooles of London.

CLERIMONT. [*aside*]—Now he's in.

LA FOOLE. They all come out of our house, the La Fooles of the north, the La Fooles of the west, the La Fooles of the east and south—we are as ancient a family as any is in Europe—but I myself am descended lineally of the French La Fooles—and we do bear for our coat yellow, or Or, checkered Azure, and Gules, and some three or four colors more,[4] which is a very noted coat, and has sometimes been solemnly worn by divers nobility of our house—but let that go, antiquity is not respected now—I had a brace of fat does sent me, gentlemen, and half a dozen of pheasants, a dozen or two of godwits, and some other fowl, which I would have eaten while they are good, and in good company—there will be a great lady or two, my Lady Haughty, my Lady Centaur, Mistress Doll Mavis—And they come o' purpose to see the silent gentlewomen, Mistress Epicoene, that honest Sir John Daw has promised to bring thither—and then, Mistress Trusty, my lady's woman, will be there, too, and this honorable knight, Sir Dauphine, with yourself, Master Clerimont—And we'll be very merry, and have fiddlers, and dance—I have been a mad wag in my time, and have spent some crowns since I was a page in court, to my Lord Lofty, and after, my Lady's gentleman–usher, who got me knighted in Ireland, since it pleased my elder brother to die—I had as fair a gold jerkin on that day as any was worn in the island voyage, or at Cadiz,[5] none dispraised; and I came over in it hither, showed myself to my friends in court, and after went down to my tenants in the country, and surveyed my lands, let new leases, took their money, spent it in the eye o' the land here, upon ladies—and now I can take up[6] at my pleasure.

3. Amphibious animals, like the frog, are equally at home on land or water. The imputation about his wife is that she is not only bossy but promiscuous.

4. The La Foole coat of arms is suspiciously like motley, a fool's many-colored garment.

5. Semi-piratical expeditions were sent out by the English, in 1596 against the Spanish seaport of Cadiz and in 1597 against "the islands"—the Azores. The adventurers, all eager for court positions and confident of booty, wore their finest clothes.

6. Borrow, but also pre-empt, take for one's own. The "eye of the land" is London.

DAUPHINE. Can you take up ladies, sir?

CLERIMONT. O, let him breathe, he has not recovered.

DAUPHINE. Would I were your half in that commodity!

LA FOOLE. No, sir, excuse me; I meant money, which can take up anything. I have another guest or two to invite, and say as much to, gentlemen. I'll take my leave abruptly, in hope you will not fail——Your servant. [*Exit.*]

DAUPHINE. We will not fail you, Sir Precious La Foole; but she shall, that your ladies come to see, if I have credit afore Sir Daw.

CLERIMONT. Did you ever hear such a windfucker as this?

DAUPHINE. Or such a rook as the other, that will betray his mistress to be seen! Come, 'tis time we prevented it.

CLERIMONT. Go. [*Exeunt.*]

Act II

SCENE 1. MOROSE'S *house*

[*Enter* MOROSE *with a tube in his hand, followed by* MUTE.]

MOROSE. Cannot I yet find out a more compendious method, than by this trunk, to save my servants the labor of speech, and mine ears the discord of sounds? Let me see: all discourses but mine own afflict me; they seem harsh, impertinent, and irksome. Is it not possible that thou shouldst answer me by signs, and I apprehend thee, fellow? Speak not, though I question you. You have taken the ring off from the street door, as I bade you? Answer me not by speech, but by silence, unless it be otherwise. [MUTE *makes a leg.*][7] Very good. And you have fastened on a thick quilt, or flock-bed, on the outside of the door, that if they knock with their daggers, or with brickbats, they can make no noise? But with your leg, your answer, unless it be otherwise. [A *leg.*] Very good.—This is not only fit modesty in a servant, but good state and discretion in a master.—And you have been with Cutbeard the barber, to have him come to me? [A *leg.*] Good. And he will come presently? Answer me not but with your leg, unless it be otherwise; if it be otherwise, shake your head, or shrug. [A *leg.*] So.—Your Italian and Spaniard are wise in these, and it is a frugal and comely gravity!—How long will it be ere Cutbeard come? Stay, if an hour, hold up your whole hand; if half an hour, two fingers; if a quarter, one. [A *finger, bent.*] Good, half a quarter? 'tis well. And have you given him a key, to come in without knocking? [A *leg.*] Good. And is the lock oiled, and the hinges, today? [A *leg.*] Good. And the quilting of the stairs nowhere worn out and bare? [A *leg.*] Very good. I see, by much doctrine and impulsion, it may be effected. Stand by.—The Turk, in this divine discipline, is admirable, exceeding all the potentates of the earth; still waited on by mutes, and all his com-

7. I.e., a perfunctory bow or scrape.

mands so executed; yea, even in the war, as I have heard, and in his marches, most of his charges and directions given by signs, and with silence—an exquisite art! And I am heartily ashamed, and angry oftentimes, that the princes of Christendom should suffer a barbarian to transcend them in so high a point of felicity. I will practice it hereafter. [*One winds*[8] *a horn without.*] How now? O! O! what villain, what prodigy of mankind is that? Look. [*Exit* MUTE. *Horn again.*] O, cut his throat, cut his throat! What murderer, hell-hound, devil can this be?

[*Re-enter* MUTE.]

MUTE. It is a post[9] from the court——

MOROSE. Out, rogue! and must thou blow thy horn, too?

MUTE. Alas, it is a post from the court, sir, that says he must speak with you, pain of death——

MOROSE. Pain of thy life, be silent!

SCENE 2

[*Enter* TRUEWIT *with a post-horn and a halter in his hand.*]

TRUEWIT. By your leave, sir,—I am a stranger here—is your name Master Morose? is your name Master Morose? Fishes![1] Pythagoreans all! This is strange. What say you, sir! nothing! Has Harpocrates[2] been here with his club, among you? Well, sir, I will believe you to be the man at this time; I will venture upon you, sir. Your friends at court commend them to you, sir——

MOROSE. O men! O manners! was there ever such an impudence?

TRUEWIT. And are extremely solicitous for you, sir.

MOROSE. Whose knave are you?

TRUEWIT. Mine own knave, and your compeer, sir.

MOROSE. Fetch me my sword——

TRUEWIT. You shall taste the one half of my dagger, if you do, groom; and you the other, if you stir, sir. Be patient, I charge you, in the King's name, and hear me without insurrection. They say you are to marry; to marry! do you mark, sir?[3]

MOROSE. How then, rude companion!

TRUEWIT. Marry, your friends do wonder, sir, the Thames being so near, wherein you may drown so handsomely; or London Bridge, at a low fall, with a fine leap, to hurry you down the stream; or such a delicate steeple i' the town, as Bow, to vault from; or a braver height, as Paul's;[4] or, if you affected to do it nearer home, and a shorter way, an excellent garret-window into the street; or a beam in the said garret, with this halter—[*shows him the halter*] which they have sent, and desire that you would sooner

8. Blows.
9. Messenger.
1. "Mute as fishes!" is understood. "Pythagoreans all!" implies that they have taken a vow of silence, like members of the ancient Greek philosophical sect.
2. Harpocrates was the Greek and Roman god of silence.
3. Most of Truewit's long and virulent diatribe against women and marriage is adapted from Juvenal's sixth satire against women.
4. St. Mary le Bow in Cheapside or St. Paul's Cathedral would provide heights to leap from.

commit your grave head to this knot, than to the wedlock noose; or take a little sublimate,[5] and go out of the world like a rat, or a fly—as one said—with a straw i' your arse; any way rather than to follow this goblin, matrimony. Alas, sir, do you ever think to find a chaste wife in these times? now? when there are so many masques, plays, Puritan preachings, mad folks, and other strange sights to be seen daily, private and public? If you had lived in King Etheldred's time, sir, or Edward the Confessor's,[6] you might perhaps have found in some cold country hamlet, then, a dull, frosty wench, would have been contented with one man. Now, they will as soon be pleased with one leg or one eye. I'll tell you, sir, the monstrous hazards you shall run with a wife.

MOROSE. Good sir, have I ever cozened[7] any friends of yours of their land? bought their possessions? taken forfeit of their mortgage? begged a reversion[8] from 'em? bastarded their issue? What have I done that may deserve this?

TRUEWIT. Nothing, sir, that I know, but your itch of marriage.

MOROSE. Why, if I had made an assassinate upon your father, vitiated your mother, ravished your sisters——

TRUEWIT. I would kill you, sir, I would kill you, if you had.

MOROSE. Why, you do more in this, sir. It were a vengeance centuple, for all facinorous[9] acts that could be named, to do that you do——

TRUEWIT. Alas, sir, I am but a messenger. I but tell you what you must hear. It seems your friends are careful after your soul's health, sir, and would have you know the danger; but you may do your pleasure for all them, I persuade not, sir. If, after you are married, your wife do run away with a vaulter, or the Frenchman that walks upon ropes, or him that dances the jig, or a fencer for his skill at his weapon; why, it is not their fault; they have discharged their consciences, when you know what may happen. Nay, suffer valiantly, sir, for I must tell you all the perils that you are obnoxious to. If she be fair, young, and vegetous,[1] no sweetmeats ever drew more flies; all the yellow doublets and great roses[2] i' the town will be there. If foul and crooked, she'll be with them, and buy those doublets and roses, sir. If rich, and that you marry her dowry, not her, she'll reign in your hour as imperious as a widow. If noble, all her kindred will be your tyrants. If fruitful, as proud as May and humorous[3] as April; she must have her doctors, her midwives, her nurses, her longings every hour, though it be for the dearest morsel of man. If learned, there was never such a parrot; all your patrimony will be too little for the guests that must be invited to hear her speak Latin and Greek; and you must lie with her in those languages too, if you will

5. Mercury chloride, a violent poison.
6. I.e., 600 or 800 years ago.
7. Deceived.
8. A right of succession to their property (which would pauperize Truewit).
9. Wicked to the highest degree.

1. Full of sap and vigor.
2. Yellow doublets and great roses stand for fancy attire.
3. Changeable (in allusion to April showers).

please her. If precise, you must feast all the silenced brethren,[4] once in three days; salute the sisters; entertain the whole family, or wood[5] of 'em; and hear long-winded exercises, singings, and catechizings, which you are not given to, and yet must give for, to please the zealous matron your wife, who, for the holy cause, will cozen you over and above. You begin to sweat, sir? But this is not half, i' faith! You may do your pleasure, notwithstanding, as I said before; I come not to persuade you. [MUTE *is stealing away.*] Upon my faith, Master Serving-man, if you do stir, I will beat you.

MOROSE. O, what is my sin? what is my sin?

TRUEWIT. Then, if you love your wife, or rather, dote on her, sir, O how she'll torture you, and take pleasure i' your torments! You shall lie with her but when she lists;[6] she will not hurt her beauty, her complexion; or it must be for that jewel, or that pearl, when she does. Every half-hour's pleasure must be bought anew, and with the same pain and charge you wooed her at first. Then you must keep what servants she please, what company she will; that friend must not visit you without her licence; and him she loves most, she will seem to hate eagerliest, to decline[7] your jealousy; or feign to be jealous of you first, and for that cause go live with her she-friend, or cousin at the College, that can instruct her in all the mysteries of writing letters, corrupting servants, taming spies; where she must have that rich gown for such a great day, a new one for the next, a richer for the third; be served in silver; have the chamber filled with a succession of grooms, footmen, ushers, and other messengers, besides embroiderers, jewellers, tire-women, sempsters, feather-men, perfumers; while she feels not how the land drops away, nor the acres melt;[8] nor foresees the change, when the mercer[9] has your woods for her velvets; never weighs what her pride costs, sir, so she may kiss a page, or a smooth chin that has the despair of a beard; be a stateswoman, know all the news, what was done at Salisbury, what at the Bath,[1] what at court, what in progress; or so she may censure poets and authors and styles, and compare 'em—Daniel with Spenser, Jonson with the tother youth,[2] and so forth; or be thought cunning in controversies or the very knots of divinity, and have often in her mouth the state of the question;[3] and then skip to the mathematics and demonstration; and answer, in religion to one, in state to another, in bawdry to a third.

MOROSE. O! O!

TRUEWIT. All this is very true, sir. And then her going in disguise

4. Puritan preachers, once in the church of England, but now censored or ejected and so dependent on the charity of sympathizers. "Precise": puritanical.
5. Tribe.
6. Chooses.
7. Lull.
8. I.e., her expenses cause her husband's estate to drop away and disappear.
9. Dealer in fabrics.
1. Salisbury and Bath are fashionable places where the latest news or scandal is likely to be heard.
2. The standard comparison was Jonson and Shakespeare, but Jonson may not want to be too particular here.
3. "The state of the question" implies formal logical disputations.

to that conjurer, and this cunning–woman,[4] where the first question is how soon you shall die? next, if her present servant[5] love her? next that, if she shall have a new servant? And how many? which of her family would make the best bawd, male or female? what precedence she shall have by her next match? and sets down the answers, and believes 'em above the scriptures. Nay, perhaps she'll study the art.

MOROSE. Gentle sir, have you done? have you had your pleasure o' me? I'll think of these things.

TRUEWIT. Yes, sir, and then comes reeking home of vapor and sweat, with going afoot, and lies in, a month, of a new face, all oil and birdlime; and rinses in asses' milk, and is cleansed with a new fucus.[6] God b'w'you, sir. One thing more, which I had almost forgot. This too, with whom you are to marry, may have made a conveyance of her virginity aforehand, as your wise widows do of their states,[7] before they marry, in trust to some friend, sir. Who can tell? Or if she have not done it yet, she may do, upon the wedding day, or the night before, and antedate you cuckold. The like has been heard of in nature. 'Tis no devised, impossible thing, sir. God b'w'you. I'll be bold to leave this rope with you, sir, for a remembrance.—Farewell, Mute! [*Exit.*]

MOROSE. Come, have me to my chamber; but first shut the door. [*The horn again.*] O, shut the door, shut the door! Is he come again?

[*Enter* CUTBEARD.]

CUTBEARD. 'Tis I, sir, your barber.

MOROSE. O Cutbeard, Cutbeard, Cutbeard! here has been a cutthroat with me. Help me in to my bed, and give me physic with thy counsel. [*Exeunt.*]

SCENE 3. SIR JOHN DAW'S *house*

[*Enter* DAW, CLERIMONT, DAUPHINE, *and* EPICOENE.]

DAW. Nay, an she will, let her refuse at her own charges; 'tis nothing to me, gentlemen. But she will not be invited to the like feasts or guests every day.

CLERIMONT. O, by no means, she may not refuse——[*they dissuade her privately*] to stay at home, if you love your reputation. 'Slight, you are invited thither o' purpose to be seen, and laughed at by the lady of the College and her shadows. This trumpeter hath proclaimed you.

DAUPHINE. You shall not go. Let him be laughed at in your stead, for not bringing you; and put him to his extemporal faculty of fooling and talking loud to satisfy the company.

CLERIMONT. He will suspect us; talk aloud.—Pray, Mistress Epicoene, let's see your verses; we have Sir John Daw's leave. Do not conceal your servant's merit, and your own glories.

4. Witch-doctress.
5. With the overtone of Italian *cavalier sirvente*, half lover, half domestic convenience.
6. Makeup.
7. Estates.

EPICOENE. They'll prove my servant's glories, if you have his leave so soon.

DAUPHINE. His vainglories, lady!

DAW. Show them, show them, mistress! I dare own them.

EPICOENE. Judge you what glories.

DAW. Nay, I'll read them myself, too; an author must recite his own works. It is a madrigal of modesty:

Modest and fair, for fair and good are near
Neighbors, howe'er.

DAUPHINE. Very good.

CLERIMONT. Ay, is't not?

DAW.

No noble virtue ever was alone,
But two in one.

DAUPHINE. Excellent!

CLERIMONT. That again, I pray, Sir John.

DAUPHINE. It has something in't like rare wit and sense.

CLERIMONT. Peace.

DAW.

No noble virtue ever was alone,
But two in one.
Then, when I praise sweet modesty, I praise
Bright beauty's rays;
And having praised both beauty and modesty,
I have praised thee.

DAUPHINE. Admirable!

CLERIMONT. How it chimes and cries tink in the close[8] divinely!

DAUPHINE. Ay, 'tis Seneca.

CLERIMONT. No, I think 'tis Plutarch.[9]

DAW. The *dor* on Plutarch and Seneca,[1] I hate it! They are mine own imaginations, by that light! I wonder those fellows have such credit with gentlemen.

CLERIMONT. They are very grave authors.

DAW. Grave asses! mere essayists! a few loose sentences, and that's all. A man would talk so his whole age. I do utter as good things every hour, if they were collected and observed, as either of 'em.

DAUPHINE. Indeed, Sir John!

CLERIMONT. He must needs, living among the wits, and braveries too.

DAUPHINE. Ay, and being president of 'em, as he is.

DAW. There's Aristotle, a mere commonplace fellow; Plato, a discourser; Thucydides and Livy, tedious and dry; Tacitus, an entire knot—sometimes worth the untying, very seldom.[2]

CLERIMONT. What do you think of the poets, Sir John?

DAW. Not worthy to be named for authors. Homer, an old, tedious,

8. Conclusion.
9. Seneca and Plutarch, grave and moral authors of antiquity, are the least appropriate authors under the circumstances.
1. I.e., "To the devil with Plutarch and Seneca."
2. Sir John Daw's opinions of the great classical authors are the trite formulas of lazy and reluctant readers.

prolix ass, talks of curriers and chines of beef;[3] Virgil, of dunging of land, and bees; Horace, of I know not what.

CLERIMONT. —I think so.

DAW. And so Pindarus, Lycophron, Anacreon, Catullus, Seneca the tragedian, Lucan, Propertius, Tibullus, Martial, Juvenal, Ausonius, Statius, Politian, Valerius Flaccus,[4] and the rest——

CLERIMONT. —What a sack-full of their names he has got!

DAUPHINE. And how he pours 'em out! Politian with Valerius Flaccus!

CLERIMONT. Was not the character right of him?[5]

DAUPHINE. As could be made, i' faith.

DAW. And Persius, a crabbed coxcomb, not to be endured.[6]

DAUPHINE. Why, whom do you account for authors, Sir John Daw?

DAW. Syntagma Juris Civilis, Corpus Juris Civilis, Corpus Juris Canonici, the King of Spain's Bible[7]——

DAUPHINE. Is the King of Spain's Bible an author?

CLERIMONT. Yes, and Syntagma.

DAUPHINE. What was that Syntagma, sir?

DAW. A civil lawyer, a Spaniard.

DAUPHINE. Sure, Corpus was a Dutchman.

CLERIMONT. Ay, both the Corpuses, I knew 'em; they were very corpulent authors.

DAW. And then there's Vatablus, Pomponatius, Symancha;[8] the others are not to be received within the thought of a scholar.

DAUPHINE. [*aside*] 'Fore God, you have a simple learned servant, lady—in titles.

CLERIMONT. I wonder that he is not called to the helm, and made a councillor!

DAUPHINE. He is one extraordinary.

CLERIMONT. Nay, but in ordinary! to say truth, the state wants such.

DAUPHINE. Why, that will follow.

CLERIMONT. I muse a mistress can be so silent to the dotes[9] of such a servant.

DAW. 'Tis her virtue, sir. I have written somewhat of her silence, too.

DAUPHINE. In verse, Sir John?

CLERIMONT. What else?

DAUPHINE. Why, how can you justify your own being of a poet, that so slight all the old poets?

DAW. Why, every man that writes in verse is not a poet; you have

3. Curriers of horses and sides of beef. Virgil in his *Georgics* writes of farm life.

4. Sir John Daw rattles off a miscellaneous list of Latin poets, concluding with Politian (Poliziano), an Italian poet of the 15th century, and Valerius Flaccus, a Roman poet of the 1st century.

5. I.e., didn't I tell you what sort of fellow he was?

6. Persius, a sharp and witty satirist, is indeed rather hard reading.

7. I.e., The Collection of Civil Law, The Body of Civil Law, The Body of Canon Law, and even The King of Spain's Bible—Sir John thinks they are all personal names.

8. Renaissance scholars: Vatable, Pomponazzi, Simancus.

9. Endowments.

of the wits that write verses, and yet are no poets. They are poets that live by it, the poor fellows that live by it.

DAUPHINE. Why, would not you live by your verses, Sir John?

CLERIMONT. No, 'twere pity he should. A knight live by his verses? He did not make them to that end, I hope.

DAUPHINE. And yet the noble Sidney lives by his,[1] and the noble family not ashamed.

CLERIMONT. Ay, he professed himself; but Sir John Daw has more caution. He'll not hinder his own rising i' the state so much! do you think he will? Your verses, good Sir John, and no poems.

DAW.

Silence in woman is like speech in man,
Deny 't who can.

DAUPHINE. Not I, believe it; your reason, sir.

DAW.

Nor is't a tale,
That female vice should be a virtue male,
Or masculine vice a female virtue be.
You shall it see
Proved with increase;
I know to speak, and she to hold her peace.

Do you conceive me, gentlemen?

DAUPHINE. No, faith; how mean you *with increase*, Sir John?

DAW. Why, *with increase* is when I court her for the common cause of mankind, and she says nothing, but *consentire videtur*, and in time is *gravida*.[2]

DAUPHINE. Then this is a ballad of procreation?

CLERIMONT. A madrigal of procreation, you mistake.

EPICOENE. Pray give me my verses again, servant.

DAW. If you'll ask them aloud, you shall.

CLERIMONT. See, here's Truewit again!

SCENE 4

[*Enter* TRUEWIT *with his horn.*]

CLERIMONT. Where hast thou been, in the name of madness, thus accoutred with thy horn?

TRUEWIT. Where the sound of it might have pierced your senses with gladness, had you been in ear-reach of it. Dauphine, fall down and worship me; I have forbid the banns,[3] lad. I have been with thy virtuous uncle, and have broke the match.

DAUPHINE. You have not, I hope.

TRUEWIT. Yes, faith, an thou shouldst hope otherwise, I should repent me. This horn got me entrance; kiss it. I had no other way to get in, but by feigning to be a post;[4] but when I got in once, I proved none, but rather the contrary, turned him into a post, or a

1. Sir Philip Sidney, living in fame through his poetry, though long dead.
2. I.e., she says nothing but seems to consent and in time is pregnant.
3. Banns are public announcements of a proposed marriage.
4. Messenger.

stone, or what is stiffer, with thundering into him the incommodities of a wife, and the miseries of marriage. If ever Gorgon[5] were seen in the shape of a woman, he hath seen her in my description. I have put him off o' that scent forever. Why do you not applaud and adore me, sirs? Why stand you mute? Are you stupid? You are not worthy of the benefit.

DAUPHINE. Did not I tell you? Mischief!

CLERIMONT. I would you had placed this benefit somewhere else.

TRUEWIT. Why so?

CLERIMONT. 'Slight, you have done the most inconsiderate, rash, weak thing, that ever man did to his friend.

DAUPHINE. Friend! if the most malicious enemy I have, had studied to inflict an injury upon me, it could not be a greater.

TRUEWIT. Wherein, for God's sake? Gentlemen, come to yourselves again.

DAUPHINE. But I presaged thus much afore to you.

CLERIMONT. Would my lips had been soldered when I spake on't! 'Slight, what moved you to be thus impertinent?

TRUEWIT. My masters, do not put on this strange face to pay my courtesy; off with this visor.[6] Have good turns done you, and thank 'em this way!

DAUPHINE. 'Fore heaven, you have undone me. That which I have plotted for, and been maturing now these four months, you have blasted in a minute. Now I am lost I may speak. This gentlewoman was lodged here by me o' purpose, and, to be put upon my uncle, hath professed this obstinate silence for my sake, being my entire friend, and one that for the requital of such a fortune as to marry him, would have made me very ample conditions; where now all my hopes are utterly miscarried by this unlucky accident.

CLERIMONT. Thus 'tis when a man will be ignorantly officious, do services and not know his why. I wonder what courteous itch possessed you! You never did absurder part i' your life, nor a great trespass to friendship, to humanity.

DAUPHINE. Faith, you may forgive it best; 'twas your cause principally.

CLERIMONT. I know it, would it had not!

[*Enter* CUTBEARD.]

DAUPHINE. How now, Cutbeard! what news?

CUTBEAD. The best, the happiest that ever was, sir. There has been a mad gentleman with your uncle this morning—I think this be the gentleman—that has almost talked him out of his wits, with threatening him from marriage——

DAUPHINE. On, I pray thee.

CUTBEARD. And your uncle, sir, he thinks 'twas done by your procurement. Therefore he will see the party you wot of presently; and if he like her, he says, and that she be so inclining to dumb

5. The Gorgons were frightful females of antiquity, the most famous being Medusa, who by her very glance turned men to stone.

6. False face.

as I have told him, he swears he will marry her today, instantly, and not defer it a minute longer.

DAUPHINE. Excellent! beyond our expectation!

TRUEWIT. Beyond your expectation! by this light, I knew it would be thus.

DAUPHINE. Nay, sweet Truewit, forgive me.

TRUEWIT. No, I was *ignorantly officious, impertinent;* this was the *absurd, weak part.*

CLERIMONT. Wilt thou ascribe that to merit now, was mere fortune?

TRUEWIT. Fortune? mere providence! Fortune had not a finger in't. I saw it must necessarily in nature fall out so; my genius is never false to me in these things. Show me how it could be otherwise.

DAUPHINE. Nay, gentlemen, contend not; 'tis well now.

TRUEWIT. Alas, I let him go on with *inconsiderate,* and *rash,* and what he pleased.

CLERIMONT. Away, thou strange justifier of thyself, to be wiser than thou wert, by the event!

TRUEWIT. Event! by this light, thou shalt never persuade me but I foresaw it as well as the stars themselves.

DAUPHINE. Nay, gentlemen, 'tis well now. Do you two entertain Sir John Daw with discourse, while I send her away with instructions.

TRUEWIT. I'll be acquainted with her first, by your favor.

CLERIMONT. Master Truewit, lady, a friend of ours.

TRUEWIT. I am sorry I have not known you sooner, lady, to celebrate this rare virtue of your silence.

[*Exeunt* DAUPHINE, EPICOENE, *and* CUTBEARD.]

CLERIMONT. Faith, an you had come sooner, you should have seen and heard her well celebrated in Sir John Daw's madrigals.

TRUEWIT. [*Advances to* DAW.] Jack Daw, God save you! when saw you La Foole?

DAW. Not since last night, Master Truewit.

TRUEWIT. That's a miracle! I thought you two had been inseparable.

DAW. He's gone to invite his guests.

TRUEWIT. God's so'! 'tis true! What a false memory have I towards that man! I am one.[7] I met him e'en now upon that he calls his delicate, fine black horse, rid into foam with posting from place to place and person to person, to give them the cue——

CLERIMONT. Lest they should forget?

TRUEWIT. Yes. There was never poor captain took more pains at a muster to show men, than he at this meal to show friends.

DAW. It is his quarter-feast, sir.[8]

CLERIMONT. What! do you say so, Sir John?

TRUEWIT. Nay, Jack Daw will not be out at the best friends he

7. I.e., I am one of the party, I am invited.

8. Held on quarter-day, when rents or allowances were paid.

has, to the talent of his wit. Where's his mistress, to hear and applaud him? is she gone?

DAW. Is Mistress Epicoene gone?

CLERIMONT. Gone afore, with Sir Dauphine, I warrant, to the place.

TRUEWIT. Gone afore! That were a manifest injury, a disgrace and a half; to refuse him at such a festival time as this, being a bravery, and a wit too!

CLERIMONT. Tut, he'll swallow it like cream. He's better read in *Jure Civili*[9] than to esteem anything a disgrace is offered him from a mistress.

DAW. Nay, let her e'en go; she shall sit alone and be dumb in her chamber a week together, for John Daw, I warrant her! Does she refuse me?

CLERIMONT. No, sir, do not take it so to heart; she does not refuse you, but a little neglect you. Good faith, Truewit, you were to blame, to put it into his head that she does refuse him.

TRUEWIT. Sir, she does refuse him, palpably, however you mince it. An I were as he, I would swear to speak ne'er a word to her today, for't.

DAW. By this light, no more I will not!

TRUEWIT. Nor to anybody else, sir.

DAW. Nay, I will not say so, gentlemen.

CLERIMONT. [*aside*]—It had been an excellent happy condition for the company, if you could have drawn him to it.

DAW. I'll be very melancholy, i' faith.

CLERIMONT. As a dog, if I were as you, Sir John.

TRUEWIT. Or a snail, or a hog-louse. I would roll myself up for this day; in,troth, they should not unwind me.[1]

DAW. By this picktooth, so I will.

CLERIMONT. [*aside*]—'Tis well done, he begins already to be angry with his teeth.

DAW. Will you go, gentlemen?

CLERIMONT. Nay, you must walk alone, if you be right melancholy, Sir John.

TRUEWIT. Yes, sir, we'll dog you; we'll follow you afar off.

[*Exit* DAW.]

CLERIMONT. Was there ever such a two yards of knighthood measured out by Time to be sold to Laughter?

TRUEWIT. A mere talking mole, hang him! No mushroom was ever so fresh. A fellow so utterly nothing, as he knows not what he would be.

CLERIMONT. Let's follow him. But first let's go to Dauphine; he's hovering about the house to hear what news.

TRUEWIT. Content. [*Exeunt.*]

9. In civil law, with a special ironic allusion to the courtesies governing behavior toward a mistress.

1. A hog-louse, when touched, rolls itself up in a ball.

SCENE 5. MOROSE'S *house*

[*Enter* MOROSE *and* MUTE, *followed by* CUTBEARD *with* EPIOCENE.]

MOROSE. Welcome, Cutbeard! Draw near with your fair charge, and in her ear softly entreat her to unmask. [EPICOENE *takes off her mask.*] So! Is the door shut? [MUTE *makes a leg.*] Enough! Now, Cutbeard, with the same discipline I use to my family, I will question you. As I conceive, Cutbeard, this gentlewoman is she you have provided, and brought, in hope she will fit me in the place and person of a wife? Answer me not but with your leg, unless it be otherwise. [CUTBEARD *makes a leg.*] Very well done, Cutbeard. I conceive besides, Cutbeard, you have been preacquainted with her birth, education, and qualities, or else you would not prefer her to my acceptance, in the weighty consequence of marriage. This I conceive, Cutbeard. Answer me not but with your leg, unless it be otherwise. [A *leg.*] Very well done, Cutbeard. Give aside now a little, and leave me to examine her condition and apitutude to my affection. [*Goes about her and views her.*] She is exceeding fair, and of a special good favor; a sweet composition, or harmony of limbs; her temper of beauty has the true height of my blood. The knave hath exceedingly well fitted me without; I will now try her within.—Come near, fair gentlewoman. Let not my behavior seem rude, though unto you, being rare, it may haply appear strange. [EPICOENE *curtsies.*]—Nay, lady, you may speak, though Cutbeard and my man might not; for of all sounds, only the sweet voice of a fair lady has the just length of mine ears. I beseech you, say, lady—out of the first fire of meeting eyes, they say, love is stricken—do you feel any such emotion suddenly shot into you, from any part you see in me? ha, lady? [*Curtsy.*] Alas, lady, these answers by silent curtsies from you, are too courtless and simple. I have ever had my breeding in court, and she that shall be my wife must be accomplished with courtly and audacious ornaments. Can you speak, lady?

EPICOENE. [*softly*] Judge you, forsooth.

MOROSE. What say you, lady? Speak out, I beseech you.

EPICOENE. Judge you, forsooth.

MOROSE. On my judgment, a divine softness! But can you naturally, lady, as I enjoin these by doctrine and industry, refer yourself to the search of my judgment, and—not taking pleasure in your tongue, which is a woman's chiefest pleasure—think it plausible to answer me by silent gestures, so long as my speeches jump right with what you conceive? [*Curtsy.*] Excellent! divine! if it were possible she should hold out thus! Peace, Cutbeard, thou art made forever, as thou hast made me, if this felicity have lasting: but I will try her further. Dear lady, I am courtly, I tell you, and I must have mine ears banqueted with pleasant and witty conferences, pretty girds, scoffs, and dalliance in her that I mean to choose for my bed-fere.[2] The ladies in court think it a most desperate impair to their quickness of wit, and good carriage, if they cannot give occasion for a man to court 'em; and when an amorous discourse is set on foot, minister as good matter to continue it as himself. And do you alone so much differ from all them, that what they, with so much circumstance, affect and toil for—to seem learned, to seem judicious, to seem sharp and conceited—you can bury in yourself with silence? and rather trust your graces to the fair conscience of virtue, than to the world's or your own proclamation?

EPICOENE. [*softly*] I should be sorry else.

MOROSE. What say you, lady? Good lady, speak out.

EPICOENE. I should be sorry else.

MOROSE. That sorrow doth fill me with gladness! O Morose, thou art happy above mankind! pray that thou mayst contain thyself. I will only put her to it once more, and it shall be with the utmost touch and test of their sex.—But hear me, fair lady: I do also love to see her whom I shall choose for my heifer[3] to be the first and principal in all fashions, precede all the dames at court by a fortnight, have her council of tailors, lineners, lace-women, embroiderers, and sit with 'em sometimes twice a day upon French intelligences;[4] and then come forth varied like Nature, or oftener than she, and better by the help of Art, her emulous servant. This do I affect. And how will you be able, lady, with this frugality of speech, to give the manifold but necessary instructions, for that bodice, these sleeves, those skirts, this cut, that stitch, this embroidery, that lace, this wire, those knots, that ruff, those roses, this girdle, that fan, the tother scarf, these gloves, ha? What say you, lady?

EPICOENE. [*softly*] I'll leave it to you, sir.

MOROSE. How, lady? Pray you rise a note.

EPICOENE. I leave it to wisdom and you, sir.

MOROSE. Admirable creature! I will trouble you no more. I will not sin against so sweet a simplicity. Let me now be bold to print on those divine lips, the seal of being mine. Cutbeard, I give thee the lease of thy house free: thank me not but with thy leg [CUTBEARD *shakes his head*.] I know what thou wouldst say: she's poor and her friends deceased. She has brought a wealthy dowry in her silence, Cutbeard; and in respect of her poverty, Cutbeard, I shall have her more loving and obedient, Cutbeard. Go thy ways, and get me a minister presently, with a soft, low voice, to marry us; and pray him he will not be impertinent, but brief as he can; away. Softly, Cutbeard. [*Exit* CUTBEARD.] Sirrah, conduct your mistress into the dining-room, your now mistress. [*Exit* MUTE, *followed by* EPICOENE.] O my felicity! How I shall be revenged on mine insolent kinsman, and his plots to fright me from marrying! This night I will get an heir, and thrust him out

2. Bed-mate.

3. In the 17th century, the word "heifer" could be used without contempt to describe a wife.

4. Talking about the latest news of French fashions.

of my blood like a stranger. He would be knighted, forsooth, and thought by that means to reign over me; his title must do it. No, kinsman, I will now make you bring me the tenth lord's and the sixteenth lady's letter, kinsman; and it shall do you no good, kinsman. Your knighthood itself shall come on its knees, and it shall be rejected; it shall be sued for its fees to execution, and not be redeemed; it shall cheat at the twelvepenny ordinary, it knighthood,[5] for its diet all the term time, and tell tales for it in the vacation to the hostess; or it knighthood shall do worse, take sanctuary in Cole Harbor,[6] and fast. It shall fright all it friends with borrowing letters; and when one of the fourscore hath brought it knighthood ten shillings, it knighthood shall go to the Cranes, or the Bear at the Bridge-foot,[7] and be drunk in fear. It shall not have money to discharge one tavern reckoning, to invite the old creditors to forbear it knighthood, or the new, that should be, to trust it knighthood. It shall be the tenth name in the bond to take up the commodity of pipkins and stone-jugs,[8] and the part thereof shall not furnish it knighthood forth for the attempting of a baker's widow, a brown baker's widow. It shall give it knighthood's name for a stallion to all gamesome citizens' wives, and be refused, when the master of a dancing-school, or—how do you call him?—the worst reveler in the town, is taken.[9] It shall want clothes, and by reason of that, wit, to fool lawyers. It shall not have hope to repair itself by Constantinople, Ireland, or Virginia;[1] but the best and last fortune to it knighthood shall be to make Doll Tearsheet[2] or Kate Common a lady; and so, it knighthood may eat. [*Exit.*]

SCENE 6. *A lane near* MOROSE's *house*

[*Enter* TRUEWIT, DAUPHINE, *and* CLERIMONT.]

TRUEWIT. Are you sure he is not gone by?

DAUPHINE. No, I stayed in the shop ever since.

CLERIMONT. But he may take the other end of the lane.

DAUPHINE. No, I told him I would be here at this end; I appointed him hither.

TRUEWIT. What a barbarian it is to stay then!

DAUPHINE. Yonder he comes.

5. The form "its" was very new in 1609, and Morose uses the archaic form sarcastically, almost as a form of baby-talk.

6. Cole (or Cold) Harbor was a sorry tenement where debtors often took sanctuary from their creditors and their bailiffs.

7. Seedy taverns in the suburbs of town. Even there, Dauphine would be drunk only in fear of bailiffs and debt-collectors.

8. Morose is straining to think of the most miserable dodges to which Dauphine can be reduced to raise a few pennies; this one involves a shabby trick on a greedy pawnbroker.

9. Dauphine, after trying to seduce a citizen's wife by using his knighthood as a lure, will be rejected in favor of a dancing-master. There's something in the phrasing that suggests Jonson had in mind a particular man named Howe.

1. Traditional places for repairing broken fortunes.

2. Since Shakespeare's *Merry Wives of Windsor*, the traditional name of a prostitute.

CLERIMONT. And his charge left behind him, which is a very good sign, Dauphine.

[*Enter* CUTBEARD.]

DAUPHINE. How now, Cutbeard! succeeds it or no?

CUTBEARD. Past imagination, sir, *omnia secunda;*[3] you could not have prayed to have had it so well. *Saltat senex,*[4] as it is in the proverb; he does triumph in his felicity, admires the party! He has given me the lease of my house, too! And I am now going for a silent minister to marry 'em, and away.

TRUEWIT. 'Slight! get one o' the silenced ministers; a zealous brother would torment him purely.[5]

CUTBEARD. *Cum privilegio,* sir.

DAUPHINE. O, by no means; let's do nothing to hinder it now. When 'tis done and finished, I am for you, for any device of vexation.

CUTBEARD. And that shall be within this half hour, upon my dexterity, gentlemen. Contrive what you can in the meantime, *bonis avibus.*[6] [*Exit.*]

CLERIMONT. How the slave doth Latin it!

TRUEWIT. It would be made a jest to posterity, sirs, this day's mirth, if ye will.

CLERIMONT. Beshrew his heart that will not, I pronounce.

DAUPHINE. And for my part. What is't?

TRUEWIT. To translate all La Foole's company and his feast hither today, to celebrate this bridal.

DAUPHINE. Ay, marry, but how will't be done?

TRUEWIT. I'll undertake the directing of all the lady-guests thither, and then the meat must follow.

CLERIMONT. For God's sake, let's effect it! It will be an excellent comedy of affliction, so many several noises.

DAUPHINE. But are they not at the other place already, think you?

TRUEWIT. I'll warrant you for the College Honors;[7] one o' their faces has not the priming color laid on yet, nor the other her smock[8] sleeked.

CLERIMONT. O, but they'll rise earlier than ordinary, to a feast.

TRUEWIT. Best go see, and assure ourselves.

CLERIMONT. Who knows the house?

TRUEWIT. I'll lead you. Were you never there yet?

DAUPHINE. Not I.

CLERIMONT. Nor I.

TRUEWIT. Where have you lived then? not know Tom Otter!

CLERIMONT. No. For God's sake, what is he?

TRUEWIT. An excellent animal, equal with your Daw or La Foole, if not transcendent, and does Latin it as much as your barber. He is his wife's subject; he calls her princess, and at such times

3. All things favorable.
4. I.e., the old man leaps for joy.
5. Puritan preachers were notoriously long talkers; they talked "with privilege" because, as clergy, they could not be interrupted.
6. Literally, with good birds; i.e., under favorable auspices.
7. I.e., the literary ladies.
8. Petticoat.

as these follows her up and down the house like a page, with his hat off, partly for heat, partly for reverence. At this instant he is marshalling of his Bull Bear, and Horse.

DAUPHINE. What be those, in the name of Sphinx?[9]

TRUEWIT. Why, sir, he has been a great man at the bear-garden[1] in his time, and from that subtle sport has ta'en the witty denomination of his chief carousing cups. One he calls his Bull, another his Bear, another his Horse. And then he has his lesser glasses, that he calls his Deer and his Ape; and several degrees of them too; and never is well, nor thinks any entertainment perfect, till these be brought out and set o' the cupboard.

CLERIMONT. For God's love! we should miss this if we should not go.

TRUEWIT. Nay, he has a thousand things as good, that will speak him all day. He will rail on his wife, with certain commonplaces, behind her back; and to her face——

DAUPHINE. No more of him. Let's go see him, I petition you. [*Exeunt.*]

Act III

SCENE 1. MISTRESS OTTER'S *house*

[*Enter* CAPTAIN OTTER *with his cups, and* MISTRESS OTTER.]

OTTER. Nay, good Princess, hear me, *pauca verba.*[2]

MISTRESS OTTER. By that light, I'll have you chained up, with your bull-dogs and bear-dogs, if you be not civil the sooner. I'll send you to kennel, i' faith. You were best bait me with your Bull, Bear, and Horse! Never a time that the courtiers or Collegiates come to the house, but you make it a Shrove Tuesday![3] I would have you get your Whitsuntide velvet cap, and your staff in your hand, to entertain them. Yes, in troth, do.

OTTER. No so, Princess, neither, but under correction, sweet Princess, give me leave—these things I am known to the courtiers by. It is reported to them for my humor, and they receive it so, and do expect it. Tom Otter's Bull, Bear, and Horse is known all over England, *in rerum natura.*[4]

MISTRESS OTTER. 'Fore me, I will na-ture 'em over to Paris Garden,[5] and na-ture you thither too, if you pronounce them again. Is a bear a fit beast, or a bull, to mix in society with great ladies? Think in your discretion, in any good policy.

OTTER. The horse then, good Princess.

9. The Sphinx, renowned for asking difficult questions.
1. The bear-garden, where the animals were baited, was familiar to Jonson; in his early acting career, he had performed at the Paris Garden.
2. A few words.
3. Mardi Gras, a riotous festival for roughnecks at the bear gardens.
4. In the nature of things, with an allusion to Lucretius's poem of that name.
5. The bear-baiting pit; it also served as a part-time theater.

MISTRESS OTTER. Well, I am contented, for the horse; they love to be well horsed, I know.[6] I love it myself.

OTTER. And it is a delicate fine horse this. *Poetarum Pegasus.*[7] Under correction, Princess, Jupiter did turn himself into a—taurus, or bull, under correction, good Princess.

[*Enter* TRUEWIT, CLERIMONT, *and* DAUPHINE *behind.*]

MISTRESS OTTER. By my integrity, I'll send you over to the Bankside, I'll commit you to the Master of the Garden,[8] if I hear but a syllable more. Must my house or my roof be polluted with the scent of bears and bulls, when it is perfumed for great ladies? Is this according to the instrument, when I married you? that I would be princess, and reign in mine own house; and you would be my subject, and obey me? What did you bring me, should make you thus peremptory? Do I allow you your half-crown a day, to spend where you will, among your gamesters, to vex and torment me at such times as these? Who gives you your maintenance, I pray you? Who allows you your horse-meat and man's-meat? your three suits of apparel a year? your four pair of stockings, one silk, three worsted? your clean linen, your bands[9] and cuffs, when I can get you to wear 'em? 'Tis mar'l[1] you have 'em on now. Who graces you with courtiers or great personages, to speak to you out of their coaches and come home to your house? Were you ever so much as looked upon by a lord or a lady before I married you, but on the Easter or Whitsun-holidays? and then out at the Banqueting House window, when Ned Whiting or George Stone[2] were at the stake.

TRUEWIT. [*aside*]—For God's sake, let's go stave her off him.

MISTRESS OTTER. Answer me to that. And did not I take you up from thence, in an old, greasy buff doublet, with points,[3] and green velvet sleeves out at the elbows? You forget this.

TRUEWIT. [*aside*]—She'll worry him, if we help not in time.

[*They come forward.*]

MISTRESS OTTER. O, here are some of the gallants! Go to, behave yourself distinctly, and with good morality; or, I protest, I'll take away your exhibition.[4]

SCENE 2

TRUEWIT. By your leave, fair Mistress Otter, I'll be bold to enter these gentlemen in your acquaintance.

MISTRESS OTTER. It shall not be obnoxious or difficil, sir.

TRUEWIT. How does my noble Captain? Is the Bull, Bear, and Horse *in rerum natura* still?

OTTER. Sir, *sic visum superis.*[5]

6. Well provided with horses, but also with an obscene meaning.
7. Pegasus is the poet's winged horse of inspiration.
8. The Master of the Garden was the keeper of the bears.
9. Strips of linen worn at the wrists.
1. Marvel.
2. Bears, named after their owners; the latter was particularly famous.
3. Laces, cords.
4. Daily allowance.
5. As it pleases the gods.

MISTRESS OTTER. I would you would but intimate 'em, do. Go your ways in, and get toasts and butter made for the woodcocks. That's a fit province for you.

[*Drives him out.*]

CLERIMONT. Alas, what a tyranny is this poor fellow married to.

TRUEWIT. O, but the sport will be anon, when we get him loose.

DAUPHINE. Dares he ever speak?

TRUEWIT. No Anabaptist[6] ever railed with the like licence. But mark her language in the meantime, I beseech you.

MISTRESS OTTER. Gentlemen, you are very aptly come. My cousin, Sir Amorous, will be here briefly.

TRUEWIT. In good time, lady. Was not Sir John Daw here, to ask for him, and the company?

MISTRESS OTTER. I cannot assure you, Master Truewit. Here was a very melancholy knight in a ruff, that demanded my subject[7] for somebody, a gentleman, I think.

CLERIMONT. Ay, that was he, lady.

MISTRESS OTTER. But he departed straight, I can resolve you.

DAUPHINE. What an excellent, choice phrase this lady expresses in!

TRUEWIT. O, sir, she is the only authentical courtier, that is not naturally bred one, in the City!

MISTRESS OTTER. You have taken that report upon trust, gentlemen.

TRUEWIT. No, I assure you, the court governs it so, lady, in your behalf.

MISTRESS OTTER. I am the servant of the court and courtiers, sir.

TRUEWIT. They are rather your idolaters.

MISTRESS OTTER. Not so, sir.

[*Enter* CUTBEARD.]

DAUPHINE. How now, Cutbeard! any cross?[8]

CUTBEARD. O no, sir, *omnia bene*. 'Twas never better o'the hinges; all's sure. I have so pleased him with a curate, that he's gone to't almost with the delight he hopes for soon.

DAUPHINE. What is he, for a vicar?

CUTBEARD. One that has catched a cold sir, and can scarce be heard six inches off; as if he spoke out of a bulrush that were not picked, or his throat were full of pith;[9] a fine, quick fellow, and an excellent barber of prayers. I came to tell you, sir, that you might '*omnem movere lapidem*,'[1] as they say, be ready with your vexation.

DAUPHINE. Gramercy, honest Cutbeard! be thereabouts with thy key to let us in.

CUTBEARD. I will not fail you, sir. *Ad manum*.[2]

[*Exit.*]

TRUEWIT. Well, I'll go watch my coaches.

CLERIMONT. Do; and we'll send Daw to you, if you meet him not.

MISTRESS OTTER. Is Master Truewit gone?

6. Traditionally a violent, ranting, radical Protestant sect.
7. I.e., her husband.
8. Accident; "*omnia bene*": all's well.
9. Phlegm. A "barber of prayers" clips the prayers short.
1. Leave no stone unturned.
2. Right at hand.

DAUPHINE. Yes, lady, there is some unfortunate business fallen out.

MISTRESS OTTER. So I judged by the physiognomy of the fellow that came in; and I had a dream last night, too, of the new pageant[3] and my Lady Mayoress, which is always very ominous to me. I told it my Lady Haughty t'other day, when her honor came hither to see some China stuffs, and she expounded it out of Artemidorus[4] and I have found it since very true. It has done me many affronts.

CLERIMONT. Your dream, lady?

MISTRESS OTTER. Yes, sir, anything I do but dream of the City.[5] It stained me a damask tablecloth, cost me eighteen pound at one time, and burnt me a black satin gown, as I stood by the fire at my Lady Centaur's chamber in the College, another time. A third time, at the Lord's masque, it dropped all my wire and my ruff[6] with wax candle, that I could not go up to the banquet. A fourth time, as I was taking coach to go to Ware, to meet a friend, it dashed me a new suit all over—a crimson satin doublet and black velvet skirts—with a brewer's horse, that I was fain to go in and shift me,[7] and kept my chamber a leash of days for the anguish of it.

DAUPHINE. These were dire mischances, lady.

CLERIMONT. I would not dwell in the City an 'twere so fatal to me.

MISTRESS OTTER. Yes, sir, but I do take advice of my doctor to dream of it as little as I can.

DAUPHINE. You do well, Mistress Otter.

[*Enter* SIR JOHN DAW, *and is taken aside by* CLERIMONT.]

MISTRESS OTTER. Will it please you to enter the house farther, gentlemen?

DAUPHINE. And your favor, lady. But we stay to speak with a knight, Sir John Daw, who is here come. We shall follow you, lady.

MISTRESS OTTER. At your own time, sir. It is my cousin, Sir Amorous, his feast——

DAUPHINE. I know it, lady.

MISTRESS OTTER. And mine together. But it is for his honor, and therefore I take no name of it, more than of the place.

DAUPHINE. You are a bounteous kinswoman.

MISTRESS OTTER. Your servant, sir.

[*Exit.*]

SCENE 3

CLERIMONT. [*coming forward with* DAW] Why, do not you know it, Sir John Daw?

DAW. No, I am a rook if I do.

3. The city government of London had a great many pageants and parades.
4. Artemidorus wrote a treatise on the interpretation of dreams.
5. London City, as contrasted with the court.
6. The large lace ruffs of fine ladies were stiffened with wires.
7. Change my clothes; "leash": couple.

CLERIMONT. I'll tell you then: she's married by this time. And whereas you were put i' the head, that she was gone with Sir Dauphine, I assure you Sir Dauphine has been the noblest, honestest friend to you, that ever gentleman of your quality could boast of. He has discovered[8] the whole plot, and made your mistress so acknowledging, and indeed so ashamed of her injury to you, that she desires you to forgive her, and but grace her wedding with your presence today—She is to be married to a very good fortune, she says, his uncle, old Morose; and she willed me in private to tell you that she shall be able to do you more favors, and with more security, now, than before.

DAW. Did she say so, i' faith?

CLERIMONT. Why, what do you think of me, Sir John? Ask Sir Dauphine!

DAW. Nay, I believe you. Good Sir Dauphine, did she desire me to forgive her?

DAUPHINE. I assure you, Sir John, she did.

DAW. Nay, then, I do with all my heart, and I'll be jovial.

CLERIMONT. Yes, for look you, sir, this was the injury to you. La Foole intended this feast to honor her bridal day, and made you the property[9] to invite the College ladies, and promise to bring her; and then at the time she should have appeared—as his friend—to have given you the dor.[1] Whereas now Sir Dauphine has brought her to a feeling of it, with this kind of satisfaction, that you shall bring all the ladies to the place where she is, and be very jovial. And there she will have a dinner, which shall be in your name; and so disappoint La Foole, to make you good again, and, as it were, a saver in the main.

DAW. As I am a knight, I honor her, and forgive her heartily.

CLERIMONT. About it then presently. Truewit is gone before to confront the coaches, and to acquaint you with so much, if he meet you. Join with him, and 'tis well. See, here comes your antagonist; but take you no notice, but be very jovial.

[*Enter* SIR AMOROUS LA FOOLE.]

LA FOOLE. Are the ladies come, Sir John Daw, and your mistress? [*Exit* DAW.]—Sir Dauphine! you are exceeding welcome, and honest Master Clerimont. Where's my cousin? Did you see no Collegiates, gentlemen?

DAUPHINE. Collegiates! do you not hear, Sir Amorous, how you are abused?

LA FOOLE. How, sir!

CLERIMONT. Will you speak so kindly to Sir John Daw, that has done you such an affront?

LA FOOLE. Wherein, gentlemen? let me be a suitor to you to know, I beseech you!

CLERIMONT. Why, sir, his mistress is married today to Sir Dauphine's uncle, your cousin's neighbor, and he has diverted all the

8. Exposed.
9. Pretext.
1. Put a disgrace on you.

ladies, and all your company thither, to frustrate your provision, and stick a disgrace upon you. He was here now to have enticed us away from you too, but we told him his own,[2] I think.

LA FOOLE. Has Sir John Daw wronged me so inhumanely?

DAUPHINE. He has done it, Sir Amorous, most malicously and treacherously; but if you'll be ruled by us, you shall quit him, i' faith.

LA FOOLE. Good gentlemen, I'll make one, believe it. How, I pray?

DAUPHINE. Marry, sir, get me your pheasants, and your godwits, and your best meat, and dish it in silver dishes of your cousin's presently; and say nothing, but clap me a clean towel about you, like a sewer;[3] and bareheaded, march afore it with a good confidence—'tis but over the way, hard by—and we'll second you, where you shall set it off the board;[4] and bid 'em welcome to 't, which shall show 'tis yours, and disgrace his preparation utterly. And for your cousin, whereas she should be troubled here at home with care of making and giving welcome, she shall transfer all that labor thither, and be a principal guest herself; sit ranked with the College Honors, and be honored, and have her health drunk as often, as bare,[5] and as loud as the best of 'em.

LA FOOLE. I'll go tell her presently. It shall be done, that's resolved. [*Exit.*]

CLERIMONT. I thought he would not hear it out but 'twould take him.

DAUPHINE. Well, there be guests and meat now; how shall we do for music?

CLERIMONT. The smell of the venison, going through the street, will invite one noise[6] of fiddlers or other.

DAUPHINE. I would it would call the trumpeters thither!

CLERIMONT. Faith, there is hope; they have intelligence of all feasts. There's good correspondence betwixt them and the London cooks. 'Tis twenty to one but we have 'em.

DAUPHINE. 'Twill be a most solemn day for my uncle, and an excellent fit of mirth for us.

CLERIMONT. Ay, if we can hold up the emulation betwixt Foole and Daw, and never bring them to expostulate.[7]

DAUPHINE. Tut, flatter 'em both, as Truewit says, and you may take their understandings in a pursenet.[8] They'll believe themselves to be just such men as we make 'em, neither more nor less. They have nothing, not the use of their senses, but by tradition.

[*Re-enter* LA FOOLE, *like a sewer.*]

CLERIMONT. See! Sir Amorous has his towel on already. Have you persuaded your cousin?

LA FOOLE. Yes, 'tis very feasible. She'll do anything, she says, rather than the La Fooles shall be disgraced.

2. Told him off.
3. Steward.
4. Put it on the table.
5. Bareheaded, in token of respect.
6. I.e., a pickup group of itinerant street musicians.
7. To explain things to one another.
8. A small sack closed by a string, fit to hold both their brains.

DAUPHINE. She is a noble kinswoman. It will be such a pestling[9] device, Sir Amorous, it will pound all your enemy's practices to powder, and blow him up with his own mine, his own train![1]

LA FOOLE. Nay, we'll give fire, I warrant you.

CLERIMONT. But you must carry it privately, without any noise, and take no notice by any means——

[*Re-enter* CAPTAIN OTTER.]

OTTER. Gentlemen, my Princess says you shall have all her silver dishes, *festinate;*[2] and she's gone to alter her tire[3] a little, and go with you——

CLERIMONT. And yourself too, Captain Otter?

DAUPHINE. By any means, sir.

OTTER. Yes, sir, I do mean it; but I would entreat my cousin Sir Amorous, and you, gentlemen, to be suitors to my Princess, that I may carry my Bull and my Bear, as well as my Horse.

CLERIMONT. That you shall do, Captain Otter.

LA FOOLE. My cousin will never consent, gentlemen.

DAUPHINE. She must consent, Sir Amorous, to reason.

LA FOOLE. Why, she says they are no decorum among ladies.

OTTER. But they are *decora,*[4] and that's better, sir.

CLERIMONT. Ay, she must hear argument. Did not Pasiphaë, who was a queen, love a bull?[5] and was not Callisto, the mother of Arcas, turned into a bear, and made a star, Mistress Ursula, i' the heavens?

OTTER. O God! that I could ha' said as much! I will have these stories painted in the bear-garden, *ex Ovidii Metamorphosi.*[6]

DAUPHINE. Where is your Princess, Captain? pray be our leader.

OTTER. That I shall, sir.

CLERIMONT. Make haste, good Sir Amorous.

[*Exeunt.*]

SCENE 4. MOROSE'S *house*

[*Enter* MOROSE, EPICOENE, PARSON, *and* CUTBEARD.]

MOROSE. Sir, there's an angel[7] for yourself, and a brace of angels for your cold. Muse not at this manage of my bounty. It is fit we should thank fortune, double to nature, for any benefit she confers upon us; besides, it is your imperfection, but my solace.

PARSON. [*Speaks as having a cold.*] I thank your worship; so is it mine now.

MOROSE. What says he, Cutbeard?

CUTBEARD. He says, presto, sir, whensoever your worship needs

9. A trick that works like a mortar and pestle.

1. I.e., a track of gunpowder leading to the enemy's bomb; ignite it and you blow him up.

2. Hasten.

3. Attire, specifically hair-do.

4. *Decora* are fine things, though they may not be decorous (i.e., suitable to the occasion).

5. Pasiphaë, queen of Crete, loved a bull, and so gave birth to the Minotaur; Callisto was turned into a bear and is now Ursa Major, a constellation in the heavens.

6. Out of Ovid's *Metamorphoses.*

7. A gold coin bearing the image of St. Michael, and worth a handsome sum of money.

him, he can be ready with the like. He got this cold with sitting up late, and singing catches[8] with cloth-workers.

MOROSE. No more. I thank him.

PARSON. God keep your worship, and give you much joy with your fair spouse! [*Coughs.*] Uh, uh!

MOROSE. O, O! Stay, Cutbeard! let him give me five shillings of my money back. As it is bounty to reward benefits, so it is equity to mulct injuries. I will have it. What says he?

CLERIMONT. He cannot change it, sir.

MOROSE. It must be changed.

CUTBEARD. [*Aside.*]—Cough again.

MOROSE. What says he?

CUTBEARD. He will cough out the rest, sir.

PARSON. [*Coughs.*] Uh, uh, uh!

MOROSE. Away, away with him! stop his mouth! away! I forgive it——.

[*Exit* CUTBEARD *thrusting out the* PARSON.]

EPICOENE. Fie, Master Morose, that you will use this violence to a man of the church!

MOROSE. How!

EPICOENE. It does not become your gravity or breeding, as you pretend in court, to have offered this outrage on a waterman,[9] or any more boisterous creature, much less on a man of his civil coat.

MOROSE. You can speak then!

EPICOENE. Yes, sir.

MOROSE. Speak out, I mean.

EPICOENE. Ay, sir. Why, did you think you had married a statue, or a motion[1] only? one of the French puppets, with the eyes turned with a wire? or some innocent out of the hospital, that would stand with her hands thus, and a plaice-mouth,[2] and look upon you?

MOROSE. O immodesty! a manifest woman! What, Cutbeard!

EPICOENE. Nay, never quarrel with Cutbeard, sir; it is too late now. I confess it doth bate[3] somewhat of the modesty I had, when I writ simply maid; but I hope I shall make it a stock still competent to the estate and dignity of your wife.

MOROSE. She can talk!

EPICOENE. Yes indeed, sir.

[*Enter* MUTE.]

MOROSE. What, sirrah! None of my knaves there? Where is this impostor Cutbeard?

EPICOENE. Speak to him, fellow, speak to him! I'll have none of this coacted,[4] unnatural dumbness in my house, in a family where I govern.

[*Exit* MUTE.]

8. Songs in several parts. Huguenot weavers, refugees from Catholic persecution in France, were celebrated for singing at their work.

9. A hired boatman on the Thames.

1. Puppet.

2. Puckered-up, wry mouth, like that of a flat-fish.

3. Abate, diminish.

4. Forced.

MOROSE. She is my regent already! I have married a Penthesilea, a Semiramis![5] sold my liberty to a distaff!

SCENE 5

[*Enter* TRUEWIT.]

TRUEWIT. Where's Master Morose?

MOROSE. Is he come again? Lord have mercy upon me!

TRUEWIT. I wish you all joy, Mistress Epicoene, with your grave and honorable match.

EPICOENE. I return you the thanks, Master Truewit, so friendly a wish deserves.

MOROSE. She has acquaintance, too!

TRUEWIT. God save you, sir, and give you all contentment in your fair choice here! Before, I was the bird of night to you, the owl;[6] but now I am the messenger of peace, a dove, and bring you the glad wishes of many friends to the celebration of this good hour.

MOROSE. What hour, sir?

TRUEWIT. Your marriage hour, sir. I commend your resolution, that —notwithstanding all the dangers I laid afore you, in the voice of a night-crow—would yet go on, and be yourself. It shows you are a man constant to your own ends, and upright to your purposes, that would not be put off with left-handed cries.[7]

MOROSE. How should you arrive at the knowledge of so much?

TRUEWIT. Why did you ever hope, sir, committing the secrecy of it to a barber, that less than the whole town should know it? You might as well have told it the conduit,[8] or the bakehouse, or the infantry that follow the court, and with more security. Could your gravity forget so old and noted a remnant as *'lippis et tonsoribus notum'*?[9] Well, sir, forgive it yourself now, the fault, and be communicable with your friends. Here will be three or four fashionable ladies from the College to visit you presently, and their train of minions and followers.

MOROSE. Bar my doors! bar my doors! Where are all my eaters,[1] my mouths, now?——

[*Enter* SERVANTS.]

Bar up my doors, you varlets!

EPICOENE. He is a varlet that stirs to such an office. Let 'em stand open. I would see him that dares move his eyes toward it. Shall I have a barricado[2] made against my friends, to be barred of any pleasure they can bring in to me with honorable visitation?

[*Exeunt* SERVANTS.]

MOROSE. O Amazonian[3] impudence!

5. Penthesilea and Semiramis were warrior queens of antiquity. A "distaff", used in spinning, is not only a stick, but one which whirs and clatters.
6. Traditional bird of ill omen.
7. The left or sinister hand is always associated with bad luck.
8. All these phrases are more or less metaphorical ways of referring to the rabble, the common herd.
9. The phrase, from a satire by Horace, means "known to everyone, to the blear-eyed and the barbers."
1. Servants, i.e., those who have all this time eaten my bread.
2. Barrier.
3. As of Amazons, fierce female warriors of antiquity.

TRUEWIT. Nay, faith, in this, sir, she speaks but reason; and, methinks, is more continent than you. Would you go to bed so presently, sir, afore noon? A man of your head and hair should owe more to that reverend ceremony, and not mount the marriage bed like a town-bull, or a mountain-goat; but stay the due season, and ascend it then with religion and fear. Those delights are to be steeped in the humor and silence of the night; and give the day to other open pleasures, and jollities of feast, of music, of revels, of discourse. We'll have all, sir, that may make your Hymen[4] high and happy.

MOROSE. O my torment, my torment!

TRUEWIT. Nay, if you endure the first half hour, sir, so tediously, and with this irksomeness, what comfort or hope can this fair gentlewoman make to herself hereafter, in the consideration of so many years as are to come——

MOROSE. Of my affliction. Good sir, depart, and let her do it alone.

TRUEWIT. I have done, sir.

MOROSE. That cursed barber!

TRUEWIT. Yes, faith, a cursed wretch indeed, sir.

MOROSE. I have married his cittern,[5] that's common to all men. Some plague above the plague——

TRUEWIT. All Egypt's ten plagues.[6]

MOROSE. Revenge me on him!

TRUEWIT. 'Tis very well, sir. If you laid on a curse or two more, I'll assure you he'll bear 'em. As that he may get the pox with seeking to cure it, sir. Or that, while he is curling another man's hair, his own may drop off. Or, for burning some male bawd's lock, he may have his brain beat out with the curling-iron.

MOROSE. No, let the wretch live wretched. May he get the itch, and his shop so lousy, as no man dare come at him, nor he come at no man!

TRUEWIT. Ay, and if ye would swallow all his balls[7] for pills, let not them purge him.

MOROSE. Let his warming-pan be ever cold!

TRUEWIT. A perpetual frost underneath it, sir.

MOROSE. Let him never hope to see fire again!

TRUEWIT. But in hell, sir.

MOROSE. His chairs be always empty, his scissors rust, and his combs mold in their cases!

TRUEWIT. Very dreadful that! And may he lose the invention, sir, of carving lanterns in paper.[8]

MOROSE. Let there be no bawd carted that year, to employ a basin of his;[9] but let him be glad to eat his sponge for bread!

4. God of marriage, hence by extension the ceremony itself.

5. A guitar, often kept in barber shops for customers to fool with while they waited; hence, a common floozie.

6. The Lord visited ten plagues on Egypt, so that the children of Israel might go free.

7. Of soap, commonly used in that form by barbers.

8. Barber-signs, for the twilight hours.

9. Bawds being whipped through the streets in a cart were preceded by a man banging on a basin to invite public attention.

TRUEWIT. And drink lotion to it, and much good do him!

MOROSE. Or, for want of bread——

TRUEWIT. Eat ear-wax, sir! I'll help you. Or draw his own teeth, and add them to the lute-string!

MOROSE. No, beat the old ones to powder, and make bread of them!

TRUEWIT. Yes, make meal of the millstones.

MOROSE. May all the botches and burns that he has cured on others, break out upon him!

TRUEWIT. And he now forget the cure of them in himself sir; or, if he do remember it, let him have scraped all his linen into lint for't, and have not a rag left him to set up with!

MOROSE. Let him never set up[1] again, but have the gout in his hands forever! Now, no more sir.

TRUEWIT. O, that last was too high set; you might go less with him, i' faith, and be revenged enough: as, that he be never able to new-paint his pole——

MOROSE. Good sir, no more. I forgot myself.

TRUEWIT. Or, want credit to take up with a comb-maker——

MOROSE. No more, sir.

TRUEWIT. Or, having broken his glass in a former despair, fall now into a much greater, of ever getting another—

MOROSE. I beseech you, no more.

TRUEWIT. Or, that he never be trusted with trimming of any but chimney-sweepers——

MOROSE. Sir——

TRUEWIT. Or, may he cut a collier's[2] throat with his razor, by chance-medley, and yet hang for't.

MOROSE. I will forgive him rather than hear any more. I beseech you, sir.

SCENE 6

[*Enter* DAW, *with* LADY HAUGHTY, LADY CENTAUR, MISTRESS MAVIS, *and* TRUSTY.]

DAW. This way, madam.

MOROSE. O, the sea breaks in upon me! another flood! an inundation! I shall be o'erwhelmed with noise. It beats already at my shores. I feel an earthquake in myself for't.

DAW. Give you joy, mistress.

MOROSE. Has she servants too!

DAW. I have brought some ladies here to see and know you. My Lady Haughty—[EPICOENE *kisses them severally, as he presents them*]—this my Lady Centaur—Mistress Doll Mavis—Mistress Trusty, my Lady Haughty's woman. Where's your husband? let's see him. Can he endure no noise? let me come to him.

MOROSE. What nomenclator is this?

1. Set up shop.
2. Literally, a coal-miner, figuratively, a rascal, worthless person; "chance-medley": accident.

TRUEWIT. Sir John Daw, sir, your wife's servant, this.

MOROSE. A Daw, and her servant! O, 'tis decreed, 'tis decreed of me, an she have such servants.

TRUEWIT. Nay, sir, you must kiss the ladies; you must not go away now. They come toward you to seek you out.

HAUGHTY. I' faith, Master Morose, would you steal a marriage thus, in the midst of so many friends, and not acquaint us? Well, I'll kiss you, notwithstanding the justice of my quarrel. You shall give me leave, mistress, to use a becoming familiarity with your husband.

EPICOENE. Your ladyship does me an honor in it, to let me know he is so worthy your favor; as you have done both him and me grace to visit so unprepared a pair to entertain you.

MOROSE. Compliment! compliment!

EPICOENE. But I must lay the burden of that upon my servant here.

HAUGHTY. It shall not need, Mistress Morose; we will all bear, rather than one shall be oppressed.

MOROSE. I know it; and you will teach her the faculty, if she be to learn it.

[*Walks aside.*]

HAUGHTY. Is this the Silent Woman?

CENTAUR. Nay, she has found her tongue since she was married, Master Truewit says.

HAUGHTY. O, Master Truewit, save you! What kind of creature is your bride here? She speaks, methinks!

TRUEWIT. Yes, madam, believe it, she is a gentlewoman of very absolute behavior, and of a good race.

HAUGHTY. And Jack Daw told us she could not speak!

TRUEWIT. So it was carried in plot, madam, to put her upon this old fellow, by Sir Dauphine, his nephew, and one or two more of us. But she is a woman of an excellent assurance, and an extraordinary happy wit and tongue. You shall see her make rare sport with Daw ere night.

HAUGHTY. And he brought us to laugh at her!

TRUEWIT. That falls out often, madam, that he that thinks himself the master-wit, is the master-fool. I assure your ladyship, ye cannot laugh at her.

HAUGHTY. No, we'll have her to the College. An she have wit, she shall be one of us! Shall she not, Centaur? We'll make her a Collegiate.

CENTAUR. Yes, faith, madam, and Mavis and she will set up a side.[3]

TRUEWIT. Believe it, madam and Mistress Mavis, she will sustain her part.

MAVIS. I'll tell you that when I have talked with her, and tried her.

HAUGHTY. Use her very civilly, Mavis.

MAVIS. So I will, madam.

[*Whispers to her.*]

3. I.e., make a pair in a game of cards.

MOROSE. [*aside*]—Blessed minute! that they would whisper thus ever!

TRUEWIT. In the meantime, madam, would but your ladyship help to vex him a little. You know his disease; talk to him about the wedding ceremonies, or call for your gloves, or——

HAUGHTY. Let me alone. Centaur, help me. Master Bridegroom, where are you?

MOROSE. [*aside*]—O, it was too miraculously good to last!

HAUGHTY. We see no ensigns[4] of a wedding here, no character of a bridal. Where be our scarfs and our gloves? I pray you, give 'em us. Let us know your bride's colors, and yours, at least.[5]

CENTAUR. Alas, madam, he has provided none.

MOROSE. Had I known your ladyship's painter,[6] I would.

HAUGHTY. He has given it you, Centaur, i' faith. But do you hear, Master Morose? a jest will not absolve you in this manner. You that have sucked the milk of the court, and from thence have been brought up to the very strong meats and wine of it; been a courtier from the biggen to the nightcap,[7] as we may say; and you to offend in such a high point of ceremony as this, and let your nuptials want all marks of solemnity! How much plate have you lost today—if you had but regarded your profit—what gifts, what friends, through your mere rusticity!

MOROSE. Madam——

HAUGHTY. Pardon me, sir, I must insinuate your errors to you; no gloves? no garters? no scarfs? no epithalamium?[8] no masque?

DAW. Yes, madam, I'll make an epithalamium, I promised my mistress. I have begun it already. Will your ladyship hear it?

HAUGHTY. Ay, good Jack Daw.

MOROSE. Will it please your ladyship command a chamber, and be private with your friend? You shall have your choice of rooms to retire to after. My whole house is yours. I know it hath been your ladyship's errand into the City at other times,[9] however now you have been unhappily diverted upon me; but I shall be loath to break any honorable custom of your ladyship's. And therefore, good madam——

EPICOENE. Come, you are a rude bridegroom, to entertain ladies of honor in this fashion.

CENTAUR. He is a rude groom[1] indeed.

TRUEWIT. By that light, you deserve to be grafted, and have your horns[2] reach from one side of the island to the other—Do not mistake me, sir, I but speak this to give the ladies some heart again, not for any malice to you.

4. I.e., special emblems.

5. The bride and her bridesmaids, the groom and his followers, wore distinctive colors.

6. Painting (wearing make-up) was not well thought of in those days; Morose indicates that if he had known Lady Centaur's make-up man, he would have had her daubed, say, green and orange.

7. I.e., from the cradle to the grave.

8. Marriage poem; masques were also performed for very fancy weddings.

9. I.e., she has gone into the city from the court to be alone in a bedroom with a jackdaw courtier.

1. Not just a rude bridegroom but rude by the standards of stableboys (grooms).

2. The cuckold's traditional antlers.

MOROSE. Is this your bravo,[3] ladies?

TRUEWIT. As God help me, if you utter such another word, I'll take Mistress Bride in, and begin to you in a very sad cup,[4] do you see? Go to, know your friends and such as love you.

SCENE 7

[*Enter* CLERIMONT *followed by a number of musicians.*]

CLERIMONT. By your leave, ladies. Do you want any music? I have brought you variety of noises—Play, sirs, all of you.

[*Music of all sorts.*]

MOROSE. O, a plot, a plot, a plot, a plot upon me! This day I shall be their anvil to work on; they will grate me asunder. 'Tis worse than the noise of a saw.

CLERIMONT. No, they are hair, rosin, and guts. I can give you the receipt.[5]

TRUEWIT. Peace, boys!

CLERIMONT. Play, I say!

TRUEWIT. Peace, rascals! You see who's your friend now, sir? Take courage, put on a martyr's resolution. Mock down all their attemptings with patience. 'Tis but a day, and I would suffer heroically. Should an ass exceed me in fortitude? No. You betray your infirmity with your hanging dull ears, and make them insult. Bear up bravely, and constantly. [LA FOOLE *passes over, serving the meat, followed by servants carrying dishes, and* MISTRESS OTTER.]—Look you here sir, what honor is done you unexpected, by your nephew; a wedding dinner come, and a knight-sewer before it, for the more reputation; and fine Mistress Otter, your neighbor, in the rump or tail of it.

MOROSE. Is that Gorgon, that Medusa[6] come? Hide me, hide me!

TRUEWIT. I warrant you, sir, she will not transform you. Look upon her with a good courage. Pray you entertain her, and conduct your guests in. No?—Mistress Bride, will you entreat in the ladies? Your bridegroom is so shamefaced here——

EPICOENE. Will it please your ladyship, madam?

HAUGHTY. With the benefit of your company, mistress.

EPICOENE. Servant, pray you perform your duties.

DAW. And glad to be commanded, mistress.

CENTAUR. How like you her wit, Mavis?

MAVIS. Very prettily, absolutely well.

MISTRESS OTTER. 'Tis my place.

MAVIS. You shall pardon me, Mistress Otter.

MISTRESS OTTER. Why, I am a Collegiate.

MAVIS. But not in ordinary.[7]

MISTRESS OTTER. But I am.

3. Bully—implying that they are whores.
4. I.e., get your marriage off to a very bad start.
5. Recipe.
6. Medusa the Gorgon had frightful features that turned men to stone.
7. The ladies have their dignities and precedences: "in ordinary" implies "with all the titles and formalities."

MAVIS. We'll dispute that within.

[*Exeunt* LADIES.]

CLERIMONT. Would this had lasted a little longer!

TRUEWIT. And that they had sent for the heralds!

[*Enter* CAPTAIN OTTER.]

Captain Otter! what news?

OTTER. I have brought my Bull, Bear, and Horse, in private, and yonder are the trumpeters without, and the drum, gentlemen.[8]

[*The drum and trumpets sound.*]

MOROSE. O, O, O!

OTTER. And we will have a rouse[9] in each of 'em, anon, for bold Britons, i' faith!

[*They sound again.*]

MOROSE. O, O, O!

[*Exit.*]

ALL. Follow, follow, follow![1]

[*Exeunt all.*]

Act IV

SCENE 1. MOROSE'S *house*

[*Enter* TRUEWIT *and* CLERIMONT]

TRUEWIT. Was there ever poor bridegroom so tormented? or man, indeed?

CLERIMONT. I have not read of the like in the chronicles of the land.

TRUEWIT. Sure, he cannot but go to a place of rest, after all this purgatory.[2]

CLERIMONT. He may presume it, I think.

TRUEWIT. The spitting, the coughing, the laughter, the sneezing, the farting, dancing, noise of the music, and her masculine and loud commanding, and urging the whole family, makes him think he has married a fury.[3]

CLERIMONT. And she carries it up bravely.

TRUEWIT. Ay, she takes any occasion to speak; that's the height on't.

CLERIMONT. And how soberly Dauphine labors to satisfy him, that it was none of his plot!

TRUEWIT. And has almost brought him to the faith, in the article. Here he comes.

[*Enter* SIR DAUPHINE.]

Where is he now? what's become of him, Dauphine?

8. At serious drinking bouts a flourish of trumpets and a ruffle of drums saluted each emptying of the glasses.

9. Toast.

1. "Follow, follow, follow" is the Elizabethan playwright's way of indicating a confused gabble of many people.

2. In Catholic theology, the place of purification after death; used here with the overtone that Morose has been purged of his humor.

3. The Furies were three frightful females, appointed, so the ancients thought, to punish human crimes: Epicoene looks like one of them.

DAUPHINE. O, hold me up a little, I shall go away in the jest[4] else. He has got on his whole nest of nightcaps, and locked himself up in the top of the house, as high as ever he can climb from the noise. I peeped in at a cranny, and saw him sitting over a cross-beam of the roof, like him on the saddler's horse in Fleet Street,[5] upright; and he will sleep there.

CLERIMONT. But where are your Collegiates?

DAUPHINE. Withdrawn with the bride in private.

TRUEWIT. O, they are instructing her in the College grammar. If she have grace with them, she knows all their secrets instantly.

CLERIMONT. Methinks the Lady Haughty looks well today, for all my dispraise of her in the morning. I think I shall come about to thee again, Truewit.

TRUEWIT. Believe it, I told you right. Women ought to repair the losses time and years have made in their features, with dressings. And an intelligent woman, if she know by herself the least defect will be most curious to hide it; and it becomes her. If she be short, let her sit much, lest, when she stands, she be thought to sit. If she have an ill foot, let her wear her gown the longer, and her shoe the thinner. If a fat hand and scald nails, let her carve the less, and act in gloves.[6] If a sour breath, let her never discourse fasting, and always talk at her distance. If she have black and rugged teeth, let her offer the less at laughter, especially if she laugh wide and open.

CLERIMONT. O, you shall have some women, when they laugh you would think they brayed, it is so rude and——

TRUEWIT. Ay, and others that will stalk in their gait like an ostrich, and take huge strides. I cannot endure such a sight. I love measure in the feet, and number in the voice.[7] They are gentlenesses that oftentimes draw no less than the face.

DAUPHINE. How camest thou to study these creatures so exactly? I would thou wouldst make me a proficient.

TRUEWIT. Yes, but you must leave to live i' your chamber, then, a month together upon Amadis de Gaul, or Don Quixote as you are wont;[8] and come abroad where the matter is frequent, to court, to tiltings,[9] public shows, and feasts, to plays, and church sometimes. Thither they come to show their new tires too, to see and to be seen. In these places a man shall find whom to love, whom to play with, whom to touch once, whom to hold ever. The variety arrests his judgment. A wench to please a man comes not down dropping from the ceiling, as he lies on his back droning a tobacco-pipe. He must go where she is.

DAUPHINE. Yes, and be never the nearer.

TRUEWIT. Out, heretic! That diffidence makes thee worthy it should be so.

4. Die laughing.
5. A bootmaker in Fleet Street evidently had a sign consisting of a wooden horse and rider.
6. I.e., if she has rough, scabby hands, she shouldn't carve at table, when everyone will be watching them.
7. Small feet and a soft voice.
8. Romantic and impractical reading.
9. Mock jousts.

CLERIMONT. He says true to you, Dauphine.

DAUPHINE. Why?

TRUEWIT. A man should not doubt to overcome any woman. Think he can vanquish them, and he shall; for though they deny, their desire is to be tempted. Penelope herself cannot hold out long. Ostend, you saw, was taken at last.[1] You must persevere and hold to your purpose. They would solicit us, but that they are afraid. Howsoever, they wish in their hearts we should solicit them. Praise them, flatter them, you shall never want eloquence or trust; even the chastest delight to feel themselves that way rubbed. With praises you must mix kisses too; if they take them, they'll take more. Though they strive, they would be overcome.

CLERIMONT. O, but a man must beware of force.

TRUEWIT. It is to them an acceptable violence, and has oft-times the place of the greatest courtesy. She that might have been forced, an you let her go free without touching, though then she seem to thank you, will ever hate you after; and, glad in the face, is assuredly sad at the heart.

CLERIMONT. But all women are not to be taken all ways.

TRUEWIT. 'Tis true. No more than all birds, or all fishes. If you appear learned to an ignorant wench, or jocund to a sad, or witty to a foolish, why, she presently begins to mistrust herself. You must approach them in their own height, their own line; for the contrary makes many that fear to commit themselves to noble and worthy fellows, run into the embraces of a rascal. If she love wit, give verses, though you borrow them of a friend, or buy them, to have good. If valor, talk of your sword, and be frequent in the mention of quarrels, though you be staunch in fighting.[2] If activity, be seen on your barbary[3] often, or leaping over stools, for the credit of your back. If she love good clothes or dressing, have your learned council about you every morning, your French tailor, barber, linener, &c. Let your powder, your glass, and your comb be your dearest acquaintance. Take more care for the ornament of your head, than the safety; and wish the commonwealth rather troubled, than a hair about you. That will take her. Then, if she be covetous and craving, do you promise anything, and perform sparingly; so shall you keep her in appetite still. Seem as you would give, but be like a barren field that yields little, or unlucky dice to foolish and hoping gamesters. Let your gifts be slight and dainty, rather than precious. Let cunning be above cost. Give cherries at time of year,[4] or apricots, and say they were sent you out of the country, though you bought them in Cheapside. Admire her tires; like her in all fashions; compare her in every habit to some deity; invent excellent dreams to flatter her, and riddles; or, if she be a great one, perform always

1. Penelope, Odysseus' wife, held out against the solicitations of her many suitors for twenty years; Ostend in Belgium held out against the Spaniards from 1601 to 1604.

2. The passage would make easier sense if it said, as it evidently means, staunch *against* fighting.

3. Arabian horse.

4. I.e., at the odd time of year, out of season.

the second parts to her: like what she likes, praise whom she praises, and fail not to make the household and servants yours, yea, the whole family, and salute them by their names—'tis but light cost, if you can purchase them so—and make her physician your pensioner; and her chief woman.[5] Nor will it be out of your gain to make love to her too, so she follow, not usher her lady's pleasure. All blabbing is taken away, when she comes to be a part of the crime.

DAUPHINE. On what courtly lap hast thou late slept, to come forth so sudden and absolute a courtling?

TRUEWIT. Good faith, I should rather question you, that are so hearkening after these mysteries. I began to suspect your diligence, Dauphine. Speak, art thou in love in earnest?

DAUPHINE. Yes, by my troth, am I! 'twere ill dissembling before thee.

TRUEWIT. With which of 'em, I pray thee?

DAUPHINE. With all the Collegiates.

CLERIMONT. Out on thee! We'll keep you at home, believe it, in the stable, an you be such a stallion.

TRUEWIT. No, I like him well. Men should love wisely, and all women: some one for the face, and let her please the eye; another for the skin, and let her please the touch; a third for the voice, and let her please the ear; and where the objects mix, let the senses so, too. Thou wouldst think it strange if I should make them all in love with thee afore night!

DAUPHINE. I would say thou hadst the best philter in the world, and couldst do more than Madam Medea,[6] or Doctor Forman.

TRUEWIT. If I do not, let me play the mountebank for my meat, while I live, and the bawd for my drink.

DAUPHINE. So be it, I say.

SCENE 2

[*Enter* OTTER, *with his three cups,* DAW, *and* LA FOOLE.]

OTTER. O Lord, gentlemen, how my knights and I have missed you here!

CLERIMONT. Why, Captain, what service, what service?

OTTER. To see me bring up my Bull, Bear, and Horse to fight.

DAW. Yes, faith, the Captain says we shall be his dogs to bait them.

DAUPHINE. A good employment.

TRUEWIT. Come on, let's see a course, then.

LA FOOLE. I am afraid my cousin will be offended, if she come.

OTTER. Be afraid of nothing. Gentlemen, I have placed the drum and the trumpets, and one to give them the sign when you are ready. Here's my Bull for myself, and my Bear for Sir John Daw, and my Horse for Sir Amorous. Now set your foot to mine, and yours to his and——

5. Bribe her doctor and maid—the former just with money, the latter with sex in addition.

6. The witch-sorceress of Greek mythology; Doctor Simon Forman was an astrologer, physician, and druggist of Jonson's day.

LA FOOLE. Pray God my cousin come not.

OTTER. Saint George and Saint Andrew, fear no cousins—Come, sound, sound!—'*Et rauco strepuerunt cornua cantu.*'[7]

[*Drum and trumpets. They drink.*]

TRUEWIT. Well said, Captain, i' faith! Well fought at the Bull.

CLERIMONT. Well held at the Bear.

TRUEWIT. Low, low, Captain!

DAUPHINE. O, the Horse has kicked off his dog already.

LA FOOLE. I cannot drink it, as I am a knight.

TRUEWIT. God's so! off with his spurs, somebody!

LA FOOLE. It goes against my conscience. My cousin will be angry with it.

DAW. I have done mine.

TRUEWIT. You fought high and fair, Sir John.

CLERIMONT. At the head.

DAUPHINE. Like an excellent bear-dog.

CLERIMONT. —You take no notice of the business,[8] I hope?

DAW. Not a word, sir, you see we are jovial.

OTTER. Sir Amorous, you must not equivocate.[9] It must be pulled down, for all my cousin.

CLERIMONT. —'Sfoot, if you take not your drink, they'll think you are discontented with something. You'll betray all, if you take the least notice.

LA FOOLE. Not I, I'll both drink and talk then.

OTTER. You must pull the horse on his knees, Sir Amorous; fear no cousins. *Jacta est alea.*[10]

TRUEWIT. —O, now he's in his vein, and bold. The least hint given him of his wife now will make him rail desperately.

CLERIMONT. Speak to him of her.

TRUEWIT. Do you, and I'll fetch her to the hearing of it.

[*Exit.*]

DAUPHINE. Captain he-Otter, your she-Otter is coming, your wife.

OTTER. Wife! buzz! Titivilitium![1] There's no such thing in nature. I confess, gentleman, I have a cook, a laundress, a house drudge, that serves my necessary turns, and goes under that title; but he's an ass that will be so uxorious to tie his affections to one circle. Come, the name dulls appetite. Here, replenish again; another bout. [*Fills the cups again.*] Wives are nasty, sluttish animals.

DAUPHINE. O, Captain.

OTTER. As ever the earth bare, *tribus verbis.*[2] Where's Master Truewit?

DAW. He's slipped aside, sir.

CLERIMONT. But you must drink and be jovial.

DAW. Yes, give it me.

7. And the trumpets gave off a roaring sound.

8. I.e., the supposed quarrel with La Foole.

9. Palter, stall; in drinking contests, no excuses were accepted till a man lay insensible.

10. "The die is cast"—as Caesar said when he crossed the Rubicon to seize imperial power.

1. Nonsense.

2. In three words.

LA FOOLE. And me too.

DAW. Let's be jovial.

LA FOOLE. As jovial as you will.

OTTER. Agreed. Now you shall have the Bear, cousin, and Sir John Daw the Horse, and I'll have the Bull still.—Sound, Tritons of the Thames!—'*Nunc est bibendum, nunc pede libero*——'[3]

MOROSE. [*Speaks from above, as the drum beats and the trumpets sound.*] Villains, murderers, sons of the earth, and traitors, what do you there?

CLERIMONT. O, now the trumpets have waked him, we shall have his company.

OTTER. A wife is a scurvy clogdogdo, an unlucky thing, a very foresaid bear-whelp, without any good fashion or breeding, *mala bestia*.[4]

[*Re-enter* TRUEWIT *behind with* MISTRESS OTTER.]

DAUPHINE. Why did you marry one then, Captain?

OTTER. A pox! I married with six thousand pound, I. I was in love with that. I have not kissed my Fury these forty weeks.

CLERIMONT. The more to blame you, Captain.

TRUEWIT. [*aside*]—Nay, Mistress Otter, hear him a little first.

OTTER. She has a breath worse than my grandmother's, *profecto!*[5]

MISTRESS OTTER. [*aside*]—O treacherous liar! Kiss me, sweet Master Truewit, and prove him a slandering knave.

TRUEWIT. I'll rather believe you, lady.

OTTER. And she has a peruke that's like a pound of hemp, made up in shoe-threads.

MISTRESS OTTER. [*aside*]—O viper, mandrake!

OTTER. A most vile face! and yet she spends me forty pound a year in mercury and hogs'-bones.[6] All her teeth were made in the Blackfriars, both her eyebrows in the Strand, and her hair in Silver Street. Every part o' the town owns a piece of her.

MISTRESS OTTER. [*Comes forward.*]—I cannot hold.

OTTER. She takes herself asunder still when she goes to bed, into some twenty boxes; and about next day noon is put together again, like a great German clock; and so come forth, and rings a tedious 'larum to the whole house, and then is quiet again for an hour, but for her quarters.—Have you done me right, gentlemen?

MISTRESS. OTTER. [*Falls upon him and beats him.*] No, sir, I'll do you right with my quarters, with my quarters!

OTTER. O, hold, good Princess.

TRUEWIT. Sound, sound!

[*Drum and trumpets.*]

CLERIMONT. A battle, a battle!

MISTRESS OTTER. You notorious stinkardly bear-ward,[7] does my breath smell?

3. From Horace: "Now's the time to drink, now we dance lightly," etc.

4. Ugly beast.

5. For a fact.

6. The disgusting ingredients entering into cosmetics were a favorite theme of satirists.

7. Bear-warden, keeper of the bears.

OTTER. Under correction, dear Princess—Look to my Bear and my Horse, gentlemen.

MISTRESS OTTER. Do I want teeth and eyebrows, thou bulldog?

TRUEWIT. Sound, sound still!

[*Trumpets again.*]

OTTER. No, I protest, under correction——

MISTRESS OTTER. Ay, now you are under correction, you protest; but you did not protest before correction, sir. Thou Judas, to offer to betray thy Princess! I'll make thee an example——

[*Beats him.*]

[MOROSE *descends with a long-sword.*]

MOROSE. I will have no such examples in my house, Lady Otter.

MISTRESS OTTER. Ah——

[*Exeunt* MISTRESS OTTER, DAW *and* LA FOOLE.]

MOROSE. Mistress Mary Ambree,[8] your examples are dangerous.—Rogues, hellhounds, Stentors![9] out of my doors, you sons of noise and tumult, begot on an ill May-day, or when the galley-foist is afloat to Westminster.[1] [*Drives out the musicians.*] A trumpeter could not be conceived but then!

DAUPHINE. What ails you, sir?

MOROSE. They have rent my roof, walls, and all my windows asunder with their brazen throats.

[*Exit.*]

TRUEWIT. Best follow him, Dauphine.

DAUPHINE. So I will.

[*Exit.*]

CLERIMONT. Where's Daw and La Foole?

OTTER. They are both run away, sir. Good gentlemen, help to pacify my Princess, and speak to the great ladies for me. Now must I go lie with the bears this fortnight, and keep out o' the way, till my peace be made, for this scandal she has taken. Did you not see my bull-head, gentlemen?

CLERIMONT. Is't not on, Captain?[2]

TRUEWIT. No; but he may make a new one, by that is on.

OTTER. O, here 'tis. An you come over, gentlemen, and ask for Tom Otter, we'll go down to Ratcliffe, and have a course, i' faith, for all these disasters. There's *bona spes*[3] left.

TRUEWIT. Away, Captain, get off while you are well.

[*Exit* OTTER.]

CLERIMONT. I am glad we are rid of him.

TRUEWIT. You had never been, unless we had put his wife upon him. His humor is as tedious at last as it was ridiculous at first.

8. A legendary English Amazon supposed to have helped defend Ghent against the Spaniards in 1584.

9. The herald of the gods in antiquity; the memory of his thunderous voice is preserved in the word "stentorian."

1. May-day and the day of the Lord Mayor's entry into office (when the official galley, loaded with musicians, firecrackers, and ceremonial artillery, carried him to Westminster), were (thinks distracted Morose) the only days on which trumpeters could have been begotten.

2. The joke is that Otter, a cuckold, wears the legendary horns.

3. Good hope. Ratcliff, in the outer suburbs, had a lot of low taverns, and so was a good place for a "course," a drinking-spree.

SCENE 3. MOROSE'S *house*

[*Enter* LADY HAUGHTY, MISTRESS OTTER, LADY MAVIS, DAW, LA FOOLE, LADY CENTAUR, *and* EPICOENE.]

HAUGHTY. We wondered why you shrieked so, Mistress Otter.

MISTRESS OTTER. O God, madam, he came down with a huge, long, naked weapon in both his hands, and looked so dreadfully! Sure, he's beside himself.

MAVIS. Why, what made you there, Mistress Otter?

MISTRESS OTTER. Alas, Mistress Mavis, I was chastising my subject, and thought nothing of him.

DAW. Faith, mistress, you must do so, too. Learn to chastise. Mistress Otter corrects her husband so, he dares not speak but under correction.

LA FOOLE. And with his hat off to her. 'Twould do you good to see.

HAUGHTY. In sadness, 'tis good and mature counsel, Practise it, Morose. I'll call you Morose still now, as I call Centaur and Mavis; we four will be all one.

CENTAUR. And you'll come to the College, and live with us?

HAUGHTY. Make him give milk and honey.

MAVIS. Look how you manage him at first, you shall have him ever after.

CENTAUR. Let him allow you your coach and four horses, your woman, your chambermaid, your page, your gentleman-usher, your French cook, and four grooms.

HAUGHTY. And go with us to Bedlam, to the chinahouses, and to the Exchange.[4]

CENTAUR. It will open the gate to your fame.

HAUGHTY. Here's Centaur has immortalized herself with taming of her wild male.

MAVIS. Ay, she has done the miracle of the kingdom.

[*Enter* CLERIMONT *and* TRUEWIT.]

EPICOENE. But, ladies, do you count it lawful to have such plurality of servants, and do 'em all graces?

HAUGHTY. Why not? Why should women deny their favors to men? Are they the poorer, or the worse?

DAW. Is the Thames the less for the dyers' water,[5] mistress?

LA FOOLE. Or a torch for lighting many torches?

TRUEWIT. Well said, La Foole.—What a new one he has got!

CENTAUR. They are empty losses women fear in this kind.

HAUGHTY. Besides, ladies should be mindful of the approach of age, and let no time want his due use. The best of our days pass first.

4. Fine ladies commonly amused themselves with trips to Bedlam (to watch the idiots), to the china shops (where they shopped for porcelain and picked up lovers), and to the Royal Exchange, where they bargained over lace and gewgaws.

5. Dyers of cloth use a lot of water, most of which they return (somewhat the worse for wear) to the source where they got it. The reference is very local, but the basic idea, like many others in this scene, comes from Horace's *Art of Love,* III.

MAVIS. We are rivers that cannot be called back, madam. She that now excludes her lovers may live to lie a forsaken beldam[6] in a frozen bed.

CENTAUR. 'Tis true, Mavis; and who will wait on us to coach then? or write, or tell us the news then? make anagrams of our names, and invite us to the Cockpit,[7] and kiss our hands all the playtime, and draw their weapons for our honors?

HAUGHTY. Not one.

DAW. Nay, my mistress is not altogether unintelligent of these things. Here be in presence have tasted of her favors.

CLERIMONT. [*aside*]—What a neighing hobby-horse is this!

EPICOENE. But not with intent to boast 'em again, servant.—And have you those excellent receipts, madam, to keep yourselves from bearing of children?

HAUGHTY. O yes, Morose. How should we maintain our youth and beauty else? Many births of a woman make her old, as many crops make the earth barren.

SCENE 4

[*Enter* MOROSE *and* DAUPHINE.]

MOROSE. O my cursed angel, that instructed me to this fate!

DAUPHINE. Why, sir?

MOROSE. That I should be seduced by so foolish a devil as a barber will make!

DAUPHINE. I would I had been worthy, sir, to have partaken your counsel; you should never have trusted it to such a minister.

MOROSE. Would I could redeem it with the loss of an eye, nephew, a hand, or any other member.

DAUPHINE. Marry, God forbid, sir, that you should geld yourself to anger your wife.

MOROSE. So it would rid me of her! and that I did supererogatory penance in a belfry, at Westminister Hall, i' the Cockpit, at the fall of a stag, the Tower Wharf,—what place is there else?—London Bridge, Paris Garden, Billingsgate when the noises are at their height and loudest.[8] Nay, I would sit out a play, that were nothing but fights at sea, drum, trumpet, and target!

DAUPHINE. I hope there shall be no such need, sir. Take patience, good uncle. This is but a day, and 'tis well worn, too, now.

MOROSE. O, 'twill be so forever, nephew, I foresee it, forever. Strife and tumult are the dowry that comes with a wife.

TRUEWIT. I told you so, sir, and you would not believe me.

MOROSE. Alas, do not rub those wounds, Master Truewit, to blood again. 'Twas my negligence. Add not affliction to affliction. I have perceived the effect of it too late in Madam Otter.

6. Crone.

7. I.e., the theater, but just as likely the pit where cock-fights were held.

8. All of these are places of excessive noise—Westminster Hall, full of loud lawyers; the Cockpit, full of noisy spectators; the stag, surrounded by howling dogs and blaring horns; Tower Wharf, covered with ordnance; Paris Garden, where bull-baitings were held; Billingsgate, where fishwives shrieked their wares.

EPICOENE. How do you, sir?

MOROSE. Did you ever hear a more unnecessary question? as if she did not see! Why, I do as you see, Empress, Empress.

EPICOENE. You are not well, sir; you look very ill; something has distempered you.

MOROSE. O horrible, monstrous impertinencies! Would not one of these have served, do you think, sir? would not one of these have served?

TRUEWIT. Yes, sir, but these are but notes of female kindness, sir, certain tokens that she has a voice, sir.

MOROSE O, is't so! Come, an't be no otherwise——What say you?

EPICOENE. How do you feel yourself, sir?

MOROSE. Again that!

TRUEWIT. Nay, look you, sir, you would be friends with your wife upon unconscionable terms—her silence.

EPICOENE. They say you are run mad, sir.

MOROSE. Not for love, I assure you, of you, do you see?

EPICOENE. O Lord, gentlemen, lay hold on him, for God's sake! What shall I do! Who's his physician—can you tell?—that knows the state of his body best, that I might send for him? Good sir, speak; I'll send for one of my doctors else.

MOROSE. What, to poison me, that I might die intestate, and leave you possessed of all?

EPICOENE. Lord, how idly he talks, and how his eyes sparkle! He looks green about the temples! Do you see what blue spots he has?

CLERIMONT. Ay, it's melancholy.

EPICOENE. Gentlemen, for Heaven's sake, counsel me. Ladies!—Servant, you have read Pliny and Paracelsus;[9] ne'er a word now to comfort a poor gentlewoman? Ay me, what fortune had I to marry a distracted man!

DAW. I'll tell you, mistress——

TRUEWIT. [*aside to* CLERIMONT]—How rarely she holds it up!

MOROSE. What mean you, gentlemen?

EPICOENE. What will you tell me, servant?

DAW. The disease in Greek is called μανία, in Latin '*insania, furor, vel ecstasis melancholica,*' that is, '*egressio,*' and a man '*ex melancholico evadit fanaticus.*'[1]

MOROSE. Shall I have a lecture read upon me alive.

DAW. But he may be but *phreneticus* yet, mistress; and *phrenesis* is only *delirium,* or so.[2]

EPICOENE. Ay, that is for the disease, servant; but what is this to the cure? We are sure enough of the disease.

MOROSE. Let me go.

TRUEWIT. Why, we'll entreat her to hold her peace, sir.

9. These are natural historians, one of Roman times, one of the Renaissance.

1. I.e., "madness, fury, or melancholy ecstasy"; that is, "being beside yourself," and a man "from being melancholy turns to a fanatic."

2. I.e., he may be only "frenetic," and "frenzy" is nothing more than "delirium," but not absolute insanity.

MOROSE. O no, labor not to stop her. She is like a conduit-pipe, that will gush out with more force when she opens again.

HAUGHTY. I'll tell you, Morose, you must talk divinity to him altogether, or moral philosophy.

LA FOOLE. Ay, and there's an excellent book of moral philosophy, madam, of Reynard the Fox and all the beasts, called 'Doni's Philosophy.'[3]

CENTAUR. There is indeed, Sir Amorous La Foole.

MOROSE. O misery!

LA FOOLE. I have read it, my Lady Centaur, all over, to my cousin here.

MISTRESS OTTER. Ay, and 'tis a very good book as any is, of the moderns.

DAW. Tut, he must have Seneca read to him, and Plutarch, and the ancients.[4] The moderns are not for this disease.

CLERIMONT. Why, you discommended them too, today, Sir John.

DAW. Ay, in some cases; but in these they are best; and Aristotle's 'Ethics.'

MAVIS. Say you so, Sir John? I think you are deceived; you took it upon trust.

HAUGHTY. Where's Trusty, my woman? I'll end this difference. I pray thee, Otter, call her. Her father and mother were both mad, when they put her to me.

MOROSE. I think so.—Nay, gentlemen, I am tame. This is but an exercise, I know, a marriage ceremony, which I must endure.

HAUGHTY. And one of 'em, I know not which, was cured with 'The Sick Man's Salve,' and the other with 'Green's Groatsworth of Wit.'[5]

TRUEWIT. A very cheap cure, madam.

HAUGHTY. Ay, it's very feasible.

[*Enter* TRUSTY.]

MISTRESS OTTER. My lady called for you, Mistress Trusty. You must decide a controversy.

HAUGHTY. O, Trusty, which was it you said, your father or your mother, that was cured with 'The Sick Man's Salve'?

TRUSTY. My mother, madam, with the 'Salve.'

TRUEWIT. Then it was the sick woman's salve.

TRUSTY. And my father with the 'Groatsworth of Wit.' But there was other means used: we had a preacher that would preach folk asleep still; and so they were prescribed to go to church, by an old woman that was their physician, thrice a week—

EPICOENE. To sleep?

3. The latter book is a collection of rag-bag lore, translated into Italian by Doni, and into English (1601) by Sir Thomas North. The story of Reynard the Fox is quite different, a good deal older, and much cleverer.

4. Seneca and Plutarch, grave moral authors, are prescribed by Sir John Daw as psychotherapy.

5. Cheap moral pamphlets of the day: *Sick Man's Salve* by Thomas Bacon was published in 1561 and many times reprinted; Robert Greene's *Groatsworth of Wit*, his deathbed autobiography, was published in 1592.

TRUSTY. Yes, forsooth, and every night they read themselves asleep on those books.

EPICOENE. Good faith, it stands with great reason. I would I knew where to procure those books.

MOROSE. O!

LA FOOLE. I can help you with one of 'em, Mistress Morose, the 'Groatsworth of Wit.'

EPICOENE. But I shall disfurnish you, Sir Amorous; can you spare it?

LA FOOLE. O yes, for a week or so; I'll read it myself to him.

EPICOENE. No, I must do that, sir; that must be my office.

MOROSE. O, O!

EPICOENE. Sure, he would do well enough if he could sleep.

MOROSE. No, I should do well enough if you could sleep. Have I no friend that will make her drunk? or give her a little laudanum, or opium?

TRUEWIT. Why, sir, she talks ten times worse in her sleep.

MOROSE. How!

CLERIMONT. Do you not know that, sir? Never ceases all night.

TRUEWIT. And snores like a porpoise.

MOROSE. O, redeem me, fate; redeem me, fate! For how many causes may a man be divorced, nephew?

DAUPHINE. I know not, truly, sir.

TRUEWIT. Some divine must resolve you[6] in that, sir, or canon lawyer.

MOROSE. I will not rest, I will not think of any other hope or comfort, till I know.

[*Exit with* DAUPHINE.]

CLERIMONT. Alas, poor man!

TRUEWIT. You'll make him mad indeed, ladies, if you pursue this.

HAUGHTY. No, we'll let him breathe now, a quarter of an hour or so.

CLERIMONT. By my faith, a large truce!

HAUGHTY. Is that his keeper, that is gone with him?

DAW. It is his nephew, madam.

LA FOOLE. Sir Dauphine Eugenie.

CENTAUR. He looks like a very pitiful knight——

DAW. As can be. This marriage has put him out of all.

LA FOOLE. He has not a penny in his purse, madam——

DAW. He is ready to cry all this day.

LA FOOLE. A very shark; he set me i' the nick t'other night at primero.[7]

TRUEWIT. [*aside*]—How these swabbers talk!

CLERIMONT. Ay, Otter's wine has swelled their humors above a spring-tide.

HAUGHTY. Good Morose, let's go in again. I like your couches exceeding well; we'll go lie and talk there.

6. I.e., settle all your doubts.

7. I.e., he won from me by cheating at primero, a card game.

[*Exeunt* LADY CENTAUR, MISTRESS MAVIS, TRUSTY, LA FOOLE, *and* DAW.]

EPICOENE. [*following them*] I wait on you, madam.

TRUEWIT. [*stopping her*] 'Slight, I will have 'em silent as signs, and their post[8] too, ere I have done. Do you hear, Lady Bride? I pray thee now, as thou art a noble wench, continue this discourse of Dauphine within; but praise him exceedingly. Magnify him with all the height of affection thou canst—I have some purpose in't—and but beat off these two rooks, Jack Daw and his fellow, with any discontentment, hither, and I'll honor thee forever.

EPICOENE. I was about it here. It angered me to the soul, to hear 'em begin to talk so malapert.[9]

TRUEWIT. Pray thee perform it, and thou winn'st me an idolater to thee everlasting.

EPICOENE. Will you go in and hear me do 't?

TRUEWIT. No, I'll stay here. Drive 'em out of your company, 'tis all I ask; which cannot be any way better done than by extolling Dauphine, whom they have so slighted.

EPICOENE. I warrant you; you shall expect one of 'em presently. [*Exit.*]

CLERIMONT. What a cast of kastrils[1] are these, to hawk after ladies thus!

TRUEWIT. Ay, and strike at such an eagle as Dauphine.

CLERIMONT. He will be mad when we tell him. Here he comes.

SCENE 5

[*Re-enter* DAUPHINE.]

O, sir, you are welcome.

TRUEWIT. Where's thine uncle?

DAUPHINE. Run out of doors in his nightcaps to talk with a casuist about his divorce. It works admirably.

TRUEWIT. Thou wouldst have said so, an thou hadst been here! The ladies have laughed at thee most comically, since thou went'st, Dauphine.

CLERIMONT. And asked if thou wert thine uncle's keeper.

TRUEWIT. And the brace of baboons answered yes; and said thou were a pitiful, poor fellow, and didst live upon posts, and hadst nothing but three suits of apparel, and some few benevolences that the lords gave thee to fool to 'em and swagger.

DAUPHINE. Let me not live, I'll beat 'em! I'll bind them both to grand Madam's bed-posts, and have them baited with monkeys.

TRUEWIT. Thou shalt not need; they shall be beaten to thy hand, Dauphine. I have an execution to serve upon them, I warrant thee shall serve; trust my plot.

8. Their messenger (Daw), with a pun on the notion of someone being deaf or mute as a post.

9. Impudently.

1. Pair of scavengers. Kastrils or kestrels were small hawks, not as noble as falcons.

DAUPHINE. Ay, you have many plots. So you had one to make all the wenches in love with me!

TRUEWIT. Why, if I do it not yet afore night, as near as 'tis, and that they do not every one invite thee, and be ready to scratch[2] for thee, take the mortgage of my wit.

CLERIMONT. 'Fore God, I'll be his witness, thou shalt have it, Dauphine!—Thou shalt be his fool forever, if thou dost not.

TRUEWIT. Agreed. Perhaps 'twill be the better estate. Do you observe this gallery, or rather lobby, indeed? Here are a couple of studies, at each end one: here will I act such a tragi-comedy between the Guelphs and the Ghibellines,[3] Daw and La Foole—Which of 'em comes out first, will I seize on. You two shall be the chorus behind the arras,[4] and whip out between the acts and speak. If I do not make them keep the peace for this remnant of the day, if not of the year, I have failed once——I hear Daw coming. Hide [*they withdraw*], and do not laugh, for God's sake!

[*Re-enter* DAW.]

DAW. Which is the way into the garden, trow?[5]

TRUEWIT. O, Jack Daw! I am glad I have met with you. In good faith, I must have this matter go no further between you. I must have it taken up.

DAW. What matter, sir? Between whom?

TRUEWIT. Come, you disguise it: Sir Amorous and you. If you love me, Jack, you shall make use of your philosophy now, for this once, and deliver me your sword. This is not the wedding the Centaurs were at,[6] though there be a she-one here. [*Takes his sword.*] The bride has entreated me I will see no blood shed at her bridal; you saw her whisper me erewhile.

DAW. As I hope to finish Tacitus,[7] I intend no murder.

TRUEWIT. Do you not wait for Sir Amorous?

DAW. Not I, by my knighthood.

TRUEWIT. And your scholarship too?

DAW. And my scholarship too.

TRUEWIT. Go to, then I return you your sword, and ask you mercy; but put it not up, for you will be assaulted. I understood that you had apprehended it, and walked here to brave him; and that you had held your life contemptible, in regard of your honor.

DAW. No, no; no such thing, I assure you. He and I parted now as good friends as could be.

TRUEWIT. Trust not you to that visor.[8] I saw him since dinner with another face. I have known many men in my time vexed with losses, with deaths, and with abuses, but so offended a wight as Sir Amorous did I never see or read of. For taking away his guests, sir, today, that's the cause; and he declares it behind your

2. Claw each other's faces.
3. Traditional opponents in Italian politics.
4. I.e., the commentators behind the curtain.
5. I.e., can you tell me?
6. In the mythological story, the Centaurs and Lapiths got into a battle royal at the marriage of Hippodamia with Peirithous.
7. Tacitus is notoriously a hard study.
8. Mask.

back with such threatenings and contempts——He said to Dauphine you were the arrant'st ass——

DAW. Ay, he may say his pleasure.

TRUEWIT. And swears you are so protested a coward, that he knows you will never do him any manly or single right, and therefore he will take his course.

DAW. I'll give him any satisfaction, sir—but fighting.

TRUEWIT. Ay, sir, but who knows what satisfaction he'll take? Blood he thirsts for, and blood he will have; and whereabouts on you he will have it, who knows but himself?

DAW. I pray you, Master Truewit, be you a mediator.

TRUEWIT. Well, sir, conceal yourself then in this study till I return. [*Puts him into the study.*] Nay, you must be content to be locked in; for, for mine own reputation, I would not have you seen to receive a public disgrace, while I have the matter in managing. God's so, here he comes. Keep your breath close, that he do not hear you sigh.—In good faith, Sir Amorous, he is not this way. I pray you be merciful, do not murder him; he is a Christian, as good as you. You are armed as if you sought a revenge on all his race. Good Dauphine, get him away from this place. I never knew a man's choler[9] so high, but he would speak to his friends, he would hear reason.—Jack Daw, Jack Daw! Asleep?

DAW. [*within*] Is he gone, Master Truewit?

TRUEWIT. Ay, did you hear him?

DAW. O God, yes!

TRUEWIT. —What a quick ear fear has!

DAW. [*Comes out of the closet.*]—But is he so armed as you say?

TRUEWIT. Armed! did you ever see a fellow set out to take possession?[1]

DAW. Ay, sir.

TRUEWIT. That may give you some light to conceive of him, but 'tis nothing to the principal. Some false brother in the house has furnished him strangely; or, if it were out of the house, it was Tom Otter.

DAW. Indeed, he's a captain, and his wife is his kinswoman.

TRUEWIT. He has got somebody's old two-hand sword, to mow you off at the knees; and that sword hath spawned such a dagger! But then he is so hung with pikes, halberds, petronels, calivers,[2] and muskets, that he looks like a Justice of Peace's hall. A man of two thousand a year is not cessed[3] at so many weapons as he has on. There was never fencer challenged at so many several foils.[4] You would think he meant to murder all Saint 'Pulchre's parish.[5] If he could but victual himself for half a year in his breeches, he is sufficiently armed to overrun a country.

9. Anger, rage.

1. I.e., of a new property, when real fighting with the old owner was not out of the question.

2. Petronels and calivers are varieties of pistol. All these weapons, supplied by the citizenry, would be lodged with the Justice of the Peace for use in time of emergency.

3. Taxed; rich men had to contribute more weapons than poor ones.

4. Champion fencers, offering to meet all comers, listed the various weapons they would be willing to use.

5. The parish of Saint Sepulchre in London City, with the additional overtone that he wants to fill a cemetery single-handed.

DAW!. Good Lord! what means he, sir? I pray you, Master Truewit, be you a mediator.

TRUEWIT. Well, I'll try if he will be appeased with a leg or an arm; if not, you must die once.

DAW. I would be loath to lose my right arm, for writing madrigals.

TRUEWIT. Why, if he will be satisfied with a thumb or a little finger, all's one to me. You must think, I'll do my best.

[*Shuts him up again.*]

DAW. Good sir, do.

[CLERIMONT *and* DAUPHINE *come forward.*]

CLERIMONT. What hast thou done?

TRUEWIT. He will let me do nothing, man, he does all afore me; he offers his left arm.

CLERIMONT. His left wing, for a jackdaw.

DAUPHINE. Take it, by all means.

TRUEWIT. How! maim a man forever, for a jest? What a conscience hast thou!

DAUPHINE. 'Tis no loss to him; he has no employment for his arms but to eat spoon-meat. Beside, as good maim his body as his reputation.

TRUEWIT. He is a scholar and a wit, and yet he does not think so. But he loses no reputation with us, for we all resolved him an ass before. To your places again.

CLERIMONT. I pray thee, let me be in it at the other a little.

TRUEWIT. Look, you'll spoil all; these be ever your tricks.

CLERIMONT. No, but I could hit off some things that thou wilt miss, and thou wilt say are good ones.

TRUEWIT. I warrant you. I pray, forbear, I'll leave it off else.

DAUPHINE. Come away, Clerimont.

[DAUPHINE *and* CLERIMONT *withdraw.*]

[*Enter* LA FOOLE.]

TRUEWIT. Sir Amorous!

LA FOOLE. Master Truewit.

TRUEWIT. Whither were you going?

LA FOOLE. Down into the court to make water.

TRUEWIT. By no means, sir, you shall rather tempt your breeches.

LA FOOLE. Why, sir?

TRUEWIT. Enter here, if you love your life.

[*Opens the door of the other study.*]

LA FOOLE. Why? why?

TRUEWIT. Question till your throat be cut, do! dally till the enraged soul find you.

LA FOOLE. Who's that?

TRUEWIT. Daw it is! Will you in?

LA FOOLE. Ay, ay. I'll in. What's the matter?

TRUEWIT. Nay, if he had been cool enough to tell us that, there had been some hope to atone[6] you; but he seems so implacably enraged!

LA FOOLE. 'Slight, let him rage! I'll hide myself.

6. Reconcile, make you at one.

TRUEWIT. Do, good sir. But what have you done to him within, that should provoke him thus? You have broke some jest upon him afore the ladies.

LA FOOLE. Not I, never in my life broke jest upon any man. The bride was praising Sir Dauphine, and he went away in snuff,[7] and I followed him—unless he took offense at me in his drink erewhile, that I would not pledge all the Horse full.

TRUEWIT. By, my faith, and that may be; you remember well. But he walks the round up and down, through every room o' the house, with a towel in his hand, crying, 'Where's La Foole? Who saw La Foole?' And when Dauphine and I demanded the cause, we can force no answer from him but, 'O revenge, how sweet art thou! I will strangle him in this towel!' Which leads us to conjecture that the main cause of his fury is for bringing your meat today with a towel about you, to his discredit.

LA FOOLE. Like enough. Why, an he be angry for that, I'll stay here till his anger be blown over.

TRUEWIT. A good, becoming resolution, sir, if you can put it on o' the sudden.

LA FOOLE. Yes, I can put it on. Or, I'll away into the country presently.

TRUEWIT. How will you get out of the house, sir? He knows you are in the house, and he'll watch you this se'nnight,[8] but he'll have you. He'll outwait a sergeant[9] for you.

LA FOOLE. Why, then I'll stay here.

TRUEWIT. You must think how to victual yourself in time, then.

LA FOOLE. Why, sweet Master Truewit, will you entreat my cousin Otter to send me a cold venison pasty, a bottle or two of wine, and a chamber-pot.

TRUEWIT. A stool were better, sir, of Sir Ajax's invention.[1]

LA FOOLE. Ay, that will be better indeed; and a pallet to lie on.

TRUEWIT. O, I would not advise you to sleep, by any means.

LA FOOLE. Would you not, sir? Why, then I will not.

TRUEWIT. Yet there's another fear——

LA FOOLE. Is there! What is't?

TRUEWIT. No, he cannot break open this door with his foot, sure.

LA FOOLE. I'll set my back against it, sir. I have a good back.

TRUEWIT. But then if he should batter.

LA FOOLE. Batter! if he dare, I'll have an action of battery against him.

TRUEWIT. Cast you the worst. He has sent for powder already, and what he will do with it no man knows—perhaps blow up the corner of the house where he suspects you are. Here he comes; in quickly. [*Thrusts in* LA FOOLE, *and shuts the door.*]—I protest, Sir John Daw, he is not this way. What will you do? Before God, you shall hang no petard[2] here! I'll die rather. Will you not take

7. In a rage.
8. For a week (seven nights).
9. Sergeants (who want to arrest one for debt) are traditionally tenacious men.
1. According to Sir John Harington's scatological farce (1596), the Homeric hero Ajax was metamorphosed into a jakes—a water closet.
2. Bomb, mortar-shell.

my word? I never knew one but would be satisfied.—Sir Amorous, there's no standing out. He has made a petard of an old brass pot, to force your door. Think upon some satisfaction, or terms, to offer him.

LA FOOLE. [*within*] Sir, I'll give him any satisfaction. I dare give any terms.

TRUEWIT. You'll leave it to me then?

LA FOOLE. Ay, sir. I'll stand to any conditions.

TRUEWIT. [*Calls forth* CLERIMONT *and* DAUPHINE.] How now! what think you, sirs? Were't not a difficult thing to determine which of these two feared most?

CLERIMONT. Yes, but this fears the bravest; the other a whinneling, dastard jackdaw! But La Foole, a brave, heroic coward! and is afraid in a great look and a stout accent. I like him rarely.

TRUEWIT. Had it not been pity these two should have been concealed?

CLERIMONT. Shall I make a motion?

TRUEWIT. Briefly, for I must strike while 'tis hot.

CLERIMONT. Shall I go fetch the ladies to the catastrophe?

TRUEWIT. Umh? ay, by my troth.

DAUPHINE. By no mortal means. Let them continue in the state of ignorance, and err still; think 'em wits and fine fellows, as they have done. 'Twere sin to reform them.

TRUEWIT. Well, I will have them fetched, now I think on't, for a private purpose of mine. Do, Clerimont, fetch them, and discourse to them all that's passed, and bring them into the gallery here.

DAUPHINE. This is thy extreme vanity, now! Thou think'st thou wert undone if every jest thou mak'st were not published.

TRUEWIT. Thou shalt see how unjust thou art presently—Clerimont, say it was Dauphine's plot. [*Exit* CLERIMONT.] Trust me not if the whole drift be not for thy good. There's a carpet in the next room; put it on, with this scarf over thy face, and a cushion on thy head, and be ready when I call Amorous. Away. [*Exit* DAUPHINE.] John Daw!

[*Goes to* DAW'S *closet, and brings him out.*]

DAW. What good news, sir?

TRUEWIT. Faith, I have followed, and argued with him hard for you. I told him you were a knight and a scholar, and that you knew fortitude did consist '*magis patiendo quam faciendo, magis ferendo quam feriendo*.'[3]

DAW. It doth so indeed, sir.

TRUEWIT. And that you would suffer, I told him. So at first he demanded, by my troth, in my conceit[4] too much.

DAW. What was it, sir?

TRUEWIT. Your upper lip and six of your foreteeth.

DAW, 'Twas unreasonable.

TRUEWIT. Nay, I told him plainly, you could not spare them all. So

3. "More in suffering than in inflicting pain, more in bearing than in striking blows."

4. In my judgment.

after long argument—*pro et con,* as you know—I brought him down to your two butter-teeth,[5] and them he would have.

DAW. O, did you so? Why, he shall have them.

TRUEWIT. But he shall not, sir, by your leave. The conclusion is this, sir: because you shall be very good friends hereafter, and this never to be remembered or upbraided; besides, that he may not boast he has done any such thing to you in his own person; he is to come here in disguise, give you five kicks in private, sir, take your sword from you, and lock you up in that study during pleasure; which will be but a little while, we'll get it released presently.

DAW. Five kicks? he shall have six, sir, to be friends.

TRUEWIT. Believe me, you shall not overshoot yourself, to send him that word by me.

DAW. Deliver it, sir, he shall have it with all my heart, to be friends.

TRUEWIT. Friends! Nay, an he should not be so, and heartily too, upon these terms, he shall have me to enemy while I live. Come, sir, bear it bravely.

DAW. O God, sir, 'tis nothing!

TRUEWIT. True. What's six kicks to a man that reads Seneca?[6]

DAW. I have had a hundred, sir.

TRUEWIT. Sir Amorous! No speaking one to another, or rehearsing old matters. [DAUPHINE *comes forth disguised, and kicks* DAW.]

DAW. One, two, three, four, five. I protest, Sir Amorous, you shall have six.

TRUEWIT. Nay, I told you you should not talk. Come, give him six, an he will needs. [DAUPHINE *kicks him again.*] Your sword. [*He takes it.*] Now return to your safe custody. You shall presently meet afore the ladies, and be the dearest friends one to another. [*Puts* DAW *in the study.*]—Give me the scarf now, thou shalt beat the other barefaced. Stand by. [DAUPHINE *retires, and* TRUEWIT *goes to the other closet and releases* LA FOOLE.]—Sir Amorous!

LA FOOLE. What's here? A sword!

TRUEWIT. I cannot help it, without I should take the quarrel upon myself. Here he has sent you his sword——

LA FOOLE. I'll receive none on't.

TRUEWIT. And he wills you to fasten it against a wall, and break your head in some few several places against the hilts.

LA FOOLE. I will not; tell him roundly. I cannot endure to shed my own blood.

TRUEWIT. Will you not?

LA FOOLE. No. I'll beat it against a fair flat wall, if that will satisfy him. If not, he shall beat it himself, for Amorous.

TRUEWIT. Why, this is strange starting off, when a man undertakes for you! I offered him another condition; will you stand to that?

LA FOOLE. Ay, what is't?

5. Front teeth; *pro et con*: for and against.

6. Seneca teaches one to endure misfortune (but not disgrace and humiliation) patiently.

TRUEWIT. That you will be beaten in private.

LA FOOLE. Yes, I am content, at the blunt.[7]

[*Enter above* LADY HAUGHTY, LADY CENTAUR, MISTRESS MAVIS, MISTRESS OTTER, EPICOENE, *and* TRUSTY.]

TRUEWIT. Then you must submit yourself to be hoodwinked in this scarf and be led to him, where he will take your sword from you, and make you bear a blow over the mouth *gules*, and tweaks by the nose, *sans nombre*.[8]

LA FOOLE. I am content. But why must I be blinded?

TRUEWIT. That's for your good, sir; because if he should grow insolent upon this, and publish it hereafter to your disgrace—which I hope he will not do—you might swear safely and protest he never beat you to your knowledge.

LA FOOLE. O, I conceive.

TRUEWIT. I do not doubt but you'll be perfect good friends upon't, and not dare to utter an ill thought, one of another, in future.

LA FOOLE. Not I, as God help me, of him.

TRUEWIT. Nor he of you, sir. If he should [*Blindfolds him.*]—Come, sir. All hid, Sir John!

[DAUPHINE *enters to tweak him by the nose.*]

LA FOOLE. Oh, Sir John, Sir John! Oh, o-o-o-o-o-oh—

TRUEWIT. Good Sir John, leave tweaking, you'll blow his nose off. —'Tis Sir John's pleasure you should retire into the study. [*Puts him back again.*] Why, now you are friends. All bitterness between you, I hope, is buried; you shall come forth, by and by, Damon and Pythias[9] upon 't, and embrace with all the rankness of friendship that can be.—I trust we shall have 'em tamer in their language hereafter. Dauphine, I worship thee. God's will, the ladies have surprised us!

SCENE 6

[*Enter* CLERIMONT, *with* LADY HAUGHTY, LADY CENTAUR, MISTRESS MAVIS, MISTRESS OTTER, EPICOENE, *and* TRUSTY.]

HAUGHTY. Centaur, how our judgments were imposed on by these adulterate[1] knights!

CENTAUR. Nay, madam, Mavis was more deceived then we; 'twas her commendation uttered them in the College.

MAVIS. I commended but their wits, madam, and their braveries.[2] I never looked toward their valors.

HAUGHTY. Sir Dauphine is valiant, and a wit too, it seems.

MAVIS. And a bravery too.

HAUGHTY. Was this his project?

MISTRESS OTTER. So Master Clerimont intimates, madam.

7. If it comes to that.

8. Numberless; *gules*, the heraldic term for scarlet, implies that the blow must draw blood.

9. Damon and Pythias were students of Pythagoras, condemned to die by Dionysus of Syracuse for their beliefs. Each, however, wanted to die for the other; and the tyrant, impressed by their devotion to one another, pardoned both.

1. Degenerate.

2. Finery.

HAUGHTY. Good Morose, when you come to the College, will you bring him with you? He seems a very perfect gentleman.

EPICOENE. He is so, madam, believe it.

CENTAUR. But when will you come, Morose?

EPICOENE. Three or four days hence, madam, when I have got me a coach and horses.

HAUGHTY. No, tomorrow, good Morose; Centaur shall send you her coach.

MAVIS. Yes, faith, do, and bring Sir Dauphine with you.

HAUGHTY. She has promised that, Mavis.

MAVIS. He is a very worthy gentleman in his exteriors, madam.

HAUGHTY. Ay, he shows he is judicial in his clothes.

CENTAUR. And yet not so superlatively neat as some, madam, that have their faces set in a brake.[3]

HAUGHTY. Ay, and have every hair in form.

MAVIS. That wear purer linen than ourselves, and profess more neatness than the French hermaphrodite.

EPICOENE. Ay, ladies, they, what they tell one of us, have told a thousand; and are the only thieves of our fame, that think to take us with that perfume, or with that lace, and laugh at us unconscionably when they have done.

HAUGHTY. But Sir Dauphine's carelessness becomes him.

CENTAUR. I could love a man for such a nose!

MAVIS. Or such a leg!

CENTAUR. He has an exceeding good eye, madam!

MAVIS. And a very good lock![4]

CENTAUR. Good Morose, bring him to my chamber first.

MISTRESS OTTER. Please your honors to meet at my house, madam.

TRUEWIT. —See how they eye thee, man! they are taken, I warrant thee.

[LADY HAUGHTY *comes forward.*]

HAUGHTY. You have unbraced our brace of knights here, Master Truewit.

TRUEWIT. Not I, madam, it was Sir Dauphine's engine;[5] who, if he have disfurnished your ladyship of any guard or service by it,[6] is able to make the place good again in himself.

HAUGHTY. There's no suspicion of that, sir.

CENTAUR. God's so, Mavis, Haughty is kissing.

MAVIS. Let us go, too, and take part.

[*They come forward.*]

HAUGHTY. But I am glad of the fortune—beside the discovery of two such empty caskets—to gain the knowledge of so rich a mine of virtue as Sir Dauphine.

CENTAUR. We would be all glad to style him of our friendship, and see him at the College.

3. A rigid form (originally from a rig used to confine a horse's feet while it was being shod).
4. Lock of hair.
5. Idea, device.
6. I.e., if he has deprived you of any servants or protectors.

MAVIS. He cannot mix with a sweeter society, I'll prophesy, and I hope he himself will think so.

DAUPHINE. I should be rude to imagine otherwise, lady.

TRUEWIT. [*aside*]—Did not I tell thee, Dauphine? Why, all their actions are governed by crude opinion, without reason or cause. They know not why they do anything; but as they are informed, believe, judge, praise, condemn, love, hate, and in emulation one of another, do all these things alike. Only they have a natural inclination sways them generally to the worst, when they are left to themselves. But pursue it, now thou hast them.

HAUGHTY. Shall we go in again, Morose?

EPICOENE. Yes, madam.

CENTAUR. We'll entreat Sir Dauphine's company.

TRUEWIT. Stay, good madam, the interview of the two friends, Pylades and Orestes.[7] I'll fetch them out to you straight.

HAUGHTY. Will you, Master Truewit?

DAUPHINE. Ay, but, noble ladies, do not confess in your countenance, or outward bearing to them, any discovery of their follies, that we may see how they will bear up again, with what assurance and erection.

HAUGHTY. We will not, Sir Dauphine.

CENTAUR, MAVIS. Upon our honors, Sir Dauphine.

TRUEWIT. [*Goes to the first closet.*] Sir Amorous! Sir Amorous! The ladies are here.

LA FOOLE. Are they?

TRUEWIT. Yes, but slip out by and by, as their backs are turned, and meet Sir John here, as by chance, when I call you [*Goes to the other closet.*] — Jack Daw!

DAW. [*within*] What say you, sir?

TRUEWIT. Whip out behind me suddenly; and no anger in your looks to your adversary. Now, now!

[LA FOOLE *and* DAW *slip out of their closets and greet each other.*]

LA FOOLE. Noble Sir John Daw! where have you been?

DAW. To seek you, Sir Amorous.

LA FOOLE. Me! I honor you.

DAW. I prevent you, sir.

CLERIMONT. They have forgot their rapiers!

TRUEWIT. O, they meet in peace, man.

DAUPHINE. Where's your sword, Sir John?

CLERIMONT. And yours, Sir Amorous?

DAW. Mine? my boy had it forth to mend the handle, e'en now.

LA FOOLE. And my gold handle was broke, too, and my boy had it forth.

DAUPHINE. Indeed, sir!—How their excuses meet!

CLERIMONT. What a consent there is, in the handles!

7. Another pair of proverbial classical friends.

TRUEWIT. Nay, there is so in the points too, I warrant you.

[*Enter* MOROSE, *with the two swords, drawn, in his hands.*]

MISTRESS OTTER. O me! madam, he comes again, the madman! Away!

[*Exeunt* LADIES, DAW, *and* LA FOOLE.]

SCENE 7

MOROSE. What make these naked weapons here, gentlemen?

TRUEWIT. O sir! here hath like to been murder since you went—a couple of knights fallen out about the bride's favors! We were fain to take away their weapons; your house had been begged[8] by this time else.

MOROSE. For what?

CLERIMONT. For manslaughter, sir, as being accessory.

MOROSE. And for her favors?

TRUEWIT. Ay, sir, heretofore, not present. Clerimont, carry them their swords now. They have done all the hurt they will do.

[*Exit* CLERIMONT *with the swords.*]

DAUPHINE. Have you spoke with the lawyer sir?

MOROSE. O no! there is such a noise in the court that they have frighted me home with more violence than I went! Such speaking and counterspeaking, with their several voices of citations, appelations, allegations, certificates, attachments, interrogatories, references, convictions, and afflictions indeed, among the doctors and proctors, that the noise here is silence to't, a kind of calm midnight!

TRUEWIT. Why, sir, if you would be resolved indeed, I can bring you hither a very sufficient lawyer, and a learned divine, that shall inquire into every least scruple for you.

MOROSE. Can you, Master Truewit?

TRUEWIT. Yes, and are very sober, grave persons, that will dispatch it in a chamber, with a whisper or two.

MOROSE. Good sir, shall I hope this benefit from you, and trust myself into your hands?

TRUEWIT. Alas, sir! your nephew and I have been ashamed and oft-times mad,[9] since you went, to think how you are abused. Go in, good sir, and lock yourself up till we call you; we'll tell you more anon, sir.

MOROSE. Do your pleasure with me, gentlemen. I believe in you, and that deserves no delusion—

[*Exit.*]

TRUEWIT. You shall find none, sir,—but heaped, heaped plenty of vexation.

DAUPHINE. What wilt thou do now, Wit?

8. Forfeit to the crown for breach of the peace; the crown would then bestow it on a third party who asked (begged) for it.

9. Angry, frustrated.

TRUEWIT. Recover me hither Otter and the barber, if you can, by any means, presently.

DAUPHINE. Why? to what purpose?

TRUEWIT. O, I'll make the deepest divine and gravest lawyer out of them two, for him——

DAUPHINE. Thou canst not, man; these are waking dreams.

TRUEWIT. Do not fear me. Clap but a civil gown with a welt on the one, and a canonical cloak with sleeves on the other, and give them a few terms in their mouths; if there come not forth as able a doctor and complete a parson, for this turn, as may be wished, trust not my election. And I hope, without wronging the dignity of either profession, since they are but persons put on, and for mirth's sake, to torment him.[1] The barber smatters Latin, I remember.

DAUPHINE. Yes, and Otter, too.

TRUEWIT. Well then, if I make them not wrangle out this case to his no-comfort, let me be thought a jackdaw, or La Foole, or anything worse. Go you to your ladies, but first send for them.

DAUPHINE. I will.

[*Exeunt*]

Act V

SCENE 1. MOROSE'S *house*

[*Enter* LA FOOLE, CLERIMONT, *and* DAW.]

LA FOOLE. Where had you our swords, Master Clerimont?

CLERIMONT. Why, Dauphine took them from the madman.

LA FOOLE. And he took them from our boys, I warrant you!

CLERIMONT. Very like, sir.

LA FOOLE. Thank you, good Master Clerimont. Sir John Daw and I are both beholden to you.

CLERIMONT. Would I knew how to make you so, gentlemen.

DAW. Sir Amorous and I are your servants, sir.

[*Enter* MISTRESS MAVIS.]

MAVIS. Gentlemen, have any of you a pen and ink? I would fain write out a riddle in Italian, for Sir Dauphine to translate.

CLERIMONT. Not I, in troth, lady, I am no scrivener.[2]

DAW. I can furnish you, I think, lady.

[*Exeunt* DAW *and* MAVIS.]

CLERIMONT. He has it in the haft of a knife, I believe.

LA FOOLE. No, he has his box of instruments.

CLERIMONT. Like a surgeon!

LA FOOLE. For the mathematics—his square, his compasses, his brass pens, and black-lead, to draw maps of every place and person where he comes.

CLERIMONT. How, maps of persons!

1. Jonson's apology for the parody of lawyers and clergymen that follows suggests that there had been some complaint.

2. Draftsmen of legal documents who might well carry pen and ink with them.

LA FOOLE. Yes, sir, of Nomentack, when he was here, and of the Prince of Moldavia, and of his mistress, Mistress Epicoene.[3]

[*Re-enter* DAW.]

CLERIMONT. Away! he hath not found out her latitude, I hope.

LA FOOLE. You are a pleasant gentleman, sir.

CLERIMONT. Faith, now we are in private, let's wanton it a little, and talk waggishly.—Sir John, I am telling Sir Amorous here, that you two govern the ladies; where'er you come, you carry the feminine gender afore you.

DAW. They shall rather carry us afore them, if they will, sir.

CLERIMONT. Nay, I believe that they do withal—But that you are the prime men in their affections, and direct all their actions——

DAW. Not I; Sir Amorous is.

LA FOOLE. I protest, Sir John is.

DAW. As I hope to rise in the state, Sir Amorous, you have the person.

LA FOOLE. Sir John, you have the person, and the discourse too.

DAW. Not I sir. I have no discourse—and then you have activity beside.

LA FOOLE. I protest, Sir John, you come as high from Tripoli[4] as I do, every whit; and lift as many joint-stools, and leap over them, if you would use it—

CLERIMONT. Well, agree on't together, knights, for between you, you divide the kingdom or commonwealth of ladies' affections. I see it, and can perceive a little how they observe you, and fear you indeed. You could tell strange stories, my masters, if you would, I know.

DAW. Faith, we have seen somewhat, sir.

LA FOOLE. That we have—velvet petticoats, and wrought smocks, or so.

DAW. Ay, and——

CLERIMONT. Nay, out with it, Sir John! Do not envy your friend the pleasure of hearing, when you have had the delight of tasting.

DAW. Why—a—do you speak, Sir Amorous.

LA FOOLE. No, do you, Sir John Daw.

DAW. I' faith, you shall.

LA FOOLE. I' faith, you shall.

DAW. Why, we have been——

LA FOOLE. In the great bed at Ware[5] together in our time. On, Sir John.

DAW. Nay, do you, Sir Amorous.

CLERIMONT. And these ladies with you, knights?

LA FOOLE. No, excuse us, sir.

3. Nomentack was an Indian chief from the colony in Virginia who visited London in 1605–9. The Prince of Moldavia was a con man who passed through England in 1607. In the text, "his" mistress clearly refers to Sir John Daw's mistress; but Lady Arabella Stuart thought it referred to the Prince of Moldavia's mistress, i.e., herself, and the more so because she had been involved in an epicene escapade, which involved her dressing up as a boy.

4. I.e., are able to skip and frisk as well. The phrase is simply a play on the word "trip"; it has nothing to do with North Africa.

5. The great Bed of Ware was a public curiosity—it measured nearly eleven feet in each direction, and naturally became a byword for erotic overachievement.

DAW. We must not wound reputation.

LA FOOLE. No matter—they were these, or others. Our bath cost us fifteen pound when we came home.

CLERIMONT. Do you hear, Sir John? You shall tell me but one thing truly, as you love me.

DAW. If I can, I will, sir.

CLERIMONT. You lay in the same house with the bride here?

DAW. Yes, and conversed with her hourly, sir.

CLERIMONT. And what humor is she of? Is she coming and open, free?

DAW. O, exceeding open, sir. I was her servant, and Sir Amorous was to be.

CLERIMONT. Come, you have both had favors from her: I know, and have heard so much.

DAW. O no, sir.

LA FOOLE. You shall excuse us, sir; we must not wound reputation.

CLERIMONT. Tut, she is married now, and you cannot hurt her with any report, and therefore speak plainly: how many times, i' faith? which of you led first? ha?

LA FOOLE. Sir John had her maidenhead, indeed.

DAW. O, it pleases him to say so, sir, but Sir Amorous knows what's what as well.

CLERIMONT. Dost thou, i' faith, Amorous?

LA FOOLE. In a manner, sir.

DAW. Why, I commend you, lads. Little knows Don Bridegroom of this; nor shall he, for me.

DAW. Hang him, mad ox!

CLERIMONT. Speak softly, here comes his nephew, with the Lady Haughty. He'll get the ladies from you, sirs, if you look not to him in time.

LA FOOLE. Why, if he do, we'll fetch them home again, I warrant you.

[*Exit with* DAW. CLERIMONT *walks aside.*]

SCENE 2

[*Enter* DAUPHINE *and* LADY HAUGHTY.]

HAUGHTY. I assure you, Sir Dauphine, it is the price and estimation of your virtue only, that hath embarked me to this adventure, and I could not but make out to tell you so. Nor can I repent me of the act, since it is always an argument of some virtue in ourselves, that we love and affect it so in others.

DAUPHINE. Your ladyship sets too high a price on my weakness.

HAUGHTY. Sir, I can distinguish gems from pebbles——

DAUPHINE. [*aside*]—Are you so skilful in stones?

HAUGHTY. And howsoever I may suffer in such a judgment as yours, by admitting equality of rank or society with Centaur or Mavis—

DAUPHINE. You do not, madam; I perceive they are your mere foils.

HAUGHTY. Then are you a friend to truth, sir. It makes me love you the more. It is not the outward but the inward man that I affect.

They are not apprehensive of an eminent perfection, but love flat, and dully.

CENTAUR. [*Calls from offstage.*] Where are you, my Lady Haughty?

HAUGHTY. I come presently, Centaur.—My chamber, sir, my page shall show you; and Trusty, my woman, shall be ever awake for you. You need not fear to communicate anything with her, for she is a Fidelia.[6] I pray you wear this jewel for my sake, Sir Dauphine.

[*Enter* LADY CENTAUR.]

Where's Mavis, Centaur?

CENTAUR. Within, madam, a-writing. I'll follow you presently. [*Exit* HAUGHTY.] I'll but speak a word with Sir Dauphine.

DAUPHINE. With me, madam?

CENTAUR. Good Sir Dauphine, do not trust Haughty, nor make any credit to her, whatever you do besides. Sir Dauphine, I give you this caution: she is a perfect courtier, and loves nobody but for her uses; and for her uses, she loves all. Besides, her physicians give her out to be none o' the clearest; whether she pay them or no, Heaven knows! And she's above fifty, too, and pargets![7] See her in a forenoon. Here comes Mavis, a worse face than she! you would not like this by candlelight.

[*Re-enter* MISTRESS MAVIS.]

If you'll come to my chamber one of these mornings early, or late in an evening, I'll tell you more.—Where's Haughty, Mavis?

MAVIS. Within, Centaur.

CENTAUR. What have you there?

MAVIS. An Italian riddle for Sir Dauphine. You shall not see it, i' faith, Centaur. [*Exit* CENTAUR.] Good Sir Dauphine, solve it for me. I'll call for it anon.

[*Exit.*]

CLERIMONT. [*coming forward*] How now, Dauphine! how dost thou quit thyself of these females?

DAUPHINE. 'Slight, they haunt me like fairies, and give me jewels here; I cannot be rid of them.

CLERIMONT. O, you must not tell though.

DAUPHINE. Mass, I forgot that! I was never so assaulted. One loves for virtue, and bribes me with this [*shows the jewel*]. Another loves me with caution, and so would possess me. A third brings me a riddle here; and all are jealous, and rail each at other.

CLERIMONT. A riddle! pray let me see't.

[*Reads the paper.*]

Sir Dauphine: I chose this way of intimation for privacy. The ladies here, I know, have both hope and purpose to make a Collegiate and servant of you. If I might be so honored as to appear at any end of so noble a work, I would enter into a fame of taking physic tomorrow,[8] *and continue it four or five days, or longer, for your visitation.*

Mavis.

6. I.e., trustworthy.

7. Uses a lot of make-up.

8. I.e., I'll give out that I'm sick and confined to my bed.

By my faith, a subtle one! Call you this a riddle? What's their plain-dealing, trow?

DAUPHINE. We lack Truewit, to tell us that.

CLERIMONT. We lack him for somewhat else, too: his knights *reformados* are wound up as high and insolent as ever they were.

DAUPHINE. You jest.

CLERIMONT. No drunkards, either with wine or vanity, ever confessed such stories of themselves. I would not give a fly's leg in balance against all the women's reputations here, if they could be but thought to speak truth; and for the bride, they have made their affidavit against her directly——

DAUPHINE. What, that they have lain with her?

CLERIMONT. Yes, and tell times and circumstances, with the cause why, and the place where. I had almost brought them to affirm that they had done it today.

DAUPHINE. Not both of them?

CLERIMONT. Yes, faith, with a sooth or two more I had effected it. They would have set it down under their hands.

DAUPHINE. Why, they will be our sport, I see, still, whether we will or no.

SCENE 3

[*Enter* TRUEWIT.]

TRUEWIT. O are you here? Come, Dauphine, go call your uncle presently. I have fitted my divine and my canonist, dyed their beards and all. The knaves do not know themselves, they are so exalted and altered. Preferment changes any man. Thou shalt keep one door and I another, and then Clerimont in the midst, that he may have no means of escape from their cavilling, when they grow hot once. And then the women—as I have given the bride her instructions—to break in upon him in the l'envoy.[9] O, 'twill be full and twanging! Away, fetch him! [*Exit* DAUPHINE]

[*Enter* OTTER, *disguised as a divine, and* CUTBEARD *as a canon lawyer.*][1]

Come, Master Doctor, and Master Parson, look to your parts now, and discharge them bravely. You are well set forth, perform it as well. If you chance to be out, do not confess it with standing still or humming or gaping one at another; but go on, and talk aloud, and eagerly; use vehement action, and only remember your terms, and you are safe. Let the matter go where it will; you have many will do so. But at first be very solemn and grave, like your garments, though you loose yourselves after, and skip out like a brace of jugglers on a table. Here he comes! Set your faces, and look superciliously, while I present you.

[*Re-enter* DAUPHINE *with* MOROSE.]

MOROSE. Are these the two learned men?

9. Afterward; "twanging": noisy and exciting.

1. Otter is a clergyman, Cutbeard a lawyer specializing in ecclesiastical cases.

TRUEWIT. Yes, sir, please you salute them.

MOROSE. Salute them! I had rather do anything than wear out time so unfruitfully, sir. I wonder how these common forms, as *God save you,* and *You are welcome,* are come to be a habit in our lives; or *I am glad to see you*—when I cannot see what the profit can be of these words, so long as it is no whit better with him whose affairs are sad and grievous, that he hears this salutation.

TRUEWIT. 'Tis true, sir; we'll go to the matter then.—Gentlemen, Master Doctor and Master Parson, I have acquainted you sufficiently with the business for which you are come hither, and you are not now to inform yourselves in the state of the question, I know. This is the gentleman who expects your resolution, and therefore, when you please, begin.

OTTER. Please you, Master Doctor.

CUTBEARD. Please you, good Master Parson.

OTTER. I would hear the canon law speak first.

CUTBEARD. It must give place to positive divinity, sir.[2]

MOROSE. Nay, good gentlemen, do not throw me into circumstances. Let your comforts arrrive quickly at me, those that are. Be swift in affording me my peace, if so I shall hope any. I love not your disputations or your court tumults. And that it be not strange to you, I will tell you: my father, in my education, was wont to advise me that I should always collect and contain my mind, not suffering it to flow loosely; that I should look to what things were necessary to the carriage of my life, and what not, embracing the one and eschewing the other; in short, that I should endear myself to rest and avoid turmoil; which now is grown to be another nature to me. So that I come not to your public pleadings, or your places of noise; not that I neglect those things that make for the dignity of the commonwealth; but for the mere avoiding of clamors, and impertinences of orators that know not how to be silent. And for the cause of noise am I now a suitor to you. You do not know in what a misery I have been exercised this day, what a torrent of evil! My very house turns round with the tumult! I dwell in a windmill! The perpetual motion is here and not at Eltham.[3]

TRUEWIT. Well, good Master Doctor, will you break the ice? Master Parson will wade after.

CUTBEARD. Sir, though unworthy, and the weaker, I will presume.

OTTER. 'Tis no presumption, *Domine* Doctor.[4]

MOROSE. Yet again!

CUTBEARD. Your question is, for how many causes a man may have

2. "Positive divinity" based on the scripture is Otter's province; canon law (Cutbeard's) is the entire body of regulations governing the church—a mass of material which already had a long and complex history before it was summarized in the 12th century by Gratian.

3. A Dutch inventor named Drebbel exhibited what he called a perpetual-motion machine at Eltham.

4. *Domine* (Master) Doctor. Much of the comedy of the following scene derives from the learned disputants' increasing intoxication with Latin. But many of their Latin phrases are either followed or preceded by a translation in the text, and so will not be annotated.

divortium legitimum, a lawful divorce? First you must understand the nature of the word 'divorce,' *a divertendo*[5]——

MOROSE. No excursions upon words, good Doctor, to the question briefly.

CUTBEARD. I answer then, the canon law affords divorce but in few cases; and the principal is in the common case, the adulterous case. But there are *duodecim impedimenta*, twelve impediments as we call 'em, all which do not *dirimere contractum*, but *irritum reddere matrimonium* as we say in the canon law, not take away the bond but cause a nullity therein.

MOROSE. I understand you before, good sir, avoid your impertinency of translation.

OTTER. He cannot open this too much, sir, by your favor.

MOROSE. Yet more!

TRUEWIT. O, you must give the learned men leave, sir.—To your impediments, Master Doctor.

CUTBEARD. The first is *impedimentum erroris*.[6]

OTTER. Of which there are several species.

CUTBEARD. Ay, as *error personae*.[7]

OTTER. If you contract yourself to one person thinking her another.

CUTBEARD. Then, *error fortunae*.[8]

OTTER. If she be a beggar, and you thought her rich.

CUTBEARD. Then, *error qualitatis*.[9]

OTTER. If she prove stubborn or headstrong, that you thought obedient.

MOROSE. How! is that, sir, a lawful impediment? One at once, I pray you, gentlemen.

OTTER. Ay, *ante copulam*, but not *post copulam*,[1] sir.

CUTBEARD. Master Parson says right. *Nec post nuptiarum benedictionem*. It doth indeed but *irrita reddere sponsalia*, annul the contract; after marriage it is of no obstancy.[2]

TRUEWIT. Alas, sir, what a hope are we fallen from by this time!

CUTBEARD. The next is *conditio*: if you thought her free-born and she prove a bondwoman there is impediment of estate and condition.

OTTER. Ay, but, Master Doctor, those servitudes are *sublatae*[3] now, among us Christians.

CUTBEARD. By your favor, Master Parson——

OTTER. You shall give me leave, Master Doctor.

MOROSE. Nay, gentlemen, quarrel not in that question; it concerns not my case. Pass to the third.

CUTBEARD. Well, then, the third is *votum*: if either party have made a vow of chastity. But that practice, as Master Parson said of the other, is taken away among us, thanks be to discipline.

5. *A divertendo*: from the word "divide," or separate. But *diverto* has a secondary sense, which is to digress.
6. The impediment of error.
7. An error of the person.
8. An error as to fortune.
9. An error of quality.

1. "Before marriage" but not "after marriage."
2. "It's grounds for breaking an engagement, but not the marriage itself." "Obstancy" (a made-up word from the Latin): obstacle.
3. Laid aside, obsolete.

The fourth is *cognatio*; if the persons be of kin within the degrees.

OTTER. Ay; do you know what the degrees are, sir?

MOROSE. No, nor I care not, sir. They offer me no comfort in the question, I am sure.

CUTBEARD. But there is a branch of this impediment may, which is *cognatio spiritualis*. If you were her godfather, sir, then the marriage is incestuous.

OTTER. That comment is absurd and superstitious, Master Doctor. I cannot endure it. Are we not all brothers and sisters, and as much akin in that as god-fathers and god-daughters?

MOROSE. O me! to end the controversy, I never was a godfather, I never was a godfather in my life, sir. Pass to the next.

CUTBEARD. The fifth is *crimen adulterii*,[4] the known case. The sixth, *cultus disparitas*, difference of religion; have you ever examined her, what religion she is of?

MOROSE. No, I would rather she were of none, than be put to the trouble of it.

OTTER. You may have it done for you, sir.

MOROSE. By no means, good sir; on to the rest. Shall you ever come to an end, think you?

TRUEWIT. Yes, he has done half, sir.—On to the rest.—Be patient, and expect, sir.

CUTBEARD. The seventh is *vis*: if it were upon compulsion or force.

MOROSE. O no, it was too voluntary, mine, too voluntary.

CUTBEARD. The eighth is *ordo*: if ever she have taken holy orders.

OTTER. That's superstitious too.

MOROSE. No matter, Master Parson; would she would go into a nunnery yet!

CUTBEARD. The ninth is *ligamen*: if you were bound, sir, to any other before.

MOROSE. I thrust myself too soon into these fetters.

CUTBEARD. The tenth is *publica honestas*: which is *inchoata quaedam affinitas*.[5]

OTTER. Ay, or *affinitas orta ex sponsalibus*; and is but *leve impedimentum*.[6]

MOROSE. I feel no air of comfort blowing to me in all this.

CUTBEARD. The eleventh is *affinitas ex fornicatione*.[7]

OTTER. Which is no less *vera affinitas* than the other, Master Doctor.

CUTBEARD. True, '*quae oritur ex legitimo matrimonio*.'[8]

OTTER. You say right, venerable Doctor; and, '*nascitur ex eo, quod per conjugium duae personae efficiuntur una caro*——[9]

4. The crime of adultery.

5. "Public probity," which is "a certain indefinite affinity" (between the parties).

6. "Ay, or an affinity rising out of the marriage itself"; but it's only "a minor impediment."

7. "Affinity by way of fornication"—just as valid an impediment as any other. In all this desperate search after grounds for divorce, Jonson's audience could hardly have avoided thinking of Henry VIII, for his marriage with Anne Boleyn was really, in canon law, void, because falling within the forbidden degree of relationship as a result of his previous affair with her sister Mary.

8. Affinity through adultery is just as valid as that which rises from legitimate marriage.

9. And derives from the fact that in marriage two persons are made one flesh.

TRUEWIT. Hey-day, now they begin!

CUTBEARD. I conceive you, Master Parson. '*Ita per fornicationem aeque est verus pater, qui sic generat*——[1]

OTTER. '*Et vere filius qui sic generatur*——'[2]

MOROSE. What's all this to me?

CLERIMONT. —Now it grows warm.

CUTBEARD. The twelfth and last is, *si forte coire nequibis*.[3]

OTTER. Ay, that is *impedimentum gravissimum*. It doth utterly annul and annihilate, that. If you have *manifestam frigiditatem*, you are well, sir.[4]

TRUEWIT. Why, there is comfort come at length, sir. Confess yourself but a man unable, and she will sue to be divorced first.

OTTER. Ay, or if there be *morbus perpetuus et insanabilis*,[5] as paralysis, elephantiasis, or so——

DAUPHINE. O, but *frigiditas* is the fairer way, gentlemen.

OTTER. You say troth, sir, and as it is in the canon, Master Doctor ——

CUTBEARD. I conceive you, sir.

CLERIMONT. [*aside*]—Before he speaks!

OTTER. That a boy, or child under years, is not fit for marriage, because he cannot *reddere debitum*.[6] So your *omnipotentes*——

TRUEWIT. [*aside to* OTTER]—Your *impotentes*, you whoreson lobster!

OTTER. Your *impotentes*, I should say, are *minime apti ad contrahenda matrimonium*.[7]

TRUEWIT. —'*Matrimonium*?' we shall have most unmatrimonial Latin with you. '*Matrimonia*, and be hanged!

DAUPHINE. —You put them out, man.

CUTBEARD. But then there will arise a doubt, Master Parson, in our case, *post matrimonium*: that *frigiditate praeditus*—do you conceive me, sir?

OTTER. Very well, sir.

CUTBEARD. Who cannot *uti uxore pro uxore*, may *habere eam pro sorore*.[8]

OTTER. Absurd, absurd, absurd, and merely apostatical!

CUTBEARD. You shall pardon me, Master Parson, I can prove it.

OTTER. You can prove a will, Master Doctor, you can prove nothing else. Does not the verse of your own canon say:

'*Haec socianda vetant connubia, facta retractant*?'[9]

CUTBEARD. I grant you; but how do they *retractare*, Master Parson?

MOROSE. O, this was it I feared.

1. And so he is a true father who begets a child in fornication.
2. And he is truly a son who is thus begotten.
3. If for some reason you cannot consummate the marriage.
4. That is "a very heavy impediment"; if you can show "manifest frigidity," you've made your case.
5. A chronic and incurable illness.
6. Perform his matrimonial duties. Otter's slip confuses "omnipotents" with "impotents."
7. Your "impotents" are "by no means fit to undertake matrimony." But again he botches the Latin.
8. Cutbeard proposes that since Morose was impotent when he entered on the marriage, and cannot be to his wife what a husband should be, he can live with her as if she were his sister ("*pro sorore*"). apostatical: heretical.
9. These associations can't be marriages, the conditions aren't met.

OTTER. *In aeternum*,[1] sir.

CUTBEARD. That's false in divinity, by your favor.

OTTER. 'Tis false in humanity to say so. Is he not *prorsus inutilis ad thorum*? Can he *praestare fidem datam*?[2] I would fain know.

CUTBEARD. Yes; how if he do *convalere*?

OTTER. He cannot *convalere*, it is impossible.

TRUEWIT. Nay, good sir, attend the learned men; they'll think you neglect them else.

CUTBEARD. Or if he do *simulare* himself *frigidum, odio uxoris*,[3] or so?

OTTER. I say he is *adulter manifestus*, then.

DAUPHINE. —They dispute it very learnedly, i' faith.

OTTER. And *prostitutor uxoris*,[4] and this is positive.

MOROSE. Good sir, let me escape.

TRUEWIT. You will not do me that wrong, sir?

OTTER. And, therefore, if he be *manifeste frigidus*, sir——

CUTBEARD. Ay, if he be *manifeste frigidus*, I grant you——

OTTER. Why, that was my conclusion.

CUTBEARD. And mine too.

TRUEWIT. Nay, hear the conclusion, sir.

OTTER. Then, *frigiditatis causa*——

CUTBEARD. Yes, *causa frigiditatis*——

MOROSE. O mine ears!

OTTER. She may have *libellum divortii* against you.

CUTBEARD. Ay, *divortii libellum* she will sure have.

MOROSE. Good echoes, forbear.

OTTER. If you confess it——

CUTBEARD. Which I would do, sir——

MOROSE. I will do anything.

OTTER. And clear myself, *in foro conscientiae*[5]——

CUTBEARD. Because you want indeed——

MOROSE. Yet more?

OTTER. *Exercendi potestate*.[6]

SCENE 4

[*Enter* EPICOENE, *followed by* LADY HAUGHTY, LADY CENTAUR, MISTRESS MAVIS, MISTRESS OTTER, DAW, *and* LA FOOLE.]

EPICOENE. I will not endure it any longer. Ladies, I beseech you, help me. This is such a wrong as never was offered to poor bride before. Upon her marriage day to have her husband conspire against her, and a couple of mercenary companions to be brought in for form's sake, to persuade a separation! If you had blood or

1. Permanent, for eternity.
2. Is he not "wholly useless in the marriage bed?" Can he "fulfill the promise he made?" But now Cutbeard questions whether he might not afterwards recover (*convalere*).
3. Or else he might be "feigning frigidity, out of hatred for his spouse."
4. In that case, says Otter, he is a "manifest adulterer" and one who "prostitutes his own wife."
5. In the forum of conscience.
6. The power of performance.

virtue in you, gentlemen, you would not suffer such earwigs about a husband, or scorpions to creep between man and wife——

MOROSE. O, the variety and changes of my torment!

HAUGHTY. Let them be cudgeled out of doors by our grooms.

CENTAUR. I'll lend you my footman.

MAVIS. We'll have our men blanket them in the hall.[7]

MISTRESS OTTER. As there was one at our house, madam, for peeping in at the door.

DAW. Content, i' faith.

TRUEWIT. Stay, ladies and gentlemen; you'll hear before you proceed?

MAVIS. I'd have the bridegroom blanketed, too.

CENTAUR. Begin with him first.

HAUGHTY. Yes, by my troth.

MOROSE. O mankind generation![8]

DAUPHINE. Ladies, for my sake forbear.

HAUGHTY. Yes, for Sir Dauphine's sake.

CENTAUR. He shall command us.

LA FOOLE. He is as fine a gentleman of his inches, madam, as any is about the town, and wears as good colors when he list.[9]

TRUEWIT. Be brief, sir, and confess your infirmity. She'll be afire to be quit of you, if she but hear that named once. You shall not entreat her to stay; she'lll fly you like one that had the marks[1] upon him.

MOROSE. Ladies, I must crave all your pardons——

TRUEWIT. Silence, ladies.

MOROSE. For a wrong I have done to your whole sex, in marrying this fair and virtuous gentlewoman——

CLERIMONT. Hear him, good ladies.

MOROSE. Being guilty of an infirmity which, before I conferred with these learned men, I thought I might have concealed——

TRUEWIT. But now being better informed in his conscience by them, he is to declare it, and give satisfaction by asking your public forgiveness.

MOROSE. I am no man, ladies.

ALL. How!

MOROSE. Utterly unabled in nature, by reason of frigidity, to perform the duties or any of the least office of a husband.

MAVIS. Now out upon him, prodigious creature!

CENTAUR. Bridegroom uncarnate!

HAUGHTY. And would you offer it to a young gentlewoman?

MISTRESS OTTER. A lady of her longings?

EPICOENE. Tut, a device, a device, this! it smells rankly, ladies. A mere comment of his own.

TRUEWIT. Why, if you suspect that, ladies, you may have him searched.

DAW. As the custom is, by a jury of physicians.

7. Toss them in a blanket.

8. I.e., O generation of vipers! "Mankind" is an old term of disapproval.

9. Choose.

1. I.e., of the plague.

LA FOOLE. Yes, faith, 'twill be brave.

MOROSE. O me, must I undergo that?

MISTRESS OTTER. No, let women search him, madam. We can do it ourselves.

MOROSE. Out on me, worse!

EPICOENE. No, ladies, you shall not need; I'll take him with all his faults.

MOROSE. Worst of all!

CLERIMONT. Why then, 'tis no divorce, Doctor, if she consent not.

CUTBEARD. No, if the man be *frigidus*, it is *parte uxoris*, that we grant *libellum divortii* in the law.[2]

OTTER. Ay, it is the same in theology.

MOROSE. Worse, worse than worst!

TRUEWIT. Nay, sir, be not utterly disheartened; we have yet a small relic of hope left, as near as our comfort is blown out.—Clerimont, produce your brace of knights.—What was that, Master Parson, you told me, in *errore qualitatis*,[3] e'en now? [*aside*]—Dauphine, whisper the bride, that she carry it as if she were guilty and ashamed.

OTTER. Marry, sir, *in errore qualitatis*,—which Master Doctor did forbear to urge—if she be found *corrupta*, that is, vitiated or broken up, that was *pro virgine desponsa*, espoused for a maid——

MOROSE. What then, sir?

OTTER. It doth *dirimere contractum*, and *irritum reddere*, too.[4]

TRUEWIT. If this be true, we are happy again, sir, once more. Here are an honorable brace of knights that shall affirm so much.

DAW. Pardon us, good Master Clerimont.

LA FOOLE. You shall excuse us, Master Clerimont.

CLERIMONT. Nay, you must make it good now, knights, there is no remedy. I'll eat no words for you, nor no men; you know you spoke it to me.

DAW. Is this gentlemanlike, sir?

TRUEWIT. [*aside to* DAW] Jack Daw, he's worse than Sir Amorous, fiercer a great deal. [*aside to* LA FOOLE]—Sir Amorous, beware, there be ten Daws in this Clerimont.

LA FOOLE. I'll confess it, sir.

DAW. Will you, Sir Amorous? will you wound reputation?

LA FOOLE. I am resolved.

TRUEWIT. So should you be too, Jack Daw. What should keep you off? She's but a woman, and in disgrace. He'll be glad on't.

DAW. Will he? I thought he would have been angry.

CLERIMONT. You will despatch, knights, it must be done, i' faith.

TRUEWIT. Why, an it must, it shall, sir, they say. They'll ne'er go back. [*aside to them*]—Do not tempt his patience.

DAW. It is true indeed, sir.

LA FOOLE. Yes, I assure you, sir.

2. No, if the man is "frigid," it's only on "the wife's complaint" that we grant a "bill of divorce."

3. About an error of quality.

4. (If she was married as a virgin, but wasn't really), it breaks the bond and renders it void too.

MOROSE. What is true, gentlemen? what do you assure me?

DAW. That we have known your bride, sir——

LA FOOLE. In good fashion. She was our mistress, or so——

CLERIMONT. You must be plain, knights, as you were to me.

OTTER. Ay, the question is, if you have *carnaliter*,[5] or no?

LA FOOLE. *Carnaliter*! what else, sir?

OTTER. It is enough; a plain nullity.

EPICOENE. I am undone, I am undone!

MOROSE. O, let me worship and adore you, gentlemen!

EPICOENE. I am undone!

MOROSE. Yes, to my hand, I thank these knights. Master Parson, let me thank you otherwise.

CENTAUR. And have they confessed?

MAVIS. Now, out upon them, informers!

TRUEWIT. You see what creatures you may bestow your favors on, madams.

HAUGHTY. I would except against them as beaten knights, wench, and not good witnesses in law.[6]

MISTRESS OTTER. Poor gentlewoman, how she takes it!

HAUGHTY. Be comforted, Morose, I love you the better for 't.

CENTAUR. So do I, I protest.

CUTBEARD. But, gentlemen, you have not known her since *matrimonium*?

DAW. Not today, Master Doctor.

LA FOOLE. No, sir, not today.

CUTBEARD. Why, then I say, for any act before, the *matrimonium* is good and perfect; unless the worshipful bridegroom did precisely, before witnesses, demand if she were *virgo ante nuptias*.[7]

EPICOENE. No, that he did not, I assure you, Master Doctor.

CUTBEARD. If he cannot prove that, it is *ratum conjugium*, notwithstanding the premises; and they do no way *impedire*.[8] And this is my sentence, this I pronounce.

OTTER. I am of Master Doctor's resolution, too, sir, if you made not that demand *ante nuptias*.[9]

MOROSE. O my heart! wilt thou break? wilt thou break? This is worst of all worst worsts that Hell could have devised! Marry a whore, and so much noise!

DAUPHINE. Come, I see now plain confederacy in this doctor and this parson, to abuse a gentleman. You study his affliction. I pray begone, companions.—And, gentlemen, I begin to suspect you for having parts with 'em.—Sir, will it please you, hear me?

MOROSE. O do not talk to me; take not from me the pleasure of dying in silence, nephew.

DAUPHINE. Sir, I must speak to you. I have been long your poor, despised kinsman, and many a hard thought has strengthened you

5. If you've had carnal knowledge of her.
6. If they have put up with affronts, they have forfeited their honor, and are not to be believed under oath.
7. A virgin before her marriage.
8. I.e., it is a valid marriage, and her affairs before marriage in no way flaw it.
9. Before marriage.

against me; but now it shall appear if either I love you or your peace, and prefer them to all the world beside. I will not be long or grievous to you, sir. If I free you of this unhappy match absolutely and instantly, after all this trouble, and almost in your despair, now——

MOROSE. It cannot be.

DAUPHINE. Sir, that you be never troubled with a murmur of it more, what shall I hope for, or deserve of you?

MOROSE. O, what thou wilt, nephew! thou shalt deserve me, and have me.

DAUPHINE. Shall I have your favor perfect to me, and love hereafter?

MOROSE. That, and anything beside. Make thine own conditions. My whole estate is thine. Manage it; I will become thy ward.

DAUPHINE. Nay, sir, I will not be so unreasonable.

EPICOENE. Will Sir Dauphine be mine enemy, too?

DAUPHINE. You know I have been long a suitor to you, uncle, that out of your estate, which is fifteen hundred a year, you would allow me but five hundred during life, and assure the rest upon me after; to which I have often, by myself and friends, tendered you a writing to sign, which you would never consent or incline to. If you please but to effect it now——

MOROSE. Thou shalt have it, nephew. I will do it, and more.

DAUPHINE. If I quit you not, presently and forever, of this cumber,[1] you shall have power instantly, afore all these, to revoke your act, and I will become whose slave you will give me to, forever.

MOROSE. Where is the writing? I will seal to it, that, or to a blank, and write thine own conditions.

EPICOENE. O me, most unfortunate, wretched gentlewoman!

HAUGHTY. Will Sir Dauphine do this?

EPICOENE. Good sir, have some compassion on me.

MOROSE. O, my nephew knows you, belike; away, crocodile![2]

CENTAUR. He does it not, sure, without good ground.

DAUPHINE. Here, sir.

[*Gives him the parchments.*]

MOROSE. Come, nephew, give me the pen. I will subscribe to anything, and seal to what thou wilt, for my deliverance. Thou art my restorer. Here I deliver it thee as my deed. If there be a word in it lacking, or writ with false orthography, I protest before God I will not take the advantage.

[*Returns the paper.*]

DAUPHINE. Then here is your release, sir: [*Takes off* EPICOENE'S *peruke.*] You have married a boy, a gentleman's son that I have brought up this half year at my great charges, and for this composition which I have now made with you. What say you, Master Doctor? This is *justum impedimentum*, I hope, *error personae*?[3]

OTTER. Yes sir, *in primo gradu*.[4]

1. Trouble.
2. Crocodile tears are proverbially hypocritical.
3. This is "a valid impediment," I hope, "a mistaken identity?"
4. Of the highest degree.

CUTBEARD. *In primo gradu.*

DAUPHINE. I thank you, good Doctor Cutbeard, and Parson Otter. [*Pulls off their beards and disguise.*] You are beholden to them, sir, that have taken this pains for you; and my friend, Master Truewit, who enabled them, for the business. Now you may go in and rest; be as private as you will, sir. [*Exit* MOROSE.] I'll not trouble you till you trouble me with your funeral, which I care not how soon it come.—Cutbeard, I'll make your lease good. *Thank me not, but with your leg, Cutbeard.* And Tom Otter, your Princess shall be reconciled to you.—How now, gentlemen, do you look at me?

CLERIMONT. A boy!

DAUPHINE. Yes, Mistress Epicoene.

TRUEWIT. Well, Dauphine, you have lurched[5] your friends of the better half of the garland, by concealing this part of the plot; but much good do it thee, thou deserv'st it, lad! And, Clerimont, for thy unexpected bringing in these two to confession, wear my part of it freely. Nay, Sir Daw and Sir La Foole, you see the gentlewoman that has done you the favors! We are all thankful to you, and so should the womankind here, specially for lying on her,[6] though not with her! You meant so, I am sure. But that we have stuck it upon you today, in your own imagined persons, and so lately, this Amazon, the champion of the sex, should beat you now thriftily,[7] for the common slanders which ladies receive from such cuckoos as you are. You are they that, when no merit or fortune can make you hope to enjoy their bodies, will yet lie with their reputations, and make their fame suffer. Away, you common moths of these and all ladies' honors. Go travel, to make legs and faces, and come home with some new matter to be laughed at. You deserve to live in an air as corrupted as that wherewith you feed rumor. [*Exeunt* DAW *and* LA FOOLE.] Madams, you are mute upon this new metamorphosis! But here stands she that has vindicated your fames. Take heed of such *insectae* hereafter.[8] And let it not trouble you that you have discovered any mysteries to this young gentleman. He is almost of years, and will make a good visitant[9] within this twelvemonth. In the meantime, we'll all undertake for his secrecy, that can speak so well of his silence.—[*Coming forward.*] *Spectators, if you like this comedy, rise cheerfully, and now Morose is gone in, clap your hands. It may be that noise will cure him, at least please him.*

THE END.

1609

5. Cheated. The "garland" is the victor's crown, imaginary in this case, for having done the best job of plotting.
6. I.e., lying about her.
7. Handsomely, thoroughly. The sense of the sentence is that if we hadn't already had our revenge, we would let Epicoene, the boy, beat you up.
8. Because she has metamorphosed so radically, Epicoene is an "insect."
9. I.e., secret lover.

The Alchemist

The Persons of the Play

SUBTLE, *the alchemist.*
FACE, *the housekeeper.*
DOL COMMON, *their colleague.*
DAPPER, *a clerk.*
DRUGGER, *a tobacco-man.*
LOVEWIT, *master of the house.*
EPICURE MAMMON, *a knight.*
SURLY, *a gamester.*
TRIBULATION, *a pastor of Amsterdam.*
ANANIAS, *a deacon there.*
KASTRIL, *the angry boy.*
DAME PLIANT, *his sister, a widow.*

NEIGHBORS, OFFICERS, MUTES.[1]

THE SCENE: *London.*

The Argument

The sickness hot, a master quit for fear
His house in town, and left one servant there.
Ease him corrupted, and gave means to know
A cheater and his punk, who, now brought low,
Leaving their narrow practice, were become
Cozeners[2] at large; and only wanting some
House to set up, with him they here contract,
Each for a share, and all begin to act.
Much company they draw, and much abuse,
In casting figures,[3] telling fortunes, news,
Selling of flies,[4] flat bawdry, with the stone:
Till it and they and all in fume[5] are gone.

Prologue

Fortune, that favors fools, these two short hours
We wish away, both for your sakes and ours,[6]

1. I.e., characters with no lines to speak: silent actors.
2. Con-men.
3. Telling fortunes.
4. Selling familiar spirits, supernatural helpers; "stone": the philosopher's stone, reputed capable of curing all diseases and converting base metals to gold.
5. Smoke.
6. In dismissing fortune for the period of the play, Jonson is appealing to more judicious and rational powers—justice for the author, grace for the actors.

Judging spectators; and desire, in place,
To th' author justice, to ourselves but grace.
Our scene is London, 'cause we would make known,
No country's mirth is better than our own:
No clime breeds better matter for your whore,
Bawd, squire, impostor, many persons more,
Whose manners, now called humors,[7] *feed the stage;*
And which have still been subject for the rage
Or spleen of comic writers. Though this pen
Did never aim to grieve, but better men;
Howe'er the age he lives in doth endure
The vices that she breeds, above their cure.
But when the wholesome remedies are sweet,
And in their working gain and profit meet,
He hopes to find no spirit so much diseased,
But will with such fair correctives be pleased:
For here he doth not fear who can apply.
If there be any that will sit so nigh
Unto the stream, to look what it doth run,
They shall find things, they'd think or wish were done;
They are so natural follies, but so shown,
As even the doers may see, and yet not own.[8]

Act I

SCENE 1. *A room in* LOVEWIT's *house*

[*Enter* FACE, *in a captain's uniform, with his sword drawn, and* SUBTLE *with a vial, quarrelling, and followed by* DOL COMMON.]

FACE. Believe't, I will.
SUBTLE. Thy worst. I fart at thee.
DOL. Have you your wits? why, gentlemen! for love—
FACE. Sirrah, I'll strip you——[1]
SUBTLE. What to do? lick figs
Out at my—[2]
FACE. Rogue, rogue! out of all your sleights.
DOL. Nay, look ye! Sovereign, General, are you madmen?
SUBTLE. O, let the wild sheep loose. I'll gum your silks
With good strong water, an you come.[3]
DOL. Will you have
The neighbors hear you? will you betray all?
Hark! I hear somebody.

7. Humors are the particular idiosyncrasies of individual temperaments, caused, according to the old medical theories (of Galen, for example), by an imbalance among the four basic humors of the body, i.e., choler, phlegm, blood, and black bile. "rage" (line 10) includes the idea of inspiration.

8. I.e., even those who share in the follies mocked onstage will be able to *see* (recognize) and yet not *own* (admit to) them.

1. I.e., strip you of your astrologer's robes.

2. An appropriate gesture goes with this invitation to "kiss my arse."

3. Subtle has corrosive acid in his vial.

FACE. Sirrah——
SUBTLE. I shall mar
All that the tailor has made, if you approach.[4]
FACE. You most notorious whelp, you insolent slave,
Dare you do this?
SUBTLE. Yes, faith; yes, faith.
FACE. Why, who
Am I, my mongrel? who am I?
SUBTLE. I'll tell you,
Since you know not yourself.
FACE. Speak lower, rogue.
SUBTLE. Yes, you were once (time's not long past) the good,
Honest, plain, livery-three-pound-thrum,[5] that kept
Your master's worship's house here in the Friars,
For the vacations—
FACE. Will you be so loud?
SUBTLE. Since, by my means, translated[6] Suburb-Captain.
FACE. By your means, Doctor Dog?
SUBTLE. Within man's memory,
All this I speak of.
FACE. Why, I pray you, have I
Been countenanced by you? or you by me?
Do but collect, sir, where I met you first.
SUBTLE. I do not hear well.
FACE. Not of this, I think it.
But I shall put you in mind, sir;—at Pie-corner,[7]
Taking your meal of steam in, from cooks' stalls,
Where, like the father of hunger, you did walk
Piteously costive, with your pinched-horn-nose,
And your complexion of the Roman wash,[8]
Stuck full of black and melancholic worms,
Like powder corns shot at the artillery-yard.
SUBTLE. I wish you could advance your voice a little.
FACE. When you went pinned up in the several rags
You had raked and picked from dunghills, before day;
Your feet in moldy slippers, for your kibes,[9]
A felt of rug, and a thin threaden cloak,
That scarce would cover your no-buttocks——
SUBTLE. So, sir!
FACE. When all your alchemy, and your algebra,
Your minerals, vegetals, and animals,

4. I.e., Face as a man is entirely the product of his tailor.
5. A drudge, working for his livery (his butler's uniform) plus three pounds a year. The Friars are the Blackfriars, an area where Jonson lived and where the play may well have had its first performance. The name came from the fact that the Dominican monks once had a monastery there; by the 17th century, it was a humdrum district of middle-class houses.
6. Transformed into.
7. I.e., a corner where pies and pasties could be bought on the street for immediate consumption. The idea of dining on steam goes back to Rabelais, *Gargantua*, III, 37.
8. Everything about Subtle's earlier estate bespoke the starved and melancholic scholar, from his constipation ("piteously costive") to his blackheads.
9. Ankles; "felt of rug": a shaggy hat.

Your conjuring, cozening, and your dozen of trades,
Could not relieve your corpse with so much linen
Would make you tinder, but to see a fire.[1]
I gave you countenance, credit for your coals,
Your stills, your glasses, your materials,
Built you a furnace, drew you customers,
Advanced all your black arts; lent you, beside,
A house to practice in——

SUBTLE. Your master's house!

FACE. Where you have studied the more thriving skill
Of bawdry since.

SUBTLE. Yes, in your master's house.
You and the rats here kept possession.
Make it not strange.[2] I know you were one could keep
The buttery-hatch still locked, and save the chippings,[3]
Sell the dole beer to aqua-vitæ men,
The which, together with your Christmas vails,[4]
At post-and-pair, your letting out of counters,
Made you a pretty stock, some twenty marks,[5]
And gave you credit to converse with cobwebs,
Here, since your mistress' death hath broke up house.

FACE. You might talk softlier, rascal.

SUBTLE. No, you scarab,
I'll thunder you in pieces. I will teach you
How to beware to tempt a fury again,
That carries tempest in his hand and voice.

FACE. The place has made you valiant.

SUBTLE. No, your clothes.
Thou vermin, have I ta'en thee out of dung,
So poor, so wretched, when no living thing
Would keep thee company, but a spider, or worse?
Raised thee from brooms, and dust, and watering-pots,
Sublimed thee, and exalted thee, and fixed thee
In the third region, called our state of grace?[6]
Wrought thee to spirit, to quintessence, with pains
Would twice have won me the philosopher's work?
Put thee in words and fashion, made thee fit
For more than ordinary fellowships?
Giv'n thee thy oaths, thy quarreling dimensions,[7]

1. Linen tow was used to light fires.
2. Don't make a mystery out of it.
3. I.e., Face kept the pantry door locked, and clung to the leftovers he should have given away. He even sold stale beer to "aqua-vitae men," so called because they accumulated dregs and droppings of all sorts, redistilled them, and sold the product as new liquor.
4. Tips. "Post and pair" was an old card game that required counters; the man who provided those got a tiny cut of the pot.
5. As a result of all these devices, Face had twenty marks—as much as $100 of our money.
6. "Sublimed," "exalted," and "state of grace" are all alchemical terms; the "philosopher's work" is, of course, the philosopher's stone. Subtle has transformed Face, as the stone transforms base metals to gold.
7. I.e., rules and regulations, not only for quarreling (provoking a duel), but for cloaking all kinds of sharp practice with a "gallant tincture," a coloring of gallantry.

Thy rules to cheat at horse-race, cock-pit, cards,
Dice, or whatever gallant tincture else?
Made thee a second in mine own great art?
And have I this for thanks! Do you rebel,
Do you fly out in the projection?[8]
Would you be gone now?

DOL. Gentlemen, what mean you?
Will you mar all?

SUBTLE. Slave, thou hadst had no name——

DOL. Will you undo yourselves with civil war?

SUBTLE. Never been known, past *equi clibanum*,[9]
The heat of horse-dung, under ground, in cellars,
Or an ale-house darker than deaf John's; been lost
To all mankind, but laundresses and tapsters,
Had not I been.

DOL. Do you know who hears you, Sovereign?

FACE. Sirrah—

DOL. Nay, general, I thought you were civil.

FACE. I shall turn desperate, if you grow thus loud.

SUBTLE. And hang thyself, I care not.

FACE. Hang thee, collier,
And all thy pots, and pans, in picture,[1] I will,
Since thou hast moved me——

DOL. O, this will o'erthrow all.

FACE. Write thee up bawd in Paul's[2] have all thy tricks
Of cozening with a hollow coal,[3] dust, scrapings;
Searching for things lost, with a sieve and shears,
Erecting figures in your rows of houses,
And taking in of shadows with a glass,
Told in red letters; and a face cut for thee,
Worse than Gamaliel Ratsey's.[4]

DOL. Are you sound?
Have you your senses, masters?

FACE. I will have
A book, but barely reckoning thy impostures,
Shall prove a true philosopher's stone to printers.[5]

SUBTLE. Away, you trencher-rascal!

FACE. Out, you dog-leech!
The vomit of all prisons——

8. Explode, just in the last stages of the process.

9. Horse manure, used in the early stages of alchemy to provide moist and moderate heat.

1. Expose him publicly as an impostor; "collier": cheat, by allusion to the dirtiness and sharp practice of charcoal dealers.

2. St. Paul's was the place for public notices, respectable and scandalous.

3. The "hollow coal" trick involved pouring a bit of molten gold into a hollow piece of charcoal and then burning off the charcoal: this would be proof of the transmutation of metals. Searching for things lost is a traditional activity of magicians; erecting figures in rows of houses is constructing a horoscope.

4. Gamaliel Ratsey was a highwayman, hanged in 1605, who wore a hideous mask while going about his business.

5. I.e., the printers will get rich off the book.

DOL. Will you be
Your own destructions, gentlemen?
FACE. Still spewed out
For lying too heavy on the basket.[6]
SUBTLE. Cheater!
FACE. Bawd!
SUBTLE. Cow-herd!
FACE. Conjurer!
SUBTLE. Cut-purse!
FACE. Witch!
DOL. O me!
We are ruined! lost! have you no more regard
To your reputations? where's your judgment? 'slight,
Have yet some care of me, of your republic—[7]
FACE. Away, this brach! I'll bring thee, rogue, within
The statute of sorcery, *tricesimo tertio*
Of Harry the eighth;[8] ay, and perhaps, thy neck
Within a noose, for laundering gold and barbing it.[9]
DOL. [*snatches* FACE'*s sword*] You'll bring your head within a cockscomb, will you?
And you, sir, with your menstrue[1] [*dashes* SUBTLE'*s vial out of his hand*]—gather it up.—
'Sdeath, you abominable pair of stinkards,
Leave off your barking, and grow one again,
Or, by the light that shines, I'll cut your throats.
I'll not be made a prey unto the marshal,[2]
For ne'er a snarling dog-bolt of you both.
Have you together cozened all this while,
And all the world, and shall it now be said,
You've made most courteous shift to cozen yourselves?
[*to* FACE] You will accuse him! You will bring him in
Within the statute! Who shall take your word?
A whoreson, upstart, apocryphal captain,
Whom not a Puritan in Blackfriars will trust
So much as for a feather. [*to* SUBTLE] And you, too,
Will give the cause, forsooth! you will insult,
And claim a primacy in the divisions!
You must be chief! as if you only had
The powder to project with, and the work
Were not begun out of equality?
The venture tripartite? all things in common?
Without priority? 'Sdeath! you perpetual curs,

6. For cheating in the distribution of food within the prison.

7. As a republic (from Latin, meaning public thing), Dol is exactly right; "brach": bitch.

8. The statute Face cites (against alchemy and multiplying metal) was passed in the thirty-third year of Henry VIII, 1541.

9. "Laundering gold" was washing coins in acid, which ate away their weight; "barbing it" was clipping. Both were hanging offenses.

1. Stinking concoction.

2. As a prostitute, Dol was always in danger from the marshal; "dog-bolt": worthless pup.

Fall to your couples again, and cozen kindly,
And heartily, and lovingly, as you should,
And lose not the beginning of a term,[3]
Or, by this hand, I shall grow factious too,
And take my part, and quit you.
FACE. 'Tis his fault;
He ever murmurs, and objects his pains,
And says, the weight of all lies upon him.
SUBTLE. Why, so it does.
DOL. How does it? do not we
Sustain our parts?
SUBTLE. Yes, but they are not equal.
DOL. Why, if your part exceed today, I hope
Ours may, tomorrow, match it.
SUBTLE. Ay, they may.
DOL. May, murmuring mastiff? ay, and do. Death on me!
Help me to throttle him. [*Seizes* SUBTLE, *by the throat*.]
SUBTLE. Dorothy! mistress Dorothy!
'Ods precious, I'll do any thing. What do you mean?
DOL. Because o' your fermentation and cibation?[4]
SUBTLE. Not I, by heaven——
DOL. Your Sol and Luna[5]——[*to* FACE]
Help me.
SUBTLE. Would I were hanged then! I'll conform myself.
DOL. Will you, sir? do so then, and quickly: swear.
SUBTLE. What should I swear?
DOL. To leave your faction, sir,
And labor kindly in the common work.
SUBTLE. Let me not breathe if I meant aught beside.
I only used those speeches as a spur
To him.
DOL. I hope we need no spurs, sir. Do we?
FACE. 'Slid, prove today, who shall shark best.
SUBTLE. Agreed.
DOL. Yes, and work close and friendly.
SUBTLE. 'Slight, the knot
Shall grow the stronger for this breach, with me.
[*They shake hands*.]
DOL. Why, so, my good baboons! Shall we go make
A sort of sober, scurvy, precise neighbors,[6]
That scarce have smiled twice since the king came in,
A feast of laughter at our follies? Rascals,
Would run themselves from breath, to see me ride,[7]

3. The first days of a court term, implying the prime time for business.
4. Moistening, in the fancy language of alchemy.
5. Alchemical terms for gold and silver.
6. "Precise" defines the neighbors as puritans, earnest to observe the law of God (as they understood it) precisely; "since the king came in": 1603, i.e., seven years before.
7. Dol would ride in a cart, stripped and whipped, to the workhouse. Face and Subtle, as pimps, would be pilloried and have their ears cut off—all this to the great delight of the neighbors.

Or you t' have but a hole to thrust your heads in,
For which you should pay ear-rent? No, agree.
And may Don Provost ride a feasting long,[8]
In his old velvet jerkin and stained scarfs,
My noble Sovereign, and worthy General,
Ere we contribute a new crewel[9] garter
To his most worsted worship.

SUBTLE. Royal Dol!
Spoken like Claridiana,[1] and thyself.

FACE. For which at supper thou shalt sit in triumph,
And not be styled Dol Common, but Dol Proper,
Dol Singular: the longest cut at night,[2]
Shall draw thee for his Dol Particular. [*Bell rings without.*]

SUBTLE. Who's that? one rings. To the window, Dol. [*Exit* DOL.] Pray heaven,
The master do not trouble us this quarter.[3]

FACE. O, fear not him. While there dies one a week
O' the plague, he's safe from thinking toward London.
Beside, he's busy at his hop-yards now;
I had a letter from him. If he do,
He'll send such word, for airing of the house,
As you shall have sufficient time to quit it.
Though we break up a fortnight, 'tis no matter.
[*Re-enter* DOL.]

SUBTLE. Who is it, Dol?

DOL. A fine young quodling.[4]

FACE. O,
My lawyer's clerk, I lighted on last night,
In Holborn, at the Dagger.[5] He would have
(I told you of him) a familiar,[6]
To rifle with at horses, and win cups.

DOL. O, let him in.

SUBTLE. Stay. Who shall do't?

FACE. Get you
Your robes on. I will meet him, as going out.

DOL. And what shall I do?

FACE. Not be seen; away! [*Exit* DOL.]
Seem you very reserved.

SUBTLE. Enough. [*Exit.*]

FACE. [*aloud and retiring*] God be wi' you, sir,

8. Don Provost, though a specific officer of the law, stands here for the whole legal apparatus, especially the public executioner, who got as part of his fee the best clothes of those he whipped or executed.

9. "Crewel": worsted, but with a pun on "cruel" and another on "worsted."

1. The heroine of a huge Spanish romance, *The Mirror of Knighthood.* The terms applied to Dol—"proper," "singular," and "particular"—are parodies of terms used in heraldry.

2. I.e., they'll draw straws to decide who sleeps with her.

3. Periods when the law courts were in session.

4. Sprout.

5. A particularly low eating- and drinking-house of the district.

6. Short for "familiar spirit," a magic spiritual helper; "rifle": gamble (a variant form of "raffle").

I pray you let him know that I was here;
His name is Dapper. I would gladly have stayed, but—
DAPPER. [*within*] Captain, I am here.

SCENE 2

FACE. Who's that?—He's come, I think, doctor.
[*Enter* DAPPER.]
Good faith, sir, I was going away.
DAPPER. In truth,
I'm very sorry captain.
FACE. But I thought
Sure I should meet you.
DAPPER. Ay, I'm very glad.
I had a scurvy writ or two to make,
And I had lent my watch last night to one
That dines today at the sheriff's, and so was robbed
Of my pass-time.[7]
[*Re-enter* SUBTLE *in his velvet cap and gown.*]
Is this the cunning-man?[8]
FACE. This is his worship.
DAPPER. Is he a doctor?
FACE. Yes.
DAPPER. And have you broke with him,[9] captain?
FACE. Aye.
DAPPER. And how?
FACE. Faith, he does make the matter, sir, so dainty,
I know not what to say.
DAPPER. Not so, good captain.
FACE. Would I were fairly rid of it, believe me.
DAPPER. Nay, now you grieve me, sir. Why should you wish so?
I dare assure you, I'll not be ungrateful.
FACE. I cannot think you will sir. But the law
Is such a thing——and then he says, Read's matter[1]
Falling so lately.
DAPPER. Read! he was an ass,
And dealt, sir, with a fool.
FACE. It was a clerk, sir.
DAPPER. A clerk!
FACE. Nay, hear me, sir, you know the law
Better, I think——
DAPPER. I should, sir, and the danger.
You know, I showed the statute to you.[2]
FACE. You did so.

7. Watches were still expensive, and conferred social prestige on the owner.
8. A country term for "magician."
9. Explained the matter to him.
1. In 1608 Simon Read was charged with necromancy; he had called up some spirits to ask them who had stolen a sum of money from his client. King James pardoned him.
2. This is the source of Face's remarkable erudition above (I,i,112–13); it is part of Jonson's point that con-men learn their trade from their victims.

DAPPER. And will I tell then? By this hand of flesh,
Would it might never write good court-hand[3] more,
If I discover. What do you think of me,
That I am a chiaus?[4]
FACE. What's that?
DAPPER. The Turk, was here.
As one would say, do you think I am a Turk?
FACE. I'll tell the doctor so.
DAPPER. Do, good sweet captain.
FACE. Come, noble doctor, pray thee let's prevail;
This is the gentleman, and he is no chiaus.
SUBTLE. Captain, I have returned you all my answer.
I would do much, sir, for your love——But this
I neither may, nor can.
FACE. Tut, do not say so.
You deal now with a noble fellow, doctor,
One that will thank you richly; and he is no chiaus:
Let that, sir, move you.
SUBTLE. Pray you, forbear—
FACE. He has
Four angels here.[5]
SUBTLE. You do me wrong, good sir.
FACE. Doctor, wherein? to tempt you with these spirits?
SUBTLE. To tempt my art and love, sir, to my peril.
'Fore heaven, I scarce can think you are my friend,
That so would draw me to apparent danger.
FACE. I draw you! a horse draw you, and a halter,
You, and your flies together—[6]
DAPPER. Nay, good Captain.
FACE. That know no difference of men.
SUBTLE. Good words, sir.
FACE. Good deeds, sir Doctor Dogs'-Meat. 'Slight, I bring you
No cheating Clim-o'-the-Cloughs, or Claribels,[7]
That look as big as five-and-fifty, and flush;[8]
And spit out secrets like hot custard—
DAPPER. Captain?
FACE. Nor any melancholic under-scribe,
Shall tell the vicar; but a special gentle,
That is the heir to forty marks a year,
Consorts with the small poets of the time,
Is the sole hope of his old grandmother;

3. The particular script used by clerks in the courts of law.
4. In Turkish, a messenger (pronounced "chouse"). In 1607 a messenger named Mustafa arrived in England as if from Turkey itself; he collected a lot of money from gullible folk, and made off with it, leaving behind a new English word for "cheat."
5. Coins bearing an image of Michael the archangel. The total bribe is about two pounds.
6. As in the Argument, familiar spirits, sometimes taking the form of flies, but just as often assuming other shapes.
7. Clim o' the Clough was one of Robin Hood's playmates, Claribel a lewd and wicked knight in Spenser; unsavory characters, in other words.
8. In the old card game of primero, this would be as good a hand as a royal straight flush today.

That knows the law, and writes you six fair hands,
Is a fine clerk, and has his ciphering perfect,
Will take his oath o' the Greek Testament,
If need be, in his pocket; and can court
His mistress out of Ovid.[9]
DAPPER. Nay, dear captain—
FACE. Did you not tell me so?
DAPPER. Yes; but I'd have you
Use master Doctor with some more respect.
FACE. Hang him, proud stag, with his broad velvet head![1]
But for your sake, I'd choke, ere I would change
An article of breath with such a puckfist—[2]
Come, let's be gone. [*Going.*]
SUBTLE. Pray you let me speak with you.
DAPPER. His worship calls you, Captain.
FACE. I am sorry
I e'er embarked myself in such a business.
DAPPER. Nay, good sir; he did call you.
FACE. Will he take then?
SUBTLE. First, hear me—
FACE. Not a syllable, 'less you take.
SUBTLE. Pray you, sir—
FACE. Upon no terms, but an *assumpsit*.[3]
SUBTLE. Your humor must be law. [*He takes the four angels.*]
FACE. Why now, sir, talk.
Now I dare hear you with mine honor. Speak.
So may this gentleman too.
SUBTLE. Why, sir—
[*Pretending to whisper to* FACE.]
FACE. No whispering.
SUBTLE. 'Fore heaven, you do not apprehend the loss
You do yourself in this.
FACE. Wherein? for what?
SUBTLE. Marry, to be so importunate for one,
That, when he has it, will undo you all.
He'll win up all the money in the town.
FACE. How!
SUBTLE. Yes, and blow up gamester after gamester,
As they do crackers[4] in a puppet-play.
If I do give him a familiar,
Give you him all you play for; never set him;[5]
For he will have it.
FACE. You are mistaken, Doctor.
Why, he does ask one but for cups and horses,

9. I.e., will have the smartest and sexiest possible things to say to her.
1. Doctors wore velvet caps, and Face also alludes to the "velvet" on a stag's antlers.
2. Literally, tightwad, but Face is accusing Subtle of being a "stingy receiver."
3. Literally, a taking. Subtle must take Dapper's money (reluctant as he is to do so) to avoid a quarrel with Face.
4. Firecrackers.
5. Never bet against him.

A rifling fly;[6] none of your great familiars.
DAPPER. Yes, Captain, I would have it for all games.
SUBTLE. I told you so.
FACE. [*taking* DAPPER *aside*] 'Slight, that's a new business!
I understood you, a tame bird, to fly
Twice in a term, or so, on Friday nights,
When you had left the office, for a nag
Of forty or fifty shillings.
DAPPER. Ay, 'tis true, sir;
But I do think now I shall leave the law,
And therefore——
FACE. Why, this changes quite the case.
Do you think that I dare move him?
DAPPER. If you please, sir;
All's one to him, I see.
FACE. What! for that money?
I cannot with my conscience; nor should you
Make the request, methinks.
DAPPER. No, sir, I mean
To add consideration.
FACE. Why then, sir,
I'll try. [*Goes to* SUBTLE.] Say that it were for all games, Doctor?
SUBTLE. I say then, not a mouth shall eat for him
At any ordinary, but on the score;[7]
That is a gaming mouth, conceive me.
FACE. Indeed!
SUBTLE. He'll draw you all the treasure of the realm,
If it be set him.
FACE. Speak you this from art?
SUBTLE. Ay, sir, and reason too, the ground of art.
He is of the only best complexion,
The Queen of Fairy loves.
FACE. What! is he?
SUBTLE. Peace,
He'll overhear you. Sir, should she but see him—
FACE. What?
SUBTLE. Do not you tell him.
FACE. Will he win at cards too?
SUBTLE. The spirits of dead Holland, living Isaac,[8]
You'd swear, were in him; such a vigorous luck
As cannot be resisted. 'Slight, he'll put
Six of your gallants to a cloak,[9] indeed.
FACE. A strange success, that some man shall be born to!
SUBTLE. He hears you, man——

6. A spirit for use in now-and-then gambling situations.
7. I.e., No gamester will have a bit of cash left to buy food at a tavern ("ordinary"); they'll all have to eat on credit.
8. John and Isaac Holland were Dutch alchemists; Subtle implies that they are masters of good luck.
9. I.e., he'll strip six gallants to their cloaks.

DAPPER. Sir, I'll not be ungrateful.
FACE. Faith, I have confidence in his good nature:
You hear, he says he will not be ungrateful.
SUBTLE. Why, as you please; my venture follows yours.
FACE. Troth, do it, Doctor; think him trusty, and make him.
He may make us both happy in an hour;
Win some five thousand pound, and send us two on't.
DAPPER. Believe it, and I will, sir.
FACE. And you shall, sir.
You have heard all? [*Takes him aside.*]
DAPPER. No, what was't? Nothing, I, sir.
FACE. Nothing?
DAPPER. A little, sir.
FACE. Well, a rare star
Reigned at your birth.
DAPPER. At mine, sir! No.
FACE. The doctor
Swears that you are—
SUBTLE. Nay, captain, you'll tell all now.
FACE. Allied to the Queen of Fairy.
DAPPER. Who? that I am?
Believe it, no such matter—
FACE. Yes, and that
You were born with a caul on your head.[1]
DAPPER. Who says so?
FACE. Come,
You know it well enough, though you dissemble it.
DAPPER. I'fac, I do not: you are mistaken.
FACE. How!
Swear by your fac,[2] and in a thing so known
Unto the Doctor? how shall we, sir, trust you
In the other matter? can we ever think,
When you have won five or six thousand pound,
You'll send us shares in't, by this rate?
DAPPER. By Jove, sir,
I'll win ten thousand pound, and send you half.
I'fac's no oath.
SUBTLE. No, no, he did but jest.
FACE. Go to. Go thank the doctor: he's your friend,
To take it so.
DAPPER. I thank his worship.
FACE. So?
Another angel.
DAPPER. Must I?
FACE Must you! 'slight,

1. A membrane on the head of a new-born child, considered a mark of good luck.

2. "In faith," but diluted to the point where it's not much more of an oath than our "Gosh" or "Golly."

What else is thanks? will you be trivial?—Doctor,
[DAPPER *gives him the money.*]
When must he come for his familiar?
DAPPER. Shall I not have it with me?
SUBTLE. O, good sir!
There must a world of ceremonies pass;
You must be bathed and fumigated first;
Besides, the Queen of Fairy does not rise
Till it be noon.
FACE. Not if she danced tonight.
SUBTLE. And she must bless it.
FACE. Did you never see
Her royal grace yet?
DAPPER. Whom?
FACE. Your aunt of Fairy?
SUBTLE. Not since she kissed him in the cradle, Captain;
I can resolve you that.
FACE. Well, see her Grace,
Whate'er it cost you, for a thing that I know.
It will be somewhat hard to compass; but
However, see her. You are made, believe it,
If you can see her. Her Grace is a lone woman,
And very rich; and if she take a fancy,
She will do strange things. See her, at any hand.
'Slid, she may hap to leave you all she has:
It is the doctor's fear.
DAPPER. How will't be done, then?
FACE. Let me alone, take you no thought. Do you
But say to me, Captain, I'll see her Grace.
DAPPER. Captain, I'll see her Grace.
FACE. Enough. [*Knocking within.*]
SUBTLE. Who's there?
Anon! [*aside to* FACE]—Conduct him forth by the back way.—
Sir, against one o'clock prepare yourself;
Till when you must be fasting; only take
Three drops of vinegar in at your nose,
Two at your mouth, and one at either ear;
Then bathe your fingers' ends and wash your eyes,
To sharpen your five senses, and cry *hum*
Thrice, and then *buz* as often; and then come. [*Exit.*]
FACE. Can you remember this?
DAPPER. I warrant you.
FACE. Well then, away. It is but your bestowing
Some twenty nobles 'mong her Grace's servants,[3]
And put on a clean shirt. You do not know
What grace her Grace may do you in clean linen.
[*Exeunt* FACE *and* DAPPER.]

3. For a man of Dapper's class, this is a stiff sum, perhaps a hundred or two of our dollars.

SCENE 3

SUBTLE. [*within*] Come in! [*He calls out through the door.*]—
Good wives, I pray you forbear me now;[4]
Troth, I can do you no good till afternoon—
[*Re-enters, followed by* DRUGGER.]
What is your name, say you, Abel Drugger?
DRUGGER. Yes, sir.
SUBTLE. A seller of tobacco?
DRUGGER. Yes, sir.
SUBTLE. Umph!
Free of the grocers?[5]
DRUGGER. Ay, an't please you.
SUBTLE. Well——
Your business, Abel?
DRUGGER. This, an't please your worship;
I am a young beginner, and am building
Of a new shop, an't like your worship, just
At corner of a street: here is the plot[6] on't.
And I would know by art, sir, of your worship,
Which way I should make my door, by necromancy,
And where my shelves; and which should be for boxes,
And which for pots. I would be glad to thrive, sir;
And I was wished to your worship by a gentleman,
One Captain Face, that says you know men's planets.
And their good angels, and their bad.
SUBTLE. I do, [*Enter* FACE.]
If I do see them—
FACE. What! my honest Abel?
Thou art well met here.
DRUGGER. Troth, sir, I was speaking,
Just as your worship came here, of your worship.
I pray you speak for me to master Doctor.
FACE. He shall do anything. Doctor, do you hear?
This is my friend Abel, an honest fellow;
He lets me have good tobacco, and he does not
Sophisticate it with sack-lees or oil,
Nor washes it in muscadel and grains,
Nor buries it in gravel, under ground,
Wrapped up in greasy leather, or pissed clouts:
But keeps it in fine lily pots, that, opened,
Smell like conserve of roses, or French beans.
He has his maple block, his silver tongs,
Winchester pipes, and fire of juniper;
A neat, spruce, honest fellow, and no goldsmith.[7]

4. Subtle is putting off tradeswomen to whom he owes money.
5. Are you a full member of the grocer's company? (I.e., have you served your apprenticeship?)
6. Plan, layout.
7. As usual, Jonson's technical details are precise: the maple block was used to shred the tobacco, the silver tongs to hold a coal of glowing juniper to get the pipe lit, and Winchester pipes were thought to be the best. The highest commendation is that Abel is no goldsmith, i.e., not a usurer, as grocers tended to be.

SUBTLE. He is a fortunate fellow, that I am sure on.
FACE. Already, sir, have you found it? Lo thee, Abel!
SUBTLE. And in right way toward riches—
FACE. Sir!
SUBTLE. This summer
He will be of the clothing of his company,[8]
And next spring called to the scarlet; spend what he can.
FACE. What, and so little beard?
SUBTLE. Sir, you must think,
He may have a receipt to make hair come.
But he'll be wise, preserve his youth, and fine for't;[9]
His fortune looks for him another way.
FACE. 'Slid, Doctor, how canst thou know this so soon?
I am amused[1] at that!
SUBTLE. By a rule, Captain,
In metoposcopy,[2] which I do work by;
A certain star in the forehead, which you see not.
Your chestnut or your olive-colored face
Does never fail; and your long ear doth promise.
I knew't, by certain spots, too, in his teeth,
And on the nail of his mercurial finger.
FACE. Which finger's that?
SUBTLE. His little finger.[3] Look.
You were born upon a Wednesday?
DRUGGER. Yes, indeed, sir.
SUBTLE. The thumb, in chiromancy, we give Venus;
The fore-finger, to Jove; the midst, to Saturn;
The ring, to Sol; the least, to Mercury,
Who was the lord, sir, of his horoscope,
His house life being Libra; which fore-showed
He should be a merchant, and should trade with balance.
FACE. Why, this is strange! Is it not, honest Nab?
SUBTLE. There is a ship now, coming from Ormuz,[4]
That shall yield him such a commodity
Of drugs [*pointing to the plan*]——This is the west, and this the south?
DRUGGER. Yes, sir.
SUBTLE. And those are your two sides?
DRUGGER. Ay, sir.
SUBTLE. Make me your door, then, south; your broad side, west;
And on the east side of your shop, aloft,
Write Mathlai, Tarmiel, and Baraborat;[5]
Upon the north part, Rael, Velel, Thiel.

8. I.e., an officer of the grocers' company, for whom the next step up would be appointment as sheriff ("called to the scarlet"). All this despite his extreme youth ("so little beard").
9. He'll be smart enough not to accept the office, with its responsibilities; he'll do better to pay a fine for refusing it.
1. Bemused, puzzled.
2. Telling of fortunes by looking in someone's face.
3. This astrological gibberish, which Drugger takes very seriously, may be understood to say that he is in particular danger from thieves—as he obviously is.
4. An island in the Persian gulf, source of many drugs.
5. Gibberish names for occult spirits which will protect Drugger's stock on the shelves.

They are the names of those mercurial spirits
That do fright flies from boxes.

DRUGGER. Yes, sir.

SUBTLE. And
Beneath your threshold, bury me a lodestone
To draw in gallants that wear spurs; the rest,
They'll seem to follow.

FACE. That's a secret, Nab!

SUBTLE. And, on your stall, a puppet, with a vice[6]
And a court-fucus, to call city-dames.
You shall deal much with minerals.

DRUGGER. Sir, I have
At home, already——

SUBTLE. Ay, I know you have arsenic,
Vitriol, sal-tartar, argaile,[7] alkali,
Cinoper: I know all.—This fellow, Captain,
Will come, in time, to be a great distiller,
And give a say[8]—I will not say directly,
But very fair—at the philosopher's stone.

FACE. Why, how now, Abel! is this true?

DRUGGER. [*aside to* FACE.] Good Captain,
What must I give?

FACE. Nay, I'll not counsel thee.
Thou hear'st what wealth he says, spend what thou canst,
Thou'rt like to come to.

DRUGGER. I would gi' him a crown.

FACE. A crown! and toward such a fortune? Heart,
Thou shalt rather gi' him thy shop. No gold about thee?

DRUGGER. Yes, I have a portague,[9] I have kept this half year.

FACE. Out on thee, Nab! 'Slight, there was such an offer—
Shalt keep't no longer, I'll give't him for thee.—Doctor,
Nab prays your worship to drink this, and swears
He will appear more grateful, as your skill
Does raise him in the world.

DRUGGER. I would entreat
Another favor of his worship.

FACE. What is't, Nab?

DRUGGER. But to look over, sir, my almanac,
And cross out my ill-days, that I may neither
Bargain, nor trust upon them.

FACE. That he shall, Nab;
Leave it, it shall be done, 'gainst afternoon.

SUBTLE. And a direction for his shelves.

FACE. Now, Nab,
Art thou well pleased, Nab?

DRUGGER. Thank, sir, both your worships.

6. Device, for making the puppet move; "court-fucus": the kind of make-up used at court, bound to sell well to city ladies who never go there.

7. Cream of tartar; "cinoper": cinnabar.

8. Essay, attempt.

9. Portuguese gold piece, worth nearly four pounds.

FACE. Away.

[*Exit* DRUGGER.]

Why, now, you smoky persecutor of nature!
Now do you see, that something's to be done,
Beside your beech-coal, and your corsive waters,
Your crosslets, crucibles, and cucurbites?[1]
You must have stuff, brought home to you, to work on.
And yet you think, I am at no expense
In searching out these veins, then following them,
Then trying them out. 'Fore God, my intelligence
Costs me more money, than my share oft comes to,
In these rare works.

SUBTLE. You are pleasant, sir.—How now?

SCENE 4

[*Re-enter* DOL.]

What says my dainty Dolkin?

DOL. Yonder fishwife
Will not away. And there's your giantess,
The bawd of Lambeth.

SUBTLE. Heart, I cannot speak with them.

DOL. Not afore night, I have told them in a voice,
Through the trunk,[2] like one of your *familiars*.
But I have spied sir Epicure Mammon——

SUBTLE. Where?

DOL. Coming along, at far end of the lane,
Slow of his feet, but earnest of his tongue
To one that's with him.

SUBTLE. Face, go you, and shift. [*Exit* FACE.]
Dol, you must presently make ready, too.

DOL. Why, what's the matter?

SUBTLE. O, I did look for him
With the sun's rising: marvel he could sleep!
This is the day I am to perfect for him
The *magisterium*,[3] our great work, the stone;
And yield it, made, into his hands, of which
He has, this month, talked as he were possessed.
And now he's dealing pieces on't away.
Methinks I see him entering ordinaries,
Dispensing for the pox, and plaguy houses,
Reaching his dose, walking Moorfields[4] for lepers,
And offering citizens' wives pomander-bracelets,
As his preservative, made of the elixir;
Searching the spittle,[5] to make old bawds young,

1. Acids, furnaces, and cupping-glasses, used in alchemical demonstrations.
2. Speaking-tube.
3. Masterwork.
4. Moorfields, in the suburbs, was a hangout for beggars, cripples, the feeble-minded, and the hopelessly diseased; "pomander-bracelets": medicine-bracelets.
5. Hospital. Sir Epicure will cure all the epidemic diseases of the time when he has the stone.

And the highways, for beggars, to make rich;
I see no end of his labors. He will make
Nature ashamed of her long sleep, when art,
Who's but a stepdame, shall do more than she,
In her best love to mankind, ever could.
If his dream last, he'll turn the age to gold. [*Exeunt.*]

Act II

SCENE 1. *An outer room in* LOVEWIT's *house*

[*Enter* SIR EPICURE MAMMON *and* SURLY.]

MAMMON. Come on, sir. Now, you set your foot on shore
In *Novo Orbe*;[1] here's the rich Peru;
And there within, sir, are the golden mines,
Great Solomon's Ophir![2] he was sailing to't,
Three years, but we have reached it in ten months.
This is the day, wherein, to all my friends,
I will pronounce the happy word, *be rich*;
This day you shall be *spectatissimi*.[3]
You shall no more deal with the hollow die
Or the frail card. No more be at charge of keeping
The livery-punk[4] for the young heir, that must
Seal, at all hours, in his shirt. No more,
If he deny, have him beaten to't, as he is
That brings him the commodity. No more
Shall thirst of satin, or the covetous hunger
Of velvet entrails for a rude-spun cloak,
To be displayed at Madam Augusta's,[5] make
The sons of Sword and Hazard fall before
The golden calf, and on their knees, whole nights,
Commit idolatry with wine and trumpets,
Or go a feasting after drum and ensign.
No more of this. You shall start up young viceroys,
And have your punks,[6] and punketees, my Surly.
And unto thee I speak it first, *be rich*.
Where is my Subtle, there? Within, ho!

FACE. [*within*] Sir,
He'll come to you by and by.

1. The New World, with all its legends of El Dorado, the mythical man of gold, whom Pizarro found to be real and actual in the Inca of Peru.
2. Solomon was understood from a Biblical text (I Kings 10:22) to have found great wealth in the Arabian city of Ophir, to which he sent a fleet every three years.
3. Most distinguished.
4. Professed pimp. The general sense is that the man with the philosopher's stone no longer has to resort to dishonest and degrading ways of making a living—such as by rounding up girls for young heirs.
5. Clearly a brothel, where the wretched servant has resorted to recruit girls for his master. The "sons of Sword and Hazard" are highwaymen and (like Surly) gamesters—alternative ways for the desperate fellow to make money. And if all else fails, he can "go a-feasting after drum and ensign"—enlist in the army.
6. Pimps; "punketees" (evidentally an invented word) bawds.

MAMMON. That is his fire-drake,[7]
His Lungs, his Zephyrus, he that puffs his coals,
Till he firk[8] nature up, in her own center.
You are not faithful,[9] sir. This night, I'll change
All that is metal, in my house, to gold;
And, early in the morning, will I send
To all the plumbers and the pewterers,
And buy their tin and lead up; and to Lothbury[1]
For all the copper.
SURLY. What, and turn that too?
MAMMON. Yes, and I'll purchase Devonshire, and Cornwall,
And make them perfect Indies![2] you admire now?
SURLY. No, faith.
MAMMON. But when you see th' effects of the great medicine,
Of which one part projected on a hundred
Of Mercury, or Venus, or the Moon,[3]
Shall turn it to as many of the Sun;
Nay, to a thousand, so *ad infinitum*—
You will believe me.
SURLY. Yes, when I see't, I will.
But if my eyes do cozen me so, and I
Giving them no occasion, sure I'll have
A whore, shall piss them out, next day.
MAMMON. Ha! why?
Do you think I fable with you? I assure you,
He that has once the flower of the sun,
The perfect ruby, which we call elixir,[4]
Not only can do that, but, by its virtue,
Can confer honor, love, respect, long life;
Give safety, valor, yea, and victory,
To whom he will. In eight and twenty days,
I'll make an old man of fourscore, a child.
SURLY. No doubt; he's that already.
MAMMON. Nay, I mean,
Restore his years, renew him, like an eagle,
To the fifth age;[5] make him get sons and daughters,
Young giants; as our philosophers have done,
The ancient patriarchs, afore the flood,
But taking, once a week, on a knife's point,
The quantity of a grain of mustard of it;
Become stout Marses,[6] and beget young Cupids.

7. A fire-dragon, supposed to live in the element of fire; all Mammon's fanciful names for Face imply his role as a stimulator of fire.
8. Stir.
9. A true believer.
1. The street of the coppersmiths in London.
2. I.e., the Americas. Tin and copper mines were found in Devon and Cornwall; Mammon will convert them to storehouses of gold.
3. Alchemically speaking, quicksilver, copper, or silver. The sun is, of course, gold itself.
4. The fluid that changes base metals to gold and cures all diseases instantly: liquefied philosopher's stone.
5. The early ages of the world, when all men were young and lusty.
6. Sturdy gods of war.

SURLY. The decayed vestals[7] of Pict-hatch would thank you,
That keep the fire alive, there.
MAMMON. 'Tis the secret
Of nature naturized[8] 'gainst all infections,
Cures all diseases coming of all causes;
A month's grief in a day, a year's in twelve;
And, of what age soever, in a month,
Past all the doses of your drugging doctors.
I'll undertake, withal, to fright the plague
Out of the kingdom in three months.
SURLY. And I'll
Be bound, the players shall sing your praises, then,[9]
Without their poets.
MAMMON. Sir, I'll do't. Meantime,
I'll give away so much unto my man,
Shall serve the whole city, with preservative,[1]
Weekly; each house his dose, and at the rate—
SURLY. As he that built the water-work, does with water?[2]
MAMMON. You are incredulous.
SURLY. Faith, I have a humor,
I would not willingly be gulled.[3] Your stone
Cannot transmute me.
MAMMON. Pertinax, my Surly,
Will you believe antiquity? records?
I'll show you a book where Moses and his sister,
And Solomon have written of the art;
Ay, and a treatise penned by Adam[4]—
SURLY. How!
MAMMON. Of the philosopher's stone, and in High Dutch.
SURLY. Did Adam write, sir, in High Dutch?
MAMMON. He did;
Which proves it was the primitive tongue.
SURLY. What paper?
MAMMON. On cedar board.
SURLY. O that, indeed, they say,
Will last 'gainst worms.
MAMMON. 'Tis like your Irish wood
'Gainst cobwebs. I have a piece of Jason's fleece, too,
Which was no other than a book of alchemy,
Writ in large sheepskin, a good fat ram-vellum.
Such was Pythagoras' thigh, Pandora's tub,

7. Virgins, sardonically. "Pict-hatch": district near Blackfriars famous for prostitutes.

8. In scholastic philosophy, "nature naturing" is nature using her own inherent powers; "nature naturized" is nature perfected and transcendent, as in the stone.

9. When the plague ran rampant, theaters closed and actors were unemployed.

1. Stuff that's good for what ails you.

2. About 1595 the first public waterworks were established in London, supplying Thames water to households at a fee.

3. Tricked.

4. Moses, Miriam, Solomon, and Adam were only a few of the early worthies whom the alchemists claimed as members of their craft.

And, all that fable of Medea's charms,
The manner of our work;[5] the bulls, our furnace,
Still breathing fire; our argent-vive, the dragon:
The dragon's teeth, mercury sublimate,
That keeps the whiteness, hardness, and the biting;
And they are gathered into Jason's helm,
The alembic,[6] and then sowed in Mars his field,
And thence sublimed so often, till they're fixed.
Both this, the Hesperian garden, Cadmus' story,
Jove's shower, the boon of Midas, Argus' eyes,
Boccace his Demogorgon, thousands more,
All abstract riddles of our stone.[7]—How now?

SCENE 2

[*Enter* FACE, *as the servant, Lungs.*]
Do we succeed? Is our day come? and holds it?
FACE. The evening will set red upon you, sir;[8]
You have color for it, crimson: the red ferment
Has done his office; three hours hence prepare you
To see projection.[9]
MAMMON. Pertinax, my Surly,
Again I say to thee, aloud, *be rich.*
This day, thou shalt have ingots; and, tomorrow,
Give lords th' affront.—Is it, my Zephyrus, right?
Blushes the bolt's-head?[1]
FACE. Like a wench with child, sir,
That were but now discovered to her master.
MAMMON. Excellent witty Lungs!—my only care is,
Where to get stuff enough now, to project on;
This town will not half serve me.
FACE. No, sir? buy
The covering off o' churches.
MAMMON. That's true.
FACE. Yes.
Let them stand bare, as do their auditory;
Or cap them, new, with shingles.

5. In addition to Pythagoras's golden thigh and Pandora's box (tub), Mammon interprets as an emblem of the stone the story of Jason and Medea. Jason had to plough a field with a pair of brazen-footed, fire-breathing bulls (the furnace), sow the furrows with dragon's teeth (mercury sublimate), kill the armed men who sprang from those teeth, and then overcome a sleepless dragon ("argent-vive," quicksilver) guarding the golden fleece. Medea, a prototype of the witch, helped him pass these various tests.

6. Jason's helmet is the retort in which ingredients were heated and distilled.

7. Like the tale of Jason and the golden fleece, the stories of Cadmus and the sowing of dragon's teeth, of Jove wooing Danae in a shower of gold, of Argus the watchman with a hundred eyes, and of Boccaccio's Demogorgon who was the original god of all gods are all versions of a single basic story: the transmutation of metals.

8. A red sky at night is a traditional omen of prosperity.

9. The twelfth and final work of the alchemist: the creation of gold.

1. A long-necked vessel, the top of which turns red ("blushes") at the height of the process.

MAMMON. No, good thatch:[2]
Thatch will lie light upon the rafters, Lungs.
Lungs, I will manumit[3] thee from the furnace;
I will restore thee thy complexion, Puff,
Lost in the embers; and repair this brain,
Hurt with the fume o' the metals.
FACE. I have blown, sir,
Hard for your worship; thrown by many a coal,
When 'twas not beech;[4] weighed those I put in, just,
To keep your heat still even; these bleared eyes
Have waked to read your several colors, sir,
Of the pale citron, the green lion, the crow,
The peacock's tail, the pluméd swan.[5]
MAMMON. And, lastly,
Thou hast descried the flower, the *sanguis agni*?[6]
FACE. Yes, sir.
MAMMON. Where's master?
FACE. At his prayers, sir, he;
Good man, he's doing his devotions
For the success.
MAMMON. Lungs, I will set a period
To all thy labors; thou shalt be the master
Of my seraglio.[7]
FACE. Good, sir.
MAMMON. But do you hear?
I'll geld you, Lungs.
FACE. Yes, sir.
MAMMON. For I do mean
To have a list of wives and concubines,
Equal with Solomon, who had the stone
Alike with me; and I will make me a back
With the elixir, that shall be as tough
As Hercules, to encounter fifty a night.—
Thou art sure thou saw'st it blood?
FACE. Both blood and spirit, sir.
MAMMON. I will have all my beds blown up, not stuffed:
Down is too hard. And then, mine oval room
Filled with such pictures as Tiberius took
From Elephantis,[8] and dull Aretine
But coldly imitated. Then, my glasses
Cut in more subtle angles, to disperse

2. Having taken the lead off church roofs, and toyed with Face's fancy of leaving them bareheaded like the audiences inside them, Mammon replaces them (in his fantasy) with cheap thatch.
3. Liberate.
4. Only beech, a particularly dense and expensive wood, yielded the right coal for alchemy.
5. The various colors through which the basic materials pass on their way to becoming the philosopher's stone.
6. Blood of the lamb, the final blood-red color of projection.
7. Harem.
8. Suetonius in his life of Tiberius describes the obscene decorations of the villa on Capri where the emperor held his orgies. Elephantis was an erotic writer of antiquity and Pietro Aretino a pornographer of more recent vintage.

And multiply the figures, as I walk
Naked between my succubae.[9] My mists
I'll have of perfume, vapored 'bout the room,
To lose ourselves in; and my baths, like pits
To fall into; from whence we will come forth,
And roll us dry in gossamer and roses.—
Is it arrived at ruby?——Where I spy
A wealthy citizen, or a rich lawyer,
Have a sublimed pure wife, unto that fellow
I'll send a thousand pound to be my cuckold.

FACE. And I shall carry it?

MAMMON. No. I'll have no bawds,
But fathers and mothers: they will do it best,[1]
Best of all others. And my flatterers
Shall be the pure and gravest of divines,
That I can get for money. My mere fools,
Eloquent burgesses,[2] and then my poets
The same that writ so subtly of the fart,[3]
Whom I will entertain still for that subject.
The few that would give out themselves to be
Court and town-stallions, and each-where belie
Ladies who are known most innocent, for them;
Those will I beg, to make me eunuchs of:
And they shall fan me with ten ostrich tails
A-piece, made in a plume to gather wind.
We will be brave,[4] Puff, now we have the medicine.
My meat shall all come in, in Indian shells,
Dishes of agate set in gold, and studded
With emeralds, sapphires, hyacinths,[5] and rubies.
The tongues of carps, dormice, and camels heels,
Boiled in the spirit of Sol,[6] and dissolved pearl,
Apicius' diet, 'gainst the epilepsy:
And I will eat these broths with spoons of amber,
Headed with diamond and carbuncle.
My foot-boy shall eat pheasants, calvered salmons,
Knots, godwits, lampreys[7]: I myself will have
The beards of barbels served instead of salads;
Oiled mushrooms; and the swelling unctuous paps
Of a fat pregnant sow newly cut off,

9. Whores with demonic overtones.

1. The detail comes from Juvenal's Tenth Satire, but the streak of perversity is Mammon's own.

2. He'll have so much money that he'll hire respectable bourgeois ("burgesses") to play the fool before him.

3. An episode of a fart let in the House of Commons created a minor stir in the session of 1607; a number of poets, including Jonson himself, took occasion to display their wit.

4. Splendid.

5. Rare blue stones.

6. I.e., liquid gold. Roman gourmets recommended these and many of the other delicacies described below as preventives of epilepsy. Apicius, the best-known of them, had a better remedy: after eating himself out of a huge fortune, he hanged himself.

7. "Calvered salmon" are simply sliced. "Knots" and "godwits" are game birds, "lampreys" eels. "Barbels" are fish like catfish, with soft, fleshy chin-whiskers.

Dressed with an exquisite and poignant sauce;[8]
For which, I'll say unto my cook, *There's gold,*
Go forth, and be a knight.
FACE. Sir, I'll go look
A little, how it heightens. [*Exit.*]
MAMMON. Do.—My shirts
I'll have of taffeta-sarsnet[9] soft and light
As cobwebs; and for all my other raiment
It shall be such as might provoke the Persian
Were he to teach the world riot[1] anew.
My gloves of fishes and bird skins perfumed
With gums of paradise and eastern air—
SURLY. And do you think to have the stone with this?
MAMMON. No, I do think t'have all this with the stone.
SURLY. Why, I have heard, he must be *homo frugi*,[2]
A pious, holy, and religious man,
One free from mortal sin, a very virgin.
MAMMON. That makes it, sir; he is so. But I buy it;
My venture brings it me. He, honest wretch,
A notable, superstitious, good soul,
Has worn his knees bare, and his slippers bald,
With prayer and fasting for it: and, sir, let him
Do it alone, for me, still. Here he comes.
Not a profane word afore him; 'tis poison.

SCENE 3

MAMMON. Good morrow, father. [*Enter* SUBTLE.]
SUBTLE. Gentle son, good morrow
And to your friend there. What is he, is with you?
MAMMON. An heretic, that I did bring along,
In hope, sir, to convert him.
SUBTLE. Son, I doubt[3]
You are covetous, that thus you meet your time
In the just point—prevent your day at morning.[4]
This argues something, worthy of a fear
Of importune and carnal appetite.
Take heed you do not cause the blessing leave you,
With your ungoverned haste. I should be sorry
To see my labors, now even at perfection,
Got by long watching and large patience,
Not prosper where my love and zeal hath placed them.
Which (heaven I call to witness with your self,
To whom I have poured my thoughts) in all my ends,

8. Many of the gastronomic details are from the *Life of Heliogabalus* by the late Roman historian Lampridius.
9. A particularly soft and luxuriant fabric.
1. Luxury. The Persians were famous for rich living.
2. A man of temperate habits. It was, of course, accepted by alchemists that a man who discovered the secret of nature's perfection must himself be perfect.
3. Suspect.
4. Anticipate the arrival of day by coming early.

Have looked no way, but unto public good,
To pious uses, and dear charity
Now grown a prodigy[5] with men. Wherein
If you, my son, should now prevaricate,
And, to your own particular lusts employ
So great and catholic[6] a bliss, be sure
A curse will follow, yea, and overtake
Your subtle and most secret ways.

MAMMON. I know, sir;
You shall not need to fear me. I but come,
To have you confute this gentleman.

SURLY. Who is,
Indeed, sir, somewhat costive[7] of belief
Toward your stone; would not be gulled.

SUBTLE. Well, son,
All that I can convince him in, is this,
The *work is done*, bright Sol is in his robe.
We have a medicine of the triple soul,
The glorified spirit. Thanks be to heaven,
And make us worthy of it!—Ulen Spiegel![8]

FACE. [*within*] Anon, sir.

SUBTLE. Look well to the register.[9]
And let your heat still lessen by degrees,
To the aludels.[1]

FACE. [*within*] Yes, sir.

SUBTLE. Did you look
O' the bolt's-head yet?

FACE. [*within*] Which? on D, sir?

SUBTLE. Aye;
What's the complexion?

FACE. [*within*] Whitish.

SUBTLE. Infuse vinegar,
To draw his volatile substance and his tincture:
And let the water in glass E be filtered,
And put into the gripe's egg.[2] Lute him well;
And leave him closed *in balneo*.

FACE. [*within*] I will, sir.

SURLY. What a brave language here is! next to canting.[3]

SUBTLE. I have another work, you never saw, son,
That three days since passed the philosopher's wheel,
In the lent heat of Athanor;[4] and's become
Sulphur of Nature.

5. Rarity.
6. Universal.
7. Reluctant to grant consent.
8. Till Eulenspiegel literally, "Owlglass") was a German joker of the Renaissance, a trickster and con-man with whom Face and Subtle recognize kinship.
9. Damper of the furnace.
1. Pots without bottoms, fitted together to form a condenser.
2. A specially shaped vessel, like a vulture's egg. Face is to pack this vessel in clay to make it airtight, and leave it "*in balneo*" in the bath of hot water.
3. Thieves' slang, but also a special jargon developed by extreme Puritans.
4. The gentle heat of a slow furnace. "Sulphur of Nature" is just pure sulphur.

MAMMON. But 'tis for me?
SUBTLE. What need you?
You have enough in that is perfect.
MAMMON. O but——
SUBTLE. Why, this is covetise!
MAMMON. No, I assure you,
I shall employ it all in pious uses,
Founding of colleges and grammar schools,
Marrying young virgins, building hospitals,
And now and then a church. [*Re-enter* FACE]
SUBTLE. How now?
FACE. Sir, please you,
Shall I not change the filter?
SUBTLE. Marry, yes;
And bring me the complexion of glass B. [*Exit* FACE.]
MAMMON. Have you another?
SUBTLE. Yes, son; were I assured
Your piety were firm, we would not want
The means to glorify it; but I hope the best.
I mean to tinct C in sand-heat tomorrow,
And give him imbibition.[5]
MAMMON. Of white oil?
SUBTLE. No, sir, of red. F is come over the helm too,
I thank my maker, in Saint Mary's bath,[6]
And shows *lac virginis*. Blessed be heaven!
I sent you of his faeces there calcined:
Out of that calx,[7] I have won the salt of mercury.
MAMMON. By pouring on your rectifiéd water?
SUBTLE. Yes, and reverberating[8] in Athanor. [*Re-enter* FACE.]
How now! what color says it?
FACE. The ground black, sir.
MAMMON. That's your crow's head?[9]
SURLY. Your cockscomb's is it not?
SUBTLE. No, 'tis not perfect. Would it were the crow.
That work wants something.
SURLY. [*aside*] O, I looked for this.
The hay's a pitching.[1]
SUBTLE. Are you sure you loosed them
In their own menstrue?[2]
FACE. Yes, sir, and then married them,
And put them in a bolt's-head nipped to digestion,
According as you bade me, when I set
The liquor of Mars to circulation
In the same heat.

5. Moistening.
6. Essentially, a double boiler; "*lac virginis*": literally, milk of the virgin, dissolved mercury.
7. "Faeces": literally, excrement, actually sediment; "calx": powder.
8. Heating in a furnace where the heat is reflected off the top of the furnace.
9. Jet-black; Surly's correction implies Mammon is a fool, a coxcomb.
1. The trap is being set; a "hay" was a snare to catch a rabbit.
2. Solvents.

SUBTLE. The process then was right.
FACE. Yes, by the token, sir; the retort brake,
And what was saved was put into the pelican,
And signed with Hermes' seal.[3]
SUBTLE. I think 'twas so.
We should have a new amalgama.[4]
SURLY. [*aside*] O, this ferret
Is rank as any pole cat.
SUBTLE. But I care not:
Let him e'en die; we have enough beside,
In embrion.[5] H has his white shirt on?
FACE. Yes sir,
He's ripe for inceration,[6] he stands warm
In his ash-fire. I would not you should let
Any die now, if I might counsel, sir,
For luck's sake to the rest: it is not good.
MAMMON. He says right.
SURLY. [*aside*] Ay, are you bolted?[7]
FACE. Nay, I know't, sir,
I have seen the ill fortune. What is some three ounces
Of fresh materials?
MAMMON. Is't no more?
FACE. No more, sir,
Of gold, t'amalgam with some six of mercury.
MAMMON. Away, here's money. What will serve?
FACE. Ask him, sir.
MAMMON. How much?
SUBTLE. Give him nine pound; you may give him ten.
SURLY. Yes, twenty, and be cozened, do.
MAMMON. There 'tis.
[*Gives* FACE *the money.*]
SUBTLE. This needs not; but that you will have it so,
To see conclusions of all; for two
Of our inferior works are at fixation,
A third is in ascension.[8] Go your ways.
Have you set the oil of luna in kemia?[9]
FACE. Yes, sir.
SUBTLE. And the philosopher's vinegar?[1]
FACE. Ay. [*Exit.*]
SURLY. We shall have a salad!

3. The "pelican" was a retort whose outlet led back into itself. "Hermes' seal" was a way of closing off a tube (hermetically, so to speak) by twisting it shut.
4. Combination.
5. Embryo. The "white shirt" signified a stage in distillation when all the ingredients appeared white.
6. The stage of waxiness.
7. Driven into the net. Surly sees the whole process of trapping Mammon as a rabbit hunt, in which the net is laid (pitched) and the rabbit driven into it.
8. The two "inferior works" are Dapper and Drugger, both set aside for the moment in "fixation"; Mammon is in "ascension"; he's getting crazier and crazier in his ambitious lust.
9. "Oil of luna" contains an allusion to the moon and to the silver of which it is an emblem; "kemia" is the process of alchemy itself. Mammon is being transmuted.
1. Some sort of corrosive.

MAMMON. When do you make projection?
SUBTLE. Son, be not hasty, I exalt our med'cine,
By hanging him *in balneo vaporoso*,[2]
And giving him solution; congeal him;
And then dissolve him; then again congeal him.
For look, how oft I iterate the work,
So many times I add unto his virtue.
As, if at first one ounce converts a hundred,
After his second loose, he'll turn a thousand;
His third solution, ten; his fourth, a hundred.
After his fifth, a thousand thousand ounces
Of any imperfect metal, into pure
Silver or gold, in all examinations
As good as any of the natural mine.
Get you your stuff here against afternoon,
Your brass, your pewter, and your andirons.
MAMMON. Not those of iron?
SUBTLE. Yes, you may bring them too:
We'll change all metals.
SURLY. I believe you in that.
MAMMON. Then I may send my spits?
SUBTLE. Yes, and your racks.
SURLY. And dripping-pans, and pot-hangers, and hooks,
Shall he not?
SUBTLE. If he please.
SURLY. —To be an ass.
SUBTLE. How, sir!
MAMMON. This gentleman you must bear withal.
I told you he had no faith.
SURLY. And little hope, sir;
But much less charity, should I gull myself.
SUBTLE. Why, what have you observed, sir, in our art,
Seems so impossible?
SURLY. But your whole work, no more.
That you should hatch gold in a furnace, sir,
As they do eggs in Egypt![3]
SUBTLE. Sir, do you
Believe that eggs are hatched so?
SURLY. If I should?
SUBTLE. Why, I think that the greater miracle.
No egg but differs from a chicken more
Than metals in themselves.
SURLY. That cannot be.
The egg's ordained by nature to that end,
And is a chicken *in potentia*.[4]
SUBTLE. The same we say of lead and other metals,
Which would be gold, if they had time.

2. In a steam bath.
3. In incubators, supposed to be an Egyptian invention.
4. Potentially.

MAMMON. And that
Our art doth further.
SUBTLE. Ay, for 'twere absurd
To think that nature in the earth bred gold
Perfect in the instant. Something went before.
There must be remote matter.
SURLY. Ay, what is that?
SUBTLE. Marry, we say—
MAMMON. Ay, now it heats; stand, father,
Pound him to dust.
SUBTLE. It is, of the one part,
A humid exhalation, which we call
Materia liquida, or the unctuous water;[5]
On the other part, a certain crass and viscous
Portion of earth; both which, concorporate,
Do make the elementary matter of gold;
Which is not yet *propria materia*,[6]
But common to all metals and all stones.
For, where it is forsaken of that moisture,
And hath more dryness, it becomes a stone;
Where it retains more of the humid fatness,
It turns to sulphur, or to quicksilver,
Who are the parents of all other metals.
Nor can this remote matter suddenly
Progress so from extreme unto extreme,
As to grow gold, and leap o'er all the means.
Nature doth first beget the imperfect, then
Proceeds she to the perfect. Of that airy
And oily water, mercury is engendered;
Sulphur of the fat and earthy part; the one,
Which is the last, supplying the place of male,
The other of the female, in all metals.
Some do believe hermaphrodeity,[7]
That both do act and suffer.[8] But these two
Make the rest ductile, malleable, extensive.
And even in gold they are; for we do find
Seeds of them, by our fire, and gold in them,
And can produce the species of each metal
More perfect thence, than nature doth in earth.[9]
Beside, who doth not see in daily practice
Art can beget bees, hornets, beetles, wasps,

5. I.e., oily water. The lecture on alchemy that Subtle delivers here had been put forward in all seriousness by the alchemists themselves. Its premise is that all inferior metals would be gold if they could; the work of the alchemist is simply to help them fulfill their basic disposition.
6. Proper material.
7. A grear deal of alchemical terminology extended a sexual principle into chemical processes; thus, gold was the product of a fortunate marriage between sulphur and mercury.
8. Acting and suffering define the active and passive energies of a relationship.
9. Outdoing mere nature, the philosopher's art could produce—or so the alchemists believed—a kind of supergold, capable of creating new gold.

Out of the carcasses and dung of creatures?[1]
Yea, scorpions of an herb, being rightly placed?
And these are living creatures, far more perfect
And excellent than metals.

MAMMON. Well said, father!
Nay, if he take you in hand, sir, with an argument,
He'll bray you in a mortar.[2]

SURLY. Pray you, sir, stay.
Rather than I'll be brayed, sir, I'll believe
That alchemy is a pretty kind of game,
Somewhat like tricks o' the cards, to cheat a man
With charming.

SUBTLE. Sir?

SURLY. What else are all your terms,
Whereon no one of your writers 'grees with other?
Of your elixir, your *lac virginis*,
Your stone, your med'cine, and your chrysosperme,
Your sal, your sulphur, and your mercury,
Your oil of height, your tree of life, your blood,
Your marchesite, your tutie, your magnesia,
Your toad, your crow, your dragon, and your panther;
Your sun, your moon, your firmament, your adrop,
Your lato, azoch, zernich, chibrit, heautarit,
And then your red man, and your white woman,
With all your broths, your menstrues, and materials,
Of piss and egg-shells, women's terms, man's blood,
Hair o' the head, burnt clouts, chalk, merds, and clay,
Powder of bones, scalings of iron, glass,
And worlds of other strange ingredients,[3]
Would burst a man to name?

SUBTLE. And all these named,
Intending but one thing; which art our writers
Used to obscure their art.

MAMMON. Sir, so I told him
Because the simple idiot should not learn it,
And make it vulgar.

SUBTLE. Was not all the knowledge
Of the Egyptians writ in mystic symbols?[4]
Speak not the Scriptures oft in parables?
Are not the choicest fables of the poets,
That were the fountains and first springs of wisdom,
Wrapped in perplexed allegories?

MAMMON. I urged that,
And cleared to him, that Sisyphus was damned

1. Aristotle had taught the reality of spontaneous generation; if that can happen, why not transmutation of metals?
2. Crush you to a powder.
3. The phrases of this vehement catalogue are all legitimate alchemical expressions. Note that the list starts with technical terms and gradually works down to ingredients that are not only common but disgusting.
4. Hieroglyphics which in spite of many pretenses, nobody could read before the 19th century.

To roll the ceaseless stone, only because
He would have made ours common.[5] [DOL *appears at the door.*]
—Who is this?

SUBTLE. God's precious!—What do you mean? go in, good lady,
Let me entreat you. [DOL *retires.*] Where's this varlet?
[*Re-enter* FACE.]

FACE. Sir.

SUBTLE. You very knave! do you use me thus?

FACE. Wherein, sir?

SUBTLE. Go in and see, you traitor. Go! [*Exit* FACE.]

MAMMON. Who is it, sir?

SUBTLE. Nothing, sir, nothing.

MAMMON. What's the matter, good sir?
I have not seen you thus distempered. Who is it?

SUBTLE. All arts have still had, sir, their adversaries;
But ours the most ignorant. [*Re-enter* FACE.] What now?

FACE. 'Twas not my fault, sir; she would speak with you.

SUBTLE. Would she, sir! Follow me.
[*Exit.*]

MAMMON. [*stopping him*] Stay, Lungs.

FACE. I dare not, sir.

MAMMON. Stay, man; what is she?

FACE. A lord's sister, sir.

MAMMON. How! pray thee, stay.

FACE. She's mad, sir, and sent hither—
He'll be mad too.

MAMMON. I warrant thee. Why sent hither?

FACE. Sir, to be cured.

SUBTLE. [*within*] Why, rascal!

FACE. Lo you!—Here, sir! [*Exit.*]

MAMMON. 'Fore God, a Bradamante,[6] a brave piece.

SURLY. Heart, this is a bawdy-house! I'll be burnt else.

MAMMON. O, by this light, no. Do not wrong him. He's
Too scrupulous that way; it is his vice.
No, he's a rare physician, do him right,
An excellent Paracelsian,[7] and has done
Strange cures with mineral physic. He deals all
With spirits, he; he will not hear a word
Of Galen,[8] or his tedious recipes.
How now, Lungs!

FACE. Softly, sir; speak softly. I meant
To have told your worship all. This[9] must not hear.

MAMMON. No, he will not be gulled; let him alone.

5. Sisyphus was condemned to roll a stone in the underworld because he betrayed the secrets of the gods: Mammon says that secret was the philosopher's stone.

6. Bradamante, a heroine of Ariosto's *Orlando Furioso* and, like Dol, as bold at war as love.

7. A follower of Theophrastus Bombastus von Hohenheim (Paracelsus), the 16th-century Swiss physician and alchemist.

8. Galen, late Roman doctor and chief authority cited by conventional physicians, whom Paracelsus and his followers despised.

9. With a gesture at Surly.

FACE. You're very right, sir; she is a most rare scholar,
And is gone mad with studying Broughton's works.[1]
If you but name a word touching the Hebrew,
She falls into her fit, and will discourse
So learnedly of genealogies,
As you would run mad too, to hear her, sir.
MAMMON. How might one do t' have conference with her, Lungs?
FACE. O divers[2] have run mad upon the conference.
I do not know, sir. I am sent in haste.
To fetch a vial.
SURLY. Be not gulled, sir Mammon.
MAMMON. Wherein? pray ye, be patient.
SURLY. Yes, as you are,
And trust confederate knaves and bawds and whores.
MAMMON. You are too foul, believe it.—Come here, Ulen,
One word.
FACE. I dare not, in good faith. [*Going.*]
MAMMON. Stay, knave.
FACE. He is extreme angry that you saw her, sir.
MAMMON. Drink that. [*Gives him money.*] What is she when she's out of her fit?
FACE. O, the most affablest creature, sir! so merry!
So pleasant! she'll mount you up, like quick-silver,
Over the helm;[3] and circulate like oil,
A very vegetal: discourse of state,[4]
Of mathematics, bawdry, anything——
MAMMON. Is she no way accessible? no means,
No trick to give a man a taste of her——wit——
Or so?
SUBTLE. [*within*] Ulen!
FACE. I'll come to you again, sir. [*Exit.*]
MAMMON. Surly, I did not think one of your breeding
Would traduce personages of worth.
SURLY. Sir Epicure,
Your friend to use; yet still, loath to be gulled.
I do not like your philosophical bawds.
Their stone is lechery enough to pay for
Without this bait.
MAMMON. 'Heart, you abuse yourself.
I know the lady, and her friends, and means,
The original of this disaster. Her brother
Has told me all.
SURLY. And yet you ne'er saw her
Till now!
MAMMON. O yes, but I forgot. I have, believe it,

1. Hugh Broughton (1549–1612) was a scholar of Hebrew whom Jonson particularly loathed, never missing an opportunity to sneer at him. In fact Broughton was a perfectly respectable scholar.
2. Various people.
3. Face's commendations of Dol are phrased in alchemical terms, but can be understood to apply to a whore.
4. Talk of politics; "vegetal": a stimulant.

One of the treacherousest memories, I do think,
Of all mankind.
SURLY. What call you her brother?
MAMMON. My lord——
He will not have his name known, now I think on't.
SURLY. A very treacherous memory!
MAMMON. On my faith——
SURLY. Tut, if you have it not about you, pass it,
Till we meet next.
MAMMON. Nay, by this hand, 'tis true.
He's one I honor, and my noble friend;
And I respect his house.
SURLY. Heart! can it be
That a grave sir, a rich, that has no need,
A wise sir, too, at other times, should thus
With his own oaths and arguments make hard means
To gull himself? An this be your elixir,
Your *lapis mineralis*,[5] and your lunary,
Give me your honest trick yet at primero,
Or gleek; and take your *lutum sapientis*,
Your *menstruum simplex*! I'll have gold before you,
And with less danger of the quicksilver,
Or the hot sulphur.[6] [*Enter* FACE, *still as Lungs*.]
FACE. [*to* SURLY] Here's one from Captain Face, sir,
Desires you meet him in the Temple-church,
Some half hour hence, and upon earnest business.
Sir, [*whispers to* MAMMON] if you please to quit us now, and come
Again within two hours, you shall have
My master busy examining o'the works;
And I will steal you in, unto the party,
That you may see her converse. [*Aloud to* SURLY.]
Sir, shall I say,
You'll meet the captain's worship?
SURLY. Sir, I will. [*Walks aside*.]
But, by attorney,[7] and to a second purpose.
Now, I am sure it is a bawdy-house;
I'll swear it, were the marshal here to thank me;
The naming this commander doth confirm it.
Don Face! Why he's the most authentic dealer
In these commodities, the superintendent
To all the quainter traffickers[8] in town!
He is the visitor, and does appoint
Who lies with whom, and at what hour; what price;
Which gown, and in what smock; what fall, what tire.[9]

5. Mineral stone. Surly is saying that if this is alchemy, he'd rather lose his money at cards.
6. "*Lutum sapientis*": wise man's glue, "*menstrum simplex*": plain solvent. Both phrases refer to Dol; Surly's road to wealth involves less danger from quicksilver or sulphur, both used to cure venereal diseases.
7. Through a representative, at second hand.
8. Traders in sex.
9. I.e., what ruff or collar the woman wears, how she dresses her hair.

Him will I prove by a third person, to find
The subtleties of this dark labyrinth;
Which if I do discover, dear sir Mammon,
You'll give your poor friend leave, though no philosopher,
To laugh; for you that are, 'tis thought, shall weep.[1]

FACE. Sir, he does pray, you'll not forget.

SURLY. I will not, sir.
Sir Epicure, I shall leave you.

MAMMON. I follow you, straight.

FACE. But do so, good sir, to avoid suspicion.
This gentleman has a parlous head.[2]

MAMMON. But wilt thou, Ulen,
Be constant to thy promise?

FACE. As my life, sir.

MAMMON. And wilt thou insinuate what I am, and praise me,
And say, I am a noble fellow?

FACE. O, what else, sir?
And that you'll make her royal with the stone,
An empress; and your self, king of Bantam.[3]

MAMMON. Wilt thou do this?

FACE. Will I, sir!

MAMMON. Lungs, my Lungs!
I love thee.

FACE. Send your stuff, sir, that my master
May busy himself about projection.

MAMMON. Thou has witched me, rogue; take, go.
[*Gives him money.*]

FACE. Your jack,[4] and all, sir.

MAMMON. Thou art a villain—I will send my jack,
And the weights too. Slave, I could bite thine ear.[5]
Away, thou dost not care for me.

FACE. Not I, sir!

MAMMON. Come, I was born to make thee, my good weasel,
Set thee on a bench, and have thee twirl a chain
With the best lord's vermin of 'em all.[6]

FACE. Away, sir.

MAMMON. A count, nay, a count palatine——

FACE. Good, sir, go.

MAMMON. Shall not advance thee better; no nor faster.
[*Exit.*]

SCENE 4

[*Enter* SUBTLE *and* DOL.]

SUBTLE. Has he bit? has he bit?

1. Surly plays on the old contrast between Democritus the laughing philosopher and Heraclitus the weeping philosopher.
2. Dangerously clever mind.
3. A rich East Indian kingdom.
4. An iron machine for turning a spit holding meat over the fire. It worked by means of weights on chains, wound up and allowed to unwind.
5. I.e., in exultant, erotic affection.
6. Lords are entitled to wear ermine trimming on their robes, playfully referred to as "vermin."

FACE. And swallowed too, my Subtle.
I have given him line, and now he plays, i' faith.
SUBTLE. And shall we twitch him?
FACE. Through both the gills.
A wench is a rare bait, with which a man
No sooner's taken, but he straights firks mad.[7]
SUBTLE. Dol, my lord What'shum's sister, you must now
Bear your self *statelich*.[8]
DOL. O let me alone.
I'll not forget my race, I warrant you.
I'll keep my distance, laugh and talk aloud,
Have all the tricks of a proud scurvy lady,
And be as rude as her woman.
FACE. Well said, sanguine![9]
SUBTLE. But will he send his andirons?
FACE. His jack, too,
And's iron shoeing-horn; I have spoke to him. Well,
I must not lose my wary gamester yonder.
SUBTLE. O monsieur Caution, that will not be gulled.
FACE. Ay,
If I can strike a fine hook into him, now!
The Temple-church, there I have cast mine angle.[1]
Well, pray for me. I'll about it. [*Knocking without.*]
SUBTLE. What, more gudgeons![2]
Dol, scout, scout! [DOL *goes to the window.*]
Stay, Face, you must go to the door.
'Pray God it be my anabaptist.[3] Who is't, Dol?
DOL. I know him not; he looks like a gold-end-man.[4]
SUBTLE. God's so! 'tis he, he said he would send——what call you him?
The sanctified elder,[5] that should deal
For Mammon's jack and andirons. Let him in.
Stay, help me off, first, with my gown. [*Exit* FACE *with the gown.*] Away
Madam, to your withdrawing chamber. [*Exit* DOL.] Now,
In a new tune, new gesture, but old language.
This fellow is sent from one negotiates with me
About the stone too; for the holy brethren
Of Amsterdam, the exiled saints,[6] that hope
To raise their discipline by it. I must use him
In some strange fashion, now, to make him admire me.

7. Runs mad, with the added overtone of sexual activity.
8. German for "stately," to suggest strangeness as well as dignity.
9. I.e., (be) confident.
1. Fishing line.
2. A proverbially simple-minded breed of small fish.
3. One of an extreme group of puritans.
4. A buyer of odds and ends of gold and silver.
5. Pastor of a puritan sect.
6. Amsterdam had a colony of English Puritans in exile who still maintained relations with the old country. Within a few years, some of them would depart for the New World, to become the Pilgrim Fathers.

SCENE 5

[*Enter* ANANIAS.]

SUBTLE. [*calling loudly*] Where is my drudge? [*Enter* FACE.]
FACE. Sir!
SUBTLE. Take away the recipient,
And rectify your menstrue from the phlegma.
Then pour it on the Sol, in the cucurbite,
And let them macerate together.[7]
FACE. Yes, sir
And save the ground?
SUBTLE. No: *terra damnata*[8]
Must not have entrance in the work. Who are you?
ANANIAS. A faithful brother, if it please you.
SUBTLE. What's that?
A Lullianist? a Ripley?[9] *Filius artis?*
Can you sublime and dulcify? calcine?
Know you the sapor pontic? sapor stiptic?[1]
Or what is homogene, or heterogene?
ANANIAS. I understand no heathen language, truly.
SUBTLE. Heathen, you Knipper-doling![2] is *Ars sacra,*
Or chrysopoeia, or spagyrica,
Or the pamphysic, or panarchic knowledge,[3]
A heathen language?
ANANIAS. Heathen Greek, I take it.
SUBTLE. How! heathen Greek?
ANANIAS. All's heathen but the Hebrew.[4]
SUBTLE. Sirrah, my varlet, stand you forth and speak to him,
Like a philosopher; answer, in the language.
Name the vexations, and the martyrizations
Of metals in the work.
FACE. Sir, putrefaction,
Solution, ablution, sublimation,
Cohobation, calcination, ceration, and
Fixation.
SUBTLE. This is heathen Greek to you, now?
And when comes vivification?
FACE. After mortification.
SUBTLE. What's cohobation?

7. This gibberish means something like, "Take a pot and develop a solvent from the mixture. Pour it on the gold in a retort and let them soak together."
8. Corrupt materials.
9. Subtle wants to know what "faith" Ananias holds to—that of Raymond Lull, the 13th-century Catalonian mystic, or George Ripley, the 15th-century English monk. Both were alchemists of renown. "Filius artis": son of the art, a general term for any alchemical devotee.
1. There are nine "sapors" or tastes in alchemy; "pontic" is very sour, "styptic" less so.
2. Bernt Knipperdoling was a leading figure in the bloody attempt of the Anabaptists to establish the kingdom of God in Münster, Germany, in 1534.
3. "Chrysopoeia" is gold-making, "spagyrica" is a fancy word for alchemy; but "pamphysic" and "panarchic knowledge" are coinages by Subtle.
4. As they preferred the Old Testament over the New, the Puritans tended to exalt Hebrew over any other tongue.

FACE. 'Tis the pouring on
Your aqua regis, and then drawing him off,
To the trine circle of the seven spheres.[5]
SUBTLE. What's the proper passion of metals?
FACE. Malleation.
SUBTLE. What's your *ultimum supplicium auri?*[6]
FACE. Antimonium.
SUBTLE. This is heathen Greek to you? And what's your mercury?
FACE. A very fugitive, he will be gone, sir.
SUBTLE. How know you him?
FACE. By his viscosity,
His oleosity, and his suscitability.[7]
SUBTLE. How do you sublime[8] him?
FACE. With the calce of egg-shells,
White marble, talc.
SUBTLE. Your *magisterium*,[9] now,
What's that?
FACE. Shifting, sir, your elements,
Dry into cold, cold into moist, moist into hot,
Hot into dry.
SUBTLE. This is heathen Greek to you still?
Your *lapis philosophicus?*[1]
FACE. 'Tis a stone,
And not a stone; a spirit, a soul, and a body;
Which if you do dissolve, it is dissolved;
If you coagulate, it is coagulated;
If you make it to fly, it flieth.
SUBTLE. Enough. [*Exit* FACE.]
This is heathen Greek to you? What are you, sir?
ANANIAS. Please you, a servant of the exiled brethren,
That deal with widows and with orphans' goods;
And make a just account unto the saints,
A deacon.
SUBTLE. O, you are sent from master Wholesome,
Your teacher?
ANANIAS. From Tribulation Wholesome,
Our very zealous pastor.
SUBTLE. Good! I have
Some orphans' goods to come here.
ANANIAS. Of what kind, sir?
SUBTLE. Pewter and brass, andirons and kitchen-ware,
Metals, that we must use our medicine on,
Wherein the brethren may have a pennyworth
For ready money.

5. Alchemical jargon is being enriched by jargon from astrology.
6. Antimony is the "final punishment of gold," because it hardens and fixes the gold.
7. Activity.
8. Sublimate, purify.
9. Masterwork.
1. Philosopher's stone.

ANANIAS. Were the orphans' parents
Sincere professors?[2]
SUBTLE. Why do you ask?
ANANIAS. Because
We then are to deal justly, and give in truth
Their utmost value.
SUBTLE. 'Slid, you'd cozen else,
And if their parents were not of the faithful?
I will not trust you, now I think on it,
'Till I have talked with your pastor. Have you brought money
To buy more coals?
ANANIAS. No, surely.
SUBTLE. No! how so?
ANANIAS. The brethren bid me say unto you, sir,
Surely they will not venture any more
Till they may see projection.
SUBTLE. How!
ANANIAS. You have had,
For the instruments, as bricks and loam and glasses,
Already thirty pound; and for materials,
They say, some ninety more; and they have heard since,
That one at Heidelberg made it of an egg,
And a small paper of pin-dust.
SUBTLE. What's your name?
ANANIAS. My name is Ananias.
SUBTLE. Out, the varlet
That cozened the apostles! Hence, away!
Flee, mischief! had your holy consistory
No name to send me, of another sound,
Than wicked Ananias?[3] send your elders
Hither, to make atonement for you, quickly,
And give me satisfaction; or out goes
The fire; and down th'alembics, and the furnace,
Piger Henricus,[4] or what not. Thou wretch!
Both sericon and bufo[5] shall be lost,
Tell them. All hope of rooting out the bishops,
Or the antichristian hierarchy, shall perish,
If they stay threescore minutes. The aqueity,
Terreity, and sulphureity[6]
Shall run together again, and all be annulled,
Thou wicked Ananias! [*Exit* ANANIAS.] This will fetch 'em,
And make them haste towards their gulling more.
A man must deal like a rough nurse, and fright
Those that are froward, to an appetite.

2. Good Puritans protestants, of our cause.
3. Ananias tried to cheat the Apostles; his failure and its consequences are described in the Acts of the Apostles, chapter 5.
4. Literally, "Lazy Henry," a many-chambered furnace heated by a single fire.
5. The red and black stages of the experiment.
6. Water, earth, and sulphur, all the ingredients of the mixture.

SCENE 6

[FACE *in his captain's uniform,* SUBTLE, DRUGGER.]

FACE. He is busy with his spirits, but we'll upon him.
SUBTLE. How now! what mates, what Bayards[7] have we here?
FACE. I told you, he would be furious. Sir, here's Nab,
Has brought you another piece of gold to look on;
[*Aside to* DRUGGER.]
—We must appease him. Give it me.—and prays you,
You would devise—what is it, Nab?
DRUGGER. A sign, sir.
FACE. Ay, a good lucky one, a thriving sign, doctor.
SUBTLE. I was devising now.
FACE. [*Aside to* SUBTLE.] 'Slight, do not say so,
He will repent he gave you any more—
What say you to his constellation, doctor,
The Balance?[8]
SUBTLE. No, that way is stale, and common.
A townsman born in Taurus, gives the bull,
Or the bull's head; in Aries, the ram.
A poor device! No, I will have his name
Formed in some mystic character, whose radii,
Striking the senses of the passers by,
Shall, by a virtual influence, breed affections,
That may result upon the party owns it:
As thus——
FACE. Nab!
SUBTLE. He shall have *a bell,* that's *Abel;*
And by it standing one whose name is *Dee,*
In a *rug* gown, there's D, and *Rug,* that's *drug;*
And right anenst him a dog snarling *Er;*[9]
There's *Drugger,* Abel Drugger. That's his sign.
And here's now mystery and hieroglyphic![1]
FACE. Abel, thou art made.
DRUGGER. Sir, I do thank his worship.
FACE. Six o' thy legs[2] more will not do it, Nab.
He has brought you a pipe of tobacco, doctor.
DRUGGER. Yes, sir.
I have another thing I would impart——
FACE. Out with it, Nab.
DRUGGER. Sir, there is lodged, hard by me,
A rich young widow——

7. The chevalier Bayard was a daredevil soldier of the early 16th century, hence any bold and reckless fellow.
8. The Scales, a zodiacal sign naturally suited to a merchant.
9. Doctor John Dee was a well-known alchemist in Jonson's London. A rug gown is one made of rough wool, and "Er" is a rather strained representation of "Grrr."
1. The ancient Egyptians, especially their mythical mage Hermes Trismegistus, were thought to be the true founders of alchemy, which they expressed in hieroglyphics. But what Subtle has made is a rebus.
2. Scrapes and bows.

FACE. Good! a bona roba?[3]
DRUGGER. But nineteen, at the most.
FACE. Very good, Abel.
DRUGGER. Marry, she's not in fashion yet; she wears
A hood, but it stands a cop.[4]
FACE. No matter, Abel.
DRUGGER. And I do now and then give her a fucus[5]—
FACE. What! dost thou deal,[6] Nab?
SUBTLE. I did tell you, captain.
DRUGGER. And physic too, sometimes, sir; for which she trusts me
With all her mind. She's come up here of purpose
To learn the fashion.
FACE. Good (his match too!)—On, Nab.
DRUGGER. And she does strangely long to know her fortune.
FACE. God's lid, Nab, send her to the doctor, hither.
DRUGGER. Yes, I have spoke to her of his worship already;
But she's afraid it will be blown abroad,[7]
And hurt her marriage.
FACE. Hurt it! 'tis the way
To heal it, if 'twere hurt; to make it more
Followed and sought. Nab, thou shalt tell her this:
She'll be more known, more talked of; and your widows
Are ne'er of any price till they be famous;
Their honor is their multitude of suitors.
Send her, it may be *thy* good fortune. What?
Thou dost not know.
DRUGGER. No, sir, she'll never marry
Under a knight; her brother has made a vow.
FACE. What! and dost thou despair, my little Nab,
Knowing what the doctor has set down for thee,
And seeing so many of the city dubbed?
One glass o' thy water, with a madam I know,
Will have it done, Nab[8]. What's her brother, a knight?
DRUGGER. No, sir, a gentleman newly warm in his land, sir,
Scarce cold in his one-and-twenty, that does govern
His sister here; and is a man himself
Of some three thousand a year, and is come up
To learn to quarrel, and to live by his wits,
And will go down again, and die in the country.
FACE. How! to quarrel?
DRUGGER. Yes, sir, to carry quarrels,
As gallants do, and manage them by line.[9]

3. Literally, "well dressed," but also implying "available" and even suggesting whoredom.
4. Hoods were out of fashion; the lady's came to a point, which amounted to making the best of a bad job.
5. The materials of make-up—cosmetics being unusual at the time, especially among young women.
6. Do you trade underhandedly or out of your field?
7. Noised about.
8. Given a specimen of Drugger's urine, a witch can enchant the lady into loving him.
9. The code of dueling had many elaborate rules, which Jonson was fond of satirizing. Alchemists didn't really give rules for getting into fights, but Jonson imagines Subtle doing so.

FACE. 'Slid, Nab, the doctor is the only man
In Christendom for him. He has made a table,
With mathematical demonstrations,
Touching the art of quarrels; he will give him
An instrument to quarrel by. Go, bring them both,
Him and his sister. And, for thee, with her
The doctor haply may persuade. Go to;
'Shalt give his worship a new damask suit
Upon the premises.[1]
SUBTLE. O, good captain!
FACE. He shall;
He is the honestest fellow, doctor.—Stay not,
No offers; bring the damask, and the parties.
DRUGGER. I'll try my power, sir.
FACE. And thy will too, Nab.
SUBTLE. 'Tis good tobacco, this! what is't an ounce?
FACE. He'll send you a pound, doctor.
SUBTLE. O, no.
FACE. He will do't.
It is the goodest soul! Abel, about it.
Thou shalt know more anon. Away, be gone. [*Exit* ABEL.]
A miserable rogue, and lives with cheese,
And has the worms.[2] That was the cause, indeed,
Why he came now. He dealt with me in private,
To get a med'cine for them.
SUBTLE. And shall, sir. This works.
FACE. A wife, a wife for one of us, my dear Subtle!
We'll e'en draw lots, and he that fails, shall have
The more in goods, the other has in tail.[3]
SUBTLE. Rather the less; for she may be so light
She may want grains.[4]
FACE. Ay, or be such a burden,
A man would scarce endure her for the whole.
SUBTLE. Faith, best let's see her first, and then determine.
FACE. Content. But Dol must have no breath on't.
SUBTLE. Mum.
Away you, to your Surly yonder, catch him.
FACE. 'Pray God I have not stayed too long.
SUBTLE I fear it.
[*Exeunt.*]

Act III

SCENE 1. *The lane before* LOVEWIT'S *house*

[*Enter* TRIBULATION WHOLESOME, *and* ANANIAS.]

TRIBULATION. These chastisements are common to the saints,

1. To get the good work started.
2. Cheese, which often had mites in it, was thought to cause worms.
3. With a sexual meaning, but also with a glance at the legal expression "entail," in the sense of a commitment of future property.
4. Need extra ballast to make legal weight.

And such rebukes we of the separation[5]
Must bear with willing shoulders, as the trials
Sent forth to tempt our frailties.

ANANIAS. In pure zeal,[6]
I do not like the man; he is a heathen,
And speaks the language of Canaan, truly.[7]

TRIBULATION. I think him a profane person indeed.

ANANIAS. He bears
The visible mark of the beast[8] in his forehead.
And for his stone, it is a work of darkness,
And with philosophy blinds the eyes of man.

TRIBULATION. Good brother, we must bend unto all means,
That may give furtherance to the holy cause.

ANANIAS. Which his cannot; the sanctified cause
Should have a sanctified course.

TRIBULATION Not always necessary.
The children of perdition are oft-times
Made instruments even of the greatest works.
Beside, we should give somewhat to man's nature,[9]
The place he lives in, still about the fire,
And fume of metals, that intoxicate
The brain of man, and make him prone to passion.
Where have you greater atheists than your cooks?
Or more profane, or choleric, than your glass-men?[1]
More antichristian than your bell-founders?
What makes the devil so devilish, I would ask you,
Satan our common enemy, but his being
Perpetually about the fire, and boiling
Brimstone and arsenic? We must give, I say,
Unto the motives, and the stirrers up
Of humors in the blood. It may be so,
When as the work is done, the stone is made,
This heat of his may turn into a zeal,
And stand up for the beauteous discipline,
Against the menstruous cloth and rag of Rome.[2]
We must await his calling, and the coming
Of the good spirit. You did fault, t' upbraid him
With the brethren's blessing of Heidelberg, weighing
What need we have to hasten on the work,

5. I.e. separated from the Church of England, which extreme Puritans considered too corrupt to be reformed.

6. Some Puritans cultivated zeal or enthusiasm in preference to reason or learning; their enemies accused all Puritans of doing so.

7. Likening themselves to the Jews as specially chosen people, the Puritans often referred to their opponents as pagans—Philistines, Canaanites, etc.

8. As a consequence of their addiction to the prophecies in the Book of Revelation, the Puritans sought in their enemies the mark of that "beast" who they thought stood in the way of Christ's second coming.

9. I.e., concede something to the frailties of human nature and the peculiar situation of the alchemist.

1. Glass-blowers, subject to unusual temptations because of their fiery calling.

2. The "beauteous discipline" is that established by John Calvin in his *Institutes,* and exemplified in the city of Geneva; the rags and tatters of Rome (i.e., Roman Catholicism) were a standard feature of Puritan rhetoric.

For the restoring of the silenced saints,[3]
Which ne'er will be, but by the philosopher's stone.
And so a learned elder, one of Scotland,
Assured me; *aurum potabile* being
The only medicine, for the civil magistrate,[4]
T' incline him to a feeling of the cause,
And must be daily used in the disease.

ANANIAS. I have not edified more, truly, by man,
Not since the beautiful light first shone on me;
And I am sad my zeal hath so offended.

TRIBULATION. Let us call on him then.

ANANIAS. The motion's[5] good,
And of the spirit; I will knock first. [*Knocks.*] Peace be within!
[*The door is opened, and they enter.*]

SCENE 2. *A room in* LOVEWIT'S *house*

[SUBTLE *opens the door to* TRIBULATION *and* ANANIAS.]

SUBTLE. O, are you come? 'Twas time. Your threescore minutes
Were at the last thread, you see; and down had gone
Furnus acediae, turris circulatorius,[6]
Limbec, bolt's-head, retort, and pelican
Had all been cinders. Wicked Ananias!
Art thou returned? Nay then, it goes down yet.

TRIBULATION. Sir, be appeased; he is come to humble
Himself in spirit, and to ask your patience,
If too much zeal hath carried him aside
From the due path.

SUBTLE. Why, this doth qualify!

TRIBULATION. The brethren had no purpose, verily,
To give you the least grievance: but are ready
To lend their willing hands to any project
The spirit and you direct.

SUBTLE. This qualifies more!

TRIBULATION. And for the orphans' goods, let them be valued,
Or what is needful else to the holy work,
It shall be numbered; here, by me, the saints
Throw down their purse before you.

SUBTLE. This qualifies most!
Why, thus it should be, now you understand.
Have I discoursed so unto you of our stone,
And of the good that it shall bring your cause?
Showed you (beside the main of hiring forces
Abroad, drawing the Hollanders, your friends,

3. I.e., those Puritan reformers who had been dismissed from their posts in the Church of England (silenced) for preaching against its ruling bishops.

4. I.e., bribery is the only way to reform the civil government.

5. Impulse, idea.

6. "*Furnus acediae,*" or the furnace of sloth, is like "Piger Henricus," or Lazy Henry, above, a furnace with several chambers but only one fire. "*Turris circulatorius,*" or circulating tower, is a kind of elaborate still.

From the Indies, to serve you, with all their fleet)[7]
That even the medicinal use shall make you a faction,
And party in the realm? As, put the case,
That some great man in state, he have the gout,
Why, you but send three drops of your elixir,
You help him straight: there you have made a friend.
Another has the palsy or the dropsy,
He takes of your incombustible stuff,[8]
He's young again: there you have made a friend.
A lady that is past the feat of body,
Though not of mind, and hath her face decayed
Beyond all cure of paintings, you restore,
With the oil of talc: there you have made a friend,
And all her friends. A lord that is a leper,
A knight that has the bone-ache,[9] or a squire
That hath both these, you make them smooth and sound,[1]
With a bare fricace[1] of your medicine: still
You increase your friends.

TRIBULATION. Ay, it is very pregnant.

SUBTLE. And then the turning of this lawyer's pewter
To plate at Christmas—

ANANIAS. Christ-tide, I pray you.[2]

SUBTLE. Yet, Ananias!

ANANIAS. I have done.

SUBTLE. Or changing
His parcel gilt[3] to massy gold. You cannot
But raise you friends. Withal, to be of power
To pay an army in the field, to buy
The king of France out of his realms, or Spain
Out of his Indies. What can you not do
Against lords spiritual or temporal,
That shall oppone you?

TRIBULATION. Verily, 'tis true.
We may be temporal lords ourselves, I take it.

SUBTLE. You may be anything, and leave off to make
Long-winded exercises; or suck up
Your *ha!* and *hum!* in a tune. I not deny,
But such as are not graced in a state,
May, for their ends, be adverse in religion,
And get a tune to call the flock together.
For, to say sooth, a tune does much with women,
And other phlegmatic people; it is your bell.[4]

7. Through Subtle's mouth, Jonson accuses the Puritans directly of treachery, in hoping to hire the Dutch to mount an attack on England.

8. I.e., so perfectly tempered it would neither decay nor burn.

9. Syphilis.

1. Rubdown.

2. Because "Christmas" included the hateful word "mass," the Puritans preferred to call it "Christ-tide" or, more elaborately, "the day of Christ's nativity."

3. Silverware covered with gold plate or simply gilded.

4. Puritans were famous for singing psalms; Subtle equates this with bell-ringing, but Ananias will have none of it, thinking bells to be rags of popery and superstition.

ANANIAS. Bells are profane; a tune may be religious.
SUBTLE. No warning with you? then farewell my patience.
'Slight, it shall down; I will not be thus tortured.
TRIBULATION. I pray you, sir.
SUBTLE. All shall perish. I have spoke it.
TRIBULATION. Let me find grace, sir, in your eyes; the man
He stands corrected; neither did his zeal,
But as yourself, allow a tune somewhere.[5]
Which now, being toward the stone, we shall not need.
SUBTLE. No, nor your holy vizard, to win widows
To give you legacies; or make zealous wives
To rob their husbands for the common cause;
Nor take the start of bonds broke but one day,
And say, they were forfeited by providence.[6]
Nor shall you need o'ernight to eat huge meals,
To celebrate your next day's fast the better,
The whilst the brethren and the sisters humbled,
Abate the stiffness of the flesh. Nor cast
Before your hungry hearers scrupulous bones;
As whether a Christian may hawk or hunt,
Or whether matrons of the holy assembly
May lay their hair out, or wear doublets,
Or have that idol starch about their linen.
ANANIAS. It is indeed an idol.
TRIBULATION. Mind him not, sir.
I do command thee, spirit of zeal, but trouble,
To peace within him! Pray you, sir, go on.
SUBTLE. Nor shall you need to libel 'gainst the prelates,
And shorten so your ears against the hearing
Of the next wire-drawn grace.[7] Nor of necessity
Rail against plays, to please the alderman
Whose daily custard you devour. Nor lie
With zealous rage till you are hoarse. Not one
Of these so singular arts. Nor call your selves
By names of Tribulation, Persecution,
Restraint, Long-patience, and such like, affected
By the whole family or wood[8] of you,
Only for glory, and to catch the ear
Of the disciple.
TRIBULATION. Truly, sir, they are
Ways that the godly brethren have invented,
For propagation of the glorious cause,
As very notable means, and whereby also

5. Tribulation tries to smooth things over by saying everyone considers "tunes" (psalms) to be lawful.

6. Puritans, being generally of the middle class and subject to the frailties of petty merchants, were often reproached with the difference between their scruples in religion and their sharp commercial practice.

7. Libeling the prelates (bishops) sometimes led Puritans to the pillory, where their ears might well be clipped. At least, Subtle says, that will make it easier for them to sit through the next long-drawn-out Puritan sermon.

8. Clutch, gang, tribe.

Themselves grow soon, and profitably, famous.
SUBTLE. O, but the stone, all's idle to it! nothing!
The art of angels, nature's miracle,
The divine secret that doth fly in clouds
From east to west; and whose tradition
Is not from men, but spirits.
ANANIAS. I hate traditions;[9]
I do not trust them——
TRIBULATION. Peace!
ANANIAS. They are popish all.
I will not peace. I will not——
TRIBULATION. Ananias!
ANANIAS. Please the profane, to grieve the godly; I may not.
SUBTLE. Well, Ananias, thou shall overcome.
TRIBULATION. It is an ignorant zeal that haunts him, sir:
But truly, else, a very faithful brother,
A botcher,[1] and a man, by revelation,
That hath a competent knowledge of the truth.
SUBTLE. Has he a competent sum there in the bag
To buy the goods within? I am made guardian,
And must, for charity, and conscience sake,
Now see the most be made for my poor orphans;
Though I desire the brethren too good gainers.
There they are within. When you have viewed and bought 'em,
And ta'en the inventory of what they are,
They are ready for projection; there's no more
To do. Cast on the medicine, so much silver
As there is tin there, so much gold as brass,
I'll give't you in by weight.
TRIBULATION. But how long time,
Sir, must the saints expect yet?[2]
SUBTLE. Let me see,
How's the moon now? Eight, nine, ten days hence,
He will be silver potate;[3] then three days
Before he citronise; some fifteen days,
The magisterium will be perfected.
ANANIAS. About the second day of the third week,
In the ninth month?[4]
SUBTLE. Yes, my good Ananias.
TRIBULATION. What will the orphans' goods arise[5] to, think you?

9. Mere human traditions (of councils, church-fathers, or other church-authorities), were of no force against the pure, undiluted word of God in the Scriptures.
1. A low-grade tailor who patches clothes.
2. The "saints" were always expecting the second coming, so their language adapts naturally to the dream of the philosopher's stone.
3. The moon must turn first to liquid silver, then yellow like a lemon ("citronise") before turning rosy red when projection is completed. Making the philosopher's stone takes just about as long as it does to make a normal human baby, and analogies are constantly implied between the two processes.
4. The Puritans avoided the normal English names of the months as "pagan."
5. Amount.

SUBTLE. Some hundred marks, as much as filled three cars,
Unladed now: you'll make six million of them.
But I must have more coals laid in.
TRIBULATION. How!
SUBTLE. Another load,
And then we've finished. We must now increase
Our fire to *ignis ardens*, we are past
Fimus equinus, balnei, cineris,[6]
And all those lenter heats. If the holy purse
Should with this draught fall low, and that the saints
Do need a present sum, I have a trick
To melt the pewter, you shall buy now, instantly,
And with a tincture make you as good Dutch dollars
As any are in Holland.[7]
TRIBULATION. Can you so?
SUBTLE. Aye, and shall 'bide the third examination.
ANANIAS. It will be joyful tidings to the brethren.
SUBTLE. But you must carry it secret.
TRIBULATION. Ay, but stay,
This act of coining, is it lawful?
ANANIAS. Lawful!
We know no magistrate; or, if we did,
This is foreign coin.
SUBTLE. It is no coining, sir.
It is but casting.
TRIBULATION. Ha! you distinguish well.
Casting of money may be lawful.
ANANIAS. 'Tis, sir.
TRIBULATION. Truly, I take it so.
SUBTLE. There is no scruple,
Sir, to be made of it; believe Ananias.
This case of conscience he is studied in.
TRIBULATION. I'll make a question of it to the brethren.
ANANIAS. The brethren shall approve it lawful, doubt not.
Where shall it be done? [*Knocking without.*]
SUBTLE. For that we'll talk anon.
There's some to speak with me. Go in, I pray you,
And view the parcels. That's the inventory.
I'll come to you straight. [*Exeunt* TRIBULATION *and* ANANIAS.]
Who is it? [*He gestures, as if conjuring.*]—Face! appear!

SCENE 3

[*Enter* FACE *in his uniform.*]
How now! good prize?

6. In the graduated series of heats, they have passed "*Fimus equinus*" (horse manure), "*balnei*" (the double boiler), and "*cineris*" (ashes), all "lenter," or more moderate, heats; now is the time for "*ignis ardens*," or glowing fire.
7. Pewter, which is tin and lead, can be made to look like silver coins.

FACE. Good pox! yond' costive[8] cheater
Never came on.
SUBTLE. How then?
FACE. I have walked the round
Till now, and no such thing.
SUBTLE. And have you quit him?
FACE. Quit him! an hell would quit him too, he were happy.
Slight! would you have me stalk like a mill-jade,
All day, for one that will not yield us grains?
I know him of old.
SUBTLE. O, but to have gulled him,
Had been a mastery.
FACE. Let him go, black boy![9]
And turn thee, that some fresh news may possess thee.
A noble count, a don of Spain (my dear
Delicious compeer, and my party-bawd),
Who is come hither private for his conscience,
And brought munition with him, six great slops,[1]
Bigger than three Dutch hoys, beside round trunks.
Furnished with pistolets, and pieces of eight,
Will straight be here, my rogue, to have thy bath[2]
(That is the color), and to make his battery
Upon our Dol, our castle, our cinque-port,[3]
Our Dover pier, our what thou wilt. Where is she?
She must prepare perfumes, delicate linen,
The bath in chief, a banquet, and her wit,
For she must milk his epididymis.[4]
Where is the doxy?
SUBTLE. I'll send her to thee,
And but dispatch my brace of little John Leydens,[5]
And come again myself.
FACE. Are they within then?
SUBTLE. Numbering the sum.
FACE. How much?
SUBTLE. A hundred marks, boy.
[*Exit.*]
FACE. Why, this is a lucky day. Ten pounds of Mammon!
Three of my clerk! a portague of my grocer!
This of the brethren! beside reversions,
And states to come in the widow, and my count!
My share today will not be bought for forty—
[*Enter* DOL.]

8. I.e., Surly.
9. Subtle wears a black academic robe, and is dark from attending his smoky furnaces.
1. Loose-fitting trousers, bigger than "Dutch hoys" (i.e., fishing boats), in addition to "round trunks," i.e., the kind of hose that puff out around the waist.
2. A specially luxurious bath, furnished in high-class whorehouses as a preliminary ceremony; "color": pretext.
3. The five channel ports, through which England could most easily be entered from the Continent. Dover pier was where most travelers from abroad first disembarked.
4. Seminal vesicles.
5. I.e., Anabaptist or Puritan leaders—after John Bockelhausen, who came from Leyden in Holland, and led the fanatical Puritan insurrection at Münster in 1534.

DOL. What?
FACE. Pounds, dainty Dorothy! art thou so near?
DOL. Yes; say, lord General, how fares our camp?
FACE. As with the few that had entrenched themselves
Safe, by their discipline, against a world, Dol;
And laughed within those trenches, and grew fat
With thinking on the booties, Dol, brought in
Daily by their small parties. This dear hour,
A doughty don is taken with my Dol;
And thou mayst make his ransom what thou wilt,
My Dousabel;[6] he shall be brought here fettered
With thy fair looks, before he sees thee; and thrown
In a down-bed, as dark as any dungeon;
Where thou shalt keep him waking with thy drum;
Thy drum, my Dol, thy drum; till he be tame
As the poor blackbirds were in the great frost,[7]
Or bees are with a basin; and so hive him
In the swan-skin coverlid, and cambric sheets,
Till he work honey and wax, my little God's-gift.[8]
DOL. What is he, General?
FACE. An adalantado,[9]
A grandee, girl. Was not my Dapper here yet?
DOL. No.
FACE. Nor my Drugger?
DOL. Neither.
FACE. A pox on 'em,
They are so long a furnishing! such stinkards
Would not be seen upon these festival days. [*Enter* SUBTLE]
How now! have you done?
SUBTLE. Done. They are gone. The sum
Is here in bank, my Face. I would we knew
Another chapman[1] now would buy 'em outright.
FACE. 'Slid, Nab shall do't against he have the widow,
To furnish household.
SUBTLE. Excellent, well thought on;
Pray God he come.
FACE. I pray he keep away
Till our new business be o'erpassed.
SUBTLE. But, Face,
How cam'st thou by this secret don?
FACE. A spirit
Brought me th' intelligence in a paper here,
As I was conjuring yonder in my circle
For Surly; I have my flies abroad.[2] Your bath
Is famous, Subtle, by my means. Sweet Dol,

6. From French *douce et belle,* "sweet and lovely"; but often used of a hoyden.
7. During the winter of 1607–8 the Thames froze over, and the blackbirds obviously suffered. Swarming bees were attracted by banging on a basin.
8. Dorothy (like its male counterpart Theodore) means "God's gift" in Greek.
9. Mayor or governor (Spanish); "grandee": dignitary.
1. Merchant.
2. What happened was simply that he was handed a written note as he walked around looking for Surly.

You must go tune your virginal,[3] no losing
O' the least time. And, do you hear? good action.
Firk, like a flounder; kiss, like a scallop, close;
And tickle him with thy mother-tongue. His great
Verdugoship[4] has not a jot of language;
So much the easier to be cozen'd, my Dolly.
He will come here in a hired coach, obscure,
And our own coachman, whom I have sent as guide,
No creature else. [*Knocking without.*] Who's that? [*Exit* DOL.]

SUBTLE. It is not he?

FACE. O no, not yet this hour.

[*Re-enter* DOL.]

SUBTLE. Who is't?

DOL. Dapper,
Your clerk.

FACE. God's will then, Queen of Fairy,
On with your tire; [*Exit* DOL.] and, Doctor, with your robes.
Let's dispatch him for God's sake.

SUBTLE. 'Twill be long.

FACE. I warrant you, take but the cues I give you,
It shall be brief enough. [*Goes to the window.*]
'Slight, here are more!
Abel, and I think the angry boy, the heir,
That fain would quarrel.

SUBTLE. And the widow?

FACE. No,
Not that I see. Away! [*Exit* SUBTLE.]

SCENE 4

[*Enter* DAPPER.]

O sir, you are welcome.
The doctor is within a moving for you;
I have had the most ado to win him to it!
He swears you'll be the darling of the dice.
He never heard her highness dote till now.
Your aunt has given you the most gracious words
That can be thought on.

DAPPER. Shall I see her grace?

FACE. See her, and kiss her too.

[*Enter* ABEL, *followed by* KASTRIL.]

What, honest Nab!
Hast brought the damask?

DRUGGER. No, sir; here's tobacco.

FACE. 'Tis well done, Nab; thou'lt bring the damask too?

DRUGGER. Yes. Here's the gentleman, Captain, master Kastril,
I have brought to see the Doctor.

FACE. Where's the widow?

3. Put your harpsichord in tune (with obvious *double-entendre*).

4. From the Spanish word for "hangman."

DRUGGER. Sir, as he likes, his sister, he says, shall come.
FACE. O, is it so? good time. Is your name Kastril, sir?
KASTRIL. Ay, and the best of the Kastrils, I'd be sorry else,
By fifteen hundred a year.[5] Where is this Doctor?
My mad tobacco-boy, here, tells me of one
That can do things: has he any skill?
FACE. Wherein, sir?
KASTRIL. To carry a business, manage a quarrel fairly,
Upon fit terms.
FACE. It seems, sir, you're but young
About the town, that can make that a question.
KASTRIL. Sir, not so young, but I have heard some speech
Of the angry boys,[6] and seen 'em take tobacco;
And in his shop; and I can take it too.
And I would fain be one of 'em, and go down
And practice in the country.
FACE. Sir, for the duello,
The doctor, I assure you, shall inform you,
To the least shadow of a hair; and show you
An instrument he has of his own making,
Wherewith no sooner shall you make report
Of any quarrel, but he will take the height on't
Most instantly, and tell in what degree
Of safety it lies in, or mortality.[7]
And how it may be borne, whether in a right line,
Or a half circle; or may else be cast
Into an angle blunt, if not acute:
All this he will demonstrate.[8] And then, rules
To give and take the lie by.
KASTRIL. How! to take it?
FACE. Yes, in oblique he'll show you, or in circle;
But never in diameter.[9] The whole town
Study his theorems, and dispute them ordinarily
At the eating academies.[1]
KASTRIL. But does he teach
Living by the wits too?
FACE. Anything whatever.
You cannot think that subtlety but he reads it.
He made me a Captain. I was a stark pimp,
Just of your standing, 'fore I met with him,
It is not two months since. I'll tell you his method.
First, he will enter you at some ordinary.[2]

5. If he weren't an elder son, he wouldn't have an estate of this value.
6. Town swaggerers and bullies; taking tobacco, as a new art, required some skill and practice.
7. Subtle's "instrument" is some kind of chart on which one can look up any particular quarrel and discover how serious it is ("the height on't"), how safely it may be embarked on, and what is the danger of getting killed in it ("mortality").
8. The art of quarreling is the art, not of encountering an opponent directly, but of coming at him on an angle, social or political.
9. I.e., the lie direct. One may adjust to being sort of a liar but not in so many words.
1. Common taverns or public houses.
2. Public eating-house, tavern.

KASTRIL. No, I'll not come there; you shall pardon me.
FACE. For why, sir?
KASTRIL. There's gaming there, and tricks.
FACE. Why, would you be
A gallant, and not game?
KASTRIL. Ay, 'twill spend[3] a man.
FACE. Spend you! it will repair you when you are spent.
How do they live by their wits there, that have vented
Six times your fortunes?
KASTRIL. What, three thousand a year!
FACE. Ay, forty thousand.
KASTRIL. Are there such?
FACE. Ay, sir,
And gallants yet. Here's a young gentleman
Is born to nothing, [*points to* DAPPER] forty marks a year,
Which I count nothing. He is to be initiated,
And have a fly[4] of the doctor. He will win you,
By unresistible luck, within this fortnight,
Enough to buy a barony. They will set him
Upmost, at the groom porter's, all the Christmas,[5]
And for the whole year through, at every place,
Where there is play, present him with the chair;
The best attendance, the best drink; sometimes
Two glasses of canary, and pay nothing;
The purest linen, and the sharpest knife,
The partridge next his trencher; and somewhere
The dainty bed in private with the dainty.
You shall have your ordinaries bid for him,
As playhouses for a poet; and the master
Pray him aloud to name what dish he affects,
Which must be buttered shrimps: and those that drink
To no mouth else, will drink to his, as being
The goodly president mouth of all the board.[6]
KASTRIL. Do you not gull one?
FACE. 'Ods my life! do you think it?
You shall have a cast commander (can but get
In credit with a glover, or a spurrier,
For some two pair of either's ware aforehand),
Will, by most swift posts, dealing with him,
Arrive at competent means to keep himself,[7]
His punk and naked boy, in excellent fashion,
And be admired for't.
KASTRIL. Will the doctor teach this?

3. Bankrupt.
4. A familiar spirit.
5. The groom porter was in charge of gambling at the court; Christmas, and the period of twelfth-night associated with it, were the gambling season. To be "set upmost" on these occasions is to head up the gambling table.
6. I.e., those who will drink a toast to nobody else will be glad to toast him.
7. I.e., a dismissed soldier, who can get credit only for a pair of gloves or spurs, will quickly make a fortune under his guidance.

FACE. He will do more, sir; when your land is gone,
(As men of spirit hate to keep earth long)[8]
In a vacation, when small money is stirring,
And ordinaries suspended till the term,
He'll show a perspective,[9] where on one side
You shall behold the faces and the persons
Of all sufficient young heirs in town,
Whose bonds are current for commodity;
On th' other side, the merchants' forms, and others,
That without help of any second broker,
Who would expect a share, will trust such parcels:
In the third square, the very street and sign
Where the commodity dwells, and does but wait
To be delivered, be it pepper, soap,
Hops, or tobacco, oatmeal, woad,[1] or cheeses.
All which you may so handle, to enjoy
To your own use, and never stand obliged.

KASTRIL. I' faith! is he such a fellow?

FACE. Why, Nab here knows him.
And then for making matches for rich widows,
Young gentlewomen, heirs, the fortunat'st man!
He's sent to, far and near, all over England
To have his counsel and to know their fortunes.

KASTRIL. God's will, my suster[2] shall see him.

FACE. I'll tell you, sir,
What he did tell me of Nab. It's a strange thing!—
(By the way, you must eat no cheese, Nab, it breeds melancholy,
And that same melancholy breeds worms; but pass it)—
He told me, honest Nab here was ne'er at tavern
But once in's life!

DRUGGER. Truth, and no more I was not.

FACE. And then he was so sick—

DRUGGER. Could he tell you that too?

FACE. How should I know it?

DRUGGER. In troth we had been a shooting,
And had a piece of fat ram-mutton to supper,
That lay so heavy o' my stomach—

FACE. And he has no head
To bear any wine; for what with the noise of the fiddlers,
And care of his shop, for he dares keep no servants—

DRUGGER. My head did so ache—

FACE. As he was fain to be brought home,

8. Land was the safest and most prestigious investment in Jonson's day; Face affects to despise it, because active and stirring people know where the action really is.

9. Image, chart.

1. A dyestuff. The racket is to discover some desperate young heir-to-be who, in his anxiety to borrow money, has been forced to accept some part of the loan in damaged commodities; having no particular use for them, he leaves them in a warehouse, where a sly operator can easily appropriate them.

2. Kastril comes from the country, probably the West Country, and tends to pronounce the *ih* sound *uh—suster* for *sister, kuss* for *kiss.*

The Doctor told me; and then a good old woman—
DRUGGER. Yes, faith, she dwells in Sea-coal-lane,—did cure me,
With sodden ale, and pellitory of the wall;[3]
Cost me but twopence. I had another sickness
Was worse than that.
FACE. Ay, that was with the grief
Thou took'st for being cessed at eighteenpence,
For the water-work.[4]
DRUGGER. In truth, and it was like
T' have cost me almost my life.
FACE. Thy hair went off?
DRUGGER. Yes, sir; 'twas done for spite.
FACE. Nay, so says the Doctor.
KASTRIL. Pray thee, tobacco-boy, go fetch my suster;
I'll see this learned boy before I go;
And so shall she.
FACE. Sir, he is busy now:
But if you have a sister to fetch hither,
Perhaps your own pains may command her sooner;
And he by that time will be free.
KASTRIL. I go. [*Exit* KASTRIL.]
FACE. Drugger, she's thine: the damask!—[*Exit* ABEL.]
[*aside*] Subtle and I
Must wrestle for her.—Come on, master Dapper,
You see how I turn clients here away,
To give your cause despatch. Have you performed
The ceremonies were enjoined you?
DAPPER. Yes, of the vinegar,
And the clean shirt.
FACE. 'Tis well; that shirt may do you
More worship than you think. Your aunt's afire,
But that she will not show it, t' have a sight of you.
Have you provided for her Grace's servants?
DAPPER. Yes, here are six score Edward shillings.[5]
FACE. Good!
DAPPER. And an old Harry's sovereign.
FACE. Very good!
DAPPER. And three James shillings, and an Elizabeth groat,
Just twenty nobles.
FACE. O, you are too just.
I would you had had the other noble in Maries.
DAPPER. I have some Philip and Maries.
FACE. Ay, those same
Are best of all. Where are they? Hark, the Doctor.

3. Boiled ale and a purgative made of local weeds.
4. The new water-work was a recent economic fact of life, and having to pay for water was a painful experience for Englishmen. "Cessed": assessed.
5. English coins varied in value according to the reign during which they were minted, because the amount of precious metal in them also varied. Dapper has to dig deep.

SCENE 5

[*Enter* SUBTLE, *disguised like a priest of Fairy, with an old petticoat.*]

SUBTLE. [*in a feigned voice*] Is yet her grace's cousin come?
FACE. He is come.
SUBTLE. And is he fasting?
FACE. Yes.
SUBTLE. And hath cried *hum*?
FACE. Thrice, you must answer.
DAPPER. Thrice.
SUBTLE. And as oft *buz*?
FACE. If you have, say.
DAPPER. I have.
SUBTLE. Then, to her coz,
Hoping that he hath vinegared his senses,
As he was bid, the Fairy Queen dispenses,
By me, this robe, the petticoat of Fortune;
Which that he straight put on, she doth importune. [*They put it on him.*]
And though to fortune near be her petticoat,
Yet nearer is her smock, the Queen doth note:
And therefore, ev'n of that a piece she hath sent,
Which, being a child, to wrap him in was rent;
And prays him for a scarf he now will wear it,
With as much love as then her Grace did tear it,
About his eyes, [*they blind him with a rag*] to show he is fortunate.
And, trusting unto her to make his state,
He'll throw away all worldly pelf about him;
Which that he will perform, she doth not doubt him.
FACE. She need not doubt him, sir. Alas, he has nothing,
But what he will part withal as willingly,
Upon her Grace' word—throw away your purse—
As she would ask it:—handkerchiefs and all—[*He throws away, as they bid him.*]
She cannot bid that thing, but he'll obey.
If you have a ring about you, cast it off,
Or a silver seal at your wrist; her grace will send
Her fairies here to search you, therefore deal
Directly with her Highness. If they find
That you conceal a mite, you are undone.
DAPPER. Truly, there's all.
FACE. All what?
DAPPER My money; truly.
FACE. Keep nothing that is transitory about you.
[*aside to* SUBTLE] Bid Dol play music.—Look, the elves are come [DOL *plays on the cittern*[6] *within.*]

6. Guitar.

To pinch you, if you tell not truth. Advise you. [*They pinch him.*]
DAPPER. O! I have a paper with a spur-ryal[7] in't.
FACE. *Ti, ti.*
They knew't, they say.
SUBTLE. *Ti, ti, ti, ti.* He has more yet.
FACE. *Ti, ti-ti-ti.* [*aside to* SUBTLE] In the other pocket?
SUBTLE. *Titi, titi, titi, titi.*
They must pinch him or he will never confess, they say. [*They pinch him again.*]
DAPPER. O, O!
FACE. Nay, pray you hold: he is her Grace's nephew,
Ti, ti, ti? What care you? good faith, you shall care.
Deal plainly, sir, and shame the fairies. Show
You are an innocent.
DAPPER. By this good light, I have nothing.
SUBTLE. *Ti, ti, ti, ti, to, ta.* He does equivocate,[8] she says:
Ti, ti do ti, ti ti do, ti da; and swears by the light when he is blinded.
DAPPER. By this good dark, I have nothing but a half-crown
Of gold about my wrist, that my love gave me;
And a leaden heart I wore since she forsook me.[9]
FACE. I thought 'twas something. And would you incur
Your aunt's displeasure for these trifles? Come,
I had rather you had thrown away twenty half-crowns.
[*Takes it off.*]
You may wear your leaden heart still. [*Enter* DOL. *hastily.*]
How now!
SUBTLE. What news, Dol?
DOL. Yonder's your knight, sir Mammon.
FACE. God's lid, we never thought of him till now.
Where is he?
DOL. Here hard by. He is at the door.
SUBTLE. And you are not ready, now! Dol, get his suit.[1]
[*Exit* DOL.]
He must not be sent back.
FACE. O by no means.
What shall we do with this same puffin[2] here,
Now he's on the spit?
SUBTLE. Why, lay him back awhile,
With some device.
[*Re-enter* DOL. *with* FACE'*s clothes.*]
—*Ti, ti, ti, ti, ti,* Would her Grace speak with me?

7. A gold coin bearing on its face a blazing sun that resembled the rowels of a spur.
8. Equivocation, or creating a false impression by saying something only technically true, or swearing by some nonexistent principle, was much in the English news after the Gunpowder Plot (1605), when some of the suspects were accused of equivocating.
9. These little love-devices were characteristic of humble middle-class citizens like Dapper.
1. Face's costume as Lungs, the alchemist's drudge.
2. I.e., Drugger, a bird and a particularly clumsy and stupid one, now in the process of being roasted over the fire.

I come.—Help, Dol! [*Knocking without.*]

FACE. [*speaks through the key-hole*] Who's there? Sir Epicure,
My master's in the way. Please you to walk
Three or four turns, but till his back be turned,
And I am for you.—Quickly, Dol!

SUBTLE. Her Grace
Commends her kindly to you, master Dapper.

DAPPER. I long to see her Grace.

SUBTLE. She now is set
At dinner in her bed, and she has sent you
From her own private trencher, a dead mouse,
And a piece of gingerbread, to be merry withal,
And stay your stomach, lest you faint with fasting.
Yet if you could hold out till she saw you, she says,
It would be better for you.

FACE. Sir, he shall
Hold out, an 'twere this two hours, for her Highness;
I can assure you that. We will not lose
All we have done.——

SUBTLE. He must not see, nor speak
To anybody, till then.

FACE. For that we'll put, sir,
A stay[3] in's mouth.

SUBTLE. Of what?

FACE. Of gingerbread.
Make you it fit. He that hath pleased her Grace
Thus far, shall not now crinkle[4] for a little.—
Gape sir, and let him fit you. [*They thrust a gag of gingerbread in his mouth.*]

SUBTLE. Where shall we now
Bestow him?

DOL. In the privy.

SUBTLE. Come along, sir,
I now must show you Fortune's privy lodgings.

FACE. Are they perfumed, and his bath ready?

SUBTLE. All.
Only the fumigation's somewhat strong.

FACE. [*speaking through the key-hole*] Sir Epicure, I am yours, sir, by and by.

[*Exeunt with* DAPPER.]

Act IV

SCENE 1. *A room in* LOVEWIT'S *house*

[*Enter* FACE *dressed as* LUNGS, *and* MAMMON.]

FACE. O sir, you are come in the only finest time—

MAMMON. Where's master?

3. Impediment, gag.

4. Give up, fall short.

FACE. Now preparing for projection, sir.
Your stuff will be all changed shortly.
MAMMON. Into gold?
FACE. To gold and silver, sir.
MAMMON. Silver I care not for.
FACE. Yes, sir, a little to give beggars.
MAMMON. Where's the lady?
FACE. At hand here. I have told her such brave things of you,
Touching your bounty, and your noble spirit—
MAMMON. Hast thou?
FACE. As she is almost in her fit to see you.
But, good sir, no divinity in your conference,[5]
For fear of putting her in rage—
MAMMON. I warrant thee.
FACE. Six men will not hold her down; and then,
If the old man should hear or see you—
MAMMON. Fear not.
FACE. The very house, sir, would run mad. You know it,
How scrupulous he is, and violent,
'Gainst the least act of sin. Physic, or mathematics,
Poetry, state, or bawdry, as I told you,
She will endure, and never startle; but
No word of controversy.
MAMMON. I am schooled, good Ulen.
FACE. And you must praise her house, remember that,
And her nobility.
MAMMON. Let me alone:
No herald, no, nor antiquary, Lungs,
Shall do it better. Go.
FACE. [*aside*] Why, this is yet
A kind of modern happiness,[6] to have
Dol Common for a great lady. [*Exit* FACE.]
MAMMON. [*alone, to himself*] Now, Epicure,
Heighten thyself, talk to her all in gold;
Rain her as many showers as Jove did drops
Unto his Danäe;[7] show the god a miser,
Compared with Mammon. What! the stone will do't.
She shall feel gold, taste gold, hear gold, sleep gold;
Nay, we will *concumbere*[8] gold: I will be puissant,
And mighty in my talk to her.
[*Enter* FACE *with* DOL. *richly dressed.*]
Here she comes.
FACE. [*aside*] To him, Dol, suckle him.—This is the noble knight,
I told your ladyship—
MAMMON. Madam, with your pardon,
I kiss your vesture.

5. I.e., don't talk religion to her.
6. Modern happiness is the vulgar sort, the only kind available nowadays.
7. Jove wooed and won Danäe in the form of a shower of gold.
8. Copulate; "puissant": overpowering.

DOL. Sir, I were uncivil
If I would suffer that; my lip to you, sir. [*Kisses him.*]
MAMMON. I hope my lord your brother be in health, lady.
DOL. My lord, my brother is, though I no lady, sir.
FACE. [*aside*] Well said, my Guinea bird.[9]
MAMMON. Right noble madam—
FACE. [*aside*] O, we shall have most fierce idolatry.
MAMMON. 'Tis your prerogative.
DOL. Rather your courtesy.
MAMMON. Were there nought else t'enlarge your virtues to me,
These answers speak your breeding, and your blood.
DOL. Blood we boast none, sir, a poor baron's daughter.
MAMMON. Poor! and gat you? profane not. Had your father
Slept all the happy remnant of his life
After that act, lain but there still, and panted,
He had done enough to make himself, his issue,
And his posterity noble.
DOL. Sir, although
We may be said to want the gilt and trappings,
The dress of honor, yet we strive to keep
The seeds and the materials.
MAMMON. I do see
The old ingredient, virtue, was not lost,
Nor the drug money used to make your compound.
There is a strange nobility in your eye,
This lip, that chin! methinks you do resemble
One of the Austriac princes.[1]
FACE. [*aside*] Very like!
Her father was an Irish costermonger.[2]
MAMMON. The house of Valois, just, had such a nose,
And such a forehead, yet, the Medici
Of Florence boast.[3]
DOL. Troth, and I have been likened
To all these princes.
FACE. [*aside*] I'll be sworn, I heard it.
MAMMON. I know not how! it is not any one,
But e'en the very choice of all their features.
FACE. [*aside*] I'll in, and laugh. [*Exit.*]
MAMMON. A certain touch, or air,
That sparkles a divinity beyond
An earthly beauty!
DOL. O, you play the courtier.
MAMMON. Good lady, give me leave—
DOL. In faith, I may not,
To mock me, sir.

9. Slang for a slut.
1. The Hapsburgs, princes of Austria, tended to a heavy jaw and hanging lower lip.
2. Pushcart salesman.
3. The Valois were the royal house of France; the Medici of Florence were never particularly handsome, but Mammon is determined to flatter.

MAMMON. To burn in this sweet flame;
The phoenix[4] never knew a nobler death.
DOL. Nay, now you court the courtier, and destroy
What you would build; this art, sir, in your words,
Calls your whole faith in question.
MAMMON. By my soul——
DOL. Nay, oaths are made of the same air, sir.
MAMMON. Nature
Never bestowed upon mortality
A more unblamed, a more harmonious feature;
She played the stepdame in all faces else.
Sweet madam, let me be particular[5]—
DOL. Particular, sir? I pray you know your distance.
MAMMON. In no ill sense, sweet lady; but to ask
How your fair graces pass the hours. I see
You are lodged here, in the house of a rare man,
An excellent artist; but what's that to you?
DOL. Yes, sir; I study here the mathematics,
And distillation.
MAMMON. O, I cry your pardon.
He's a divine instructor! can extract
The souls of all things by his art; call all
The virtues, and the miracles of the sun,
Into a temperate furnace: teach dull nature
What her own forces are. A man, the Emperor
Has courted above Kelly;[6] sent his medals
And chains, to invite him.
DOL. Ay, and for his physic, sir—
MAMMON. Above the art of Æsculapius,
That drew the envy of the thunderer![7]
I know all this, and more.
DOL. Troth, I am taken, sir,
Whole with these studies, that contémplate nature.
MAMMON. It is a noble humor; but this form
Was not intended to so dark a use.
Had you been crooked, foul, of some coarse mould,
A cloister had done well; but such a feature
That might stand up the glory of a kingdom,
To live recluse! is a mere solecism,[8]
Though in a nunnery. It must not be.
I muse, my lord your brother will permit it:
You should spend half my land first, were I he.
Does not this diamond better on my finger,
Than in the quarry?

4. The fabulous bird that builds itself a special pyre on which to enact its own death.
5. Mammon means "precise," "detailed"; Dol thinks, or affects to think, he is making a pass.
6. Edward Kelly (1555–95) worked with Doctor John Dee very much as Face works with Subtle. The Holy Roman Emperor Rudolph II invited Kelly to his court, where he promised to make gold; after failing, he was jailed, and died while trying to escape.
7. Aesculapius the Greek physician was so successful in his cures that Zeus ("the thunderer") destroyed him lest he render men immortal.
8. Anomaly, absurdity.

DOL. Yes.

MAMMON. Why, you are like it.
You were created, lady, for the light.
Here, you shall wear it; take it, the first pledge
Of what I speak, to bind you to believe me.

DOL. In chains of adamant?[9]

MAMMON. Yes, the strongest bands.
And take a secret too—here, by your side,
Doth stand this hour, the happiest man in Europe.

DOL. You are contented, sir?

MAMMON. Nay, in true being,
The envy of princes and the fear of states.

DOL. Say you so, sir Epicure?

MAMMON. Yes, and thou shalt prove it,
Daughter of honor. I have cast mine eye
Upon thy form, and I will rear this beauty
Above all styles.

DOL. You mean no treason, sir?

MAMMON. No, I will take away that jealousy.[1]
I am the lord of the philosopher's stone,
And thou the lady.

DOL. How, sir! have you that?

MAMMON. I am the master of the mastery.[2]
This day the good old wretch here o' the house
Has made it for us; now he's at projection.
Think therefore thy first wish now, let me hear it;
And it shall rain into thy lap, no shower,
But floods of gold, whole cataracts, a deluge,
To get a nation on thee.[3]

DOL. You are pleased, sir,
To work on the ambition of our sex.

MAMMON. I am pleased the glory of her sex should know
This nook, here, of the Friars[4] is no climate
For her to live obscurely in, to learn
Physic and surgery, for the constable's wife
Of some odd hundred in Essex;[5] but come forth,
And taste the air of palaces; eat, drink
The toils of empirics,[6] and their boasted practice,
Tincture of pearl, and coral, gold and amber;
Be seen at feasts and triumphs; have it asked,
What miracle she is? set all the eyes
Of court afire, like a burning glass,
And work 'em into cinders, when the jewels
Of twenty states adorn thee, and the light
Strikes out the stars! that, when thy name is mentioned,
Queens may look pale; and we but showing our love,

9. Literally, diamond; practically, a very hard metal.
1. Suspicion.
2. I own the masterwork, i.e., the stone.
3. Beget a whole population.
4. Blackfriars.
5. I.e., the wife of a modest rural official in a country town.
6. The alchemical followers of Paracelsus were called "empirics" because they disregarded Galen's rules and followed what they saw as "experience."

Nero's Poppæa may be lost in story![7]
Thus will we have it.
DOL. I could well consent, sir.
But, in a monarchy, how will this be?
The prince will soon take notice, and both seize
You and your stone, it being a wealth unfit
For any private subject.
MAMMON. If he knew it.
DOL. Yourself do boast it, sir.
MAMMON. To thee, my life.
DOL. O, but beware, sir! you may come to end
The remnant of your days in a loathed prison,
By speaking of it.
MAMMON. 'Tis no idle fear.
We'll therefore go withal,[8] my girl, and live
In a free state, where we will eat our mullets,
Soused in high-country wines, sup pheasants' eggs,
And have our cockles boiled in silver shells;
Our shrimps to swim again, as when they lived,
In a rare butter made of dolphins' milk,
Whose cream does look like opals; and with these
Delicate meats set ourselves high for pleasure,
And take us down again, and then renew
Our youth and strength with drinking the elixir,
And so enjoy a perpetuity
Of life and lust! And thou shalt have thy wardrobe
Richer than nature's, still to change thyself,
And vary oftener, for thy pride, than she,
Or art, her wise and almost-equal servant. [*Re-enter* FACE.]
FACE. Sir, you are too loud. I heard you every word
Into the laboratory. Some fitter place;
The garden, or great chamber above. How like you her?
MAMMON. Excellent, Lungs! There's for thee. [*Gives him money.*]
FACE. But do you hear?
Good sir, beware, no mention of the rabbins.[9]
MAMMON. We think not on 'em.
[*Exeunt* MAMMON *and* DOL.]
FACE. O, it is well, sir.—Subtle!

SCENE 2

[*Enter* SUBTLE.]
Dost thou not laugh?
SUBTLE. Yes; are they gone?
FACE. All's clear.
SUBTLE. The widow is come.
FACE. And your quarreling disciple?

7. Poppaea was the second wife of Nero; she will be lost in history when the newer and greater love of Mammon and Dol is made manifest.

8. At once.

9. Rabbis, Hebrew commentators on the Old Testament.

SUBTLE. Ay.
FACE. I must to my Captainship again then.
SUBTLE. Stay, bring them in first.
FACE. So I meant. What is she?
A bonnibel?[1]
SUBTLE. I know not.
FACE. We'll draw lots;
You'll stand to that?[2]
SUBTLE. What else?
FACE. O, for a suit
To fall now like a curtain, flap![3]
SUBTLE. To the door, man.
FACE. You'll have the first kiss, 'cause I am not ready. [*Exit* FACE.]
SUBTLE. Yes, and perhaps hit you through both the nostrils.[4]
FACE. [*within*] Who would you speak with?
KASTRIL. [*within*] Where's the Captain?
FACE. [*within*] Gone, sir,
About some business.
KASTRIL. [*within*] Gone!
FACE. [*within*] He'll return straight.
But master Doctor, his lieutenant, is here.
[*Enter* KASTRIL, *followed by* DAME PLIANT.]
SUBTLE. Come near, my worshipful boy, my *terræ fili*,[5]
That is, my boy of land; make thy approaches.
Welcome; I know thy lusts, and thy desires,
And I will serve and satisfy them. Begin,
Charge me from thence, or thence, or in this line;
Here is my center; ground thy quarrel.
KASTRIL. You lie.
SUBTLE. How, child of wrath and anger! the loud lie?
For what, my sudden boy?
KASTRIL. Nay, that look you to,
I am afore-hand.[6]
SUBTLE. O, this's no true grammar,
And as ill logic! You must render causes, child,
Your first and second intentions, know your canons[7]
And your divisions, moods, degrees, and differences,
Your predicaments, substance, and accident,
Series extern and intern, with their causes,
Efficient, material, formal, final,
And have your elements perfect—

1. Beauty.
2. Agree to that.
3. Face needs his captain's uniform and is getting tired of the frequent quick-changes required by his many plots.
4. Perhaps from the old poacher's sport of fish-spearing: "get the best of you before you're ready." Cf. above Act II, Scene 4, "Twitch him through both gills."
5. Subtle translates this Latin phrase in the next line; Kastril possesses broad acres, but he's also a boy of the earth in being lumpish and common.
6. To be "aforehand" in a quarrel was to gain certain advantages in the duel which was bound to follow.
7. "First and second intentions," "canons," "divisions, moods, degrees," and so forth are all Aristotelian categories—terms of art for dressing nature in learned jargon.

KASTRIL. What is this
The angry tongue he talks in?
SUBTLE. That false precept,
Of being afore-hand, has deceived a number,
And made them enter quarrels, oftentimes,
Before they were aware; and afterward,
Against their wills.
KASTRIL. How must I do then, sir?
SUBTLE. I cry this lady mercy: she should first
Have been saluted. [*Kisses her.*] I do call you lady,
Because you are to be one, ere 't be long,
My soft and buxom widow.
KASTRIL. Is she, i'faith?
SUBTLE. Yes, or my art is an egregious liar.
KASTRIL. How know you?
SUBTLE. By inspection on her forehead,
And subtlety of her lip, which must be tasted
Often to make a judgment. [*Kisses her again.*]—'Slight, she melts
Like a myrobolane.[8]—Here is yet a line,
In *rivo frontis*, tells me he is no knight.
DAME PLIANT. What is he then, sir?
SUBTLE. Let me see your hand.
O, your *linea fortunæ* makes it plain;
And stella here in *monte Veneris*.
But, most of all, *junctura annularis*.[9]
He is a soldier, or a man of art, lady,
But shall have some great honor shortly.
DAME PLIANT. Brother,
He's a rare man, believe me!
[*Enter* FACE, *in his Captain's uniform.*]
KASTRIL. Hold your peace.
Here comes the t' other rare man.—'Save you, Captain.
FACE. Good master Kastril! Is this your sister?
KASTRIL. Ay, sir.
Please you to kuss her, and be proud to know her.
FACE. I shall be proud to know you, lady. [*Kisses her.*]
DAME PLIANT. Brother,
He calls me lady too.
KASTRIL. Ay, peace; I heard it.
[KASTRIL *takes her aside.*]
FACE. The Count is come.
SUBTLE. Where is he?
FACE. At the door.
SUBTLE. Why, you must entertain him.

8. Candied plum from the East that melted in the mouth. "*rivo frontis*": a line on the forehead, supposed to be significant in fortune-telling.
9. The "*linea fortunae*" or line of fortune is one of the main lines in the palm of the hand; the "*stella*" or star on the mount of Venus at the base of the thumb and loose joints on the ring finger ("*junctura annularis*") are evidence of sexual appetite.

FACE. What will you do
With these the while?
SUBTLE. Why, have them up, and show them
Some fustian[1] book, or the dark glass.
FACE. 'Fore God,
She is a delicate dabchick! I must have her. [*Exit* FACE.]
SUBTLE. Must you! ay, if your fortune will, you must.
Come, sir, the Captain will come to us presently.
I'll have you to my chamber of demonstrations,
Where I will show you both the grammar and logic
And rhetoric of quarreling; my whole method
Drawn out in tables;[2] and my instrument,
That hath the several scales upon't, shall make you
Able to quarrel at a straw's breadth by moonlight.[3]
And, lady, I'll have you look in a glass,
Some half an hour, but to clear your eyesight,
Against you see your fortune; which is greater,
Than I may judge upon the sudden, trust me.
[*Exit, followed by* KASTRIL *and* DAME PLIANT.]

SCENE 3

[*Enter* FACE, *as Captain.*]
FACE. Where are you, Doctor?
SUBTLE. [*within*] I'll come to you presently.
FACE. I will have this same widow, now I've seen her,
On any composition.[4] [*Enter* SUBTLE.]
SUBTLE. What do you say?
FACE. Have you disposed of them?
SUBTLE. I've sent them up.
FACE. Subtle, in troth, I needs must have this widow.
SUBTLE. Is that the matter?
FACE. Nay, but hear me.
SUBTLE. Go to,
If you rebel once, Dol shall know it all.
Therefore be quiet, and obey your chance.
FACE. Nay, thou art so violent now—Do but conceive,
Thou art old, and canst not serve—
SUBTLE. Who cannot? I?
'Slight, I will serve her with thee, for a—
FACE. Nay,
But understand: I'll give you composition.[5]
SUBTLE. I will not treat with thee; what! sell my fortune?
'Tis better than my birthright. Do not murmur.
Win her, and carry her. If you grumble, Dol
Knows it directly.

1. Pompous and phony; "the dark glass": the crystal ball.
2. Diagrams.
3. I.e., able to pick a quarrel over something ordinary folk can't even see.
4. On any terms whatever.
5. Make a deal with you.

FACE. Well, sir, I am silent.
Will you go help to fetch in Don in state?
SUBTLE. I follow you, sir. [*Exit* FACE.] We must keep Face in awe,
Or he will over-look[6] us like a tyrant.
[*Enter* FACE, *introducing* SURLY *disguised as a Spaniard.*]
Brain of a tailor! who comes here? Don John![7]
SURLY. *Señores, beso las manos à vuestras mercedes.*[8]
SUBTLE. Would you had stooped a little, and kissed our *anos*!
FACE. Peace, Subtle.
SUBTLE. Stab me; I shall never hold, man.[9]
He looks in that deep ruff like a head in a platter,
Served in by a short cloak upon two trestles.
FACE. Or, what do you say to a collar of brawn,[1] cut down
Beneath the souse, and wriggled with a knife?
SUBTLE. 'Slud, he does look too fat to be a Spaniard.
FACE. Perhaps some Fleming or some Hollander got him
In d'Alva's time; count Egmont's bastard.[2]
SUBTLE. Don,
Your scurvy, yellow Madrid face is welcome.
SURLY. *Gratia.*
SUBTLE. He speaks out of a fortification.
Pray God he have no squibs in those deep sets.[3]
SURLY. *Por dios, señores, muy linda casa!*[4]
SUBTLE. What says he?
FACE. Praises the house, I think;
I know no more but's action.
SUBTLE. Yes, the *casa*,
My precious Diego, will prove fair enough
To cozen you in. Do you mark? you shall
Be cozened, Diego.
FACE. Cozened, do you see,
My worthy Donzel, cozened.
SURLY. *Entiendo.*[5]
SUBTLE. Do you intend it? so do we, dear Don.
Have you brought pistolets, or portagues,
My solemn Don?—Dost thou feel any?
FACE. [*feels his pockets*] Full.
SUBTLE. You shall be emptied, Don, pumped and drawn
Dry, as they say.
FACE. Milked, in troth, sweet Don.
SUBTLE. See all the monsters; the great lion of all, Don.[6]

6. Domineer.
7. Don John was a common name for a Spaniard. Both as a disguise and because Spaniards were understood to be elaborate dressers, Surly wears an ornate costume.
8. Gentlemen, I kiss the hands of your honors.
9. I shall never keep a straight face.
1. Pig's head and neck; "souse": ears.
2. Dutchmen and Flemings, over whom the Spanish had ruled for years, were supposed to be fat.
3. The folds of his ruff; "squibs": firecrackers, i.e., unpleasant surprises.
4. By heaven, gentlemen, a very fine house.
5. I understand.
6. Subtle pretends to be master of an amusement park; the Don will see all the sideshows.

SURLY. *Con licencia, se puede ver à esta señora?*[7]
SUBTLE. What talks he now?
FACE. Of the señora.
SUBTLE. O, Don,
That is the lioness, which you shall see
Also, my Don.
FACE. 'Slid, Subtle, how shall we do?
SUBTLE. For what?
FACE. Why, Dol's employed, you know.
SUBTLE. That's true.
'Fore heaven, I know not; he must stay, that's all.
FACE. Stay! that he must not by no means.
SUBTLE. No, why?
FACE. Unless you'll mar all. 'Slight, he will suspect it,
And then he will not pay, not half so well.
This is a traveled punk-master,[8] and does know
All the delays; a notable hot rascal,
And looks already rampant.[9]
SUBTLE. 'Sdeath, and Mammon
Must not be troubled.
FACE. Mammon! in no case.
SUBTLE. What shall we do then?
FACE. Think: you must be sudden.
SURLY. *Entiendo que la señora es tan hermosa, que codicio tan verla, como la bien aventuránza de mi vida.*[1]
FACE. *Mi vida!* 'Slid, Subtle, he puts me in mind o' the widow.
What dost thou say to draw her to it? ha!
And tell her 'tis her fortune? All our venture
Now lies upon't. It is but one man more,
Which of us chance to have her; and beside,
There is no maidenhead to be feared or lost.
What dost thou think on't, Subtle?
SUBTLE. Who, I? why—
FACE. The credit of our house too is engaged.
SUBTLE. You made me an offer for my share ere-while.
What wilt thou give me, i' faith?
FACE. O, by that light
I'll not buy now. You know your doom[2] to me.
"E'en take your lot, obey your chance, sir; win her,
And wear her out, for me."
SUBTLE. 'Slight, I'll not work her then.
FACE. It is the common cause; therefore bethink you.
Dol else must know it, as you said.
SUBTLE. I care not.
SURLY. *Señores, porqué se tarda tanto?*[3]
SUBTLE. Faith, I am not fit, I am old.
FACE. That's now no reason, sir.

7. Please, can this lady be seen?
8. An experienced whoremaster.
9. Up on his hind legs and ready to go.
1. I understand the lady is so lovely that seeing her will be the greatest piece of good luck in my life.
2. Expression. Face quotes Subtle back at himself.
3. Gentlemen, what's all the delay?

SURLY. *Puede ser de hazer burla de mi amor?*[4]
FACE. You hear the Don too? by this air, I call,
And loose the hinges. Dol!
SUBTLE. A plague of hell——
FACE. Will you then do?
SUBTLE. You're a terrible rogue!
I'll think of this: will you, sir, call the widow?
FACE. Yes, and I'll take her too with all her faults,
Now I do think on't better.
SUBTLE. With all my heart, sir;
Am I discharged o' the lot?
FACE. As you please.
SUBTLE. Hands.
[*They shake hands.*]
FACE. Remember now, that upon any change,
You never claim her.
SUBTLE. Much good joy, and health to you, sir.
Marry a whore! fate, let me wed a witch first.
SURLY. *Por estas honradas barbas*[5]——
SUBTLE. He swears by his beard.
Despatch, and call the brother too. [*Exit* FACE.]
SURLY. *Tengo dùda, señores,*
Que no me hágan alguna trayción.[6]
SUBTLE. How, issue on? Yes, *presto, señor*. Please you
Enthratha the *chambratha*, worthy Don:
Where if you please the fates, in your *bathada*,
You shall be soaked, and stroked, and tubbed, and rubbed,
And scrubbed, and fubbed,[7] dear Don, before you go.
You shall in faith, my scurvy baboon Don,
Be curried, clawed and flawed, and tawed,[8] indeed.
I will the heartlier go about it now,
And make the widow a punk so much the sooner,
To be revenged on this impetuous Face.
The quickly doing of it, is the grace.
[*Exeunt* SUBTLE *and* SURLY.]

SCENE 4. *Another room in* LOVEWIT'S *house*

[*Enter* FACE, KASTRIL, *and* DAME PLIANT.]
FACE. Come, lady; I knew the Doctor would not leave,
Till he had found the very nick[9] of her fortune.
KASTRIL. To be a countess, say you?
FACE. A Spanish countess, sir.
DAME PLIANT. Why, is that better than an English countess?

4. Perhaps you're making game of my love?
5. By this honorable beard—
6. I'm afraid, gentlemen, that you may be playing some trick on me.
7. Tricked.
8. Beaten with the taws, i.e., whipped; "flawed": flayed.
9. Exact character.

FACE. Better! 'Slight, make you that a question, lady?
KASTRIL. Nay, she is a fool, Captain, you must pardon her.
FACE. Ask from your courtier, to your inns-of-court-man,
To your mere milliner; they will tell you all,
Your Spanish jennet is the best horse; your Spanish
Stoup[1] is the best garb: your Spanish beard
Is the best cut; your Spanish ruffs are the best
Wear; your Spanish pavanne the best dance;
Your Spanish titillation in a glove
The best perfume; and for your Spanish pike,
And Spanish blade, let your poor Captain speak.
Here comes the Doctor. [*Enter* SUBTLE, *with a paper.*]
SUBTLE. My most honored lady,
(For so I am now to style you, having found
By this my scheme, you are to undergo
An honorable fortune, very shortly)
What will you say now, if some—
FACE. I have told her all, sir;
And her right worshipful brother here, that she shall be
A countess; do not delay them, sir. A Spanish countess!
SUBTLE. Still, my scarce-worshipful Captain, you can keep
No secret! Well, since he has told you, madam,
Do you forgive him, and I do.
KASTRIL. She shall do that, sir;
I'll look to't, 'tis my charge.
SUBTLE. Well then, nought rests
But that she fit her love now to her fortune.
DAME PLIANT. Truly I shall never brook[2] a Spaniard.
SUBTLE. No?
DAME PLIANT. Never since eighty-eight[3] could I abide them,
And that was some three year afore I was born, in truth.
SUBTLE. Come, you must love him, or be miserable;
Choose which you will.
FACE. By this good rush,[4] persuade her;
She will cry strawberries else within this twelve-month.[5]
SUBTLE. Nay, shads and mackerel, which is worse.
FACE. Indeed, sir!
KASTRIL. Od's lid, you shall love him, or I'll kick you.
DAME PLIANT. Why,
I'll do as you will have me, brother.
KASTRIL. Do,
Or by this hand I'll maul you.
FACE. Nay, good sir,
Be not so fierce.
SUBTLE. No, my enragéd child;

1. Probably an article of clothing.
2. Endure.
3. 1588, the year of the Spanish Armada.
4. He picks up a rush from the floor.
5. I.e., peddle strawberries in the street as an itinerant huckster—only one stage above selling fish from a fish-stall.

She will be ruled. What, when she comes to taste
The pleasures of a countess! to be courted—
FACE. And kissed, and ruffled!
SUBTLE. Ay, behind the hangings.
FACE. And then come forth in pomp!
SUBTLE. And know her state!
FACE. Of keeping all the idolaters of the chamber
Barer to her, than at their prayers![6]
SUBTLE. Is served
Upon the knee!
FACE. And has her pages, ushers,
Footmen, and coaches—
SUBTLE. Her six mares—
FACE. Nay, eight!
SUBTLE. To hurry her through London, to the Exchange,[7]
Bedlam, the china-houses—
FACE. Yes, and have
The citizens gape at her, and praise her tires,
And my lord's goose-turd[8] bands, that ride with her!
KASTRIL. Most brave! By this hand, you are not my suster,
If you refuse.
DAME PLIANT. I will not refuse, brother. [*Enter* SURLY.]
SURLY. *Qué es esto, señores, que non se venga?*
Esta tardanza me mata![9]
FACE. It is the Count come;
The Doctor knew he would be here, by his art.
SUBTLE. *En gallanta madama, Don! gallantissima!*
SURLY. *Par tódos los dioses, la más acabada*
Hermosura, que he visto en mi vida![1]
FACE. Is't not a gallant language that they speak?
KASTRIL. An admirable language! Is't not French?
FACE. No, Spanish, sir.
KASTRIL. It goes like law-French,[2]
And that, they say, is the courtliest language.
FACE. List, sir.
SURLY. *El sol ha perdido su lumbre, con el*
Resplandor que trae esta dama! Válgame dios![3]
FACE. He admires your sister.
KASTRIL. Must not she make curtsey?
SUBTLE. God's will, she must go to him, man, and kiss him!
It is the Spanish fashion, for the women

6. I.e., the courtiers will remove their caps to her more reverently than at their prayers.

7. The Exchange in the Strand was where fashionable ladies went shopping; Bedlam (the madhouse) was where they went for amusement.

8. Ribbons of a fashionable shade of greenish-yellow.

9. How is it she doesn't come, gentlemen? The delay is killing me.

1. A fine lady, Don! very fine! By all the gods, the most gorgeous creature I've ever seen in my life.

2. The variety of Norman French long spoken in English law courts, of which we still have remnants in words like "Oyez," "torts," and "mortgage." "Courtliest" is a pun.

3. The sun has lost its glitter before the splendor of this lady. Lord bless me.

To make first court.
FACE. 'Tis true he tells you, sir;
His art knows all.
SURLY. *Porqué no se acùde?*[4]
KASTRIL. He speaks to her, I think.
FACE. That he does, sir.
SURLY. *Por el amor de Dios, que es esto que se tarda?*[5]
KASTRIL. Nay, see: she will not understand him! Gull!
Noddy!
DAME PLIANT. What say you, brother?
KASTRIL. Ass, my suster,
Go kiss him, as the cunning man would have you;
I'll thrust a pin in your buttocks else.
FACE. O no, sir.
SURLY. *Señora mia, mi persona muy indigna está*
A llegar á tanta hermosura.[6]
FACE. Does he not use her bravely?
KASTRIL. Bravely, i' faith!
FACE. Nay, he will use her better.
KASTRIL. Do you think so?
SURLY. *Señora, si sera servida, entremos.*[7]
[*Exit with* DAME PLIANT.]
KASTRIL. Where does he carry her?
FACE. Into the garden, sir;
Take you no thought: I must interpret for her.
SUBTLE. [*Aside to* FACE, *who goes out*] Give Dol the word.—
Come, my fierce child, advance,
We'll to our quarreling lesson again.
KASTRIL. Agreed.
I love a Spanish boy with all my heart.
SUBTLE. Nay, and by this means, sir, you shall be brother
To a great count.
KASTRIL. Ay, I knew that at first.
This match will advance the house of the Kastrils.
SUBTLE. 'Pray God your sister prove but pliant!
KASTRIL. Why,
Her name is so, by her other husband.
SUBTLE. How!
KASTRIL. The widow Pliant. Knew you not that?
SUBTLE. No, faith, sir;
Yet, by erection of her figure,[8] I guessed it.
Come, let's go practice.
KASTRIL. Yes, but do you think, doctor,
I e'er shall quarrel well?
SUBTLE. I warrant you. [*Exeunt.*]

4. Why doesn't she come to me?
5. For the love of God, why is she holding back?
6. My lady, my person is altogether unworthy of approaching such loveliness.
7. Lady, if you will, let us retire.
8. By casting her horoscope; but there's an obvious pun.

SCENE 5

[*Enter* DOL *in her fit of raving, followed by* MAMMON.]
DOL. *For after Alexander's death*[9]—
MAMMON. Good lady—
DOL. *That Perdiccas and Antigonus were slain,*
The two that stood, Seleuc', and Ptolomee—
MAMMON. Madam.
DOL. *Made up the two legs, and the fourth beast,*
That was Gog-north, and Egypt-south; which after
Was called Gog-iron-leg, and South-iron-leg—
MAMMON. Lady—
DOL. *And then Gog-hornéd. So was Egypt, too;*
Then Egypt-clay-leg, and Gog-clay-leg—
MAMMON. Sweet madam.
DOL. *And last Gog-dust, and Egypt-dust, which fall*
In the last link of the fourth chain. And these
Be stars in story, which none see, or look at—
MAMMON. What shall I do?
DOL. *For, as he says, except*
We call the rabbins and the heathen Greeks—
MAMMON. Dear lady.
DOL. *To come from Salem, and from Athens,*
And teach the people of Great Britain—
[*Enter* FACE *hastily, dressed as* LUNGS.]
FACE. What's the matter, sir?
DOL. *To speak the tongue of Eber, and Javan*—
MAMMON. O,
She's in her fit.
DOL. *We shall know nothing*—
FACE. Death, sir,
We are undone!
DOL. *Where then a learned linguist*
Shall see the ancient used communion
Of vowels and consonants—
FACE. My master will hear!
DOL. *A wisdom, which Pythagoras held most high*—
MAMMON. Sweet honorable lady!
DOL. *To comprise*
All sounds of voices, in few marks of letters—
FACE. Nay, you must never hope to lay[1] her now.

9. Dol's ravings come mostly from Hugh Broughton's book *The Consent of Scripture* (1590), which tried to establish a conclusive, comprehensive chronology of the Bible. It is neither necessary nor possible to understand the gibberish she recites. Nor is it necessary to suppose that Broughton's work was as silly as Jonson represents it; this kind of comparative chronology had a long and honorable tradition behind it.

1. Quiet.

[*They all speak together.*]

DOL. *And so we may arrive by Talmud skill,*
And profane Greek, to raise the building up
Of Helen's house,[2] *against the Ishmaelite,*
King of Thogarma, and his habergions[3]
Brimstony, blue, and fiery; and the force
Of king Abaddon, and the beast of Cittim;
Which rabbi David Kimchi, Onkelos,
And Ibn Ezra do interpret Rome.

FACE. How did you put her into't?
MAMMON. Alas, I talked
Of a fifth monarchy I would erect,[4]
With the philosopher's stone, by chance, and she
Falls on the other four straight.
FACE. Out of Broughton!
I told you so. 'Slid, stop her mouth.
MAMMON. Is't best?
FACE. She'll never leave else. If the old man hear her,
We are but faeces, ashes.
SUBTLE. [*within*] What's to do there?
FACE. O, we are lost! Now she hears him, she is quiet.

[*Enter* SUBTLE; *they run different ways.*]

MAMMON. Where shall I hide me!
SUBTLE. How! what sight is here?
Close deeds of darkness, and that shun the light!
Bring him again. Who is he? What, my son!
O, I have lived too long.
MAMMON. Nay, good, dear father,
There was no unchaste purpose.
SUBTLE. Not! and flee me,
When I come in?
MAMMON. That was my error.
SUBTLE. Error?
Guilt, guilt, my son. Give it the right name. No marvel,
If I found check in our great work within,
When such affairs as these were managing!
MAMMON. Why, have you so?
SUBTLE. It has stood still this half hour:
And all the rest of our less works gone back.
Where is the instrument of wickedness,
My lewd false drudge?
MAMMON. Nay, good sir, blame not him;
Believe me, 'twas against his will or knowledge.
I saw her by chance.
SUBTLE. Will you commit more sin,
To excuse a varlet?
MAMMON. By my hope, 'tis true, sir.
SUBTLE. Nay, then I wonder less, if you, for whom
The blessing was prepared, would so tempt heaven,
And lose your fortunes.
MAMMON. Why, sir?
SUBTLE. This'll retard
The work, a month at least.

2. I.e., the house of the Hellenes.
3. Coats of mail, but senseless in this context.
4. The fifth monarchy, predicted in the book of Revelation, was a concept dear to the Puritans; it was the period of Christ's second coming, hence of divine perfection. Mammon anticipates its emergence through application of the philosopher's stone.

MAMMON. Why, if it do,
What remedy? But think it not, good father;
Our purposes were honest.
SUBTLE. As they were,
So the reward will prove. [*A loud explosion within.*] How now! Ay me!
God, and all saints be good to us. [*Enter* FACE.] What's that?
FACE. O sir, we are defeated! all the works
Are flown *in fumo*,[5] every glass is burst.
Furnace and all rent down! as if a bolt
Of thunder had been driven through the house.
Retorts, receivers, pelicans, bolt-heads,
All struck in shivers!
[SUBTLE *falls down as in a swoon.*]
Help, good sir! alas,
Coldness and death invades him. Nay, sir Mammon,
Do the fair offices of a man! you stand,
As you were readier to depart than he. [*Knocking within.*]
Who's there? My lord her brother is come.
MAMMON. Ha, Lungs!
FACE. His coach is at the door. Avoid his sight,
For he's as furious as his sister's mad.
MAMMON. Alas!
FACE. My brain is quite undone with the fume, sir,
I ne'er must hope to be mine own man again.
MAMMON. Is all lost, Lungs? will nothing be preserved
Of all our cost?
FACE. Faith, very little, sir;
A peck of coals or so, which is cold comfort, sir.
MAMMON. O my voluptuous mind! I am justly punished.
FACE. And so am I, sir.
MAMMON. Cast from all my hopes—
FACE. Nay, certainties, sir.
MAMMON. By mine own base affections.
SUBTLE. [*seeming to come to himself*] O, the cursed fruits of vice and lust!
MAMMON. Good father,
It was my sin. Forgive it.
SUBTLE. Hangs my roof
Over us still, and will not fall? O justice
Upon us, for this wicked man!
FACE. Nay, look, sir,
You grieve him now with staying in his sight.
Good sir, the nobleman will come too, and take you,
And that may breed a tragedy.
MAMMON. I'll go.
FACE. Ay, and repent at home, sir. It may be,

5. In smoke.

For some good penance you may have it yet;
A hundred pound to the box at Bedlam[6]—

MAMMON. Yes.

FACE. For the restoring such as—have their wits.

MAMMON. I'll do't.

FACE. I'll send one to you to receive it.

MAMMON. Do.
Is no projection left?

FACE. All flown, or stinks, sir.

MAMMON. Will nought be saved that's good for medicine, think'st thou?

FACE. I cannot tell, sir. There will be perhaps,
Something about the scraping of the shards,
Will cure the itch [*aside*]—though not your itch of mind, sir.—
It shall be saved for you, and sent home. Good sir,
This way for fear the lord should meet you. [*Exit* MAMMON.]

SUBTLE. [*raising his head*] Face!

FACE. Ay.

SUBTLE. Is he gone?

FACE. Yes, and as heavily
As all the gold he hoped for were in's blood.
Let us be light, though.

SUBTLE. [*leaping up*] Ay, as balls, and bound
And hit our heads against the roof for joy.
There's so much of our care now cast away.

FACE. Now to our Don.

SUBTLE. Yes, your young widow by this time
Is made a countess, Face; she's been in travail[7]
Of a young heir for you.

FACE. Good, sir.

SUBTLE. Off with your case,[8]
And greet her kindly, as a bridegroom should,
After these common hazards.

FACE. Very well, sir.
Will you go fetch Don Diego off, the while?

SUBTLE. And fetch him over too, if you'll be pleased, sir;
Would Dol were in her place, to pick his pockets now!

FACE. Why, you can do't as well, if you would set to't.
I pray you prove your virtue.[9]

SUBTLE. For your sake, sir.

[*Exeunt.*]

SCENE 6

[*Enter* SURLY *and* DAME PLIANT.]

SURLY. Lady, you see into what hands you are fallen;
'Mongst what a nest of villains! and how near

6. Giving money for support of lunatics was a common gesture of repentance, very appropriate here.

7. At work on.

8. His costume as Lungs.

9. Talents.

Your honor was t'have catched a certain clap,
Through your credulity, had I but been
So punctually forward, as place, time,
And other circumstances would have made a man;
For you're a handsome woman. Would you were wise too!
I am a gentleman come here disguised,
Only to find the knaveries of this citadel;
And where I might have wronged your honor, and have not,
I claim some interest in your love. You are,
They say, a widow, rich; and I'm a bachelor,
Worth nought. Your fortunes may make me a man,
As mine have preserved you a woman. Think upon it,
And whether I have deserved you or no.

DAME PLIANT. I will, sir.

SURLY. And for these household-rogues, let me alone
To treat with them.

[*Enter* SUBTLE.]

SUBTLE. How doth my noble Diego,
And my dear madam countess? hath the count
Been courteous, lady? liberal, and open?
Donzel, methinks you look melancholic,
After your *coitum*, and scurvy! truly,
I do not like the dulness of your eye;
It hath a heavy cast, 'tis upsee Dutch,[1]
And says you are a lumpish whoremaster.
Be lighter, I will make your pockets so.
[*Attempts to pick them.*]

SURLY. [*Throws open his cloak.*] Will you, don bawd and pick-purse? [*Strikes him down.*] How now! Reel you?
Stand up, sir, you shall find, since I'm so heavy,
I'll give you equal weight.

SUBTLE. Help! murder!

SURLY. No, sir,
There's no such thing intended: a good cart,
And a clean whip[2] shall ease you of that fear.
I am the Spanish don *that should be cozened*,
Do *you see, cozened*? Where's your Captain Face,
That parcel broker,[3] and whole-bawd, all rascal?

[*Enter* FACE *in his uniform.*]

FACE. How, Surly!

SURLY. O, make your approach, good Captain.
I have found from whence your copper rings and spoons
Come, now, wherewith you cheat abroad in taverns.
'Twas here you learned t' anoint your boot with brimstone,
Then rub men's gold on't for a kind of touch,
And say 'twas naught, when you had changed the color,

1. Dull, stupefied, like a man who's drunk too much strong beer.
2. Cart and whip were the usual fate of bawds.
3. Part-time pimp.

That you might have't for nothing.[4] And this doctor,
Your sooty, smoky-bearded compeer, he
Will close you so much gold, in a bolt's-head,
And, on a turn, convey in the stead another
With sublimed mercury, that shall burst in the heat,
And fly out all *in fumo*'![5] Then weeps Mammon;
Then swoons his worship. [FACE *slips out*.] Or, he is the Faustus,[6]
That casteth figures and can conjure, cures
Plagues, piles, and pox, by the ephemerides,[7]
And holds intelligence with all the bawds
And midwives of three shires: while you send in—
Captain!—what! is he gone?—damsels with child,
Wives that are barren, or the waiting-maid
With the green sickness.[8] [*Seizes Subtle as he is slipping off*.]
—Nay, sir, you must tarry,
Though he be scaped; and answer by the ears, sir.

SCENE 7

[*Enter* FACE *with* KASTRIL.]

FACE. Why, now's the time, if ever you will quarrel
Well, as they say, and be a true-born child.[9]
The doctor and your sister both are abused.
KASTRIL. Where is he? Which is he? He is a slave,
Whate'er he is, and the son of a whore. Are you
The man, sir, I would know?
SURLY. I should be loath, sir,
To confess so much.
KASTRIL. Then you lie in your throat.[1]
SURLY. How!
FACE. [*to* KASTRIL] A very arrant rogue, sir, and a cheater,
Employed here by another conjurer
That does not love the Doctor, and would cross him,
If he knew how.
SURLY. Sir, you are abused.
KASTRIL. You lie;
And 'tis no matter.
FACE. Well said, sir! He is
The impudent'st rascal—
SURLY. You are indeed. Will you hear me, sir?
FACE. By no means: bid him be gone.

4. The swindle seems to involve persuading men that the real gold they have is worthless, and then buying it cheaply.
5. This trick is to take real gold from a sucker, pretend to use it in an experiment, and when the experiment fails, keep the original gold.
6. I.e., magician.
7. The astrological calendar; "holds intelligence": keeps in touch with.
8. Female troubles provide a favorite field for the operation of frauds, in the 20th century as in the 16th.
9. I.e., knight-errant.
1. All Kastril knows is the assault direct.

KASTRIL. Be gone, sir, quickly.

SURLY. This's strange! Lady, do you inform your brother.

FACE. There is not such a foist[2] in all the town,
The Doctor had him presently;[3] and finds yet,
The Spanish count will come here. [*aside*]—Bear up, Subtle.

SUBTLE. Yes, sir, he must appear within this hour.

FACE. And yet this rogue would come in a disguise,
By the temptation of another spirit,
To trouble our art, though he could not hurt it!

KASTRIL. Ay,
I know. [DAME PLIANT *whispers to her brother*.]—Away, you talk like a foolish mauther.[4]

SURLY. Sir, all is truth she says.

FACE. Do not believe him, sir.
He is the lyingest swabber! Come your ways, sir.

SURLY. You are valiant, out of company![5]

KASTRIL. Yes, how then, sir?

[*Enter* DRUGGER *with a piece of damask*.]

FACE. Nay, here's an honest fellow, too, that knows him,
And all his tricks. [*aside to* DRUGGER]—Make good what I say, Abel,
This cheater would have cozened thee o' the widow.—
He owes this honest Drugger here, seven pound,
He has had on him, in two-penny'orths of tobacco.

DRUGGER. Yes, sir. And he's damned himself three terms to pay me.[6]

FACE. And what does he owe for *lotium*?

DRUGGER. Thirty shillings, sir;
And for six syringes.

SURLY. Hydra of villainy![7]

FACE. Nay, sir, you must quarrel him out o'the house.

KASTRIL. I will.
—Sir, if you get not out o' doors, you lie;
And you are a pimp.

SURLY. Why, this is madness, sir,
Not valor in you; I must laugh at this.

KASTRIL. It is my humor: you are a pimp and a trig,[8]
And an *Amadis de Gaul*, or a *Don Quixote*.

DRUGGER. Or a knight o' the curious coxcomb, do you see?

[*Enter* ANANIAS.]

ANANIAS. Peace to the household.

KASTRIL. I'll keep peace for no man.

ANANIAS. Casting of dollars is concluded lawful.

KASTRIL. Is he the constable?

SUBTLE. Peace, Ananias.

2. Cheating rogue.
3. Caught on to him at once.
4. Stupid girl.
5. Brave, now that you have someone to back you up.
6. I.e., has sworn for the last three terms (of court) to pay me back.
7. The Hydra was a many-headed dragon of mythology; the more heads Hercules cut off, the more grew back again.
8. Coxcomb.

FACE. No, sir.
KASTRIL. Then you are an otter, and a shad, a whit,
A very tim.[9]
SURLY. You'll hear me, sir?
KASTRIL. I will not.
ANANIAS. What is the motive?
SUBTLE. Zeal in the young gentleman,
Against his Spanish slops.[1]
ANANIAS. They are profane,
Lewd, superstitious, and idolatrous breeches.
SURLY. New rascals!
KASTRIL. Will you be gone, sir?
ANANIAS. Avoid,[2] Satan!
Thou art not of the light! That ruff of pride
About thy neck, betrays thee; and is the same
With that which the unclean birds, in seventy seven,[3]
Were seen to prank it with on divers coasts.
Thou look'st like antichrist, in that lewd hat.
SURLY. I must give way.
KASTRIL. Be gone, sir.
SURLY. But I'll take
A course with you—
ANANIAS. Depart, proud Spanish fiend!
SURLY. Captain and Doctor—
ANANIAS. Child of perdition!
KASTRIL. Hence, sir!
[*Exit* SURLY.]
Did I not quarrel bravely?
FACE. Yes, indeed, sir.
KASTRIL. Nay, an I give my mind to't, I shall do't.
FACE. O, you must follow, sir, and threaten him tame.
He'll turn again else.
KASTRIL. I'll re-turn him then. [*Exit* KASTRIL.]
[SUBTLE *takes* ANANIAS *aside.*]
FACE. Drugger, this rogue prevented[4] us, for thee;
We had determined that thou shouldst have come
In a Spanish suit, and have carried her so; and he,
A brokerly[5] slave! goes, puts it on himself.
Hast brought the damask?
DRUGGER Yes, sir.
FACE. Thou must borrow
A Spanish suit. Hast thou no credit with the players?
DRUGGER. Yes, sir; did you never see me play the Fool?[6]

9. Country words of uncertain application.
1. Breeches.
2. Be gone.
3. Perhaps a reference to Spanish troops which in 1567, under the duke of Alva, invaded Holland to put down a Protestant rising there.
4. Forestalled.
5. Meddling.
6. There may be an in-company joke here, if the part of Drugger was taken in the first production by the man who generally took fools' roles for the King's Men.

FACE. I know not, Nab. [*aside*]—Thou shalt, if I can help it.—
Hieronimo's[7] old cloak, ruff, and hat will serve;
I'll tell thee more when thou bring'st 'em. [*Exit* DRUGGER.]
ANANIAS. Sir, I know
The Spaniard hates the brethren,[8] and hath spies
Upon their actions; and that this was one
I make no scruple.[9] But the holy synod
Have been in prayer and meditation for it;
And 'tis revealed no less to them than me,
That casting of money is most lawful.
SUBTLE. True,
But here I cannot do it; if the house
Should chance to be suspected, all would out,
And we be locked up in the Tower[1] forever,
To make gold there for the state, never come out;[2]
And then are you defeated.
ANANIAS. I will tell
This to the elders and the weaker brethren
That the whole company of the separation
May join in humble prayer again.
SUBTLE. And fasting.
ANANIAS. Yea, for some fitter place. The peace of mind
Rest with these walls! [*Exit* ANANIAS.]
SUBTLE. Thanks, courteous Ananias.
FACE. What did he come for?
SUBTLE. About casting dollars,
Presently out of hand.[3] And so I told him,
A Spanish minister came here to spy,
Against the faithful—
FACE. I conceive. Come, Subtle,
Thou art so down upon the least disaster!
How wouldst thou have done, if I had not helped thee out?
SUBTLE. I thank thee, Face, for the angry boy, i' faith.
FACE. Who would have looked it should have been that rascal
Surly? he had dyed his beard and all. Well, sir,
Here's damask come to make you a suit.
SUBTLE. Where's Drugger?
FACE. He is gone to borrow me a Spanish habit;
I'll be the count, now.
SUBTLE. But where's the widow?
FACE. Within, with my lord's sister; madam Dol
Is entertaining her.
SUBTLE. By your favor, Face,
Now she is honest, I will stand again.
FACE. You will not offer it?

7. Hieronimo was a figure in Kyd's old play *The Spanish Tragedy*.
8. I.e., the Puritan brethren.
9. Have no doubt.
1. The Tower of London, reserved for traitors and criminals of distinction—not the common jail where vulgar con-men would really be held.
2. If they were ever arrested, the government would use their magical powers for its own advantage.
3. On the spot, right away.

SUBTLE. Why?
FACE. Stand to your word,
Or—here comes Dol!—she knows—
SUBTLE. You're tyrannous still.
[*Enter* DOL *hastily.*]
FACE. Strict for my right. How now, Dol! Hast told her,
The Spanish count will come?
DOL. Yes; but another is come,
You little looked for!
FACE. Who's that?
DOL. Your master;
The master of the house.
SUBTLE. How, Dol!
FACE. She lies,
This is some trick. Come, leave your quiblins,[4] Dorothy.
DOL. Look out, and see. [FACE *goes to the window.*]
SUBTLE. Art thou in earnest?
DOL. 'Slight,
Forty o' the neighbors are about him, talking.
FACE. 'Tis he by this good day.
DOL. 'Twill prove ill day
For some on us.
FACE. We are undone and taken.
DOL. Lost, I'm afraid.
SUBTLE. You said he would not come,
While there died one a week within the liberties.[5]
FACE. No: 'twas within the walls.
SUBTLE. Was't so? cry you mercy;
I thought the liberties. What shall we do now, Face?
FACE. Be silent. Not a word, if he call or knock.
I'll into mine old shape again and meet him,
Of Jeremy, the butler. In the mean time,
Do you two pack up all the goods and purchase,[6]
That we can carry in the two trunks. I'll keep him
Off for today, if I cannot longer; and then
At night, I'll ship you both away to Ratcliff,[7]
Where we will meet tomorrow, and there we'll share.
Let Mammon's brass and pewter keep the cellar;
We'll have another time for that. But, Dol,
'Prithee go heat a little water quickly;
Subtle must shave me. All my Captain's beard
Must off, to make me appear smooth Jeremy.
You'll do it?
SUBTLE. Yes, I'll shave you, as well as I can.
FACE. And not cut my throat, but trim me?
SUBTLE. You shall see, sir.
[*Exeunt.*]

4. Jokes.
5. The suburbs, outside the city itself, and so at "liberty" from its regulations. "Within the walls": within the city proper.
6. Booty, loot.
7. Down the Thames, to the East.

Act V

SCENE 1. *The lane before* LOVEWIT'*s door*

[*Enter* LOVEWIT, *with several of the* NEIGHBORS.]

LOVEWIT. Has there been such resort,[8] say you?
1 NEIGHBOR. Daily, sir.
2 NEIGHBOR. And nightly, too.
3 NEIGHBOR. Ay, some as brave as lords.
4 NEIGHBOR. Ladies and gentlewomen.
5 NEIGHBOR. Citizens' wives.
1 NEIGHBOR. And knights.
6 NEIGHBOR. In coaches.
2 NEIGHBOR. Yes, and oyster-women.
1 NEIGHBOR. Beside other gallants.
3 NEIGHBOR. Sailors' wives.
4 NEIGHBOR. Tobacco men.
5 NEIGHBOR. Another Pimlico![9]
LOVEWIT. What should my knave advance,
To draw this company? he hung out no banners
Of a strange calf with five legs to be seen?
Or a huge lobster with six claws?
6 NEIGHBOR. No, sir.
3 NEIGHBOR. We had gone in then, sir.
LOVEWIT. He has no gift
Of teaching in the nose that e'er I knew of.[1]
You saw no bills set up that promised cure
Of agúes, or the tooth-ache?
2 NEIGHBOR. No such thing, sir.
LOVEWIT. Nor heard a drum struck for baboons or puppets?
5 NEIGHBOR. Neither, sir.
LOVEWIT. What device should he bring forth now?
I love a teeming wit as I love my nourishment.
'Pray God he have not kept such open house,
That he hath sold my hangings, and my bedding!
I left him nothing else. If he have eat them,
A plague o' the moth,[2] say I! Sure he has got
Some bawdy pictures to call all this ging;[3]
The friar and the nun; or the new motion
Of the knight's courser covering the parson's mare,
The boy of six year old with the great thing.
Or't may be, he has the fleas that run at tilt[4]
Upon a table, or some dog to dance.
When saw you him?
1 NEIGHBOR. Who, sir, Jeremy?

8. Throng of visitors.
9. A popular carnival held at Hogsden, now Hoxton, outside London.
1. Teaching how to cant or preach through the nose, was not a real activity, but Jonson lists it as another stroke against the Puritans.
2. The locution was proverbial; it implies irritation but not deep distress.
3. Gang; "motion": show.
4. In a flea circus, creatures trained to imitate a tournament.

2 NEIGHBOR. Jeremy butler?
We saw him not this month.

LOVEWIT. How!

4 NEIGHBOR. Not these five weeks, sir.

1 NEIGHBOR. These six weeks at the least.

LOVEWIT. You amaze me, neighbors!

5 NEIGHBOR. Sure, if your worship know not where he is,
He's slipped away.

6 NEIGHBOR. Pray god, he be not made away!

LOVEWIT. Ha! it's no time to question, then. [*Knocks at the door.*]

6 NEIGHBOR. About
Some three weeks since, I heard a doleful cry,
As I sat up a-mending my wife's stockings.

LOVEWIT. 'Tis strange that none will answer! Didst thou hear
A cry, sayst thou?

6 NEIGHBOR. Yes, sir, like unto a man
That had been strangled an hour, and could not speak.

2 NEIGHBOR. I heard it too, just this day three weeks, at two o'clock
Next morning.

LOVEWIT. These be miracles, or you make 'em so!
A man an hour strangled, and could not speak,
And both you heard him cry?

3 NEIGHBOR. Yes, downward, sir.

LOVEWIT. Thou art a wise fellow. Give me thy hand, I pray thee.
What trade are thou on?

3 NEIGHBOR. A smith, an't please your worship.

LOVEWIT. A smith! then lend me thy help to get this door open.

3 NEIGHBOR. That I will presently, sir, but fetch my tools—
[*Exit*]

1 NEIGHBOR. Sir, best to knock again, afore you break it.

LOVEWIT. [*Knocks again.*] I will.

SCENE 2

[*Enter* FACE, *in his butler's livery.*]

FACE. What mean you, sir?

1. 2. 4. NEIGHBORS. O, here's Jeremy!

FACE. Good sir, come from[5] the door.

LOVEWIT. Why, what's the matter?

FACE. Yet farther, you are too near yet.

LOVEWIT. In the name of wonder,
What means the fellow?

FACE. The house, sir, has been visited.

LOVEWIT. What, with the plague? stand thou then farther.

FACE. No, sir,
I had it not.

LOVEWIT. Who had it then? I left
None else but thee in the house.

5. Step away from.

FACE. Yes, sir, my fellow,
The cat that kept the buttery, had it on her
A week before I spied it; but I got her
Conveyed away in the night: and so I shut
The house up for a month—
LOVEWIT. How!
FACE. Purposing then, sir,
T'have burnt rose-vinegar, treacle, and tar,
And have made it sweet, that you should ne'er have known it;
Because I knew the news would but afflict you, sir.
LOVEWIT. Breathe less, and farther off! Why this is stranger!
The neighbors tell me all here that the doors
Have still been open—
FACE. How, sir!
LOVEWIT. Gallants, men, and women,
And of all sorts, tag-rag, been seen to flock here
In threaves,[6] these ten weeks, as to a second Hogsden,
In days of Pimlico and Eye-bright.
FACE. Sir,
Their wisdoms will not say so.
LOVEWIT. Today they speak
Of coaches, and gallants; one in a French-hood
Went in, they tell me; and another was seen
In a velvet gown at the window! divers more
Pass in and out!
FACE. They did pass through the doors then,
Or walls, I assure their eyesights, and their spectacles;
For here, sir, are the keys, and here have been,
In this my pocket, now above twenty days!
And for before, I kept the fort alone there.
But that 'tis yet not deep in the afternoon,
I should believe my neighbors had seen double
Through the black pot,[7] and made these apparitions!
For, on my faith to your worship, for these three weeks
And upwards, the door has not been opened.
LOVEWIT. Strange!
1 NEIGHBOR. Good faith, I think I saw a coach.
2 NEIGHBOR. And I too,
I'd have been sworn.
LOVEWIT. Do you but think it now?
And but one coach?
4 NEIGHBOR. We cannot tell, sir; Jeremy
Is a very honest fellow.
FACE. Did you see me at all?
1 NEIGHBOR. No; that we are sure on.
2 NEIGHBOR. I'll be sworn o' that.
LOVEWIT. Fine rogues to have your testimonies built on!
[*Enter third* NEIGHBOR, *with his tools.*]

6. Throngs. Pimlico and Eye-bright were places where cakes and ale could be consumed by holiday crowds.
7. I.e., of liquor.

3 NEIGHBOR. Is Jeremy come!
1 NEIGHBOR. O, yes; you may leave your tools;
We were deceived, he says.
2 NEIGHBOR. He has had the keys;
And the door has been shut these three weeks.
3 NEIGHBOR. Like enough.
LOVEWIT. Peace, and get hence, you changelings.
[*Enter* SURLY *and* MAMMON.]
FACE. [*aside*] Surly come!
And Mammon made acquainted! they'll tell all.
How shall I beat them off? what shall I do?
Nothing's more wretched than a guilty conscience.

SCENE 3

SURLY. No, sir, he was a great physician. This,
It was no bawdy-house, but a mere chancel![8]
You knew the lord and his sister.
MAMMON. Nay, good Surly—
SURLY. *The happy word, be rich—*
MAMMON. Play not the tyrant—
SURLY. *Should be today pronounced to all your friends.*
And where be your andirons now? and your brass pots,
That should have been golden flagons, and great wedges?
MAMMON. Let me but breathe. What, they have shut their doors,
Methinks!
SURLY. Ay, now 'tis holiday with them.
MAMMON. Rogues,
[*He and* SURLY *knock.*]
Cozeners, impostors, bawds!
FACE. What mean you, sir?
MAMMON. To enter if we can.
FACE. Another man's house!
Here is the owner, sir. Turn you to him,
And speak your business.
MAMMON. Are you, sir, the owner?
LOVEWIT. Yes, sir.
MAMMON. And are those knaves within your cheaters?
LOVEWIT. What knaves? what cheaters?
MAMMON. Subtle and his Lungs.
FACE. The gentleman is distracted, sir! No lungs,
Nor lights[9] have been seen here these three weeks, sir,
Within these doors, upon my word.
SURLY. Your word,
Groom arrogant?

8. I.e., the house was not a bawdy-house but pure as a church (Surly reminds Mammon of his own words).

9. Pretending to mistake the word "lungs," Face says there have been no lights (inner organs, as in the expression "liver and lights") on the street for three weeks.

FACE. Yes, sir, I am the housekeeper,
And know the keys have not been out of my hands.
SURLY. This's a new Face.
FACE. You do mistake the house, sir:
What sign was't at?
SURLY. You rascal! this is one
Of the confederacy. Come, let's get officers,
And force the door.
LOVEWIT. Pray you stay, gentlemen.
SURLY. No, sir, we'll come with warrant.
MAMMON. Ay, and then
We shall have your doors open. [*Exeunt* MAMMON *and* SURLY.]
LOVEWIT. What means this?
FACE. I cannot tell, sir.
1 NEIGHBOR. These are two of the gallants
That we do think we saw.
FACE. Two of the fools!
You talk as idly as they. Good faith, sir,
I think the moon has crazed 'em all. [*Aside.*]—O me,
[*Enter* KASTRIL.]
The angry boy come too! He'll make a noise,
And ne'er away till he have betrayed us all.
KASTRIL. [*knocking*] What, rogues, bawds, slaves, you'll open the door, anon!
Punk, cockatrice,[1] my suster! By this light
I'll fetch the marshal to you. You are a whore
To keep your castle—
FACE. Who would you speak with, sir?
KASTRIL. The bawdy Doctor, and the cozening Captain,
And puss my suster.[2]
LOVEWIT. This is something, sure!
FACE. Upon my trust, the doors were never open, sir.
KASTRIL. I have heard all their tricks told me twice over,
By the fat knight and the lean gentleman.[3]
LOVEWIT. Here comes another.
[*Enter* ANANIAS *and* TRIBULATION.]
FACE. Ananias too?
And his pastor!
TRIBULATION. [*beating at the door*] The doors are shut against us.
ANANIAS. Come forth, you seed of sulphur, sons of fire![4]
Your stench it is broke forth; abomination
Is in the house.
KASTRIL. Ay, my suster's there.
ANANIAS. The place,
It is become a cage of unclean birds.

1. Slang for a prostitute. A whore in a house was often spoken of as keeping a castle.
2. "Puss" is as likely to refer to a rabbit as a cat.
3. I.e. Mammon and Surly.
4. Much of Ananias' language is from the Book of Revelation.

KASTRIL. Yes, I will fetch the scavenger,[5] and the constable.
TRIBULATION. You shall do well.
ANANIAS. We'll join to weed them out.
KASTRIL. You will not come then, punk device,[6] my sister.
ANANIAS. Call her not sister; she's a harlot verily.
KASTRIL. I'll raise the street.
LOVEWIT. Good gentleman, a word.
ANANIAS. Satan avoid, and hinder not our zeal!
[*Exeunt* ANANIAS, TRIBULATION, *and* KASTRIL.]
LOVEWIT. The world's turned Bedlam.[7]
FACE. These are all broke loose
Out of St. Katherine's, where they use to keep
The better sort of mad-folks.
1 NEIGHBOR. All these persons
We saw go in and out here.
2 NEIGHBOR. Yes, indeed, sir.
3 NEIGHBOR. These were the parties.
FACE. Peace, you drunkards! Sir,
I wonder at it! Please you to give me leave
To touch the door, I'll try an the lock be changed.
LOVEWIT. It 'mazes me!
FACE. [*Goes to the door.*] Good faith, sir, I believe
There's no such thing. 'Tis all *deceptio visus*.[8]—
[*Aside.*] Would I could get him away.
DAPPER. [*within*] Master Captain! master Doctor!
LOVEWIT. Who's that?
FACE. [*aside*] Our clerk within, that I forgot!
—I know not, sir.
DAPPER. [*within*] For God's sake, when will her Grace be at leisure?
FACE. Ha!
Illusions, some spirit o' the air! [*aside*]—His gag is melted,
And now he sets out the throat.
DAPPER. [*within*] I am almost stifled—
FACE. [*aside*] Would you were altogether.
LOVEWIT. 'Tis in the house.
Ha! list.
FACE. Believe it, sir, in the air.
LOVEWIT. Peace, you—
DAPPER. [*within*] Mine aunt's grace does not use me well.
SUBTLE. [*within*] You fool,
Peace, you'll mar all.
FACE. [*speaks through the key-hole, while* LOVEWIT *advances to the door unobserved*] Or you will else, you rogue.
LOVEWIT. O, is it so? then you converse with spirits!—
Come, sir. No more of your tricks, good Jeremy,
The truth, the shortest way.

5. Street-sweeper.
6. She is a prostitute proclaimed by her device, i.e., her heraldic emblem, with a play on the old French phrase for perfection, *point devise*.
7. Run mad. St. Katherine's was another, older, madhouse.
8. Optical illusion.

FACE. Dismiss this rabble, sir.—
[*aside.*] What shall I do? I am catched.
LOVEWIT. Good neighbors,
I thank you all. You may depart. [*Exeunt* NEIGHBORS.]—Come sir,
You know that I am an indulgent master;
And therefore, conceal nothing. What's your medicine,
To draw so many several sorts of wild fowl?[9]
FACE. Sir, you were wont to affect mirth and wit:
(But here's no place to talk on't in the street)
Give me but leave to make the best of my fortune,
And only pardon me the abuse of your house;
It's all I beg. I'll help you to a widow,
In recompense, that you shall give me thanks for,
Will make you seven years younger, and a rich one.
'Tis but your putting on a Spanish cloak.
I have her within. You need not fear the house;
It was not visited.[1]
LOVEWIT. But by me, who came
Sooner than you expected.
FACE. It is true, sir.
'Pray you forgive me.
LOVEWIT. Well; let's see your widow.
[*Exeunt.*]

SCENE 4. *A room in* LOVEWIT'S *house*

[*Enter* SUBTLE, *leading in* DAPPER, *with his eyes bound as before.*]
SUBTLE. How! have you eaten your gag?
DAPPER. Yes, faith, it crumbled
Away in my mouth.
SUBTLE. You have spoiled all then.
DAPPER. No,
I hope my aunt of Fairy will forgive me.
SUBTLE. Your aunt's a gracious lady; but in troth
You were to blame.
DAPPER. The fume did overcome me,
And I did do't to stay my stomach. 'Pray you
So satisfy her Grace.[2] [*Enter* FACE *in his uniform*].
Here comes the Captain.
FACE. How now! is his mouth down?[3]
SUBTLE. Ay, he has spoken!
FACE. [*aside*] A pox, I heard him, and you too.—[*loudly*]
He's undone then.—
[*He pushes* DAPPER *away and whispers to* SUBTLE.]
I have been fain to say, the house is haunted
With spirits, to keep churl[4] back.

9. Geese and ducks to be snared.
1. Touched by the plague.
2. Explain it all to her Grace.
3. Has he opened his mouth?
4. I.e., Lovewit, the man from the country.

SUBTLE. And hast thou done it?
FACE. Sure, for this night.
SUBTLE. Why, then triumph and sing
Of Face so famous, the precious king
Of present wits.
FACE. Did you not hear the coil[5]
About the door?
SUBTLE. Yes, and I dwindled with it.
FACE. Show him his aunt, and let him be dispatched;
I'll send her to you. [*Exit* FACE.]
SUBTLE. Well, sir, your aunt her Grace
Will give you audience presently, on my suit,[6]
And the Captain's word that you did not eat your gag
In any contempt of her highness. [*Unbinds his eyes.*]
DAPPER. Not I, in troth, sir.

[*Enter* DOL *like the queen of Fairy.*]

SUBTLE. Here she is come. Down o' your knees and wriggle.
She has a stately presence. [DAPPER *kneels and shuffles towards her.*] Good! Yet nearer,
And bid, God save you!
DAPPER. Madam!
SUBTLE. And your aunt.
DAPPER. And my most gracious aunt, God save your Grace.
DOL. Nephew, we thought to have been angry with you;
But that sweet face of yours hath turned the tide.
And made it flow with joy, that ebbed of love.
Arise, and touch our velvet gown.
SUBTLE. The skirts,
And kiss 'em. So!
DOL. Let me now stroke that head.
Much, nephew, shalt thou win, much shalt thou spend;
Much shalt thou give away, much shalt thou lend.
SUBTLE. [*aside*] Ay, much indeed—Why do you not thank her Grace?
DAPPER. I cannot speak for joy.
SUBTLE. See, the kind wretch!
Your Grace's kinsman right.[7]
DOL. Give me the bird.
Here is your fly in a purse, about your neck, cousin;
Wear it, and feed it about this day se'en-night,[8]
On your right wrist—
SUBTLE. Open a vein with a pin,
And let it suck but once a week; till then,
You must not look on't.
DOL. No. And, kinsman,
Bear yourself worthy of the blood you come on.
SUBTLE. Her Grace would have you eat no more *Woolsack* pies,[9]

5. Racket.
6. At my request.
7. True kinsman; "kind": tender-hearted.
8. A week from today.
9. Subtle advises against the kind of pies sold at the Woolsack, a London tavern, and "frumety," a kind of spiced pudding sold at the Dagger, another tavern.

Nor *Dagger* frumety.
DOL. Nor break his fast
In *Heaven* and *Hell.*[1]
SUBTLE. She's with you everywhere!
Nor play with costermongers, at mum-chance, tray-trip,[2]
God-make-you-rich (when as your aunt has done it); but keep
The gallant'st company, and the best games—
DAPPER. Yes, sir.
SUBTLE. Gleek and primero; and what you get, be true to us.
DAPPER. By this hand, I will.
SUBTLE. You may bring's a thousand pound
Before tomorrow night, if but three thousand
Be stirring, an you will.
DAPPER. I swear I will then.
SUBTLE. Your fly will learn you all games.
FACE. [*within*] Have you done there?
SUBTLE. Your Grace will command him no more duties?
DOL. No;
But come, and see me often. I may chance
To leave him three or four hundred chests of treasure,
And some twelve thousand acres of Fairyland,
If he game well and comely with good gamesters.
SUBTLE. There's a kind aunt! kiss her departing part.—
But you must sell your forty mark a year, now.
DAPPER. Ay, sir, I mean.
SUBTLE. Or, give't away; pox on't!
DAPPER. I'll give't mine aunt: I'll go and fetch the writings. [*Exit.*]
SUBTLE. 'Tis well, away. [*Enter* FACE.]
FACE. Where's Subtle?
SUBTLE. Here; what news?
FACE. Drugger is at the door, go take his suit,
And bid him fetch a parson, presently;
Say, he shall marry the widow. Thou shalt spend
A hundred pound by the service![3] [*Exit* SUBTLE.] Now, Queen Dol,
Have you packed up all?
DOL. Yes.
FACE. And how do you like
The lady Pliant?
DOL. A good dull innocent. [*Enter* SUBTLE.]
SUBTLE. Here's your Hieronimo's cloak and hat.
FACE. Give me them.
SUBTLE. And the ruff too?
FACE. Yes; I'll come to you presently. [*Exit.*]

1. Heaven and Hell were a pair of low taverns in Westminster; there was a third nearby, known as Purgatory.
2. "Mum-chance," "tray-trip," and "God-make-you-rich" were simple games of chance, on the general level of "go fish."
3. You'll gain a hundred pounds by doing this.

SUBTLE. Now he is gone about his project, Dol,
I told you of, for the widow.
DOL. 'Tis direct
Against our articles.[4]
SUBTLE. Well, we will fit him, wench.
Hast thou gulled her of her jewels or her bracelets?
DOL. No; but I'll do't.
SUBTLE. Soon at night, my Dolly,
When we are shipped, and all our goods aboard,
Eastward for Ratcliff; we will turn our course
To Brainford,[5] westward, if thou sayst the word,
And take our leaves of this o'erweening rascal,
This peremptory Face.
DOL. Content, I'm weary of him.
SUBTLE. Thou'st cause, when the slave will run a wiving, Dol,
Against the instrument that was drawn between us.
DOL. I'll pluck his bird as bare as I can.
SUBTLE. Yes, tell her,
She must by any means address some present
To the cunning man, make him amends for wronging
His art with her suspicion; send a ring,
Or chain of pearl; she will be tortured else
Extremely in her sleep, say, and have strange things
Come to her. Wilt thou?
DOL. Yes.
SUBTLE. My fine flitter-mouse,[6]
My bird o' the night! we'll tickle it at the *Pigeons*,[7]
When we have all, and may unlock the trunks,
And say, this's mine, and thine; and thine, and mine. [*They kiss.*]
[*Enter* FACE.]
FACE. What now! a-billing?
SUBTLE. Yes, a little exalted
In the good passage of our stock-affairs.
FACE. Drugger has brought his parson; take him in, Subtle,
And send Nab back again to wash his face.
SUBTLE. I will: and shave himself? [*Exit.*]
FACE. If you can get him.
DOL. You are hot upon it, Face, whate'er it is!
FACE. A trick that Dol shall spend ten pound a month by.
[*Enter* SUBTLE.]
Is he gone?
SUBTLE. The chaplain waits you in the hall, sir.
FACE. I'll go bestow him.[8] [*Exit* FACE.]
DOL. He'll now marry her, instantly.

4. Articles of incorporation by which Face, Dol, and Subtle formed their original league.

5. Instead of going down the Thames to Ratcliff, and hence presumably outward-bound, Dol and Subtle will go upriver to Brainford (Brentford), heading to the West Country.

6. Bat (cf. German *Fledermaus*); as a prostitute, Dol is a night-bird.

7. The Three Pigeons Inn at Brentford, famous into the first years of the 20th century.

8. Get him ready.

SUBTLE. He cannot yet, he is not ready. Dear Dol,
Cozen her of all thou canst. To deceive him
Is no deceit, but justice, that would break
Such an inextricable tie as ours was.
DOL. Let me alone to fit him.[9] [*Enter* FACE.]
FACE. Come, my venturers,[1]
You have packed up all? where be the trunks? bring forth.
SUBTLE. Here.
FACE. Let us see them. Where's the money?
SUBTLE. Here,
In this.
FACE. Mammon's ten pound; eight score before.
The brethren's money, this. Drugger's and Dapper's.
What paper's that?
DOL. The jewel of the waiting maid's,
That stole it from her lady, to know certain—
FACE. If she should have precedence of her mistress?
DOL. Yes.
FACE. What box is that?
SUBTLE. The fishwives' rings, I think;
And the alewives' single money.[2] Is't not, Dol?
DOL. Yes; and the whistle that the sailor's wife
Brought you to know an her husband were with Ward.[3]
FACE. We'll wet it tomorrow; and our silver beakers
And tavern cups. Where be the French petticoats,
And girdles and hangers?
SUBTLE. Here, in the trunk,
And the bolts of lawn.
FACE. Is Drugger's damask there,
And the tobacco?
SUBTLE. Yes.
FACE. Give me the keys.
DOL. Why you the keys?
SUBTLE. No matter, Dol; because
We shall not open them before he comes. [*She gives them.*]
FACE. 'Tis true, you shall not open them, indeed;
Nor have them forth, do you see? not forth, Dol.
DOL. No!
FACE. No, my smock-rampant.[4] The right is, my master
Knows all, has pardoned me, and he will keep 'em;
Doctor, 'tis true—you look—for all your figures;[5]
I sent for him, indeed. Wherefore, good partners,
Both he and she, be satisfied; for here

9. I.e., I'll manage to give him what he deserves.
1. Partners.
2. Loose change.
3. A notorious pirate. The whistle was evidently a silver bosun's whistle, and Face puns off it: i.e., we'll wet our whistles tomorrow.
4. In mock-heraldic language, Dol's smock or slip is the emblem of her trade, and she is rampant, i.e., rearing up to attack Face.
5. I.e., Doctor—there's no need to stare—it's true in spite of all your calculations.

Determines the *indenture tripartite*[6]
'Twixt Subtle, Dol, and Face. All I can do
Is to help you over the wall, o' the backside,
Or lend you a sheet to save your velvet gown, Dol.
Here will be officers presently; bethink you
Of some course suddenly to 'scape the dock:[7]
For thither you'll come else. [*Loud knocking.*] Hark you, thunder.

SUBTLE. You are a precious fiend!

OFFICERS. [*without*] Open the door.

FACE. Dol, I am sorry for thee i' faith; but hearest thou?
It shall go hard but I will place thee somewhere:
Thou shalt have my letter to mistress Amo[8]—

DOL. Hang you!

FACE. Or madam Cæsarean.

DOL. Pox upon you, rogue,
Would I had but time to beat thee!

FACE. Subtle,
Let's know where you set up next; I will send you
A customer now and then, for old acquaintance.
What new course have you?

SUBTLE. Rogue, I'll hang myself;
That I may walk a greater devil than thou,
And haunt thee in the flock-bed and the buttery.[9]

[*Exeunt.*]

SCENE 5. *An outer room in* LOVEWIT'S *house*

[*Enter* LOVEWIT *in Spanish dress, with the* PARSON. *Loud knocking at the door.*]

LOVEWIT. What do you mean, my masters?

MAMMON. [*without*] Open your door,
Cheaters, bawds, conjurers.

OFFICERS. [*without*] Or we'll break it open.

LOVEWIT. What warrant have you?

OFFICERS. [*without*] Warrant enough, sir, doubt not,
If you'll not open it.

LOVEWIT. Is there an officer, there?

OFFICERS. [*without*] Yes, two or three for failing.[1]

LOVEWIT. Have but patience,
And I will open it straight. [*Enter* FACE, *as butler.*]

FACE. Sir, have you done?
Is it a marriage? perfect?

LOVEWIT. Yes, my brain.

FACE. Off with your ruff and cloak, then; be yourself, sir.

6. Here ends ("determines") the three-way agreement.
7. The prisoner's dock, perhaps also the executioner's dock.
8. Mistress Amo(retta) or Madam Caesarean are obviously brothel-keepers.
9. Ghosts would haunt a victim in his bed and at his board.
1. I.e., for good measure.

SUBTLE. [*without*] Down with the door.
KASTRIL. [*without*] Slight, ding it open.[2]
LOVEWIT. [*opening the door*] Hold,
Hold, gentlemen, what means this violence?
[MAMMON, SURLY, KASTRIL, ANANIAS, TRIBULATION, *and* OFFICERS *rush in.*]
MAMMON. Where is this collier?[3]
SURLY. And my Captain Face?
MAMMON. These day owls.
SURLY. That are birding in men's purses.
MAMMON. Madam suppository.
KASTRIL. Doxy,[4] my suster.
ANANIAS. Locusts
Of the foul pit.
TRIBULATION. Profane as Bel and the dragon.[5]
ANANIAS. Worse than the grasshoppers, or the lice of Egypt.
LOVEWIT. Good gentlemen, hear me. Are you officers,
And cannot stay this violence?
1 OFFICER. Keep the peace.
LOVEWIT. Gentlemen, what is the matter? whom do you seek?
MAMMON. The chemical cozener.
SURLY. And the Captain pander.
KASTRIL. The nun[6] my suster.
MAMMON. Madam Rabbi.
ANANIAS. Scorpions,
And caterpillars.
LOVEWIT. Fewer at once, I pray you.
2 OFFICER. One after another, gentlemen, I charge you,
By virtue of my staff.[7]
ANANIAS. They are the vessels
Of pride, lust, and the cart.
LOVEWIT. Good zeal, lie still
A little while.
TRIBULATION. Peace, deacon Ananias.
LOVEWIT. The house is mine here, and the doors are open;
If there be any such persons as you seek for,
Use your authority, search on o' God's name.
I am but newly come to town, and finding
This tumult 'bout my door, to tell you true,
It somewhat 'mazed me; till my man, here, fearing
My more displeasure, told me he had done
Somewhat an insolent part, let out my house
(Belike presuming on my known aversion
From any air o' the town while there was sickness)

2. Break it down.
3. Cheat.
4. Slut. "Madam suppository" is, of course, Dol.
5. One of the apocryphal books of the Bible bears this title. Daniel wars upon a pagan deity (Baal) and a dragon. The grasshoppers and lice of Egypt were plagues visited on that land before the exodus of Moses.
6. Cant term for a prostitute in a house.
7. The officers carry long rods as emblems of authority.

To a Doctor and a Captain: who, what they are
Or where they be, he knows not.
MAMMON. Are they gone?
LOVEWIT. You may go in and search, sir. [MAMMON, ANANIAS *and* TRIBULATION *go in.*] Here, I find
The empty walls worse than I left them, smoked,
A few cracked pots and glasses, and a furnace;
The ceiling fill'd with poesies of the candle,[8]
And madam with a dildo writ o' the walls:
Only one gentlewoman, I met here,
That is within, that said she was a widow—
KASTRIL. Ay, that's my suster; I'll go thump her. Where is she?
[*Goes in.*]
LOVEWIT. And should have married a Spanish count, but he,
When he come to't, neglected her so grossly,
That I, a widower, am gone through with her.
SURLY. How! have I lost her then?
LOVEWIT. Were you the don, sir?
Good faith, now, she does blame you extremely, and says
You swore, and told her you had ta'en the pains
To dye your beard, and umber o'er your face,
Borrowed a suit, and ruff, all for her love;
And then did nothing. What an oversight,
And want of putting forward, sir, was this!
Well fare an old harquebusier,[9] yet,
Could prime his powder, and give fire, and hit,
All in a twinkling! [*Enter* MAMMON.]
MAMMON. The whole nest are fled!
LOVEWIT. What sort of birds were they?
MAMMON. A kind of choughs,[1]
Or thievish daws, sir, that have picked my purse
Of eight score and ten pounds within these five weeks,
Beside my first materials; and my goods,
That lie in the cellar, which I am glad they have left,
I may have home yet.
LOVEWIT. Think you so, sir?
MAMMON. Ay.
LOVEWIT. By order of law, sir, but not otherwise.
MAMMON. Not mine own stuff?
LOVEWIT. Sir, I can take no knowledge
That they are yours, but by public means.
If you can bring certificate that you were gulled of 'em,
Or any formal writ out of a court,
That you did cozen yourself, I will not hold them.
MAMMON. I'll rather lose 'em.
LOVEWIT. That you shall not, sir,
By me, in troth. Upon these terms, they're yours.

8. I.e., poems traced on the walls in candle smoke; madam with a dildo is obviously a dirty picture.

9. Musketeer.

1. Thievish magpies.

What should they have been, sir, turned into gold, all?
MAMMON. No.
I cannot tell. It may be they should. What then?
LOVEWIT. What a great loss in hope have you sustained!
MAMMON. Not I, the commonwealth has.
FACE. Ay, he would have built
The city new; and made a ditch about it
Of silver, should have run with cream from Hogsden;[2]
That, every Sunday, in Moorfields, the younkers,
And tits and tom-boys should have fed on, gratis.
MAMMON. I will go mount a turnip-cart, and preach
The end of the world, within these two months. Surly,
What! in a dream?
SURLY. Must I needs cheat myself,
With that same foolish vice of honesty!
Come, let us go and hearken out the rogues.
That Face I'll mark for mine, if e'er I meet him.
FACE. If I can hear of him, sir, I'll bring you word,
Unto your lodging; for in troth, they were strangers
To me, I thought 'em honest as myself, sir.
[*Exeunt* MAMMON *and* SURLY.]
[*Enter* ANANIAS *and* TRIBULATION.]
TRIBULATION. 'Tis well, the saints shall not lose all yet. Go,
And get some carts—
LOVEWIT. For what, my zealous friends?
ANANIAS. To bear away the portion of the righteous
Out of this den of thieves.
LOVEWIT. What is that portion?
ANANIAS. The goods sometime the orphans', that the brethren
Bought with their silver pence.
LOVEWIT. What, those in the cellar,
The knight sir Mammon claims?
ANANIAS. I do defy
The wicked Mammon, so do all the brethren,
Thou profane man! I ask thee with what conscience
Thou canst advance that idol against us,
That have the seal? Were not the shillings numbered,
That made the pounds? Were not the pounds told out,
Upon the second day of the fourth week,
In the eighth month, upon the table dormant,
The year of the last patience of the saints,
Six hundred and ten?[3]
LOVEWIT. Mine earnest vehement botcher,
And deacon also, I cannot dispute with you:
But if you get you not away the sooner,
I shall confute you with a cudgel.
ANANIAS. Sir!

2. Mammon's dream is described in terms of the Land of Cockayne, where all good things come for free.

3. I.e., the last Tuesday of August in 1610.

TRIBULATION. Be patient, Ananias.
ANANIAS. I am strong,
And will stand up, well girt, against an host,
That threaten Gad in exile.[4]
LOVEWIT. I shall send you
To Amsterdam, to your cellar.
ANANIAS. I will pray there,
Against thy house. May dogs defile thy walls,
And wasps and hornets breed beneath thy roof,
This seat of falsehood, and this cave of cozenage!
[*Exeunt* ANANIAS *and* TRIBULATION.]
[*Enter* DRUGGER.]
LOVEWIT. Another, too?
DRUGGER. Not I, sir, I am no brother.
LOVEWIT. [*beats him*] Away, you Harry Nicholas![5] do you talk?
[*Exit* DRUGGER.]
FACE. No, this was Abel Drugger. Good sir, [*to the* PARSON] go,
And satisfy him; tell him all is done:
He stayed too long a washing of his face.
The Doctor, he shall hear of him at Westchester;[6]
And of the Captain, tell him, at Yarmouth, or
Some good port-town else, lying for a wind. [*Exit* PARSON.]
If you get off the angry child, now, sir—
[*Enter* KASTRIL *dragging in his sister*.]
KASTRIL. Come on, you ewe, you have matched most sweetly, have you not?
Did not I say, I would never have you tupped[7]
But by a dubbed boy, to make you a lady-tom?
'Slight, you are a mammet![8] O, I could touse you, now.
Death, mun' you marry with a pox?
LOVEWIT. You lie, boy;
As sound as you; and I'm aforehand with you.
KASTRIL. Anon!
LOVEWIT. Come, will you quarrel? I will feize[9] you, sirrah;
Why do you not buckle to your tools?
KASTRIL. God's light,
This is a fine old boy as e'er I saw!
LOVEWIT. What, do you change your copy[1] now? Proceed,
Here stands my dove; stoop[2] at her, if you dare.
KASTRIL. 'Slight, I must love him! I cannot choose, i' faith,
An I should be hanged for't! Suster, I protest,
I honor thee for this match.
LOVEWIT. O, do you so, sir?

4. The persecuted saints, with an allusion to Genesis 49:19.
5. Lovewit mistakes Drugger for another Puritan, and calls him "Harry Nicholas" by allusion to the Dutch founder of a radical protestant sect, the Family of Love.
6. Face's messsage sends Drugger off on a couple of hopeless wild-goose chases.
7. Mated (the term is commonly applied to sheep); "a dubbed boy": a knight; "lady-tom": the wife of a knight, any knight.
8. Doll, puppet, idiot; "touse": beat.
9. Beat, fight.
1. Style.
2. As a hawk stoops (dives) to clutch its prey.

KASTRIL. Yes, an thou canst take tobacco and drink, old boy,
I'll give her five hundred pound more to her marriage,
Than her own state.[3]
LOVEWIT. Fill a pipe full, Jeremy.
FACE. Yes; but go in and take it, sir.
LOVEWIT. We will.
I will be ruled by thee in anything, Jeremy.
KASTRIL. 'Slight, thou art not hide-bound, thou art a jovy boy.[4]
Come, let us in, I pray thee, and take our whiffs.
LOVEWIT. Whiff in with your sister, brother boy.
[*Exeunt* KASTRIL *and* DAME PLIANT.] That master
That had received such happiness by a servant,
In such a widow, and with so much wealth,
Were very ungrateful, if he would not be
A little indulgent to that servant's wit,
And help his fortune, though with some small strain
Of his own candor. [*advancing*]—*Therefore, gentlemen,*
And kind spectators, if I have outstripped
An old man's gravity, or strict canon, think
What a young wife and a good brain may do;
Stretch age's truth sometimes, and crack it too.
Speak for thyself, knave.
FACE. *So I will, sir.*
[*Advancing to the front of the stage.*] *Gentlemen,*
My part a little fell in this last scene,
Yet 'twas decorum.[5] *And though I am clean*
Got off from Subtle, Surly, Mammon, Dol,
Hot Ananias, Dapper, Drugger, all
With whom I traded; yet I put myself
On you, that are my country:[6] *and this pelf,*
Which I have got, if you do quit me, rests
To feast you often, and invite new guests.

THE END

1610

3. I.e., five hundred pounds in dowry, beyond what she already has from her first marriage.
4. Jovial good fellow.
5. I.e., the rule that a character must not violate the nature assigned him at the start of the play. He was a bold rogue as Face, he is a sly rogue as Jeremy, but always a rogue.
6. I.e., appeal to a jury of my peers.

The Sad Shepherd

or

A Tale of Robin Hood

The Persons of the Play

ROBIN HOOD, *the chief woodman, master of the feast*
MARIAN, *his lady, the mistress*

THEIR FAMILY

FRIAR TUCK, *the chaplain and steward*
LITTLE JOHN, *bow bearer*
SCARLET, SCATHLOCK } *two brothers, huntsmen*
GEORGE A GREENE, *usher*[1] *of the bower*
MUCH, *Robin Hood's bailiff or acater*[2]

THE GUESTS INVITED

CLARION, *the rich*
LIONEL, *the courteous*
ALKEN, *the sage*
EGLAMOUR, *the sad*
KAROLIN, *the kind* } *shepherds*
MELLIFLEUR, *the sweet*
AMIE, *the gentle*
EARINE, *the beautiful* } *shepherdesses*

THE TROUBLES UNEXPECTED

MAUDLIN, *the envious, the Witch of Papplewick*
DOUCE, *the proud, her daughter*
LOREL, *the rude, a swineherd, the witch's son*
PUCK-HAIRY, *or Robin Foodfellow, their hine*[3]

THE RECONCILER

REUBEN, *a devout hermit*

The scene is Sherwood, consisting of a landscape of forest, hills, valleys, cottages, a castle, a river, pastures, herds, flocks, all full of

1. I.e., butler and overseer; the term "usher" is oddly formal in a gang of outlaws.
2. I.e., caterer, the person in charge of provisions.
3. Servant.

country simplicity. ROBIN HOOD'S *bower; his well; the witch's dimble;*[4] *the swineherd's oak; the hermit's cell.*

Prologue

He[5] that hath feasted you these forty years,
And fitted fables for your finer ears,
Although at first he scarce could hit the bore,[6]
Yet you, with patience hearkening more and more,
At length have grown up to him, and made known
The working of his pen is now your own.
He prays you would vouchsafe, for your own sake,
To hear him this once more, but sit awake.
And, though he now present you with such wool
As from mere English flocks his muse can pull,
He hopes when it is made up into cloth,
Not the most curious head here will be loath
To wear a hood of it, it being a fleece
To match or those of Sicily or Greece.
His scene is Sherwood, and his play a tale
Of Robin Hood's inviting from the Vale
Of Belvoir[7] all the shepherds to a feast,
Where by the casual absence of one guest
The mirth is troubled much, and in one man
As much sadness shown as passion can—
The sad young shepherd, whom we here present,
[*The* SAD SHEPHERD *passeth silently over the stage.*]
Like his woes' figure, dark and discontent
For his lost love, who in the Trent is said
To have miscarried. 'Las! What knows the head[8]
Of a calm river whom the feet have drowned?
Hear what his sorrows are, and, if they wound
Your gentle breasts, so that the end crown all,
Which in the scope of one day's chance may fall,
Old Trent will send you more such tales as these,
And shall grow young again as one doth please.

[*Here the Prologue, thinking to end, returns upon a new purpose and speaks on.*]

But here's an heresy of late let fall,
That mirth by no means fits a pastoral.[9]

4. Dingle, a secluded grove.
5. I.e., the author, Jonson in his own person.
6. Match the caliber of your wit.
7. The Vale of Belvoir and many other features of the theatrical landscape, particularly the river Trent and its small tributaries, identify the place of the action as the North Country. The "low" characters speak a kind of broad Yorkshire or Low Scots dialect that will be annotated only when the basic word seems hard to identify.
8. The "head" of a stream is its source; Jonson plays with the idea by assuming that its mouth is the "feet."
9. That pastorals cannot be comic is a heresy indeed: it's not clear whom Jonson has in mind. Both antiquity and the Renaissance freely admitted comic effects in their pastorals.

Such say so, who can make none, he presumes;
Else there's no scene more properly assumes
The sock.[1] For whence can sport in kind arise
But from the rural routs[2] and families?
Safe on this ground then, we not fear today
To tempt your laughter by our rustic play;
Wherein if we distaste, or be cried down,
We think we therefore shall not leave the town,
Nor that the forewits,[3] that would draw the rest
Unto their liking, always like the best.
The wise and knowing critic will not say,
This worst, or better is, before he weigh
Where[4] every piece be perfect in the kind,
And then, though in themselves he difference find,
Yet, if the place require it where they stood,
The equal fitting makes them equal good.
You shall have love and hate and jealousy,
As well as mirth and rage and melancholy,
Or whatsoever else may either move
Or stir affections,[5] and your likings prove.
But that no style for pastoral should go
Current but what is stamped with "Ah" and "O,"
Who judgeth so, may singularly err,
As if all poesy had one character
In which what were not written, were not right,
Or that the man who made such one poor flight
In his whole life, had with his wingéd skill
Advanced him upmost on the muses' hill,
When he like poet yet remains, as those
Are painters who can only make a rose.[6]
From such your wits redeem you, or your chance,
Lest to a greater height you do advance
Of folly, to contemn those that are known
Artificers, and trust such as are none.

The Argument of the First Act

Robin Hood, having invited all the shepherds and shepherdesses of the Vale of Belvoir to a feast in the Forest of Sherwood, and, trusting to his mistress, Maid Marian, with her woodmen, to kill him venison against the day, having left the like charge with Friar Tuck, his chaplain and steward, to command the rest of his merry men to see the bower made ready and all things in order for the

1. Traditional low slipper worn by comic actors in antiquity, as against the high-heeled buskin worn by tragic actors; "in kind": in nature, naturally.
2. Gatherings, parties.
3. Forward wits, critics.
4. Whether; "perfect in the kind": correct in terms of the genre.
5. Emotions.
6. Jonson argues, not only against limitations on the freedom of the poet, but for his duty to choose many diverse subjects.

entertainment, meeting with his guests at their entrance into the wood, welcomes and conducts them to his bower, where, by the way, he receives the relation of the Sad Shepherd, Eglamour, who is fallen into a deep melancholy for the loss of his beloved Earine, reported to have been drowned in passing over the Trent some few days before. They endeavor in what they can to comfort him, but, his disease having taken so strong root, all is in vain, and they are forced to leave him. In the meantime Marian is come from hunting with the huntsmen, where the lovers interchangeably express their loves. Robin Hood inquires if she hunted the deer at force[7] *and what sport he made, how long he stood, and what head he bore; all which is briefly answered with a relation of breaking him up, and the raven and her bone, the suspect*[8] *had of that raven to be Maudlin, the Witch of Papplewick, whom one of the huntsmen met i' the morning at the rousing of the deer, and is confirmed by her being then in Robin Hood's kitchen, i' the chimney corner broiling the same bit which was thrown to the raven at the quarry*[9] *or fall of the deer. Marian, being gone in to show the deer to some of the shepherdesses, returns instantly to the scene discontented, sends away the venison she had killed to her they call the Witch, quarrels with her love, Robin Hood, abuseth him and his guests, the shepherds, and so departs, leaving them all in wonder and perplexity.*

Act I.

SCENE 1. ROBIN HOOD'S *bower*

EGLAMOUR

EGLAMOUR. Here she was wont to go, and here, and here—
Just where those daisies, pinks, and violets grow!
The world may find the spring by following her,
For other print her airy steps ne'er left.
Her treading would not bend a blade of grass,
Or shake the downy blowball[1] from his stalk!
But like the soft west wind she shot along,
And, where she went, the flowers took thickest root,
As she had sowed them with her odorous foot.

SCENE 2

[*To him,*] MARIAN, TUCK, JOHN, WOODMEN, *etc.*

MARIAN. Know all, or can you guess, my merry men,
What 'tis that keeps your master Robin Hood
So long both from his Marian and the wood?

7. I.e., with dogs, in open country; "what head he bore": how many points were in his horns.
8. Suspicion.
9. I.e., cutting up.
1. Dandelion-thistle.

TUCK. Forsooth, madám, he will be here by noon,
And prays it of your bounty, as a boon,
That you by then have killed him venison some
To feast his jolly friends, who hither come
In threaves[2] to frolic with him and make cheer.
Here's Little John hath harbored[3] you a deer,
I see by his tackling.
JOHN. And a hart of ten[4]
I trow he be, madám, or blame your men;
For by his slot, his entries, and his port,
His frayings, fewmets[5] he doth promise sport
And standing 'fore the dogs; he bears a head
Large and well-beamed, with all rights summed and spread.[6]
MARIAN. Let's rouse him quickly, and lay on the hounds.
JOHN. Scathlock is ready with them on the grounds;
So is his brother Scarlet. Now they have found
His lair, they have him sure within the pound.
MARIAN. Away then! When my Robin bids a feast,
'Twere sin in Marian to defraud a guest.
[*Exeunt* MARIAN *and* JOHN *with the* WOODMEN.]

SCENE 3

TUCK, GEORGE A GREENE, MUCH, EGLAMOUR

TUCK. And I, the chaplain, here am left to be
Steward today, and charge you all in fee[7]
To don your liveries, see the bower dressed,
And fit the fine devices for the feast.
You, George, must care to make the baldric[8] trim,
And garland that must crown or her or him
Whose flock this year hath brought the earliest lamb.
GEORGE. Good Father Tuck, at your commands I am
To cut the table out o' the greensward,
Or any other service for my lord,
To carve the guests large seats and these laid in
With turf so soft and smooth as the mole's skin,
And hang the bulléd[9] nosegays 'bove their heads . . .
The piper's bank whereon to sit and play,
And a fair dial[1] to mete out the day.
Our master's feast shall want no just delights;
His entertainments must have all the rites.

2. Throngs.
3. Tracked down; "tackling": equipment (bow and arrows).
4. A stag with ten tines on his antlers.
5. "Slot": footprint; "entries"; the tracks left by a deer in the underbrush; "port": the depth of his track, indicative of his weight; "frayings": the places where he has rubbed his antlers on trees, to get rid of the velvet; "fewmets": his dung.
6. With all his tines completed and his horns well grown.
7. In fealty, on your loyalty.
8. A decorative belt, given to the person whose ewe lambed first.
9. Budding. A line, perhaps more, seems to have been accidentally omitted at this. point.
1. Clock or sun-dial to measure the day.

MUCH. Ay, and all choice that plenty can send in—
Bread, wine, acates,[2] fowl, feather, fish, or fin,
For which my father's nets have swept the Trent.
[EGLAMOUR *falls in with them.*]
EGLAMOUR. And ha' you found her?
MUCH. Whom?
EGLAMOUR. My drownéd love,
Earine! The sweet Earine!
The bright and beautiful Earine!
Have you not heard of my Earine?
Just by your father's mills (I think I am right—
Are not you Much the Miller's son?)—
MUCH. I am.
EGLAMOUR. And baily[3] to brave Robin Hood?
MUCH. The same.
EGLAMOUR. Close by your father's mills, Earine,
Earine was drowned! O my Earine!
(Old Maudlin tells me so, and Douce, her daughter.)
Ha' you swept the river, say you, and not found her?
MUCH. For fowl and fish we have.
EGLAMOUR. O, not for her?
You are goodly friends, right charitable men!
Nay, keep your way and leave me; make your toys,
Your tales, your poesies, that you talked of—all
Your entertainments. You not injure me.
Only if I may enjoy my cypress[4] wreath,
And you will let me weep, 'tis all I ask,
Till I be turned to water as was she!
And, troth, what less suit can you grant a man?
TUCK. His fantasy[5] is hurt; let us now leave him;
The wound is yet too fresh to admit searching. [*Exit.*]
EGLAMOUR. Searching? Where should I search, or on what track?
Can you, slow drop of tears or this dark shade
About my brows, enough describe her loss?
Earine! O, my Earine's loss!
No, no, no, no; this heart will break first.
GEORGE. How will this sad disaster strike the ears
Of bounteous Robin Hood, our gentle master! [*Exit.*]
MUCH. How will it mar his mirth, abate his feast,
And strike a horror into every guest! [*Exit.*]
EGLAMOUR. If I could knit whole clouds about my brows,
And weep like Swithin[6] or those watery signs,
The Kids[7] that rise then, and drown all the flocks
Of those rich shepherds dwelling in this vale,
Those careless shepherds that did let her drown,

2. Provisions in general.
3. Bailiff, deputy.
4. Cypress, emblem of mourning and death.
5. Imagination.
6. St. Swithin, whose day is July 15, is supposed to presage summer storms.
7. A group of stars in Auriga, supposed to influence hurricanes.

Then I did something; or could make old Trent
Drunk with my sorrow, to start out in breaches
To drown their herds, their cattle, and their corn,
Break down their mills, their dams, o'erturn their weirs,
And see their houses and whole livelihood
Wrought into water with her, all were good—
I'd kiss the torrent and those whirls of Trent
That sucked her in, my sweet Earine!
When they have cast her body on the shore,
And it comes up as tainted as themselves,
All pale and bloodless, I will love it still,
For all that they can do, and make them mad
To see how I will hug it in mine arms,
And hang upon the looks, dwell on her eyes,
Feed round about her lips, and eat her kisses,
Suck of her drownéd flesh!—and where's their malice?
Not all their envious sousing[8] can change that.
But I will study some revenge past this!
I pray you, give me leave, for I will study,
Though all the bells, pipes, tabors, tambourines ring,
That you can plant about me; I will study.

SCENE 4

To him, ROBIN HOOD, CLARION, MELLIFLEUR, LIONEL, AMIE, ALKEN, TUCK, SERVANTS, *with music of all sorts*

ROBIN. Welcome, bright Clarion and sweet Mellifleur,
The courteous Lionel, fair Amie, all
My friends and neighbors, to the jolly bower
Of Robin Hood and to the greenwood walks!
Now that the shearing of your sheep is done,
And the washed flocks are lighted[9] of their wool,
The smoother ewes are ready to receive
The mounting rams again; and both do feed,
As either promised, to increase your breed
At eaning[1] time, and bring your lusty twins.
Why should or you or we so much forget
The season in ourselves as not to make
Use of our youth and spirits to awake
The nimble hornpipe and the tambourine,
And mix our songs and dances in the wood,
And each of us cut down a triumph bough?[2]
Such were the rites the youthful June allow.
CLARION. They were, gay Robin; but the sourer sort
Of shepherds[3] now disclaim in all such sport,

8. Drenching, drowning.
9. Lightened (by shearing).
1. Yeaning, i.e., lambing time.
2. Since time out of mind, green branches, cut on May Day or at harvest festivals, had been emblems of fertility.
3. I.e., Puritans, bitterly hostile to the folk festivals and celebrations of rural England as either papist, pagan, or both.

And say our flocks the while are poorly fed,
When with such vanities the swains are led.

TUCK. Would they, wise Clarion, were not hurried more
With covetise and rage, when to their store
They add the poor man's eanling, and dare sell
Both fleece and carcass, not gi'ing him the fell;[4]
When to one goat they reach that prickly weed,
Which maketh all the rest forbear to feed,
Or strew tods' hairs, or with their tails[5] do sweep
The dewy grass, to doff the simpler sheep,
Or dig deep pits their neighbor's neat[6] to vex,
To drown the calves and crack the heifers' necks,
Or with pretense of chasing thence the brock[7]
Send in a cur to worry the whole flock!

LIONEL. O friar, those are faults that are not seen;
Ours open and of worst example been.[8]
They call ours pagan pastimes, that infect
Our blood with ease, our youth with all neglect,
Our tongues with wantonness, our thoughts with lust;
And what they censure[9] ill, all others must.

ROBIN. I do not know what their sharp sight may see
Of late, but I should think it still might be,
As 'twas, a happy age, when on the plains
The woodmen met the damsels, and the swains,
The neat-herds, plowmen, and the pipers loud,
And each did dance, some to the kit or crowd,[1]
Some to the bagpipe; some the tabret[2] moved,
And all did either love or were beloved.

LIONEL. The dextrous shepherd then would try his sling,
Then dart his hook at daisies, then would sing,
Sometimes would wrastle.

CLARION. Ay, and with a lass,
And give her a new garment on the grass[3]
After a course at barleybreak or base.

LIONEL. And all these deeds were seen without offense,
Or the least hazard o' their innocence.

ROBIN. Those charitable times had no mistrust;
Shepherds knew how to love and not to lust.

CLARION. Each minute that we lose thus, I confess,
Deserves a censure on us, more or less,
But that a sadder chance hath given allay[4]
Both to the mirth and music of this day.

4. I.e., take the poor man's lamb (his only increase for the year), and sell both fleece and carcass, not leaving him even the shorn skin ("fell"). Puritans were often accused of sharp business practice.
5. Foxes' hairs or tails, which, being scattered in the grass, will so terrify the sheep that they won't graze.
6. Cattle.
7. Badger.
8. Are. Lusty shepherds don't hide their faults hypocritically.
9. Disapprove.
1. Rural stringed instruments, cousins to the violin.
2. Taboret, a small drum.
3. I.e., a roll in the hay. "Barleybreak" and "base" are rural variations of "tag."
4. Mixture (of sadness).

Our fairest shepherdess we had of late,
Here upon Trent, is drowned, for whom her mate,
Young Eglamour, a swain, who best could tread
Our country dances, and our games did lead,
Lives like the melancholy turtle,[5] drowned
Deeper in woe than she in water, crowned
With yew[6] and cypress, and will scarce admit
The physic[7] of our presence to his fit.

LIONEL. Sometimes he sits, and thinks all day, then walks,
Then thinks again, and sighs, weeps, laughs, and talks,
And twixt his pleasing frenzy and sad grief[8]
Is so distracted as no sought relief
By all our studies can procure his peace.

CLARION. The passion finds in him that[9] large increase
As we doubt hourly we shall lose him too.

ROBIN. You should not cross him then, whate'er you do,
For fancy stopped will soon take fire and burn
Into an anger, or to a frenzy turn.

CLARION. Nay, so we are advised by Alken here,
A good sage shepherd, who, although he wear
An old worn hat and cloak, can tell us more
Than all the forward fry that boast their lore.

LIONEL. See, yonder comes the brother of the maid,
Young Karolin! How curious and afraid
Here is at once, willing to find him out,
And loath to offend him.

ALKEN. Sure he's here about.

SCENE 5

ROBIN HOOD, CLARION, MELLIFLEUR, LIONEL, AMIE, ALKEN, KAROLIN; EGLAMOUR, *sitting upon a bank by them.*

CLARION. See where he sits.

EGLAMOUR. It will be rare, rare, rare!
An exquisite revenge! But peace, no words—
Not for the fairest fleece of all the flock!
If it be known afore, 'tis all worth nothing.
I'll carve it on the trees and in the turf,
On every greensworth[1] and in every path,
Just to the margin of the cruel Trent.
There will I knock the story in the ground,
In smooth great pebble and moss fill it round,[2]
Till the whole country read how she was drowned,
And with the plenty of salt tears there shed

5. The turtle dove, a proverbially amorous and melancholy bird.
6. Like cypress, yew is a dark evergreen, associated with mourning.
7. Medicine.
8. The pleasing frenzy (i.e., madness) is that she still lives; the sad grief that she doesn't.
9. Such.
1. Greensward.
2. I.e., make a picture of the tragedy by laying stones in the earth.

Quite alter the complexion of the spring.
Or I will get some old, old grandam thither,
Whose rigid foot, but dipped into the water,
Shall strike that sharp and sudden cold throughout
As it shall lose all virtue;[3] and those nymphs,
Those treacherous nymphs, pulled in Earine,
Shall stand curled up like images of ice,
And never thaw. Mark, never! A sharp justice!
Or, stay, a better! When the year's at hottest,
And that the Dog Star foams, and the stream boils
And curls and works and swells ready to sparkle,
To fling a fellow with a fever in,
To set it all on fire till it burn
Blue as Scamander 'fore the walls of Troy[4]
When Vulcan leaped into him to consume him!

ROBIN. A deep-hurt fancy! [*They approach him.*]

EGLAMOUR. Do you not approve it?

ROBIN. Yes, gentle Eglamour, we all approve,
And come to gratulate your just revenge,
Which, since it is so perfect, we now hope
You'll leave all care thereof and mix with us
In all the proffered solace of the spring.

EGLAMOUR. A spring, now she is dead! Of what? Of thorns?
Briars and brambles? Thistles? Burrs and docks?[5]
Cold hemlock?[6] Yew? The mandrake or the box?
These may grow still; but what can spring beside?
Did not the whole earth sicken when she died?
As if there since did fall one drop of dew
But what was wept for her, or any stalk
Did bear a flower, or any branch a bloom,
After her wreath was made! In faith, in faith,
You do not fair to put these things upon me,
Which can in no sort be. Earine,
Who had her very being and her name[7]
With the first knots or buddings of the spring,
Born with the primrose and the violet,
Or earliest roses blown, when Cupid smiled,
And Venus led the Graces out to dance,
And all the flowers and sweets in nature's lap
Leaped out, and made their solemn conjuration
To last but while she lived! Do not I know
How the vale withered the same day, how Dove,
Dean, Eye, and Erwash, Idel, Snite, and Soare

3. The water will lose not only its merit but its character as water—i.e., it will be ice. The old grandam will evidently be not only frigid but a witch, known for icy temperatures.

4. Scamander was one of two streams flowing before Troy; Hephaestus (Vulcan, god of the forge) dried it up by breathing hotly on it in *Iliad* XXI.

5. Coarse and prickly weeds.

6. Hemlock is a poison; the mandrake is a magical herb with sinister implications; and the box tree, a dark evergreen shrub, is both hardy and gloomy.

7. Earine is associated in Jonson's mind with Greek ἔαρ, ἔαροσ, the season of spring; "knots": swellings.

Each broke his urn,[8] and twenty waters more
That swelled proud Trent shrunk themselves dry? That, since,
No sun or moon or other cheerful star
Looked out of heaven, but all the cope[9] was dark,
As it were hung so for her exequies!
And not a voice or sound to ring her knell
But of that dismal pair, the scritching[1] owl
And buzzing hornet! Hark, hark, hark, the foul
Bird! How she flutters with her wicker wings![2]
Peace! You shall hear her scritch.

CLARION. Good Karolin, sing.
Help to divert this fancy.

KAROLIN. All I can.

The Song, which while KAROLIN *sings, Eglamour reads:*

Though I am young and cannot tell
Either what Death or Love is well,
Yet I have heard they both bear darts,
And both do aim at human hearts.
And then again I have been told,
Love wounds with heat, as Death with cold,
So that I fear they do but bring
Extremes to touch, and mean one thing.

As in a ruin[3] *we it call*
One thing to be blown up or fall,
Or to our end like way may have
By a flash of lightning or a wave,
So Love's inflamèd shaft or brand
May kill as soon as Death's cold hand,
Except[4] *Love's fires the virtue have*
To fright the frost out of the grave.

EGLAMOUR. Do you think so? Are you in that good heresy,
I mean opinion? If you be, say nothing.
I'll study it as a new philosophy,
But by myself alone. Now you shall leave me.
Some of these nymphs here will reward you—this,
This pretty maid, although but with a kiss.
[*He forces* AMIE *to kiss* KAROLIN.]
Lived my Earine, you should have twenty;
For every line here, one I would allow them
From mine own store, the treasure I had in her.
Now I am as poor as you.

KAROLIN. And I a wretch!

CLARION. Yet keep an eye upon him, Karolin.
[EGLAMOUR *goes out and* KAROLIN *follows him.*]

8. These various brooks and rivers which swell the current of the River Trent all ceased to flow at the death of Earine.
9. Vault of heaven.
1. Screech.
2. Barred (?) wings.
3. With the specific sense of Latin *ruina*, collapse.
4. Unless.

MELLIFLEUR. Alas, that ever such a generous spirit
As Eglamour's should sink by such a loss!
CLARION. The truest lovers are least fortunate:
Look't all their lives and legends, what they call
The lovers' scriptures, Heliodore's or Tatii,
Longi, Eustathii, Prodomi,[5] you'll find it!
What think you, father?

ALKEN. I have known some few,
And read of more, who've had their dose, and deep,
Of these sharp bittersweets.
LIONEL. But what is this
To jolly Robin, who the story is
Of all beatitude in love?
CLARION. And told
Here every day with wonder on the wold.[6]
LIONEL. And with Fame's voice.
ALKEN. Save that some folk delight
To blend all good of others with some spite.
CLARION. He and his Marian are the sum and talk
Of all that breathe here in the greenwood walk.
MELLIFLEUR. Or Belvoir Vale.
LIONEL. The turtles of the wood.
CLARION. The billing pair.
ALKEN. And so are understood
For simple loves, and sampled lives[7] beside.
MELLIFLEUR. Faith, so much virtue should not be enviéd.
ALKEN. Better be so than pitied, Mellifleur,
For 'gainst all envy virtue is a cure,
But wretched pity ever calls on scorns.—
[*Horns within.*]
The deer's brought home; I hear it by their horns.

SCENE 6

To ROBIN, *etc.*, MARIAN, JOHN, SCARLET, SCATHLOCK

ROBIN. My Marian, and my mistress!
MARIAN. My loved Robin!
MELLIFLEUR. The moon's at full; the happy pair are met.
MARION. How hath this morning paid me for my rising—
First, with my sports, but most with meeting you.
I did not half so well reward my hounds
As she hath me today, although I gave them
All the sweet morsels called tongue, ears, and dowcets![8]
ROBIN. What, and the inchpin?

5. Authors of Greek romances dealing with idyllic love.
6. The fortunate loves of Robin Hood and Maid Marian are a legend in the countryside.
7. I.e., exemplary lives.
8. Testicles; "inchpin": sweetbreads.

MARION. Yes.
ROBIN. Your sports then pleased you?
MARION. You are a wanton.
ROBIN. *One,* I do confess.
I *wanted* till you came; but now I have you
I'll grow to your embraces, till two souls,
Distilléd into kisses through our lips.
Do make one spirit of love. [*Kisses her.*]
MARIAN. O Robin, Robin!
ROBIN. Breathe, breathe awhile. What says my gentle Marian?
MARIAN. Could you so long be absent?
ROBIN. What, a week?
Was that so long?
MARIAN. How long are lovers' weeks,
Do you think, Robin, when they are asunder?
Are they not prisoners' years?
ROBIN. To some they seem so,
But, being met again, they are schoolboys' hours—
MARIAN. That have got leave to play, and so we use them.
ROBIN. Had you good sport i' your chase today?
JOHN. O, prime!
MARIAN. A lusty stag.
ROBIN. And hunted ye at force?
MARIAN. In a full cry.
JOHN. And never hunted change![9]
ROBIN. You had stanch hounds then?
MARIAN. Old and sure; I love
No young rash dogs, no more than changing friends.
ROBIN. What relays set you?
JOHN. None at all; we laid not
In one fresh dog.
ROBIN. He stood not long then?
SCARLET. Yes,
Five hours and more. A great, large deer!
ROBIN. What head?
JOHN. Forkéd! A hart of ten.
MARIAN. He is good venison,
According to the season i' the blood,[1]
I'll promise all your friends for whom he fell.
JOHN. But at his fall there happed a chance.
MARIAN. Worth mark.
ROBIN. Ay, what was that, sweet Marian? [*He kisses her.*]
MARIAN. You'll not hear?
ROBIN. I love these interruptions in a story; [*He kisses her again.*]
They make it sweeter.
MARIAN. You do know as soon

9. Brought in fresh hounds. To hunt with relays of dogs would be a kind of foul play.

1. In rutting season, venison was not supposed to make good eating.

As the assay[2] is taken. [*He kisses her again.*]
ROBIN. On, my Marian.
I did but take the assay.
MARIAN. You stop one's mouth,
And yet you bid them speak!—When the arbor's made—[3]
ROBIN. Pulled down, and paunch turned out—
MARIAN. he that undoes him[4]
Doth cleave the brisket bone, upon the spoon
Of which a little gristle grows; you call it—
ROBIN. The raven's bone.[5]
MARIAN. Now o'erhead sat a raven
On a sere[6] bough—a grown, great bird, and hoarse,
Who, all the while the deer was breaking up,[7]
So croaked and cried for 't as all the huntsmen,
Especially old Scathlock, thought it ominous,
Swore it was mother Maudlin, whom he met
At the day-dawn just as he roused the deer
Out of his lair; but we made shift to run him
Off his four legs, and sunk him ere we left.
[*Enter* SCATHLOCK.]
Is the deer come?
SCATHLOCK. He lies within o' the dresser.[8]
MARIAN. Will you go see him, Mellifleur?
MELLIFLEUR. I attend you.
MARIAN. Come, Amie, you'll go with us?
AMIE. I am not well.
LIONEL. She's sick o' the young shepherd that bekissed her.
MARIAN. Friend, cheer your friends up; we will eat him merrily.
[*Exeunt* MARIAN, MELLIFLEUR, *and* AMIE.]
ALKEN. Saw you the raven, friend?
SCATHLOCK. Ay, quha suld let me?[9]
I suld be afraid o' you, sir, suld I?
CLARION. Huntsman,
A dram more of civility would not hurt you.
ROBIN. Nay, you must give[1] them all their rudenesses;
They are not else themselves without their language.
ALKEN. And what do you think of her?
SCATHLOCK. As of a witch.
They call her a wise woman, but I think her
An arrant witch.
CLARION. And wherefore think you so?

2. Sample. Some details of the lover's badinage appear to have got mixed up in the printing: Marian jokes on a word Robin hasn't yet spoken.
3. After the death, the deer is hung from a tree or trestle ("arbor") to be cleaned and dressed.
4. Cuts him up.
5. Gristle, offal, and inedible bits of the deer were left for the ravens.
6. Dry.
7. Being dismembered.
8. Butcher's block, on which the meat was dressed.
9. I.e., "Ay, who should prevent me?" The back-country dialect of Scathlock and his fellows can generally be understood by pronouncing it aloud, broadly and slowly.
1. Forgive.

SCATHLOCK. Because I saw her since, broiling the bone
Was cast her at the quarry.
ALKEN. Where saw you her?
SCATHLOCK. I' the chimley nuik,[2] within; she's there now.
ROBIN. Marian!

SCENE 7

To them, MARIAN

ROBIN. Your hunt holds in his tale[3] still, and tells more.
MARIAN. My hunt? What tale?
ROBIN. How! Cloudy, Marian!
What look is this?
MARIAN. A fit one, sir for you.
Hand off, rude ranger!—[*To* SCATHLOCK.] Sirrah, get you in,
And bear the venison hence. It is too good
For these coarse, rustic mouths that cannot open,
Or spend a thank for 't. A starved mutton's carcass
Would better fit their palates. See it carried
To mother Maudlin's, whom you call the witch, sir.
Tell her I sent it to make merry with.
She'll turn[4] us thanks at least! Why stand'st thou, groom?
ROBIN. I wonder he can move, that he's not fixed,
If that his feeling be the same with mine!
I dare not trust the faith of mine own senses;
I fear[5] mine eyes and ears. This is not Marian!
Nor am I Robin Hood! I pray you ask her,
Ask her, good shepherds, ask her all for me—
Or rather ask yourselves—if she be she,
Or I be I.
MARIAN. Yes, and you are the spy,
And the spied spy that watch upon my walks
To inform what deer I kill or give away!
Where! When! To Whom! But spy your worst, good spy.
I will dispose of this where least you like!
Fall to your cheesecakes, curds, and clawted cream,[6]
Your fools, your flauns, and of ale a stream
To wash it from your livers. Strain ewes' milk
Into your cider sillabubs,[7] and be drunk
To him whose fleece hath brought the earliest lamb
This year, and wears the baudric[8] at your board,
Where you may all go whistle, and record
This i' your dance, and foot it lustily. [*She leaves them.*]
ROBIN. I pray you, friends, do you hear and see as I do?

2. Chimney nook.
3. I.e., your huntsman sticks to his story.
4. Render.
5. Suspect.
6. I.e., clotted cream. Like "fools" (stewed fruit with whipped cream) and "flauns" (flans, custards), clotted cream is a dairy delicacy.
7. Milk mixed with cider—watery stuff for a hunter's feast.
8. Baldric, a decorative belt.

Did the same accents strike your ears, and objects
Your eyes, as mine?
ALKEN. We taste the same reproaches.
LIONEL. Have seen the changes.
ROBIN. Are we not all changed,
Transformèd from ourselves?
LIONEL. I do not know.
The best is silence.
ALKEN. And to await the issue.
ROBIN. The dead or lazy wait for 't! I will find it. [*Exeunt.*]

The Argument of the Second Act

The Witch Maudlin, having taken the shape of Marian to abuse Robin Hood and perplex his guests, cometh forth with her daughter, Douce, reporting in what confusion she hath left them, defrauded them of their venison, made them suspicious each of the other, but most of all Robin Hood so jealous of his Marian as she hopes no effect of love would ever reconcile them, glorying so far in the extent of her mischief as she confesseth to have surprised Earine, stripped her of her garments to make her daughter appear fine at this feast in them, and to have shut the maiden up in a tree as her son's prize, if he could win her, or his prey, if he would force her. Her son, a rude, bragging swineherd, comes to the tree to woo her (his mother and sister stepping aside to overhear him) and first boasts his wealth to her and his possessions—which move not. Then he presents her gifts such as himself is taken with, but she utterly shows a scorn and loathing both of him and them. His mother is angry, rates[9] him, instructs him what to do the next time, and persuades her daughter to show herself about the bower, tells how she shall know her mother, when she is transformed, by her broidered belt. Meanwhile the young shepherdess Amie, being kissed by Karolin, Earine's brother, before, falls in love, but knows not what love is, but describes her disease so innocently that Marian pities her. When Robin Hood and the rest of his guests invited, enter to Marian, upbraiding her with sending away their venison to mother Maudlin by Scathlock, which she denies, Scathlock affirms it, but, seeing his mistress weep and to forswear it, begins to doubt his own understanding rather than affront her farder,[1] which makes Robin Hood and the rest to examine themselves better. But Maudlin, entering like herself, the witch, comes to thank her for her bounty, at which Marian is more angry, and more denies the deed. Scathlock enters, tells he has brought it again, and delivered it to the cook. The witch is inwardly vexed the venison is so recovered from her by the rude huntsman, and mur-

9. Scolds, berates.

1. Farther.

murs and curses, bewitches the cook, mocks poor Amie and the rest, discovereth[2] *her ill nature, and is a mean of reconciling them all. For the Sage Shepherd suspecteth her mischief, if she be not prevented,*[3] *and so persuadeth to seize on her. Whereupon Robin Hood despatcheth out his woodmen to hunt and take her, which ends the act.*

Act II

SCENE 1. *The* WITCH'S *dimble, with the* SWINEHERD'S *oak at one side*

MAUDLIN, DOUCE [*dressed in* EARINE'*s clothes*]

MAUDLIN. Have I not left 'em in a brave confusion,
Amazed their expectation; got their venison,
Troubled their mirth and meeting, made them doubtful
And jealous of each other, all distracted,
And, i' the close, uncertain of themselves?
This can your mother do, my dainty Douce:
Take any shape upon her, and delude
The senses best acquainted with their owners!
The jolly Robin, who hath bid this feast,
And made this solemn invitation,
I ha' possesséd so with syke[4] dislikes
Of his own Marian that, albee he know her
As doth the vauting hart his venting hind,[5]
He ne'er fra hence sall nase[6] her i' the wind,
To his first liking.
DOUCE. Did you so distaste him?
MAUDLIN. As far as her proud scorning him could bate,
Or blunt the edge of any lover's temper.
DOUCE. But were ye like her, mother?
MAUDLIN. So like, Douce,
As, had she seen me herself, herself had doubted
Whether had ben the liker of the twa!
This can your mother do, I tell you, daughter!
I ha' but dight[7] ye yet i' the outdress
And 'parel of Earine; but this raiment,
These very weeds, sall make ye as, but coming
In vew or ken of Eglamour, your form
Shall show too slippery[8] to be looked upon,
And all the forests swear you to be she!
They shall rin[9] after ye, and wage the odds,
Upo' their own deceivéd sights, ye are her,[1]
Whilst she, poor lass, is stocked up[2] in a tree—

2. Discloses.
3. Forestalled.
4. Such.
5. Doe in heat; "vaunting hart": proud stag.
6. Nose, sniff.
7. Dressed; "outdresss": outer garments.
8. Uncertain, hazy.
9. Run.
1. The deceived watchers will prove by their own senses, against all probability, that Douce is Earine.
2. Imprisoned in the tree-trunk.

Your brother Lorel's prize! For so my largess
Hath 'lotted her to be your brother's mistress,
Gif she can be reclaimed[3]—gif not, his prey!
And here he comes new claithéd,[4] like a prince
Of swineherds. Syke he seems, dight i' the spoils
Of those he feeds[5]—a mighty lord of swine!
He is command[6] now to woo. Let's step aside,
And hear his lovecraft. See, he opes the door,
And takes her by the hand, and helps her forth.
This is true courtship, and becomes his ray.[7]

SCENE 2. *The same*

LOREL, EARINE, MAUDLIN, DOUCE

LOREL. Ye kind to others, but ye coy to me,
Deft mistress, whiter than the cheese new pressed,
Smoother than cream, and softer than the curds,
Why start ye from me ere ye hear me tell
My wooing errand and what rents I have?
Large herds and pastures! Swine and ky[8] mine own!
And though my nase be camused,[9] my lips thick,
And my chin bristled, Pan,[1] great Pan, was such,
Who was the chief of herdsmen, and our sire!
I am na fay, na incubus, na changelin',[2]
But a good man that lives o' my awn gear.
This house, these grounds, this stock is all mine awn.
EARINE. How better 'twere to me, this were not known!
MAUDLIN. [*aside*] She likes it not; but it is boasted well.
LOREL. An hundred udders for the pail I have,
That gi' me milk and curds, that make me cheese
To cloy the markets! Twenty swarm of bees,
Whilk[3] all the summer hum about the hive,
And bring me wax and honey in bilive.[4]
An aged oak, the king of all the field,
With a broad beech there grows afore my dur,
That mickle mast[5] unto the farm doth yield.
A chestnut, whilk hath larded mony a swine,
Whose skins I wear to fend me fra' the cold;
A poplar green, and with a carvéd seat,
Under whose shade I solace in the heat,
And thence can see gang out and in my neat.[6]

3. If she can be persuaded.
4. Clothed.
5. Such he seems, dressed in the skins of pigs.
6. Coming (substituting "and" for "ing" is frequent in North Country dialect).
7. I.e., suits his array (dress).
8. Kine, cattle.
9. Short and flat.
1. Roman rural god of flocks and fields—goat-footed, hairy, horned, as much animal as human in his shape.
2. I.e., no fairy, no diabolic spirit, no imp slipped mischievously into a human cradle.
3. Which.
4. At once, hastily.
5. Much food—beechnuts for swine, but also for people.
6. Cattle.

Twa trilland brooks each from his spring doth meet
And make a river to refresh my feet,
In which each morning, ere the sun doth rise,
I look myself, and clear my pleasant eyes,
Before I pipe, for therein I have skill
'Bove other swineherds. Bid me, and I will
Straight play to you, and make you melody.

EARINE. By no means. Ah, to me all minstrelsy
Is irksome, as are you.

LOREL. Why scorn you me?
Because I am a herdsman, and feed swine!

[*He draws out other presents.*]

I am a lord of other gear. This fine
Smooth bauson's cub, the young grice of a gray,
Twa tiny urshins, and this ferret gay.[7]

EARINE. Out on 'em! What are these?

LOREL. I give 'em ye
As presents, Mrs.[8] —

EARINE. O, the fiend and thee!
Gar[9] take them hence; they fewmand all the claithes,
And prick my coats.[1] Hence with 'em, limmer lown,[2]
Thy vermin and thyself; thyself art one!
Ay, lock me up—all's well when thou art gone.

[*Lorel shuts her in the tree again.*]

SCENE 3. *The same*

LOREL, MAUDLIN, DOUCE

LOREL. Did you hear this? She wished me at the fiend
With all my presents!

MAUDLIN. A too lucky end
She wishend[3] thee, foul limmer, dritty lown!
Gude faith, it dules[4] me that I am thy mother.
And see, thy sister scorns thee for her brother.
Thou woo thy love, thy mistress, with twa hedgehogs,
A stinkand brock,[5] a polecat? Out, thou howlet!
Thou shouldst ha' given her a madge-owl,[6] and then
Tho' hadst made a present o' thyself, owlspiegle![7]

DOUCE. Why, mother, I have heard ye bid to give,
And often as the cause calls.

MAUDLIN. I know well,
It is a witty[8] part sometimes to give;

7. I.e., a baby badger, a couple of hedgehogs, and a weasel.
8. Pronounced Mistress—a title of respect, but not implying marriage.
9. You must.
1. Make holes in my petticoats.
2. Clumsy clod.
3. Wished for you; "dritty": dirty.
4. Grieves.
5. Badger; "howlet": baby owl, with the implication of a solemn fool.
6. Barn-owl.
7. From German *Eulenspiegel* or owl-glass, the name of a medieval buffoon and joker.
8. Shrewd.

But what? To wham?[9] No monsters, nor to maidens.
He suld present them with mare[1] pleasand things,
Things natural, and what all women covet
To see: the common parent of us all,
Which maids will twire[2] at tween their fingers thus;
With which his sire gat him, he s' get another,
And so beget posterity upon her.
This he should do! False gelden,[3] gang thy gait,
And do thy turns betimes; or I s' gar take
Thy new breikes fra thee,[4] and thy duiblet too.
The talleur and the souter sall undo
All they ha' made,[5] except thou manlier woo!

[LOREL *goes out.*]

DOUCE. Gud mother, gif you chide him, he'll do wairs.[6]
MAUDLIN. Hang him! I geif him to the devil's erse.
But ye, my Douce, I charge ye, show yoursel'
To all the shepherds baudly.[7] Gang amang hem,
Be mickel i' their eye, frequent and fugeand,[8]
And, gif they ask ye of Earine,
Or of these claithes, say I ga' hem ye,
And say no more. I ha' that wark in hand,
That web upo' the luime,[9] shall gar hem think
By then, thy feelin' their own frights and fears,
I s' pu'[1] the world or nature 'bout their ears.
But hear ye, Douce, bycause ye may meet me
In mony shapes today, where'er you spy
This brodered belt with characters, 'tis I.
A Gypsan lady, and a right beldame,[2]
Wrought it by moonshine for me, and starlight,
Upo' your grannam's[3] grave, that very night
We earthed her in the shades, when our dame Hecate[4]
Made it her gang-night over the kirkyard,
With all the barkand parish-tikes[5] set at her,
While I sat whirland of my brazen spindle.
At every twisted thrid my rock let fly[6]
Unto the sewster, who did sit me nigh,
Under the town turnpike, which ran each spell
She stitchéd in the work, and knit it well.

9. Whom.
1. More.
2. Peek.
3. False gelding, go your ways (get lost).
4. I.e., I'll have to take away all your fine pig-skin clothing; "breikes": breeches; "duiblet": doublet.
5. The tailor and cobbler (souter), who have made him whatever sort of man he is, will unmake him.
6. Worse.
7. Boldly.
8. I.e. be much in their eye, often and active.
9. Loom.
1. Shall pull.
2. I.e., an old (and presumably wise) gypsy lady.
3. Grandmother's.
4. Goddess of the moon and witchcraft; her "gang-night over the kirk-yard" is her special night for haunting the graveyard.
5. The dogs of the parish.
6. I.e., every twisted thread my spindle let fly. As Hecate watches, Maudlin spins the thread, the gypsy lady weaves it; between the three of them, they suggest the ancient Fates or Norns, weaving the magic threads of human life. "Sewster": seamstress.

See ye take tent[7] to this, and ken your mother.
[*Exeunt*.]

SCENE 4. *Before* ROBIN HOOD'S *bower*

MARIAN, MELLIFLEUR, AMIE

MARIAN. How do you, sweet Amie? Yet?
MELLIFLEUR. She cannot tell;
If she could sleep, she says, she should do well.
She feels a hurt, but where, she cannot show
Any least sign that she is hurt or no.
Her pain's not doubtful to her, but the seat
Of her pain is. Her thoughts, too, work and beat,
Oppressed with cares, but why she cannot say.
All matter of her care is quite away.
MARIAN. Hath any vermin[8] broke into your fold?
Or any rot seized on your flock, or cold?
Or hath your fighting ram burst his hard horn,
Or any ewe her fleece or bag[9] hath torn,
My gentle Amie?
AMIE. Marian, none of these.
MARIAN. Ha' you been stung by wasps or angry bees,
Or rased[1] with some rude bramble or rough brier?
AMIE. No, Marian, my disease is somewhat nigher.
I weep, and boil away myself in tears;
And then my panting heart would dry those fears.
I burn, though all the forest lend a shade,
And freeze, though the whole wood one fire were made.[2]
MARIAN. Alas!
AMIE. I often have been torn with thorn and brier,
Both in the leg and foot, and somewhat higher,
Yet gave not then such fearful shrieks as these. Ah!
I often have been stung too with curst[3] bees,
Yet not remember that I then did quit
Either my company or mirth for it. Ah!
And therefore what it is that I feel now,
And know no cause of it, nor where, nor how
It entered in me, nor least print can see,
I feel, afflicts me more than brier or bee. O!
How often when the sun, heaven's brightest birth,
Hath with his burning fervor cleft the earth,
Under a spreading elm or oak hard by
A cool, clear fountain could I sleeping lie,

7. Heed.
8. I.e., polecats or wolves. In rural England, vermin, which can be exterminated by fair means or foul, are sharply distinguished from game animals, to be hunted only with full formalities by the gentry.
9. Udder.
1. Scraped.
2. Amie's disease has all the traditional symptoms and traditional rhetoric of Petrarchan love.
3. Mischieveous, malicious.

Safe from the heat! But now no shady tree
Nor purling brook can my refreshing be.
Oft when the meadows were grown rough with frost,
The rivers ice-bound, and their currents lost,
My thick, warm fleece I wore was my defense;
Or large, good fires I made drave[4] winter thence.
But now my whole flock's fells,[5] nor this thick grove,
Enflamed to ashes, can my cold remove.
It is a cold and heat that doth outgo
All sense of winter's and of summer's so.

SCENE 5. *The same*

To them, ROBIN HOOD, CLARION, LIONEL, ALKEN

ROBIN. O, are you here, my mistress?
MARIAN. Ay, my love!
[*She, seeing him, runs to embrace him. He puts her back.*]
Where should I be but in my Robin's arms,
The sphere which I delight in so to move?
ROBIN. What, "the rude ranger" and "spied spy"? Hand off!
You are "for no such rustics."
MARINA. What means this?
Thrice worthy Clarion, or wise Alken, know ye?
ROBIN. 'Las, no, not they! "A poor, starved mutton's carcass
Would better fit their palates than your venison."
MARIAN. What riddle is this? Unfold yourself, dear Robin.
ROBIN. You ha' not sent your venison hence by Scathlock
To mother Maudlin?
MARIAN. I to mother Maudlin!
Will Scathlock say so?
ROBIN. Nay, we will all swear so.
For all did hear it when you gave the charge so,
Both Clarion, Alken, Lionel, myself.
MARIAN. Good honest shepherds, masters of your flocks,
Simple and virtuous men, no others' hirelings,
Be not you made to speak against your conscience
That which may soil the truth. I send the venison
Away? By Scathlock, and to mother Maudlin?
I came to show it here to Mellifleur,
I do confess; but Amie's falling ill
Did put us off it. Since, we employed ourselves
In comforting of her.
[SCATHLOCK *enters.*]
O, here he is!—
Did I, sir, bid you bear away the venison
To mother Maudlin?

4. Drove.
5. I.e., neither all the wool of my flock, nor all the wood of the forest if it were burned, could remove my cold.

SCATHLOCK. Ay, gude faith, madám,
Did you, and I ha' done it.
MARIAN. What ha' you done?
SCATHLOCK. Obeyed your hests,[6] madám, done your commands.
MARIAN. Done my commands, dull groom? Fetch it again,
Or kennel with the hounds.—Are these the arts,
Robin, you rede[7] your rude ones o' the wood
To countenance your quarrels and mistakings?
Or are the sports to entertain your friends
Those forméd jealousies?[8] Ask of Mellifleur
If I were ever from her here, or Amie,
Since I came in with them; or saw this Scathlock
Since I related to you his tale o' the raven.
SCATHLOCK. Ay, say you so? [SCATHLOCK *goes out.*]
MELLIFLEUR. She never left my side
Since I came in here, nor I hers.
CLARION. This 's strange!
Our best of senses were deceived, our eyes, then!
LIONEL. And ears too.
MARIAN. What you have concluded on,
Make good, I pray you.
AMIE. O my heart, my heart!
MARIAN. My heart it is, is wounded, pretty Amie.
Report not you your griefs; I'll tell for all.
MELLIFLEUR. Somebody is to blame there is a fault.
MARIAN. Try if you can take rest. A little slumber
Will much refresh you, Amie. [AMIE *sleeps.*]
ALKEN. What's her grief?
MARIAN. She does not know; and therein she is happy.

SCENE 6. *The same*

To them, JOHN, MAUDLIN, *and* SCATHLOCK *after*

JOHN. Here's mother Maudlin come to give you thanks,
Madam, for some late gift she hath received—
Which she's not worthy of, she says, but crakes[9]
And wonders of it, hops about the house,
Transported with the joy.
MAUDLIN. Send me a stag, [*she danceth*]
A whole stag, madam, and so fat a deer!
So fairly hunted, and at such a time too,
When all your friends were here!
ROBIN. Do you mark this, Clarion?
Her own acknowledgment?
MAUDLIN. 'Twas such a bounty
And honor done to your poor beadswoman,[1]

6. Orders.
7. Teach.
8. Contrived, deliberate jealousies.
9. Croaks, cackles.
1. Literally, one who will say prayers for you; a grateful recipient.

I know not how to owe[2] it but to thank you;
And that I come to do. I shall go round
And giddy with the toy[3] of the good turn.
Look out, look out,
Gay folk about,
She turns round
And see me spin
The ring I am in
Of mirth and glee,
With thanks for fee
The heart puts on,
For th' venison
My lady sent,
Which shall be spent
In draughts of wine,
To fume up fine
till she falls.
Into the brain,
And down again
Fall in a swoun,[4]
Upo' the groun'.

ROBIN. Look to her; she is mad.
MAUDLIN. [*rising*] My son hath sent you
A pot of strawberries gathered i' the wood
(His hogs would else have rooted up or trod);
With a choice dish of wildings[5] here to scald
And mingle with your cream.
MARIAN. Thank you, good Maudlin,
And thank your son. Go, bear 'em in to Much,
Th' acater; let him thank her. Surely, mother,
Your were mistaken, or my woodmen more,
Or most myself, to send you all our store
Of venison, hunted for ourselves this day.
You will not take it, mother, I dare say,
If we'd entreat you, when you know our guests;
Red deer is head still of the forest feasts.
MAUDLIN. But I knaw[6] ye, a right free-hearted lady,
Can spare it out of superfluity.
I have departit[7] it 'mong my poor neighbors,
To speak your largess.
MARIAN. I not gave it, mother;
You have done wrong then. I know how to place
My gifts, and where; and when to find my seasons
To give, not throw away my courtesies.
MAUDLIN. Count you this thrown away?
MARIAN. What's ravished from me
I count it worse, as stolen; I lose my thanks.
But leave this quest. They fit not you nor me,

2. Own, acknowledge.
3. Delight. (Perhaps "toy" is a misprint for "joy".)
4. Swoon, faint.
5. Crab apples.
6. Know.
7. Distributed.

Maudlin, contentions of this quality.—
[SCATHLOCK *enters.*]
How now?

SCATHLOCK. Your stag's returned upon my shoulders;
He has found his way into the kitchen again
With his two legs, if now your cook can dress him.
'Slid, I thought the swineherd would ha' beat me,
He looks so big,[8] the sturdy karl, lewd Lorel!

MARIAN. There, Scathlock, for thy pains; thou hast deserved it.
[MARIAN *gives him gold.*]

MAUDLIN. Do you give a thing, and take a thing, madam?

MARIAN. No, Maudlin, "you had imparted to your neighbors;"
As much good do 't them! I ha' done no wrong.

THE FIRST CHARM

MAUDLIN.

The spit stand still, no broaches turn
Before the fire, but let it burn
Both sides and haunches till the whole
Converted be into one coal!

CLARION. What devil's paternoster[9] mumbles she?

ALKEN. Stay, you will hear more of her witchery.

MAUDLIN.

The swilland dropsy enter in
The lazy cuke[1] *and swell his skin;*
And the old mortmal on his shin
Now prick and itch withouten blin.[2]

CLARION. Speak out, hag, we may hear your devil's matins.

MAUDLIN.

The pain we call Saint Anton's fire,[3]
The gout, or what we can desire,
To cramp a cuke in every limb,
Before they dine yet, seize on him.

ALKEN. A foul, ill spirit hath possesséd her.

AMIE. [*from her sleep*] O Karol, Karol, call him back again!

LIONEL. Her thoughts do work upon her in her slumber,
And may express some part of her disease.

ROBIN. Observe and mark, but trouble not her ease.

AMIE. O, O!

MARIAN. How is 't, Amie?

MELLIFLEUR. Wherefore start you?

AMIE. [*awakening*] O Karol! He is fair and sweet.

MAUDLIN. What then?
Are there not flowers as sweet and fair as men?
The lily is fair, and rose is sweet.

8. Surly; "karl": churl; "lewd": gross.
9. Prayer, spell.
1. I.e., may the swelling dropsy enter into the lazy knave.
2. Without relief; "mortmal": ulcer.
3. Saint Anthony's fire, erysipelas.

AMIE. Ay, so!
Let all the roses and the lilies go.
Karol is only fair to me.
MARIAN. And why?
AMIE. Alas, for Karol, Marian, I could die!
Karol, he singeth sweetly too.
MAUDLIN. What then?
Are there not birds sing sweeter far than men?
AMIE. I grant the linnet, lark, and bullfinch sing,
But best the dear, good angel of the spring,
The nightingale.
MAUDLIN. Then why, then why, alone,
Should his notes please you?
AMIE. I not long agone
Took a delight with wanton kids to play,
And sport with little lambs a summer's day,
And view their frisks. Methought it was a sight
Of joy to see my two brave rams to fight!
Now Karol only all delight doth move;
All that is Karol, Karol I approve!
This very morning but,[4] I did bestow
(It was a little gainst my will, I know)
A single kiss upon the seely[5] swain,
And now I wish that very kiss again.
His lip is softer, sweeter than the rose;
His mouth and tongue with dropping honey flows;
The relish of it was a pleasing thing.
MAUDLIN. Yet, like the bees, it had a little sting.
AMIE. And sunk, and sticks yet in my marrow deep;
And what doth hurt me I now wish to keep.
MARIAN. Alas, how innocent her story is!
AMIE. I do remember, Marian, I have oft
With pleasure kissed my lambs and puppies soft;
And once a dainty, fine roe-fawn I had,
Of whose outskipping bounds I was as glad
As of my health, and him I oft would kiss;
Yet had his no such sting or pain as this.
They never pricked or hurt my heart; and, for
They were so blunt and dull, I wish no more.
But this, that hurts and pricks, doth please; this sweet
Mingled with sour I wish again to meet;
And that delay, methinks, most tedious is
That keeps or hinders me of Karol's kiss.
MARIAN. We'll send for him, sweet Amie, to come to you.
MAUDLIN. But I will keep him off, if charms will do it.
[*She goes murmuring out.*]
CLARION. Do you mark the murmuring hag, how she doth mutter?
ROBIN. I like her not; and less her manners now.

4. Just this very morning.
5. Simple, silly.

ALKEN. She is a shrewd, deforméd piece, I vow.
LIONEL. As crooked as her body.
ROBIN. I believe
She can take any shape, as Scathlock says.
ALKEN. She may deceive the sense, but really
She cannot change herself.
ROBIN. Would I could see her
Once more in Marian's form, for I am certain
Now it was she abused us, as I think
My Marian, and my love, now innocent—
Which faith I seal unto her with this kiss,
And call you all to witness of my penance. [*Kisses* MARIAN.]
ALKEN. It was believed before, but now confirmed,
That we have seen the monster.

SCENE 7. *The same*

To them, TUCK, JOHN, MUCH, SCARLET

TUCK. Hear you how
Poor Tom, the cook, is taken! All his joints
Do crack, as if his limbs were tied with points;[6]
His whole frame slackens; and a kind of rack
Runs down along the spondils[7] of his back;
A gout or cramp now seizeth on his head,
Then falls into his feet; his knees are lead;
And he can stir his either hand no more
Than a dead stump, to his office,[8] as before.
ALKEN. He is bewitched.
CLARION. This is an argument
Both of her malice and her power, we see.
ALKEN. She must by some device restrained be,
Or she'll go far in mischief.
ROBIN. Advise how,
Sage Shepherd, we shall put it straight in practice.
ALKEN. Send forth your woodmen then into the walks,
Or let 'em prick[9] her footing hence; a witch
Is sure a creature of melancholy,
And will be found or sitting in her fourm,[1]
Or else at relief, like a hare.
CLARION. You speak,
Alken, as if you knew the sport of witch-hunting,
Or starting of a hag.
[*Enter* GEORGE *to the* HUNTSMEN, *who by themselves continue the scene, the rest going off.*]
ROBIN. Go, sirs, about it.
Take George here with you; he can help to find her.

6. Laces, strings.
7. Joints.
8. To carry out his functions.
9. Track.
1. The nest of a hare, her burrow; "relief": feeding.

Leave Tuck and Much behind to dress the dinner
I' the cook's stead.

MUCH. We'll care to get that done.

ROBIN. Come, Marian, let's withdraw into the bower.

SCENE 8. *The same*

JOHN, SCARLET, SCATHLOCK, GEORGE; *to them,* ALKEN

JOHN. Rare sport, I swear, this hunting of the witch
Will make us.

SCARLET. Let's advise upon 't like huntsmen.

GEORGE. An[2] we can spy her once, she is our own.

SCATHLOCK. First, think which way she fourmeth, on what wind—
Or north or south.

GEORGE. For, as the shepherd said,
A witch is a kind of hare.

SCATHLOCK. And marks the weather,
As the hare does.

JOHN. Where shall we hope to find her?

[ALKEN *returns.*]

ALKEN. I have asked leave to assist you, jolly huntsmen,
If an old shepherd may be heard among you,
Not jeered or laughed at.

JOHN. Father, you will see
Robin Hood's household know more courtesy.

SCATHLOCK. Who scorns at eld,[3] peels off his own young hairs.

ALKEN. Ye say right well. Know ye the Witch's Dell?

SCATHLOCK. No more than I do know the walks of hell.

ALKEN. Within a gloomy dimble she doth dwell
Down in a pit, o'ergrown with brakes and briers,
Close by the ruins of a shaken abbey,
Torn with an earthquake down unto the ground,
'Mongst graves and grots, near an old charnel house,[4]
Where you shall find her sitting in her fourm
As fearful and melancholic as that
She is about, with caterpillars' kells[5]
And knotty cobwebs, rounded in with spells.
Thence she steals forth to relief, in the fogs
And rotten mists, upon the fens and bogs,
Down to the drownéd lands of Lincolnshire,
To make ewes cast their lambs, swine eat their farrow,
The housewife's tun[6] not work, nor the milk churn!
Writhe children's wrists, and suck their breath in sleep,
Get vials of their blood! And, where the sea
Casts up his slimy ooze, search for a weed
To open locks with, and to rivet charms,

2. If.
3. Old age.
4. A house to hold dead bones.
5. Cocoons.
6. The keg in which she brews the family beer.

Planted about her in the wicked feat[7]
Of all her mischiefs, which are manifold.
JOHN. I wonder such a story could be told
Of her dire deeds.
GEORGE. I thought a witch's banks
Had enclosed nothing but the merry pranks
Of some old woman.
SCARLET. Yes, her malice more.
SCATHLOCK. As it would quickly appear had we the store
Of his collects.[8]
GEORGE. Ay, this gude, learned man
Can speak her right.
SCARLET. He knows her shifts and haunts.
ALKEN. And all her wiles and turns; the venomed plants
Wherewith she kills; where the sad mandrake grows,
Whose groans are deathful;[9] the dead-numbing nightshade,
The stupefying hemlock, adder's tongue,
And martagan;[1] the shrieks of luckless owls
We hear, and croaking night crows in the air;
Green-bellied snakes; blue firedrakes[2] in the sky,
And giddy flittermice[3] with leather wings;
The scaly beetles, with their habergeons,[4]
That make a humming murmur as they fly!
There in the stocks of trees white fays[5] do dwell,
And span-long elves that dance about a pool,
With each a little changeling in their arms!
The airy spirits play with falling stars,
And mount the sphere of fire to kiss the moon,
While she sits reading by the glowworm's light
Or rotten wood, o'er which the worm hath crept,
The baneful schedule of her nocent[6] charms,
And binding characters through which she wounds
Her puppets,[7] the sigilla of her witchcraft.
All this I know, and I will find her for you,
And show you her sitting in her fourm. I'll lay
My hand upon her, make her throw her scut[8]
Along her back, when she doth start before us.
But you must give her law;[9] and you shall see her
Make twenty leaps and doubles, cross the paths,
And then squat down beside us.

7. Performance.
8. I.e., if we knew as much as he does.
9. When plucked, the mandrake root shrieks so dreadfully that the sound kills anyone who hears it—so, at least, legend declares. The nightshade really is deadly poison and so is hemlock; but adder's tongue just sounds and looks sinister—it's a harmless fern.
1. Lily with medicinal roots. The owls are not luckless themselves, but omens of ill luck for those who hear them.
2. Literally, fire dragons, will-o-the-wisps.
3. Bats (cf. German, *Fledermaus*).
4. Literally helmets, actually scaly carapaces.
5. Fairies or wood-nymphs lurking in tree-trunks.
6. Harmful.
7. Wax or cloth dolls, used to hex people; "sigilla": seals.
8. Hare's tail.
9. A fair start.

JOHN. Crafty crone!
I long to be at the sport, and to report it.
SCARLET. We'll make this hunting of the witch as famous
As any other blast of venery.[1]
SCATHLOCK. Hang her, foul hag! She'll be a stinking chase.
I had rather ha' the hunting of her heir.
GEORGE. If we could come to see her, cry "so haw"[2] once.
ALKEN. That I do promise, or I am no good hag-finder.
[*Exeunt.*]

The Argument of the Third Act

Puck-Hairy discovers himself in the forest, and discourseth his offices, with their necessities, briefly; after which, Douce, entering in the habit of Earine, is pursued by Karol, who, mistaking her at first to be his sister, questions her how she came by those garments. She answers, by her mother's gift. The Sad Shepherd coming in the while, she runs away affrighted, and leaves Karol suddenly; Eglamour, thinking it to be Earine's ghost he saw, falls into a melancholic expression of his fancy to Karol, and questions him sadly about that point, which moves compassion in Karol of his mistake still. When Clarion and Lionel enter to call Karol to Amie, Karol reports to them Eglamour's passion with much regret. Clarion resolves to seek him, Karol to return with Lionel. By the way, Douce and her mother, in the shape of Marian, meet them, and would divert them, affirming Amie to be recovered, which Lionel wondered at to be so soon. Robin Hood enters; they tell him the relation of the witch, thinking her to be Marian; Robin, suspecting her to be Maudlin, lays hold of her girdle suddenly, but, she striving to get free, they both run out, and he returns with the belt broken. She, following in her own shape, demanding it, but at a distance, as fearing to be seized upon again, and seeing she cannot recover it, falls into a rage and cursing, resolving to trust to her old arts, which she calls her daughter to assist in. The shepherds, content with this discovery, go home triumphing, make the relation to Marian. Amie is gladded with the sight of Karol, etc. In the meantime, enters Lorel, with purpose to ravish Earine, and, calling her forth to that lewd end, he, by the hearing of Clarion's footing,[3] is stayed and forced to commit her hastily to the tree again, where Clarion, coming by and hearing a voice singing, draws near unto it; but Eglamour, hearing it also and knowing it to be Earine's, falls into a superstitious commendation of it, as being an angel's, and in the air; when Clarion espies a hand put forth from the tree, and makes towards it, leaving Eglamour to his wild fancy, who quitteth

1. I.e., any other famous hunting-story.
2. An early form of the view-halloo, the shout raised at sight of the prey.
3. Footsteps.

the place; and, Clarion beginning to court the hand and make love to it, there ariseth a mist suddenly, which darkening all the place, Clarion loseth himself and the tree where Earine is enclosed, lamenting his misfortune, with the unknown nymph's misery. The air clearing, enters the witch with her son and daughter, tells them how she had caused that late darkness to free Lorel from surprisal, and his prey from being rescued from him, bids him look to her, and lock her up more carefully, and follow her to assist a work she hath in hand of recovering her lost girdle, which she laments the loss of, with cursings, execrations, wishing confusion to their feast and meeting; sends her son and daughter to gather certain simples[4] *for her purpose, and bring them to her dell. This Puck, hearing, prevents, and shows her error still. The huntsmen, having found her footing, follow the tract,*[5] *and prick after her. She gets to her dell, and takes her form.*[6] *Enter* [*the huntsmen*]. *Alken has spied her sitting with her spindle, threads, and images. They are eager to seize her presently,*[7] *but Alken persuades them to let her begin her charms, which they do. Her son and daughter come to her; the huntsmen are affrighted as they see her work go forward; and, over-hasty to apprehend her, she escapeth them all by the help and delusions of Puck.*

Act III

SCENE 1. *The forest*

PUCK-HAIRY

[PUCK.] The fiend[8] hath much to do that keeps a school,
Or is the father of a family,
Or governs but a country academy.
His labors must be great, as are his cares,
To watch all turns, and cast how to prevent 'em.
This dame of mine here, Maud, grows high in evil,
And thinks she does all, when 'tis I, her devil,
That both delude her and must yet protect her.
She's confident in mischief, and presumes
The changing of her shape will still[9] secure her;
But they may fail, and divers hazards meet
Of other consequence, which I must look to—
Not let her be surprised on the first catch.
I must go dance about the forest now,
And firk[1] it like a goblin till I find her.
Then will my service come worth acceptation,

4. Herbs.
5. Track; "prick": trail, pursue.
6. It's not clear whether she assumes the form of Old Maudlin, the form of a witch, or simply gets into her house, i.e., her fourm.
7. At once.
8. Spirit.
9. Always.
1. Frisk, caper.

When not expected of her; when the help
Meets the necessity, and both do kiss,
'Tis called the timing of a duty, this. [*Exit*.]

SCENE 2

KAROL, DOUCE [*in the dress of* EARINE]. *To them*, EGLAMOUR

KAROL. Sure, you are very like her! I conceived
You had been she, seeing you run afore me,
For such a suit she made her gainst this feast,
In all resemblance, or the very same;
I saw her in it. Had she lived t' enjoy it,
She had been there an acceptable guest
To Marian and the gentle Robin Hood,
Who are the crown and garland of the wood.
DOUCE. I cannot tell; my mother gave it me,
And bade me wear it.
KAROL. Who, the wise, good woman,
Old Maud of Papplewick?
DOUCE. Yes—[*Aside*.] This sullen man,
I cannot like him.—I must take my leave.
[EGLAMOUR *enters and* DOUCE *goes out*.]
EGLAMOUR. What said she to you?
KAROL. Who?
EGLAMOUR. Earine.
I saw her talking with you, or her ghost,
For she indeed is drowned in old Trent's bottom.
Did she not tell who would ha' pulled her in,
And had her maidenhead upon the place,
The river's brim, the margin of the flood?
No ground is holy enough (you know my meaning);
Lust is committed in kings' palaces,
And yet their majesty's not violated!
No words!
KAROL. How sad and wild his thoughts are! Gone?
[EGLAMOUR *goes out, but comes in again*.]
EGLAMOUR. But she, as chaste as was her name, Earine,[2]
Died undeflowered; and now her sweet soul hovers
Here in the air above us, and doth haste
To get up to the moon and Mercury,
And whisper Venus in her orb; then spring
Up to old Saturn, and come down by Mars,
Consulting Jupiter, and seat herself
Just in the midst with Phoebus, tempering all
The jarring spheres, and giving to the world
Again his first and tuneful planeting.[3]

2. Earine is named after the spring.
3. In the golden age of the earth's first existence, the music of the spheres was audible to humanity.

O, what an age will here be of new concords!
Delightful harmony! to rock old sages,
Twice infants, in the cradle o' speculation,
And throw a silence upon all the creatures!
[*He goes out again but returns as soon as before.*]

KAROL. A cogitation of the highest rapture!

EGLAMOUR. The loudest seas and most engragéd winds
Shall lose their clangor; tempest shall grow hoarse,
Loud thunder dumb, and every spece[4] of storm,
Laid in the lap of listening nature, hushed
To hear the changéd chime of this eighth sphere.
Take tent,[5] and hearken for it; lose it not. [EGLAMOUR *departs.*]

SCENE 3

CLARION, LIONEL, KAROL.

CLARION. O, here is Karol! Was not that the Sad
Shepherd slipped from him?

LIONEL. Yes, I guess it was.—
Who was that left you, Karol?

KAROL. The lost man,
Whom we shall never see himself again,
Or ours, I fear; he starts away from hand so,
And all the touches or soft stroke of reason
Ye can apply! No colt is so unbroken,
Or hawk yet half so haggard or unmanned![6]
He takes all toys that his wild fancy proffers,
And flies away with them. He now conceives
That my lost sister, his Earine,
Is lately turned a sphere amid the seven,
And reads a music lecture to the planets!
And with this thought he's run to call them hearers.

CLARION. Alas, this is a strained but innocent fancy!
I'll follow him, and find him if I can.
Meantime, go you with Lionel, sweet Karol;
He will acquaint you with an accident,[7]
Which much desires your presence on the place. [*Exit.*]

SCENE 4

KAROL, LIONEL

KAROL. What is it, Lionel, wherein I may serve you?
Why do you so survey and circumscribe me,
As if you stuck one eye into my breast,
And with the other took my whole dimensions?

4. Sort.
5. Take note.
6. I.e., untamed or unmastered.
7. Event.

LIONEL. I wish you had a window i' your bosom,
Or i' your back, I might look through you,
And see your in-parts, Karol, liver, heart;
For there the seat of Love is, whence the boy,
The wingéd archer, hath shot home a shaft
Into my sister's breast, the innocent Amie,
Who now cries out, upon her bed, on Karol,
Sweet-singing Karol, the delicious Karol,
That kissed her like a Cupid! In your eyes,
She says, his stand is, and between your lips
He runs forth his divisions[8] to her ears,
But will not bide there, 'less yourself do bring him.
Go with me, Karol, and bestow a visit
In charity upon the afflicted maid,
Who pineth with the langour of your love.

To them, MAUDLIN *and* DOUCE, *but* MAUDLIN *appearing like* MARIAN

MARIAN. [*who is really* MAUDLIN] Whither intend you? Amie is recovered,
Feels no such grief as she complained of lately.
This maiden hath been with her from her mother
Maudlin, the cunning woman, who hath sent her
Herbs for her head, and simples[9] of that nature
Have wrought upon her a miraculous cure,
Settled her brain to all our wish and wonder.
LIONEL. So instantly? You know I now but left her,
Possessed with such a fit almost to a frenzy;
Yourself, too, feared her,[1] Marian, and did urge
My haste to seek out Karol and to bring him.
MARIAN. I did so. But the skill of that wise woman,
And her great charity of doing good,
Hath by the ready hand of this deft lass,
Her daughter, wrought effects beyond belief,
And to astonishment; we can but thank,
And praise, and be amazed, while we tell it. [*They go out.*]
LIONEL. 'Tis strange that any art should so help nature
In her extremes.
KAROL. Then it appears most real,
When th' other is deficient.
[*Enter* ROBIN HOOD.]
ROBIN. Wherefore stay you
Discoursing here, and haste not with your succors
To poor afflicted Amie, that so needs them?
LIONEL. She is recovered well, your Marian told us
But now here. See, she is returned t' affirm it!

8. Rapid, melodic passages of music.
9. Herbs.
1. Feared for her.

[*Enter* MAUDLIN *like* MARIAN. MAUDLIN, *espying* ROBIN HOOD, *would run out, but he stays her by the girdle, and runs in with her.*]

ROBIN. My Marian?
MARIAN. Robin Hood! is he here?
ROBIN. Stay;
What was 't you ha' told my friend?

[*He returns with the girdle broken and she in her own shape.*]

MAUDLIN. Help, murder, help!
You will not rob me, outlaw? Thief, restore
My belt that ye have broken!
ROBIN. Yes, come near.
MAUDLIN. Not i' your gripe.
ROBIN. Was this the charméd circle,[2]
The copy that so cozened and deceived us?
I'll carry hence the trophy of your spoils.
My men shall hunt you too upon the start,[3]
And course you soundly.
MAUDLIN. I shall make 'em sport,
And send some home without their legs or arms.
I'll teach 'em to climb stiles, leap ditches, ponds,
And lie i' the waters, if they follow me.
ROBIN. Out, murmuring hag! [*Exeunt all but* MAUDLIN.]
MAUDLIN. I must use all my powers,
Lay all my wits to piecing of this loss.
Things run unluckily. Where's my Puck-Hairy?

SCENE 5

MAUDLIN, PUCK

[MAUDLIN.] Hath he forsook me?
PUCK. At your beck, madám.
MAUDLIN. O Puck, my goblin! I have lost my belt;
The strong thief, Robin Outlaw, forced it from me.
PUCK. They are other clouds and blacker threat you, dame;
You must be wary, and pull in your sails,
And yield unto the weather of the tempest.
You think your power's infinite as your malice,
And would do all your anger prompts you to;
But you must wait occasions, and obey them—
Sail in an eggshell, make a straw your mast,
A cobweb all your cloth,[4] and pass unseen,
Till you have 'scaped the rocks that are about you.

2. Magicians and witches traditionally made a charmed circle to protect themselves from the effects of their own enchantments. "Copy": counterfeit.

3. Without giving you any lead-time; instantly. "Course": chase.

4. Sail.

MAUDLIN. What rocks about me?
PUCK. I do love, madám,
To show you all your dangers, when you are past 'em!
Come, follow me; I'll once more be your pilot.
And you shall thank me. [*Exit.*]
MAUDLIN. Lucky, my loved goblin!
[LOREL *meets her.*]
Where are you gaang now?
LOREL. Unto my tree,
To see my maistress.
MAUDLIN. Gang thy gait, and try
Thy turns with better luck, or hang thysel'.[5]

5. The play breaks off, incomplete. F. G. Waldron published one completion of it in 1783, and Alan Porter another in 1944; but, apart from the Argument of Act III and the presence in the "Persons of the Play" of Reuben the Reconciler, there's no knowing how Jonson would have made it come out.

The Staging of Jonson's Plays and Masques

The plays in this volume which were mounted on the stage (*The Sad Shepherd*, being incomplete and posthumous, was never performed in the 17th century) were exhibited to paying audiences in theaters of two different sorts. *Volpone* and *The Alchemist* were staged, in 1606 and 1610 respectively, by the King's Men at the Globe Theater on the Bankside: this was a public theater. *Epicoene* was first acted in 1609 by the Children of the Queen's Revels, at the Whitefrairs Theater; this was a private theater. The masques were not staged for a paying audience at all; each had a single performance in a large assembly-room at court, which served a number of functions besides theatrical display. All these circumstances call for a bit of explanation.

The King's Men were the oldest and most successful company of actors in London; under several earlier titles, they had been active since 1572, taking the name of the King's Men at the accession of James in 1603. Though they were nominally "his" men, and occasionally by particular request put on a play at court, the King actually had very little to do with them. They took his name and were under his protection largely because, years before, when actors were mainly strolling players and so liable to the laws against vagabonds, a custom had sprung up among them of claiming to be some nobleman's servants. But by now the King's Men were substantial citizens. They owned their own theater, in which the principal players held shares; they had a library of plays which they had already performed and could mount from time to time as a venture promised profit; they had an assortment of props and costumes. Shakespeare was of their number, and they produced most of his plays; for example, between 1606 and 1610, they put on *Antony and Cleopatra* and *King Lear*. It was a good time, obviously, to be an actor; and with plays like these to sink their teeth into, the King's Men were a practiced repertory company. Both Jonson's plays at the Globe were resounding successes, and *Volpone* was repeated twice the following year, when the King's Men went visiting to Oxford and Cambridge.

Working in their own open-air theater, the Globe, the King's Men had a large raised stage facing a substantial auditorium, without, however, any sort of artificial lighting or any proscenium curtain. Plays were performed in the afternoon, and in both *Volpone* and *The Alchemist* Jonson is careful (far beyond the wont of his contemporaries) to confine the time of the action to a single day: thus the sun would be setting in stage time just as it was in real time. A full house would have consisted of about two thousand spectators, running the social gamut, from lords and knights who sat in boxes or on chairs at the side of the stage, down to the lowest-priced admissions, the "groundlings," who had standing room in what we would call the "orchestra" and they called the "pit." As the play began, there being no special way to signal that the action had started, the actors onstage had to assert themselves over the audience noise—hence the noisy quarrel with which *The Alchemist* begins, and the audacious blasphemies with which Volpone unveils his gold-hoard and performs devotions before it.

Because the stage protruded quite far out into the "pit" or "ground," a good deal of the action onstage must have been essentially "in the round," as we now say. Looking out over the upturned faces of the groundlings (just about the level of his feet), the actor would face three tiers of boxes. The audience, as they looked back at him, would see him against a wall or backdrop, which might be of one story or two; over his head would be a small roof or hut, covering the central part of the stage. Characters entered and exited through doors set in the rear wall: probably there were two of them, though some stage directions seem to imply three—the third might be a door in a screen placed onstage for the occasion. In the center of the rear wall there was often a hanging or curtain, which could be raised or drawn aside, as when Volpone uncovers his gold-hoard. Behind the wall (and invisible, of course, to the audience) was the "tiring room," in which the actors donned or changed their costumes. (During the performance of *The Alchemist*, it must have been a frantic place.) As for the roofed hut overhead, it served in the first place to keep brief rain showers off the actors —the groundlings got wet, but serious storms cancelled the show entirely —and it may also have had acoustical advantages. Besides, the hut may have had a second story, from which Celia, for example, could flutter her handkerchief coyly to "Scoto" atop his platform erected on the main stage.

Perhaps too much has been made of the plainness of the Elizabethan stage, its lack of scenic props—Puritan moralists of the day were apt to complain of its excessive and gaudy decoration. None of Jonson's plays call for palatial luxury or elaborate visual effects, but the rudiments of scenic differentiation were clearly available; the officers of the Scrutineo must have sat on some sort of raised bench, perhaps behind a desk; when the laboratory blows up in *The Alchemist*, it would be a very poor stage manager who couldn't contrive, in addition to crashing noises on tin sheets and a couple of gunshots offstage, a puff of smoke through the door leading to the laboratory. The well-known producer Philip Henslowe has left us an inventory of the props available on March, 1598, in his theater, the Rose. They include such sizable items as numerous trees, a chariot, a little altar, "the cloth of the Sun & the Moon," dragons, lions, a rainbow, a good deal of armor, "the City of Rome," plus lesser items like cloaks, visors, crowns, and so forth. One wouldn't need much more than a fair selection of this stuff to make as much of Venice or London as Jonson's two plays were likely to require.

In some respects, the Elizabethans had more appetite for stage realism than we give them credit for. Battles might indeed by represented by "armies" of a few actors on a side, clad in tin armor and waving wooden swords; but in formal duels (like that in Act V of *Hamlet*), the audience clearly wanted a good show, the playwright drew out the scene to give them one, and it is very likely that at the height of the struggle a little bladder of pig's blood, hidden under the actor's outer garments, was punctured to procure a gory climax. Thunder was simulated by rolling a cannonball down a wooden trough, and boys touched off flashes of powder to suggest lightning. Rain on a roof was represented by pouring peas from a height onto a tin plate, and sailors just rescued from drowning in *The Tempest* were instructed to come onstage dripping wet. But Jonson, as we've said, was notably conservative about using these scenic devices; both *Volpone* and *The Alchemist* require very little state machinery. Perhaps a screen pushed onstage could represent the door through which Lovewit parleys with Jeremy, and Bonario could be shoved, like Dapper, behind the hanging till it was time for him to interrupt the action onstage.

Though some plays were much more successful than others, it is not clear how, or even if, the more successful playwright was more largely rewarded. Publication of a play was not automatic, nor did publication imply (in those days before copyright and royalties) reward for the author. Jonson was the object of much ridicule when in 1616 he published his *Works*. English authors were not supposed to have "Works"; the word was applied only to Latin authors, whose works were called "Opera." In any case, during his last years when he was sick and poor, Jonson got some help from the King, some from the government of London city, and some from loyal patrons, but from those who had published his books and produced his plays he got nothing at all.

On the stage of the Globe, female parts were of course taken by boys; not till after the Restoration (1660) did actresses appear on the English stage. Because boys lost their clean chins and soprano voices in the natural course of time, their stage careers were relatively short, and skillful ones were not in large supply. In the plays done for the King's Men, Jonson makes use of a few female characters, whereas in *Epicoene,* which was acted by and written for a company of boys, male and female characters are about equally balanced.

Where did these boys in the company known as "Children of the Queen's Revels" come from? Historically, they had begun as a boys' choir, selected and trained for the musical delight of the court; under certain circumstances and during certain periods, boys could even be impressed (that is, forcibly removed from their parents) for service in the choir. Gradually they began putting on plays; then they largely ceased to sing (much to the distress of their parents, who often shared middle-class prejudices against actors, and thought they were being forced into a vagabond, ne'er-do-well existence); and by the turn of the century they were a regularly established theatrical company. Shakespeare speaks of them with ill-concealed bitterness in the second act of *Hamlet*:

> but there is, sir, an eyrie [nest] of children, little eyases [eaglets], that cry out on the top of the question and are most tyrannically clapped for it; these are now the fashion, and so berattle the common stages—so they call them—that many wearing rapiers are afraid of goose-quills [pens], and dare scarce come hither.

The children's companies did not act at the Globe, across the river in the suburbs, but in "private" theaters within the city limits. These were smaller houses, roofed in so they were more available during the winter months, using artificial lighting, and on the whole attracting a more select audience than the raffish crowd that attended the Globe. The best known of them were a pair constructed in old abbey buildings lying between Fleet Street and the river Thames: from the monks who used to inhabit them, they were known as Blackfriars (Dominicans) and Whitefriars (Carmelites)—but it was many years since friars of any shade had occupied the buildings. They were used for storage depots and record offices, rented out to storekeepers, and adapted to playhouses. The relation of the "private" to the "public" theaters was not altogether antagonistic; for example, the Burbage family, who took the lead in building the Globe and its predecessor (known simply as The Theater) also built the Blackfriars Theater, and the King's Men sometimes played there. Perhaps they also recruited from the children's company; for these boys were not by any means fringe performers. They had excellent coaching, and by all accounts they were trained professionals; several, we know, went on to adult careers on the stage. Before *Epicoene*, they had staged several of Jonson's earlier plays (*Cynthia's Revels, The Case Is Altered*); other playwrights wrote for them, and plays of their performance were just as likely to make the author's reputation, and earn him money, as any others.

Whatever the theater in which they were staged, or the company producing them, Elizabethan plays did not generally have long consecutive runs because the supply of available spectators was not very large. When everyone who wanted to had seen the play, the script was placed in the company's library of reserve scripts, where it would be available in case a revival was called for or a road company wanted to take it on tour. When they were unusually successful in London, like *Volpone*, plays might be performed in the universities, and they sometimes went out into the provinces (especially when the plague grew hot in London) to be performed in inn yards and the main halls of country houses. If he could interest a publisher, the author might get his play printed. The seventeenth-century stage represented one of the few ways to make money by writing, but nobody, not even the prolific and popular Shakespeare, got really rich at it; and Jonson died destitute.

The masque as it flourished in England in the early 17th century was a brief artistic growth, ephemeral if not exotic. There had been very primitive court-entertainments as early as the late 13th and early 14th centuries; they were called "mummings" or "disguisings." Early in the 16th century, they started to be called "masks" or "masques"; there may have been a Continental influence, but its extent is not clear. Sometimes the participants wore false faces, sometimes not; they generally figured or represented an imaginary personage or an abstraction. Masques reached a climax of complexity and beauty under James I, and withered under the chill blasts of Puritanism, disappearing for all-but-good with the outbreak of the Civil Wars in 1640.*

Because they were written by many different authors under a great variety of circumstances, because they had no classical precedents to follow, nor any critical canons to observe, masques took many diverse forms. They were, after all, not literary forms so much as courtly entertainments; poets and men of letters got involved with them only by the side door, as it were,

* A few small exceptions must be made for later works like Dryden's *Secular Masque* (1700), which deliberately revived for a momentary occasion a form that was essentially dead.

and incidentally. The first and most important element of the masque was the practice of dressing up and showing off. Already this distinguishes them sharply from stage plays, where the actors, though they wear costumes and assume characters not their own, are precisely *not* showing off, *not* calling attention to their own qualities, *not* involving themselves in their own persons with the audience. Masques are analogies if not allegories, deliberately fantastic and unrealistic in their mode, so that they can more accurately mirror the ideals of a courtly audience. They grow out of three other courtly ceremonies, the *tournament*, the *pageant*, and the *triumph*, each of which is related to the others.

As tournaments ceased to consist of real or mock battles, they took on a kind of allegorical or didactic structure. The ladies were labeled Truth, Modesty, Virtue, etc.; the knights, Honor, Temperance, Fortitude, etc. The triumphant knight got to dance with the lady of his choice; each was complimented, and both joined to present their compliments to the person in whose honor the tournament, gradually being converted to a pageant, was being held. All the participants wore their finest and fanciest costumes: they carried out some minimal instructive action, for they were all amateur actors, and not up to complex emotions or elaborate speeches. Dancing was a natural consequence of the choosing of partners, and music accompanied, inevitably, the dance. The whole structure led toward the presentation of the supreme compliment to the most important person present. And then the audience was called on to mingle with the masquers in a way that the playhouses would have found socially unthinkable and physically impossible. The final dance circled around the central luminary of the occasion; everyone took part in it because no one was present who was not part of the court, and everyone in the court was bound, by ties of loyalty and reverence, to its supreme figure. In this way the tournament-become-pageant easily melted into the pageant-become-triumph. Dignitaries visiting at country houses, monarchs on tour or celebrating a birthday, princes being crowned or princesses getting married, all could easily be made the centers of a festive event in which they were welcomed, reverenced, felicitated—in a word, flattered. By our rough democratic standards the flattery often appears fulsome; in the 17th century, within the narrow circles of the court, it was an expression of normal good manners and social propriety. One called King James the fountain of honor and the wellspring of nobility or one described Queen Anne as the paragon of feminine beauty, on the same principle that, nowadays, one tells a Hollywood actor that his latest film is "sensational," or an actress that she's looking "divine."

Words, it is important to recall, were only one element in a masque; and though Ben Jonson ultimately made them equal partners, they never overbalanced their fellow-ingredients, music, dance, and spectacle. There was a lot of singing and dancing in every masque; professional composers wrote the melodies, instrumentalists were hired, and good voices were picked for the singing parts. The masquers were ladies and gentlemen of the court, that is, of the idle rich class. As they commonly dressed with great elegance in everyday life, when they dressed up for a masque they were bound to indulge in high fantasy and extravagant costuming. The masque was an occasion for the ladies in particular to show off, and some masques had much the character of a fashion show. Participation in them was very expensive; indeed, its cost was one of the limiting and exclusive features of the form. Finally, the masques generally called for the introduction of elaborate and costly "machinery." Even though the anticipated run of a masque was for only one night, the sets were much more elaborate and expensive than those of the playhouses. Inigo Jones, the great architect and designer of the age, had brought back from his Italian travels ideas for perspective sets, which produced the illusion of three dimensions. One had to have rather a sophisticated eye to understand this principle. Most Englishmen had seen very little of the art of the Renaissance; their eyes didn't readily compose a set of receding flats—that is painted canvas backdrops—into a deep landscape. And because a perspective stage has to be looked at fairly straight on, to produce its effect, perspectives couldn't be used on the Elizabethan stage. Most of the audience in the Globe would have seen sets as we know them from an impossibly acute angle, and some would have seen them, actually, from behind. But the masque focused so closely on one figure in the audience that perspectives could be used, and the King at least could enjoy them.

In addition, the masques made liberal use of onstage scenery. Mountains opened up into caves, witches' dens turned abruptly into the House of Fame. Generally, these effects were achieved by machines that actually rotated, their operation perhaps concealed by a puff of smoke. Sometimes characters or groups of musicians could be made to appear in moving chariots, or individuals could be made to descend from the sky, dangling on cords run over pulleys and worked by stagehands in the wings. New and surprising effects were much in demand; in the matter of stage machinery, the masques were far in advance of the playhouses. Engineers, painters, musicians, choreographers, poets, and stage designers made up a sizable troop of artists; a really ambitious masque, like *The Masque of Queens*, cost the royal treasury over £ 3,000, not to speak of the sums that the masquers themselves spent on their costumes. Money equivalents are extremely hard to estimate, but in those days a hundred pounds a year was comfort, a thousand pounds a nice fortune, and three thousand pounds for a single evening's entertainment inconceivable extravagance.

Being essentially so lofty and aristocratic a form, the masque inevitably required material for contrast and relief, and this led Jonson, with his strong theatrical sense, to develop anti-masques. These were simply counter-figures, either grotesque or comic, who appeared in the first part of the show: gentry, of course, never took these parts. They might be pygmies, satyrs, witches, Irishmen, alchemists; like Vices in the old morality plays, they were half-comic antagonists of the Virtues, Macabre, funny, or actively sinister, they performed their antics and displayed their characters onstage for a while, until (inevitably) the forces of Virtue appeared and triumphed over them. In some ways they are like the villains of stage plays, but without intrigue or motivation. The conflict is heraldic, not dramatic; good appears, declaring itself, and the figures of evil withdraw like the shades of night when the sun rises.

The masque was thus a deliberately limited and exclusive form; though some masques were performed at country houses and under domestic circumstances (i.e., as family festivals), the great majority were performed at court, where vast halls, gorgeously attired courtiers, fine ladies, musical and artistic talent, and immense sums of money could be woven into a short-lived but stunning theatrical complex. But these various elements were not easily reconciled. Like the court itself, where "favor" was sought with ferocious intensity, the masques easily became occasions for jealous resentment. Jonson quarrelled with Chapman over assignments; and after a short period of fruitful collaboration, he quarrelled bitterly and permanently with Inigo Jones, the architect and scene designer, who had contributed largely to Jonson's first masques.

Jones (1573–1652) was a remarkable man. Though born in humble circumstances, he was pensioned in his late twenties by William Herbert, third earl of Pembroke, to travel in Italy and study the works of painting and architecture, as well as the classical ruins, to be found there. The experience was not lost on Jones; he not only learned a great deal about the art of building in the neo-classical mode, he developed a taste for the painting of the Italian Renaissance such as few Englishmen possessed, and investigated the arts of theatrical design and scenic representation. One of the chief influences on his thinking was the Italian architect Andrea Palladio (1518–80), whose book on architecture he annotated and translated; and one of Palladio's outstanding achievements was the Teatro Olimpico in Vicenza, which certainly helped to make Jones what he was, the foremost scenic artist in England. His quarrel with Jonson, which became open warfare in the 1620's, was stirred more, it would seem, by personal than by artistic differences. The two men were strong, outspoken, even truculent characters; their collaboration ended in a welter of recriminations. In any event, Jones's real career was in architecture; and in the last part of his life, when masques had fallen out of fashion, and Jonson himself was old and neglected, Inigo Jones continued to carry on a busy career as builder and designer of stately homes and public edifices.

Because only a few aristocrats got to see them performed, masques naturally aroused a good deal of curiosity in the public at large; Jonson was proud of his part in them, and put forth the text of several in tiny quarto pamphlets. But even with their stage directions, masques were never long enough to constitute a proper volume, and most of Jonson's are known simply from their appearance in the several folio editions of his *Works* (1616, 1640). Several also survive in manuscript form, and one in particular, *The Masque of Queens*, in a manuscript of Jonson's own writing, with particularly elaborate stage instructions and footnotes. Jonson prepared it as a gift to Prince Henry, the eldest son of Queen Anne and King James. Within three years' time, Prince Henry was to die abruptly of typhoid fever (November 6, 1612), but at the time of *The Masque of Queens* (1609) he was a lively and inquisitive lad of 15. Apparently he asked Jonson for a copy of the masque composed in his mother's honor, and Jonson, who had a broad pedagogic streak in him, gave him this richly annotated version to show him that in these gaudy trifles too there could be found a good deal of tough intellectual and scholarly work. We don't by any means reproduce in this volume all of Jonson's classical learning, but the text of *The Masque of Queens* includes about as much of it as the modern student is likely to want; and from the text of *Oberon*, which Jonson also annotated for Prince Henry, we have eliminated the erudite documentation altogether.

The Texts of
The Masques

The Masque of Queens

It increasing now to the third time of my being used in these services to her majesty's personal presentations,[1] *with the ladies whom she pleaseth to honor, it was my first and special regard to see that the nobility of the invention should be answerable to the dignity of their persons. For which reason I chose the argument to be,* A Celebration of Honorable and True Fame, Bred Out of Virtue; *observing that rule of the best artist, to suffer no object of delight to pass without his mixture of profit and example.*[2]

And because her majesty (best knowing that a principal part of life in these spectacles lay in their variety) had commanded me to think on some dance or show that might precede hers, and have the place of a foil or false masque, I was careful to decline not only from others but mine own steps in that kind, since the last year I had an anti-masque of boys,[3] *and therefore now devised that twelve women in the habit of hags or witches,*[4] *sustaining the persons of Ignorance, Suspicion, Credulity, etc., the opposites to good fame,*[5] *should fill that part; not as a masque, but a spectacle of strangeness producing multiplicity of gesture and not unaptly sorting with the current and whole fall of the device.*

First then, his majesty being set and the whole company in expectation, that which presented itself was an ugly hell, which, flaming beneath, smoked unto the top of the roof. And, in respect all evils are (morally) said to come from hell, as also from that saying of Torrentius upon Horace his Canidia,[6] *that she was so learned in poisons that she might seem to have come straight from the jaws of hell; these witches, with a kind of hollow and infernal music, came forth from thence. First one, then two, and three, and more, till their number increased to eleven, all differently attired: some with rats on their heads, some on their shoulders; others with ointment-pots at their girdles; all with spindles, timbrels,*[7] *rattles, or other venefical instruments, making a confused noise with strange gestures. The device of their attire was Mr. Jones's,*[8] *with the inven-*

1. The masque was presented at Whitehall on February 2, 1609.
2. The precept is that of Horace in his *Art of Poetry*.
3. In the masque made the year before for the marriage of Viscount Hadington. On the anti-masque see, above, "The Staging of Jonson's Plays and Masques."
4. Jonson doesn't mention among the reasons for having an anti-masque of witches the presence of King James, who had written a book on withcraft and was obsessed with the subject.
5. Good Fame or reputation (like Bad Fame or scandal) was an important concept for the Renaissance, where court societies could make or mar one's social prestige with a breath.
6. Several of Horace's Epodes (V, XII, XIII) deal with a witch named Canidia. Torrentius was an editor who had recently written a commentary on Horace, from which Jonson quotes.
7. Tambourines; "venefical": in the literal sense, poisonous, in this context, simply magical.
8. On Inigo Jones, stage-designer and architect, see, above, "The Staging of Jonson's Plays and Masques."

tion and architecture of the whole scene and machine. Only I prescribed them their properties, of vipers, snakes, bones, herbs, roots, and other ensigns[9] *of their magic out of the authority of ancient and late writers. Wherein the faults are mine, if there be any found, and for that cause I confess them.*

These eleven witches beginning to dance (which is a usual ceremony at their convents[1] *or meetings, where sometimes also they are vizarded*[2] *and masked), on the sudden one of them missed their chief, and interrupted the rest with this speech:*

Sisters, stay; we want[3] our Dame.
Call upon her by her name,
And the charm we use to say,
That she quickly anoint,[4] and come away.

1 *Charm*

Dame, Dame, the watch is set,
Quickly come, we all are met.
From the lakes and from the fens,
From the rocks and from the dens,
From the woods and from the caves,
From the church-yards, from the graves,
From the dungeon, from the tree[5]
That they die on, here are we.

Comes she not yet?
Strike another heat.

2 *Charm*

The weather is fair, the wind is good,
Up, Dame, on your horse of wood;
Or else, tuck up your gray frock,
And saddle your goat, or your green cock,
And make his bridle a bottom of thrid
To roll up how many miles you have rid.[6]
    Quickly, come away,
    For we all stay.

    Nor yet? Nay then,
    We'll try her again.

9. Emblems.
1. From the Latin, coming together.
2. Vizards or visors are half-masks.
3. Lack.
4. Anointing, an indispensable preliminary to flight on broomstick. goat, or hog.
5. Gallows-tree.
6. Most of the witches' mounts are traditional, but Jonson's note confesses that the green cock and the "bottom of thrid" (bobbin of thread) came from "a vulgar fable" that he heard as a schoolboy.

3 Charm

The owl is abroad, the bat and the toad,
And so is the cat-a-mountain;[7]
The ant and the mole both sit in a hole,
And frog peeps out of the fountain;
The dogs they do bay and the timbrels play,
The spindle is now a-turning;
The moon it is red, and the stars are fled,
But all the sky is a-burning:
The ditch is made, and our nails the spade,
With pictures full, of wax and of wool,
Their livers I stick with needles quick,[8]
There lacks but the blood to make up the flood.
Quickly, Dame, then, bring your part in,
Spur, spur upon little Martin,[9]
Merrily, merrily make him sail,
A worm in his mouth and a thorn in his tail,
Fire above and fire below,
With a whip in your hand to make him go.
Oh now she's come!
Let all be dumb.

At this the Dame entered to them, naked-armed, barefooted, her frock tucked, her hair knotted and folded with vipers; in her hand a torch made of a dead man's arm, lighted, girded with a snake. To whom they all did reverence, and she spake, uttering by way of question the end wherefore they came: which, if it had been done either before or otherwise, had not been so natural. For to have made themselves their own decipherers, and each one to have told upon their entrance what they were and whither they would, had been a most piteous hearing, and utterly unworthy any quality of a poem, wherein a writer should always trust somewhat to the capacity of the spectator, especially at these spectacles; where men, besides enquiring eyes, are understood to bring quick ears, and not those sluggish ones of porters and mechanics that must be bored through at every act with narrations.

DAME, HAGS

Well done, my hags. And come we, fraught with spite,
To overthrow the glory of this night?
Holds our great purpose? HAGS. Yes. DAME. But wants there none
Of our just number? HAGS. Call us, one by one,

7. The witch's pet, a wild cat.

8. To cast a spell on someone, the witch made an image of wax or wool, dug a trench with her own fingernails and filled it with blood, then stuck needles in the image or burnt it, to the accompaniment of incantations.

9. A disguise of the devil—a buck goat with a human voice who carries the witches to their meeting-places.

And then our Dame shall see. DAME. First then advance
My drowsy servant, stupid Ignorance,
Known by thy scaly vesture; and bring on
Thy fearful sister, wild Suspicion,
Whose eyes do never sleep; let her knit hands
With quick Credulity that next her stands,
Who hath but one ear, and that always ope;
Two-facéd Falsehood follow in the rope,[1]
And lead on Murmur, with the cheeks deep-hung,
She Malice, whetting of her forkéd tongue,
And Malice Impudence, whose forehead's lost;[2]
Let Impudence lead Slander on, to boast
Her oblique look; and to her subtle side,
Thou, black-mouthed Execration, stand applied;
Draw to thee Bitterness, whose pores sweat gall,
She flame-eyed Rage; Rage, Mischief.[3] HAGS. Here we are all.
DAME. Join now our hearts, we faithful opposites
To Fame and Glory. Let not these bright nights
Of Honor blaze, thus to offend our eyes.
Show ourselves truly envious; and let rise
Our wonted rages. Do what may beseem
Such names and natures. Virtue, else, will deem
Our powers decreased, and think us banished earth
No less than heaven. All her antique[4] birth,
As Justice, Faith, she will restore; and, bold
Upon our sloth, retrieve her Age of Gold.[5]
We must not let our native manners thus
Corrupt with ease. Ill lives not but in us.
I hate to see these fruits of a soft peace,
And curse the piety gives it such increase.
Let us disturb it then, and blast the light,
Mix hell with heaven, and make nature fight
Within herself; loose the whole hinge of things,
And cause the ends run back into their springs.

HAGS. What our Dame bids us do
We are ready for. DAME. Then, fall to.
But first relate me what you have sought,
Where you have been, and what you have brought.

HAGS

1

I have been all day looking after
A raven, feeding upon a quarter;[6]

1. Order, chain.
2. I.e., who's lost to shame (from a blush appearing on the forehead).
3. Jonson's note emphasizes the careful ordering of these vices, Ignorance being the first and fundamental one, Suspicion and Credulity being consequences of Ignorance, and so on down the line.
4. Ancient.
5. The original age of universal innocence and virtue under Saturn.
6. At a time when drawing and quartering were often part of an execution, the nature of the quarter would be evident.

And soon as she turned her beak to the south,
I snatched this morsel out of her mouth.

2

I have been gathering wolves' hairs,
The mad dog's foam, and the adder's ears,
The spurging[7] of a dead man's eyes,
And all since the evening star did rise.

3

I last night lay all alone
On the ground, to hear the Mandrake[8] groan,
And plucked him up, though he grew full low,
And as I had done, the cock did crow.

4

And I have been choosing out this skull
From charnel-houses[9] that were full,
From private grots, and public pits,
And frighted a sexton[1] out of his wits.

5

Under a cradle I did creep
By day; and when the child was asleep,
At night I sucked the breath; and rose,
And plucked the nodding nurse by the nose.

6

I had a dagger, what did I with that?
Killed an infant to have his fat.
A piper it got, at a church-ale,[2]
I bade him again blow wind in the tail.

7

A murderer yonder was hung in chains,
The sun and the wind had shrunk his veins;
I bit off a sinew, I clipped his hair,
I brought off his rags that danced in the air.

8

The screech-owl's eggs and the feathers black,
The blood of the frog and the bone in his back,
I have been getting, and made of his skin
A purset, to keep Sir Cranion in.[3]

9

And I have been plucking, plants among,
Hemlock, henbane, adders' tongue,
Nightshade, moonwort, leopard's bane,[4]
And twice by the dogs was like to be ta'en.

10

I from the jaws of a gardener's bitch
Did snatch these bones, and then leaped the ditch,

7. Oozing.
8. A dangerous aphrodisiac, a root with a human voice which was death to hear.
9. Houses for storing old dead bones.
1. Guardian of a graveyard.
2. Church-ales were church-festivals, often quite alcoholic. To "blow wind in the tail" is a vague but clearly contemptuous expression.
3. Her familiar spirit, perhaps in the form of a spider.
4. These are all vegetables of evil omen.

Yet went I back to the house again,
Killed the black cat—and here's the brain.

11

I went to the toad breeds under the wall,
I charmed him out, and he came at my call;
I scratched out the eyes of the owl, before;
I tore the bat's wing; what would you have more?

12

DAME

Yes, I have brought (to help our vows)
Hornèd poppy, cypress boughs,
The fig-tree wild, that grows on tombs,
And juice that from the larch-tree comes,
The basilisk's blood and the viper's skin.[5]
And now our orgies let's begin.

Here the Dame put herself into the midst of them and began her following invocation; wherein she took occasion to boast all the power attributed to witches by the ancients, of which every poet (or the most) doth give some. Homer to Circe in the Odyssey; *Theocritus to Simatha in Idyll II The Sorceress; Virgil to Alphesiboeus in his Eighth Eclogue. Ovid to Dipsas in his* Amores, *to Medea and Circe in the* Metamorphoses. *Tibullus to Saga. Horace to Canidia, Sagana, Veia, Folia. Seneca to Medea and the Nurse in* Hercules on Oeta. *Petronius Arbiter to his Saga in the fragment known as* Satyricon, *and Claudian to his Megaera in book one of his poem* On Rufinus, *who takes the habit of a witch as these do, and supplies that historical part in the poem, besides her moral person of a Fury.*[6] *Confirming the same drift in ours.*

DAME

You Fiends and Furies (if yet any be
Worse than our selves), you that have quaked to see
These knots untied, and shrunk when we have charmed
You that (to arm us) have yourselves disarmed,
And to our powers resigned your whips and brands
When we went riding forth, the scourge of men and lands;
You that have seen me ride, when Hecatè[7]
Durst not take chariot, when the boisterous sea

5. The basilisk was a fabulous creature which could destroy its foe at a glance. All the other ingredients are in one way or another poisonous or malignant. "Orgies": ceremonies.

6. As explained in "The Staging of Jonson's Plays and Masques," above, the text of this particular masque is taken from a particularly elaborate manuscript in Jonson's own hand which he prepared for the instruction of Prince Henry. All the witchly learning of this stage direction, which the editor has considerably abridged and simplified for the benefit of a modern reader, represents but a fraction of that which Jonson stuffed into marginal notes or stage directions throughout the masque.

7. Hecate (pronounced with three syllables): goddess of witchcraft in classical times.

Without a breath of wind hath knocked the sky,
And that hath thundered, Jove not knowing why;
When we have set the elements at wars,
Made midnight see the sun, and day the stars;
When the wing'd lightning in the course hath stayed;
And swiftest rivers have run back, afraid
To see the corn remove,[8] the groves to range,
Whole places alter, and the seasons change.
When the pale moon at the first voice down fell
Poisoned, and durst not stay the second spell.
You that have oft been conscious of these sights,
And thou, three-formèd star, that on these nights
Art only powerful, to whose triple name
Thus we incline; once, twice, and thrice the same:[9]
If now with rites profane and foul enough,
We do invoke thee; darken all this roof,
With present[1] fogs. Exhale earth's rott'nest vapors
And strike a blindness through these blazing tapers.[2]
Come, let a murmuring charm resound
The whilst we bury all i'the ground.
But first, see every foot be bare,
And every knee. HAGS. Yes, Dame, they are.

4 Charm

Deep, oh deep, we lay thee to sleep;
We leave thee drink by, if thou chance to be dry,
Both milk and blood, the dew and the flood.
We breathe in thy bed at the foot and the head,
We cover thee warm that thou take no harm;
And when thou dost wake,
Dame Earth shall quake,
And the houses shake,
And her belly shall ache,
As her back were brake,
Such a birth to make
As is the blue drake
Whose form thou shalt take.[3]

DAME

Never a star yet shot?
Where be the ashes? HAGS. Here, i'the pot.

8. Even the fields of grain are moved about by the forces of enchantment.

9. Being connected with the moon, Hecate has three phases (waxing, waning, and full); as an embodiment of Diana (another classical moon-goddess), she is patroness of virginity, of childbirth, and of magic. Three is, in any case, a magic number, and all invocations to witches or their presiding goddesses have to be made three times.

1. Instant.

2. The candles lighting the hall.

3. By burying their materials and saying spells over them, the witches imitate the process of creation; the malignant spirit they are forming will take the form of a "blue drake," a comet or meteor. "Drake" comes from Latin *draco,* dragon.

DAME. Cast them up; and the flint stone
Over the left shoulder bone
Into the west. HAGS. It will be best.

5 Charm

The sticks are a cross, there can be no loss,
The sage is rotten, the sulphur is gotten
Up to the sky, that was in the ground.
Follow it then, with our rattles, round.
Under the bramble, over the brier,
A little more heat will set it on fire.
Put it in mind, to do it kind,
Flow water, and blow wind.[4]
Rouncy is over, *Robble* is under,[5]
A flash of light and a clap of thunder,
A storm of rain, and another of hail,
We all must home in the egg-shell sail;
The mast is made of a great pin,
The tackle of cobweb, the sail as thin,
And if we go through, and not fall in—

DAME

Stay: all our charms do nothing win
Upon the night; our labor dies!
Our magic feature[6] will not rise,
Nor yet the storm! We must repeat
More direful voices far, and beat
The ground with vipers till it sweat.

6 Charm

Bark dogs, wolves howl,
Seas roar, woods roll.
Clouds crack, all be black,
But the light our charms do make.

DAME

Not yet? My rage begins to swell;
Darkness, Devils, Night, and Hell,
Do not thus delay my spell.
I call you again, and I call you twice,
I beat you again if you stay me thrice;
Through these crannies where I peep,

4. This ceremony is intended to raise a storm.

5. "*Rouncy*" and "*Robble*" are nonsense terms, but they suggest the sound of thunder.

6. Demonic creature.

I'll let in the light, to see your sleep;
And all the secrets of your sway
Shall lie as open to the day
As unto me. Still are you deaf?
Reach me a bough that ne'er bare leaf
To strike the air; and aconite
To hurl upon this glaring light;[7]
A rusty knife to wound mine arm,
And as it drops, I'll speak a charm
Shall cleave the ground as low as lies
Old shrunk-up Chaos; and let rise
Once more his dark and reeking head
To strike the world and nature dead
Until my magic birth be bred.

7 Charm

Black go in, and blacker come out,
At thy going down, we give thee a shout:
Hoo!
At thy rising again, thou shalt have two,
And if thou dost what we would have thee do,
Thou shalt have three, thou shalt have four,
Thou shalt have ten, thou shalt have a score.
Hoo, Har, Har, Hoo.

8 Charm

A cloud of pitch, a spur and a switch,
To haste him away, and a whirlwind play
Before and after, with thunder for laughter,
And storms for joy of the roaring boy,
His head of a drake, his tail of a snake.

9 Charm

About, about, and about,
Till the mist arise, and the lights fly out,
The images neither be seen nor felt,
The woolen burn and the waxen melt.
Sprinkle your liquors upon the ground,
And into the air; around, around.
Around, around,
Around, around,
Till a music sound,

7. A branch that never sprouted leaves would be particularly deadly in its influence; aconite is a deadly poison which Ovid says sprang from the foam of Cerberus, the three-headed hound of hell. By shedding her own blood with a rusty knife, the witch seals the curse she is pronouncing.

And the pace be found
To which we may dance
And our charms advance.

At which, with a strange and sudden music, they fell into a magical dance full of preposterous change and gesticulation, but most applying to their property;[8] *who at their meetings do all things contrary to the custom of men, dancing back to back, hip to hip, their hands joined, and making their circles backward to the left hand, with strange fantastic motions of their heads and bodies.*[9] *All which were excellently imitated by the maker of the dance, Mr. Jerome Herne, whose right it is here to be named.*

In the heat of their dance, on the sudden, was heard a sound of loud music, as if many instruments had given one blast. With which not only the hags themselves but their hell into which they ran, quite vanished; and the whole face of the scene altered, scarce suffering the memory of any such thing. But in the place of it appeared a glorious and magnificent building, figuring the House of Fame, in the upper part of which were discovered the twelve masquers sitting upon a throne triumphal, erected in form of a pyramid, and circled with all store of light. From whom a person by this time descended in the furniture of Perseus,[1] *and expressing heroical and masculine virtue began to speak.*

HEROIC VIRTUE

So should, at Fame's loud sound and Virtue's sight,
All poor and envious witchcraft fly the light.
I did not borrow Hermes'[2] wings, nor ask
His crooked sword, nor put on Pluto's casque,
Nor on mine arm advanced wise Pallas's shield
(By which, my face aversed, in open field
I slew the Gorgon) for an empty name:
When Virtue cut off Terror, he gat Fame.[3]
And if, when Fame was gotten, Terror died,
What black Erinyes[4] or more hellish pride
Durst arm these hags, now she's grown and great,

8. I.e., the things they did were appropriate to their dramatic characters.

9. In this ceremony, as in ceremonies of the black mass, the point is to do everything backwards.

1. Perseus, who killed Medusa the witch-like Gorgon, is a fit figure for Heroic Virtue to assume against the hags. His "furniture" would include winged sandals, a magic wallet, the helmet of Hades, the mirror-shield of Pallas, and a sickle-shaped sword. All these identifying emblems are to be seen on Cellini's famous statue of Perseus in Florence, which Inigo Jones had seen and Jonson surely heard about.

2. As messenger of the gods, Hermes had wings, which he contributed to Perseus, as the other gods did their various emblems.

3. By "cutting off Terror," the speaker refers specifically to his cutting off the head of Medusa, the Gorgon whose very sight turned men to stone. Perseus overcame her by looking at her only in the mirror-shield given him by Pallas, goddess of wisdom.

4. Furies.

To think they could her glories once defeat?
I was her parent and I am her strength.
Heroic Virtue sinks not under length
Of years or ages, but is still the same
While he preserves, as when he got, Good Fame.
My daughter[5] then, whose glorious house you see
Built all of sounding[6] brass, whose columns be
Men-making poets, and those well made men
Whose strife it was to have the happiest pen
Renowme[7] them to an after-life and not
With pride to scorn the Muse and die, forgot:—
She, that enquireth into all the world
And hath about her vaulted palace hurled
All rumors and reports, or true or vain,
What utmost lands or deepest seas contain
(But only hangs great actions on her file),[8]
She to this lesser world and greatest isle
Tonight sounds honor, which she would have seen
In yon bright bevy, each of them a queen.
Eleven of them are of times long gone.
Penthesilea, the brave Amazon,
Swift-foot Camilla, Queen of Volscia,
Victorious Tomyris of Scythia,
Chaste Artemisia, the Carian dame,
And fair-haired Berenice, Egypt's fame,
Hypsicratea, Glory'of Asia,
Candace, pride of Ethiopia,
The Britain honor, Boadicea,
The virtuous Palmyrene, Zenobia,
The wise and warlike Goth, Amalasunta,
And bold Valasca of Bohemia.[9]
These, in their lives as fortunes, crowned the choice
Of womankind, and 'gainst all opposite voice
Made good to time, had after death the claim
To live eternized in the House of Fame,
Where hourly hearing (as what is there old?)
The glories of Bel-Anna[1] so well told,
Queen of the ocean; how that she alone
Possessed all virtues, for which, one by one,
They were so famed; and, wanting then a head
To form that sweet and gracious pyramid
Wherein they sit, it being the sovereign place
Of all that palace, and reserved to grace
The worthiest queen: these, without envy,'on her
In life desired that honor to confer

5. The daughter of Heroic Virtue is Fame.
6. Resounding, resonant.
7. The old form of renown, used here as a verb meaning "convey their names."
8. List or line of heroes.
9. For the deeds and characters of these distinguished ladies, see Jonson's description of them below.
1. James's wife, Queen Anne; "Bel-" to imply her beauty.

Which with their death no other should enjoy.[2]
She this embracing with a virtuous joy
Far from self-love, as humbling all her worth
To him that gave it,[3] hath again brought forth
Their names to memory, and means this night
To make her once more visible to light.
And to that light, from whence her truth of spirit
Confesseth all the lustre of her merit.
To you, most royal and most happy king,
Of whom Fame's house in every part doth ring
For every virtue; but can give no'increase,
Not though her loudest trumpet blaze your peace.
To you that cherish every great example
Contracted in your self; and being so ample
A field of honor, cannot but embrace
A spectacle so full of love and grace
Unto your court, where every princely dame
Contends to be as bounteous of her fame
To others, as her life was good to her.
For by their lives they only did confer
Good on themselves, but by their fame, to yours
And every age, the benefit endures.

Here the throne wherein they sat, being Machina versatilis,[4] *suddenly changed, and in the place of it appeared* Fama bona *as she is described in* Iconolog. *di Cesare Ripa, attired in white, with white wings, having a collar of gold about her neck and a heart hanging at it—which Horus Apollo in his* Hieroglyp. *interprets the note of a good fame.*[5] *In her right hand she bore a trumpet, in her left an olive branch, and for her state, it was as Virgil describes her, at the full, her feet on the ground and her head in the clouds.*[6] *She, after the music had done, which waited on the turning of the machine, called from thence to Virtue, and spake thus:*

FAME

Virtue, my father and my honor; thou
That mad'st me good as great, and darest avow
No Fame for thine but what is perfect: aid
Tonight the triumphs of thy white-winged maid.
Do those renownéd queens all utmost rites
Their states can ask. This is a night of nights.

2. Jonson's flattery seems excessive but was perfectly well understood in 1609 for what it was.
3. Probably God, though perhaps King James as well, who is duly flattered below.
4. I.e., a kind of revolving stage.
5. Cesare Ripa's book *Iconologia* was very popular in the Renaissance. "Horus Apollo" was the name assigned to the author of a book called *Hieroglyphica*, which purported to interpret the images of the gods created by the Egyptians. (It was largely fanciful, since nobody really could decipher hieroglyphics till the 19th century.)
6. Virgil, *Aeneid*, IV, 173 ff.

In mine own chariots let them crownéd ride,
And mine own birds and beasts in gears[7] applied
To draw them forth. Unto the first car, tie
Far-sighted eagles, to note Fame's sharp eye;
Unto the second, Griffons,[8] that design
Swiftness and strength, two other gifts of mine;
Unto the last, our lions, that imply
The top of graces,[9] State and Majesty.
And let those hags be led as captives, bound,
Before their wheels, whilst I my trumpet sound.[1]

At which the loud music sounded as before, to give the masquers time of descending. And here, we cannot but take the opportunity to make some more particular description of the scene, as also of the persons they presented; which, though they were disposed rather by chance than election, yet it is my part to justify them all virtuous, and then the lady that will own her presentation, may.[2]

To follow therefore the rule of chronology which we have observed in our verse, the most upward[3] *in time was Penthesilea. She was queen of the Amazons, and succeeded Otrera, or (as some will) Orythyia. She lived and was present at the war of Troy, on their part against the Greeks, where (as Justin gives her testimony) she gave great proofs of her power against the very strongest men.*[4] *She is nowhere mentioned but with the preface of honor and virtue, and is always advanced in the head of the worthiest women. Diodorus Siculus makes her the daughter of Mars.*[5] *She was honored in her death to have it the act of Achilles; of which Propertius sings this triumph to her beauty:*

After the golden helm laid bare her brow,
Her candid beauty laid the victor low.[6]

Next follows Camilla, queen of the Volscians, celebrated by Virgil about the end of the seventh book; than whose verses nothing can be imagined more exquisite or more honoring the person

7. Harness.
8. Fabulous creatures, half eagle and half lion.
9. I.e., the highest graces, state and majesty, because they are peculiar to royalty.
1. With the appearance of the hags as prisoners, the masque takes on aspects of a favorite Renaissance ceremony, the triumphal procession.
2. Evidently, the court ladies were told they were to be queens, then each chose (perhaps with the aid of a learned counselor) which queen she wanted to be.
3. I.e., the earliest.
4. Though she is associated with the Trojan war, Penthesilea does not appear in Homer. She arrived after the death of Hector, was slain by Achilles and, so the story goes, much regretted by him. When Thersites mocked the grief of Achilles, the hero killed him with a blow of his fist. "Justin" is Junianus Justinus, who in the 2d century A.D. wrote a summary, or epitome, of an earlier general history by Pompeius Trogus which told the tale of Penthesilea. Trogus' book is lost; Jonson cites Book 2 of Justin's epitome.
5. Jonson cites Book 2 of the history of Diodorus of Sicily, a Greek historian who lived about the period of Caesar and Augustus, just before the birth of Christ.
6. The lines are from Elegy 10 of Book 3 (translated by the present editor).

they describe. They are these, where he reckons up those that came on Turnus's part against Aeneas.[7]

With these there came, from the Volscian people, Camilla
Leading her horsemen on, aglitter with bronze,
A warrior girl; not for her hands the distaff,[8]
Or baskets of wool; she was a girl for savage
Skirmishes, and for outrunning the winds.
She might have fled over the uncut stalks
Of waving wheat without once bending them down,
Or fled lightfoot across the surges of ocean,
And yet never wet the soles of her flying feet.

And afterward tells her attire and arms; with the admiration that the spectators had of her. All which if the poet created out of himself, without nature, he did but show how much so divine a soul could exceed her.

The third lived in the age of Cyrus, the great Persian monarch, and made him leave to live: Tomyris, queen of the Scythians or Massagetes, a heroine of a most invincible and unbroken fortitude. Who, when Cyrus had invaded her and, taking her only son (rather by treachery than war, as she objected), had slain him; not touched with the grief of so great a loss, in the juster comfort she took of a greater revenge, pursued not only the occasion and honor of conquering so great an enemy, with whom fell two hundred thousand soldiers; but (what was right memorable in her victory), left not a messenger surviving of his side to report the massacre. She is remembered both by Herodotus and Justin to the great renown and glory of her kind with this eulogy.[9] *"That she waged war on the most powerful monarch of the Persians, and deprived him both of his army and his life, in order to gain a just revenge for the disgraceful murder of her son."*

The fourth was honored to live in the time of Xerxes,[1] *and present at his great expedition into Greece, Artemisia the queen of Caria, whose virtue Herodotus, not without some wonder, records. That was a woman, a queen, without a husband, her son a ward, and she administering the government occasioned by no necessity but a mere excellence of spirit, should embark herself for such a war, and there so to behave her, as Xerxes, beholding her fight, should say: "My men behaved like women, but my women like men."*[2] *She is no less renowned for her chastity and love to her husband, Mausolus, whose bones (after he was dead) she preserved in*

7. *Aeneid*, VII, 803 ff. (translated by the present editor). The lines describe all the armies that assembled to help Turnus, the native Italian prince, against Aeneas, the invading prince from Troy, who was to found the Roman Empire.

8. Household implements for spinning; metaphorically, womens' work.

9. Herodotus, Book I toward the end; Justin, Book 10 of the summary.

1. The Persian prince who invaded Greece in the 5th century B.C.

2. Herodotus, Book VIII.

ashes and drank in wine, making herself his tomb; and yet built to his memory a monument deserving a place among the seven wonders of the world, which could not be done by less than a wonder of women.[3]

The fifth was the fair-haired daughter of Ptolemaeus Philadelphus by the elder Arsinoë, who (married to her brother Ptolemaeus, surnamed Euergetes) was afterwards queen of Egypt. I find her written both Beronice and Berenice. This lady, upon an expedition of her new-wedded lord into Assyria, vowed to Venus, if he returned safe and conqueror, the offering of her hair; which vow of hers (exacted by the success)[4] *she afterwards performed. But her father missing it, and taking it to heart, Conon, a mathematician who was then in the household with Ptolemy and knew well to flatter him, persuaded the king that it was taken up to heaven and made a constellation; showing him those seven stars near the tail of Leo which are since called Berenice's hair. Which story, then presently celebrated by Callimachus in a most elegant poem, Catullus more elegantly converted;*[5] *wherein they call her magnanimous from girlhood: alluding (as Hyginus saith) to a rescue she made of her father in his flight, and restoring the honor and courage of his army, even to a victory. The words are,*

> *I knew you from a little girl a magnanimous heroine.*[6]

The sixth, that famous wife of Mithridates and queen of Pontus, Hypsicratea, no less an example of virtue than the rest; who so loved her husband, as she was assistant to him in all labors and hazards of the war in a masculine habit. For which cause (as Valerius Maximus observes), she departed with a chief ornament of her beauty. "For she cut off her hair and hardened herself to live on horseback and under arms, that she might be more involved in his labors and perils."[7] *And afterwards in his flight from Pompey, accompanies his misfortune with a mind and body equally unwearied. She is solemnly registered by that grave author as a notable precedent of marriage-loyalty and love—virtues that might raise a mean person to the equality with a queen, but a queen to the state and honor of a deity.*

The seventh, that renown of Ethiopia, Candace; from whose excellency, the succeeding queens of that nation were ambitious to be called so. A woman of most haughty spirit against enemies, and

3. Ever since Artemisia's time, a large memorial tomb has been known as a mausoleum.

4. I.e., the success of her husband's expedition required that she fulfill her vow.

5. The poem of Callimachus has been lost; Catullus's translation of it is numbered 66 in the standard arrangement of his poems.

6. Gaius Julius Hyginus was a mythographer of the Augustan age; he tells the two stories about Berenice in Chapter XXIV of his *Poeticon Astronomicon.* The line of verse is from Catullus.

7. Valerius Maximus, who lived in the first century A.D., compiled *Nine Books of Memorable Deeds and Sayings,* which the Renaissance found useful to illustrate moral commonplaces, because the stories were arranged topically. Hypsicratea appears in Book 4, Chapter 6, as an instance of conjugal affection.

singular affection to her subjects. I find her celebrated by Dion and Pliny,[8] *invading Egypt in the time of Augustus; who, though she were enforced to a peace by his lieutenant Petronius, doth not the less worthily hold her place here, when everywhere his eulogy remains of her fame, that she was "A woman of the highest spirit, so devoted to her own people that all the queens of Ethiopia desired to be called by her name." She governed in Meroë.*[9]

The eighth, our own honor, Voadicea or Boodicia, by some Bunduica and Bunduca, queen of the Iceni. A people that inhabited that part of the island which was called East Anglia, and comprehended Suffolk, Norfolk, Cambridge, and Huntingdon Shires.[1] *Since she was born here at home, we will first honor her with a home-born testimony, from the grave and diligent Spenser:*

Bunduca Britoness,

* * *

Bunduca, that victorious conqueress,
That, lifting up her brave heroic thought
'Bove women's weakness, with the Romans fought,
Fought, and in field against them thrice prevailed,[2] *etc.*

To which, see her orations in story made by Tacitus and Dion,[3] *wherein is expressed all magnitude of a spirit breathing to the liberty and redemption of her country. The later of whom doth honest*[4] *her, beside, with a particular description. 'Bunduica, a British woman of royal blood, who not only ruled the Britons with great dignity, but administered the whole country; her mind was more manly than womanly.' And afterwards, 'A woman of most impressive appearance, severe of expression,' etc. All which doth weigh the more to her true praise in coming from the mouths of Romans and enemies. She lived in the time of Nero.*[5]

The ninth in time, but equal in fame and (the cause of it) virtue, was the chaste Zenobia, queen of the Palmyrans, who, after the death of her husband Odenatus had the name to be reckoned among the thirty that usurped the Roman Empire from Galienus.[6] *She continued a long and brave war against several chiefs, and was at length triumphed on by Aurelian;*[7] *but 'after such a fashion*

8. Dion is Dionysus Halicarnassus, who describes Candace in Book 54 of his *Roman History*; Pliny mentions her in the *Natural History*, Book 6, Chapter 29. The "time of Augustus" is between 27 B.C. and 14 A.D.

9. The quotation is from "Dion"; Meroë, capital of Ethiopia, was a city on the Nile (it is now in the Sudan); the pyramid of Candace is still said to be visible there.

1. This is the Fen Country of east-central England.

2. "The Ruins of Time," lines 106–11.

3. Tacitus mentions Boadicea in the *Annals*, Book 14; "Dion" in this case refers to the Greek historian Dio Cassius, whose history Jonson cites from the epitome made of it by John Xiphilinus, an 11th-century Byzantine monk.

4. Favor.

5. Nero reigned from 37 to 68 A.D.

6. Jonson's authority for Zenobia is Trebellius Pollio, one of the group of writers known collectively as "the writers of Augustan history," who described events of the later, or lower, Roman Empire.

7. Aurelian was Emperor of Rome in the latter part of the third century A.D.

that the Roman people saw nothing triumphant about it.' Her chastity was such 'that she never even knew her own husband, except in order to have children.' She lived in a most royal manner, and was adored to the custom of the Persians. When she made orations to her soldiers, she had always her casque on. A woman of a most divine spirit, and incredible beauty. In Trebellius Pollio, read the most noble description of a queen and her, that can be uttered with the dignity of an historian.

The tenth, succeeding, was that learned and heroic Amalasunta, queen of the Ostrogoths, daughter to Theodoric, that obtained the principality of Ravenna and almost all Italy.[8] *She drove the Burgundians and Almaynes out of Liguria, and appeared in her government rather an example than a second. She was the most eloquent of her age, and cunning in all languages, of any nation that had commerce with the Roman Empire. It is recorded of her that 'no man could see her without reverence, and it was like a miracle to hear her speak; and so great was her gravity as a judge that even hardened criminals in the agony of their punishment never let drop a bitter word against her.'*

The eleventh was that brave Bohemian queen, Valasca, who for her courage had the surname of Bold. That, to redeem herself and her sex from the tyranny of men, which they lived in under Primislaus, on a night and however appointed, led on the women to the slaughter of their barbarous husbands and lords. And, possessing themselves of their horses, arms, treasure, and places of strength, not only ruled the rest, but lived many years after with the liberty and fortitude of Amazons. Celebrated (by Raphael Volterranus, and in an elegant tract of an Italian's, in Latin, who names himself Philalethes, Citizen of Polytopiensis) as 'among the most distinguished of women.'[9]

The twelfth and worthy sovereign of all, I make Bel-Anna, royal queen of the ocean; of whose dignity and person, the whole scope of the invention doth speak throughout; which, to offer you again here, might but prove offense to that sacred majesty which hears any testimony of others iterated with more delight than her own praise. She being placed above the need of such ceremony, and safe in her princely virtue against the good or ill of any witness. The name of Bel-Anna I devised to honor hers proper, by, as adding to it the attribute of fair; and is kept by me in all my poems wherein I mention her majesty with any shadow or figure. Of which some may come forth with a longer destiny than this age commonly gives

8. Jonson cites the authority of Cassiodorus, chief minister of the Ostrogoth King Theodoric who reigned from 474 to 526; Amalasunta herself lived in the 6th century A.D. "Almaynes": Germans.

9. Queen Valasca seems to belong to the dark and confused history of early Bohemia (i.e., modern Czechoslovakia); Jonson's authority for her is the geographer Raphael Volterranus, Book 7.

the best births, if but helped to light by her gracious and ripening favor.

But here I discern a possible objection arising against me, to which I must turn: As, how can I bring persons of so different ages to appear properly together? Or why (which is more unnatural) with Virgil's Mezentius,[1] *I join the living with the dead? I answer to both these at once, Nothing is more proper, nothing more natural. For these all live, and together in their fame; and so I present them. Besides, if I would fly to the all-daring power of poetry, Where could I not take sanctuary? or in whose poem?*

There rests now that we give the description we promised of the scene, which was the House of Fame. The structure and ornament of which (as is professed before) was entirely Mr. Jones his invention and design.[2] *First for the lower columns he chose the statues of the most excellent poets, as Homer, Virgil, Lucan, &c., as being the substantial supporters of Fame. For the upper, Achilles, Aeneas, Caesar, and those great heroes which those poets had celebrated. All which stood as in massy gold. Between the pillars underneath were figured land battles, sea fights, triumphs, loves, sacrifices, and all magnificent subjects of honor, in brass and heightened with silver. In which he professed to follow that noble description made by Chaucer of the like place.*[3] *Above were placed the masquers over whose heads he devised two eminent figures, of Honor and Virtue, for the arch. The friezes, both below and above, were filled with several-colored lights, like emeralds, rubies, sapphires, carbuncles, &c. The reflex of which, with other lights placed in the concave, upon the masquers' habits, was full of glory. These habits had in them the excellency of all device and riches, and were worthily varied by his invention to the nations whereof they were queens. Nor are these alone his due, but divers other accessions to the strangeness and beauty of the spectacle, as the hell, the going about of the chariots, the binding of the witches, the turning machine, with the presentation of Fame: all which I willingly acknowledge for him, since it is a virtue planted in good natures that what respects they wish to obtain fruitfully from others they will give ingenuously themselves.*

By this time, imagine the masquers descended and again mounted into three triumphant chariots, ready to come forth. The first four were drawn with eagles (whereof I gave the reason, as of the rest, in Fame's speech), their four torch-bearers attending on

1. Mezentius, in the *Aeneid*, is Turnus's most terrifying lieutenant in the war against Aeneas; he despises the gods and is hated by his own people but in what sense he joins the living with the dead is not clear.
2. Inigo Jones was indeed the most talented stage designer in England; but he had better than £2,000 to spend on this spectacle—an enormous sum of money for those days.
3. Jones followed in many details the third book of Chaucer's *Hous of Fame*, but without Chaucer's satiric intent.

the chariot sides, and four of the hags bound before them. Then followed the second, drawn by griffons, with their torch-bearers and four other hags. Then the last, which was drawn by lions and more eminent (wherein her majesty was) and had six torch-bearers more (peculiar to her), with the like number of hags. After which a full triumphant music,[4] *singing this song while they rode in state about the stage:*

Song

Help, help all tongues to celebrate this wonder;
The voice of Fame should be as loud as thunder.
  Her house is all of echo made,
    Where never dies the sound;
  And as her brows the clouds invade,
    Her feet do strike the ground.
Sing then Good Fame, that's out of Virtue born,
For who doth Fame neglect doth Virtue scorn.

Here they alighted from their chariots and danced forth their first dance, then a second immediately following it; both right curious and full of subtle and excellent changes, and seemed performed with no less spirits than those they personated. The first was to the cornets, the second to the violins. After which, they took out the men[5] *and danced the measures, entertaining the time almost to the space of an hour with singular variety. When, to give them rest, from the music which attended the chariots, by that most excellent tenor voice and exact singer (her majesty's servant, Mr. John Allen) this ditty was sung:*

Song

When all the ages of the earth
Were crowned, but in this famous birth;
And that when they would boast their store
Of worthy queens, they knew no more:
How happier is that age, can give
A queen in whom all they do live!

After which, they danced their third dance, than which a more numerous composition could not be seen; graphically disposed into letters and honoring the name of the most sweet and ingenious prince, Charles, Duke of York.[6] *Wherein, besides that principal grace of perspicuity, the motions were so even and apt, and their*

4. Consort of instruments and singers.
5. I.e., called up men from the audience.
6. This is the future King Charles the First, just eight years old at the moment. The dancers seem to have spelled out Charles's name, letter by letter. The adjective "ingenious," applied to Charles, is probably synonymous with "ingenuous"; the two words were often interchanged.

expression so just, as if mathematicians had lost their proportion, they might have found it. The author was Mr. Thomas Giles. After this, they danced galliards and corrantos.[7] *And then their last dance, no less elegant (in the place) than the rest. With which they took their chariots again, and triumphing about the stage had their return to the House of Fame celebrated with this last song, whose notes (as to the former) were the work and honor of my excellent friend Alfonso Ferrabosco:*

Song

Who, Virtue, can thy power forget,
That sees these live and triumph yet?
Th'Assyrian pomp, the Persian pride,
Greeks' glory and the Romans' died;
And who yet imitate
Their noises, suffer the same fate.
Force greatness all the glorious ways
You can, it soon decays;
But so Good Fame shall never:
Her triumphs, as their causes, are for ever.[8]

To conclude which, I know no worthier way of epilogue than the celebration of who were the celebrators:

The Queen's Majesty
Countess of Arundel
Countess of Derby
Countess of Huntingdon
Countess of Bedford
Countess of Essex
Countess of Montgomery
Lady Cranborne
Lady Ellen Guilford
Lady Anne Winter
Lady Windsor
Lady Anne Clifford

THE END

1609

1609

7. Literally, galliards are gay dances and corrantos are running dances; in reality they are stately, slow, and formal performances.

8. The pomp, pride, and glory of political power (noises) perish, but good fame endures forever, as evidenced by the presence of the queens in the masque.

Oberon,

The Faery Prince.

a Masque

of Prince Henry's[1]

The first face of the scene appeared all obscure, and nothing perceived but a dark rock with trees beyond it; and all wildness that could be presented: till, at one corner of the cliff, above the horizon, the moon began to show,[2] and rising, a satyr was seen (by her light) to put forth his head and call.

SATYR 1

Chromis, Mnasyl?[3] None appear?
See you not, who riseth here?
You saw Silenus late, I fear![4]
I'll prove, if this can reach your ear.

He wound his cornet,[5] and thought himself answered; but was deceived by the echo.

Oh, you wake then; come away,
Times be short, are made for play;
The hum'rous[6] moon too will not stay,
What doth make you thus delay?
Hath his tankard touched your brain?
Sure, they're fal'n asleep again:
Or I doubt it was the vain
Echo did me entertain.[7]

He wound the second time, and found it.[8]

Prove again, I thought 'twas she.
Idle Nymph, I pray thee, be
Modest, and not follow me;
I nor love my self, nor thee.[9]

1. At the time of this masque (1 January 1611), Henry Prince of Wales was but 16 years old; he appears in the action simply as a solemn, silent young Prince of Faery who leads the masquers in paying homage to his father, King James. He would die the very next year of typhoid fever.
2. The first impression of the viewers. As masques were staged indoors and at night (unlike plays), it was perfectly possible to have a moon, painted on a cloth and lit from behind by candles, rise slowly in the "sky."
3. The names of two satyrs in Virgil's sixth eclogue—as Jonson's note points out. Jonson's satyrs are half little boys and half wild animals.
4. I.e., you were up drinking till late last night; "prove": try.
5. I.e., blew a blast on his horn.
6. Fickle, various.
7. Delude.
8. Verified his supicion.
9. Narcissus, whom Echo loved, loved only himself; after he turned into a flower, she turned into a hollow, repetitive voice (see Ovid, *Metamorphoses* III).

Here he wound the third time, and was answered by another satyr, who likewise showed himself; to which he spoke.

Ay, this sound I better know:
List![1] I would I could hear mo.

At this they came running forth, severally, from divers parts of the rock, leaping and making antic action and gestures, to the number of ten; some of them speaking, some admiring: and among them a Silene, who is ever the prefect[2] of the satyrs, and so presented in all their Chori[3] and meetings.

SATYR 2

Thank us, and you shall do so.

SATYR 3

Ay, our number soon will grow.

SATYR 2

See Silenus!

SATYR 3

Cercops,[4] too!

SATYR 4

Yes. What is there now to do?

SATYR 5

Are there any nymphs to woo?

SATYR 4

If there be, let me have two.

SILENUS

Chaster language! These are nights
Solemn to the shining rites

1. Listen; "mo": more.
2. Ruler, pedagogue—but also master of the revels. Silenus is generally represented as an obese, drunken old man with a fondness for little boys; but Jonson improves him considerably for purposes of this masque, and cites many learned precedents for doing so, including notably the sixth eclogue of Virgil.
3. Revels.
4. The Cercopes took part in one of Hercules's minor adventures. They were a hairy, ape-like people who bothered him, so he caught them, tied them up, and slung them over his back on a stick. But the jokes they made as they hung there upside-down so entertained the strong man that at last he let them all go.

Of the Faery Prince and Knights:
While the moon their orgies[5] lights.

SATYR 2

Will they come abroad anon?

SATYR 3

Shall we see young Oberon?[6]

SATYR 4

Is he such a princely one
  As you speak him long agone?

SILENUS

Satyrs, he doth fill with grace
  Every season, every place;
  Beauty dwells but in his face;
  He's the height of all our race.
Our Pan's father,[7] god of tongue,
  Bacchus, though he still be young,
  Phoebus, when he crownéd sung,
  Nor Mars,[8] when first his armor rung,
Might with him be named, that day.
  He is lovelier than in May
  Is the spring, and there can stay
  As little as he can decay.[9]

CHORUS

Oh, that he would come away!

SATYR 3

Grandsire, we shall leave to play
With Lyaeus[1] now, and serve
Only Ob'ron.

5. Dances and frolics (without any necessary implication of license.)
6. Oberon, prince of Faery in Jonson's flimsy mythological scheme, represents Prince Henry; his father is therefore King Arthur, i.e., King James. The reader shouldn't look for either logic or history in these fantastic genealogies.
7. Mercury turned himself into a goat to seduce Penelope (not Odysseus's wife, but another Penelope); upon her he begot Pan, the goat-god. "Tongue": eloquence.
8. Bacchus, god of the vine, Phoebus (Apollo), god of the sun, and Mars, god of war, were traditionally handsome gods, comparable to Mercury.
9. Like the spring, he can neither stop short nor retrogress; he must go forward to be a great king. The prophecy is particularly pathetic in light of Henry's actual fate.
1. One of the names of Bacchus.

SILENUS

He'll deserve
All you can and more, my boys.

SATYR 4

Will he give us pretty toys
To beguile the girls withal?

SATYR 3

And to make 'em quickly fall?

SILENUS

Peace, my wantons: he will do
More than you can aim unto.

SATYR 4

Will he build us larger caves?

SILENUS

Yes, and give you ivory staves
When you hunt, and better wine—

SATYR 1

Than the master of the vine?

SATYR 2

And rich prizes to be won
When we leap or when we run?

SATYR 1

Ay, and gild our cloven feet?

SATYR 3

Strew our head with powders sweet?

SATYR 1

Bind our crooked legs in hoops,
Made of shells with silver loops?

SATYR 2

Tie about our tawny wrists
Bracelets of the faery twists?

SATYR 4

And, to spite the coy nymphs' scorns,
Hang upon our stubbéd horns
Garlands, ribbons, and fine posies—

SATYR 3

Fresh as when the flower discloses?

SATYR 1

Yes, and stick our pricking ears
With the pearl that Tethys[2] wears.

SATYR 2

And to answer all things else,
Trap our shaggy thighs with bells
That as we do strike a time
In our dance shall make a chime

SATYR 3

Louder than the rattling pipes
Of the wood-gods,

SATYR 1

or the stripes
Of the taber[3] when we carry
Bacchus up, his pomp to vary.

CHORUS

Oh, that he so long doth tarry!

SILENUS

See, the rock begins to ope,
Now you shall enjoy your hope;
'Tis about the hour, I know.

2. Wife of Oceanus, hence adorned with pearls.
3. I.e., drumbeats; Bacchus's rites were celebrated with much loud and rhythmic music.

There the whole scene opened, and within was discovered the frontispiece[4] of a bright and glorious palace, whose gates and walls were transparent. Before the gates lay two sylvans[5] armed with their clubs and dressed in leaves, asleep. At this, the satyrs wondering, Silenus proceeds.

Look! does not his palace show
Like another sky of lights?
Yonder with him live the knights,
Once the noblest of the earth,
Quickened by a second birth;
Who for prowess and for truth
There are crowned with lasting youth:
And do hold, by Fate's command,
Seats of bliss in Faery land.
But their guards (methinks) do sleep!
Let us wake 'em. Sirs, you keep
Proper watch, that thus do lie
Drowned in sloth.

SATYR 1

They've ne'er an eye
To wake withal.[6]

SATYR 2

Nor sense, I fear;
For they sleep in either ear.

SATYR 3

Holla, Sylvans! Sure, they're caves
Of sleep, these—or else they're graves!

SATYR 4

Hear you, friends, who keeps the keepers?

SATYR 1

They're the eighth and ninth sleepers.[7]

SATYR 2

Shall we cramp 'em?

4. Façade.
5. I.e., denizens of the forest. Akin to satyrs, fauns, and sileni, sylvans were natives of Italy (they had no Greek existence). They were shy little wild creatures.
6. I.e., they don't have eyes to wake up with.
7. The famous seven sleepers of legend dozed off in a cave near Ephesus around 250 A.D. and woke up 187 years later.

SILENUS

Satyrs, no.

SATYR 3

Would we'd Boreas[8] here, to blow
Off their leafy coats, and strip 'em.

SATYR 4

Ay, ay, ay; that we might whip 'em.

SATYR 3

Or that we had a wasp or two
For their nostrils.

SATYR 1

Hairs will do
Even as well: take my tail.

SATYR 2

What do you say to'a good nail
Through their temples?[9]

SATYR 3

Or an eel
In their guts, to make 'em feel?

SATYR 4

Shall we steal away their beards?

SATYR 3

For Pan's goat, that leads the herds?

SATYR 2

Or try whether is more dead,
His club, or th'other's head?

SILENUS

Wags, no more: you grow too bold.

8. The north wind.
9. Jael killed Sisera in this way (Judges iv).

SATYR 1

I would fain now see 'em rolled
Down a hill, or from a bridge
Headlong cast, to break their ridge-
Bones;[1] or to some river take 'em:
Plump! and see if that would wake 'em.

SATYR 2

There no motion yet appears.

SILENUS

Strike a charm into their ears.

At which the satyrs fell suddenly into this catch[2]:

Buz, quoth the blue fly,
  Hum, quoth the bee:
Buz and hum they cry,
  And so do we.
In his ear, in his nose,
  Thus, do you see?
He ate the dormouse,
  Else it was he.

The two Sylvans, starting up amazed and betaking themselves to their arms, were thus questioned by Silenus.

How now, Sylvans! can you wake?
I commend the care you take
In your watch. Is this your guise
To have both your ears and eyes
Sealed so fast, as these my elves
Might have stol'n you from yourselves?

SATYR 3

We had thought we must have got
Stakes, and heated 'em red-hot,
And have bored you through the eyes
(With the Cyclops) ere you'd rise.[3]

SATYR 2

Or have fetched some trees, to heave

1. Backbones.
2. Song, round.
3. The story of blinding the one-eyed giant Cyclops with a glowing stake is told in *Odyssey* IX.

Up your bulks that so did cleave
To the ground, there.

SATYR 4

Are you free
Yet of sleep, and can you see
Who is yonder up aloof?[4]

SATYR 1

Be your eyes yet moon-proof?

SYLVAN

Satyrs, leave your petulance,
And go frisk about and dance,
Or else rail upon the moon;
Your expectance is too soon.
For before the second cock
Crow, the gates will not unlock.
And till then, we know we keep
Guard enough, although we sleep.

SATYR 1

Say you so? then let us fall
To a song or to a brawl.
Shall we, grandsire? Let us sport,
And make expectation short.

SILENUS

Do, my wantons, what you please.
I'll lie down and take mine ease.

SATYR 1

Brothers, sing then, and upbraid
(As we use) yon seeming maid.[5]

Song

Now, my cunning lady Moon,
Can you leave the side so soon
Of the boy you keep so hid?

4. They point to the rising moon.
5. The moon, whose chastity the satyrs impugn (with some justice) on the score of her intimacy with the shepherd Endymion.

Midwife Juno[6] sure will say
This is not the proper way
  Of your paleness to be rid.
But perhaps it is your grace
To wear sickness in your face
  That there might be wagers laid
  Still by fools you are a maid.[7]

Come, your changes overthrow
What your look would carry so;
Moon, confess then what you are,
And be wise and free to use
Pleasures that you now do lose.
  Let us satyrs have a share;
Though our forms be rough and rude,
Yet our acts may be endued
  With more virtue: every one
  Cannot be Endymion.

The song ended, they fell suddenly into an antic dance full of gesture and swift motion, and continued it till the crowing of the cock, at which they were interrupted by Silenus.

SILENUS

Stay, the cheerful Chanticlere[8]
Tells you that the time is near:
See the gates already spread!
Every satyr bow his head.

There the whole palace opened, and the nation of Fays were discovered, some with instruments, some bearing lights, others singing; and within, afar off in perspective, the knights masquers sitting in their several sieges.[9] *At the further end of all, Oberon, in a chariot which to a loud triumphal music began to move forward, drawn by two white bears, and on either side guarded by three Sylvans, with one going in front.*

Song

Melt earth to sea, sea flow to air,
  And air fly into fire,

6. Juno, wife of Jupiter, is goddess of marriage, hence of childbirth.
7. The "green sickness," or chlorosis, was a form of anemia common among young women, and naturally attributed by men to sexual cravings.
8. Proverbial name for a cock.
9. Benches. The gates and walls of the palace, we recall, were transparent. Evidently some of the doors and windows opened, and lights appeared behind the façade, so the masquers could be seen through the walls. The perspectives, which Jonson emphasizes, were provided by Inigo Jones, on whom see, above, "The Staging of Jonson's Plays and Masques." The two white bears may have been trained animals (such were available), but they were probably just men wearing bearskins.

Whilst we in tunes to Arthur's chair
  Bear Oberon's desire;
  Than which there can be nothing higher,
Save JAMES, to whom it flies:
But he the wonder is of tongues, of ears, of eyes.

Who hath not heard, who hath not seen,
    Who hath not sung his name?
The soul that hath not, hath not been,
    But is the very same
    With buried sloth, and knows not fame,
Which him doth best comprise:
For he the wonder is of tongues, of ears, of eyes.

By this time the chariot was come as far forth as the face of the scene.[1] *And the Satyrs beginning to leap and express their joy for the un-used state and solemnity, the foremost Sylvan began to speak.*

SYLVAN

Give place, and silence; you were rude too late.
This is a night of greatness and of state,
Not to be mixed with light and skipping sport:
A night of homage to the British court,
And ceremony, due to Arthur's chair
From our bright master, Oberon the fair;
Who, with these knights attendants, here preserved
In Faery land, for good they have deserved
Of yon high throne are come of right to pay
Their annual vows, and all their glories lay
At's[2] feet, and tender to this only great
True majesty,[3] restorèd in this seat;
To whose sole power and magic they do give
The honor of their being; that they live
Sustained in form, fame, and felicity
From rage of fortune or the fear to die.

SILENUS

And may they well. For this indeed is he,
My boys, whom you must quake at when you see.
He is above your reach, and neither doth
Nor can he think within a Satyr's tooth.[4]

1. I.e., out to the front gate of the palace, where the Satyrs and Sylvans would be waiting in attitudes of reverence.
2. I.e., at his.
3. All the masquers, including Oberon, Sylvans, Satyrs, and Silenus, here turn their attention to King James on his throne in the front of the "audience." But it isn't really an audience, and he isn't a member of it: he is the most significant actor present.
4. "Toothed" and "toothless" satires were distinguished in the early 17th century by Joseph Hall, who called himself the first English satirist. *Satires* don't

Before his presence you must fall or fly.
He is the matter of virtue,[5] and placed high.
His meditations to his height are even,[6]
And all their issue is akin to heaven.
He is a god o'er kings, yet stoops he then
Nearest a man when he doth govern men,
To teach them by the sweetness of his sway,
And not by force. He's such a king as they,
Who're tyrants' subjects, or ne'er tasted peace,
Would in their wishes form for their release.
'Tis he that stays the time from turning old,
And keeps the age up in a head of gold;[7]
That in his own true circle still doth run,
And holds his course, as certain as the sun.
He makes it ever day and ever spring
Where he doth shine, and quickens everything
Like a new nature: so that, true to call
Him by his title, is to say, He's all.

SYLVAN

I thank the wise Silenus for this praise.
Stand forth, bright Fays and Elves, and tune your lays[8]
Unto his name. Then let your nimble feet
Tread subtle circles, that may always meet
In point to him;[9] and figures, to express
The grace of him and his great empress.[1]
That all that shall tonight behold the rites
Performed by princely Oberon and these knights
May, without stop, point out the proper heir
Designed so long to Arthur's crowns and chair.[2]

The Song, by two Fays

1. Seek you majesty to strike?[3]
   Bid the world produce his like.
2. Seek you glory to amaze?
   Here let all eyes stand at gaze

have any special connection with *satyrs* (the word *satire* comes from Latin *satura,* meaning a full dish, a mishmash); but in Jonson's day the two words were supposed to be connected.
5. I.e., the substance itself of virtue.
6. I.e., his ideas are as lofty as his station.
7. The age of gold was that of Saturn's reign; James fancied himself a philosopher, and was vulnerable to flattery on that score. Literally, the circle of gold on his head, the crown, sustains the historic age in a state of perfection.
8. I.e., turn your songs.
9. The circles of your dances will always have him at their center; "figures": emblems.
1. Three syllables: emperess.
2. As King of England, Ireland, Scotland, and Wales, James inherited all Arthur's crowns.
3. I.e., a striking image of majesty.

CHORUS. Seek you wisdom to inspire?
Touch, then, at no others' fire.

1. Seek you knowledge to direct?
Trust to his without suspect.
2. Seek you piety to lead?
In his footsteps only tread.

CHORUS. Every virtue of a king,
And of all, in him we sing.

Then the lesser fays dance forth their dance; which ended, a full song follows by all the voices.

Song

The solemn rites are well begun;
And though but lighted by the moon,
They show as rich as if the sun
Had made this night his noon.
But may none wonder that they are so bright,
The moon now borrows from a greater light:
Then, princely Oberon,
Go on,
This is not every night.

There Oberon and the knights dance out the first masque-dance, which was followed with this song.

Song

Nay, nay,
You must not stay,
Nor be weary, yet;
This's no time to cast away,
Or for fays so to forget
The virtue of their feet.
Knotty legs and plants[4] of clay
Seek for ease or love delay.
But with you it still should fare
As with the air of which you are.

After which, they danced forth their second masque-dance, and were again excited[5] by a song.

Song

1. Nor yet, nor yet, Oh you in this night blest,
Must you have will or hope to rest.

4. Feet. As "fays" (fairies), the dancers are creatures of air, not clay.

5. Roused to motion.

2. If you use the smallest stay,
You'll be overta'en by day.
1. And these beauties[6] will suspect
That their forms you do neglect,
If you do not call them forth:
2. Or that you have no more worth
Than the coarse and country Faery
That doth haunt the hearth or dairy.

Then followed the measures, corantos, galliards, &c. till Phosphoros the day-star appeared, and called them away; but first they were invited home by one of the Sylvans with this song.

Song

Gentle knights,
Know some measure[7] of your nights.
Tell the high-graced Oberon,
It is time that we were gone.
Here be forms so bright and airy,
And their motions so they vary,
As they will enchant the faery
If you longer here should tarry.

PHOSPHORUS

To rest, to rest! the Herald of the Day,
Bright Phosphorus commands you hence; obey.
The moon is pale and spent; and wingéd night
Makes headlong haste to fly the morning's sight,
Who now is rising from her blushing wars,[8]
And with her rosy hand puts back the stars,
Of which myself, the last, her harbinger,
But stay to warn you that you not defer
Your parting longer. Then do I give way,
As night hath done, and so must you, to day.

After this, they danced their last dance into the work.[9] *And with a full song the star vanished and the whole machine closed.*

Song

Oh yet how early and before her time
The envious Morning up doth climb,
Though she not love her bed!

6. I.e., ladies of the court, now singled out by the knights of the masque for what we would call social dancing.
7. Limit, moderation.
8. Tithonus, husband of Aurora, the goddess of dawn, became immortal as a result of her prayers, but without eternal youth; she gets up early every morning to escape his chilly bed.
9. I.e., the dances led back into the stage-palace, and the doors closed on them.

What haste the jealous Sun doth make
His fiery horses[1] up to take,
  And once more show his head!
Lest, taken with the brightness of this night,
The world should wish it last, and never miss his light.

THE END

1611 1616

1. Classic myth figures the sun's career across the sky as that of a chariot drawn by fiery horses.

Mercury Vindicated from the Alchemists at Court

By Gentlemen the King's Servants

After the loud music, the scene discovered; being a laboratory, or Alchemist's workhouse: Vulcan looking to the Registers,[1] *while a Cyclops tending the fire to the cornets began to sing.*

CYCLOPS

Soft, subtle fire, thou soul of Art,
  Now do thy part
On weaker Nature, that through age is lamed.
  Take but thy time, now she is old,
  And the Sun, her friend, grown cold,
She will be no more in strife with thee be named.[2]
Look but how few confess her now,
  In cheek or brow!
From every head, almost, how she is frighted!
  The very age abhors her so,
  That it learns to speak and go
As if by Art alone it could be righted.

The song ended, Mercury[3] *appeared, thrusting out his head and afterward his body at the tunnel of the middle furnace; which Vulcan espying, cried out to the Cyclops.*

VULCAN

Stay, see! our Mercury is coming forth. Art and all the elements assist! Call forth our philosophers! He will be gone, he will evaporate! Dear Mercury! Help! He flies! He is 'scaped! Precious, golden Mercury, be fixed; be not so volatile! Will none of the Sons of Art[4] appear?

In which time Mercury, having run once or twice around the room, takes breath and speaks.

1. Vulcan, as classical god of the forge, is dressed like a blacksmith, and tending the "registers," or dampers, of the alchemical furnace. Cyclops is a one-eyed giant (he must have worn a mask, and perhaps high-heeled shoes); he sings to a trumpet obbligato.

2. The contrast between Nature and Art was a commonplace of the age, fueled by the thought that Nature was decaying.

3. Throughout the masque, Mercury is both the classical deity and the metal quicksilver, a major ingredient in the process by which the alchemists proposed to make gold.

4. "Philosophers" and "Sons of Art" were cant names assumed by alchemists.

MERCURY

Now the place and goodness of it protect me. One tender-hearted creature or other, save Mercury and free him. Ne'er an old gentlewoman in the house that has a wrinkle about her to hide me in? I could run into a serving-woman's pocket now; her glove, any little hole. Some merciful farthingale[5] among so many, be bounteous and undertake me; I will stand close up anywhere to escape this polt-footed philosopher, old Smug here of Lemnos,[6] and his smoky family. Has he give me time to breathe? Oh, the variety of torment that I have endured in the reign of the Cyclops, beyond the exquisite wit of tyrants! The whole household of 'em are become Alchemists (since their trade of armor-making failed them)[7] only to keep themselves in fire for this winter; for the mischief of a secret that they know, above the consuming of coals and drawing of usquebaugh.[8] Howsoever they may pretend under the specious names of Geber, Arnold, Lully, Bombast of Hohenheim[9] to commit miracles in art and treason against nature. And, as if the title of philosopher, that creature of glory, were to be fetched out of a furnace, abuse the curious and credulous nation of metal-men through the world, and make Mercury their instrument. I am their crude and their sublimate; their precipitate and their unctuous; their male and their female; sometimes their hermaphrodite; what they list to style me.[1] It is I that am corroded and exalted and sublimed and reduced and fetched over and filtered and washed and wiped; what between their salts and their sulphurs, their oils and their tartars, their brines and their vinegars, you might take me out now a soused Mercury, now a salted Mercury, now a smoked and dried Mercury, now a powdered and pickled Mercury. Never herring, oyster, or cucumber passed so many vexations. My whole life with 'em hath been an exercise of torture; one, two, three, four, and five times an hour have they made me dance the philosophical circle, like an ape through a hoop or a dog in a wheel.[2] I am their turnspit indeed; they eat or smell no roast meat but in my name. I am their bill of credit still, that passes for their victuals and house-room. It is through me they have got this corner of the court to cozen in, where they shark for a hungry diet below stairs, and cheat upon your under-officers, promising mountains for their meat, and

5. Hoop-skirt.
6. I.e., Vulcan, "smug" because a complacent cuckold (as a result of Mars's intrigue with Venus), and "of Lemnos" because he fell on that Aegean island when Jove threw him out of Olympus. He is "polt-footed" or lame because of his hard landing on that occasion.
7. Vulcan was a maker of armor for heroes like Achilles and Aeneas.
8. Coals and "usquebaugh" (whiskey) are two ways to keep warm in winter.
9. Geber (Abu Abdallah Jaber ben Hayyam ben Abdallah al-Kufi), Arnoldus de Villa Nova, Raymond Lull or Lully, and Paracelsus (Philippus Aureolus Theophrastus Bombastus ab Hohenheim) were well-known alchemists.
1. Mercury overflows with terms of alchemical art.
2. Dogs in wheels connected to spits were used to turn roasting meat.

all upon Mercury's security.[3] A poor page of the larder they have made obstinately believe he shall be physician for the household next summer: they will give him a quantity of the quintessence shall serve him to cure kibes or the mort-mal of the shin, take away the pustules in the nose,[4] and Mercury is engaged for it. A child of the scullery steals all their coals for 'em too, and he is bid sleep secure, he shall find a corner of the philosopher's stone for it under his bolster one day, and have the proverb inverted.[5] Against which one day I am to deliver the buttery in so many firkins of *Aurum potabile*, as it delivers out bombards of budge to them, between this and that.[6] For the pantry, they are at a certainty with me, and keep a tally, an ingot, a loaf, or a wedge of some five pound weight, which is a thing of nothing, a trifle. And so the black guard are pleased with a toy, a lease of life (for some 999),[7] especially those of the boiling house, they are to have Medea's kettle[8] hung up, that they may souse into it when they will, and come out renewed like so many striped snakes at their pleasure. But these are petty engagements and (as I said) below the stairs; marry, above here, perpetuity of beauty (do you hear, Ladies), health, riches, honors, a matter of immortality is nothing. They will calcine[9] you a grave matron (as it might be a mother of the maids) and spring up a young virgin out of her ashes, as fresh as a phoenix:[1] lay you an old courtier on the coals like a sausage or a bloat-herring, and after they have broiled him enough, blow a soul into him with a pair of bellows, till he start up into his galliard,[2] that was made when Monsieur was here. They profess familiarly to melt down all the old sinners of the suburbs once in half a year into fresh gamesters again—get all the cracked maidenheads and cast 'em into new ingots; half the wenches of the town are Alchemy. See, they begin to muster again, and draw their forces out against me! The Genius[3] of the

3. The alchemists are accused of dealing with the cooks and butlers ("under-officers") of the court, promising them a share in the philosopher's stone in return for a free meal in the pantry. The philosopher's stone was, of course, supposed to turn any common metal to gold at a touch. "Cozen": cheat.

4. "Pustules of the nose" were from syphilis, cured (sometimes) by injections of mercury; "kibes": chilblains; "mort-mal": gangrene.

5. An old proverb says one may mistake a stone for a treasure: the scullery boy is promised by the alchemists that he will find a treasure in the stone.

6. Mercury delivers tubs of potable gold, the buttery hands out in return leather sacks ("bombards") of foodstuffs to the hungry alchemists.

7. Leases on land were written sometimes for life, sometimes for 999 years; the kitchen help ("black guard") have, so to speak, mortgaged themselves for life to the alchemists.

8. Medea, the archetypical witch of antiquity, had a kettle of herbs in which she immersed Aeson, Jason's father; it bestowed on him eternal youth.

9. Reduce to chalk.

1. The phoenix, a fabulous bird, was supposed to rise afresh from its own ashes every thousand years.

2. A sprightly dance. The Duke of Anjou, known as "Monsieur," visited England as a potential suitor of Queen Elizabeth, in 1579.

3. Mercury here comes forward and importunes the King directly for help. James is the "Sol" (Sun) of the cosmos within which Mercury is a planet, and "Jupiter" (father of the gods) in the family of which Mercury is a member; on both scores he is the "Genius," guiding spirit, or tutelary guardian, of the troubled speaker.

place defend me! You that are both the Sol and Jupiter of this sphere, Mercury invokes your majesty against the sooty tribe here; for in your favor only, I grow recovered and warm.

At which time Vulcan entering with a troop of threadbare Alchemists, prepares them to the first Antimasque.

VULCAN

Begin your charm, sound music, circle him in and take him: if he will not obey, bind him.

They all danced about Mercury with variety of changes, while he defends himself with his Caduceus,[4] *and after the dance spake.*

MERCURY

It is in vain, Vulcan, to pitch your net in the sight of the fowl, thus; I am no sleepy Mars to be catched in your subtle toils.[5] I know what your aims are, sir, to tear the wings from my head and heels, and lute[6] me up in a glass with my own seals, while you might wrest the caduceus out of my hand, to the adultery and spoil of Nature, and make your accesses by it to her dishonor more easy. Sir,[7] would you believe it should be come to that height of impudence in mankind that such a nest of fire-worms as these are (because their patron Mulciber heretofore has made stools stir and statues dance, a dog of brass to bark, and—which some will say was his worst act—a woman to speak)[8] should therefore with their heats called *Balnei, Cineris,* or horse-dung,[9] profess to outwork the sun in virtue, and contend to the great act of generation, nay, almost creation? It is so, though. For in yonder vessels which you see in their laboratory they have enclosed materials to produce men, beyond the deeds of Deucalion or Prometheus (of which one, they say, had the philosopher's stone and threw it over his shoulder, the other the fire, and lost it.)[1] And what men are they, they are so busy about, think you? not common or ordinary creatures, but of rarity and excellence, such as the times wanted, and the age had a special deal of need of: such, as there was a necessity they should be

4. The serpent-entwined, winged wand traditionally carried by Mercury.
5. Mars, sleeping with Venus, was netted by Vulcan, her husband.
6. Fasten. Hermes's seals are traditional means of sealing a container, as we say, "hermetically."
7. Again the address is directly to King James.
8. Mulciber is a secondary name of Vulcan, the arch-artificer, who made moving chairs and dancing statutes (*Iliad* 18), barking dogs (*Odyssey* 7) and a talking woman in the person of Pandora.
9. A traditional source of slow alchemical heat. *Balnei*: of the bath; *Cineris*: of ashes.
1. In classical mythology, Deucalion created men by throwing stones over his shoulder, and Prometheus by stealing fire out of heaven. These interpretations of classical fables are reminiscent of those in *The Alchemist*, II, 1.

artificial, for Nature could never have thought or dreamt of their composition. I can remember some of their titles to you and the ingredients. Do not look for Paracelsus' man among them,[2] that he promised you out of white bread and dele-wine,[3] for he never came to light. But of these, let me see: the first that occurs, a master of the duel, a carrier of the differences.[4] To him went spirit of ale, a good quantity, with the amalgam of sugar and nutmegs, oil of oaths, sulphur of quarrel, strong waters, valor precipitate, vapored o'er the helm with tobacco and the rosin of Mars, with a dram of the business,[5] for that's the word of tincture, the business. Let me alone with the business, I will carry the business. I do understand the business. I do find an affront in the business. Then another is a fencer in the mathematics or the town's cunning-man, a creature of art too, a supposed secretary to the stars;[6] but indeed a kind of lying intelligencer from those parts. His materials, if I be not deceived, were juice of almanacs, extraction of ephemerides,[7] scales of the *Globe*, filings of figures, dust of the twelve houses,[8] conserve of questions, salt of confederacy, a pound of adventure, a grain of skill, and a drop of truth. I saw vegetals too as well as minerals, put into one glass there, as adder's tongue,[9] title-bane, nitre of clients, tartar of false conveyance, *Aurum palpabile*,[1] with a huge deal of talk, to which they added a tincture of conscience, with the faeces of honesty;[2] but for what this was I could not learn, only I have overheard one of the artists say, Out of the corruption of a lawyer was the best generation of a broker in suits:[3] whether this were he or no, I know not.

VULCAN

Thou art a scorner, Mercury, and out of the pride of thy protection here makest it thy study to revile Art, but it will turn to thine own contumely soon. Call forth the creatures of the first class,[4] and let them move to the harmony of our heat, till the slanderer have sealed up his own lips to his own torment.

2. Paracelsus in his book *On the Nature of Things* gave a recipe for creating a man.
3. A kind of Rhine wine.
4. Among the special men created by alchemists is the master of quarreling (very reminiscent of Subtle in *The Alchemist*).
5. "Business" is mocked as a catch-all word; any quarrel is "the business."
6. The universal shyster-about-town, Mr. Know-It-All.
7. Records of trivial, momentary happenings. The *Globe* was the public theater, where gossip could be picked up; but the "scales" are a lost allusion.
8. The dust of the twelve (astrological) houses is trivial nonsense.
9. The adder's tongue is forked as well as poisonous; "title-bane" is a poison that destroys not only titles of honor but legal titles too—a lawyer's poisonous tongue.
1. Palpable, i.e., tangible gold.
2. The dregs of truth.
3. "The corruption of *this* is the generation of *that*" was a favorite, semi-serious formula of Renaissance popular scientists. A "broker in suits" is a seller of second-hand clothes.
4. I.e., the phony men I and my alchemists are alleged to have created.

MERCURY

Let 'em come, let 'em come, I would not wish a greater punishment to thy impudence.

There enters the second Antimasque *of imperfect creatures, with helms of limbecks*[5] *on their heads: whose dance ended,*

MERCURY *proceeded*

Art thou not ashamed, Vulcan, to offer in defense of thy fire and Art, against the excellence of the Sun and Nature, creatures more imperfect than the very flies and insects that are her trespasses and 'scapes? Vanish with thy insolence, thou and thy impostors, and all mention of you melt before the Majesty of this light[6] whose Mercury henceforth I profess to be, and never again the philosphers'. Vanish, I say, that all who have but their senses may see and judge the difference between thy ridiculous monsters and his absolute features.

At which the whole scene changed to a glorious bower, wherein Nature was placed, with Prometheus at her feet; and the twelve masquers standing about them. After they had been a while viewed, Prometheus descended, and Nature after him, singing.

NATURE

How young and fresh am I tonight
To see't kept day by so much light,
And twelve my sons stand in their Maker's sight.
Help, wise Prometheus, something must be done
To show they are the creatures of the Sun,
That each to other
Is a brother,
And Nature here no stepdame, but a mother.

CHORUS { Come forth, come forth, prove all the numbers then,[7]
That make perfection up, and may absolve you men.

NATURE

But show thy winding ways and arts,
Thy risings and thy timely starts
Of stealing fire from Ladies' eyes and hearts.[8]

5. I.e., with retorts on their heads.
6. Once more the reference is to King James.
7. Arrange all the numerical combinations that make toward perfection. The Chorus invites the masquers (not without some hyperbole) to form the dance that figures ideal man.
8. Prometheus as stealer of fire and inspirer of men is in his element with the ladies' eyes.

Those softer circles are the young man's heaven,
And there more orbs and planets are than seven,
To know whose motion
Were a notion
As worthy of youth's study as devotion.
CHORUS } Come forth, come forth, prove all the time will gain,
For Nature bids the best, and never bade in vain.

The first dance;
After which this song:

PROMETHEUS, NATURE

PROMETHEUS How many, 'mongst these Ladies here
Wish now they such a mother were!
NATURE Not one, I fear,
And read it in their laughters.
There's more, I guess, would wish to be my daughters.
PROMETHEUS You think they would not be so old
For so much glory.
NATURE I think that thought so told
Is no false piece of story.
'Tis yet with them but beauty's noon,
They would not grandames be too soon.
PROMETHEUS Is that your sex's humor?[9]
'Tis then since Niobe was changed that they have left that tumor.[1]
CHORUS Move, move again, in forms as heretofore.
NATURE 'Tis form allures.
Then move, the Ladies here are store.
PROMETHEUS Nature is motion's mother, as she's yours.
CHORUS The spring whence order flows, that all directs,
And knits the causes with th'effects.

The main dance.
Then dancing with the Ladies;
Then their last dance.
After which, Prometheus calls to them in song.

PROMETHEUS

What, have you done
So soon?
And can you from such beauty part?
You'll do a wonder more than I.
I woman with her ills did fly,
But you their good and them deny.
CHORUS Sure each hath left his heart
In pawn to come again, or else he durst not start.

9. Taste, preference.
1. Vanity. Niobe was the mother of fourteen, or perhaps fifty, children, all of whom were killed by Apollo. Since then, ladies have not been so eager to have many children.

NATURE

They are loath to go,
I know,
Or sure they are no sons of mine.
There is no banquet, boys, like this,
If you hope better, you will miss;
Stay here, and take each one a kiss.[2]
CHORUS Which, if you can refine,
The taste knows no such cates, nor yet the palate wine.
No cause of tarrying shun,
They are not worth his light, go backward from the Sun.[3]

THE END

1615 1616

2. At the end of the dance, each gentleman received a kiss from his lady.

3. I.e., they are not worthy of the sun's light who go backward from it.

Pleasure Reconciled to Virtue

A Masque as It Was Presented at Court Before King James. 1618.

The scene was the mountain Atlas, who had his top ending in the figure of an old man, his head and beard all hoary and frost as if his shoulders were covered with snow; the rest wood and rock. A grove of ivy at his feet, out of which, to a wild music of cymbals, flutes and tabors, is brought forth Comus,[1] *the god of cheer, or the belly, riding in triumph, his head crowned with roses and other flowers, his hair curled; they that wait upon him crowned with ivy, their javelins done about with it; one of them going with Hercules his bowl bare before him, while the rest presented him with this*

Hymn

Room, room! make room for the bouncing belly,
First father of sauce, and deviser of jelly;
Prime master of arts, and the giver of wit,
That found out the excellent engine, the spit,
The plow and the flail, the mill and the hopper,
The hutch and the bolter, the furnace and copper.
The oven, the bavin, the mawkin, the peel,
The hearth and the range, the dog and the wheel.[2]
He, he first invented the hogshead and tun,
The gimlet and vice too, and taught them to run.
And since, with the funnel, an Hippocras bag
He's made of himself, that now he cries swag.[3]
Which shows, though the pleasure be but of four inches,
Yet he is a weasel, the gullet that pinches,
Of any delight, and not spares from the back
Whatever to make of the belly a sack.[4]
Hail, hail, plump paunch! O the founder of taste
For fresh meats, or powdered, or pickle, or paste;

1. Comus is the traditional classical and Renaissance figure of sensual indulgence; many of his properties here (ivy, wild music, and the flowing bowl) suggest his kinship with Dionysus. The bowl of Hercules, given him by the Sun-god, was so big that the hero sailed across the ocean in it. At the root of the masque is the ancient story that early in his life Hercules had to choose between a life of easy pleasure and one of strenuous virtue. But now, under King James, the two principles are at last going to be reconciled. Jonson's stage directions, being partly descriptive (for the reader), partly instructive (for the performer), are rather casual about observing consistency of tense.

2. "Hutch" (bin), "mill," and "hopper" were used in grinding grain; bavin, mawkin, and peel are different sorts of apparatus used in a bake-shop. A dog harnessed to a wheel served to keep a roasting spit turning.

3. "Gimlet" and "vice" are tools for tapping a keg. A "Hippocras bag" is a cloth filter for clearing wine, and to "cry swag" is to reveal a drooping, pendulous belly.

4. The gullet, though only four inches long, is a harsh master; it imposes the belly's great weight on the back.

Devourer of broiled, baked, roasted or sod,[5]
And emptier of cups, be they even or odd;
All which have now made thee so wide i' the waist
As scarce with no pudding thou art to be laced;
But eating and drinking until thou dost nod,
Thou break'st all thy girdles, and break'st forth a god.

To this, the BOWL-BEARER

Do you hear, my friends? to whom did you sing all this now? Pardon me only that I ask you, for I do not look for an answer; I'll answer myself. I know it is now such a time as the Saturnals[6] for all the world, that every man stands under the eaves of his own hat and sings what pleases him; that's the right and the liberty of it. Now you sing of god Comus here, the Belly-god. I say it is well, and I say it is not well. It is well as it is a ballad, and the belly worthy of it, I must needs say, an 'twere forty yards of ballad more—as much ballad as tripe. But when the belly is not edified by it, it is not well; for where did you ever read or hear that the belly had any ears? Come, never pump for an answer, for you are defeated. Our fellow Hunger there, that was as ancient a retainer to the belly as any of us, was turned away for being unseasonable—not unreasonable, but unseasonable—and now is he (poor thin-gut) fain to get his living with teaching of starlings, magpies, parrots and jackdaws, those things he would have taught the belly. Beware of dealing with the belly; the belly will not be talked to, especially when he is full. Then there is no venturing upon Venter;[7] he will blow you all up; he will thunder indeed, la: some in derision call him the father of farts. But I say he was the first inventor of great ordnance, and taught us to discharge them on festival days. Would we had a fit feast for him, i' faith, to show his activity: I would have something now fetched in to please his five senses, the throat; or the two senses, the eyes. Pardon me for my two senses; for I that carry Hercules' bowl[8] in the service may see double by my place, for I have drunk like a frog today. I would have a tun now brought in to dance, and so many bottles about him. Ha! You look as if you would make a problem of this. Do you see? Do you see? a problem: why bottles? and why a tun? and why a tun? and why bottles to dance? I say that men that drink hard and serve the belly in any place of quality (as *The Jovial Tinkers*, or *The Lusty Kindred*[9]) are living measures of drink, and can transfom themselves, and do every

5. Boiled.
6. The Roman Saturnalia, which came about the end of the year, were a time of license; Jonson compares them to the twelfth-night festivities in the English court, at which this masque was produced.
7. Belly, in Latin.
8. To carry Hercules' bowl would clearly imply drinking a lot. "Tun": barrel.
9. These seem to be names of taverns.

day, to bottles or tuns when they please; and when they have done all they can, they are, as I say again (for I think I said somewhat like it afore) but moving measures of drink; and there is a piece in the cellar can hold more than all they. This will I make good if it please our new god but to give a nod; for the belly does all by signs, and I am for the belly, the truest clock in the world to go by.

Here the first antimasque[1] *danced by men in the shape of bottles, tuns, etc., after which,* HERCULES:

What rites are these? Breeds earth more monsters yet?
Antacus[2] scarce is cold: what can beget
This store?—and stay such contraries upon her?
Is earth so fruitful of her own dishonor?
Or 'cause his vice was inhumanity,
Hopes she by vicious hospitality
To work an expiation first?[3] and then
(Help, Virtue!) these are sponges and not men.
Bottles? mere vessels? half a tun of paunch?
How? and the other half thrust forth in haunch?
Whose feast? the belly's! Comus'! and my cup
Brought in to fill the drunken orgies up
And here abused! that was the crowned reward
Of thirsty heroes after labor hard!
Burdens and shames of nature, perish, die;
For yet you never lived, but in the sty
Of vice have wallowed, and in that swine's strife
Been buried under the offense of life.
Go, reel and fall under the load you make,
Till your swoll'n bowels burst with what you take.
Can this be pleasure, to extinguish man?
Or so quite change him in his figure? Can
The belly love his pain, and be content
With no delight but what's a punishment?
These monsters plague themselves, and fitly, too.
For they do suffer what and all they do.
But here must be no shelter, nor no shroud
For such: sink grove, or vanish into cloud!

After this the whole grove vanished, and the whole music was discovered, sitting at the foot of the mountain, with Pleasure and Virtue seated above them. The choir invited Hercules to rest with this

1. The antimasque, or antic masque, was a group of dancers, grotesquely or comically dressed, who served to contrast with the main group of masquers.
2. Antaeus, an earth-born giant, whom Hercules destroyed in the course of his labors. As his favored sport was wrestling, and he grew stronger every time he touched the ground, Hercules had to kill him by holding him in the air till he died.
3. Hercules thinks that Comus is another child of earth. Earth, he supposes, is trying to expiate her guilt by producing one monster after another.

Song

Great friend and servant of the good,
Let cool awhile thy heated blood,
And from thy mighty labor cease.
Lie down, lie down,
And give thy troubled spirits peace,
Whilst Virtue, for whose sake
Thou dost this godlike travail take,
May of the choicest herbage[4] make,
Here on this mountain bred,
A crown, a crown
For thy immortal head.

Here Hercules lay down at their feet, and the second antimasque, which was of pygmies, appeared.

1ST PYGMY. Antaeus dead and Hercules yet live!
Where is this Hercules? What would I give
To meet him now? Meet him? nay three such other,
If they had hand in murder of our brother![5]
With three? with four, with ten, nay, with as many
As the name yields! Pray anger there be any
Whereon to feed my just revenge, and soon!
How shall I kill him? Hurl him 'gainst the moon,
And break him in small portions! Give to Greece
His brain, and every tract of earth a piece!
2ND PYGMY. He is yonder.
1ST PYGMY. Where?
3RD PYGMY. At the hill foot, asleep.
1ST PYGMY. Let one go steal his club.
2ND PYGMY. My charge; I'll creep.
4TH PYGMY. He's ours.
1ST PYGMY. Yes, peace.
3RD PYGMY. Triumph, we have him, boy.
4TH PYGMY. Sure, sure, he's sure.
1ST PYGMY. Come, let us dance for joy.

At the end of their dance they thought to surprise him, when suddenly, being awaked by the music, he roused himself, and they all ran into holes.

Song

CHOIR. Wake, Hercules, awake: but heave up thy black eye,
'Tis only asked from thee to look and these will die,

4. Plants and branches; "travail": labor, trouble.

5. Pygmies and giants, minimals and maximals, are disproportioned offspring of mere earth, therefore brothers to one another. The pygmies don't know how many Hercules-figures there are, because so many tales were told about the hero that even Renaissance mythographers were forced to think there must have been several persons of that name.

Or fly.
Already they are fled,
Whom scorn had else left dead.

At which Mercury descended form the hill with a garland of poplar to crown him.

MERCURY. Rest still, thou active friend of Virtue: these
Should not disturb the peace of Hercules.
Earth's worms and honor's dwarfs, at too great odds,
Prove or provoke the issue of the gods.
See here a crown the agèd hill hath sent thee,
My grandsire Atlas, he that did present thee
With the best sheep that in his fold were found,
Or golden fruit in the Hesperian ground,
For rescuing his fair daughters, then the prey
Of a rude pirate, as thou cam'st this way;
And taught thee all the learning of the sphere,
And how, like him, thou might'st the heavens up-bear,
As that thy labor's virtuous recompense.[6]
He, though a mountain now, hath yet the sense
Of thanking thee for more, thou being still
Constant to goodness, guardian of the hill;
Antaeus, by thee suffocated here,
And the voluptuous Comus, god of cheer,
Beat from his grove, and that defaced. But now
The time's arrived that Atlas told thee of: how
By unaltered law, and working of the stars,
There should be a cessation of all jars[7]
'Twixt Virtue and her noted opposite,
Pleasure; that both should meet here in the sight
Of Hesperus, the glory of the west,[8]
The brightest star, that from his burning crest
Lights all on this side the Atlantic seas
As far as to thy pillars, Hercules.[9]
See where he shines, Justice and Wisdom placed
About his throne, and those with Honor graced,
Beauty and Love! It is not with his brother
Bearing the world, but ruling such another
Is his renown.[1] Pleasure, for his delight,
Is reconciled to Virtue, and this night
Virtue brings forth twelve princes have been bred

6. When Hercules was seeking the golden apples of the Hesperides, he took for a while Atlas' job of holding up the heavens, so the giant could wade out in the ocean and get the apples. Atlas himself was originally an astronomer, and thus knew "all the learning of the sphere."

7. Quarrels.

8. Jonson followed the mythographers in making Hesperus a brother of Atlas; as the evening star and guardian of the western isles, he identifies easily with King James.

9. The "pillars of Hercules" are the straits of Gibraltar.

1. As Hesperus, King James does not hold up the sky, like his brother Atlas, but rules over a special world of his own, England.

In this rough mountain and near Atlas' head,
The hill of knowledge; one and chief of whom
Of the bright race of Hesperus is come,
Who shall in time the same that he is be,
And now is only a less light than he.[2]
These now she trusts with Pleasure, and to these
She gives an entrance to the Hesperides,
Fair Beauty's garden; neither can she fear
They should grow soft or wax effeminate here,
Since in her sight and by her charge all's done,
Pleasure the servant, Virtue looking on.[3]

Here the whole choir of music called the twelve masquers forth from the lap of the mountain, which then opened with this

Song

Ope, agèd Atlas, open then thy lap,
And from thy beamy bosom strike a light,
That men may read in thy mysterious map
All lines
And signs
Of royal education and the right,
See how they come and show,
That are but born to know.
Descend,
Descend,
Though pleasure lead,
Fear not to follow:
They who are bred
Within the hill
Of skill
May safely tread
What path they will:
No ground of good is hollow.

In their descent from the hill Daedalus[4] *came down before them, of whom Hercules questioned Mercury.*

HERCULES. But Hermes, stay a little, let me pause:
Who's this that leads?
MERCURY. A guide that gives them laws
To all their motions: Daedalus the wise.
HERCULES. And doth in sacred harmony comprise
His precepts?

2. Tradition has it that Prince Charles was one of the masquers; he was just 18 at the time, and it was his first masque.
3. Having grown up inside Atlas itself, so that virtue comes naturally to them, the masquers can now be allowed to mingle freely with the daughters of Hesperus, in pursuit of pleasure.
4. Daedalus, the mythical Greek maker of mazes, acts here as master of the intricate steps of the dance which interweaves pleasure with virtue under the guidance of art.

MERCURY. Yes.
HERCULES. They may securely prove[5]
Then, any labyrinth, though it be of love.

Here, while they put themselves in form, Daedalus has his first

Song

Come on, come on! and where you go,
So interweave the curious knot,
As ev'n th' observer scarce may know
Which lines are Pleasure's and which not.

First, figure out the doubtful way
At which awhile all youth should stay,[6]
Where she and Virtue did contend
Which should have Hercules to friend.

Then, as all actions of mankind.
Are but a labyrinth or maze,
So let your dances be entwined,
Yet not perplex men unto gaze;

But measured, and so numerous too,
As men may read each act you do,
And when they see the graces meet,
Admire the wisdom of your feet.

For dancing is an exercise
Not only shows the mover's wit,
But maketh the beholder wise,
As he hath power to rise to it.

The first dance.

After which Daedalus again.

Song 2

O more, and more! this was so well
As praise wants half his voice to tell;
Again yourselves compose;
And now put all the aptness on
Of figure, that proportion
Or color can disclose.

That if those silent arts were lost,
Design and picture, they might boast
From you a newer ground;[7]

5. Experience.

6. The dancers are to "figure out" the doubtful moment of Hercules' choice in the sense of illustrating it; they are beyond the occasion of making it themselves, having already reconciled pleasure with virtue.

7. Put on the "aptness of figure," i.e., significance of expression, of which art (proportion or color) is capable; thus, if design and picture, the silent arts, were lost, they could be rebuilt out of the dance alone.

Instructed to the height'ning sense
Of dignity and reverence
In your true motions found:

Begin, begin; for look, the fair
Do longing listen to what air
You form your second touch;[8]

That they may vent their murmuring hymns
Just to the tune you move your limbs,
And wish their own were such.

Make haste, make haste, for this
The labyrinth of beauty is.

The second dance:

That ended, DAEDALUS:

Song 3

It follows now you are to prove
The subtlest maze of all, that's love,
And if you stay too long,
The fair will think you do 'em wrong,

Go choose among—but with a mind
As gentle as the stroking wind
Runs o'er the gentler flowers.
And so let all your actions smile
As if they meant not to beguile
The ladies, but the hours.

Grace, laughter and discourse may meet,
And yet the beauty not go less:
For what is noble should be sweet,
But not dissolved in wantonness.

Will you that I give the law
To all your sport, and sum it?
It should be such should envy draw,
But ever overcome it.

Here they danced with the ladies, and the whole revels followed;[9] *which ended, Mercury called to Daedalus in this following speech, which was after repeated in song by two trebles, two tenors, a bass, and the whole chorus.*

Song 4

An eye of looking back were well,
Or any murmur that would tell

8. Endeavor.

9. Group of onlookers and courtiers.

Your thoughts, how you were sent
And went,
To walk with Pleasure, not to dwell.

These, these are hours by Virtue spared
Herself, she being her own reward,
But she will have you know
That though
Her sports be soft, her life is hard.

You must return unto the hill,
And there advance
With labor, and inhabit still
That height and crown
From whence you ever may look down
Upon triúmphed Chance.

She, she it is, in darkness shines.
'Tis she that still herself refines
By her own light, to every eye
More seen, more known when Vice stands by.
And though a stranger here on earth,
In heaven she hath her right of birth.
There, there is Virtue's seat,
Strive to keep her your own;
'Tis only she can make you great,
Though place here make you known.

After which, they danced their last dance, and returned into the scene, which closed and was a mountain again as before.

And so it ended.

This pleased the king so well, as he would see it again; when it was presented with these additions.[1]

1618 1640

1. The "additions" were another short masque, *For the Honor of Wales*.

A Note on the Texts

By the standards of his day, Jonson was a meticulous corrector of proof, and he had ample opportunity to correct most of the texts reprinted here. *Volpone*, printed as a separate quarto in 1607, and *The Alchemist*, similarly printed in 1612, were included in two folio editions of Jonson's *Works* published during his lifetime (1616, 1631), as well as the posthumous folio of 1640. *Epicoene*, first published in the folio of 1616, was reprinted as a separate quarto in 1620, as well as in the *Works* of 1631 and 1640. Only *The Sad Shepherd* never underwent Jonsonian revision for the press; as a posthumous fragment, it first appeared in the 1640 folio. "The Masque of Queens" was published in quarto the year it was produced at court (1609), and was included in all the folio editions of the *Works*; but the basic text is a fine handwritten copy with copious notes, made by Jonson himself for presentation to Prince Henry and now in the British Museum. "Oberon" and "Mercury Vindicated" were first printed in the 1616 folio, and "Pleasure Reconciled to Virtue" in the 1640 folio. In the absence of positive evidence to the contrary, the authority of anything appearing in the 1640 *Works* is very good, for though Jonson never read proof on it, the editors had full access to his papers. The most careful and accurate reprint of all these texts is that of C. H. Herford, and Percy and Evelyn Simpson, in their classic 11 volume edition of the *Works* (Oxford, 1925–52).

To make a proper text for modern American students, however, Jonson's page has to be considerably altered. A lot of extra *e*'s have dropped off words like "selfe" and "heire"; *u* has set itself up as a separate letter from *v*, so that words like "enuie" and "deuill" look odd; *i* and *j* have similarly parted ways, so that "iuyce," "iest," and "iustice" are also strange; and Jonson's system of colloquial contractions has grown obsolete, so that forms like "I'am," "do's," "I'le," and "ha's" disturb the eye, though the intent is clear. Besides, some words have changed form with the years. Jonson is constant in spelling "window" as "windore," and "ostrich" as "estrich"; and his system of punctuation often does not agree with modern conventions. He or his printer uses an occasional ampersand (&) for "and"; he prints numbers ("a 1000 crowns") where we would spell out the word; he capitalizes and italicizes much more freely, and erratically, than we do. In these respects and a few others, like removing the extra *u* from "humour," "honour," etc., the text has been silently restyled in order to render it as accessible as possible to a modern American reader. Seventeenth-century texts had very few stage-directions and made few scene-divisions; for ease in following the action and referring to specific passages of the text, the present editor has copied or modified these pieces of apparatus, as first introduced by Jonson's major 19th-century editor, William Gifford. On the same principle, though not on the same authority, lines of poetry have been numbered.

Textual Notes: Major Variants

Volpone

IV,v,43	1616 *substitutes* goodness *for* virtue
IV,v,130	1616 *substitutes* catholic *for* Christian
V,iv,55	1616 *substitutes* fitted *for* apted

The Alchemist

I,i,48	1616 *substitutes* Death on me! *for* God's will!
I,ii,56	1616 *substitutes* Xenophon *for* Testament
I,ii,135	1616 *substitutes* Jove *for* Gad
II,ii,58–59	1616 *adds* They will do it best, Best of all others.
III,i,2–5	1616 *substitutes* And such rebukes we of the separation Must bear with willing shoulders as the trials Sent forth to tempt our frailties. *for* 1612 And such rebukes th' elect must bear with patience; They are the exercises of the spirit, And sent to tempt our frailties.
V,iii,44	1616 *substitutes* Come forth you seed of sulphur, sons of fire *for* 1612 Come forth you seed of vipers, sons of Belial
V,v,23–24	1616 *substitutes* They are the vessels Of pride, lust, and the cart *for* 1612 They are the vessels Of shame and of dishonor
V,v,99	1616 *substitutes* Idol *for* Nimrod

Epicoene

The basic text of this play is that reproduced in the Folio of 1616. The Quarto of 1620 is a careless reprint of this original text, and the Folio of 1640 also reproduces it, faithfully copying the consequences of an accident that occurred in the course of the 1616 printing. One large tray (forme) of type was apparently spilled on the floor after a number of examples had been printed; it was picked up and put together, very carelessly, by someone about the print shop, and more copies of the 1616 folio were then printed off, containing about 280 changes from the original, correct version. It was one of these careless copies that was used as the basis for the 1640 Folio. The present editor has not thought it necessary to record these variants, or the other unimportant variants introduced by 1620 and 1640.

Ben Jonson: His Life, His Plays, His Masques—An Outline Chronology

Jonson was such an active man, so deeply engaged with life on such a variety of fronts, that it has seemed best to present a schematic outline of his career in three parallel columns, representing the events of his life, his plays, and his major masques, arranged in order of time.

Year	Life	Plays
1572	Born, probably in Westminster, of North Country parents.	
1591–92	Soldiering in Holland and Belgium.	
1592	Married to Anne Lewis.	
1597	Acting for Philip Henslowe's company, with some writing.	
1598	Kills Gabriel Spenser in a duel; jailed, branded, and (while in jail) converted to Roman Catholicism.	*Every Man in his Humor* *The Case Is Altered*
1599		*Every Man Out of His Humor*
1600		*Cynthia's Revels*
1601		*Poetaster*

1603	Elizabeth dies, James succeeds: Jonson's oldest son dies of the plague.	*Sejanus*	*The Satyr*, also known as *The Entertainment at Althorpe*
1605	Imprisoned for slurs on the Scots in *Eastward Ho*: perhaps some involvement in the Gunpowder Plot.	*Eastward Ho* (with Marston and Chapman)	*The Masque of Blackness*
1606		*Volpone*	*Hymenaei*
1608			*The Masque of Beauty*
1609		*Epicoene*	*The Masque of Queens*
1610	Returns to Church of England.	*The Alchemist*	
1611		*Catiline*	*Oberon, the Faery Prince* *Love Freed from Ignorance and Folly*
1612–13	Travels to France as tutor to Sir Walter Raleigh's son.		
1613			*The Irish Masque*
1614		*Batholomew Fair*	
1615			*Mercury Vindicated from the Alchemists*
1616	Granted a 100-mark pension by the King: publishes his *Works* in folio.	*The Devil Is an Ass*	*The Golden Age Restored* *Christmas his Masque*
1617			*The Vision of Delight*
1618	Walking trip to Scotland, conversations with Drummond.		*Pleasure Reconciled to Virtue*
1619	Honorary degree from Oxford.		

1621			*News from the New World* *The Gypsies Metamorphosed*
1622			*The Masque of Augurs*
1623	His personal library and manuscripts destroyed by fire.		*Time Vindicated*
1624			*Neptune's Triumph*
1625		*The Staple of News*	*The Fortunate Isles*
1628	Appointed city chronologer.		
1629		*The New Inn*	
1631			*Chloridia*
1632		*The Magnetic Lady*	
1633		*A Tale of a Tub*	*The King's Entertainment at Welbeck*
1634			*Love's Welcome at Bolsover*
1637	Dies and is buried in Westminster Abbey.		
1640	Second edition of the *Works*, including one posthumous fragment, and a few lines of another play.	*The Sad Shepherd* *The Fall of Mortimer*	

Jonson on His Work

Discourses on Poetry

Jonson's relation to his readers was always peculiarly direct and personal: far from rhapsodizing in a vacuum, he always conceived of himself as a man talking to other men. Part of the poet's duty, as he saw it (and a long tradition helped him see it this way) was to provide his readers with instruction about both life and art, and he was rarely devious or indirect in doing so. In his prologues, his plays, his poems, and his prose he often went out of his way to lay down a set of ethical and esthetic principles. These allocutions tell us a great deal about the character of the man, something too about the best way to approach his work; with both these ends in view, we have arranged a selection of representative passages.

From *Every Man in His Humour* (first version, 1598)[1]

LORENZO SENIOR. * * * Go to; you see
How abjectly your poetry is ranked
In general opinion.
LORENZO JUNIOR. Opinion! O God, let gross opinion
Sink and be damned as deep as Barathrum.[2]
If it may stand with your most wished content,
I can refell[3] opinion, and approve
The state of poesy, such as it is,
Blesséd, eternal, and most true divine.
Indeed, if you will look on poesy
As she appears in many, poor and lame,
Patched up in remnants and old worn rags,
Half starved for want of her peculiar food,
Sacred invention, then I must confirm
Both your conceit and censure of her merit.
But view her in her glorious ornaments,
Attired in the majesty of art,
Set high in spirit with the precious taste
Of sweet philosophy, and, which is most,
Crowned with the rich traditions of a soul
That hates to have her dignity profaned
With any relish of an earthly thought:
Oh, then how proud a presence doth she bear!

1. The play, first performed in 1598, exists in two versions, the Quarto of 1601 and the heavily revised Folio of 1616. In the first version, Lorenzo junior is having trouble with his father, Lorenzo senior, who wants his son to give up poetry and devote himself to something practical like making money. His assertion that poetry is not highly valued by "the general opinion" provokes a long and earnest rebuttal by his son—through whose voice one can surely hear that of Jonson himself. The passage is found in Act V, scene 3, lines 309 and following.
2. A pit in ancient Athens into which criminals condemned to death were thrown.
3. Refute; "approve": prove.

Then is she like herself, fit to be seen
Of none but grave and consecrated eyes;
Nor is it any blemish to her fame
That such lean, ignorant, and blasted wits,
Such brainless gulls,[4] should utter their stol'n wares
With such applauses in our vulgar[5] ears,
Or that their slubbered lines have current pass
From the fat judgments of the multitude,
But that this barren and infected age
Should set no difference 'twixt these empty spirits
And a true poet: than which reverend name
Nothing can more adorn humanity.

Prologue to *Every Man in His Humour* (second version, 1616)[1]

Though need make many Poets, and some such
As art and nature have not bettered[2] much,
Yet ours, for want, hath not so loved the stage
As he dare serve th'ill customs of the age,
Or purchase your delight at such a rate
As for it he himself must justly hate:
To make a child, now swaddled, to proceed
Man, and then shoot up, in one beard and weed[3]
Past threescore years; or with three rusty swords
And help of some few foot-and-half-foot words
Fight over *York* and *Lancaster*'s long jars,
And in the tiring-house[4] bring wounds to scars.
He rather prays you will be pleased to see
One such today as other plays should be:
Where neither *Chorus* wafts you o'er the seas,[5]
Nor creaking throne comes down, the boys to please,
Nor nimble squib is seen, to make afeared
The gentlewomen,[6] nor rolled bullet heard,
To say, *It thunders*; nor tempestuous drum
Rumbles to tell you when the storm doth come:
But deeds and language, such as men do use,
And persons such as *Comedy* would choose

4. Simpletons.
5. Gross, undiscriminating: from Latin *vulgus*, mob.
1. In this second version of the play, Lorenzo junior's defence of poetry has disappeared, along with Lorenzo junior (his name is now Edward Kno'well); but the Prologue introduces the play with a forthright account of what Jonson thinks a play should and should not be.
2. Improved over their original ignorance.
3. Suit of clothing.
4. Dressing and make-up room.
5. Jonson is reflecting on Shakespeare's *Henry V*, where the Chorus invites the audience to imagine themselves aboard a fleet crossing the Channel to invade France; his previous allusion is to stage-battles like that of Shrewsbury in *Henry IV*, Part I.
6. Squibs were firecrackers, sometimes let off onstage or amid the audience, as in Marlowe's *Doctor Faustus*; to imitate thunder, a cannonball was rolled down a wooden trough.

When she would show an image of the times,
And sport with human follies, not with crimes—
Except, we make 'em such by loving still
Our popular errors, when we know they're ill.
I mean such errors as you'll all confess
By laughing at them, they deserve no less:
Which when you heartily do, there's hope left then,
You that have so graced monsters may like men.

Prologue to *Cynthia's Revels* (produced 1600, published 1601)[1]

If gracious silence, sweet attention,
Quick sight, and quicker apprehension
(The lights of judgment's throne) shine anywhere,
Our doubtful[2] author hopes this is their sphere,
And therefore opens he himself to those,
To other weaker beams his labors close,
As loth to prostitute their virgin strain
To every vulgar and adulterate brain.
In this alone his Muse her sweetness hath,
She shuns the print of any beaten path,
And proves[3] new ways to come to learned ears:
Pied ignorance[4] she neither loves nor fears.
Nor hunts she after popular applause,
Or foamy praise, that drops from common jaws.
The garland that she wears their hands must twine
Who can both censure, understand, define
What merit is: then cast those piercing rays
Round as a crown, instead of honored bays,[5]
About his poesy; which (he knows) affords
Words above action, matter above words.

From *Poetaster* (1601)[1]

CAESAR. Say then, loved Horace, thy true thought of Virgil.
HORACE. I judge him of a rectified spirit,

1. *Cynthia's Revels* is a satirical comedy in which satire all but overwhelms its comic partner. In declaring here that only the knowing few can judge him, Jonson comes close to arrogance; and in placing "matter," i.e., thought, far above "action," he comes close to disdaining the first commandment of the storyteller, "Dramatize!"
2. Uncertain (of the success of his play).
3. Attempts.
4. Fools wore a harlequin jacket, and ignorance was associated with motley ("pied").
5. Bays, or laurel, traditionally composed the poet's crown.

1. *Poetaster* (the word means "mini-poet" or "pseudo-poet") carries forward the set of literary quarrels which animated *Cynthia's Revels*. Its action centers on a plot to defame Horace, which is exposed and defeated; in the course of rendering judgment, Caesar asks Horace what he thinks of Virgil, and the answer turns into an extended description, if not quite a definition, of what Horace (i.e., Jonson) thinks a real poet should be. The passage is found in Act V, scene 1, lines 99 and following.

By many revolutions of discourse
(In his bright reason's influence) refined
From all the tartarous moods of common men;[2]
Bearing the nature and similitude
Of a right heavenly body; most severe
In fashion and collection of himself,
And then as clear and confident as Jove.
GALLUS. And yet so chaste and tender is his ear,
In suffering any syllable to pass
That he thinks may become the honored name
Of issue to his so examined self,[3]
That all the lasting fruits of his full merit
In his own poems, he doth so distaste
As if his mind's peace, which he strove to paint,
Could not with fleshly pencils have her right.
TIBULLUS. But, to approve his works of sovereign worth,
This observation (methinks) more than serves,
And is not vulgar;[4] That which he hath writ
Is with such judgment labored and distilled
Through all the needful uses of our lives,
That could a man remember but his lines,
He should not touch at any serious point,
But he might breathe his spirit out of him.
CAESAR. You mean, he might repeat part of his works,
As fit for any conference he can use?
TIBULLUS. True, royal Caesar. CAESAR. Worthily observed,
And a most worthy virtue in his works.
What thinks material[5] Horace of his learning?
HORACE. His learning labors not the school-like gloss
That most consists in echoing words and terms
And soonest wins a man an empty name,
Nor any long or far-fetched circumstance
Wrapped in the curious generalties of arts;
But a direct and analytic sum
Of all the worth and first effects of arts.
And for his poesy, 'tis so rammed with life
That it shall gather strength of life with being,
And live hereafter more admired than now.

2. The basic metaphor is that he is a heavenly body, a star, purified of the earthy deposits ("tartarous moods") of ordinary humans.

3. I.e., he is so careful of letting anything pass that might be attributed to him as its author, that he criticizes sharply his own writings.

4. Commonplace.

5. Substantial, solid.

Jonson's Shoptalk

A spacious, talkative, and opinionated man, Jonson frequently unburdened himself on a wide variety of miscellaneous topics. We have two compendia of these sayings. The first consists of a manuscript or group of manuscripts, found after his death by Jonson's literary executor, Sir Kenelm Digby, and by him bundled into the 1640 Folio edition of Jonson's *Works*. The material has at least three titles—*Timber, Explorata, Discoveries*—but the subtitle of the original edition best describes the contents. They are discoveries "made upon men and matter as they have flowed out of his daily readings or had their reflux to his peculiar notion of the times"—a sort of commonplace book, as it were, in which he made notes and observations as things struck him. They constitute, effectually, our first glimpse inside an English poet's workshop. We see here what he thought about his trade, what his stylistic aims were and how he trained himself to carry them out. Many of his ideas are not really his, but are transcribed out of the classical and continental authors whom he read avidly; but that doesn't lessen their interest, or his sincerity in professing them.

The second collection of Jonson's talk is more picturesque in its origins. In mid-summer of 1618 he took off on a walking trip to Scotland, having a mind to see the country and write a poetical account of his adventures on the way. Against all the odds, for he was a corpulent man in his middle years and since the military days of his youth given more to eating and drinking than to exercise, he completed the tour, and was feted royally by the literary society of Edinburgh. Among his hosts on the trip was the Anglo-Scottish poet William Drummond, at whose estate of Hawthornden Jonson lingered for a couple of weeks. Drummond wasn't altogether enchanted with his English guest, who seemed to drink a lot, boast of his own doings, and run down everybody else. But he jotted down the memoranda of his conversations with Jonson—or rather, of Jonson's monologues to him. These notes lay hidden for many years but were discovered in 1833 by David Laing and published. They furnish a vivid and intimate picture—unique in the early history of our literature—of Jonson talking off the top of his head and through a growing army of empty bottles.

From *Discoveries*

For a man to write well, there are required three necessaries: to read the best authors, observe the best speakers, and much exercise of his own style. In style, to consider what ought to be written, and after what manner. He must first think and excogitate his matter, then choose his words and examine the weight of either. Then take care in placing and ranking both matter and words that the composition be comely; and to do this with diligence, and often. No matter how slow the style be at first, so it be labored and accurate; seek the best, and be not glad of the forward conceits or first words that offer themselves to us, but judge of what we invent and order what we approve. Repeat often what we have formerly written, which besides that it helps the consequence and makes the juncture better, it quickens the heat of imagination that often cools in the time of setting down, and gives it new strength as if it grew lustier by the going back. As we see in the contention of leaping, they jump farthest that fetch their race largest; or, as in throwing a dart or javelin, we force back our arms to make our loose[1] the stronger. Yet, if we have a fair gale of wind, I forbid not the steering out of our sail,[2] so the favor of the gale deceive us not. For all that we invent doth please us in the conception or birth, else we would never set it down. But the safest is to return to our judgment and handle over again those things the easiness of which might make them justly suspected.

So did the best writers in their beginnings; they imposed upon themselves care and industry. They did nothing rashly. They obtained first to write well, and then custom made it easy and a habit. By little and little their matter showed itself to them more plentifully; their words answered, their composition followed; and all, as in a well-ordered family, presented itself in the place. So that the sum of all is: Ready writing makes not good writing, but good writing brings on ready writing. Yet when we think we have got the faculty, it is even then good to resist it, as to give a horse a check sometimes with a bit, which doth not so much stop his course as stir his mettle. Again, whither a man's genius is best able to reach, thither it should more and more contend, lift, and dilate[3] itself, as men of low stature raise themselves on their toes, and so ofttimes get even, if not eminent. Besides, as it is fit for grown and able writers to stand of themselves and work with their own strength, to trust and endeavor by their own faculties, so it is fit for the beginner and learner to study others, and the best. For the mind and memory are more sharply exercised in comprehending another man's things than our own, and such as accustom themselves and are familiar with the best authors shall ever and anon find somewhat of them in themselves, and in the expression of their minds, even when they feel it not, be able to utter something like theirs, which hath an authority above their own. Nay, sometimes it is the reward of a man's study, the praise of quoting another man fitly. And though a man be more prone and able for one kind of writing than another, yet he must exercise all. For as in an instrument, so in style, there must be a harmony and consent of parts.

1. Release.
2. Letting out the sheet, running before the wind.
3. Expand, puff up.

* * * Talking and eloquence are not the same: to speak and to speak well are two things. A fool may talk but a wise man speaks, and out of the observation, knowledge, and use of things. Many writers perplex their readers and hearers with mere nonsense. Their writings need sunshine. Pure and neat language I love, yet plain and customary. A barbarous phrase hath often made me out of love with a good sense, and doubtful writing hath racked me beyond my patience. The reason why a poet is said that he ought to have all knowledges is that he should not be ignorant of the most, especially of those he will handle. And indeed when the attaining of them is possible, it were a sluggish and base thing to despair. For frequent imitation of anything becomes a habit quickly. If a man should prosecute[4] as much as could be said of every thing, his work would find no end.

Speech is the only benefit man hath to express his excellency of mind above other creatures. It is the instrument of society. Therefore Mercury, who is the president[5] of language is called *Deorum hominumque interpres.*[6] In all speech, words and sense are as the body and the soul. The sense is as the life and soul of language, without which all words are dead. Sense is wrought out of experience, the knowledge of human life and actions, or of the liberal arts which the Greeks called *Encyclopaideian.*[7] Words are the people's, yet there is a choice of them to be made. For *Verborum delectus, origo est eloquentiae.*[8] They are to be chosen according to the persons we make speak, or the things we speak of. Some are of the camp, some of the council-board, some of the shop, some of the sheep-cote,[9] some of the pulpit, some of the bar, etc. And herein is seen their elegance and propriety, when we use them fitly and draw them forth to their just strength and nature by way of translation or metaphor.[1] But in this translation we must only serve necessity . . . or commodity, which is a kind of necessity. * * * Metaphors far-fetched hinder to be understood, and, affected, lose their grace. * * * All attempts that are new in this kind are dangerous and somewhat hard before they be softened with use. A man coins not a new word without some peril and less fruit; for if it happen to be received, the praise is but moderate; if refused, the scorn is assured. Yet we must adventure, for things at first hard and rough are by use made tender and gentle. It is an honest error that is committed, following great chiefs.

Custom is the most certain mistress of language, as the public stamp makes the current money. But we must not be too frequent

4. Follow out, give expression to.
5. Presiding deity.
6. "The interpreter of Gods and men."
7. The Greek word means, literally, "instruction in a circle," the complete corpus of what a man needs to know.
8. "Choice of words is the source of eloquence."
9. Sheep-fold.
1. "Metaphor" is derived from Greek words, "translation" from Latin, but the root sense of both is the same: to carry across.

with the mint, every day coining, nor fetch words from the extreme and utmost ages, since the chief virtue of a style is perspicuity, and nothing so vicious in it as to need an interpreter. Words borrowed of antiquity do lend a kind of majesty to style, and are not without their delight sometimes. For they have the authority of years, and out of their intermission do win to themselves a kind of grace like newness. But the eldest of the present and newness of the past language is best. For what was the ancient language, which some men so dote upon, but the ancient custom? Yet when I name custom, I understand not the vulgar custom, for that were a precept no less dangerous to language than life, if we should speak or live after the manners of the vulgar. But that I call custom of speech which is the consent of the learned; as custom of life, which is the consent of the good. * * *

Our composition must be more accurate in the beginning and end, than in the midst, and in the end more than in the beginning; for through the midst the stream bears us. And this is attained by custom more than care or diligence. We must express readily and fully, not profusely. There is a difference between a liberal and a prodigal hand. As it is a great point of art, when our matter requires it, to enlarge and veer out all sail, so to take it in and contract it is of no less praise when the argument doth ask it. Either of them hath their fitness in the place. A good man always profits by his endeavor, by his help—yea, when he is absent, nay when he is dead by his example and memory. So good authors in their style.

A strict and succinct style is that where you can take away nothing without loss, and that loss to be manifest. The brief style is that which expresseth much in little. The concise style, which expresseth not enough, but leaves somewhat to be understood. The abrupt style, which hath many breaches and doth not seem to end, but fall. The congruent and harmonious fitting of parts in a sentence hath almost the fastening and force of knitting and connexion: as in stones well squared, which will rise strong a great way without mortar. Periods[2] are beautiful when they are not too long, for so they have their strength too, as in a pike or javelin. As we must take the care that our words and sense be clear, so if the obscurity happen through the hearer's or reader's want of understanding, I am not to answer for them, no more than for their not listening or marking—I must neither find them ears nor mind. * * * Whatsoever loseth the grace and clearness converts into a riddle; the obscurity is marked, but not the value. That perisheth and is passed by, like the pearl in the fable. Our style should be like a skein of silk to be carried and found by the right thread, not raveled and perplexed; then all is a knot, a heap.

* * *

2. Sentences.

The parts of a comedy are the same with a tragedy, and the end is partly the same. For they both delight and teach; the comics are called *didaskaloi*[3] of the Greeks, no less than the tragics.

Nor is the moving of laughter always the end of comedy, that is rather a fowling for the people's delight, or their fooling. For, as Aristotle says rightly, the moving of laughter is a fault in comedy, a kind of turpitude that depraves some part of man's nature without a disease.[4] As a wry face without pain moves laughter, or a deformed vizard,[5] or a rude clown dressed in a lady's habit and using her actions: we dislike and scorn such representations, which made the ancient philosophers ever think laughter unfitting in a wise man. And this induced Plato to esteem of Homer as a sacrilegious person, because he presented the gods sometimes laughing.[6] As also it is divinely said of Aristotle, that to seem ridiculous is a part of dishonesty and foolish.

So that what, either in the words or sense of an author, or in the language or actions of men, is awry or depraved, doth strangely stir mean affections and provoke for the most part to laughter. And therefore it was clear that all insolent and obscene speeches; jest upon the best men; injuries to particular persons; perverse and sinister sayings (and the rather unexpected) in the old comedy[7] did move laughter, especially where it did imitate any dishonesty. And scurrility came forth in the place of wit, which who understands the nature and genius of laughter cannot but perfectly know.

Of which Aristophanes[8] affords an ample harvest, having not only outgonc Plautus or any othcr in that kind, but expressed all the moods and figures of what is ridiculous, oddly. In short, as vinegar is not accounted good until the wine be corrupted, so jests that are true and natural seldom raise laughter with the beast, the multitude. They love nothing that is right and proper; the farther it runs from reason or possibility, with them, the better it is.

What could have made them laugh like to see Socrates presented, that example of all good life, honesty, and virtue, to have him hoisted up with a pulley and there play the philosopher in a basket, measure how many foot a flea could skip geometrically by a just scale, and edify the people from the engine?[9] This was theatrical wit, right stage-jesting, and relishing a playhouse, invented for scorn and laughter; whereas, if it had savored of equity, truth, per-

3. Teachers.
4. Jonson has here misinterpreted badly a statement in the *Poetics,* V, i.
5. Mask.
6. *Ethics,* IV, 9.
7. The "old" comedy is that of Aristophanes, satirical and personal; the "new" that of Menander, presenting primarily types not individuals.
8. Aristophanes (448–385 B.C.) was the greatest of the Greek comic poets; Jonson's own work was often compared with that of Aristophanes on the score of its bitter personalities, so it is curious to see him raising this objection against his predecessor.
9. In *The Clouds,* Aristophanes introduces Socrates onstage in an aerial basket, thinking airy and useless thoughts.

spicuity, and candor, to have tasted a wise or a learned palate, spit it out presently. "This is bitter and profitable, this instructs and would inform us; what need we know anything, that are nobly born, more than a horse race or a hunting match, our day to break with citizens, and such innate mysteries."[1]

This is truly leaping from the stage to the tumbril again, reducing all wit to the original dung-cart.[2]

From *Ben Jonson's Conversations with William Drummond of Hawthornden* (1619)[1]

* * *

of his owne lyfe, education, birth, actions

His Grandfather came from Carlifle & he thought from Anandale to it,[2] he ferved King Henry 8 & was a Gentleman his father Lofed all his eftate under Queen Marie, having been caft in prifson and forfaitted, at last turn'd Minifter So he was a Minifters fon, he himfelf was Posthūmoūs born a moneth after his fathers deceafe, brought up poorly, putt to fchool by a friend (his mafter Cambden)[3] after taken from it, and put to ane other Craft (I thinke was to be a Wright or Bricklayer) which he coūld not endure, then went he to ye low Countries būt returning foone he betook himfelf to his wonted ftudies. In his fervuce in the Low Countries, he had jn the face of both the Campes Killed ane Enimie & taken opima fpolia[4] from him, and fince his comming to England being appealed to the fields he had Killed his adverfarie, which had hurt him jn the arme & whose fwordd was 10 Inches Longer than his, for the which he was Emprifsoned and almoft at the Gallowes.[5] then took he his Religion by truft of a prieft who Vifited him jn Prifson. thereafter he was 12 years a Papift.

1. Jonson imagines Greek audiences of complacent aristocrats, approving of Aristophanes because he doesn't teach them anything (they know it all anyway): the animus in his mind is clearly against contemporary English audiences. "Our day to break with the citizens" is the gentleman's day to renege on his debts to the tradesman.
2. Tradition says the first dramas were performed on wagons or carts, drawn up in village marketplaces; Jonson thinks savage personal satire reduces comedy to the crudity of its original.
1. The conversations with Drummond were held at the latter's estate of Hawthornden in the course of Jonson's walking tour to Scotland. We print Drummond's record of these talks as it was transcribed from the manuscript, with its casual spellings, capricious capitalizations, and untrussed grammar. As a Scotsman, Drummond spelled English (and no doubt pronounced it) differently than a native Englishman; but not much differently.
2. At the mouth of Solway Firth leading into the Irish Sea, Carlisle is just a few miles from the Scottish border. There are no Jonsons or Johnsons recorded as living in the hamlet of Annandale, but there are many Johnstones; Jonson may have been of their stock.
3. William Camden, famous antiquary, is reported to have taught Jonson himself and paid his way through Westminster School.
4. I.e., the armor of an enemy whom one has killed in hand-to-hand combat.
5. This is the duel with Gabriel Spenser; Jonson pleaded his "clergy" to escape, that is, by proving his ability to read he got himself tried by more lenient laws.

He was Maſter of Arts jn both ye Univerſities by yr[6] favour not his ſtūdie.
he maried a wyfe who was a ſhrew yet honeſt, 5 yeers he had not bedded wt her but remained wt my Lord Aulbanie.[7]
jn the tyme of his cloſe Impriſsonment under Queen Eliſabeth his judges coūld gett nothing of him to all yr demands bot I[8] and No, they placed two damn'd Villans to catch advantage of him, wt him, but he was advertiſed by his Keeper, of the Spies he hath ane Epigrame.
When the King came jn England, at that tyme the Peſt was jn London, he being jn the Coūntry at Sr Robert Cottons hoūſe with old Cambden, he saw jn a viſion his eldeſt ſone (yn[9] a child and at London) appear unto him wt ye Marke of a bloodie croſse on his forehead as if it had been cutted wt a ſūord, at which amazed he prayed ūnto God, and jn ye morning he came to Mr. Cambdens chamber to tell him, who perſuaded him it was but ane appreehenſion of his fantaſie at which he ſould not be disjected. jn ye mean tyme comes yr letters from his wife of ye death of yt Boy jn ye plague. he appeared to him he ſaid of a Manlie ſhape & of yt[1] Grouth that he thinks he ſhall be at the reſurrection.
he was delated[2] by Sr James Murray to the King for writing ſomething against the Scots jn a play Eaſtward hoe & voluntarly Impriſſonned himſelf wt Chapman[3] and Marſton, who had written it amongſt ym. the report was that they ſhoūld then had their ears cūtt & noſes. after yr delivery he banqūeted all his friends, yr was Camden Selden and others. at the midſt of the Feaſt his old Mother Dranke to him & ſhew him a paper which ſhe had (if the Sentence had taken execution) to have mixed jn ye Priſson among his drinke, which was full of Lustie ſtrong poiſon & that ſhe was no chūrle ſhe told ſhe minded firſt to have Drunk of it herſelf.
he had many quarrells with Marſton beat him & took his Piſtol from him, wrote his Poetaſter[4] on him the beginning of ym were that Marſton repreſented him jn the ſtage.
jn his youth given to Venerie.[5] he thought the ūſe of a maide, nothing in compariſon to ye wantoneſs of a wyfe & would never haue ane other Miſtreſs. he ſaid two accidents ſtrange befell him,

6. The old Anglo-Saxon *thorn* (standing for "th") was transformed in 17th-century English to a "y"; thus "ye olde inne" would have been pronounced exactly as if it were written "the old inn," and "yr" in this passage stands for "their."
7. Esmé Stewart, Lord of Aubigny, a Scottish lord with estates in France, resident in London.
8. Aye.
9. Then.
1. That.
2. Accused.
3. George Chapman (best known for his translations of Homer) and John Marston, satirical playwright: *Eastward Ho* was a joint production of all three men.
4. *Poetaster* (1601), one of the most savagely satirical of Jonson's plays.
5. Lust.

one that a man made his own wyfe to Coūrt him, whom he enjoyed two yeares erre he knew of it, & one day finding them by chance Was paſsingly delighted with it, one other lay diverſe tymes with a woman, who ſhew him all that he wiſhed except the laſt act, which ſhe woūld neuer agree unto.

S. W. Raulighe ſent him Governour w^{t} his ſon anno 1613 to France.[6] this Yoūth being knaviſhly jnclyned, among other paſtimes (as the ſetting of the favour of Damoſells on a Cod piece)[7] caūſed him to be Drunken & dead drunk, ſo that he knew not wher he was, thereafter laid him on a Carr which he made to be Drawen by Pioners[8] through the ſtreets, at every corner ſhowing his Governoūr ſtreetched out & telling them that was a more Lively jmage of ye Crucifix than any they had, at which Sporte young Raughlies mother delyghted much (ſaying his father young was ſo jnclyned) though the father abhorred it.

He can ſet Horoſcopes, but truſts not jn y^{m}, he with ye conſent of a friend Couſened a lady, with whom he had made ane apointment to meet ane old Aſtrologer jn the ſūburbs, which ſhe Keeped & it was himſelf diſguyſed jn a Longe Gowne & a whyte beard at the light of a Dimm burning Candle up jn a litle Cabjnet reached unto by a Ledder.

every firſt day of the new year he had 20lb ſent him from the Earl of Pembrok to buy bookes.

after he was reconciled with the Chūrch & left of to be a recuſant[9] at his firſt communion jn token of trūe Reconciliation, he drank out all the full cup of wyne.

being at ye end of my Lord Saliſburie's table with Inigo Jones & demanded by my Lord, why he was not glad My Lord ſaid he yow promiſed I ſhould dine with yow, bot I doe not, for he had none of his meate, he eſteamed only y^{t} his meate which was of his owne diſh.

he heth conſumed a whole night jn lying looking to his great toe, about which he hath ſeen tartars & turks Romans and Carthaginions feight in his jmagination.

6. Sir Walter Raleigh's last name was spelt, in his own time, almost every conceivable way except "Raleigh." Since 1603 he had been living with his family in the Tower of London, under suspicion of treason for conspiring against James. In 1616 he was released to head an expedition after El Dorado in America; the expedition failing, he returned to England and was executed in 1618. Jonson's story is part of a large body of legends, a few funny, many dirty, and the majority false, that clustered round the Raleigh name.

7. A damsel's "favor" is her handkerchief or garter; a codpiece is a conspicuous ornamented flap in the front of men's breeches.

8. Soldiers with engineering training and equipment, i.e., shovels.

9. A "recusant" refuses to attend the services of the Church of England; in those days it was taken to be proof that one belonged to the Church of Rome. Drinking the full cup at communion would be taken as a sign of full reconciliation to the English Church.

Northampton was his mortall enimie for brauling on a St Georges day one of his attenders, he was called befor ye Coũncell for his Sejanus[1] & accused both of popperie and treaſon by him.
Sundry tymes he heth devoured his bookes .j.[2] ſold y^m all for Neceſsity.
he heth a minde to be a churchman, & ſo he might have favour to make one sermon to the King, he careth not what y^r after ſould befall him, for he would not flatter though he ſaw Death. at his hither comming Sr Francis Bacon ſaid to him, he loved not to ſie poeſy goe on other feet y^n poetical dactils & ſpondae.

* * *

Drummond's Summary of Jonson's Character (January 19, 1619)

He is a great lover and praiser of himself, a contemner and Scorner of others, given rather to loſse a friend, than a Jest, jealous of every word and action of those about him (eſpeciallie after drink) which is one of the Elements jn which he liveth) a diſsembler of ill parts which raigne jn him, a bragger of ſome good that he wanteth, thinketh nothing well bot what either he himſelf, or ſome of his friends and Countrymen hath ſaid or done. he is paſsionately kynde and angry, careleſse either to gaine or keep, Vindicative, but if he be well anſwered, at himſelf.
for any religion as being verſed[3] jn both.
jnterpreteth beſt ſayings and deeds often to the worſt:
oppressed with fantaſie, which hath ever maſtered his reason, a generall diſeaſe jn many poets. his jnventions are ſmooth and eaſie, but above all he excelleth jn a tranſlation. when his Play of a Silent woman was firſt acted, ther was found Verſes after on the ſtage againſt him, concluding that, that play was well named the Silent Woman. ther was never one man to ſay plaũdite[4] to it.

1. Saint George's day is April 23; as he is patron saint of England, it is a festive day. Henry Howard, Earl of Northampton, was a tough and tricky antagonist; and *Sejanus*, Jonson's first Roman tragedy (1603) contains many passages suggestive of a resentful and even conspiratorial disposition.
2. "j." stands for i.e., meaning "that is."
3. Practiced. The two religions are Protestantism and Catholicism.
4. Bravo, well done: from the Latin.

Contemporary Readers on Jonson

Jonson himself was a generous as well as a judicious appreciator of other men's work; his poems on Shakespeare, Donne, Beaumont, Selden, and Camden are ample evidence of his gift for warm yet dignified praise. In return he received from a choir of lesser poets tributes of complimentary verse which swelled to a chorus the year after his death with the appearance of a volume, *Jonsonius Virbius* (Jonson Reborn). Much of this verse is simply social or ceremonial in character, but from the best of it we may learn what qualities in Jonson and his work appealed most deeply to his own times.

SIDNEY GODOLPHIN

On Ben Jonson[1]

The Muses' fairest light in no dark time,
The wonder of a learnèd age; the line
Which none can pass; the most proportioned wit
To nature; the best judge of what was fit;
The deepest, plainest, highest, clearest pen;
The voice most answered by consenting[2] men,
The soul which answered best to all well said
By others, and which most requital made;
Tuned to the highest key of ancient Rome,
Returning all her music with his own;
In whom, with nature, study claimed a part,
And yet who to himself owed all his art:
  Here lies Ben Jonson. Every age will look
  With sorrow here, with wonder on his book.

EDMUND WALLER

Upon Ben Jonson[1]

Mirror of poets! mirror of our age!
Which her whole face beholding on stage,
Pleased and displeased with her own faults, endures
A remedy like those whom music cures.[2]

1. Sidney Godolphin (1610–43) was more a politician and diplomat than a man of letters; but with his friend Lord Falkland he was of the group that admired and helped support Jonson in his last years; and he contributed this eloquent poem to the memorial volume.
2. The metaphor, which works throughout the poem, is of two stringed instruments, one of which vibrates in response to chords played on the other.

1. Edmund Waller (1606–87) survived the Civil Wars to exercise a strong influence on the polished and graceful poetry fashionable during the Restoration. His contribution to *Jonsonius Virbius* emphasizes the universality of Jonson's vision and the therapeutic powers of his dramas.
2. Music was thought to cure madness by driving out one frenzy with another.

Thou hast alone those various inclinations
Which Nature gives to ages, sexes, nations
So tracéd with thy all-resembling pen,
That whate'er custom has imposed on men,
Or ill-got habits (which distort them so
That scarce the brother can the brother know)
Is represented to the wondering eyes
Of all that see or read thy comedies.
Whoever in those glasses looks, may find
The spots returned, or graces, of his mind,
And by the help of so divine an art,
At leisure view and dress[3] his nobler part.
Narcissus, cozened by that flattering well
Which nothing could but of his beauty tell,
Had here, discov'ring the deformed estate
Of his fond mind, preserved himself with hate.[4]
But virtue too, as well as vice, is clad
In flesh and blood so well, that Plato had
Beheld what his high fancy once embraced,[5]
Virtue with colors, speech, and motion graced.
The sundry postures of thy copious Muse
Who would express, a thousand tongues must use,
Whose fate's no less peculiar than thy art;
For as thou couldst all characters impart,
So none could render thine, which still escapes,
Like Proteus,[6] in variety of shapes—
Who was nor this nor that, but all we find
And all we can imagine in mankind.

JASPER MAYNE

From To the Memory of Ben. Jonson[1]

He that writes well, writes quick, since the rule's true,
Nothing is slowly done, that's always new.
So when thy FOX had ten times acted been,
Each day was first, but that 'twas cheaper seen.[2]
And so thy ALCHEMIST, played o'er and o'er,

3. Not simply adorn, but in the stronger sense of correct, redress.
4. Narcissus fell in love with his own image and starved to death; had he recognized his vanity (as Jonson's plays could have taught him to do), he would have hated that vice, and so been preserved.
5. Looking at Jonson's plays, Plato would have seen the pure and ideal form, the idea, of virtue clothed in flesh and blood.
6. Proteus, the old man of the sea, had the power to assume an infinite variety of shapes.

1. Jasper Mayne or Maine (1604–72) was a lively if not particularly gifted divine, poet, playwright, translator, controversialist, and man of letters, who contributed to the Jonson memorial volume. Precisely because they're not very original, his comments express with clarity and force the literary standards of the time.
2. In the 17th century, as in the 20th, tickets to the first performance cost more than those for the regular run of the play.

Was new o'th' Stage when 'twas not at the door.[3]
We like the Actors did repeat, the Pit
The first time saw, the next conceived thy Wit:
Which was cast in those forms, such rules, such Arts,
That but to some not half thy Acts were parts:
Since of some silken judgments we may say,
They filled a Box two hours, but saw no Play.[4]
So that th'unlearned lost their money, and
Scholars saved only, that could understand.
   Thy Scene was free from Monsters, no hard Plot
Called down a God t'untie th'unlikely knot.[5]
The Stage was still a Stage, two entrances
Were not two parts o'th' World, disjoined by Seas.
Thine were land-Tragedies, no prince was found
To swim a whole Scene out, then o'th' stage drowned;[6]
Pitched fields, as Red-Bull wars,[7] still felt thy doom,
Thou laidst no sieges to the Music-Room;[8]
Nor wouldst allow to thy best Comedies
Humors that should above the people rise:
Yet was thy language and thy style so high,
Thy Sock to th'Ankle, Buskin reached to th'thigh;[9]
And both so chaste, so 'bove Dramatic clean,
That we both safely saw and lived thy Scene.
No foul loose line did prostitute thy wit,
Thou wrot 'st thy Comedies, did not commit.[1]
We did the vice arraigned not tempting hear,
And were made Judges, not bad parts,[2] by th'ear.
For thou ev'n sin didst in such words array,
That some who came bad parts went out good play.
Which ended not with th' Epilogue; the Age
Still acted, which grew innocent from th' stage.
'Tis true thou hadst some sharpness, but thy salt
Served but with pleasure to reform the fault.
Men were laughed into virtue, and none more
Hated Face acted than were such before.
So did thy sting not blood, but humors draw,
So much doth satire more correct than law.

* * *

3. The title over the theater entrance was old when the play on the boards was still new. The "pit," where admission was cheapest, is understood to contain the dullest spectators.

4. The "silken" judgments are clearly those of the fine gentlemen, to whom Jonson himself was often hostile.

5. Having a god float down from heaven to resolve a knotty plot is a cheap theatrical device, known as a *deus ex machina*, a god out of the machine.

6. Shipwrecks and drownings onstage (as in Shakespeares' *Pericles* and *The Tempest*) taxed the credulity of spectators in ways that Jonson did not accept.

7. The Red Bull was a theater famous for putting on loud, swashbuckling shows.

8. The phrase implies that there may have been a special room on some Elizabethan stages for musicians: sieges of cities might then be sketchily represented by a couple of actors in armor attacking the music room.

9. The comic "sock" or slipper is a metaphor for the "low" style of comedy, as the high-heeled boot or "buskin" represents the exalted style of tragedy.

1. Mayne plays on the familiar prohibition, "Thou shalt not commit—adultery."

2. "Bad parts" would be the equivalent of "a bad lot"; "good play" implies what we would call "a good sort," with a punning compliment on Jonson's dramatic workmanship.

THOMAS CAREW

To Ben Jonson upon Occasion of His Note of Defiance Annexed to His Play of *The New Inn*[1]

'Tis true, dear Ben, thy just chastising hand
Hath fixed upon the sotted age a brand
To their swoll'n pride and empty scribbling due;
It cannot judge nor write;—and yet, 'tis true
Thy comic muse from the exalted line
Touched by thy *Alchemist* doth since decline
From that her zenith, and foretells a red
And blushing evening when she goes to bed,
Yet such as shall out-shine the glimmering light
With which all stars shall gild the following night.
Nor think it much (since all thy eaglets may
Endure the sunny trial)[2] if we say
This hath the stronger wing, or that doth shine
Tricked up in fairer plumes, since all are thine.
Who hath his flock of cackling geese compared
With thy tuned choir of swans? or else who dared
To call thy births deformed? but if thou bind
By city-custom or by gavelkind[3]
In equal shares thy love on all thy race,
We may distinguish of their sex and place.
Though one hand from them, and though one brain strike
Souls into all, they are not all alike.
Why should the follies then of this dull age
Draw from thy pen such an immodest rage
As seems to blast thy (else-immortal) bays[4]
When thine own tongue proclaims thy itch of praise?
Such thirst will argue drouth. No, let be hurled
Upon thy works by the detracting world
What malice can suggest; let the rout say,
The running sands that ere thou make a play
Count the slow minutes might a *Goodwin* frame[5]
To swallow when th'hast done thy shipwrecked name.
Let them the dear[6] expense of oil upbraid,

1. Thomas Carew (1594–1640) was a brilliant, charming man who hung about the fringes of the Stuart court, chasing girls and writing verses. His poem to Jonson, whose play *The New Inn* had been a catastrophic failure (1629), and who promptly wrote a poem denouncing the taste of the whole audience, neatly combines truth with tact.
2. To make sure the young birds in his nest are genuine eaglets, the eagle is reputed to fly with them up toward the sun; any bird that isn't an authentic eagle is blinded by the rays.
3. City-custom (i.e., London city custom) and gavelkind (a system of land tenure once common in Kent) were two legal ways of dividing an estate equally among all the heirs—as opposed to the normal English rule of primogeniture (everything to the eldest son).
4. Bays or laurel make up the poet's crown.
5. Goodwin-sands was a sand-bar, shifty and treacherous, on which many ships were lost. Jonson's slowness in composition was proverbial.
6. Extravagant.

Sucked by thy watchful lamp, that hath betrayed
To theft the blood of martyred authors, spilt
Into thy ink, whilst thou growest pale with guilt.[7]
Repine not at the taper's thrifty waste
That sleeks thy terser poems, nor is haste
Praise but excuse; and if thou overcome
A knotty writer, bring the booty home;
Nor think it theft if the rich spoils so torn
From conquered authors be as trophies worn.
Let others glut on the extorted praise
Of vulgar breath, trust thou to after days:
Thy labored works shall live when Time devours
Th'abortive offspring of their hasty hours.
Thou art not of their rank, the quarrel lies
Within thine own verge.[8] Then let this suffice:
The wiser world doth greater thee confess
Then all men else, than thyself only less.

7. The other great charge against Jonson was that he copied or translated too liberally from other authors.

8. I.e., within your own territory, against yourself. Duels cannot properly take place between two men of different rank, and as Jonson is out of everyone else's class, he can fight only himself.

Criticism

JONAS A. BARISH

The Double Plot in *Volpone*†

For more than two centuries literary critics have been satisfied to dismiss the subplot of *Volpone* as irrelevant and discordant, because of its lack of overt connection with the main plot. Jonson's most sympathetic admirers have been unable to account for the presence of Sir Politic Would-be, Lady Would-be, and Peregrine any more satisfactorily than by styling them a "makeweight" or a kind of comic relief to offset the "sustained gloom" of the chief action. Without questioning the orthodox opinion that the links of intrigue between the two plots are frail, one may nevertheless protest against a view of drama which criticizes a play exclusively in terms of physical action. What appears peripheral on the level of intrigue may conceal other kinds of relevance. And it is on the thematic level that the presence of the Would-be's can be justified and their peculiar antics related to the major motifs of the play.

John D. Rea, in his edition of *Volpone*, seems to have been the first to notice that Sir Politic Would-be, like the characters of the main plot, has his niche in the common beast fable:[1] he is Sir Pol, the chattering poll parrot, and his wife is a deadlier specimen of the same species. Rea's accurate insistence on the loquaciousness of the parrot, however, must be supplemented by recalling that parrots not only habitually chatter, they mimic. This banal but important little item of bird lore offers a thread whereby we may find our way through the complex thematic structure of the play. For Sir Politic and Lady Would-be function to a large extent precisely as mimics. They imitate their environment, and without knowing it they travesty the actions of the main characters. In so doing, they perform the function of burlesque traditional to comic subplots in English drama, and they make possible the added density and complexity of vision to which the device of the burlesque subplot lends itself.

His effort to Italianize himself takes the form, with Sir Politic, of an obsession with plots, secrets of state, and Machiavellian intrigue. His wife, on the other hand, apes the local styles in dress and cosmetics, reads the Italian poets, and tries to rival the lascivious Venetians in their own game of seduction.

Further, and more specifically, however, Sir Politic and Lady Would-be caricature the actors of the main plot. Sir Pol figures as a

† From *Modern Philology* 51 (1953), pp. 83–92. For purposes of this edition some of Professor Barish's copious and informative notes have been truncated. References to *Volpone* have been made by act and scene of the present edition, though actual quotations are from the old-spelling text of Herford and Simpson.

1 (New Haven, 1919), p. xxxiii.

comic distortion of Volpone. As his name implies, he is the would-be politician, the speculator *manqué*, the unsuccessful enterpriser. Volpone, by contrast, is the real politician, the successful enterpriser, whose every stratagem succeeds almost beyond expectation. Sir Pol, like Volpone, is infatuated with his own ingenuity, and like Volpone he nurses his get-rich-quick schemes; but none of these ever progresses beyond the talking stage. While Volpone continues to load his coffers with the treasures that pour in from his dupes, Sir Pol continues to haggle over vegetables in the market and to annotate the purchase of toothpicks.

Lady Would-be, for her part, joins the dizzy game of legacy-hunting. Her antics caricature the more sinister gestures of Corvino, Voltore, and Corbaccio. She is jealous, like Corvino, as meaninglessly and perversely erudite as Voltore, and like Corbaccio, she makes compromising proposals to Mosca which leave her at the mercy of his blackmail. But, like her husband, Lady Would-be is incapable of doing anything to the purpose, and when she plays into Mosca's hands in the fourth act, she becomes the most egregious of the dupes because she is the blindest.

We do not learn of the existence of the Would-be's until the close of the first act,[2] and then only in a scrap of dialogue between Mosca and Volpone. Mosca's panegyric on Celia, following his sarcasms about Lady Would-be, serves to initiate a contrast which prevails throughout the play, between the households of Corvino and Sir Politic. If Corvino's besetting vice is jealousy, that of Sir Pol is uxoriousness, and the contrast enlarges itself into a difference between the brutal, obsessive passions of Italy and the milder eccentricities, the acquired follies or humors, of England. The contrast continues to unfold in the opening scene of Act II, where Sir Politic talks to his new acquaintance, Peregrine. Peregrine, it should be mentioned, probably belongs to the beast fable himself, as the pilgrim falcon. A case for this possibility would have to be based on the habits of hawks, commonly trained to hunt other birds. One then might find propriety in the fact of the falcon's hunting the parrot in the play. In Jonson's Epigram LXXXV (Herford and Simpson, VIII, 55), the hawk is described as a bird sacred to Apollo, since it pursues the truth, strikes at ignorance, and makes the fool its quarry. All these activities are performed by Peregrine vis-à-vis Sir Politic.

In the initial scene between them, three chief ideas are developed, all of cardinal importance to the play and all interrelated. The first is the notion of monstrosity. Monstrosity has already made

2. For the sake of brevity, this discussion will confine itself as closely as possible to the scenes actually involving the Would-be's. Jonson's sources, which are legion for this play, have been assembled both by Rea and by Herford and Simpson in their editions but will not be considered here.

its spectacular appearance in the person of Androgyno and in the passage on Volpone's misbegotten offspring. We are, thereby, already familiar with the moral abnormality of Venice and its inhabitants. The present passage, with its reports of strange marvels sighted in England—a lion whelping in the Tower, a whale discovered in the Thames, porpoises above the bridge—introduces us to an order of monsters more comic than those to be met with in Venice, but to monsters nonetheless, in the proper sense of the word. Sir Pol's prodigies are distant echoes of the moral earthquake rocking Venice, a looking glass for England whereby that country is warned to heed the lesson of the Italian state lest its own follies turn to vices and destroy it.

The enactment of the interlude in the first act, by placing the soul of the fool in the body of the hermaphrodite, has already established an identification between folly and monstrosity.[3] Appropriately enough, then, having discussed monsters, Peregrine and Sir Pol turn to speak of the death of a famous fool, thus reinforcing the link between the two ideas. Sir Pol's excessive reaction to the event prompts Peregrine to inquire maliciously into a possible parentage between the two, and his companion innocently to deny it. The joke here, that Sir Pol is kin to the dead fool through their mutual folly if not through family, merges into a larger reflection on the ubiquity of folly, picking up that suggestion by ricochet, as it were, from the interlude in Act I. When Peregrine asks, "I hope / You thought him not immortall?" (Act II, scene 1, lines 55–56), the question implies its own Jonsonian answer: Master Stone, the fool, is not immortal, but his folly lives on incarnate in hundreds of fools like Sir Politic, much as the soul of Pythagoras, in the interlude, invested the body of one fool after another for thousands of years, only to reach its final and most fitting avatar in the person of Androgyno.

The colloquy concerning the Mamuluchi introduces the third chief motif of the scene, that of mimicry. This passage, where baboons are described in various quasi-human postures,[4] acquires added irony from the fact that it is recited by the parrot, the imitative animal par excellence, and also from the fact that the activities of the baboons, like those of Master Stone, the fool, consist chiefly of spying and intriguing and therefore differ so little from the way Sir Pol himself attempts to imitate the Italians.

3. For an analysis of the first interlude and its importance to the play as a whole see Harry Levin, "Jonson's Metempsychosis." [See below, p. 415—*Editor*.]

4. Rea quotes from Edward Topsel's chapter "Of the Cynocephale, or Baboun" in *The Historie of Four-footed Beastes* (1607): "It is the error of vulgar people to think that *Babouns* are men, differing only in the face or visage. . . . They will imitate all humane actions, loving wonderfully to wear garments. . . . they are as lustful and venerous as Goats, attempting to defile all sorts of women" (Rea, p. 178).

The arrival of Volpone disguised as a mountebank produces the expected confrontation between the archknave and the complete gull, the latter hopelessly hypnotized by the eloquence of the former. Volpone commences by disdaining certain imputations that have been cast on him by professional rivals. By way of counterattack, he accuses them of not knowing their trade, of being mere "*ground* Ciarlitani," or spurious mountebanks. If there is any doubt about the application of the passage to Sir Politic, it is settled by that individual's cry of admiration: "Note but his bearing, and contempt of these" (II, 2). Sir Politic thus plays charlatan to Volpone's mountebank as, within the larger frame of the play, he plays parrot to Volpone's fox. But Volpone has brought along his own misshapen child, the dwarf Nano, as an accredited imitator. Nano, who fills the role of Zan Fritada, the zany, is the domesticated mimic, the conscious mimic, as Androgyno is the conscious fool, while Sir Pol remains the unconscious mimic and the unconscious fool.

Volpone, pursuing his attack on imitators, assails them for trying to copy his elixir: "*Indeed, very many have assay'd, like apes in imitation of that, which is really and essentially in mee, to make of this oyle*" (II, 2). What is "really and essentially" in Volpone we know already to be monstrosity, so that to imitate Volpone (as Sir Politic does) is to imitate the unnatural, and therefore, in a sense, to place one's self at two removes from nature. But Volpone believes himself, not without justification, to be inimitable. The wretched practitioners who try to duplicate his ointment end in disaster. "*Poore wretches!*" he concludes, "*I rather pittie their folly, and indiscreation, then their losse of time, and money; for those may be recouered by industrie: but to bee a foole borne, is a disease incurable*" (II, 2). At this moment all that would be needed to drive home the application of Volpone's *sententia*[5] would be a pause on his part, followed by a significant look from Peregrine to Sir Pol.[6] But the situation conceals a further irony. Volpone's aphorism applies to himself. Before long, he, the archknave, will have proved the greatest fool, and this despite the versatility which enables him to transcend for the moment his own preferences, in order to cater to the prejudices of the public. Paradoxically, in this scene, speaking out of character, Volpone utters truths which reverse the premises of his former behavior. In Act I, gold, the great goddess, served him as sovereign remedy and omnipotent healer. For the saltimbanco Scoto of Mantua, peddling his

5. Aphorism [*Editor.*]

6. A proper staging of the scene would involve, I think, placing Sir Pol fairly close to Volpone, so that the two stare each other in the face, the one collecting with ardor every flower of rhetoric that falls from the other. At this moment, Volpone himself might stop to gaze into the infatuated countenance before him: by now Sir Pol's credulity is as apparent to him as it is to Peregrine.

fraudulent elixir, newer and relatively truer axioms celebrate the treasure of health: "O, *health! health! the blessing of the rich! the riches of the poore!*" (II, 2). But with the application of this facile maxim, error descends again. The new truth proves to be only a distorted half-truth. In place of gold, Volpone offers only his humbug ointment as the "*most soueraigne, and approued remedie*" (II, 2). The real point, and he has made it himself, escapes him: to be a fool born is a disease incurable, and it is this disease to which he himself is destined to succumb.

The "*little remembrance*" which Volpone now presents to Celia proves to be a cosmetic powder with virtues more miraculous than those of the *oglio* itself. It is the powder "*That made* VENVS *a goddesse (given her by* APOLLO*) that kept her perpetually yong, clear'd her wrincles, firm'd her gummes, fill'd her skin, colour'd her haire; from her, deriu'd to* HELEN, *and at the sack of* Troy *(unfortunately) lost: till now, in this our age, it was as happily recouer'd, by a studious* Antiquarie . . . *who sent a moyetie of it, to the court of* France . . . *wherewith the ladies there, now, colour theire haire*" (II, 2). Thus the history of the powder parallels the metempsychoses of Pythagoras. Like Pythagoras' soul, the powder began its career as a gift from Apollo, and in its transmigrations through the goddess of love, the whore of Sparta, and the court ladies of France, it serves to underline the ancient lineage of vanity as a special case of the folly rehearsed in the interlude.

Mosca's opening soliloquy in Act III shows that this excellent counterfeiter is himself, like his master, obsessed by the notion of imitators. His contempt for ordinary parasites suggests that there is a hierarchy of counterfeits, ranging from those who are deeply and essentially false (like himself) to those who practice falsity out of mere affectation, who are, so to speak, falsely false and therefore, again, at two removes from nature. The shift of scene back to Volpone's house produces still another variation on the theme of mimicry. In order to beguile their master from his boredom, the trio of grotesques stage an impromptu interlude, dominated by Nano, who claims that the dwarf can please a rich man better than the eunuch or the hermaphrodite. The dwarf, explains Nano, is little, and pretty:

Else, why doe men say to a creature of my shape,
So soone as they see him, it's a pritty little ape?
And, why a pritty ape? but for pleasing imitation
Of greater mens action, in a ridiculous fashion?
[III, 3, 11–14]

The first interlude, it may be recalled again, established an identification between folly and the unnatural. The present fragment confirms a further identity between mimicry and deformity, already hinited at in the mountebank scene where Nano appeared as the zany, or mimic, to Volpone's Scoto. At this point one may represent some of the relationships in the play diagrammatically as follows:

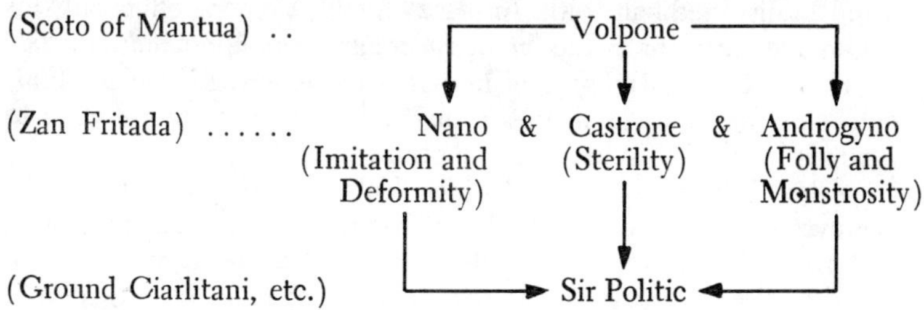

Since Volpone has (presumptively at least) sired both Nano and Androgyno, and since Sir Pol combines the chief attributes of both, one may, with the aid of the diagram, infer what is already emerging plainly in context, that mimicry itself is something monstrous and abnormal. It is unnatural for baboons and apes and parrots to counterfeit human behavior. It is equally unnatural for men to imitate beasts. It argues a perversion of their essential humanity. It is not for nothing, then, that the chief characters of the play fit into one zoölogical classification or another. As men, they duplicate the habits of beasts; as beasts, they brutishly travesty humanity. They belong to the genus *monster*—half man, half brute—that order of fabulous creatures whose common denominator is their unnaturalness, their lack of adherence to whatever category of being nature has assigned them.

The arrival of Lady Would-be, fuming and fussing over her toilet, and snapping at her servingwomen, provides still a further object-lesson in falsity. Here, as so often in Jonson, face physic symbolizes the painted surface hiding the rotten inside; the cosmetic care of the face signifies the neglect of the soul. It signifies equally an attachment to appearances, an incapacity to look beyong the superficies of life or truth. The powder which Volpone offered to Celia and which Celia did not need, since her beauty was of the platonic sort that revealed the purity of her soul, might with more justice have been given to Lady Would-be, and it is Lady Would-be who deserves the epithet of "lady *vanitie*" (II, 5, 21) with which Corvino, in his jealous tantrum, has stigmatized Celia.

The scene between Lady Would-be and Volpone serves partly as a burlesque of the parallel scenes in Act I between Volpone and the other *captatores*.[7] All the essential ingredients of those scenes reappear, but scrambled and topsy-turvy. Once again Volpone feigns sickness, but this time it is in self-defense against the terrible oratory of Lady Would-be. Once again remedies are prescribed, but

7. Legacy-hunters [*Editor*].

these are neither Corbaccio's deadly opiate nor his *aurum palpabile* offered as pump-priming, but the fantastic assortment of old wives' restoratives dredged up from Lady Would-be's infernal memory. She rains down the hailstones of her learning on the helpless Volpone, until the arch-rogue, anticipating the judgment to be rendered on him in Act V, cries out in despair: "Before I fayned diseases, now I haue one" (III, 4, 62). The whole episode is a rich application of the principle of comic justice. If in the final denouement Volpone suffers the penalty of vice, here he reaps the more ludicrous reward of his own folly. Trapped by Lady Would-be's rhetoric, itself a consequence of his own scheming, he is finally driven to pronounce himself cured. But the talking machine grinds on, and only Mosca's happy notion of exciting her jealousy, as he has previously aroused Corvino's, and for the same purpose, succeeds in getting rid of her. As her contribution to Volpone's coffers, she leaves behind a wrought cap of her own making; this forms a suitably ridiculous contrast to the treasures earlier offered by Corvino, Corbaccio, and Voltore.

The same scene serves as introduction and comic distortion of the scene immediately to follow between Volpone and Celia. Celia's unearthly purity is made to seem even more unearthly by its contrast to Lady Would-be's lecherousness, this latter apparent in the lady's addiction to cosmetics, in her slips of the tongue, and in her barely disguised sexual overtures. Lady Would-be's attempted seduction of Volpone having been thwarted, the stage is set for Volpone's attempted seduction of Celia. Volpone commences his wooing with a characteristic boast: "I, before / I would haue left my practice, for thy loue," he swears, "In varying figures, I would haue contended / With the blue PROTEVS, or the horned *Floud*" (III, 7, 150–53). Justifiably proud of his powers of disguise, Volpone emphasizes them further by citing a past occasion on which he masqueraded in the ambiguous role of Antinous, Hadrian's favorite. Embarking on an enumeration of the exotic splendors in store for Celia, he reserves as his final inducement the promise that she will participate, with him, in transmutations without end: "Whil'st we, in changed shapes, act OVIDS tales" (the *Metamorphoses*, of course),

> Thou, like EVROPA now, and I like IOVE,
> Then I like MARS, and thou like ERYCINE,
> So, of the rest, till we haue quite run through
> And weary'd all the fables of the gods.
> Then will I haue thee in more moderne formes,
> Attired like some sprightly dame of *France*,
> Braue *Tuscan* lady, or proud *Spanish* beauty.
>
> [III, 7, 221–28]

We have already witnessed, in the first interlude, the metempsychosis of folly and, in the powder offered to Celia in Act II, the transmigrations of vanity. Now, as a climax to his eloquence, Volpone rehearses the metamorphoses of lust. Jonson thus endows his central themes with vertical depth in time as well as horizontal extension in space. Folly, vanity, lust, have been, are, will be. At any given moment their practitioners are legion, and often interchangeable.

It is at this point that Celia's refusal crystallizes into a repudiation of folly, vanity, and lust combined and that her behavior contrasts most sharply with that of Lady Would-be. The recollection of Lady Would-be lacquering her face and making indecent advances to Volpone brings into sharper focus Celia's sudden horror at her own beauty, and her plea that her face be flayed or smeared with poison, in order to undo the lust she has aroused. If, for Lady Would-be, the cosmetic art is a necessary preliminary to sexual conquest, its opposite, the disfigurement of the face, becomes for Celia the badge of chastity. Where Lady Would-be strives to adopt Italian vices for her own, Celia's gestures as well as her name demonstrate her alienation from the moral and spiritual province of Venice.

Act IV carries us back into the open street, where Sir Pol, ignorant of the plot developing at Volpone's house, continues babbling of plots in terms which ordinarily have one meaning for him and another for the audience. After a patronizing recital of "instructions" to Peregrine on methods of deportment in Venice, he confides suddenly that his money-making projects need only the assistance of one trusty henchman in order to be put into instant execution. Evidently he is hinting that Peregrine undertake that assignment and thus play Mosca to his Volpone. But Peregrine contents himself with inquiring into the particulars of the plots. The most elaborate of these proves to be a way to protect Venice from the plague by using onions as an index to the state of infection on ships entering the harbor. This mad scheme, with its echo of Volpone's claim to have distributed his *oglio* under official patent to all the commonwealths of Christendom, serves chiefly to remind us again of the moral plague prevailing in Venice and of the incomprehension of that fact on the part of those characters who prattle most about disease and cure.

The ensuing scene parodies the episode in Act II where Corvino discovers his wife in conversation with the mountebank. Just as Corvino interrupts Volpone while the latter is advertising his medicine, so Lady Would-be bursts in on Sir Politic as the knight is dilating on his schemes and projects. As Corvino babbles jealously of lechers and satyrs, so Lady Would-be jabbers of land sirens, lewd harlots, and fricatrices. Corvino beats away the mountebank. Lady

Would-be rails at Peregrine. Both harp on "honor," and both discard that term as soon as it becomes an inconvenience, Corvino when it becomes an obstacle to his plan of inheritance, Lady Would-be when she discovers that Peregrine is no harlot in disguise, but a young gentleman. As for Sir Politic, though he too plays his part in the little impromptu from the *commedia dell' arte*, he remains, unlike Volpone, quite oblivious to the fact. Actually, Sir Pol reenacts not the role of "Signior FLAMINIO," the lover in disguise—that part, however reluctantly assumed, belongs to Peregrine—but the female role, the "FRANCISCINA," guarded by a jealous "PANTALONE *di besogniosi*" (II, 3, 3–8). The confusion of sexes symbolized in Androgyno, in the indiscriminate journeyings of the soul of Pythagoras, in Volpone's masquerade as Antinous, in Lady Would-be's error, as well as in the reversed masculine-feminine roles of Sir Pol and Lady Would-be, contributes its own kind of abnormality to the deformity of the moral atmosphere chiefly figured by the metamorphoses of beasts into men. And if one regards Sir Politic's uxoriousness as a kind of metaphoric emasculation, one may then equate him with Castrone, as he has already been equated with Nano and Androgyno, to make the pattern of mimicry complete.[8]

The fourth-act trial starts with justice and concludes with a perversion of it. The monsters begotten by Volpone, the prodigies and portents that exercised such a hypnotic effect on Sir Pol, now make a lavish and climactic reappearance in the language of the scene. First they designate their proper objects. But as Voltore begins to exercise his baleful rhetoric, the parlance of unnaturalness, appropriate to the guilty, begins to turn against the innocent. Corbaccio disavows his son for "the meere portent of nature"; he is "an vtter stranger" to his loins, a "Monster of men, swine, goate, wolfe, parricide" (IV, 5, 108-11). Finally Lady Would-be arrives, the eternal parrot, to give testimony which virtually clinches the case against Celia:

> Out, thou *chameleon* harlot; now, thine eies
> Vie teares with the *hyaena*. [IV, 6, 2–3]

The beast characters in the play display an unerring faculty for describing the innocent as beasts. Corvino has already called Celia a crocodile, referring to that animal's notorious ability to imitate human tears, and Lady Would-be, though she has her unnatural

8. Actually, Florio's *Worlde of Wordes* (1598) defines *Castrone* not only as "a gelded man," but as "a noddie, a meacocke, a cuckold, a ninnie, a gull" (quoted in Rea, p. 144). Any of these will serve as accurate epithets for Sir Pol, with the possible exception of "cuckold," and if that designation does not fit it is not owing to any lack of effort on Lady Would-be's part. [Florio's *Worlde of Words* is an Italian-English dictionary. "Noddie," "meacock," "ninnie," and "gull" are all variant ways of calling a man a fool.—*Editor*.]

natural history somewhat confused, invokes another creature famous for its powers of mimicry, the hyena, as well as the even more versatile chameleon.

The juxtaposition of the hyena and the chameleon reminds one that there is a point at which the ideas of metamorphosis and mimicry coalesce. The chameleon, shifting its colors to blend itself with its environment, indulges in a highly developed form of protective mimicry. Volpone carries the principle a step further. He goes through his restless series of transformations not as a shield but in order to prey on his own kind, to satisfy something in his unnatural nature which demands incessant changing of shape and form. But knavery and credulity, mimicry and metamorphosis, alike reflect aspects of one basic folly: the folly of becoming, or trying to become, what one is not, the cardinal sin of losing one's nature. Only Bonario and Celia, of all the creatures in the play, never ape others, never change their shapes, never act contrary to their essential natures. And in the unnatural state of Venice it is chiefly they, the unchanging ones, who are attacked as hyenas and chameleons.

Volpone, in short, may be read as a comic restatement of a theme familiar in Shakespeare's plays of the same period, the theme of disorder. Order figures here not as social balance or political hierarchy, but as a principle of differentiation in nature whereby each species, each sex, maintains its separate identity. With the loss of clear-cut divisions between man and beast, between beast and beast, between male and female, all creatures become monsters. The basic structure of nature is violated. The astronomical portents discussed earlier by Sir Pol and Peregrine in connection with animal prodigies reflect the upheaval of the cosmos itself following the degeneracy of man.

But by this time, justice has become as monstrous as its participants, and the *avocatori* close the session piously intoning their horror at the unnaturalness of Celia and Bonario. Volpone's last and greatest hoax is destined to set the balance of nature right again. It starts, however, with one more act of unnaturalness. Volpone, a monster, who therefore occupies no fixed place in the order of created beings, feigns death and thus symbolically demonstrates his lack of status. One by one the inheritors file in for the legacy, only to find that they have been duped by Mosca.

The first to receive her dismissal is Lady Would-be. Having made overtures to both Mosca and Volpone, she is in a position to be summarily blackmailed. "Goe home," advises Mosca, "and vse the poore sir POL, your knight, well; / For feare I tell some riddles; go, be melancholique" (V, 3, 44–45). Thus the learned lady who knew so many bizarre ways of curing Volpone's melancholy now has the opportunity to treat herself for the same ailment, and so do her colleagues. The value of this scene consists partly in its inflicting comic justice on the legacy-hunters before the *avocatori* render their sterner legal judgments, just as Volpone has already, in Lady Would-be, met a comic foretaste of the retribution which overtakes him at the *Scrutineo*. But since the parrot, for all its shrillness, remains less venal than the crow or vulture, the untrussing of Lady Would-be goes no further. In the realm of the severer truths, vice and folly may appear as different aspects of a similar spiritual malaise. In the realm of poetic justice, however, a distinction continues to be practiced. Vice, which is criminal and attacks others, must suffer public correction, whereas folly, a disease essentially self-destructive, may be dealt with in private and without the assistance of constituted authority. For Lady Would-be it is sufficient that, awakened to some sense of her own folly, she vows to quit Venice and take to sea "for physick."

And so with her preposterous knight, Sir Politic, whom we now encounter for the last time, the victim of a private plot which performs the same service of mortification for him that the final trial scene does for Volpone. The *mercatori* enlisted by Peregrine perform the office of the *avocatori* who pronounce sentence on Volpone, and the divulging of the pathetic notebook, with its scraps from playbooks, becomes the burlesque substitute for the exposure of Volpone's will, in bringing on the disaster. Peregrine, echoing Voltore's suggestion that Volpone be tested on the strappado, warns Sir Pol that his persecutors will put him to the rack. Whereupon the knight remembers an "engine" he has designed against just such emergencies, a tortoise shell. And to the disgust of three hundred years of literary critics he climbs into the ungainly object, playing possum after the fashion of his model, Volpone, who has feigned death in the foregoing scene. The arrival of the merchants brings on the catastrophe:

MER. 1: What
Are you, sir? PER: I' am a merchant, that came heere
To looke vpon this tortoyse. MER. 3: How? MER. 1: S^t^. MARKE!
What beast is this? PER: It is a fish. MER. 2: Come out, here.
PER: Nay, you may strike him, sir, and tread vpon him:
Hee'll beare a cart.

[V, 4, 62–67]

Eventually, by stamping and poking, they goad Sir Politic out of his exoskeleton. The scene thus rephrases in a vein of broadest tomfoolery the essential question of the play: "What kind of creatures are these?" Throughout the action one has seen beasts aping men and men imitating beasts on the moral and psychological levels. Here the theme of mimicry reaches its literal climax in an episode of farce, where the most imitative of the characters puts on the physical integument of an animal and the hired pranksters stand about debating its probable zoölogical classification. The final unshelling of the tortoise, a parallel to the uncasing of the fox in the last scene, arouses further comment from the merchants:

Mer. 1: 'Twere a rare motion, to be seene, in *Fleet-street!*
Mer. 2: I, i'the terme. Mer. 1. Or *Smithfield*, in the faire.
[V, 4, 77–78]

Sir Politic, thus, so inquisitive about prodigies, has finally become one himself, a specimen fit to be housed among the freaks of Smithfield or amid the half-natural, half-artificial curiosities of Fleet Street. With the knowledge that he is destined to become a victim of the kind of curiosity he himself has exhibited, his disillusionment is complete and his chastisement effected. He and Lady Would-be, the only survivors, in this play, of Jonson's earlier humor characters, are now "out of their humor," purged of their imitative folly by the strong medicine of ridicule.[9]

Public punishment, however, awaits the actors of the main plot. Jonson is not sporting here with human follies like those of the Would-be's, but dealing grimly with inhuman crimes. The names of fabulous monsters, basilisks and chimeras, continue to echo in our ears as the catastrophe approaches, fastening themselves at last onto their proper objects, the conspirators in the game of *captatio*. Voltore's spurious fit spells out in concrete theatrical terms his unnatural status and the lesson pointed by the *avocatori*: "These possesse wealth, as sicke men possesse feuers, / Which, trulyer, may be said to possesse them" (V, 12, 101–2). The delivery of Volpone's substance to the *Incurabili* places a final and proper valuation on the medicinal powers of gold. The imprisonment of Volpone is specifically designed to give him the opportunity to acquire in reality the diseases he has mimicked and the leisure to ponder the accuracy of his own text: to be a fool born is a disease incurable. Voltore and Corbaccio are henceforth to be secluded from their fellow-men like the unnatural specimens they are, while Corvino's animality is to be the object of a public display more devastating than Sir Politic's brief masquerade as a tortoise.

Thus on successive levels of low comedy and high justice, the monsters of folly and the monsters of vice suffer purgation, exposed as the sort of misshapen marvels they themselves have chattered about so freely. The relative harmlessness of Sir Pol's downfall serves to differentiate his folly from the viciousness of the Venetians, but the many parallels between his catastrophe and theirs warn us that his kind of folly is sufficiently virulent after all, is

9. Several of Jonson's early plays involve purging characters of their "humors," i.e., correcting an imbalance of their basic dispositions [*Editor.*]

closely related to graver sins, and if it persists in imitating them, must ultimately fall under the same condemnation.

If these observations are accurate, it should be clear in what sense the subplot of the Would-be's is relevant to the total structure of *Volpone*. Starting from a contrast between Italian vice and English folly, Jonson personifies the latter in two brainless English travelers, makes their folly consist chiefly in mimicry of Italian vice, and Italian vice itself, in its purest form, consist of the more comprehensive form of mimicry we have termed "metamorphosis," thus bringing the two aspects of evil together into the same moral universe and under a common moral judgment; with the use of the beast fable he binds the two together dramatically, and by the distribution of poetic justice he preserves the distinction between them. Each of the episodes involving the Would-be's, including the much despised incident of the tortoise, thus serves a definite dramatic purpose, and one may conclude, then, that the subplot adds a fresh dimension and a profounder insight without which *Volpone*, though it might be a neater play, would also be a poorer and a thinner one.

HARRY LEVIN

Jonson's Metempsychosis†

Ben Jonson often professed to be more concerned with men than with monsters. Yet the chorus of *Volpone* is a trio of deformed servants—Nano, the dwarf, Castrone, the eunuch, and Androgyno, the hermaphrodite. If Mosca is Volpone's parasite, they are Mosca's "Sub-parasites." And their monstrous antics seem almost innocent, by comparison with the moral deformities of Voltore, Corbaccio, and Corvino. At intervals throughout the play, most spectacularly in the second act, they appear as the zanies of their mountebank master, and reduce his intrigues to their own level of absurdity. In the first act, after the expository monologue in praise of gold and before the introduction of the three fortune-hunters, they perform a limping jig, which only Volpone could find "'very, very pretty" and only Mosca could claim credit for inventing.[1] Out of hand it is easiest to consider this scene an excrescence; a French critic would even call for its suppression.[2] So painstaking a playwright as Jonson, however, deserves to have his intentions more sympathetically

† From *Philological Quarterly*, XXII, 3 (July, 1943), pp. 231–39. For the purposes of this edition, some of Levin's notes have been abridged or omitted. References to the plays included in this edition have been changed to conform with the scene and line numbering used here; references to other plays and poems are to the edition of Herford and Simpson (Oxford, 1925–41).

1. *Volpone*, I. ii, 63–66.

2. Maurice Castelain, *Ben Jonson, l'homme et l'oeuvre* (Paris, 1907), p. 301.

explored; more recent scholarship would look to this very episode for a statement of his theme.[3] In that case it must be admitted that the development is clearer than the theme, for the passage in question is undeniably obscure. I venture to suggest that this obscurity may be clarified by relating the subject of Mosca's interlude to the thought of Jonson's age—which was also Donne's.

Mosca's interlude has already been related to literary tradition. Jonson's commentators, always more sensitive to classical echoes than to vernacular allusions, have debated at length whether "*the false pase of the verse*" should be classified as anapestic, spondaic, dactylic, or the *pes proceleusmaticus.*[4] Actually it is a four-stress doggerel couplet, which had been one of the commonest measures in the old English moralities, and was to be the meter of the Vice's speeches in *The Devil is an Ass.*[5] In the latter play it is a vehicle for bringing old-fashioned ideas of good and evil to bear upon the new commercial enterprises of the Jacobean period. In *Volpone* too, though somewhat more deviously, the play-within-the-play presents the point of view from which the play itself is about to launch its satirical attack. The classics, as usual, supply the ammunition for Jonson's contemporary satire. It was Horace, in the fifth poem of his second book of satires, who first coupled the beast-fable of the fox and the crow with the *captatio*, the Roman practice of legacy-hunting. It was Petronius, in the last surviving chapters of the *Satyricon*, who showed how this morbid pursuit might be organized into a series of swindling operations on a grand scale. And it was Lucian, in several of his *Dialogues of the Dead*, who sketched out the motives and cross-plots of Jonson's *dramatis personae.*[6]

The Lucianic influence has penetrated to the core of the drama. With the exception of a few details, which seem to have been gathered from Diogenes Laertius,[7] Mosca's interlude is based on Lucian's *Gallus*, otherwise known as *The Dream*. But Jonson, who had great Latin and less Greek, was most familiar with this dialogue in the translation of Erasmus.[8] It was largely *The Praise of Folly*, as Professor Rea has pointed out, which served as the intermediary between *Volpone* and Jonson's classical sources. Thus Jonson's dedi-

3. J. D. Rea, ed., *Volpone, or the Fox* (Yale Studies in English, LIX) (New Haven, 1919), pp. xxvii, 194.

4. John Upton, *Remarks on Three Plays of Ben Jonson* (London, 1749), pp. 8–10. Cf. William Gifford, ed., *The Works of Ben Jonson* (1816), III, 174–175n. [The *"pes proceleusmaticus"* is a metrical foot of infrequent occurrence in the classical tongues: it makes use of four short accents—*Editor.*]

5. E.g., *The Devil Is an Ass*, I, i. 44–53.

6. Horace, Petronius, and Lucian were classical satirists, respectively of the first century B.C. and the first and second centuries A.D. All mention the theme of fortune-hunting, but only Lucian develops it extensively, *Dramatis personae*: cast of characters [*Editor*].

7. Diogenes Laertius wrote in the second century A.D. ten simple-minded but amusing books on the lives of the philosophers; Lucian's *Gallus* is also known by a third title, *The Cock*, because it deals with a rooster who says he was once Pythagoras [*Editor*].

8. Rea, pp. xvii–xix, 160, 161. See also C. R. Thompson, *The Translations of Lucian by Erasmus and St. Thomas More* (Ithaca, N.Y., 1940).

catory epistle to the two universities borrows whole paragraphs from the *Epistola Apologetica* of Erasmus to Sir Thomas More.[9] The English comedy is more preoccupied with economic abuses; the Latin satire is more encyclopedic in its reduction of all would-be wisdom to the various forms of foolishness. Nevertheless Erasmus begins by making Folly the daughter of the god of riches, and ends by providing Jonson with instances of chicanery to adapt to his favorite formula of "The Cheater Cheated." Folly's most eloquent ironies, on the pleasures of being a fool, find an English paraphrase in the song, "Fooles, they are the onely nation."[1] The serious business which follows is designed to exhibit what happens "When wit waites upon the foole." The song completes the interlude because Folly—before arguing that fools are happier than so-called wise men —has argued that animals are happier than human beings, and has taken Lucian's *Dream* as her example:

> Therefore I shall never praise enough that cock, who was really Pythagoras: though but one, he had been all things—a philosopher, a man, a woman, a king, a subject, a fish, a horse, a frog, I think even a sponge—and he came to the conclusion that no creature is more miserable than man; for all the others are satisfied with their natural limitations, but man alone strives to go beyond the bounds proper to his station.[2]

Jonson might have found in *The Dream* what Shakespeare was finding in Lucian's *Timon*, an object-lesson in the blessings of poverty and the corruptions of wealth. "The Coblers cock," by crowing at the wrong moment, arouses its indigent master from his dream of a luxurious banquet, at which he has been celebrating the inheritance of a vast fortune. In response to the cobbler's surprise at hearing a bird speak, the cock confesses that it harbors the reincarnate soul of Pythagoras, and offers an account of its successive transmigrations—a series of Cynic jibes against the other philosophers. This has become a *locus classicus*[3] on the subject of metempsychosis, and is instanced by Robert Burton, along with a parallel passage from Ovid's *Metamorphoses*, as a far-fetched proof of the immortality of the soul.[4] Now the main theme of *Volpone* is a comic distortion of a theme that is tragic in *Hamlet* and tragicomic in *The Malcontent*,[5] the pervasive Jacobean theme of disinheritance. Volpone's suitors, cheated of their legacies in the fifth act, are

9. A phrase from this letter, which has not been pointed out, may well have suggested the character of Mosca. To justify his learned trifling Erasmus cites a number of literary burlesques, including two of Lucian's *The Fly* and *The Parasite*. This association (*"muscam et parasiticam Lucianus"*) tends to support the view * * * that Mosca's eulogy of parasites at the beginning of the third act is also founded on Lucian.

1. Rea, pp. 161–63.
2. Erasmus, *The Praise of Folly*, tr. H. H. Hudson (New York: Random House [Modern Library]), pp. 46–47 [*Editor*].
3. Classic passage [*Editor*].
4. A. R. Shilleto, ed., *The Anatomy of Melancholy* (London, 1893), I, 186.
5. Written by John Marston and John Webster, this play was produced in 1604 [*Editor*].

adumbrated in Lucian's cobbler, rudely awakened from his illusory banquet. Here, then, is the connexion between the interlude and the play, but the connexion has been left out of the interlude, which concentrates on metempsychosis. The cobbler has disappeared altogether, and Pythagoras has migrated from the cock to the epicene person of Androgyno, who seems to be both a fool and a hermaphrodite, and therefore an appropriately grotesque habitation for a soul that has already lodged in so many different men and monsters.

Jonson has added one significant new stage to this protean career. The last incarnation has been spent as

> *. . . a very strange beast, by some writers cal'd an asse;*
> *By others, a precise, pure, illuminate brother,*
> *Of those deuoure flesh, and sometimes one another:*
> *And will drop you forth a libell, or a sanctified lie,*
> *Betwixt euery spoonefull of a natiuitie-pie.*[6]

In other words, as a Puritan. Fully endowed at this stage with all the gluttony and hypocrisy that Jonson associates with the type, he will eat a Christmas pie as readily as Zeal-of-the-Land Busy, but will refuse to call it by its popish name, just as Ananias later avoids mentioning the mass by speaking of "*Christ-tide*."[7] "*Pythagoreans* all!" as Truewit exclaims, exasperated by the rule of silence in the household of the puritanical Morose.[8] This intermixture of Puritanism and Pythagoreanism does not seem to have been peculiar to Jonson. Shakespeare himself, in a farcical scene, condemns Malvolio to imprisonment until such time as he shall hold the opinion of Pythagoras: "That the soul of our grandam might happily inhabit a bird."[9] But Jonson had his own reasons for accusing the Puritans of shifting their coats as often as the soul of Pythagoras changed its shape, and of "Counting all old doctrine heresie." Jonson, "in these dayes of reformation," was for twelve years a convert to Roman Catholicism.[1] *Volpone* was written at the height of this period, and in the immediate aftermath of the Gunpowder Plot. Sir Politick Wouldbe, with his genius for spying plots everywhere and his fear lest a tinder-box explode the Arsenale, is a caricature of the kind of suspicions from which Jonson must have been suffering. His own relations with the chaplain to the Venetian ambassador may have suggested the locale of the play,[2] though Venice would seem to be an inevitable background for sharp mercantile practice and effete Italianate luxury.

The best chance of finding out anything about Jonson's personal

6. *Volpone*, I, ii, 42–46.
7. *The Alchemist*, III, ii. 43.
8. *Epicoene*, II, ii.
9. *Twelfth Night*, IV, ii, 54–65. "happily": haply, by chance.

1. "Ben Jonson's Conversations with William Drummond of Hawthornden," in Herford and Simpson, I, 139.
2. See Jonson's letter to Lord Salisbury, H&S, I, 202.

preoccupations is to turn to his criticism of his fellow poets. In 1619, thirteen years after the composition of *Volpone,* he paid his publicized visit to Hawthornden. While there he frequently expressed, in his conversations with William Drummond, his fascination and exasperation with the poetry of John Donne. He went out of his way to explain a poem which has continued to perplex Donne's admirers and critics:

> the Conceit of Dones transformation or μετεμΨυχοσις was that he sought the soule of that Aple which Eva pulled, and thereafter made it the soule of a Bitch, then of a sheewolf & so of a woman. his generall purpose was to have brought in all the bodies of the Hereticks from ye soule of Cain & at last left it in ye body of Calvin. of this he never wrotte but one sheet, & now since he was made Doctor repenteth highlie & seeketh to destroy all his poems.[3]

Jonson's explanation does not quite fit the poem that has come down to us entitled *The Progress of the Soul* and dated 1601. "This sullen Writ," though it remains a fragment, was the most ambitious poem that Donne had composed by that date. Its fifty-two ten-line stanzas could scarcely have been crowded into a single sheet. They specifically mention Mahomet and Luther, but not Calvin; instead, they darkly intimate that the soul's final destination is to be the body of Queen Elizabeth.[4] Small wonder that Donne left his project unfinished. A prefatory epistle, *obscurum per obscurius*[5] refers the reader to "the Pithagorian doctrine," and pursues the subject back to a vegetable state, when it may have been served at some "lascivious banquet."[6] The poem itself, in picaresque fashion, traces the wandering spirit of heresy from the Garden of Eden through various flora and faunas as far as Cain's wife. Much discursive satire, Professor Grierson has noted, is directed against women and courtiers—like the contemporaneous satire of *Hamlet.*[7] Hamlet, it should also be noted, is obsessed with a perverse notion of metempsychosis: his conceits follow the progress of a king through the guts of a beggar, and dwell upon the metamorphoses of Alexander and Caesar.[8] Indeed, Hamlet's cynical belief that "there is nothing either good or bad but thinking makes it so"[9] is the burden of Donne's abrupt conclusion:

> Ther's nothing simply good, nor ill alone,
> Of every quality comparison,
> The onely measure is, and judge, opinion.[1]

3. "Conversations with Drummond," H&S, I, 136.
4. H. J. C. Grierson, ed., *The Poems of John Donne* (Oxford, 1912), I, 297.
5. Explaining the dark by the darker [*Editor*].
6. *The Poems of John Donne*, I, 294.
7. *Ibid.*, II, 219.
8. *Hamlet,* IV, iii, 32–33; V, i, 224–39.
9. *Hamlet,* II, ii, 255–57.
1. Grierson, I, 316.

The Progress of the Soul bears all the stigmata of having been written in what Donne's biographer calls "a feverish crisis of intellectual pride."[2] Having lost the Catholic faith of his fathers a few years before, he was not to find a haven in the Anglican church until he had spent several years in spiritual limbo. The Essex *débâcle,* which moved Cyril Tourneur to elaborate the tortuous allegory of *The Transformed Metamorphosis,*[3] must have prompted Donne to express his profound sense of the transformation from one age to another. The scheme of his poem was probably derived from Lucian's *Dream.*[4] But in Donne's mind, the mind of a skeptical theologian, Lucian's fantasy was only the point of departure for his own explorations into the problem of evil. Rashly he undertook to account for the maladies of the new age by following them back, through a chain of being, to the original fruit of the tree of knowledge. To reconcile the values of this world with the ethics of traditional Christianity, or to justify the ways of men to God—these were problems as insoluble as to tell where all past years are, or who cleft the devil's foot. The logical solution was an ethical relativism, which accepted the Reformation as a necessary evil and regarded the aging queen as neither good nor bad but great. This was "greatness" in Fielding's sense of the word,[5] a greatness closely allied to roguery. But it was not Donne's ultimate solution; from the pulpit of his later years we find him reverting to "this transmigration of sin." So Dr. Faustus, having denied absolute sin, recognized its existence in his final outcry, and prayed to be reborn as a brutish beast: "Ah *Pythagoras metemsucosis.*"[6]

Satire springs from some perception of the disparities between the real and the ideal. Hence the satirist's position is always shifting; sooner or later he must embrace one extreme or the other. Donne, in choosing religion, chose the idealistic extreme. Jonson chose realism, and *Volpone* marks this crucial phase of his development. Possibly Mosca's interlude was written before the rest of the play, like the puppet-show in *Bartholomew Fair.*[7] At all events, it is a product of the mood that produced *The Progress of the Soul.* That mood had not abated from 1601 to 1605, but Jonson's animus against the Puritans had extended to the professions of medicine and law, and to the whole world of finance. On the relations

2. Edmund Gosse, *The Life and Letters of John Donne* (London, 1899), I, 141. p. 58.
3. Robert Devereux, second Earl of Essex, after standing high in Queen Elizabeth's favor, fell into deep disgrace in 1599 and was executed in 1601: Cyril Tourneur's obscure allegorical satire is said to mirror this event [*Editor*].
4. M. P. Ramsay, *Les doctrines médiévales chez Donne* (Oxford, 1917), p. 58.
5. C. M. Coffin, *John Donne and the New Philosophy* (New York, 1937), p. 252. [Fielding's sense of the word "great" is that implied by his title, *Jonathan Wild the Great*: Wild was a great, an extraordinary, thief—*Editor*]
6. C. F. T. Brooke, ed., *The Works of Christopher Marlowe* (Oxford, 1910), p. 193.
7. Gifford, IV, 509 n.

between early protestantism and modern business, which social historians have been calling to our attention, he is a shrewd and voluble witness. In *Volpone* he is still willing to sacrifice comedy to morality; he is still embittered by the failure of the tragedy of *Sejanus* and the mood of the "Comicall Satyres"—his three unsuccessful attempts to make the theatre an instrument of reform and put John Marston out of his humour. *Volpone* is Jonson's last experiment in poetic justice, and his own reservations about the final arraignment are confirmed by Dryden's criticism.[8] In his next play, *Epicoene*, the mood is relaxed; the earlier satire is burlesqued in a legalistic *dénouement*; and the scene is set, for the first time, in no "fustian countrie" but on English soil. All that was needed, before the consummate realism of *Bartholomew Fair*, was to naturalize the Italian comic types of *Every Man in his Humour*, and to announce in the prologue to *The Alchemist*:

> Our *Scene* is *London*, 'cause we would make knowne,
>   No countries mirth is better then our owne.
> No clime breeds better matter, for your whore,
>   Bawd, squire, impostor, many persons more,
> Whose manners, now call'd humors, feed the stage.[9]

In some respects *The Alchemist* is a realistic version of *Volpone*. The germ of the mature comedy is the mountebank scene, where Sir Politick is gulled by Volpone's medicine-show, and Peregrine comments:

> But *Alchimy*,
> I neuer heard the like: or BROUGHTONS bookes.[1]

Here, reading between the lines, we can see the plot already hatching that will pit the jargon of the alchemists against the rival cant of the Puritans, and confuse everything—in the nick of time—with the ravings of the Reverend Hugh Broughton. The motive power of *The Alchemist*, the device of the philosophers' stone, may likewise have been furnished by Erasmus. It is a greater hoax than Volpone's will, for the sinister magnificence of *Volpone* is supposed to be real, even though it is never inherited by the Venetian conspirators. Whereas the pretensions of *The Alchemist* are spurious from the start, and the London conspirators—delineated by a more tough-minded realist—are a familiar and threadbare pack of coney-catchers and gulls. Sir Epicure Mammon, perhaps, is a gull extraordinary. His very name is a compound of luxury and wealth. But the only fortune that he inherits is the legacy of Lucian's cobbler—the harsh reality that wakes him from his golden visions and epicurean banquets. He is a voluptuary, like Volpone, and he speaks the same

8. W. P. Ker, ed., *Essays of John Dryden* (Oxford, 1926), I, 73.

9. Prologue to *The Alchemist*, lines 5–9.

1. *Volpone*, II, ii.

magnificent language; but unlike Volpone, who is a great rogue, Mammon is a great fool. Yet Mammon is the more comic figure, and it may be argued that *The Alchemist* is the greater comedy. If folly and roguery are the two staples of Jonsonian comedy, then the follies of *Volpone* are too sinister, while the rogueries of *The Alchemist* are comparatively genial. By the time that he was ready to revise *Every Man in his Humour*, Jonson has learned that the true function of comedy is "to sport with humane follies, not with crimes."[2] As his powers of realistic depiction came into full play, he gradually relinquished his loudly proclaimed moral purposes. Vainly Face apologizes for the amoral ending of *The Alchemist*. Shakespeare and Donne had discovered that good and evil, in this world, are matters of opinion. So, finally, had Jonson. Mankind was subdivided, it now seemed, not into good men and bad, but into rogues and fools. Consequently, the rôle of the comic playwright was not to judge but to observe. After *Volpone*, it may be said that Jonson's genius underwent a metempsychosis of its own and, having died with a stern satirist, was reborn in a genial observer.

JOHN DRYDEN

Examen of the *Silent Woman*†

To begin first with the length of the action, it is so far from exceeding the compass of a natural day that it takes not up an artificial one.[1] 'Tis all included in the limits of three hours and an half, which is no more than is required for the presentment on the stage. A beauty perhaps not much observed; if it had, we should not have looked on the Spanish translation of *Five Hours* with so much wonder.[2] The scene of it is laid in London; the latitude of place is almost as little as you can imagine: for it lies all within the compass of two houses, and after the first act in one. The continuity of

2. Prologue to *Every Man in His Humour*, line 24.

† Dryden (1631–1700) was the most influential poet and critic of the second half of the 17th century. From his *Essay on Dramatic Poesy* (1668) we present a set piece. Dryden's *Essay* is a four-way dialogue among friends who, as they drift down the Thames in a barge, spend the cool and quiet evening talking about literature. They are gentlemen, not scholars or divines; the literature they discuss is for and about gentlemen; and it is natural that one of them turns his attention to *Epicoene*. The speaker is called Neander in the dialogue: the name means New Man, and Neander represents Dryden himself. His "Examen" is a casual but incisive account of a play, nearly sixty years old, and the product of very different circumstances, but which for its neatness of construction and elegance of wit seemed to Dryden an important precursor of the comedies of his own day. (All footnotes are by the editor.)

1. The speaker knows about the doctrine of the "unities" of time, place, and action; though he isn't rigid about them, he does value tight construction.

2. In 1663 Sir Samuel Tuke had adapted from the Spanish of Calderón a play called in English *The Adventures of Five Hours*.

scenes is observed more than in any of our plays, excepting his own *Fox* and *Alchemist*. They are not broken above twice or thrice at most in the whole comedy;[3] and in the two best of Corneille's plays, the *Cid* and *Cinna*, they are interrupted once apiece. The action of the play is entirely one; the end or aim of which is the settling Morose's estate on Dauphine. The intrigue of it is the greatest and most noble of any pure unmixed comedy in any language; you see in it many persons of various characters and humors, and all delightful: as first, Morose, or an old man, to whom all noise but his own talking is offensive. Some who would be thought critics say this humor of his is forced: but to remove that objection, we may consider him first to be naturally of a delicate hearing, as many are to whom all sharp sounds are unpleasant; and secondly, we may attribute much of it to the peevishness of his age, or the wayward authority of an old man in his own house, where he may make himself obeyed; and this the poet seems to allude to in his name *Morose*. Besides this, I am assured from divers persons that Ben Jonson was actually acquainted with such a man, one altogether as ridiculous as he is here represented. Others say it is not enough to find one man of such an humor; it must be common to more, and the more common the more natural. To prove this, they instance in the best of comical characters, Falstaff;[4] there are many men resembling him; old, fat, merry, cowardly, drunken, amorous, vain, and lying. But to convince these people, I need but tell them that humor is the ridiculous extravagance of conversation, wherein one man differs from all others. If then it be common, or communicated, to many, how differs it from other men's? or what indeed causes it to be ridiculous so much as the singularity of it? As for Falstaff, he is not properly one humor, but a miscellany of humors or images, drawn from so many several men: that wherein he is singular is his wit, or those things he says *præter expectatum*,[5] unexpected by the audience; his quick evasions when you imagine him surprised, which, as they are extremely diverting of themselves, so receive a great addition from his person; for the very sight of such an unwieldy, old, debauched fellow is a comedy alone. And here, having a place so proper for it, I cannot but enlarge somewhat upon this subject of humor into which I am fallen. The Ancients had little of it in their comedies; for the τὸ γελοῖον[6] of the Old Comedy, of which Aristophanes was chief, was not so much to imi-

3. "Continuity of scenes" was a structural principle much prized in the 17th century; the playwright started a new scene not with a whole new set of characters, but, by adding new characters and dismissing old ones, led into new actions. Jonson is by no means as careful of this principle in *Epicoene* as, for example, in the third act of *The Alchemist.*

4. Shakespeare's fat knight was so popular that he had to be brought back in several different plays.

5. Beyond expectation.

6. "The ridiculous" (Aristotle, *Poetics*, V). Old Comedy was invidious and personal; Dryden seems to be following here in the footsteps of Jonson himself; see above, p. 388.

tate a man as to make the people laugh at some odd conceit which had commonly somewhat of unnatural or obscene in it. Thus, when you see Socrates brought upon the stage,[7] you are not to imagine him made ridiculous by the imitation of his actions, but rather by making him perform something very unlike himself: something so childish and absurd as, by comparing it with the gravity of the true Socrates, makes a ridiculous object for the spectators. In their New Comedy, which succeeded,[8] the poets sought indeed to express the ’ηθος, as in their tragedies the πάθος of mankind. But this πάθος contained only the general characters of men and manners; as old men, lovers, serving-men, courtesans, parasites, and such other persons as we see in their comedies; all which they made alike: that is, one old man or father, one lover, one courtesan, so like another as if the first of them had begot the rest of every sort: *ex homine hunc natum dicas*.[9] The same custom they observed likewise in their tragedies. As for the French, though they have the word *humeur* among them, yet they have small use of it in their comedies or farces; they being but ill imitations of the *ridiculum*, or that which stirred up laughter in the Old Comedy. But among the English ’tis otherwise:[1] where by humor is meant some extravagant habit, passion, or affection, particular (as I said before) to some one person, by the oddness of which he is immediately distinguished from the rest of men; which being lively and naturally represented, most frequently begets that malicious pleasure in the audience which is testified by laughter; as all things which are deviations from common customs are ever the aptest to produce it: though, by the way, this laughter is only accidental, as the person represented is fantastic or bizarre; but pleasure is essential to it, as the imitation of what is natural. The description of these humors, drawn from the knowledge and observation of particular persons, was the peculiar genius and talent of Ben Jonson; to whose play I now return.

Besides Morose, there are at least nine or ten different characters and humors in *The Silent Woman*, all which persons have several concernments of their own, yet are all used by the poet to the conducting of the main design to perfection. I shall not waste time in commending the writing of this play, but I will give you my opinion that there is more wit and acuteness of fancy in it than in any of Ben Jonson's. Besides, that he has here described the conversation of gentlemen in the persons of True-Wit and his friends, with

7. Socrates was ridiculed in Aristophanes' *The Clouds*; it is the same example used by Jonson, of the philosopher hoisted aloft in a basket, to think airy thoughts.

8. I.e., followed. New Comedy dealt with types, not individuals. Dryden's contrast between *ethos* and *pathos* is one between "character" and "suffering."

9. "You would say this man was born from that"; from Terence (2nd century B.C.), *Eunuch*, line 460.

1. Dryden's description of "humors" defines accurately enough the common usage of the term.

more gaiety, air, and freedom, than in the rest of his comedies. For the contrivance of the plot, 'tis extreme elaborate, and yet withal easy; for the λύσις,[2] or untying of it, 'tis so admirable that, when it is done, no one of the audience would think the poet could have missed it; and yet it was concealed so much before the last scene that any other way would sooner have entered into your thoughts. But I dare not take upon me to commend the fabric of it, because it is altogether so full of art that I must unravel every scene in it to commend it as I ought. And this excellent contrivance is still the more to be admired because 'tis comedy, where the persons are only of common rank, and their business private, not elevated by passions or high concernments as in serious plays. Here every one is a proper judge of all he sees; nothing is represented but that with which he daily converses: so that by consequence all faults lie open to discovery, and few are pardonable. 'Tis this which Horace has judiciously observed:

> creditur, ex medio quia res arcessit, habere
> sudoris minimum; sed habet Comedia tanto
> plus oneris, quanto veniæ minus.[3]

But our poet, who was not ignorant of these difficulties, had prevailed himself of all advantages; as he who designs a large leap takes his rise from the highest ground. One of these advantages is that which Corneille has laid down as the greatest which can arrive to any poem, and which he himself could never compass above thrice in all his plays; viz. the making choice of some signal and long-expected day, whereon the action of the play is to depend. This day was that designed by Dauphine for the settling of his uncle's estate upon him; which to compass, he contrives to marry him. That the marriage had been plotted by him long beforehand is made evident by what he tells True-Wit in the second act, that in one moment he had destroyed what he had been raising many months.

There is another artifice of the poet which I cannot here omit, because by the frequent practice of it in his comedies he has left it to us almost as a rule: that is, when he has any character or humor wherein he would show a *coup de maistre*,[4] for his highest skill, he recommends it to your observation by a pleasant description of it before the person first appears. Thus, in *Bartholomew Fair* he gives you the pictures of Numps and Cokes, and in this those of Daw, Lafoole, Morose, and the Collegiate Ladies; all which you hear described before you see them. So that before they come upon the

2. The resolution (*lusis*) is the disclosure of Epicoene's true identity.

3. "Comedy's easy, people say; its actions flow
From common life. It's harder, though;
You get no breaks from viewers."
[Horace, *Epistles*, II, 1, 168–70; tr. R.M.A.]

4. Master-stroke.

stage you have a longing expectation of them, which prepares you to receive them favorably; and when they are there, even from their first appearance you are so far acquainted with them that nothing of their humor is lost to you.

I will observe yet one thing further of this admirable plot: the business of it rises in every act.[5] The second is greater than the first, the third than the second, and so forward to the fifth. There too you see, till the very last scene, new difficulties arising to obstruct the action of the play; and when the audience is brought into despair that the business can naturally be effected, then, and not before, the discovery is made. But that the poet might entertain you with more variety all this while, he reserves some new characters to show you, which he opens not till the second and third act. In the second, Morose, Daw, the Barber, and Otter; in the third, the Collegiate Ladies: all which he moves afterwards in by-walks, or under-plots, as diversions to the main design, lest it should grow tedious, though they are still naturally joined with it, and somewhere or other subservient to it. Thus, like a skilful chess-player, by little and little he draws out his men, and makes his pawns of use to his greater persons.

If this comedy, and some others, of his were translated into French prose (which would now be no wonder to them, since Molière has lately given them plays out of verse which have not displeased them[6]), I believe the controversy would soon be decided betwixt the two nations, even making them the judges. But we need not call our heroes to our aid; be it spoken to the honor of the English, our nation can never want in any age such who are able to dispute the empire of wit with any people in the universe. And though the fury of a civil war, and power for twenty years together abandoned to a barbarous race of men, enemies of all good learning, had buried the Muses under the ruins of monarchy; yet, with the restoration of our happiness, we see revived poesy lifting up its head, and already shaking off the rubbish which lay so heavy on it. We have seen since his Majesty's return[7] many dramatic poems which yield not to those of any foreign nation, and which deserve all laurels but the English. I will set aside flattery and envy: it cannot be denied but we have had some little blemish either in the plot or writing of all those plays which have been made within these seven years (and perhaps there is no nation in the world so quick to discern them, or so difficult to pardon them, as ours): yet if we can persuade ourselves to use the candor of that poet who (though the most severe

5. I.e., the tension continually increases.

6. One of Molière's first and greatest successes, *Les Précieuses Ridicules* (1659), was in prose: Dryden's implication that in 1668 this was a recent innovation is quite wrong.

7. I.e., since the restoration of Charles II in 1660.

of critics) has left us this caution by which to moderate our censures:

> ubi plura nitent in carmine, non ego paucis
> offendar maculis;[8]

if, in consideration of their many and great beauties, we can wink at some slight and little imperfections; if we, I say, can be thus equal to ourselves, I ask no favor from the French. And if I do not venture upon any particular judgment of our late plays, 'tis out of the consideration which an ancient writer gives me: *vivorum, ut magna admiratio, ita censura difficilis*:[9] betwixt the extremes of admiration and malice, 'tis hard to judge uprightly of the living. Only I think it may be permitted me to say that as it is no lessening to us to yield to some plays, and those not many, of our own nation in the last age, so can it be no addition to pronounce of our present poets that they have far surpassed all the Ancients, and the modern writers of other countries.

IAN DONALDSON

A Martyr's Resolution†

* * *

In following Scaliger's[1] account of the various stages in which a well-made play unfolded—Protasis, Epitasis, Catastasis, and Catastrophe—Dryden was in fact using a traditional division and terminology which Jonson had used before him.[2] Like Jonson, Dryden recognized the importance of the temporal factor in a play, of 'what happens next'. Jonson's interest in this factor becomes all the more evident if we contrast his methods with those of Marlowe. In watching Jonson's plays we seldom experience the uncertainty about

8. "When, in a poem, beauty's everywhere,
I do not mind a few spots here and there." [Horace, *Art of Poetry*, line 351; tr. R.M.A.]

9. Dryden translates the Latin immediately in the text; his source is the Roman historian Velleius Paterculus, who lived under Tiberius (*Historia romana* II, 36).

† From Ian Donaldson, *The World Upside Down* (Oxford University Press, 1970), pp. 24–45. Donaldson begins by contrasting Dryden's view of *Epicoene* as expressed in the "Examen" (above, pp. 422–27), with more modern views. Dryden places primary emphasis on the plot as the unifying element of the play; the modern critics see the unity as flowing from the centrality of certain themes, and deny that there's any real unity of plot at all. Donaldson's argument is, in effect, that Dryden was right in principle when he tried to define a leading action for the play, though mistaken in saying what that leading action actually was. (Some of Donaldson's notes have been shortened or deleted.)

1. Julius Caesar Scaliger, influential neo-Latin polymath, wrote a book on poetry which appeared in 1561, three years after his death. Protasis, Epitasis, Catastasis, and Catastrophe are Greek terms for introduction, development, climax, and conclusion [*Editor*].

2. *The Magnetic Lady* (1632), "Chorus" between Acts I and II; and elsewhere.

the value to be attached to 'what happens next' that we may when watching, say, the second part of *Tamburlaine the Great*;[3] the sequence of scenes is deliberate and significant, as Probee and the Boy continually insist to Damplay as they watch the action of *The Magnetic Lady*:

> . . . our parts that are the Spectators, or should heare a *Comedy*, are to await the processe, and events of things, as the *Poet* presents them, not as wee would corruptly fashion them. . . . Stay, and see his last *Act*, his *Catastrophe*, how hee will perplexe that, or spring some fresh cheat, to entertaine the *Spectators*, with a convenient delight, till some unexpected, and new encounter breake out to rectifie all, and make good the *Conclusion*. [*Chorus* between Acts IV and V: 10–13, 27–31]

And perhaps nowhere in Jonson's work (unless it be in *The New Inn*) do we find a greater 'cheat' than in the last scene of *Epicoene*, when Dauphine discloses, to the surprise not only of the other characters but also—one must assume—of the audience too, the real sex of Mistress Epicoene. It is a 'cheat' which some critics have held to be a flaw in the play, but it is not made simply for the sake of a cheap narrative surprise. First, there is the effect which the disclosure creates: a stunned silence. Morose, paradoxically one of the most garrulous characters of the play, simply leaves the stage without saying a word; the College ladies are for once 'mute, vpon this new *metamorphosis*' (V. iv.), and even Truewit and Clerimont are temporarily dumbfounded. It is the last and most spectacular of a series of twists and surprises in the play which have produced either a tumult of noise (e.g. Mistress Otter descending upon her husband in IV, ii) or utter silence (e.g. Dauphine's first entrance in I. ii, Truewit's invasion of Morose II. ii., and his return to tell Dauphine and Clerimont of the apparent success of his interview II. iv). The forward movement of the plot, with its surprises and 'cheats', constantly enacts what Heffner sees as the main 'symbol' of the play, noise, and its opposite, silence.[4] Plot and symbol can hardly be separated.

Furthermore, the 'cheat' of Act V of *Epicoene* finally makes evident an important fact about Dauphine: his secrecy. The idea of secrecy runs right through the play, even to the final speech where Truewit recommends to the favours of the College ladies the boy who has played the part of Mistress Epicoene, vouching for his 'secrecie'. It is the secrecy of so many of the characters of the play which results in the profusion of 'plots' (a word constantly used,

3. In the second part of Marlowe's *Tamburlaine the great* (1590), the audience is primarily concerned with the question: How long will Tamburlaine get away with it? [*Editor*].

4. Ray L. Heffner, Jr., "Unifying Symbols in the Comedy of Ben Jonson," in *English Stage Comedy*, ed. W. K. Wimsatt, Jr. (New York, 1954), pp. 74 ff.

and having obvious dramatic connotations): Morose's plot against his nephew, and the various plots of the three conspirators, Truewit, Clerimont, and Dauphine, against Morose, the Otters, Daw and La-Foole, and the College ladies; drawing together these various plots is the masterplot of Jonson himself. The three conspirators conceal aspects of their own plots from each other, and each is secretive to a different degree: Dauphine, the most guarded, considers Clerimont 'a strange open man' (I. iii), and tells him that Truewit's 'franke nature' is 'not for secrets' (I. iii). The contrast between 'secret' people and 'open' people is central to the play. *Epicoene*, like Jane Austen's *Emma*, is partly an examination of the way in which certain kinds of people enjoy what Emma calls 'disguise, equivocation, mystery' (Ch. LIV), and about the various degrees to which people are outspoken or reserved, and why.[5] Jonson's theme, like Miss Austen's, could only be fully explored by the means of a fairly complicated and surprising plot. 'Plot' is thus not simply a vehicle for theme, but actually becomes part of the theme itself. One cannot properly examine the one without the other.

And yet even if this is granted, Heffner's main objection still remains. His emphasis on the importance of theme or symbol seems to arise very largely out of the fact that there are simply too many plots in the play to make it possible to accept Dryden's view that 'the action of the Play is entirely one; the end or aim of which is the settling of Morose's estate on Dauphine'.[6] It is, he says,

> much more accurate to consider *The Silent Woman* as consisting not of a Terentian plot depending upon the delayed completion of a single, well-defined objective but of a number of separable though related actions which are initiated and brought to completion at various points in the play and are skilfully arranged to overlay and interlock,[7]

and he goes on to show how each act in the play (except the first) is centred on a separate major action. First, it should be remembered—for Heffner does, I think, allow this fact to recede—that Dryden himself goes to pains to indicate the variety as well as the unity of the play, its luxuriance of 'by-walks, or under-Plots' which distinguishes it from the single, relentlessly purposeful plots of the French dramatists; it is even possible that in defining the way in which a play can have both variety of plot and unity of action Dryden was remembering a passage in Jonson's *Discoveries*.[8]

Once this is said, however, it must be admitted that the simple financial motive which Dryden sees as the single driving force of the

5. *Emma* (1816) is a novel of matrimonial managing, mistakes, and incomprehension [*Editor*].
6. See above, p. 423 [*Editor*].
7. Heffner, op. cit., pp. 77–78.
8. Herford and Simpson, VIII, 645 ff. [*Editor*].

play is hardly prominent and seems in itself insufficient to account for the elaborately inventive actions of Morose's tormentors. Unlike *Volpone* or *The Alchemist*, *Epicoene* does not seem to be a play about the acquisition of money. It seems more accurate to see it as a play about the persecution of a misanthrope. The central fact of the play is Morose's misanthropy: his disinheriting of Dauphine is merely one of several manifestations of this characteristic. Even before it is known that Morose has disinherited his nephew, Truewit and Clerimont discuss and ridicule Morose's 'disease', his hatred of noise. Throughout the play this obsession is presented not simply as something that can conveniently be exploited by the wits to recover Dauphine's inheritance, but as a monstrous and ludicrous 'humour', patently symbolic of Morose's misanthropy, and ripe for punishment. There is also Morose's conviction that he is martyred by Dauphine and his company, whom he sees as 'authors of all ridiculous acts, and moniments are told of him'; it is this which persuades them that he must be made a martyr in fact: 'Thou art bound in conscience, when hee suspects thee without cause, to torment him'; it gives 'law of plaguing him' (I. ii.). Later Truewit tells Morose that he is persecuted for nothing but his 'itch of marriage'; the general absurdity of an old misanthrope seeking a young silent wife is as prominent as the specific consequences of disinheritance. (Clerimont declares that Truewit himself is driven on simply by a 'courteous itch' for interference: tormentor is as irrational as victim.) There is one more curious and significant fact about Morose; his hatred of festival and of festival days. 'He was wont to goe out of towne euery satterday at ten a clock, or on holy-day-eues', says Clerimont (I. i.); 'He would haue hang'd a Pewterer's prentice once vpon a shrouetuesdaies riot, for being o' that trade, when the rest were quit' (I. i.). Truewit's first plan for plaguing Morose is to draw up a false almanac so that Morose will not know which are festival days and which are not: 'and then ha' him drawne out on a coronation day to the *tower*-wharfe, and to kill him with the noise of the ordinance' (I ii.). And later in the play Morose is to turn on his persecutors and describe them as the very children of festival: 'Rogues, Hellhounds, *Stentors*, out of my dores, you sonnes of noise and tumult, begot on an ill *May*-day, or when the Gallyfoist is a-floate to *Westminster!* A trumpetter could not be conceiu'd but then!' (IV. ii.). Each of these obsessions and acts of Morose emphasizes his absurd isolation. The leading action of the play is the breaking down of that isolation, and the punishment of misanthropy. This is effected principally through the means of a viciously high-spirited festive ceremony, which Morose is invited to endure with 'a martyrs resolution' (III. vii.). The motives of the wits are neither as simple nor as sympathetic as Dryden thought; nor is the play as 'gay' and as 'genial' as it is usually said to be.[9]

If this new 'end or aim' is accepted, the play's various 'by-walks, or under-Plots' begin to take on a new relevance. For all the action of the play after III. iv takes place within Morose's house: the exposure of Captain Otter to his wife, and the fooling of Daw, La-Foole, and the College ladies are not simply diversions but also additional torments for Morose, forming a continuous invasion of his privacy and driving him to take refuge at the top of his house, from which he descends at unexpected moments to terrify the revellers below; driving him eventually to 'run out o'dores in's night-caps (IV. v.). The calm insolence with which the guests take over Morose's house ('I like your couches exceeding well: we'll goe lie, and talke there' (IV. iv.)) is not unlike that of Subtle and Face in *The Alchemist* as they take over Lovewit's house; in each case the fact that the guests almost forget that the house is not their own adds to the surprise and terror as the master returns. The episode with Daw and La-Foole in Act IV is rather feeble in itself, but succeeds because of its placing. The centre of attention switches temporarily from Morose—'wee'll let him breathe, now, a quarter of an houre, or so' (IV. iv.)—to the multiple plans against Daw, La-Foole, and the ladies, and the highest point of excitement is in fact reached when Morose enters unexpectedly at the end of IV. vi with the abandoned swords of the two knights drawn in either hand. Moments such as these, which are placed with great skill in the latter part of the play, continually remind us of the way Morose is being harassed. There are no reminders of the fact that Dauphine wants his money.

The invasion of Morose's house acts out in yet another way the theme of secrecy and openness, of things done in private and things done in public. As so often in Jonson's plays, the setting takes on an almost metaphorical quality; the setting of a house or room, with its door safely shut or thrown dangerously open. In the first scene of the play Clerimont and his page discuss why the door of the Collegiates' house should be shut to Clerimont but open to the page, who is free to make himself at home with the most private things of the ladies, their beds, their gowns, their perukes. While this discussion is proceeding, Clerimont is himself dressing, with his own door evidently standing open, for Truewit enters abruptly and unannounced in the middle of the boy's song. Truewit reprimands Clerimont for spending too much of his time in private, and tells him

9. M. Castelain described *Epicoene* as 'la plus gaie des comédies de Jonson' (*Ben Jonson, L'Homme et Oeuvre* (Paris, 1907), p. viii); for J. Palmer it was 'the most genial of the works of Jonson—the freak of a happy mood' (*Ben Johnson* (London, 1934), p. 176); C. H. Herford remarked upon its 'gaiety' (*Works*, ed. cit. ii. 76).

he should give himself more to public entertainments (I. i.), just as he tells Dauphine later in the play that he must 'leaue to liue i' your chamber then a month together vpon AMADIS *de Gaule*, or *Don* QVIXOTE, as you are wont; and come abroad where the matter is frequent, to tiltings, publique showes, and feasts, to playes, and church sometimes . . .' (IV. i.). The contrast between the two ways of life, public and private, is continued in the rest of this first scene. The lady of Clerimont's song is powdered and perfumed as if '*going to a feast*'; her 'public' face and dress Clerimont distrusts, Truewit defends. Women may practise any art, declares Truewit,

> . . . to mend breath, clense teeth, repaire eye-browes, paint, and professe it.
>
> *Clerimont*. How? publiquely?
>
> *Truewit*. The doing of it, not the manner; that must bee priuate. Many things, that seeme foule i' the doing, doe please, done. A lady should, indeed, studie her face, when wee thinke shee sleepes; nor, when the dores are shut, should men bee inquiring, all is sacred within, then. [I. i.]

What is under discussion is not simply the propriety of using Art to mend Nature, but also the propriety of doing certain things in public and others in private, 'when the dores are shut'. This is the first of several such discussions in the play, discussions which are really simply airings of opposite views which seldom reach resolution or agreement; the effect here is to create a general feeling of uncertainty about these proprieties, and about the whole relation of public and private life. This feeling is continued a little later on in the description of La-Foole, who shatters these proprieties with a gay, lunatic abandon: 'He will salute a Iudge vpon the bench, and a Bishop in the pulpit, a Lawyer when he is pleading at the barre, and a Lady when shee is dauncing in a masque, and put her out. He do's giue playes, and suppers, and inuites his guests to 'hem, aloud, out of his windore, as they ride by in coaches' (I. iii.). And when La-Foole speaks of his relatives, the La-Fooles of Essex and the La-Fooles of London—'They all come out of our house' (I. iv.)—his words seem to pick up one of the leading metaphors of the play; the prolific family of La-Fooles seems to spill out of a house as real as the one in which the solitary Morose confines himself.

The action of the sub-plots, as well as accentuating Morose's suffering, repeats in a minor key the major theme of the play, as private actions are exposed to public gaze. Thus Daw and La-Foole receive their kicks and nose-tweakings 'in priuate' as it seems to them, but in fact before an unseen audience of the College ladies, brought in to serve 'a priuate purpose' of Truewit. The two men are closeted at the very moment when Morose is forced to run out of his house, and their privacy is ludicrously threatened by Truewit in a way that recalls the invasion of Morose's privacy: 'Sir AMOROVS, there's no standing out. He has made a *petarde* of an old brasse pot, to force your dore' (IV. v.). Mavis's private letter to Dauphine (beginning '*I chose this way of intimation for priuacie*') is seized and read aloud by Clerimont. Captain Otter confesses—in private, as he thinks, but actually in his wife's hearing—what his wife does when she thinks *she* is in private. The drinking-match between Daw and La-Foole organized earlier in this scene by Captain Otter with his various tankards—his 'bull, beare, and horse'—and described (as Herford and Simpson note) in the terminology of bull- and bear-baiting, seems to bring the popular holiday entertainments of Southwark into the very house of Morose.[1]

We may notice in passing the way in which Captain Otter's liberties are usually described in 'holiday' terms. The calendar days loathed by Morose are the days of Otter's glory. Before their marriage, Mrs. Otter has declared, it was only at holiday entertainments that Captain Otter enjoyed his brief moments of distinction: 'Were you euer so much as look'd vpon by a lord, or a lady, before I married you: but on the Easter, or Whitson-holy-daies? and then out at the banqueting-house windore, when NED WHITING, or GEORGE STONE, were at the stake? (III. i.). And now they are married we are told that it is only on holidays that Captain Otter regains his liberty; at such times 'No Anabaptist euer rail'd with the like licence' (III. ii.). This licence Mrs. Otter describes in terms of holiday freedom: 'Neuer a time, that the courtiers, or collegiates come to the house, but you make it a *shrouestuesday*! I would haue you get your *whitsontide*-veluet-cap, and your staffe i' your hand, to intertaine 'hem; yes introth, doe' (III. i.). Appropriately, the day on which the action of the play takes place, on which Otter gains his liberty and Morose loses his, is a festive day. It is one of the four annual quarter-days, on which La-Foole is having his 'quarter-feast' (II. iv.); it is also, of course, the day of Morose's 'wedding'.

The tormenting of Morose is carried out by the simple device of moving La-Foole's feast and his guests to Morose's house to celebrate the wedding. At the centre of the play is this festive invasion by the public world—rowdy, licentious, and apparently sociably united, though in fact divided by individual envy and plotting—of the private world of Morose; a world he would have silent, subjected to discipline, and solitary. The invasion exposes the absurdi-

1. Bull- and bear-baiting were the common amusements of the London populace; being rowdy and noisy scenes, they were carried on in the suburbs of Southwark, where the Globe Theatre stood [*Editor*].

ties not only of the private world of Morose, but also of the public world of the revellers; it exposes, too, the disharmony that exists *between* the private and the public worlds. This invasion begins in III. v, with Morose crying in vain for his doors to be barred, Epicoene insisting they be left open, and Truewit counselling Morose to 'giue the day to other open pleasures, and jollities of feast, of musique, of reuells, of discourse: wee'll haue all, sir, that may make your *Hymen* high, and happy' (III. v.). These 'open pleasures' reach their climax in III. vi and III. vii. The nature and significance of this revelry is best understood in relation to certain festive and wedding customs common in Jonson's time; it is in the light of these we must now examine these central scenes.

That Jonson was interested in such customs may be inferred from his own detailed notes to his Twelfth Night wedding masque of 1606, *Hymenaei* (written for the marriage of the daughter of the Earl of Suffolk, Frances Howard, with the Earl of Essex), where he drew on a variety of classical sources to explain the origin and nature of Roman wedding customs, some of which survived into his own time;[2] and again from *A Tale of a Tub* where he declared his authorities were:

> *old Records*
> *Of antique Proverbs, drawne from* Whitson-Lord's,[3]
> *And their Authorities, at* Wakes *and* Ales,
> *With countrey precedents,* and *old* Wives *Tales.* [*Prologue,* 7–10]

The celebrations in *Epicoene* begin as a kind of parody of a courtly wedding masque, such as *Hymenaei,* and rapidly change into something else: the form of a popular ceremony used to deride ridiculous or irregular marriages.

Lady Haughty begins by asking—at Truewit's prompting—why this wedding is not being celebrated with all the traditional customs and 'markes of solemnitie': 'Wee see no ensignes of a wedding, here; no character of a brideale; where be our skarfes, and our gloues? I pray you, giue 'hem vs. Let's know your brides colours, and yours, at least' (III. vi.). Lady Haughty is asking, in short, for the wedding to be celebrated in the courtly style; Jonson himself had written three years earlier an epithalamion and a masque for Frances Howard's marriage; in his masque for her

2. ***Hymenaei*** **was a very learned masque indeed—the audience couldn't stand more than one verse of Jonson's epithalamion (marriage song), but in the printed text he gave the whole thing, with a condescending pardon for those who, at the performance, had been unable to relish it [*Editor*].**

3. **Whitsun-ales are parish festivals celebrating Pentecost, the "birthday of the church." Lord of such a festival would be a man of years and prudence, learned in local tradition and popular lore [*Editor*].**

remarriage in 1614, A *Challenge at Tilt,* he was to introduce the device of the married couple's colours. But this travesty marriage can have only a travesty epithalamion (promised by Sir John Daw) and a travesty masque; a kind of wild antimasque, now led in by Clerimont:

> *Clerimont.* By your leaue, ladies. Doe you want any musique? I haue brought you varietie of noyses. Play, sirs, all of you.
>
> *Morose.* O, a plot, a plot, a plot, a plot vpon me! This day, I shall be their anvile to worke on, they will grate me asunder. 'Tis worse than the noyse of a saw.
>
> *Musique of all sorts.*
>
> *Clerimont.* No, they are haire, rosin, and guts. I can giue you the receipt.
>
> *Truewit.* Peace, boyes.
>
> *Clerimont.* Play, I say.
>
> *Truewit.* Peace, rascalls. You see who's your friend now sir? Take courage, put on a martyrs resolution. Mocke downe all their attemptings, with patience. 'Tis but a day, and I would suffer heroically. [III. vii.]

Jonson has engineered the events of this and preceding scenes brilliantly to this climax (lost in Colman's later rearrangement);[4] it is a climax beyond language, producing—like the explosion in Act IV of *The Alchemist*—sheer noise. 'Noyse' is a term for a band of musicians (Tobie Turfe in A *Tale of a Tub* commands 'all noises of *Finsbury,* in our name' to celebrate his daughter's wedding (I. iv. 50–1)), but the word reverts here to its general meaning as well: 'varietie of noyses' is made as Clerimont's musicians strike up discordantly and independently to produce '*Musique of all sorts*', against which the short quarrel of Clerimont and Truewit proceeds. The incident quite obviously carries symbolic implications; and to understand those implications one is tempted by the general masque-like atmosphere of this part of the play to a comparison with Jonson's use of discordant music in his masques,[5] in particular with the '*kind of contentious Musique*' raised in the early part of *Hymenaei* by the four Humors and four Affections which threaten to disturb the ceremonies.[6] These, Jonson explains, 'were *tropically* brought in, before *Marriage*, as disturbers of that *mysticall bodie*,

4. George Colman the elder was an 18th-century dramatist who patched and adapted many earlier plays, including *Epicoene*, to suit the taste of his own times. [*Editor*].

5. *Love Freed from Ignorance and Folly*, 2; *The Masque of Queens*, 29–36; *Time Vindicated*, 220, etc. Crites in *Cynthias' Revels* (V. v. 11–12) likens the courtiers to 'a sort of jarring instruments, / All out of tune'. The symbolism of marital discord appears again in the introductory description of the uxorious Deliro in *Every Man Out of His Humour,* who wakes his wife every morning with 'villainous-out-of-tune-music'.

6. The Four Humors and Four Affections (Passions) which threaten to disturb the wedding in *Hymenaei* are a kind of embryonic anti-masque. Their appearance is "tropical," i.e., metaphorical, as tropes or figures of speech, not active threats [*Editor*].

and the *rites*, which were *soule* vnto it; that afterwards, in *Marriage*, being dutifully tempered by her *power*, they might more fully celebrate the happiness of such as liue in that sweet *union*, to the harmonious lawes of Nature and Reason' (Note on l. 112). And in *Hymenaei* this discordant music gives way to 'sacred concords', concords which, of course, never enter the jarring and disunited world of *Epicoene*.

The symbolic nature of the incident in *Epicoene* under discussion would not, I think, have been lost on an unlearned audience at Whitefriars.[7] For the ceremony to which Morose is subjected is also very similar, both in its form and its occasion, to certain festive ceremonies which that audience almost certainly would have known. That which it most resembles is the *charivari* or *chevauchée*, described as follows by Cotgrave in his Dictionary of 1632: 'A public defamation, or traducing of; a foule noise made, blacke *Santus*[8] rung, to the shame, and disgrace of another; hence, an infamous (or infaming) ballade sung, by an armed troup, under the window of an old dotard married, the day before, unto a young wanton, in mockery of them both.' The 'foule noise' in question was usually made by the beating of kettles, marrow-bones, and cleavers. E. K. Chambers explains the various 'offences' which could be punished by this ceremony: 'A miser, a henpecked husband or a wife-beater, especially in May, and on the other hand, a shrew or an unchaste woman, are liable to visitation, as are the parties to a second or third marriage, or to one perilously long delayed, or one linking May to December.'[9] There was a similar kind of musical cacophony in the related ceremony of the skimmington, in which the victims, often represented by neighbours or by effigies, were tied back-to-back on a horse and accompanied through the streets by a crowd of revellers playing discordantly on musical instruments.[1] The primary purpose of such ceremonies as the *charivari* and the skimmington was to punish through ridicule what was thought to be the absurdest of marital aberrations, the dominance of the wife:

When wives their sexes shift, like hares
And ride their husbands, like night-mares . . . [*Hudibras*, II. ii. 705–6]

The *charivari*-like scene in *Epicoene* in fact celebrates (though all the celebrants are not aware of the fact) the larger theme of sexual reversal in the play, so well discussed by Edward Partridge in *The*

7. *Epicoene* was first performed at the Whitefriars Theatre. The audience there was likely to be less erudite than that for a masque [*Editor*].

8. A black *Sanctus* would be the climax of a black mass [*Editor*].

9. E. K. Chambers, *The Mediaeval Stage* (Oxford 1903), i. 154.

1. The skimmington is described in detail by Samuel Butler in *Hudibras*, Part II, Canto ii, 565 ff. [*Hudibras* is a burlesque satire on Puritanism, very popular in the late 17th century—*Editor*.]

Broken Compass (London, 1958), and as such has application not just to Morose and Epicoene, but also to the Otters and to the Collegiates. The wider purpose of such ceremonies as the *charivari* seems to have been to punish social eccentricity in its different manifestations: miserliness, misanthropy, refusal to join in holiday revelry (the ceremonies took place on holidays or on the days immediately surrounding a wedding). Morose, being a miser, a misanthrope, an enemy of holiday revelry, and 'an old dotard married [it seems] unto a young wanton' is a natural victim for such a visitation. His punishment, like the different punishment of Pinnacia Stuffe, the tailor's wife in *The New Inn*, can only be fully understood by reference to the traditions of contemporary festive customs. That such traditions were found obscure even in the eighteenth century is evident from Thomas Davies's comments upon the play's revival in 1752: '. . . the frequent allusions to forgotten customs and characters render it impossible to be ever revived with any probability of success. To understand Jonson's comedies perfectly, we should have before us a satirical history of the age in which he lived.'[2]

At many points *Epicoene* reminds one of *The Merchant of Venice*; to Shylock music is 'vile squealing' and 'shallow fopp'ry' (II. v. 30, 35), as to Morose discourse itself, is 'harsh, impertinent, and irksome' (II. i.); Shylock shuts his casements against the sounds of revelry as Morose tries to bar his doors against the wedding guests. That discourse, music, and revelry are the things that traditionally draw men together needs no pointing out; but what is conspicuously absent in *Epicoene* is any equivalent to the Belmont scenes in *The Merchant of Venice*, any equivalent to the 'concord of sweet sounds' of which Lorenzo speaks (v.i.84), or of the 'sacred concords' which come in *Hymenaei* as masque replaces antimasque. The play ends not as comedy traditionally does, in marriage, but in divorce. It is notable that when in *The Old Bachelor*[3] Congreve takes over this idea of a fifth act 'divorce'—and the verbal echoes of *Epicoene* are clear as Heartwell cries for a release from Silvia—he removes the powerful Jonsonian feeling of continuing disharmony and isolation by allowing the play to close with the conventional promises of marriage; Bellmour will marry Belinda, and Vainlove, Araminta. Jonson's ending is uncompromising and harsh. George Colman in his adaptation of the play in 1776 apparently wanted, like Congreve, to temper this harshness when he cut Dauphine's last stinging sentence to his uncle: 'Now you may goe in and rest, and be as priuate as you will, sir. I'll not trouble you, till you trou-

2. *Dramatic Miscellanies* (London, 1784), ii. 101–2.

3. Written in 1693 by William Congreve (1670–1729), master, in English, of the comedy of manners [*Editor*].

ble me with your funerall, which I care not how soone it come' (v. iv.). 'Privacy' could not be more contemptuously restored. Morose may now look forward to the ultimate and only privacy that can be obtained, that of the grave; after his 'wedding', his funeral will be the next and only occasion to draw people together again on his behalf. The final isolation of Morose may bring to mind the words of Sir John Daw's madrigal (II. iii.):

No noble vertue ever was alone,
But two in one—

words which seem to echo those which Jonson gave to 'Truth' in the Barriers of *Hymenaei*:

Know then, the first *production* of things
Required *two*, from mere *one* nothing springs . . . [724–25]

What the revelry of the play 'celebrates', indeed, is a complex and pervasive notion of isolation and disunity, the opposite qualities to those which wedding revelry should celebrate; to those qualities, in fact, celebrated in *Hymenaei*. As D. J. Gordon's excellent study of that masque shows,[4] *Hymenaei* celebrates the perfect union of soul and body and of their humours and affections; of individual and individual, family and family, kingdom and kingdom, and of the divine plan itself. Private and public virtues are celebrated together, because private and public worlds are seen to be in perfect harmony with each other. Outward emblems—the 'show' of the masque, the colours and costumes of the masquers, the very bodies of the married couple—are perfect indexes of inward grace in the spirit of the masque and the masquers. 'Peace' extends outwards from the marriage of two individuals to that of their families and of the different parts of the kingdom, and to King James's peaceful policy abroad; a peace likened to that of Christ himself.[5] In *Epicoene* there is no such harmonious union between public and private worlds, between outward appearance and inward truth, between individual and individual; instead of peace, there is 'strife and tumult', 'disease', and isolation.

Comparison of the themes of stage play and masque suggests, finally, the possibility of comparing the nature of the decorum

4. '*Hymenaei*: Ben Jonson's Masque of Union', *Journal of the Warburg and Courtauld Institutes*, viii (1945), pp. 107–45.

5. The actual outcome of the marriage celebrated in this masque was, of course, less happy. Gifford was in fact reminded by the 'divorce' scene of *Epicoene* of the real-life divorce of Essex: 'If it were not ascertained beyond a doubt that the *Silent Woman* appeared on the stage in 1609, four years at least prior to the date of that most infamous transaction, it would be difficult to persuade the reader that a strong burlesque of it was not here intended.' *The Works of Ben Jonson*, ed. W. Gifford (London, 1816), iii. 485–86 [The divorce proceedings which so scandalized Gifford involved Lady Essex (who had meanwhile had an affair with Sir Robert Carr) obtaining an annulment from her husband on the grounds of his impotence—*Editor*.]

which controls and gives unity to each work. The 'matter' of Jonson's Court masques is normally appropriate to the special nature of the festive days upon which they were presented, as we have in part already seen—Christmas, Twelfth Night, Shrovetide, May Day, etc. As I suggested in the last chapter, this kind of occasional appropriateness is not confined to the masques. *Cynthia's Revels,* for instance, designed for presentation at Court on Twelfth Night, 1601, takes an occasion of Court revels as its theme; its appropriatness to the day it celebrates is as obvious as that of, say, *Time Vindicated to Himself and to His Honours.* As Jonson's stage plays, unlike his masques, were intended for repeated performance, such exact occasional appropriateness as that in *Cynthia's Revels* or, say *Christmas His Masque* was not always possible. But it seems not without significance that the action of several of Jonson's avowedly 'popular' plays takes place upon a holiday, and is appropriate to the holiday spirit. This is true, for instance, of *Bartholomew Fair, The New Inn,* and A *Tale of a Tub,* as well as of *Epicoene.* The popular, festive aim of *Epicoene* is acknowledged (not without irony) by Jonson in the Prologue:

> Our wishes, like to those make publique feasts
> Are not to please the cookes taste, but the guests.

The play is festive in mood, and depicts a festive occasion; a quarter-day feast[6] merging with a wedding. In her treatment of Morose, Epicoene seems to be claiming both the traditional liberties of a bride upon her wedding-day, and the traditional holiday liberties of which Pan speaks in Jonson's May Day *Entertainment at Highgate* (1604):

> The young Nymph, that's troubled with an old man,
> Let her laugh him away, as fast as she can. [239–40]

A similar wedding 'licence' (to use Jonson's own pun) falls unexpectedly to Grace Wellborn in *Bartholomew Fair,* the occasion of which is both her wedding-day and a holiday, St. Bartholomew's Day; Awdrey Turfe in A *Tale of a Tub* enjoys similar freedoms on her St. Valentine's Day wedding-day, when—in Tobie Turfe's phrase—'All things run *Arsie-Varsie;* upside downe' (III. i. 2). In each of these plays, as in *The New Inn,* the action seems to be confined to one day, not simply because this was what the classical laws required, but because one day was also the duration of the 'laws' of holiday. Hence Dryden's observation about Jonson's 'making choice' in *Epicoene* 'of some signal and long-expected day, whereon the action of the play is to depend'[7] begins to take on an additional sig-

6. Sir John Daw's feast is in honor of his "quarter-day," when he collects his rents [*Editor*].

7. Cf. above, p.425.

nificance. At the end of this 'signal and long-expected day' Morose's torments will be over, and he may live as 'priuate' as he pleases:

> Take patience, good vncle. This is but a day, and 'tis well worne too now. [IV. iv.]

> Take courage, put on a martyrs resolution. Mocke downe all their attemptings, with patience. 'Tis but a day, and I would suffer heroically. [III. vii.]

EDWARD B. PARTRIDGE

The Alchemist†

A poet re-enacts the roles of God and Adam: he creates a world and names the animals. The naming of the animals in Jonson's plays is, as anyone can recognize, particularly important. So are the epithets, the names which the animals give each other. Mammon calls Face,

> [Subtle's] fire-drake,
> His lungs, his *Zephyrus*, he that puffes his coales,
> Till he firke nature vp, in her owne center. [II. i. 26–28]

This immense blower of bellows blows so hard on the coals of the plot that the whole thing explodes in his face. '*Till it* [the stone], *and they, and all in* fume *are gone.*' The explosion of the furnace in the fourth act is an objectification of what happens to the plot. More than one play of Jonson's seems to work on the same principle of an explosion. Jonson's favorite rhetorical device—hyperbole—radiates into all parts of his plays so that the dialogue trembles on the edge of bombast, the situations move close to burlesque or mock-heroic, the characters become grotesques, and the plot explodes.

This inflation and explosion of the plot is apparent in the way epithets are used throughout *The Alchemist*. In the first scene two motifs are developed side by side; both help to establish the atmosphere of the play. One is the motif of abusive epithets which Subtle, Face, and Dol fling at each other. They call each other rogue, slave, cheater, cut-purse, bawd, and witch. That is all very well; at least all of these fine fellows are human beings. But the vehicles have a wider reference.[1] The impostors are compared to

† From Edward B. Partridge, *The Broken Compass* (New York: Columbia University Press, 1958), pp. 114–20, 139–52, 156–60. (References to plays have been changed to confirm with the line numbering used here, and some of the footnotes have been deleted.)

1. By 'vehicle' Partridge means the imagistic form through which the content ('tenor') of a metaphor is conveyed [*Editor*].

mongrels, scarabs, vermin, curs. These, in their several ways, suggest animals which live in a lower plane than men, or insects which prey on other beings. The dog imagery recurs most often. Dol is a bitch, and Face and Subtle are mastiffs. In short, we are among the snarling animals that live on other beings or each other. We are in that world which Jonson creates so authoritatively—that ambiguous world between the animal and the human.

The second motif in the first scene is developed by Dol's euphemistic epithets for her partners. They are 'gentlemen' (Subtle has just said, 'I fart at thee') and 'masters' who, according to her, ought to have more regard for their reputations. Dol addresses Face, who is in a captain's uniform, as 'Generall', and Subtle as 'Soueraigne'. At the end of the quarrel they are 'My noble Soueraigne, and worthy Generall' (I. i. 172). These royal and martial allusions are absurdly high-flown and comically inappropriate when applied to the impostors and their thievery. After Dol advises them to avoid Don Provost, the hangman, Subtle hails her as 'Royall DOL! / Spoken like CLARIDIANA, and thy selfe!' (I.i. 174–75). The quarrel to Dol is a major historical event: 'Will you vn-doe your selues with ciuill warre?' (I. i. 82). And Dol has grandiose ideas about herself: 'Haue yet, some care of me, o' your *republique*—' (I. i. 110). This republic becomes aristocratic again in the hands of Mammon who compares Dol to 'One o' the *Austriack* princes' (IV. i. 56).

After the first scene and until the next to the last scene almost all of the epithets are inflated. The grandeur of their political and martial references works itself into even casual remarks. Subtle says to himself that 'we must keepe FACE in awe' or he will overlook us 'like a tyranne' (IV. iii. 18–19). Which is more pretentious here—that Face could overlook like a tyrant or that Subtle, even using the royal 'we', could keep anyone in awe? But from the first Subtle has thought of himself as awful.

No, you *scarabe*,
I'll thunder you, in peeces. I will teach you
How to beware, to tempt a *furie*'againe
That carries tempest in his hand, and voice. [I. i. 59–62]

Subtle oscillates somewhere between 'the father of hunger' and a Fury, a bawd and a learned doctor, until he and his '*republique*' escape over the back wall.

Before the whole plot blows up in their faces, this royal trio have almost convinced themselves and certainly convinced others of their importance. To others Face and Subtle are 'your worship'. To Subtle, Face is 'so famous, the precious king / Of present wits' (V. iv. 13–14). Dol, who has been the Queene of Faery' to Dapper, becomes 'Queene Dol' to Face (V. iv. 65). She is in line for a promotion, too, because Face has exacted from Mammon a promise that he will 'make her royall, with the *stone*, / An Empresse' (II. iii. 319–20). When Face plans to marry Dame Pliant, Dol, with fine perception, notes that ''Tis direct / Against our articles' (V. iv. 71–72). Each of the distinct points of a treaty was called an 'article'; 'articles' in the plural meant a 'formal agreement' (*OED*[2]). The word scarcely seems appropriate for the usual agreement between thieves. Subtle, too, is righteously indignant because such a marriage was 'Against the instrument, that was drawne between vs' (V. iv. 81). An 'instrument' was 'a formal legal document whereby a right is created or confirmed, or a fact recorded; a formal writing of any kind, as an agreement, deed, charter, or record, drawn up and executed in technical form so as to be of legal validity' (*OED*). When the word is defined in these high-sounding terms, the pretentiousness of Subtle's language is thrown into relief. Three cozeners agree to rob as many fools as possible; they call this 'drawing up an instrument'. They are thieves, but they throw a specious air of legality over their activities by euphemistic terms, believing in the common fallacy that, if one refers to low things in high words, one raises them legally and aesthetically. In short, Dol, Subtle, and Face speak as though they had set up a commonwealth ('confederacie' to Surly [V. iii. 23]), with an instrument and articles, a King and a Queen, and a whole world of subjects.

Then, suddenly, the bubble bursts. 'Lungs' has blown so hard that he blows the confederacy and himself right out of existence Dol, inflated to the 'Queene of Faerie', shrinks to 'my smock-rampant' (V. iv. 126), whom Face will be glad to recommend to 'mistris AMO' or 'madame *Caesarean*', brothel-keepers. Subtle, who thought of Face as 'the precious king / Of present wits' now finds him a 'precious fiend' (V. iv. 138). As for himself, he is no longer a Fury 'That carries tempest in his hand, and voice', but one who will 'hang my selfe' (V. iv. 146). Subtle has already admitted that he has fallen from his majesty. When Face asked him if he heard the disturbance at the door, he answered, 'Yes, and I dwindled with it' (V. iv. 00). This movement from dogs up to kings, queens, and Furies, and back to rogues and whores reminds one of the final lines of *Volpone* where a similar swelling and bursting of the beasts occur. The circular effect of the epithets is completed, not so much by another quarrel between Face and Subtle (neither has time for a quarrel) as by the chorus of fools who thunder on the door of Love-Wit's house.

MAM. Where is this Colliar?
SVR. And my Captaine FACE?

2. **Oxford English Dictionary [*Editor*].**

MAM. These day-Owles.
SVR. That are birding in mens purses.
MAM. Madame *Suppository.*
KAS. *Doxey*, my suster.
ANA. Locusts
Of the foule pit.
TRI. Profane as BEL, and the *Dragon.*
ANA. Worse then the Grass-hoppers, or the Lice of *Egypt.*
MAM. The *Chymicall* cousoner.
SVR. And the Captaine *Pandar.*
KAS. The *Nun*, my suster.
MAM. Madame *Rabbi.*
ANA. Scorpions. [V. v. 11 ff.]

If anything, the quack, the rascal, and the whore have descended even lower than the level of the curs in the opening scene. Now they have become hawk-owls, locusts, scorpions, and caterpillars: that is, parasites which live on higher beings. Furthermore, Ananias's Biblical allusions make them appear as plagues.

Mammon's language shows the same deflation. Gone are the classical allusions which had characterized his speech when he was under the spell of the elixir. Zephyrus, Jove's shower, the boon of Midas, and all the gods have been blown up, along with his hopes. Mammon himself, who was to have been 'King of Bantam', now has humbler plans: he will mount a turnip-cart and preach the end of the world (V. v. 81–82). The picture of the gluttonous Mammon, who wanted shrimps 'In a rare butter, made of dolphins milke' and his 'beds blowne vp; not stuft', so deflated that he takes to a turnip-cart, is a magnificent absurdity.

In one sense Face alone remains what he was—that is, nothing in himself, but living only in the disguises or 'faces' which he assumes: Jeremy, the butler; Captain Face, the pander; Lungs and Zephyrus, the blower; the Spanish count; and always the 'king' of a commonwealth of fools.[3] His kingdom includes even Love-Wit, who says, 'I will be rul'd by thee in any thing, IEREMIE' (V. v. 143) and who, just before, called Face 'my braine'. Surly suggests the variety of Face when, confronted by the smooth Jeremy, he mutters, 'This's a new FACE? (V. iii. 21). But in another sense Face has blown himself out of existence. He too has come down from a Captain to a butler and is aware that his part fell a little in the final scene (V. v. 158).

3. The *OED* defines face as 'command of countenance, especially with reference to freedom from indication of shame; a bold front; impudence, effrontery, "cheek" '. There is some hint that Face is really only the clothes he has on. During his quarrel with Face, Subtle threatens to mar 'All that the taylor has made' (I.i. 9–10). Note also his remark (I.i. 63). In his dedication to Lady Mary Wroth Jonson commented on '*the ambitious Faces of the time: who, the more they paint are the lesse themselues.*'

Actually, of course, these two motifs of abuse and pretension exist side by side throughout the play. Thus at the very time that Mammon addresses Dol as 'Right noble madame', Face in an aside calls her 'my *Guiny*-bird', a slang term for a prostitute (IV. i. 38). But, normally, now one, now the other of these strains is dominant. In the first act and in the last two scenes of the final act the abusive epithets are dominant, while during most of the rest of the play the pretentious epithets are dominant. But at both times the subordinate strain remains as counterpoint to the principal melody, contrasting with it for an ironic effect.

Furthermore, both the abusive and the euphemistic names are perfectly characteristic of the speakers because they are typical of thieves' cant. Such cant was originally a peculiar slang devised for secrecy. For example, a brothel was called variously an Academy, Corinth, school of Venus, vaulting school, smuggling ken, pushing school.[4] The same impulse which caused thieves to invent such slang makes Face refer to Dol as 'my smock-rampant' or Dol call Face 'Soueraigne'. The pretentious epithets, then, as well as the abusive, are not mere rhetorical flourishes, but names which, while serving a poetic purpose, remain true to the impulse behind thieves' cant.

One of the poetic purposes of these epithets is to show Subtle, Face, and Dol on more than one level. On one level we see them as the rogues they are; on another, we see them as the insects or animals they are compared to; on still another, we see them as the higher beings that they and others think they are. The simultaneous existence of multiple levels helps create some of the humour and much of the irony which gather about a whore who thinks of herself as a '*republique*', a quack who will 'thunder' a man in pieces, and a pander who wears a uniform and calls himself 'Captaine'.

* * *

Even as the imagery is instrumental in relating alchemy to religion, medicine, and sex, so also does it suggest a relationship between all of these and business. This connection strikes one on hearing in 'The Argument' that '*A cheater, and his punque*';

> *Leauing their narrow practise, were become*
> *Cos'ners at large: and, onely wanting some*
> *House to set vp, with him they here contract,*
> *Each for a share, and all begin to act.*
> *Much company they draw, and much abuse,*
> *In casting figures, telling fortunes, newes,*
> *Selling of flyes, flat bawdry, with the* stone:
> *Till it, and they, and all in* fume *are gone.*

4. Francis Grose, *A Classical Dictionary of the Vulgar Tongue* (London, 1785).

The commercial implications, latent in the central situation of cheating and prostitution, come out in such words as '*practise*', '*House to set vp*', '*contract*', '*share*', '*company they draw*', '*selling*'. Each of these alone might not attract attention to its commercial sense, but, when these words are used together in the same passage, the commercial sense tends to rise above the other senses. The final impression is that Subtle, Dol, and Face have gone into business, with a contract, shares, and an expanding practice—all somewhat dubious, perhaps, but still flourishing. The complexity of this business can be noted in one line, '*Selling of flyes, flat bawdry, with the* stone:' where religion, sex, and gold all come together.

Such commercial terms are used throughout the play. Even in the midst of the opening quarrel Face speaks as a business partner who has drawn 'customers' to Subtle for his 'dosen of trades', given him 'credit' for his 'coales' and a 'house to practise in' where he has 'studied the more thriuing skill of bawdrie, since' (I. i. 40–49). Dol reminds them of their business obligations when she breaks up their quarrel by denouncing Subtle for claiming

a primacie, in the diuisions?
You must be chiefe? as if you, onely, had
The poulder to proiect with? and the worke
Were not begun out of equalitie?
The venter *tripartite*? All things in common?
Without prioritie? [I. i. 131–136]

From one point of view such a passage is only another example of Dol's pretentious language. But what strikes one about it is that this whore describes their catch-as-catch-can agreement as a 'venter *tripartite*', 'worke,' 'begun out of equalitie,' 'without prioritie'. 'Venter *tripartite*' is the most interesting phrase in the passage, partly because it is echoed in several places later. In this context 'venter' (or venture) principally means a commercial speculation. Later, just before the partnership breaks up, Face uses this meaning of the word when he calls Subtle and Dol 'venturers'. A 'venturer' in the early seventeenth century meant either an adventurer or 'one who undertakes or shares in a commercial or trading venture, especially by sending goods or ships beyond seas' (*OED*). It was used particularly of the trading companies such as the Merchant Venturers of Bristol. 'All things in common!' Dol cries, damning herself in doing so, for the line, read in one way, means all things in Common: that is, a three-fold commercial speculation in Common stock without priority. Dol really is a republic to these speculators, a 'common-wealth', indeed. But no matter how the passage is read, it seems to imply commercial dealings on a high plane.

The high plane is kept right to the end. Just as they are dissolving the company, Face formally ends the '*indenture tripartite*' (V. iv. 130–132). Figuratively, '*indenture*' meant contract or mutual engagement. Literally, an indenture was 'a deed between two or more parties with mutual covenants, executed in two or more copies' (*OED*). There are legal and aristocratic dimensions to the term, as well as commercial, for kings and king-makers have used it. In *Henry IV, Part I*, for instance, when Hotspur, Worcester, Mortimer, and Glendower are dividing up England, Mortimer says that their 'indentures tripartite' are drawn (III. i. 80–82). Seen through the lens of such a definition and such a use as this, Face's use of the phrase is comic, as he may mean it to be, because he is at that moment able to stand back and laugh at their absurd pretension to legality and high finance.

Between the time Dol calls it a 'venter *tripartite*' and Face, an '*indenture tripartite*', commercial terms are frequently used to refer to sex or cheating or the religion of the elixir. Dol settles the quarrel between Subtle and Face by making Subtle swear to leave his 'faction' 'And labour, kindly, in the commune worke' (I. i. 156). She really means that they should cheat fools cheerfully and cooperatively. But, since such a naked way of looking at reality offends her pretentious nature, she generally uses martial or commercial terms to disguise what is called, in plain speech, cheating and whoring. The result is that, when she and others use words like 'worke', 'labour', 'venter', and 'venturers' to refer to activities that, for one thing, are generally not thought of as commercial speculations and, for another, are not legal, then the identification of a tenor (such as whoring) and a vehicle (such as 'venter') appears indecorous and ludicrous, yet illuminating. We are asked to consider to what extent prostitution or cheating can be called a business venture (and possibly even to what extent a business venture involves some kind of prostitution or cheating). The degree to which we can equate business and cheating or business and prostitution or business and religion, as well as the degree to which such tenors and vehicles resist identification, provides some of the humour and meaning of the play.

Let us observe how the imagery suggests connections between business and sex. We have already seen that, in Mammon's world, money and sex are assumed to be monstrous twins of the same bitch goddess. Once money and sex are brought as close together as this, many connections between business (whose blood is money) and sex spring up. Some of these only depend on the nature of things in a world in which some people take money in exchange for sexual experience. The Queen of Mammon's world is, after all, a prostitute whose business is sex. Other connections only capitalize on the ambiguity of many words which have one reference to business and pick up another reference to sex. For instance, both 'venter' and 'venturer' mean 'prostitute' as well as, respectively, 'commercial speculation' and 'commercial speculator' (*OED*). But many of the connections are made simply by the force of the imagery in which commercial vehicles are related to tenors dealing with sex.

Note how commercial vehicles are used in referring to Dame Pliant and Dol. Face and Subtle speak of Dame Pliant in these extraordinary terms:

> FAC. A wife, a wife, for one on'vs, my deare SVBTLE:
> Wee'll eene draw lots, and he, that failes, shall haue
> The more in goods, the other has in taile.
> SVB. Rather the lesse. For shee may be so light
> Shee may want graines. [II. vi. 85–89]

Drawing lots seems to be their normal way of determining the fate of women, for that, one supposes, is what Face referred to in a previous speech: 'the longest cut, at night, / Shall draw thee for his DOL Particular (I. i. 178-79). There is a certain gay detachment about Face's method of settling erotic problems; getting a wife and sleeping with a whore can be settled in the same simple way—just draw lots. But the interesting aspect of this passage is the compensation suggested: if you miss the wife, you get the goods. 'In taile' is a play on the legal word 'tail', which referred to limiting the inheritance of an estate to descendants in a particular line, and on the obscene word 'tail' which meant then as now—the posterior, or the female pudend. This witty union of sex and inheritance is extended by the assertion that whatever one gets 'in taile', the other ought to get in goods. Money or property, then, becomes a possible substitution for a wife or rather for the sexual experience of having a wife.

This same substitution is emphasized later in a somewhat different way. When Surly, disguised as a Spaniard, enters, Face and Subtle forget their quarrel over marrying Dame Pliant and decide to put the Dame to more useful work.

> FAC. 'Slid, SVBTLE, he puts me in minde o'the widow,
> What dost thou say to draw her to it? ha?
> And tell her, it is her fortune. All our venter
> Now lies vpon't. It is but one man more,
> Which on's chance to haue her: . . .
> The credit of our house too is engag'd.
> SVB. You made me an offer for my share e're while.
> What wilt thou gi' me, i-faith?
> FAC. O, by that light,
> Ile not buy now . . .

E'en take your lot, obey your chance, sir; winne her,
And weare her, out for me.
SVB. 'Slight. I'll not worke her then.
FAC. It is the common cause. [IV. iii. 63 ff.]

Face has the spirit of the true capitalist—business before pleasure. Or, perhaps, a better way of putting it is to say—pleasure and business together—because Face's chief pleasure is evidently not sex, but alchemizing people; sex is only one of his many ways of doing so. There is a business terminology in this exchange pretentious enough for even Dol: 'The credit of our house too is engag'd'; 'an offer for my share': 'the common cause'. When the situation is explained in terms as high flown as these, who can blame them for putting that glorious adventure, commerce, before that mean duty, marriage? The burden of the whole passage is, as Face later puts it, that Dame Pliant is to be 'used' (IV. iv. 79) even as Dol is 'emploi'd' (IV. iii. 51). As sexual beings, they both are commodities to be bought, sold, used, worn, and worked.

One scene especially reveals how Dol is to be used—the third scene in the third act, where Dol's profession and Subtle's fraud are thought of in terms of warfare. Face announces the arrival of 'A noble *Count*, a *Don of Spaine*', who has brought his 'munition' with him and is ready

too make his battry
Vpon our DOL, our Castle, our *cinque*-Port,
Our *Douer* pire, our what thou wilt. Where is shee?
Shee must prepare perfumes, delicate linnen,
The bath in chiefe, a banquet and her wit,
For shee must milke his *Epididimis*
Where is the *Doxie*? [III. iii. 17–23]

Face's speech might be the type of the whole play: both begin in abuse, inflate by pretension, and sink into obscenity. The martial imagery, which is quite in keeping with Dol's previous 'Soueraigne' and 'Generall', moves in a kind of graduated expansion from Dol (the tenor) to 'our Castle' (one vehicle); then to '*cinque*-Port' and '*Douer* pire'; and finally, blown apart entirely, to 'what thou wilt'. Face may be making fun of their own tendency (necessary in the profession of passing a whore off as a noble lady) to think of Dol in pretentious terms. Whether he is or not, there is extravagant humour in picturing Dol first as a castle, then as Dover or Sandwich or what you will—'This fortress built by Nature for herself / Against infection and the hand of war'—Dol, ready to receive the battery of that Spanish Armada which has

brought munition with him, sixe great slopps,
Bigger then three *Dutch* hoighs, beside round trunkes,
Furnish'd with pistolets, and pieces of eight. [III. iii. 13–15]

The munition is money, the danger is infection, England will fall. The ludicrous end of the whole passage is that Dol, the doxy, 'must milke his *Epididimis*'.[5]

Once Face has introduced the theme that sexual aggression is a kind of warfare, he proceeds to vary it in another involved figure, which has a movement similar to the one just analysed. With her customary ceremony Dol asks him (and ludicrously echoes the King's opening question in *The Spanish Tragedy*),[6]

lord *Generall*, how fares our campe?
FAC. As, with the few, that had entrench'd themselues
Safe by their discipline, against a world, DOL:
And laugh'd, within those trenches, and grew fat
With thinking on the booties, DOL, brought in
Daily, by their small parties. This deare houre,
A doughtie *Don* is taken, with my DOL;
And thou maist make his ransome, what thou wilt,
My *Dousabell*: He shall be brought here, fetter'd
With thy faire lookes, before he sees thee; and throwne
In a downe-bed, as darke as any dungeon;
Where thou shalt keepe him waking, with thy drum;
Thy drum, my DOL; thy drum; till he be tame
As the poore black-birds were i' the great frost,
Or bees are with a bason: and so hiue him
I'the swan-skin couerlid, and cambrick sheets,
Till he worke honey, and waxe, my little Gods-*guift*.
[III. iii. 33–49]

Here Face extends the martial imagery to include more than sex. The impostors, it appears, are at war with the world and have fortified themselves in their castle, from which, daily, they send out small sorties. Any enemies captured are held for ransom and possibly tortured into submission by Dol's drum. This sardonic picture of economic survival of the fittest which brings together sex, business, and warfare ends with a figure as outrageous as milking the epididymis. Dol's bed first becomes a dungeon and then a beehive in which the 'doughtie *Don*' produces honey. 'Honey' obviously has a sexual meaning and partly from its colour and partly from the context acquires the meaning of gold.

Face is undeniably a virtuoso in erotic imagery. Sexual intercourse has been compared, in succession, to a battery on a castle and seaports, to milking, to keeping awake with a drum, and to extracting honey from a bee. His final erotic image in this passage follows the musical motif suggested by 'drum'.

5. The epididymis is an organ at the back of the testicles. 'Milke', as a vulgar term, also meant extract all possible profit from someone by illicit means. This sense appears later in Face's declaration that the don will be 'Milked' by them (IV. iii. 45).

6. In the opening line of Kyd's *Spanish Tragedy* the Spanish King asks resonantly "Now say, Lord General, how fares our camp?" [*Editor*].

Sweet DOL,
You must goe tune your virginall, no loosing
O' the least time. And, doe you heare? good action.
Firke, like a flounder; kisse, like a scallop, close:
And tickle him with thy mother-tongue. [III. iii. 66–70]

This cluster of violently indecorous images is about as absurd as any in the play. The name, 'virginall', applied to a whore, has its ironic humour, which is doubled when she is advised to keep it in tune lest she waste time.[7] Face, as a bawd, has a twentieth century sense of efficiency. Though 'firke' has alchemic (see II. i. 28) and financial connotations, it seems primarily to echo Face's previous remark about Dol: 'A wench is a rare bait, with which a man / No sooner's taken, but he straight firkes mad' II. iv. 4–5). The obvious erotic allusion in both places may be reinforced by the pronunciation of 'firke'.[8] 'Tickle him with thy mother-tongue' is one of the wittiest images in the whole passage. 'Mother' could then mean 'womb'. 'Mother-tongue' means either one's native language or an original language from which others spring (*OED*). Besides the obvious erotic innuendo, Face may be suggesting that sex is that universal language which even the Spanish don, who knows not a word of English, can understand. Mammon unconsciously takes up this image later when he says he will 'talke to her, all in gold' (IV. i. 25). Poor Mammon had no way of knowing what an expert conversationalist he was going to talk to.

Such obscenity is very far from being aphrodisiac because the ludicrousness and lack of taste both within the images themselves and in the relationship of the images to each other neutralize any possible pornography. That Dol should 'Firke, like a flounder' and 'kisse, like a scallop' does not make her particularly seductive. Such an indecorous mixture of vehicles applied to the same tenor helps maintain a continuous comic tone so that never for a moment do we feel close to the characters. The distance between the tenor and vehicle tends to keep us at a distance. Seen through the eyes of Mammon or Dapper, Dol is a heroine and, like the prostitutes in Plautus's plays,[9] can seem a heroine—of a sort—even to us. But she is not romanticized. The exaggerated absurdity of Dol as a Dover pier makes her whoredom ludicrous, not erotically attractive, nor even pitiful.

Martial imagery throws a cloak of authority and high matters of

7. Perhaps the implication of 'virginall' in this passage may be clarified by an image of Prospero's from the Quarto *Every Man in his Humor* (II. iii. 183–85): 'I can compare him to nothing more happely, then a Barbers virginals; for euery one may play vpon him.'

8. This unmentionable word was first brought into a dictionary by John Florio in *A World of Wordes* (1598), but it was almost certainly in common speech long before that. See Allen Walker Read, 'An Obscenity Symbol', *American Speech* (December 1934), IX, 264 ff.; and Eric Partridge, *Shakespeare's Bawdy* (New York, 1948), 113.

9. The Roman comic poet Plautus has in his plays quite a number of girls, politely called "courtesans" in the old translations, who are both clever and sympathetic [*Editor*].

state over other scenes than this one. When the furnace explodes and Subtle swoons, Face says, 'Coldnesse and death inuades him' (IV. v. 63). Supposing that Mammon is about to assault her virtue, Dol, with her high sense of honour, says, 'You meane no treason, sir!' (IV. i. 118). Love-Wit's house is a 'fort' to Face (V. ii. 29), a '*Citadell*' to Surly (IV. vi. 9), and a 'castle' to Kastril (V. iii. 36). This martial pretentiousness in part explains why Face calls himself 'Captaine' as well as why Dol constantly promotes him to 'Generall'. A Captaine in the seventeenth century was a commander of a body of troops or of a fortress or castle. The exact function of a Captain in this war with the world can be inferred from the dialogue between Subtle, who announces the arrival of Dame Pliant and Kastril, and Face:

FAC. I must to my Captaine-ship againe, then.
SVB. Stay, bring 'hem in, first.
FAC. So I meant. [IV. ii 3–4]

A captain is one who brings the customers in. Business is a war, and Face is an Intelligence officer in active service.

Mammon's language is, aside from Face's, the best example of how thoroughly the implications of the imagery relate business, religion, and sex. His name is an example of this. According to the *OED*, Mammon, the Aramaic word for 'riches', was taken by medieval writers as the proper name of the devil of covetousness. Even in the Elizabethan age Thomas Lodge in *Wits Miserie, or the Worlds Madnesse* (1596) used Mammon as the devil incarnate who tempted man by avarice. After the sixteenth century it was current as a term of opprobrium for wealth regarded as an idol or evil influence. Loosely, 'Epicure' meant 'one who disbelieves in the divine government, and in a future life'. More particularly, it came to mean one who gives himself up to sensual pleasure, especially eating. This idea of a refined taste for the pleasures of the table began as early as 1586 (*OED*). Some sense of what Epicure meant by the time of *The Alchemist* can be gained from the *Nosce Teipsum* (1599) of Sir John Davies. In the passage on the immortality of the soul Davies describes those 'light and vicious persons' who claim that the soul is 'but a smoke or airy blast' and who say, 'Come, let us eat and drink' before we die.

Therefore no heretics desire to spread
Their light opinions like these Epicures;[1]

In short, Epicure carries with it a sense of atheism and materialism, just as Mammon symbolized covetousness, riches, and worldliness. 'Epicure,' which comes from Greek, and 'Mammon', which is exclusively a Christian term, unite to form a name which is at once a

1. Part Two, "The Soul of Man," lines 1083–84.

humanistic and Christian comment on impious wealth and immorality.

The geographical allusions of this immense symbol of worldliness and sensuality reveal him to be a more romantic merchant venturer than Face.

> Now, you set your foot on shore
> In *nouo orbe*; Here's the rich *Peru*:
> And there within, sir, are the golden mines,
> Great SALOMON's *Ophir*! He was sayling to't,
> Three yeeres, but we haue reach'd it in ten months. [II. i. 1–5]

Mammon is not merely the explorer setting his foot on the shore of the New World—not even primarily the explorer—but essentially the merchant venturer. His primary interest is in the 'golden mines' within which shall make him rich. Not the least of many ironies in this scene is that Face has been thinking of Mammon himself as a 'vein' to be mined (I. iii. 106). This idea of exploiting distant lands is brought even closer home when Mammon declares that he will purchase Devonshire and Cornwall and make them 'perfect *Indies*' (II. i. 35–36). These counties were noted for tin and copper mines, which Mammon would transmute into 'golden mines'. The commercial note which opens the scene is brought in most emphatically in his lines on Subtle who makes the stone, 'But I buy it. / My venter brings it me' (II. ii. 100–101). The use of the commercial terms—'buy' and 'venter'—in reference to the stone shows how intimate is the connection between religion and business in Mammon's world. Mammon can buy his god, the elixir. Divinity and immortality can be bargained for. There is a certain justice, as Mammon himself admits, in the fate to which this business venture in religion comes. The sensual dreams which had drawn him on and his pursuit of Dol are said by Subtle to be the cause of the bursting of the glass and the failure of all his hopes. He cries, 'O my voluptuous mind! I am justly punish'd' (IV. v. 74). It is characteristic of Mammon that he should consider the loss of the power of making gold a just punishment for a voluptuous mind.

Mammon's psychic sensuality is its own best criticism. As L. C. Knights says, each of his speeches 'implicitly refers to a traditional conception of the Mean'.[2] The images he uses more than once betray the essential meanness of his vision. Not simply their constant extravagance—though that is one way of indicating hollowness—but also the action within the image itself shows this. For instance:

> My mists
> I'le haue of perfume, vapor'd 'bout the roome,

2. Knights, *Drama and Society in the Age of Jonson*, 190.

> To loose our selues in; and my baths, like pits
> To fall into: [II. ii. 48–51]

Other associations with losing one's self or falling into pits suddenly betray such lines, suggesting that Mammon may have lost himself already and calling up memories of an Inferno where sinners have fallen into pits of fire. Or the dramatic irony implicit in the imagery he uses may reveal him. Thus he explains to Surly that, once his friends are rich, they shall not have to deal with 'the hollow die' or 'the fraile card', nor keep a 'liuery-punke', nor worship 'the golden calfe', nor 'Commit idolatrie with wine, and trumpets' (II. i. 9 ff.). But we know, from the previous act, that the dice are loaded, that Dol is a punk, that Mammon is worshipping a golden calf and committing idolatry with words if not wine. Or when Mammon, to convince Surly of the authenticity of the elixir, alludes to a classical myth, the myth itself betrays him.

> SISIPHVS was damn'd
> To roule the ceaslesse stone, onely, because
> He would haue made ours common.[3] [II. iii. 208–10]

Sisyphus was punished for his fraud and avarice. Mammon, who is avaricious, if not fraudulent, suddenly turns into Sisyphus, rolling the ceaseless stone of alchemy.

* * *

The imagery of *The Alchemist* is perfectly functional in several ways. First, it develops, as alchemy develops, beginning with base metals, such as a whore, a pander, and a quack, which it tries grandiloquently to transmute into finer beings—a Faery Queen, a precious king of present wits, and a divine instructor—finally ending, as the dream of the philosopher's stone ends, in a return to the state of base metals. The various vehicles which alchemize the base situation—the inflated epithets, the erotic allusions, the religious and commercial terms—ultimately show how thoroughly mean the situation is by bringing into the context the very standards by which it could be measured: the Christian and humanistic civilization of rational men. Against the immense background the three impostors and their commonwealth of fools play out their mock-heroic life, their violent little actions contrasting sharply with the permanent values suggested by the imagery. When Subtle is compared to a priest, the comparison itself shows how much he disappoints the ideal. When Dol calls herself Queen of Faeries, we see how far she really is from the Faery Queen.

The imagery is functional in another way. The images work on

3. The stage direction may be important here: '*Dol is seene*', exactly on the word 'common'. Is this another way to suggest an equation between the stone and Dol Common?

the same principle that the play as a whole and usually each scene work. They are extravagant, inflated, and ludicrous, because the tenors (gold, Dol, Mammon) are related to great vehicles (god, Queen, Jove). The monstrous gap that opens between the tenor that we know to be mean and the vehicle that we assume to be great, and the demand that we find some similarities between them to bridge that gap, outrages our sense of decency and decorum. That outrage, within the imagery, produces part of the comic tone of the play.

A third function of the imagery is to extend and develop the multiple references that alchemy had in actual life—especially the religious, medical, and commercial references. The alchemic process in this play has religious implications because the desire for gold is thought of as a religion; it has medical implications because the elixir is thought of as a sovereign remedy; it has sexual implications because the elixir is thought to have a sexual power; it has commercial implications because business terms are used in reference to the whole fraudulent practice. When gold or the power of producing gold is spoken of as one normally speaks of a deity, we are expected to question whether this has any connections with reality. Do some people make gold their god? What is the sense in saying that man's nature can be alchemized? Is money in any sense the great healing power of the world? Does the great god, gold, have a sexual power? What is the relation of business to this religion of gold? Is sex to some people a business? Is religion? And so on. In other words, the imagery suggests that, in the Alchemist's world, the acquisition of gold is a religion, a cure-all, a sexual experience, and a commercial enterprise. The world that opens before us, once we understand these multiple references of alchemy, is outrageously obscene, crude in metaphysic and vulgar in emotion. Since this world is, in part, a caricature of the real world, one can make numerous connections between its crudity and obscenity and the crudity and obscenity latent in human experience. But as a universe of discourse, it exists in its own right, comic because it is a caricature, solid and substantial because it has a religion, an ethic, a government, and a flourishing business.

The imagery also suggests that the various peoples whose lives are dedicated to the acquisition of gold—whether they be in secular or religious life, in prostitution or other kinds of business—bear some relation to the alchemists of old. Dol Common is metaphorically an alchemist because she, too, is trying to turn base metals into gold. Mammon's cook is an alchemist in the same way; the reward of all his cooking is the accolade—'there's gold, / Goe forth and be a knight'. Perhaps the true philosopher's stone is not the stone itself;

but simply business—that is, selling the public the things it wants. Face's threatening of Subtle is pertinent:

> I will haue
> A booke, but barely reckoning thy impostures,
> Shall proue a true *philosophers stone*, to printers.
> [I. i. 100–102]

The Golden Age comes when you find that you have what someone else wants—a sensational book or a new medicine, a shiny gadget or an old fraud. The true alchemist may be Face, that 'parcell-broker, and whole-bawd' who always has something someone wants and who perpetually finds the elixir of life in Drugger, Mammon, Dame Pliant, Subtle, Dol, and finally Love-Wit. Face may be the face of the future, the prophetic vision of the super-salesman who can sell anything to anyone. All that he needs to work on is man—man who, himself another Face, will sell even things he needs in order to buy things he wants. With naked impudence he expresses his philosophy early in the game.

> You [Subtle] must have stuffe, brought home to you, to worke on?
> And, yet, you thinke, I am at no expence,
> In searching out these veines, then following 'hem,
> Then trying 'hem out. 'Fore god, my intelligence
> Costs me more money, then my share oft comes too,
> In these rare workes. [I. iii. 104–109]

That little world, man, contains the base metals on which an alchemist can work. The seams or lodes may lie deep, but they can be searched out and followed. The 'golden mines' of Mammon, his '*nouo orbe*' and 'rich *Peru*' are only new names for this old world of man—new names, ironically, for Sir Epicure Mammon. Though alchemy itself is a fraud, Subtle, Dol, and Face are successful alchemists in that they have found this golden secret. All who discover this secret—all whores like Dol, all quacks like Subtle, all shrewd rascals like Face, all unscrupulous opportunists like Love-Wit—these are the true alchemists.

This conviction that in man's nature lie the base metals of alchemy appears in a different form in an image that Face uses in speaking of his futile search for Surly.

> 'Slight would you haue me stalke like a mill-iade,
> All day, for one, that will not yeeld vs. graines? [III. iii. 5–6]

Man could be harvested as well as transmuted. Once ground down in the mill, he could yield 'graines.' This kind of gain was the 'common way' which Volpone avoided: '[I] have no mills for yron, / Oyle, corne, or men, to grinde 'hem into poulder' (I.i. 35–36). But the final source of money for Face is the final source of food for Volpone—man.

WILLIAM BLISSETT

The Venter Tripartite in *The Alchemist*†

The "judging spectator"[1] of the two most generally esteemed and most similar of Ben Jonson's comedies is required to be extraordinarily agile when, at the end of *Volpone* and of *The Alchemist*, the playwright makes equal claims for his nod of assent and pleasure. The laws of Venice are applied so stringently to Volpone, Mosca, and the other delinquents as to lead some to say that the play verges on tragedy; whereas the hubbub at the end of *The Alchemist* verges on farce: comparable dupes lose only cash and other metal moveables and, of the cheaters, two escape without gain or loss and the third appears to profit himself and is the undoubted agent of another's profit.

In mitigation of the harsh outcome of *Volpone* it may be argued that, since the law has been not only contravened but invoked by the contraveners, judicial consequences must be expected; further, that the animal characterization of the base persons makes their punishment quite unlike any judgment of souls and hence still appropriate to comedy, while Celia and Bonario are deliberately under-characterized so as to preclude any expectation that they will shine forth—and demand to be paired off—at the end; and further, that Volpone's springing up yet once more to speak the epilogue prevents the shock of the sentence from lingering: he will retire to the wings, not to the Incurabili. To all these considerations must be added the words of the playwright in his dedication to the two universities:

> *And though my* catastrophe *may, in the strict rigour of* comick *law, meet with censure, as turning back to my promises: J desire the learned, and charitable critick to have so much faith in me, to thinke it was done off industrie: For, with what ease J could have varied it, neerer his scale (but that I feare to boast my owne faculty) J could here insert. But my speciall ayme being to put the snaffle in their mouths, that crie out, we neuer punish vice in our enterludes, &c. I tooke the more liberty; though not without some lines of example, drawne euen in the ancients themselues,*

† From *Studies in English Literature 1500–1900*, 8 (1968), 323–34.

1. Prologue to *The Alchemist*, line 3 [*Editor*].

> *the goings out of whose* comoedies *are not alwaies ioyfull, but oft-times, the bawdes, the seruants, the riuals, yea, and the masters are mulcted: and fitly, it being the office of a* comick-Poet, *to imitate iustice, and instruct to life, as well as puritie of language, or stirre vp gentle affections.*[2]

But this very claim to "imitate justice" in *Volpone* makes more acute the problem of *The Alchemist.* For two centuries Jonson was deemed pre-eminent in the possession and exercise of "judgment,"[3] yet he devised a play in which, to be sure, fools are shown to be the fools they are and made to pay the price of their folly, but in which the law appears to be broken with impunity and a certain kind of wrong-doer is commended by a late-introduced "straight" character who seems to embody not only the good humor but the good sense of the audience.

Of course, it is no new thing for a playwright to work within a certain pattern and yet suddenly, on occasion, to reverse it. The festive outcome of Shakespearean comedy in the 1590's, with its wedding music and dance, is such a pattern, but *Love's Labour Lost* gains its piquancy and distinction by contravening expectation and, through the application of a sort of comic anti-matter, suddenly disappearing, along with its baffled audience, "you, that way: we, this way." But *The Alchemist* does not give the impression of simply taking a holiday from the judicious world, as *Bartholomew Fair* does. Festivity at the end of *Love's Labour Lost* is dissolved and dispelled, but *The Alchemist* still invites, still requires judgment.

Perhaps the way into the play will eventually issue into a way out. Three players enter, and two are characterized at once. It would be a sad actress indeed who could not by makeup, style of speech, and appropriate bumps and grinds, build her role to substantial fullness before the name of Dol Common is spoken or she is claimed by her companions as "our republic."[4] In such a case, *déformation professionnelle*[5] is usually quite pronounced, and, the moral condition of the character being a *donnée*,[6] she is from the

2. C. H. Herford and Percy and Evelyn Simpson, ed., *Ben Jonson* (Oxford, 1937) V, 20. All quotations from Ben Jonson are taken from this edition.
3. G. E. Bentley, *Shakespeare & Jonson* (Chicago, 1945), passim.
4. Bentley, I, 125: "Why should Doll Common be more familiar than Face or Subtle or Sejanus, Volpone, Morose, or Rabbi Zeal-of-the-Land Busy? Two possible answers are suggested by the general character of the allusions to Doll. A number of them refer to her violence in the play, and several others use her name as a generic term for a prostitute. There is some implication here that Doll was more noteworthy on the stage than in the library, and a further suggestion that her name may have been a familiar one for a wanton before Jonson used it." The name of Doll Tearsheet suggests itself, as a partial anticipation. The *Oxford English Dictionary* adds, from *Nice Wanton* (1560), "But ich tell your minion doll, by Gog's body," and from Cooper's *Thesaurus* (1578), "O pleasant companion: O common'st creature"; *Much Ado,* IV.i.66, "To link my dear friend to a common stale."
5. Professional distortion [*Editor*].
6. Given [*Editor*].

beginning analogous to a figure in a morality play, whether or not individualizing traits such as a humorous disposition or a quick wit or a heart of gold are subsequently filled in.

Naturally, we look first at Dol Common, and our summing-up is instantaneous and, as it falls out, never altered. But we listen first to a thin, noisy, foul-spoken man whom we recognize from his threadbare and starveling appearance to be the alchemist of the play's title.[7] An immediate question arises: why is the playwright at pains to make him so noisy that the quiet-voiced third member of the group must frequently and apprehensively beg him to lower his voice?

FAC. You might talk softlier, rascall.
SVB. No, you *scarabe*,
Ill thunder you, in peeces. I will teach you
How to beware, to tempt a *furie*'againe
That carries tempest in his hand, and voice. [I.i.59–62]

In terms of realistic detail, the initial answer is that the Alchemist is somewhat deaf, but why this detail? The real answer, I think, is bound up with the Alchemist's astounding first line—"Thy worst. I fart at thee." The theaters of the world must wait nearly three centuries for Père Ubu to match it for audacity and emphasis.[8] It will certainly make any audience sit up; it establishes the thorough bass of the play's style and decorum; it precludes the possibility of the play's magic being benevolent, theurgic, highbrow. But put noise and stink together in a context of necromancy and the black arts—and keep them together, for the climax of the play's action is a loud explosion, and the air is not cleared until the plague has lifted and the Alchemist has departed—and there is enough evidence to associate this closely-observed Jacobean charlatan with a morality prototype. Jonson himself is to give us the master-clue in *The Staple of News*: in one of the choric episodes one chattering playgoing woman says to another, who hopes to see a devil on the stage: "That was the old way, Gossip, when *Iniquity* came in like *Hokos Pokos*, in a *Iuglers* ierkin, with false skirts, like the *Knaue* of *Clubs*! but now they are attir'd like men and women o' the time, the *Vices*, male and female!"[9]

In the first scene of *The Alchemist*, then, three characters enter into a plot or business agreement or "venter tripartite" to waylay

7. Chaucer, *Canon's Yeoman's Prologue*, 890 897; in Jonson's masque, *Mercurie Vindicated from the Alchemists at Court*, Vulcan enters "with a troupe of threedbare Alchymists" (Herford and Simpson, VII, 412); one recalls also his epigram, "To Alchymists": "If all you boast of your great art be true; / Sure, willing povertie liues most in you." (H.&S., VIII,29).

8. In Alfred Jarry's farce *Ubu Roi* (1896) the first word spoken by the main character, in a voice of thunder, is *Merdre!* It translates, roughly, *Shritt!* [*Editor*].

9. Herford and Simpson, VI, 323; also 302 and 303.

various specimens of humanity, and one is at once recognizable as a figure of the Flesh, the second as a figure of the Devil. The third, Jeremy the Housekeeper, known as Face, is much less strongly characterized at the outset, but this again is appropriate, for who has as clear a conception of the World as of the more alluring or fascinating enemies of the soul?

Morality characterization is largely based on the old phrase "*nomina-numina*"—the name is the nature or spirit of the thing named. To name Dol Common is to know her, and the subsequent variations on her name are merely the arpeggios of concupiscence. The name "Subtle" must detain us longer. First actually named by Sir Epicure Mammon early in the second act, the Alchemist has been called Sirrah, rogue, whelp, slave, mongrel, doctor dog by Face; sovereign—and stinkard—by Dol; and doctor by Dapper and Drugger. Subtle may have been intended by the humanist playwright as a satiric jab at scholasticism and its Doctor Subtilis; but a perusal of the various forms of the word current in the Renaissance encourages a reference at once wider and more to our purpose. Two of the basic meanings of "subtle" are "rarefied" or "penetrating" and "skilful" or "crafty." The *Oxford English Dictionary* gives (1398) "The ayre and brethe drawen in by the mouth is amended and puryd, and made subtyll therein," and (1617) "The subtileness of the Ayre." Shakespeare seems to draw on both meanings, directly and as transferred epithet, in Juliet's exclamation: "What if it be a poison which the friar / Subtly hath minister'd to have me dead?" (*Romeo and Juliet*, IV.iii.25). Usually he employs the second: "Am I politic, am I subtle, am I a Machiavel?" (*Merry Wives of Windsor*, III.i.103) and, very memorably, Richard of Gloucester's "As I am subtle, false, and treacherous" (*Richard III*, I.i.37). This last-quoted line, by one who is determined to prove a villain, should serve as a reminder that the word is regularly used in a context of spiritual malice. "He's the devil," says a Volscian soldier of Coriolanus. "Bolder," replies Aufidius, "though not so subtle" (*Coriolanus*, I.x.17).

The Devil is subtle: he is devious, and he is prince of the powers of the air. Caxton (1471) says, "He chaunged hymself in guyse of a serpent this is to vnderstand in subtyllesse and in malice," and Coverdale's translation of Genesis iii.1. is to fix the word in subsequent translations (and in *Paradise Lost*): "The serpent was sotyller then all the beastes of the felde." The same word carries over from the devil to the devilish arts. Caxton (c. 1489) writes of one who was "the subtillest nygromancer that ever was in the world," and *The Institution of a Christian Man* (1537) warns against "charmes, wytch-craftes, or any other false artes subtiles and inuented by the dyuell." Very close to the time of the play, in 1603, Archbishop

Samuel Harsnet declared against "Egregious Popish Impostures" by attacking "our subtiliated, sublimated new spirits of the Sorbon."[1]

But it is not necessary to go beyond the works of Ben Jonson himself to see how closely packed is the parcel of associations. The Prologue to *The Devil is an Ass* says, "Though you presume SATAN a subtill thing, / And may haue heard hee's worne in a thumbe-ring . . ." (5–6), and clearly he is drawing on both senses. Both senses also come into play when a senior devil says to a junior who is assuming a dead man's body, "And, looke, how farre your subtility can worke / Thorough those organs, with that body . . ." (I.i.144–145). Without in this instance using the word "subtle" Jonson explicitly assigns alchemy to the domain of the Devil when Manly asks Wittipol why Fitz-Dottrell loves the Devil so:

O Sir! for hidden treasure,
Hee hopes to finde: and has propos'd himselfe
So infinite a Masse, as to recouer,
He cares not what he parts with, of the present,
To his men of Art, who are the race, may coyne him,
Promise gold-mountaines, and the coueteous
Are still most prodigall! [I.v. 16–22]

In *The Alchemist* itself, Kastril asks Face, "But do's he teach / Liuing, by the wits, too?" and Face replies, "Any thing, what euer, / You cannot thinke that subtiltie but he reads it. / He made me a Captain. I was a starke pimpe" (III.iv.41–44). The comic irony of this passage depends on our knowing that Subtle is a rogue without supernatural powers, and yet it draws sustenance from the covert association with the devil, as does Surly's threat "to find / The subtilties of this darke *labyrinth*" (II.iii.308). We come to realize that this dark labyrinth has "Fortune's privy lodging" at its center. Alchemy (like chemistry, which is still jocularly called "stinks") was a smelly business with its concoctions and menstrues;[2] around the Devil too clung a cloud of brimstone.[3] Dol calls her quarrelling associates "you abominable pair of stinkards" and Face later calls Subtle "you smoky persecutor of nature!"—both phrases calling to

1. The Sorbonne, the University of Paris [*Editor*].

2. The Canon's Yeoman in Chaucer says of alchemists:

And everemoore, where that evere they goon,
Men may hem knowe by smel of brimstoon.
For al the world they stinken as a goot:
Hir savour is so rammissh and so hoot
That though a man from hem a mile be,
The savour wole infecte him, trusteth me.
And thus by smel, and by threedbare array,
If that men liste, this folk they knowe may. [884–891]

Here and elsewhere, they are associated with the Devil (916–918, 984, 1071) and called "sutiltee" (1091, 1247).

3. A stage-direction in *The Castle of Perseverance* (c. 1425) states: "He that schal playe Belyal, loke that he haue gunne-powder brennyn[ge] In pypys in his hands and in his eris and in his ers, whanne he gothe to bat[tel]. . . ." J. Q. Adams, ed., *Chief Pre-Shakespearean Dramas* (Boston, 1924), p. 264. Firecrackers, with their noise and stench, figure of course in *Doctor Faustus;* Jonson's Pug leaves a stench of brimstone when he disappears from prison in *The Devil is an Ass.*

mind the evil-smelling perversities of the Devil and of the alchemist. Ananias speaks better than he knows at the end of the play when he and Tribulation Wholesome beat at the door:

> Come forth, you seed of sulphure, sonnes of fire,
> Your stench, it is broke forth: abomination
> Is in the house. [V.iii.44–46]

The poet that "writ so subtly of the fart" is Ben Jonson.[4]

Before the third member of this infernal trinity[5] can be more fully characterized, the clients begin to arrive, and he must busy himself in a Mosca-like role as Subtle's agent in the complications of the intrigue. (The Devil is very busy, as Latimer[6] used to say, and those who renounce him must renounce "all his works.") This intrigue consists in the cozening of a realistically-conceived sampling of the citizenry of contemporary London.[7] The two small-timers move easily within the power of the cozeners: as their names tell us, Dapper's life is circumscribed within clothes that cut a flashy figure, and Drugger's within the bounds of his trade. The engine of deception turns over in low gear as Sir Epicure Mammon pauses at the door of the house before making one of the superb entrances of drama.

With such a name, it might be expected that Sir Epicure Mammon would step in to fill the incompletely sketched third role, except for two insurmountable reservations. One is that Jeremy, who has been acquitting himself with great dispatch as Captain Face, now adds to himself a second disguise as Lungs, and begins to occupy the central position as the manipulator not only of the

4. Jonson did in fact write a poem on a fart let in the House of Commons [*Editor*].

5. The phrase "infernal trinity" is from Samuel C. Chew, *The Pilgrimage of Life* (Yale, 1962), p. 75. Three of the scaffolds about the 15th-century Castle of Perseverance are assigned to Caro, Mundus, and Belyal [the Flesh, the World, and the Devil—*Editor*] and it is perhaps relevant to note that after the three enemies fail to take the Castle, Mankind relapses seriously into sin through the temptation of Covetousness at the instance of Mundus. The fifteenth-century Morality, *Mary Magdalene,* has eight stages, including one for each of the infernal trinity. The King of the World lays claim to domination over the seven metals in a lengthy speech; later it is on the Stage of the World that the three enemies conspire. The Devil, the Flesh, and the World are the enemies respectively of Mind, Will, and Understanding in the morality play of that name. In *Mankind* there is a brief warning by Mercy against "The World, the Flesh and the Fell"; in *Mundus et Infans,* while the three do not appear, it is significant that the World (and his agent, Folly) besets the figure of mankind in all his manifestations from infancy to old age; in Henry Medwall's *Nature* (Tudor facsimile texts, 1908, sig. B, iv, verso) World says to Man:

Thynke that ye be here / a worldly man
And must do as man / that in the world dwell.

6. Hugh Latimer (1485–1555) was a powerful preacher of the early Reformation period [*Editor*].

7. See the useful article by Alan C. Dessen, "*The Alchemist*, Jonson's 'Estates' Play," *Renaissance Drama*, VII (1964), 35–54, especially his central argument concerning Jonson's making literal a previously allegorical pattern: "Significantly, Jonson has not only transformed the campaign of the Vices against humanity into the campaign of these three rogues against the Jacobean public but has also endowed his realistic conspirators with attitudes and pretensions that implicitly establish their affinity to contemporary business men." (38) In this connection Dessen refers to E. B. Partridge, *The Broken Compass* (London, 1958), pp. 139–44.

dupes but of Dol and Subtle, who act on his cues and shift their shapes less daringly and dangerously than he does. Dol appears and disappears fleetingly through most of the play, and Subtle, after his canting virtuoso pieces in the debates with Surly and Ananias, retires to busy himself with the magisterium behind scenes. "Face" may be defined as "command of countenance, especially with reference to freedom from indication of shame; a bold front; impudence, effrontery, 'cheek.' "[8] "Lungs," realistically appropriate to the plier of the bellows, is also where deep lies come from. Face, then, is in rapid process of growing into this third role, and that is one reason for the exclusion of Sir Epicure as a candidate for it; the other is that Sir Epicure simply will not do as an embodiment of the World.

For all his "pomps and vanities," Sir Epicure Mammon bears about as much resemblance to Mammon, god of worldlings,[9] as he does to Epicurus, the high-minded and frugal philosopher of refined pleasure: the name is a double travesty. One cannot listen to and share the sensual excitement of his great speeches without realizing that such glorious tumidity is not a property of the calculating World. A real worldling, like Shaw's Andrew Undershaft,[1] employs a very different rhetoric. Undershaft, reverting to explicit morality, could indeed play the World, but Sir Epicure would then play Carnal Imagination. That he is carnal in the sense of spiritually undiscerning is proved by his dealing with sorcery yet supposing all the while the sorcerer to be devout. Surly shares this delusion with him, but Mammon goes further in self-deception:

> SVR. Why, I haue heard, he must be *homo frugi*,
> A pious, holy, and religious man,
> One free from mortall sinne, a very virgin.
> MAM. That makes it, sir, he is so. But I buy it. [I.ii.97–100]

That he is carnal in the sense of being given to fleshly motions is amply shown by his dealings with Dol. As for imagination, the connotations of which in the Renaissance are usually pejorative, Mammon is (if one may allude to one great phrase) scattered in the imagination of his heart,[2] for he is (to gather in another) of imagination all compact.[3] Something of a lunatic ("He has, this

8. Partridge, 118–118, note 1.

9. See Upton's note on *The Faerie Queen*, II.vii.8., in the *Variorum Spenser* (Baltimore, 1933), II, 254.

1. Andrew Undershaft is a character in Shaw's *Major Barbara* [*Editor*].

2. The dozen uses of the word "imagination" in the King James Version are all tainted with scheming, vanity, wickedness: Genesis vi.5 and viii.22; Deut. xxix.19 and xxxi.21; Chron. xxviii.9 and xxix.18; Proverbs vi.18; Jer. xxiii.17; Lam. iii.60 and 61; Luke i.51; Romans i.21; II Chron. x.5.

3. Shakespeare's range of association for the word is wider, and often it is used simply for the faculty, without any ill connotation. As well as *A Midsummer Night's Dream* V.i.8, 14, 18, [where we find the allusion to Theseus—*Editor*] we should recall in Mammon's context Angelo's "salt imagination" (*Measure for Treasure* V.i.397) and, of Malvolio "how imagination blows him!" *Twelfth Night* II.v.48).

month, talk'd, as he were possess'd"—I.iv.16), he is more of a lover and poet in Theseus's self-deluding sense, as is demonstrated in the fourth act. At its inception he addresses himself: "Now, EPICVRE, / Heighten thy selfe, talke to her, all in gold" (IV.i.24–25). At the height of the excitement he is still cockering up his genius, though ostensibly addressing Dol:

> and then renew
> Our youth, and strength, with drinking the *elixir*,
> And so enjoy a perpetuitie
> Of life, and lust. [IV.i.163–166]

And at the end he exclaims, "O my voluptuous mind! I am iustly punish'd" (IV.v.74).

Acid resentment and unctuous hypocrisy are both sins of the World, but vinegary Ananias and oily Tribulation belong to a simpler order of satire not immediately relevant to our discussion. That leaves the role of World to Face—unless Surly cares to claim it. He does. But the cards are stacked and the dice loaded against the petty gamester in the big game. "You are incredulous," observes Mammon, and Surly replies:

> Faith, I haue a humor,
> I would not willingly be gull'd. Your *stone*
> Cannot transmute me. [II.i.77–79]

Later, Mammon explains to the Alchemist,

> This gent'man, you must beare withall,
> I told you, he had no faith. SVR And little hope, sir,
> But, much lesse charitie, should I gull my selfe.
> [II.ii.122–124]

Perhaps a little faith and hope and charity might be just the thing to prevail against the World, the Flesh, and the Devil. The name Pertinax means obstinate, and Surly means surly[4]: at no point must director or actor allow the audience a moment of sympathy or fellow-feeling with this spoil-sport. It's possible, but that would be another play; all Surly can see is

> That *Alchemie* is a pretty kind of game,
> Somewhat like tricks o'the cards, to cheat a man,
> With charming. [II.iii.180–182]

His must be the cheerless position of being "nobody's fool," and as this world goes we greatly prefer the slimmer and more ingratiating out-and-out rogue. We are depressed when he thinks he has deserved and won Dame Pliant, exhilarated when his machinations

4. Both names appear in the Epigrams—Don Surly and Pertinax Cob: see Herford and Simpson, VIII, 35–36, 50.

are foiled by Face, and Kastril roars at him the unroarable "pimp!" and "trig!" No, when it comes to the true spirit of this world, Face is your only man.

Or so it seems while the venter tripartite is in operation. But no sooner has the difficulty with Surly been dispatched than the ever-present but forgotten eventuality occurs: Lovewit the master has returned to the city and is in the neighborhood. "Yes, and I dwindled with it," says Subtle when asked if he has heard the hubbub at the door. "Dwindled" is the word: Subtle flourishes only in the bad air of the plague; he is a pest in time of pestilence; rid of one, rid of the other. "Dwindled" we know him to be, but "a little exalted / In the good passage of our stock-affaires" he still declares himself as he kisses Dol, the "fly" and "Queen of Faery" of this malodorous Lord of the Flies, the "fine flitter-mouse" of this threadbare prince of the powers of the air. He has yet one more scheme that may retrieve everything even this late in the day:

> Soone at night, my DOLLY,
> When we are shipt, and all our goods aboord,
> East-ward for *Ratcliffe*; we will turne our course
> To *Brainford*, westward, if thou saist the word:
> And take our leaues of this ore-weaning raskall,
> This peremptorie FACE. [V.iv.74–79]

It is not to be. Face stands possessed of the keys of the trunks, and, as far as this play is concerned, we shall see that possession is the whole of the law. He turns the tables finally on his confederates:

> The right is, my master
> Knowes all, has pardon'd me, and he will keepe 'hem.
> Doctor, 'tis true (you looke) for all your figures:
> I sent for him, indeed. Wherefore, good partners,
> Both hee, and shee, be satisfied: for, here
> Determines the *indenture tripartite*,
> Twixt SVBTLE, DOL, and FACE. [V.iv.126–132]

"Some knock," says the stage-direction. "Harke you, thunder," says Face. It is the devil's own racket, and Subtle exclaims from the heart, "You are a precious fiend!" and Dol, with similar propriety, "Poxe vpon you, rogue." Face is all smug expansiveness:

> SVBTLE,
> Let's know where you set vp next; I'll send you
> A customer, now and then, for old acquaintance:
> What new course ha' you? [V.iv.143–146]

Subtle in reply clinches the allusion to his morality-role:

> Rogue, I'll hang my selfe:
> That I may walke a greater diuell, then thou,
> And haunt thee i'the flock-bed, and the buttery.
> [V.iv.146–148]

This is certainly an adumbration of the title and theme of *The Devil is an Ass*: the clever worldling will outdevil the poor devil every time.[5]

But it is not quite the point and not quite the end of this play. We must reckon at last with the respectable man of the world. This master, in a tangential and crooked reference to a parable already sufficiently puzzling,[6] commends his unjust steward because he has done wisely, for the children of darkness are in their generation wiser than the children of light. "The world will love his own," is a proverb-like phrase in an Elizabethan play.[7] Among the children of darkness (and who, in this play, is not a child of darkness?) one must be wisest or shrewdest of all, and it is Lovewit. Lovewit breaks no law, indeed offers to return any misappropriated property to whoever undertakes to prove his title to it; meanwhile, he keeps all goods and chattles, including "puss my suster" (for what she is worth); and he has the pleasure of being a good fellow, freely forgiving all those who have amused and enriched him.

To this the "judging spectator" must nod his head in assent: yes, the World is like that. Lovewit? You have to hand it to him. And as for Face, let's give him a hand.

ALGERNON CHARLES SWINBURNE

[*Volpone* and *The Alchemist*—Contrast and Comparison]†

In 1605 the singular and magnificent coalition of powers which served to build up the composite genius of Jonson displayed in a single masterpiece the consummate and crowning result of its marvellous energies. No other of even his very greatest works is at once so admirable and so enjoyable. The construction or composition of *The Alchemist* is perhaps more wonderful in the perfection and

5. A minor devil named Pug comes to earth in *The Devil Is an Ass*, but finds that humans are far more wicked than he can be [*Editor*].

6. Luke xvi.1–13.

7. W. Carew Hazlitt, ed., *The Three Ladies of London* by R[obert] W[ilson] (1584), in *A Select Collection of Old English Plays* (London, 1874), VI, 274: Mercatore, the Italian trader says, "For he dat will live in the world must be of the world sure; / And de world will love his own, so long as the world endure." Later, Mercatore falls into the hands of a Jewish usurer but escapes payment by abjuring allegiance to church and state and declaring his intention to become a Turk. The Jew is so shocked that he drops the charge, whereupon Mercatore remains a Christian, proving (I take it) that the worldling is worse than the devilish Jew. It should be noted that Lady Lucre chooses Dissimulation (cf. Face) for her steward.

† From *A Study of Ben Jonson* (London, 1889), pp. 35–42. Swinburne (1837–1909) is better known as poet than critic, and his real gift was for sympathetic appreciation. Still, he did a great deal to revive an interest in the Elizabethan age and its major figures, and his evident pleasure in Jonson's masterpieces may be more likely to send us back to them than wire-drawn analyses of textual details (All footnotes to this essay are by the editor.)

combination of cumulative detail, in triumphant simplicity of process and impeccable felicity of result: but there is in *Volpone* a touch of something like imagination, a savour of something like romance, which gives a higher tone to the style and a deeper interest to the action. The chief agents are indeed what Mr. Carlyle[1] would have called 'unspeakably unexemplary mortals': but the serious fervour and passionate intensity of their resolute and resourceful wickedness give somewhat of a lurid and distorted dignity to the display of their doings and sufferings, which is wanting to the less gigantic and heroic villainies of Subtle, Dol, and Face. The absolutely unqualified and unrelieved rascality of every agent in the later comedy—unless an exception should be made in favour of the unfortunate though enterprising Surly—is another note of inferiority; a mark of comparative baseness in the dramatic metal. In *Volpone* the tone of villainy and the tone of virtue are alike higher. Celia is a harmless lady, if a too submissive consort; Bonario is an honourable gentleman, if too dutiful a son. The Puritan and shopkeeping scoundrels who are swindled by Face and plundered by Lovewit are viler if less villainous figures than the rapacious victims of Volpone.

As to the respective rank or comparative excellence of these two triumphant and transcendent masterpieces, the critic who should take upon himself to pass sentence or pronounce judgment would in my opinion display more audacity than discretion. The steadfast and imperturbable skill of hand which has woven so many threads of incident, so many shades of character, so many changes of intrigue, into so perfect and superb a pattern of incomparable art as dazzles and delights the reader of *The Alchemist* is unquestionably unique—above comparison with any later or earlier example of kindred genius in the whole range of comedy, if not in the whole world of fiction. The manifold harmony of inventive combination and imaginative contrast—the multitudinous unity of various and concordant effects—the complexity and the simplicity of action and impression, which hardly allow the reader's mind to hesitate between enjoyment and astonishment, laughter and wonder, admiration and diversion—all the distinctive qualities which the alchemic cunning of the poet has fused together in the crucible of dramatic satire for the production of a flawless work of art, have given us the most perfect model of imaginative realism and satirical comedy that the world has ever seen; the most wonderful work of its kind that can ever be run upon the same lines. Nor is it possible to resist a certain sense of immoral sympathy and humorous congratulation, more keen than any Scapin or Mascarille[2] can awake in

1. Thomas Carlyle, the Victorian sage. The source of the three words quoted has not been found.

2. Scapin is the central intriguer of Molière's *Les Fourberies de Scapin* (1671); Mascarille is one of the two jokers who animate *Les Précieuses Ridicules* (1659).

the mind of a virtuous reader, when Face dismisses Surly with a promise to bring him word to his lodging if he can hear of 'that Face' whom Surly has sworn to mark for his if ever he meets him. From the date of Plautus to the date of Sheridan[3] it would surely be difficult to find in any comedy a touch of glorious impudence which might reasonably be set against this. And the whole part is so full of brilliant and effective and harmonious touches or strokes of character or of humour that even this crowning instance of serene inspiration in the line of superhuman audacity seems merely right and simply natural.

And yet, even while possessed and overmastered by the sense of the incomparable energy, the impeccable skill, and the indefatigable craftsmanship, which combined and conspired together to produce this æsthetically blameless masterpiece the reader whose instinct requires something more than merely intellectual or æsthetic satisfaction must recognize even here the quality which distinguishes the genius of Ben Jonson from that of the very greatest imaginative humourists—Aristophanes or Rabelais, Shakespeare or Sterne, Vanbrugh or Dickens, Congreve or Thackeray. Each of these was evidently capable of falling in love with his own fancy—of rejoicing in his own imaginative humour as a swimmer in the waves he plays with: but this buoyant and passionate rapture was controlled by an instinctive sense which forbade them to strike out too far or follow the tide too long. However quaint or queer, however typical or exceptional, the figure presented may be—Olivia's or Tristram Shandy's uncle Toby, Sir John Brute or Mr. Peggotty, Lady Wishfort or Lady Kew,[4]—we recognize and accept them as lifelike and actual intimates whose acquaintance has been made for life. Sir Sampson Legend might undoubtedly find himself as much out of place in the drawingroom of the Countess Dowager of Kew as did Sir Wilful Witwoud, on a memorable occasion, in the saloon of his aunt Lady Wishfort[5]: Captain Toby Shandy could hardly have been expected to tolerate the Rabelaisian effervescences of Sir Toby Belch[6]: and Vanbrugh's typical ruffians of rank have little apparently in common with Dickens's representative heroes of the poor. But in all these immortal figures there is the lifeblood of eternal life which can only be infused by the sympathetic faith of the creator in

3. Plautus lived in the third and second centuries B.C., Sheridan in the late 18th century.

4. Swinburne runs together comic figures from different genres: Olivia's uncle Sir Toby Belch from Shakespeare's *Twelfth Night* with Uncle Toby from Sterne's novel *Tristram Shandy;* Sir John Brute from Vanbrugh's play *The Provok'd Wife* (1697) and Mr. Peggotty from Dickens's novel *David Copperfield* (1849); Lady Wishfort from Congreve's play *The Way of the World* (1700) and Lady Kew from Thackeray's novel *The Newcomes* (1855).

5. I.e., Sir Sampson Legend of Congreve's play *Love for Love* would not fit in the drawing-room of Thackeray's Countess Dowager. Sir Wilful Witwoud appears drunk and disorderly in Act IV, scene 10, of Congreve's *Way of the World.*

6. I.e., Captain Toby Shandy (of Sterne's novel) is a good deal better mannered and more tender of disposition than Sir Toby Belch of *Twelfth Night.*

his creature—the breath which animates every word, even if the word be not the very best word that might have been found, with the vital impulse of infallible imagination. But it is difficult to believe that Ben Jonson can have believed, even with some half sympathetic and half sardonic belief, in all the leading figures of his invention. Scorn and indignation are but too often the motives of the mainsprings of his comic art; and when dramatic poetry can exist on the sterile and fiery diet of scorn and indignation, we may hope to find life sustained in happiness and health on a diet of aperients and emetics. The one great modern master of analytic art is somewhat humaner than Jonson in the application of his scientific method to the purpose of dramatic satire. The study of Sludge[7] is finer and subtler by far than the study of Subtle; though undoubtedly it is, in consequence of that very perfection and sublimation of exhaustive analysis, less available for any but a monodramatic purpose. No excuse, no plea, no pretext beyond the fact of esurience[8] and the sense of ability, is suggested for the villainy of Subtle, Dol, and Face. But if we were to see what might possibly be said in extenuation of their rogueries, to hear what might possibly be pleaded in explanation or condonation of their lives, the comedy would fall through and go to pieces: the dramatic effect would collapse and be dissolved. And to this great, single, æsthetic end of art the consummate and conscientious artist who created these immortal figures was content to subdue or to sacrifice all other and subordinate considerations. Coleridge, as no reader will probably need to be reminded, 'thought the *Œdipus Tyrannus, The Alchemist,* and *Tom Jones,* the three most perfect plots ever planned.'[9] With the warmest admiration and appreciation of Fielding's noble and immortal masterpiece, I cannot think it at all worthy of comparison, for blameless ingenuity of composition and absolute impeccability of design, with the greatest of tragic and the greatest of comic triumphs in construction ever accomplished by the most consummate and the most conscientious among ancient and modern artists. And when we remember that this perfection of triumphant art is exhibited, not on the scale of an ordinary comedy, whether classic or romantic, comprising a few definite types and a few impressive situations, but on a scale of invention so vast and so various as to comprise in the course of a single play as many characters and as many incidents, all perfectly adjusted and naturally developed out of each other, as would amply suffice for the entire dramatic furniture, for the entire poetic equipment, of a great dramatic poet, we

7. Robert Browning's dramatic monologue "'Mr. Sludge, the Medium" is a deep study of an accomplished hypocrite.

8. Hunger, but with an overtone from Juvenal, who says there is nothing that a "hungry Greeklet" (*Graeculus esuriens*) won't pretend to know (Satire 3, verse 78).

9. Samuel Taylor Coleridge, the romantic poet, made this remark on July 5, 1834; it is included in his *Table Talk*.

feel that Gifford's[1] expression, a 'prodigy of human intellect,' is equally applicable to *The Fox* and to *The Alchemist*, and is not a whit too strong a term for either. Nor can I admit, as I cannot discern, the blemish or imperfection which others have alleged that they descry in the composition of *Volpone*—the unlikelihood of the device by which retribution is brought down in the fifth act on the criminals who were left at the close of the fourth act in impregnable security and triumph. So far from regarding the comic Nemesis or rather Ate[2] which infatuates and impels Volpone to his doom as a sacrifice of art to morality, an immolation of probability and consistency on the altar of poetic justice, I admire as a master-stroke of character the haughty audacity of caprice which produces or evolves his ruin out of his own hardihood and insolence of exulting and daring enjoyment. For there is something throughout of the lion as well as of the fox in this original and incomparable figure. I know not where to find a third instance of catastrophe comparable with that of either *The Fox* or *The Alchemist* in the whole range of the highest comedy; whether for completeness, for propriety, for interest, for ingenious felicity of event or for perfect combination and exposition of all the leading characters at once in supreme simplicity, unity, and fullness of culminating effect.

* * *

STEPHEN ORGEL

More Removed Mysteries†

We have now considered the Jonsonian masque in relation to its tradition, its audience, and its theater. From the Tudor disguisings,[1] the Jacobean poet received a form that was primarily spectacular and choreographic. Dialogue, in the early years, was strictly secondary if it appeared at all—we have seen how small the function of the speeches was even in so complex an entertainment as Katherine of Aragon's wedding masque in 1501. But the tradition also included something that made the masque a very special kind of entertainment, and this was the convention of bringing the monarch, and later other members of the audience, into the action of the work. This element, so central to the Jonsonian form,

1. William Gifford (1756–1826), English critic and man of letters, was an early and influential editor of Jonson's works.
2. Nemesis is doom or fate, a protentous goddess; Ate (pronounced with two syllables) is simply the goddess of mischief.
† From *The Jonsonian Masque* (Cambridge: Harvard University Press, 1965), pp. 186–202. Footnotes are by the editor, unless otherwise noted.
1. Primitive shows, because of the masks and costumes worn, were called "disguisings."

appears in English court entertainments as early as 1377, when a group of masked mummers[2] interrupted a banquet to cast loaded dice with the young Richard II; and Lydgate in 1430 virtually uses Henry VI to conclude a dramatic contention. The court entertainment under Henry VIII changed in character from a show to a game as the king himself danced in the revels; we have traced the development of the Tudor disguising through the works of William Cornysshe and William Crane. *Riches and Love* (1527) displays all the qualities of a mature work of art, and the form developed by Crane remained basically unchanged until Elizabethan times.

It is the discreteness of its parts that most distinctly characterizes the Tudor masque. By 1527, dialogue had clearly become important and even necessary to a form of some complexity. Crane employs three elements in his work: speeches, symbolic action in pantomime, and dance. But he keeps them rigidly separate and unifies the masque by thematic and structural means. His followers under Edward VI and Mary preserved the discreteness more than the unity of the form, and for many years drama and the revels were two different kinds of entertainment. The masque retained its pageants and dances and gave up its dialogue to literature.

It was through literature that the Elizabethan masque continued to develop as a form. William Hunnis employed the basic device of the tradition when, at Kenilworth in 1575, he made Queen Elizabeth an active figure in his drama of the lady of the lake. And in the greatest of the Elizabethan entertainments, Sidney's *The Lady of May*, the monarch was asked—not merely figuratively, but actually—to solve the central contention of the work. Finally, Francis Davison's *Masque of Proteus* attempted to bring together again the parts of the old Tudor disguising by uniting dialogue with dance and by concluding with the revels.[3]

If the type of masque Davison developed looks back to an earlier tradition, it also looks forward to Jonson's work. For the Jacobean poet was deeply concerned with the unity of his form, and he achieved that unity by treating the masques as literature. Jonson transmuted the occasional elements of his commission into integral parts of what was, for him, a poem. We have examined in some detail what constitutes a "successful" Jonsonian masque by looking at both the poet's intentions and his achievement. If *Oberon* is a failure as a masque, it is the failure of a great artist who is still unsure of his form. There is no trace of such uncertainty in *Neptunes Triumph*.[4]

We have considered three masques as steps toward the develop-

2. Players.
3. Sidney's *Lady of May* was presented before Elizabeth in 1578; Francis Davison's *Masque of Proteus* dates from 1595.
4. *Oberon* is dated 1611, *Neptune's Triumph* 1624.

ment of a form in which all elements were integrated into a literary work. Jonson's task as a masque writer was to join a number of totally disparate artistic disciplines; to satisfy the seemingly irreconcilable demands of his audience and his own poetic sense; to merge spectator and actor in a single mimetic illusion. We have seen just how rigidly conventional the form was as he received it. But conventions were his tools; and the way in which he analyzed and used them creatively is as much a triumph of his critical ability as of his theatrical skill.

When a culture accepts the conventions of art without understanding them, the sensibility of the age is in danger of stagnation. The mind then responds not to aesthetic experiences, but to mere formulas, automatically; and the time is ripe for the artist to revitalize both his tradition and his culture through a reinterpretation of the forms of art. Essentially this is what Jonson is doing with the masque. Though he is working on a small scale—the form is unusually rigid, and the audience unusually limited—the problems he encounters are basically the problems of all art. We cannot doubt that, by the time of *Neptunes Triumph*, the masque has become in every sense a viable form.

A striking illustration of the automatic response to art is preserved in Queen Elizabeth's reaction to *The Lady of May*. Sidney's work was a critical examination of convention—in rejecting the shepherd for the forester, he was implying that pastoral was not merely a pleasant romance, but a significant comment on human activity. The queen, however, was too well versed in the convention to follow the poet's argument. Shepherds are the heroes of pastoral, and therefore Espilus must win the lady.

We may consider the dances in a similar light, as a conventional element of the Jacobean masque. When the primary function of the form was to provide an excuse for the revels, the masque in a sense became subservient to its conventions. A notable example is Gascoigne's Montacute entertainment (1572), in which the poet accepts the requirements of his form so uncritically that his avowed purpose is simply "to devise some verses . . . convenient to render a good cause of the . . . [masquers'] presence."[5] Davison's *Proteus* retains much of this quality, and we find it even in Jonson's masques of *Blacknesse* and *Queenes*. But Jonson is clearly moving in a new direction, making a living art of a set of conventions by using them organically in his work. And by 1618 he had found a way to make even the conventional dances functional. At the culmination of *Pleasure Reconcild to Vertue*, they are not only dramatically possible, but structurally necessary.

5. *The Posies*, ed. J. W. Cunliffe (Cambridge, England, 1907), p. 75 [Orgel's note].

Not that *Pleasure Reconcild* is the ideal masque-as-poem. It is rather more diffuse than we, as readers, could wish, and its verse is occasionally uneven in quality. But in it, nevertheless, Jonson has solved all the basic problems. He no longer relies on descriptions of setting; there are no gaps in the text, and no breaches of dramatic decorum. And the final dance-songs are such striking examples of the Jonsonian method at its most successful that we may fairly take this masque as marking the beginning of the great period of his career that produced *The Gypsies Metamorphos'd* and *Neptunes Triumph* and ended only with the end of the reign.

In other ways, too, *Pleasure Reconcild to Vertue* provides a useful vantage point from which to survey our study of the masque form. If we compare it with the solidly realized drama of *Oberon*, the 1618 work will seem almost a throwback to the Tudor entertainments. In structure, it is like a pageant;[6] and though in it Jonson has unified the theatrical and literary elements, the masque is conceived in sections that are very nearly as discrete as those of *Riches and Love* had been ninety years earlier. Interestingly enough, both works also use their dances in much the same way, as a ballet on a poetically stated theme. The questions with which the masques are concerned are finally resolved in the revels—the action, that is, does not simply allow a choreographic conclusion, but requires one. The Jonsonian masque moves away from drama as the antimasque moves toward it.

The ultimate significance of the masque, however, is not defined simply by the antithetical worlds of antimasque and revels. Neither Comus nor Daedalus presides over the court in which we find ourselves at the end of *Pleasure Reconcild to Vertue*. Rather, it is a middle realm, existing somewhere between the extremes of the antimasque's misrule and the revels' order, but including both as possibilities. Indeed, this masque asserts with equal strength both the power of the individual will to overcome disorder and the insubstantiality of the ideal vision. The final song clearly implies the difficulties and uncertainties attendant upon the choice of virtue as a way of life, and Jonson's metaphors provide us with nothing so easy to follow as the conventional pathway. Nevertheless, the choice *is* possible to the resolved mind, and it constitutes the only truly heroic action in the world Jonson has created.

Jonsonian drama presents no image of heroic virtue; but the poetry of the *Epigrammes*, *The Forrest*, and *The Underwood* celebrates numerous figures who have, like Hercules,[7] made the exemplary choice and stand as models to mankind. It is, in fact, in this

6. A pageant is a succession of scenes or tableaux.

7. In his youth Hercules had to choose between pleasure and virtue; the Renaissance was fascinated with this decision, and often represented it in paintings; the story of course underlies Jonson's *Pleasure Reconciled to Virtue*.

world and with this kind of heroic potential that the mature Jonsonian masque leaves us. The heroes of Jonson's poetry are—sometimes literally—simply masquers unmasked. Lady Mary Worth, a nymph in *The Masque of Blacknesse*, thus becomes a prototype of womanly virtue, capable of replacing the traditional sources of poetic inspiration:

> Madame, had all antiquitie beene lost,
> All historie seal'd up, and fables crost;
> That we had left us, nor by time, nor place,
> Least mention of a *Nymph*, a *Muse*, a *Grace*,
> But even their names were to be made a-new,
> Who could not but create them all, from you? [lines 1–6][8]

Jonson then presents her, appropriately disgused, as several mythological figures:

> He, that but saw you wear the wheaten hat,
> Would call you more then CERES, if not that:
> And, drest in shepheards tyre, who would not say:
> You were the bright OENONE, FLORA, or *May*?
> If dancing, all would cry th'*Idalian* Queene,
> Were leading forth the *Graces* on the greene:
> And, armed to the chase, so bare her bow
> DIANA'alone, so hit, and hunted so.
> There's none so dull, that for your stile would aske,
> That saw you put on PALLAS plumed caske:
> Or, keeping your due state, that would not cry,
> There JUNO sate, and yet no Peacock by.
> So are you *Natures Index*, and restore,
> I'your selfe, all treasure lost of th'age before. [lines 12–20][9]

Here, as in the masque, the disguise is only an expression of the inner reality. It is what establishes the figure as a valid symbol, making the heroine "Natures Index," in whom all the lost virtues are preserved. But at the same time, the disguise also serves to convey those virtues to a world of spectators, and thereby to recreate in the present the heroism of the past.

Similarly, to the Countess of Bedford—another nymph in the masques of *Blacknesse* and *Beautie* and a queen in *The Masque of Queenes*—Jonson not only gives all the social graces, but allows her to be untouched by the vicissitudes of sublunary life:

> a learned, and a manly soule
> I purpos'd her; that should, with even powers,

8. "To Mary Lady Wroth," Herford and Simpson, VIII, 67–68.

9. *Ibid.*, p. 68. Of the pagan goddesses mentioned in the passage, Ceres is goddess of the harvest, Oenone was the daughter of a river god and mistress of Paris, Flora was the goddess of flowers, and the "Idalian Queen" is Aphrodite. Pallas is recognized by her plumed helmet ("caske") and Juno despite the fact that there is no peacock near to identify her, as there properly should be.

> The rock, the spindle, and the sheeres controule
> Of destinie, and spin her owne free houres.[1]

Sir William Roe, returning from a journey, has the character of a classic hero:

> This is that good AENEAS, past through fire,
> Through seas, stormes, tempests: and imbarqu'd for hell,
> Came back untouch'd.[2]

And Sir Lucius Cary and Sir Henry Morison, in the great ode written near the end of Jonson's career, become explicit heroic examples in a world that barely makes room for virtue:

> You liv'd to be the great surnames,
> And titles, by which all made claimes
> Unto the Vertue. Nothing perfect done,
> But as a CARY, or a MORISON.
> And such a force the faire example had,
> As they that saw
> The good, and durst not practise it, were glad
> That such a Law
> Was left yet to Man-kind[3]

Such figures fill the poems, safeguarding the classic truths in a society that has forgotten them. They embody the ideals of the masque in settings that suggest the plays.

There is one particularly striking instance where the masque itself is included in Jonson's poetic vision. In the espistle to Sir Robert Wroth,[4] the hero's moral choice is seen in the traditional terms of the rejection of a court world for a pastoral idyll:

> How blest art thou, canst love the countrey, WROTH,
> Whether by choice, or fate, or both;
> And, though so neere the citie, and the court,
> Art tane with neithers vice, nor sport. [lines 1–4]

Here, ironically, the masque, reduced to its most momentary and spectacular aspects, exemplifies the vices of society, and provides a center for Jonson's satiric comment:

> Nor throng'st (when masquing is) to have a sight
> Of the short braverie of the night;
> To view the jewells, stuffes, the paines, the wit
> There wasted, some not paid for yet!
> But canst, at home, in thy securer rest,
> Live, with un-bought provisions blest. [lines 9–14]

1. "On Lucy Countess of Bedford," lines 13 16, H&S, VIII, 52. The distaff "rock"), spindle, and shears are attributes of the three Fates, who spin, measure, and cut the thread of life.
2. "To William Roe," lines 12–14, H&S, VIII, 81.
3. "To the immortal memory . . . of . . . Cary and Morison," lines 113–21, H&S, VIII, 247.
4. "To Sir Robert Wroth," H&S, VIII, 96–100.

The poem then modulates into the richness of a pastoral landscape, equally artificial, but also fruitful and lasting:

> Among'st the curled woods, and painted meades,
>   Through which a serpent river leades
> To some coole, courteous shade, which he calls his,
>   And makes sleepe softer then it is! . . .
> The whil'st, the severall seasons thou has seene
>   Of flowrie fields, of cop'ces greene,
> The m[illegible]ed meddowes, with the fleeced sheepe,
>   And feasts, that either shearers keepe;
> The ripened eares, yet humble in their height,
>   And furrows laden with their weight;
> The apple-harvest, that doth longer last;
>   The hogs return'd home fat from mast;
> The trees cut out in log; and those boughes made
>   A fire now, that lent a shade! [lines 17–46]

Here, within the pastoral world, the masque is summoned up again. Now it is an expression of order and bounty, and it relates the virtuous man to whatever is mythical and divine:

>   COMUS puts in, for new delights;
> And fills thy open hall with mirth, and cheere,
>   As if in SATURNES raigne it were;
> APOLLO's harpe, and HERMES lyre resound,
>   Nor are the *Muses* strangers found:
> The rout of rurall folke come thronging in,
>   (Their rudenesse then is thought no sinne)
> Thy noblest spouse affords them welcome grace;
>   And the great *Heroes*, of her race,
> Sit mixt with losse of state, or reverence. [lines 48–57]

The hosts have, with the entrance of the gods, become a race of heroes. Comus is not a villain in this setting, and the appearance of "the rout of rurall folk"—like the cook's antimasque of sailors in *Neptunes Triumph*—is here "thought no sinne." In fact, both appetite and rudeness, natural simplicity and good humor, belong to this life. It is the city (on which the masque is "wasted," a mere diversion) that denies and destroys what is human, and from which nature is excluded:

> Let this man sweat, and wrangle at the barre,
>   For every price, in every jarre,
> And change possessions, oftner with his breath,
>   Then either money, warre, or death:
> Let him, then hardest sires, more disinherit,
>   And each where boast it as his merit,
> To blow up orphanes, widdowes, and their states;
>   And thinke his power doth equall *Fates*.

Let that goe heape a masse of wretched wealth,
  Purchas'd by rapine, worse then stealth,
And brooding o're it sit, with broadest eyes,
  Not doing good, scarce when he dyes.
Let thousands more goe flatter vice, and winne,
  By being organges to great sinne,
Get place, and honor, and be glad to keepe
  The secrets, that shall breake their sleepe:
And, so they ride in purple, eate in plate,
  Though poyson, thinke it a great fate. [lines 73–90]

This might be an anthology of evils from Jonsonian comedy and represents the realities with which the hero is faced. But the hero, in such poems as this, has a more evident and more important kind of reality even than the world of Jonson's satire: he has the reality of the masquer, the nobleman beneath the symbolic disguise, who is capable of learning, choosing, and acting. It is such figures, steadfast in a world of vice, misrule, and decay, who provide the links between the ideal vision of Jonsonian masque and the satiric vision of Jonsonian drama.

Drama exists in time: things happen and characters act on each other. Conversely, the world of the volatile and spectacular masque is a world of ideas, untouched by change, Often, as the antimasque is banished, we hear an invocation to the forces of nature to stay their motion; and the scene is lifted out of time. The end of *Love Freed from Ignorance and Folly* (1611) makes explicit the value of this poetic device:

What just excuse had aged *Time*,
  His wearie limbes now to have eas'd,
And sate him downe without his crime,
  While every thought was so much pleas'd!
For he so greedie to devoure
  His owne, and all that hee brings forth,
Is eating every piece of houre
  Some object of the rarest worth.
Yet this is rescued from his rage
  As not to die by time, or age.[5]

The poet's very concern that the masque be valid as literature has been metaphorically incorporated into the work.

I remarked in an earlier chapter that, in the two late masques written for King Charles, Jonson was unable to transmute the occasional elements into poetry, and I have suggested some reasons for their comparative failure as literature. To recapitulate briefly, both *Loves Triumph Through Callipolis* and *Chloridia* are essentially

5. *Love Freed from Ignorance and Folly,* lines 358–67, H&S, VII, 370.

accounts of theatrical spectacles, with occasional dialogue and song. Although what verse they contain is often excellent, the form is clearly no longer the poet's. So marked is the ascendancy of architect and choreographer over the aging Jonson that the antimasque of *Loves Triumph* includes no text at all. The poet's function was now to provide a description of a work conceived largely in visual terms, and he vented his dissatisfaction with this new position in the famous expostulation.[6]

> O Showes! Showes! Mightly Showes!
> The Eloquence of Masques! What need of prose
> Or Versee, or Sense t'express Immortall you?
> You are the Spectacles of State!

In *Pleasure Reconcild*, we saw how effectively Jonson could use literary terminology to express the other elements of the masque. Here the same device is employed for satiric ends; but the irony of "The Eloquence of Masques!" implies all too clearly that the poet is out of a job. The form has new conventions, the audience new expectations:

> Oh, to make Boardes to speake! There is a task!
> Painting and Carpentry are the Soule of Masque!
> Pack with your pedling Poetry to the Stage!
> This is the money-gett, Mechanick Age![7]

Jonson—and not Jonson alone—has been replaced by Jones,[8] the master-surveyor,

> The maker of the Propertyes! in summe
> The Scene! The Engine! but he now is come
> To be the Musick-Master! Fabler too!
> He is, or would be the mayne Dominus doe
> All in the Worke!

We have already looked at the circumstances surrounding Jonson's return to the stage. It is hardly surprising that the return was not a triumphant one, for both external considerations and the poet's own development worked against a new dramatic success. *The Staple of Newes*, produced in 1626, was Jonson's first play in ten years; its appearance nearly coincided with the coronation of King Charles. We may assume that between Twelfth Night 1625, when the old king's court witnessed *The Fortunate Isles*, and February 1626, when the new king's servants performed *The Staple of Newes*, Jonson gained a good notion of what he might expect at the

6. "An Expostulation with Inigo Jones," lines 39–42, H&S VIII, 403.
7. *Ibid.*, lines 49–52.
8. On Inigo Jones, the architect and scene-designer with whom Jonson quarreled so fiercely, see "The Staging of Jonson's Plays and Masques," above. The lines that follow are 61–65 of the "Expostulation."

Whitehall of Charles and Henrietta Maria. But the conventions of the stage and the expectations of the viewers were no longer what they had been fifteen years ealier, the time of the poet's greatest dramatic successes—nor could Jonson have written another *Alchemist* if he had wished. His art had moved beyond the great plays of the decade before 1614, and we shall be ignoring the evidence of the masques and the poetry if we decide that it had not progressed.

To put the case in very simple terms, during the period when Jonson was creating his court entertainments, he was also creating an audience for them. As we have seen, the masques show a remarkable comprehension of the demands of that audience—of all his rivals at court, Jonson alone was regularly commissioned to produce the Twelfth-Night entertainment—and it is a comprehension that grows in depth and subtlety over the years. If we think of Jonson as primarily a court poet and scholar after 1616, we shall not find it strange that he should have been less in touch with the interests of the paying spectator than with those of what was essentially a captive audience. But this is only part of the story. In the last decade of the old reign, Jonson's dramatic art developed entirely through the masque form. And the concept of theater that crystallized in the masque had also made the drama rigid.

The masque is a world of absolutes, in which all action is inherent in the nature of the individual figures. What we would call the drama of the form (what happens on stage) is predetermined by the structure of such a world: we have examined an extreme case in *The Masque of Queenes*, where Good banishes Evil without even a confrontation. I have briefly suggested that the same tendency is apparent in Jonsonian comedy; for the humors theory supposes that characteristics determine action, and thus what a character will do is as much a part of his nature as the particular humor that makes him a subject for comedy. Roughly, then, there are two kinds of people in the "normal" Jonsonian comedy: the cheats and the cheated. These two fit in with each other as gears in a machine; when they are made to mesh, the play begins to move. Yet, of course, drama involves interaction of characters, conflict—a condition, in short, in which the gears cease to mesh and the play's predetermined movement is violated. Thus, for example, the central action of *The Alchemist* is built around a fight between Subtle and Face, a situation in which one figure refuses to fulfill the role ordained for him. I have grossly oversimplified what is in Jonson's hands a complex and malleable form. Nevertheless, the concept is basic to all Jonsonian comedy.

But Jonsonian comedy is satire—so, indeed, is Jonsonian tragedy—and the masque has different ends. If in the humors plays characteristics are absolutes, they are only absolutes on the human scale.

There are fools and there are swindlers; but the figures of Virtue, Beauty, Fame, that fill the masques and are intermittently visible in the poems are largely missing from the plays. To a satirist, of course, it is human vice that is eternal, but vice is as absent from the world of the revels as virtue is from the drama. In a sense, Jonson produced the best masques because he had produced the best humors comedies: the courtly form shows us the humors theory applied to universals.

The difficulty with the late plays is that the violation of the movement I have described as mechanical never takes place. The fantastic complexity of the plot of *The New Inne* (1629) only testifies to the trouble Jonson was having in getting anything to happen on stage; the play remains a collection of characters, and not very clearly drawn characters at that. It seems obvious that, for a dramatist experiencing this sort of difficulty, the masque provided not only an ideal solution, but a medium in which he had a freer hand. As we have seen throughout our consideration of the form, whatever happens in the masque happens not so much between the characters themselves as between the characters and the viewers. Jonson sees the revels as the moment when the masquer breaks through the limits of his stage, when the illusion moves out into the audience. This is the point toward which the action of the masque moves, and there could be no such climax in a play.

Nevertheless, there are analogous elements in Jonson's drama. It is a commonplace to say that the plays tend to be self-conscious—we are constantly being presented with characters who comment on the action, with plays within plays, with critical inductions and epilogues to explain the drama. The *point* of a drama, Shakespeare might have objected, is that it acts out its meaning, and no explanation can do it justice. And yet, as early as *Every Man Out of His Humour* (1599), Jonson was experimenting with nondramatic means of getting closer to his audiences—and critics. After a brief opening dialogue, Asper looks out into the Globe theater:

> I not observ'd this thronged round till now.
> Gracious and kind spectators, you are welcome, [I.i.51–52]

and he continues to expound the purpose of the play he is presenting. He even provides stand-ins for an audience he cannot bring on stage:

> What? are you ready there! MITIS sit downe:
> And my CORDATUS. Sound hough, and begin.
> I leave you two, as censors, to sit here:
> Observe what I present, and liberally
> Speake your opinions, upon every Scene,
> As it shall passe the view of these spectators. [I.i.151–156]

This is undeniably a way for the playwright to move closer to his viewers, but paradoxically it also keeps the viewers at a considerable distance from the dramatic action. In the great comedies, Jonson manages to effect the necessary rapport through the more usual means of dramatic irony. But in the later plays, the move off stage has become all-important; it is as if the poet can no longer express himself through drama. *The Magnetick Lady*, which one would think was clear enough, has not only an induction but an explanatory chorus to conclude every act except the last. *The New Inne*, which proved incomprehensible to its first—and last—contemporary audience, had to be provided with arguments not only of the whole play but of each act individually, with even a note marking the point where "the Epitasis, or businesse of the Play" begins (incidentally, it does not begin until the third act), and a list of the dramatis personae "With some short Characterisme of the chiefe Actors."

These brief notes should suggest in what way the masques are a link between the playwright of *Volpone* and that of *The New Inne*. The idea of theater that Jonson conceived, he could perfect only in the masque. The unmediated confrontation of actor and spectator was impossible in the playhouse, though the conventions of French drama came closer to allowing it than did the English. Thus Molière's miser, Harpagon, can turn to the audience and beg for information of the thief who has robbed him.[9] This is, admittedly, an atypical instance: even French characters do not generally go quite this far. But if we wish more usual examples, we have only to consider the ease and frequency with which Molière brings a single actor on stage to explain his intentions or feelings. Such a scene has the quality of an extended aside; in contrast, the Elizabethan soliloquy is a more formal device, usually the place for some very serious thinking. Neither one actually acknowledges the audience, though often the French dramatist, without breaking the framework of the play's illusion, does directly involve the spectator in the stage action.

For example, in *L'Ecole des Femmes*, Arnolphe's remarks on husbands are strictly relevant to the dramatic situation, but they are also obviously pronounced with an oblique gesture toward the audience: "Fort bien: est il au monde une autre ville aussi / Où il ait des maris si patients qu'ici?"[1] Arnolphe is not, like a Jonsonian explicator, speaking out of context; he is not a chorus, but a character. We see the flaws in his reasoning, just as his friend Chrysalde

9. This is the concluding scene of Act IV of *L'Avare*.

1. "You're right: is there a nation anywhere, / Where husbands serve as patiently as here?" [*L'Ecole des Femmes*, I, 1, tr. R.M.A.]

does, and thus the playwright gives us the same reality as he has given his stage figures. We have also seen this quality achieved by Sidney in *The Lady of May*, and by Jonson himself in the opening of *Love Restored*, through the use of direct addresses to the audience. We might briefly contrast the effect of an Elizabethan soliloquy on the spectator. Prince Hal's revelation, "I know you all, and will awhile uphold / The unyok'd humour of your idleness," tells us things about him that no other mere character can know.[2] The soliloquy enables us to see into the speaker; it gives him another dimension, a depth of a sort that is, on the whole, alien to the characters of comedy. Hal exposes his motives, and, though we may not approve, we understand and sympathize. Arnolphe exposes his motives, and we understand and criticize. If we see into Hal, we see through Arnolphe. In Hal's case, we are in collusion with a character; in Arnolphe's, with the author.

As a concluding note, it is interesting to remark that what I have defined as the masque movement has borne fruit in the modern theatre. Jonson's age was developing conventions of the stage and the nature of the illusion it contains that have persisted until the present century. If the Jacobean poet was to see the climax of his work as a point at which the actor broke through the limits of his stage, those limits had to be very firmly defined. Thus, Inigo Jones regularly used the proscenium arch for masques, though not for plays,[3] and through the use of perspective stressed visual realism in his settings. It is this illusion of reality that the masque is able to extend out into its audience. But, placed on such a stage, the drama had to remain behind its proscenium; and we may date the end of the Shakespearean age in the theater from the time when a masque setting could also contain the action of a play. The necessity for scenic realism precludes the fluidity attained by Shakespeare's drama, with its frequent short scenes and changes of location. Even so simple a convention as the soliloquy, which was perfectly unexceptionable in an Elizabethan playhouse, is troublesome on a realistic stage where we have a tendency to see a man alone talking to himself. Burbage's Hamlet was far closer to his viewers than Garrick's.[4] But our own age is beginning to conceive of another kind of theater. Pirandello's[5] actors cannot quite merge with their audience as did the Tudor masquers when they unmasked; but they

2. I *Henry IV*, I, 2.
3. See E. K. Chambers, *The Elizabethan Stage* (Oxford, 1923), I, 234 [Orgel's note].
4. Richard Burbage played Hamlet in the original production, David Garrick in the 18th century.
5. Luigi Pirandello (1867–1936) wrote many plays in which the line between artifice ("acting") and life ("reality") is blurred or overstepped.

come very close to it when, in *Tonight We Improvise,* they appear and chat in the theater lobby during intermission. Thornton Wilder uses his stage manager in *Our Town*[6] as a similar means to more conventional ends. Indeed, we could choose examples ranging from Chekhov to Adamov.[7] If the drama is approaching its audience again after three hundred years, it must have something to say that cannot be expressed from behind a proscenium wall. No longer confronted by an illusion of reality, we may find, like the courtly spectator at the moment of the revels, that the world of theater is one in which we play a new kind of part.

ROBERT M. ADAMS

On the Bulk of Ben

He was a heavy man. Everyone felt it, and he said so himself, heavily. What other lover, in the course of recommending himself to his mistress, ever took occasion to remind her of his mountain belly and rocky face (Herford and Simpson, VIII, 150)? Earth and the earthy are always close at hand in Jonson's work, as if, like Antaeus the fabled opponent of Hercules, he drew strength from tangible, ingestible things through the mere act of naming them. Joyce's foil Stephen Dedalus, lecturing professorially in *Ulysses,* describes Shakespeare's art as that of surfeit (Random House, 1934, p. 199): Jonson deserves the epithet better. The impulses of the gut and groin, if generally subject to some limit or correction, are given voice throughout his work to a degree unparalleled. Gross voluptuaries like Volpone and Sir Epicure Mammon ransack the records of antiquity as compiled in awe-struck detail by the chroniclers of Roman decadence; they puff their fantasies on tales of legendary gluttons like Heliogabalus, Nero, and Apicius, multiplying their identities under the incitements of Ovid in order to multiply their sensual pleasures. But these monstrous animated appetites do not stand alone in Jonson's world. *Bartholomew Fair* (1614) reeks with the grease and steam of cooking pig; a fine oily pig-woman occupies the very center of the intrigue. In the masque *Pleasure Reconciled to Virtue* (1618), the belly-god Comus bounces across the stage, related in only the loosest possible way to an action that the viewers have not yet seen, chanting the delights of puddings

6. Thornton Wilder's *Our Town* (1938) has a stage manager who mediates between audience and actors, explaining the actions, providing transitions and commentaries, etc.

7. Anton Chekhov (1860–1904) is often taken as the figure who set the modern theater on its present path; Arthur Adamov (1908–70), is, or was when Orgel wrote, an example of the avant-garde French drama.

and meats, and of the paunch they stuff. Praise of the Sidney estate at Penshurst is praise of the way one eats there; a poem inviting a friend to dinner emphasizes the modesty of the repast to be expected, but it's one on which a man as lean as Macilente (of *Every Man Out of His Humour*) could quickly grow plump (H&S, VIII, 93, 64). The digestive tract is one major focus of Jonson's interest; people on his stage eat and are motivated by the desire to eat, they excrete, fart, burp, and suffer from heartburn; when they're not actually eating, they talk about it, and the playwright defines their characters by their attitude to food and drink.

In his learning as well, Jonson tended to come on strong. His respect for fact was great, maybe excessive, and he commonly laid down his authorities, whether for a marriage-entertainment like *Hymenaei* (1606) or in a private commonplace-book like *Discoveries*, with a certain loving fullness which reminds us that his education was at the hands of an antiquarian. The weighty footnoting of *Sejanus* (1603) and *Catiline* (1611) is only to be expected; as Roman tragedies, they were written by the book, out of books, and could hardly be otherwise. Besides, Jonson was on his mettle; there had been Roman tragedies before, like those of Shakespeare, in which the author committed gross anachronisms. Jonson in his big showpieces about antiquity was bound to make much of his authenticity. But the anti-masque of witches in the *Masque of Queens* also rests on a substantial foundation of learning, the full extent of which we can now appreciate only because of the accident that led Prince Henry to ask for Jonson's documentation. Ben brought the same archaeologizing turn of mind to Bartholomew Fair, whose sprawling, squalid, vital tangle of intrigues only a man fascinated with details would have tried to put onstage. When he was *into* a subject, such as alchemy, will-chasing, street-life, or talkative women, Jonson tended to work it up, as if sorting his vast miscellaneous erudition into topical piles. Some of the best aphorisms in *Volpone* are from Seneca, and they stand out as if he wanted them (and he did) to be recognized behind the Venetian surfaces. This is what gives Jonson's plays the semblance, often attributed in the 19th century to the plays of Henrik Ibsen, of being costume dramas in modern dress. They are bifocal plays, with a long perspective and a very close one;[1] between the two a constant reflex action is sensed.

Again, Jonson loves language for its own sake, in a way that makes his plays particularly heavy. Terms of art flood *The Alche-*

1. Among Jonson's poems, the fiercely contemptuous and denunciatory "Epistle to a Friend to Persuade Him to the Wars" contrasts strangely with the poems of compliment and flattery. Even more curiously, plays like *Bartholomew Fair* and *Epicoene* have produced almost schizoid reactions among the critics, some seeing them as gay, others as grim. See also the remarkable double attitude toward masques noted by Orgel, above, pp. 474 ff.

mist as if to stun and bewilder the audience as in fact they are intended to stun and bewilder the characters onstage. They thunder forth, not single file, but in battalions, like a deliberate act of aggression. Though it's not always built into the plot this way, linguistic overkill crops out elsewhere in Jonson's plays, with or without overt justification. For example, when Ursula is persuading Captain Whit the bawd that he should convert Win-the-Fight Littlewit to become "a bird o' the game," she puts the matter like this:

> Dost thou hear, Whit? Is't not a pity my delicate dark chestnut here, with the fine lean head, large forehead, round eyes, even mouth, sharp ears, long neck, thin crest, close withers, plain back, deep sides, short fillets, and full flanks; with a round belly, a plump buttock, large thighs, knit knees, straight legs, short pasterns, smooth hoofs, and short heels, should lead a dull honest woman's life, that might lead the life of a lady?[2]

The speech evidently parodies the speech of a horse-auctioneer, but the point about flesh-dealers is made early and hammered unremittingly; it doesn't consort particularly with Ursula's character elsewhere in the play, and her command of the patter does more to remind us that an actor is speaking than to deepen her stage presence.

In fact, Jonson has something of Rabelais' fondness for lists and verbiage. He pursues the ideal of fullness and fluency (the Renaissance phrase was *copia*), and many of his characters become, if only for a moment, mouthpieces through whom an enormous pressure of language releases itself. Juniper, in *The Case Is Altered* (1598), is quite unbearably talkative: drunk or sober, with something to say or without, his tongue ceases only when he leaves the stage. Out of sheer exuberance Face and Subtle ring all the changes they can think of on the name of Doll Common (Mistress Dorothy, Royal Doll, Doll Proper, Doll Singular, Doll Particular, My Dousabel, My Little God's-Gift, My Dolly); and for sheer vituperative invention there's no passage in English to equal the slanging-match with which they open the play. All these arabesques of words, festooned over the structure of the plays, add a specific gravity to Jonson's writing; they choke the poetic line, they weigh down the syntax, making verbs do multiple duty, suspending assertions over long periods, with many subordinate clauses and modifiers, and falling often enough into the paratactic structure of a list. Even when he has chastened his diction to lyric formality, that weight continues to be felt. We hardly have language to describe the pace of lyric poetry, but it is an impression to be recorded that Jonson's lyrics are pre-

2. *Bartholomew Fair,* Act IV, scene 5.

vailingly slow and measured. The last song of Aurora in "The Vision of Delight" is famous:

> I was not wearier where I lay
> By frozen Tithon's side tonight
> Than I am willing now to stay
> And be a part of your delight.
> But I am urgèd by the day
> Against my will, to bid you come away.[3]

The song starts off as if it were going to compare degrees of weariness, but shifts to compare a degree of weariness with a degree of willingness; it's a beautiful but strained sequence of thought, that forces the hearer to abstract one stage beyond what he expected, and holds him back to do that. And the last line, which might be merely perfunctory if it were another tetrameter, is lengthened by the emphatic "Against my will" and the only intralinear punctuation of the stanza, to a grave, reluctant enactment of unwilling consent. That weight of controlled force is felt again and again in Jonson's poetry; like Milton, he often lets us feel the heavy Latin philology behind his English, but unlike Milton he often rejoices in the comic effects of incredible abundance. Lady Politic Would-Be and the learned collegians of *Epicoene* are sisters under the skin to Volpone as he impersonates the mountebank Scoto, or to Subtle as he lectures with fluent and obviously interminable assurance on the principles of alchemical art.

Finally, Jonson's moral judgments, for all their sense of Senecan severity and critical self-consciousness, are often so heavy that they give the impression of being quite out of control. The most uncomfortable evidence of this excess appears in early performances like *Everyman Out*, *Cynthia's Revels*, and *Poetaster* (1599, 1600, 1601) which aren't so much plays as public arraignments of Jonson's enemies and contemptible emulators. As far as the scenarios are concerned, these unfortunates are dead horses to begin with, and by now they are ossified as well. Jonson flogs them unmercifully. The same zest for punishment has often formed the basis of critical comment directed against *Volpone.* At the end of that play the fox and the parasite are dragged off to punishment far in excess of what they really deserve. For they have not only been the mainsprings of the action, they have harmed nobody who did not richly deserve it, and have purged of their contemptible humors a great many who did. The worst of their doing is Volpone's attempt to rape Celia, and Corvino is an all but irresistible temptation to that action—greater than Celia's beauty, as Volpone himself declares. You could

3. Lines 198–203, H&S, VII, 471.

argue that Volpone and Mosca, though not without faults of their own, are really the only forces of morality active in Venice. At the end of Act IV, as he completes some dealings with Corbaccio, Mosca utters an exclamation that lights up, as in a flash, the whole perspective from which he sees the depraved and ignominious tribe on whom he preys:

> Bountiful bones! what horrid, strange offence
> Did he commit 'gainst nature, in his youth,
> Worthy this age? [IV, 6, 89–91]

The moral that Mosca and Volpone inculcate, and brilliantly, is the con-man's byword, "You can't cheat an honest man." Yet at the end of the play, Jonson's virtue comes onstage wearing the black robes of official justice, and sends off the honest tricksters to a punishment far worse than that of their crooked victims—a punishment which, in that day at least, everyone understood to be hideous beyond description. Everything about it is wrong. For Mosca the torment is made worse than for Volpone (though the latter was clearly the principal, and the former simply the agent) on no better principle than his inferior caste status. Yet we've already seen vividly, through the actions of the Fourth Avocatore, who is frantically impatient to marry his daughter to Mosca the instant he seems to have money, what these class distinctions are worth.

The tone of punishment and correction runs through a lot of Jonson's dramatic work; there are passages which don't come far short of suggesting that he thought the work itself a form of correction, if not punishment, for the audience: "physic of the mind" was one of his terms. In so thinking, he was, as the evidence indicates, quite different from most other members of his flighty, helter-skelter profession. Very few of them hectored their audiences as Ben did; very few of them found it necessary to spend as much time as he did in building around themselves a wall of learned, verbal values.

Praise and blame are the staple of his writing; a somewhat surly virtue allied with Senecan self-knowledge formed the hard carapace on which he relied to be himself. The "Epistle to One that Asked to Be Sealed of the Tribe of Ben" puts it succinctly:

> Well, with mine own frail pitcher what to do
> I have decreed; keep it from waves and press,
> Lest it be justled, cracked, made naught, or less:
> Live to that point I will, for which I am man,
> And dwell as in my center as I can.[4]

His real center of gravity was the shell of his learned Senecan virtue. Without his learning and craft, without his solid judgment

4. H&S, VIII, 219, lines 56–60.

founded on both, he was next to nothing, a mere foundling of the earth. Who was his father? Immediately we must distinguish. His father in the flesh was a minister from somewhere, perhaps in the north of England (tradition hints at this, and the long foot-trip into Scotland does something to confirm it); but we don't know what he was doing in London, where Jonson was evidently born, nor even what church he was a minister of. His mother promptly remarried, giving him a second father—the bricklayer of popular legend; but we don't even know for sure which of these two men was named Jonson, if either. Despite the two of them, Ben apparently did not feel adequately fathered, so he elected others to the office. Sergeant John Hoskins, who had taught him something like basic manners, became one of his "fathers"; Vincent Corbet, a Surrey nurseryman who was the natural father of Jonson's schoolfellow at Westminster (Richard Corbet, later a bishop) became another. William Camden, who as headmaster at Westminster taught him Latin and Greek, became his father in learning. These were cultural as opposed to natural fathers, elected as opposed to given affinities; a second nature, not a first, after the pattern set on the continent by J. C. Scaliger, who also had numerous metaphorical "sons." The cultural affinity had to be learned, announced enacted, exemplified, asserted in the form of a challenge; it involved learning a code of letters and a code of manners that could not help setting one among the elite, who know themselves and have adjusted to the austere general truth about human nature. The exponent of stoic virtue has trained himself to expect very little, especially from his own undisciplined nature, over which his learned nature must stand constant, vigilant guard. The moral circle in which Jonson dwells is that scribed by Seneca, the sphere of his dramatic actions is verbal or rhetorical under a cloak of factual realism, and beneath all these modes of artifice lies a deep ground of gourmandize streaked with fecality. Varying a few necessary variables, the whole construct most resembles that found in Rabelais. Gut and groin lie at the center of the circle, a severe stoic ethic rings the periphery; the ambiguous, fluctuating, tricksy element of this psychic cosmos is the imagination.

Especially in stoic terms, the imagination is almost purely negative, a Bad Thing. It puffs men up to ridiculous proportions, making vulgar English knights think themselves decadent Roman emperors, and stupid, stubborn sectarians think themselves vehicles of Divine Grace. Imagination is a philosopher's stone (fake, like all of them), which promises to turn the dross of men's real lives to gold. It is the business of Jonsonian comedy to shrink these delusions down to size, reducing Captain Face to the reality of Jeremy Butler, and Mosca from his moment of glory as a rich Venetian dignitary to a piece of human vermin chained to his bench and groaning at his oar. Jonsonian comedy is prevailingly reductive and corrective; it ends with a true judgment, or a series of true judgments, in which the characters get what they deserve, or a little worse. Shakespeare's last comedies end typically with a festival or sacrament in which everybody participates and no damn nonsense about merit. The bad are forgiven or reconciled or allowed to join silently with the circle of celebrating humanity. But in Jonson there is justice or a simulacrum of it, supplemented by precious little mercy, or none at all; and in this judgment imagination is far from being a redeeming grace, even when used for severely therapeutic effects.

Undercover agents in Jonson's plays make up an interesting group. Brainworm of *Everyman in His Humor* is closest, I think, to the wily slave of Plautine comedy;[5] he manages the intrigue throughout, tests the patience of authority to the limit, but is pardoned in the end on the score that he's arranged things well for his master and shown great wit in doing so. Face turns out to be this sort of character, but only at the last minute. Subtle and Doll make their getaways, and go back to a raggletaggle life in the liberties; their sharking has gone for nothing, but they are not turned directly over to the law, like Volpone and Mosca. Finally, there is a group of undercover truth-tellers or truth-knowers, who through most of the action lurk behind the scenes or in disguise, and then step forward triumphantly, but are somehow balked of an anticipated reward. Such is Justice Overdo of *Bartholomew Fair*, Surly of *The Alchemist*; and such, though a little less neatly, is the figure of Macilente in *Everyman Out*. There is no categorical right or wrong among all these various figures. In a world teeming with self-deceivers ("gulls" is Jonson's favorite word), even systematic deceit of others can lead to honest perceptions (as in Mosca), and an excess of honesty can result in self-delusion (as in Justice Overdo). But the shrinking of delusions is a constant preoccupation of the comedy, whether the agents who perform that action are rewarded for their labors or punished. And indeed, much the same pattern prevails in the tragedies as well; the obsessions of Sejanus and Catiline are more somber and threatening than those of the comedies, but they are no less swellings to be punctured. Overwhelmingly, imagination is a delusive enemy to be reduced or managed, if not humiliated; the laughter that results from this action, like the laughter of Rabelais, has frequently a harsh, metallic sound.

Very likely Jonson's emphasis on correction and deflation grew out of his uneasy relation to the unruly Elizabethan playhouse audience. That audience, as everyone has recognized, had an appetite

5. Plautus gets credit for establishing this type, though in fact almost all his plays were translated from the Greek.

for novelty, for vulgarity, for marvellous and sensational effects. As a condition of the profession, Jonson had to cater to the appetite, but he also aspired to correct and improve it. Many of his prologues and separate poems speak flatly of a desire to refine public taste; and the sharpness with which he assailed self-delusion may have been due to a recognition that among the public before whom he had to make it, such an assault was not likely to be very popular. Nor indeed, was he, as a purveyor of known illusions, in an ideal position to inveigh against illusion. As a man of the theater, a branded murderer, and a Roman Catholic, he had no recognized standing among the educated classes of his time: as a man with a classical background, he felt superior to the common ruck of the playhouse; and he had as yet no connection or position at court. His fringe position as entertainer, mimer, juggler of appearances, actually a mock-person who forged the identities of others (so an old and grudging view of actors proclaimed) was so questionable in society's eyes, and perhaps in his own, that it's no wonder he felt compelled to insist, all too belligerently, on an authenticity for which Cicero and Seneca, Juvenal and Tacitus could be made to stand as guartors.

When he turned to writing masques for the court, Jonson's case was a good deal altered. He now had an audience of aristocrats who didn't want to be lectured, didn't need to be lectured, whom he was in no position whatever to lecture. His rewards took the form of patronage, that is, free and substantial gifts bestowed by courtiers, noblemen, the king himself. He had a position, he was not obliged to shark for the accumulated sixpences of artisans and prentices. The masque was by no means a money-making proposition; on the contrary, as a form of conspicuous consumption, its aim was to squander the money of its noble participants, as ostentatiously as possible. Courtiers were the actors, courtiers were the audience, magnificence was the common theme. Playing ordinarily for a single night before a non-paying audience, the masques customarily cost enormous sums of money for costumes, machinery, musicians, and of course writers such as Jonson. But it was not salary. He was in the position not of lowering himself to make money (about that he always felt uneasy) but of participating in a ceremony of fealty to which money was incidentally attached as a tangible evidence of honor.

Most important of all, the masque form legitimized Jonson's position as a perpetrator of authentic make-believe. Proteus the god of transformation and metamorphosis is the genius of the masque form, which aims to present a magnified and authenticated reflection of an artifice before people who understand because they are already themselves part of that artifice. Learned compliment is the order of the day, rather than learned lectures; not because the truth is already in the audience, but because the audience is already in the truth. In masque after masque, the turn of thought is that a mythological pattern of action is presented, at the end of which the actors turn to the audience and declare that their action achieves its perfect form and meaning in the audience that has been watching it. Correction had been the essence of the action in the plays; the masques involve very little correction. What leading can be felt is implicit in the formality of the verse, the decorum of the occasion. But there's no real teaching, because no need for it. The aim of the masque is to allow the court to admire itself. There is a revelation onstage which widens to include the audience; in the dances that follow, audience and actors are interwoven, fantasy becomes fact, and vice versa. The mood of the masque is predictive, visionary; in one voice it declares that this is how things were, are, should be, and are going to be.

Standing outside space and time, and equally outside any vectors based on inwardness or sensitivity of character, the masque doesn't have a moral dimension in the sense familiar from plays or narratives. Its conflicts are not conflicts of character at all, they are heraldic in nature—so broadly defined as to ensure the outcome. Most commonly, vice in one flat personification or other, is set against an equally two-dimensional virtue—set "against" in the sense of contrast, not of struggle, for customarily there's no more external contestation in the masque than there is exercise of inward character. Most often the Jonsonian masque hinges on a discovery. In the *Masque of Queens,* Hell dissolves and disappears: the House of Fame takes its place. In *Oberon* the satyrs serve not at all to advance or impede the action, they simply frisk aimlessly till their attention is focused and their reverence stirred by the luminous appearance of Oberon. What happens in both masques is simply that a felt void is filled by a process outside the intent of the "characters," a force not to be better defined than as "the nature of things." The law of compliment would not have it otherwise. Aristocracies don't in the least like to be told that they are the fruit of a process, far less a painful process, least of all a recent process. Such ideas imply that anyone who takes equal pains may join or supplant them. What they like to be told is that they are the capstone of a structure that has long felt itself incomplete without them, that they are authenticated by the acclaim of an entire historical or natural order. The satyrs, though freakish and lawless, obey Oberon instinctively; the queens of history feel themselves completed and fulfilled by Anne of Denmark. The masque cannot question, negate, or even argue a point; it is a self-terminating mechanism that fulfills itself by coming to a halt and inviting the court to discover the pattern of itself in its own intricate dances.

Where, in this scenario of flats and mirrors, superficialities and formalities, this fancy-dress tissue of artifice, is there room for the bulk of Ben? He's such an intrusive, emphatic, solid man in the plays, so voluble in his delivery of facts, so forceful in his judgments, that there seems no place for him in the heroic dream-world of the Stuart aristocracy. Beyond question, his presence is in some measure subdued. In almost any masque, the real show belongs to the audience, not the author, and Jonson like any other courtier had to efface himself in order to make his master glitter. But he remains present nonetheless, in a capacity just as important as that of the plays, and in some ways more interesting. Very often one finds him at work subsurface, shaping a linguistic chaos toward ultimate order. The anti-masque with which the spectacle begins generally represents a principle of counter-order or disorder, and especially in its language. For example, Comus in *Pleasure Reconciled to Virtue* and Fancy in the *Vision of Delight* both speak a kind of harum-scarum, ranting dialect which gives the impression that the speaker is saying the first thing that comes into his head. Indeed, Fancy speaks something very close to unmetrical gibberish, an airy stream of images with little logical or syntactical connection to one another:

> The political pudding hath still his two ends,
> Though the bellows and the bagpipe were ne'er so good friends;
> And who can report what offense it would be
> For the squirrel to see a dog climb a tree?
> If a dream should come in now, to make you afeard,
> With a windmill on's head, and bells at his beard,
> Would you straight wear your spectacles here at your toes,
> And your boots on your brows, and your spurs on your nose?
> Your whale he will swallow a hogshead for a pill;
> But the maker o' the mouse-trap is he that hath skill.
> And the nature of the onion is to draw tears,
> As well as the mustard; peace, pitchers have ears,
> And shuttlecocks wings; these things, do not mind 'em.
> If the bell have any sides, the clapper will find 'em, etc., etc.
> [lines 56–69]

But with the advent of James, all this chaos changes to the rich and ordered progression of the seasons, figured in the breaking forth of spring, the glories of which the masquers represent. Wonder can only ask questions about this sudden blossoming of the scene:

> Whose power is this? What God?

But Fancy knows the answers:

> Behold a king
> Whose presence maketh this perpetual spring,
> The glories of which spring grow in that bower,
> And are the marks and beauties of his power. [lines 170–73]

And this transformation leads directly into the concluding songs and dances, which do not describe or declare, but simply enact, the concept of ordered complexity. These songs are much alike in all the masques; they are built primarily of the very simplest metrical materials, regular tetrameter lines rhymed in couplets or in alternating quatrains (*abab*). But in the four songs of Daedalus, for example, at the end of *Pleasure Reconciled to Virtue,* these simple meters are increasingly syncopated by the interspersion of trimeters, dimeters, and even monometer lines. At the same time, the plain sense of the line is increasingly diffused; as their pattern gets more complex, less and less attention is paid to their meaning. One stanza reads:

> An eye of looking back were well,
>   Or any murmur that would tell
>   Your thoughts, how you were sent,
>   And went,
> To walk with Pleasure, not to dwell. [lines 257–261]

The basic idea is obviously that it would be good always to keep in the back of one's mind that pleasure is only a temporary respite from the arduous pursuit of virtue. But the first wandering lines seem to suggest only loosely what they mean; "an eye of looking back" is only vaguely a retrospective eye; even after some reflection, it's impossible to know whether "tell" carries the meaning of "express" or "admonish." The third and fourth lines can be read separately as they are printed, or else combined into a single strongly emphatic tetrameter with an internal rhyme: no doubt the music would help to control this. However they are heard, the lines represent a break in the meter, but also a fulfillment of it. As for "what it is saying," Jonson's song, like many of Shakespeare's, doesn't rise much above the level of platitude; but its increasing complexity of texture, its recurrent yet increasingly varied rhythms, its steady and effortless movement, all enact the weight and fullness of Jonson's mind.

Admittedly, it's a little odd to think of heavy Jonson as a dancer. But dancing is done with an inner ear, as well as with feet, and inside there Jonson is light as a feather. One could adapt to his verses the lines that Sir John Davies applied to the wandering river Maeander:

> Such winding slights—such tricks and turns he hath,
> Such creeks, such wrenches, and such dalliance,
> That (whether it be hap or heedless chance)
>   In his indented course and wringing play,
>   He seems to dance a perfect cunning Hey.[6]

6. "Orchestra, a Poem of Dancing," lines 367–71.

T. S. ELIOT

Ben Jonson†

The reputation of Jonson has been of the most deadly kind that can be compelled upon the memory of a great poet. To be universally accepted; to be damned by the praise that quenches all desire to read the book; to be afflicted by the imputation of the virtues which excite the least pleasure; and to be read only by historians and antiquaries—this is the most perfect conspiracy of approval. For some generations the reputation of Jonson has been carried rather as a liability than as an asset in the balance-sheet of English literature. No critic has succeeded in making him appear pleasurable or even interesting. Swinburne's book on Jonson satisfies no curiosity and stimulates no thought. For the critical study in the "Men of Letters Series" by Mr. Gregory Smith there is a place;[1] it satisfies curiosity, it supplies many just observations, it provides valuable matter on the neglected masques; it only fails to remodel the image of Jonson which is settled in our minds. Probably the fault lies with several generations of our poets. It is not that the value of poetry is only its value to living poets for their own work; but appreciation is akin to creation, and true enjoyment of poetry is related to the stirring of suggestion, the stimulus that a poet feels in his enjoyment of other poetry. Jonson has provided no creative stimulus for a very long time; consequently we must look back as far as Dryden—precisely, a poetic practitioner who learned from Jonson—before we find a living criticism of Jonson's work.[2]

Yet there are possibilities for Jonson even now. We have no difficulty in seeing what brought him to this pass; how, in contrast, not with Shakespeare, but with Marlowe, Webster, Donne, Beaumont, and Fletcher,[3] he has been paid out with reputation instead of enjoyment. He is no less a poet than these men, but his poetry is of the surface. Poetry of the surface cannot be understood without study; for to deal with the surface of life, as Jonson dealt with it, is to deal so deliberately that we too must be deliberate, in order to understand. Shakespeare, and smaller men also, are in the end more difficult, but they offer something at the start to encourage the student or to satisfy those who want nothing more; they are suggestive, evocative, a phrase, a voice; they offer poetry in detail as well

† From *The Sacred Wood* (London, 1920, 1960), pp. 104–7, 113–22. All footnotes are by the editor.

1. *Ben Jonson* (London, 1919).

2. See the "Examen of the *Silent Woman*," above, pp. 422–27.

3. Eliot's list is of poets and playwrights from the Elizabethan and Jacobean ages who, without aspiring to Shakespearean universality, continue to be read and enjoyed.

as in design. So does Dante offer something, a phrase everywhere (*tu se' ombra ed ombra vedi*)[4] even to readers who have no Italian; and Dante and Shakespeare have poetry of design as well as of detail. But the polished veneer of Jonson reflects only the lazy reader's fatuity; unconscious does not respond to unconscious; no swarms of inarticulate feelings are aroused. The immediate appeal of Jonson is to the mind; his emotional tone is not in the single verse, but in the design of the whole. But not many people are capable of discovering for themselves the beauty which is only found after labour; and Jonson's industrious readers have been those whose interest was historical and curious, and those who have thought that in discovering the historical and curious interest they had discovered the artistic value as well. When we say that Jonson requires study, we do not mean study of his classical scholarship or of seventeenth-century manners. We mean intelligent saturation in his work as a whole; we mean that in order to enjoy him at all, we must get to the centre of his work and his temperament, and that we must see him unbiased by time, as a contemporary. And to see him as a contemporary does not so much require the power of putting ourselves into seventeenth-century London as it requires the power of setting Jonson in our London: a more difficult triumph of divination.

It is generally conceded that Jonson failed as a tragic dramatist; and it is usually agreed that he failed because his genius was for satiric comedy and because of the weight of pedantic learning with which he burdened his two tragic failures. The second point marks an obvious error of detail; the first is too crude a statement to be accepted; to say that he failed because his genius was unsuited to tragedy is to tell us nothing at all. Jonson did not write a good tragedy, but we can see no reason why he should not have written one. If two plays so different as *The Tempest* and *The Silent Woman* are both comedies,[5] surely the category of tragedy could be made wide enough to include something possible for Jonson to have done. But the classification of tragedy and comedy, while it may be sufficient to mark the distinction in a dramatic literature of more rigid form and treatment—it may distinguish Aristophanes from Euripides—is not adequate to a drama of such variations as the Elizabethans. Tragedy is a crude classification for plays so different in their tone as *Macbeth, The Jew of Malta,* and *The Witch of Edmonton;*[6] and it does not help us much to say that *The Mer-*

4. Dante, *Purgatorio,* xxi, line 132: Statius, recognizing Virgil, wants to kiss his feet in homage; but Virgil, raising him up, says gently, "You are a shade and see a shade before you."

5. Shakespeare's *The Tempest* (1611) is contrasted as a type of the loose, romantic comedy of sentiment, with *Epicoene* (1609) as a type of the tightly constructed comedy of intrigue.

6. The odd play in this comparison is *The Witch of Edmonton,* commonly classified as a tragi-comedy, and listed on its title-page as by Thomas Dekker, John Ford, William Rowley, "etc." Certainly Shakespeare's *Macbeth* is a very different play from Marlowe's *The Jew of Malta.*

chant of Venice and *The Alchemist* are comedies.[7] Jonson had his own scale, his own instrument. The merit which *Catiline*[8] possesses is the same merit that is exhibited more triumphantly in *Volpone*; *Catiline* fails, not because it is too laboured and conscious, but because it is not conscious enough; because Jonson in this play was not alert to his own idiom, not clear in his mind as to what his temperament wanted him to do. In *Catiline* Jonson conforms, or attempts to conform, to conventions; not to the conventions of antiquity, which he had exquisitely under control, but to the conventions of tragico-historical drama of his time. It is not the Latin erudition that sinks *Catiline*, but the application of that erudition to a form which was not the proper vehicle for the mind which had amassed the erudition.

* * *

Whereas in Shakespeare the effect is due to the way in which the characters *act upon* one another, in Jonson it is given by the way in which the characters *fit in* with each other. The artistic result of *Volpone* is not due to any effect that Volpone, Mosca, Corvino, Corbaccio, Voltore have upon each other, but simply to their combination into a whole. And these figures are not personifications of passions; separately, they have not even that reality, they are constituents. It is a similar indication of Jonson's method that you can hardly pick out a line of Jonson's and say confidently that it is great poetry; but there are many extended passages to which you cannot deny that honour.

> I will have all my beds blown up, not stuft;
> Down is too hard; and then, mine oval room
> Fill'd with such pictures as Tiberius took
> From Elephantis, and dull Aretine
> But coldly imitated. Then, my glasses
> Cut in more subtle angles, to disperse
> And multiply the figures, as I walk. . . .[9]

Jonson is the legitimate heir of Marlowe. The man who wrote, in *Volpone*:

> for thy love,
> In varying figures, I would have contended
> With the blue Proteus, or the hornèd flood. . . .[1]

and

> See, a carbuncle
> May put out both the eyes of our Saint Mark;

7. In casual parlance, a play that ends happily for the main characters is a comedy; Eliot is making the somewhat allusive point that neither Shylock nor Volpone is very happy at the end of the comedies in which they appear.

8. Of Jonson's two Roman tragedies, *Sejanus* (1603) and *Catiline* (1611), the first has been very generally respected, but the second was a failure in its own time and (on the whole) since.

9. *The Alchemist*, Act II, scene 2, lines 41–47.

1. *Volpone*, Act III, scene 7, lines 151–53.

> A diamond would have bought Lollia Paulina,
> When she came in like star-light, hid with jewels. . . .[2]

is related to Marlowe as a poet; and if Marlowe is a poet, Jonson is also. And, if Jonson's comedy is a comedy of humours, then Marlowe's tragedy, a large part of it, is a tragedy of humours. But Jonson has too exclusively been considered as the typical representative of a point of view toward comedy. He has suffered from his great reputation as a critic and theorist, from the effects of his intelligence. We have been taught to think of him as the man, the dictator (confusedly in our minds with his later namesake),[3] as the literary politician impressing his views upon a generation; we are offended by the constant reminder of his scholarship. We forget the comedy in the humours, and the serious artist in the scholar. Jonson has suffered in public opinion, as anyone must suffer who is forced to talk about his art.

If you examine the first hundred lines or more of *Volpone* the verse appears to be in the manner of Marlowe, more deliberate, more mature, but without Marlowe's inspiration. It looks like mere "rhetoric," certainly not "deeds and language such as men do use"![4] It appears to us, in fact, forced and flagitious bombast. That it is not "rhetoric," or at least not vicious rhetoric, we do not know until we are able to review the whole play. For the consistent maintenance of this manner conveys in the end an effect not of verbosity, but of bold, even shocking and terrifying directness. We have difficulty in saying exactly what produces this simple and single effect. It is not in any ordinary way due to management of intrigue. Jonson employs immense dramatic constructive skill: it is not so much skill in plot as skill in doing without a plot. He never manipulates as complicated a plot as that of *The Merchant of Venice*; he has in his best plays nothing like the intrigue of Restoration comedy. In *Bartholomew Fair* it is hardly a plot at all; the marvel of the play is the bewildering rapid chaotic action of the fair; it is the fair itself, not anything that happens to take place in the fair. In *Volpone*, or *The Alchemist*, or *The Silent Woman*, the plot is enough to keep the players in motion; it is rather an "action" than a plot. The plot does not hold the play together; what holds the play together is a unity of inspiration that radiates into plot and personages alike.

We have attempted to make more precise the sense in which it was said that Jonson's work is "of the surface"; carefully avoiding the word "superficial." For there is work contemporary with Jonson's which is superficial in a pejorative sense in which the word

2. *Ibid.*, lines 193–96.
3. Dr. Samuel Johnson of the later 18th century, quite distinct from Ben Jonson of the early 17th.
4. From the Prologue to the second version of *Every Man in His Humour*, line 21.

cannot be applied to Jonson—the work of Beaumont and Fletcher. If we look at the work of Jonson's great contemporaries, Shakespeare, and also Donne and Webster and Tourneur (and sometimes Middleton), have a depth, a third dimension,[5] as Mr. Gregory Smith rightly calls it, which Jonson's work has not. Their words have often a network of tentacular roots reaching down to the deepest terrors and desires. Jonson's most certainly have not; but in Beaumont and Fletcher we may think that at times we find it. Looking closer, we discover that the blossoms of Beaumont and Fletcher's imagination draw no sustenance from the soil, but are cut and slightly withered flowers stuck into sand.

> Wilt thou, hereafter, when they talk of me,
> As thou shalt hear nothing but infamy,
> Remember some of these things? . . .
> I pray thee, do; for thou shalt never see me so again.

> Hair woven in many a curious warp,
> Able in endless error to enfold
> The wandering soul; . . .[6]

Detached from its context, this looks like the verse of the greater poets; just as lines of Jonson, detached from their context, look like inflated or empty fustian. But the evocative quality of the verse of Beaumont and Fletcher depends upon a clever appeal to emotions and associations which they have not themselves grasped; it is hollow. It is superficial with a vacuum behind it; the superficies of Jonson is solid. It is what it is; it does not pretend to be another thing. But it is so very conscious and deliberate that we must look with eyes alert to the whole before we apprehend the significance of any part. We cannot call a man's work superficial when it is the creation of a world; a man cannot be accused of dealing superficially with the world which he himself has created; the superficies *is* the world. Jonson's characters conform to the logic of the emotions of their world. It is a world like Lobatchevsky's;[7] the worlds created by artists like Jonson are like systems of non-Euclidean geometry. They are not fancy, because they have a logic of their own; and this logic illuminates the actual world, because it gives us a new point of view from which to inspect it.

A writer of power and intelligence, Jonson endeavoured to promulgate, as a formula and programme of reform, what he chose to do himself; and he not unnaturally laid down in abstract theory

5. Another term for the quality after which Eliot is reaching here would be "resonance." But the distinction between fake and true resonance is all but impossible to formulate.

6. The lines are in Beaumont and Fletcher, somewhere. Between them, Beaumont and Fletcher wrote more than thirty plays.

7. Nikolai Lobachevsky (1792–1856) was one of the first mathematicians to publish the outlines of a non-Euclidean geometry.

what is in reality a personal point of view. And it is in the end of no value to discuss Jonson's theory and practice unless we recognize and seize this point of view, which escapes the formulæ, and which is what makes his plays worth reading. Jonson behaved as the great creative mind that he was: he created his own world, a world from which his followers, as well as the dramatists who were trying to do something wholly different, are excluded. Remembering this, we turn to Mr. Gregory Smith's objection—that Jonson's characters lack the third dimension, have no life out of the theatrical existence in which they appear—and demand an inquest. The objection implies that the characters are purely the work of intellect, or the result of superficial observation of a world which is faded or mildewed. It implies that the characters are lifeless. But if we dig beneath the theory, beneath the observation, beneath the deliberate drawing and the theatrical and dramatic elaboration, there is discovered a kind of power, animating Volpone, Busy, Fitzdottrel, the literary ladies of *Epicoene*, even Bobadil,[8] which comes from below the intellect, and for which no theory of humours will account. And it is the same kind of power which vivifies Trimalchio, and Panurge, and some but not all of the "comic" characters of Dickens.[9] The fictive life of this kind is not to be circumscribed by a reference to "comedy" or to "farce"; it is not exactly the kind of life which informs the characters of Molière or that which informs those of Marivaux[1]—two writers who were, besides, doing something quite different the one from the other. But it is something which distinguishes Barabas from Shylock, Epicure Mammon from Falstaff, Faustus from—if you will—Macbeth; Marlowe and Jonson from Shakespeare and the Shakespearians, Webster, and Tourneur.[2] It is not merely Humours: for neither Volpone nor Mosca is a humour. No theory of humours could account for Jonson's best plays or the best characters in them. We want to know at what point the comedy of humours passes into a work of art, and why Jonson is not Brome.[3]

8. Busy is Zeal-of-the-Land Busy, a puritan preacher in *Bartholomew Fair*; Fitzdottrel is a credulous squire in *The Devil Is an Ass;* Captain Bobadill is the braggart soldier of *Every Man in His Humour*.

9. Trimalchio is the rich vulgarian of Petronius's *Satyricon* (about 60 A.D.), Panurge the unscrupulous playmate of Gargantua and Pantagruel in the fantasy of Rabelais (1530–50). Mr. Micawber, of *David Copperfield*, would perhaps best exemplify a "powerful" comic character in Dickens.

1. Molière, of the 17th century, and Marivaux, of the 18th, make, as Eliot recognizes, a rather odd couple; the latter is a much more strained and fanciful stylist than the former, and his characters, to the extent they "live" at all, do so very largely through conceits of language.

2. Barabas, the central character of Marlowe's *Jew of Malta*, is seen from the outside, as Shylock (of *The Merchant of Venice*) is not; the contrast set up here is carried through the other pairings, i.e., Mammon is more exterior than Falstaff, and one doesn't enter into the thought-processes of Faustus as into those of Macbeth.

3. Richard Brome, originally Jonson's servant, later became a workmanlike but uninspired dramatist.

The creation of a work of art, we will say the creation of a character in a drama, consists in the process of transfusion of the personality, or, in a deeper sense, the life, of the author into the character. This is a very different matter from the orthodox creation in one's own image. The ways in which the passions and desires of the creator may be satisfied in the work of art are complex and devious. In a painter they may take the form of a predilection for certain colours, tones, or lightings; in a writer the original impulse may be even more strangely transmuted. Now, we may say with Mr. Gregory Smith that Falstaff or a score of Shakespeare's characters have a "third dimension" that Jonson's have not. This will mean, not that Shakespeare's spring from the feelings or imagination and Jonson's from the intellect or invention; they have equally an emotional source; but that Shakespeare's represent a more complex tissue of feelings and desires, as well as a more supple, a more susceptible temperament. Falstaff is not only the roast Manningtree ox with the pudding in his belly; he also "grows old," and, finally, his nose is as sharp as a pen.[4] He was perhaps the *satisfaction* of more, and of more complicated feelings; and perhaps he was, as the great tragic characters must have been, the offspring of deeper, less apprehensible feelings: deeper, but not necessarily stronger or more intense, than those of Jonson. It is obvious that the spring of the difference is not the difference between feeling and thought, or superior insight, superior perception, on the part of Shakespeare, but his susceptibility to a greater range of emotion, and emotion deeper and more obscure. But his characters are no more "alive" than are the characters of Jonson.

The world they live in is a larger one. But small worlds—the worlds which artists create—do not differ only in magnitude; if they are complete worlds, drawn to scale in every part, they differ in kind also. And Jonson's world has this scale. His type of personality found its relief in something falling under the category of burlesque or farce—though when you are dealing with a *unique* world, like his, these terms fail to appease the desire for definition. It is not, at all events, the farce of Molière: the latter is more analytic, more an intellectual redistribution. It is not defined by the word "satire." Jonson poses as a satirist. But satire like Jonson's is great in the end not by hitting off its object, but by creating it; the satire is merely the means which leads to the aesthetic result, the impulse which projects a new world into a new orbit. In *Every Man in his Humour* there is a neat, a very neat, comedy of humours. In discovering and proclaiming in this play the new genre Jonson was simply recognizing, unconsciously, the route which opened out in the proper direction for his instincts. His characters are and remain, like Marlowe's,

4. I *Henry IV*, Act II, scene 4; *Henry V*, Act II, scene 3.

simplified characters; but the simplification does not consist in the dominance of a particular humour or monomania. That is a very superficial account of it. The simplification consists largely in reduction of detail, in the seizing of aspects relevant to the relief of an emotional impulse which remains the same for that character, in making the character conform to a particular setting. This stripping is essential to the art, to which is also essential a flat distortion in the drawing; it is an art of caricature, of great caricature, like Marlowe's. It is a great caricature, which is beautiful; and a great humour, which is serious. The "world" of Jonson is sufficiently large; it is a world of poetic imagination; it is sombre. He did not get the third dimension, but he was not trying to get it.

If we approach Jonson with less frozen awe of his learning, with a clearer understanding of his "rhetoric" and its applications, if we grasp the fact that the knowledge required of the reader is not archæology but knowledge of Jonson, we can derive not only instruction in non-Euclidean humanity—but enjoyment. We can even apply him, be aware of him as a part of our literary inheritance craving further expression. Of all the dramatists of his time, Jonson is probably the one whom the present age would find the most sympathetic, if it knew him. There is a brutality, a lack of sentiment, a polished surface, a handling of large bold designs in brilliant colours, which ought to attract about three thousand people in London and elsewhere. At least, if we had a contemporary Shakespeare and a contemporary Jonson, it would be the Jonson who would arouse the enthusiasm of the intelligentsia! Though he is saturated in literature, he never sacrifices the theatrical qualities—theatrical in the most favourable sense—to literature or to the study of character. His work is a titanic show. But Jonson's masques, an important part of his work, are neglected; our flaccid culture lets shows and literature fade, but prefers faded literature to faded shows. There are hundreds of people who have read *Comus*[5] to ten who have read the *Masque of Blackness*. *Comus* contains fine poetry, and poetry exemplifying some merits to which Jonson's masque poetry cannot pretend. Nevertheless, *Comus* is the death of the masque; it is the transition of a form of art—even of a form which existed for but a short generation—into "literature," literature cast in a form which has lost its application. Even though *Comus* was a masque at Ludlow Castle, Jonson had, what Milton came perhaps too late to have, a sense for living art; his art was applied. The masques can still be read, and with pleasure, by anyone who will take the trouble—a trouble which in this part of

5. Milton's masque *Comus* (1634) contains a much higher proportion of verbal to scenic effects than does the average masque by Jonson; Eliot suggests that for Milton the form was losing its vitality.

Jonson is, indeed, a study of antiquities—to imagine them in action, displayed with the music, costumes, dances, and the scenery of Inigo Jones. They are additional evidence that Jonson had a fine sense of form, of the purpose for which a particular form is intended; evidence that he was a literary artist even more than he was a man of letters.

Selected Bibliography

The library-sized edition of Jonson's *Works* in eleven volumes edited by C. H. Herford and Percy and Evelyn Simpson (Oxford, 1925–52) is basic to all work on Jonson. It is not always convenient to use: the poetry in Volume VIII is indexed only by first lines, and a good deal of poetry from the masques and plays is scattered through the other volumes. Moreover, commentary is always in one volume, text in another. Yet if one has a complete set to work with, it is an extraordinary mine of detailed information; and if one can adjust to the severely unmodernized texts, one can be confident of coming about as close as possible to the materials as Jonson wanted them to appear. The *Life of Jonson* in the first two volumes is on a par with the whole project. It is a kingly performance.

Less overpowering editions are those of William Gifford (first edition 1816, many times reprinted) which, though old, is of interest for its shrewd, learned, and often vituperative notes, and of F. E. Schelling (1910). The non-dramatic poetry is available in several handy paperbacks: the complete poetry edited by W. B. Hunter, Jr., for Anchor Books (AC–4), and a selection of Jonson's poems, combined with selections from the Cavalier poets, careful textual notes, and a body of critical materials, under the editorship of Hugh Maclean (*Ben Jonson and the Cavalier Poets,* a Norton Critical Edition).

Among the many books about Jonson, apart from those represented in the present collection of critical materials, these should be mentioned:

Bamborough, J. B. *Ben Jonson* (London, 1970).

Baum, H. W. *The Satiric and the Didactic in Ben Jonson's Comedy* (Chapel Hill, N.C., 1942).

Bentley, G. E. *Shakespeare and Jonson* (Chicago, 1945).

Blissett, W., Patrick, J. M., and Van Fossen, R. *A Celebration of Ben Jonson* (Toronto, 1973).

Bush, Douglas. *Mythology and the Renaissance Tradition* (New York, 1963).

Castelain, Maurice. *Ben Jonson, l'homme et l'oeuvre* (Paris, 1909).

Doran, Madeleine. *Endeavors of Art* (Madison, Wis., 1954).

Enck, J. J. *Jonson and Comic Truth* (Madison, Wis., 1957).

Jackson, G. B. *Vision and Judgment in Ben Jonson's Drama* (New Haven, Conn., 1968).

Knights, L. C. *Drama and Society in the Age of Jonson* (London, 1937).

Knoll, R. E. *Ben Jonson's Plays* (Lincoln, Neb., 1964).

Noyes, R. G. *Ben Jonson on the English Stage* (New York, 1935).

Sackton, A. H. *Rhetoric as a Dramatic Language in Ben Jonson* (New York, 1948).

Smith, G. G. *Ben Jonson* (London, 1919).

Thayer, C. G. *Ben Jonson, Studies in the Plays* (Norman, Okla., 1963).

Any selection among the hundreds of articles written about aspects of Jonson and his work is bound to be arbitrary; I have found the following to be useful and suggestive.

Beaurline, L. A. "Ben Jonson and the Illusion of Completeness." *PMLA* 84 (1969), 51–59.

Cunningham, D. "The Jonsonian Masque as a Literary Form." *ELH* 21 (1955), 123–30.

Gordon, D. J. "Poet and Architect." *Journal of the Warburg and Courtauld Institutes,* 12 (1949), 152–78.

Hawkins, H. "Folly, Incurable Disease, and *Volpone.*" *Studies in English Literature 1500–1900,* 8 (1968), 335–48.

Perkinson, R. H. "*Volpone* and the Reputation of Venetian Justice." *Modern Language Review,* 35 (1940), 11–18.

Peterson, Richard S. "The Iconography of Jonson's *Pleasure Reconciled to Virtue,*" in *Journal of Medieval and Renaissance Studies,* Vol. 5, no. 1 (Spring 1975), pp. 123–53.

Salinger, L. G. "Farce and Fashion in *The Silent Woman.*" *Essays and Studies,* 20 (1967), 29–46.

Slights, W. W. E. "*Epicoene* and the Prose Paradox." *Philological Quarterly* 49 (1970), 179–87.

Wilson, E. "Morose Ben Jonson." *The Triple Thinkers.* New York, 1948.